W9-ATE-875

LENIN

COLLECTED WORKS

32

THE RUSSIAN EDITION WAS PRINTED
IN ACCORDANCE WITH A DECISION
OF THE NINTH CONGRESS OF THE R.C.P.(B.)
AND THE SECOND CONGRESS OF SOVIETS
OF THE U.S.S.R.

ИНСТИТУТ МАРКСИЗМА-ЛЕНИНИЗМА при ЦК КПСС

В. И. ЛЕНИН

СОЧИНЕНИЯ

Издание четвертое

ГОСУДАРСТВЕННОЕ ИЗДАТЕЛЬСТВО
ПОЛИТИЧЕСКОЙ ЛИТЕРАТУРЫ

МОСКВА

V. I. LENIN

COLLECTED WORKS

VOLUME
32

December 1920 – August 1921

PROGRESS PUBLISHERS
MOSCOW

TRANSLATED FROM THE RUSSIAN
EDITED BY YURI SDOBNIKOV

First printing 1965
Second printing 1973
Third printing 1975

11-17-78

Л $\frac{10102 - 514}{014(01) - 75}$ 60 - 75

Printed in the Union of Soviet Socialist Republics

CONTENTS

ILLUSTRATIONS

PREFACE

Volume 32 contains the works V. I. Lenin wrote between December 30, 1920, and August 14, 1921.

These works show Lenin's Party and government activities—his leadership of the Bolshevik Party and guidance of the Soviet state—in the period of transition from the policy of War Communism to the New Economic Policy.

The volume contains his articles and speeches, "The Trade Unions, the Present Situation and Trotsky's Mistakes", "The Party Crisis", and the report and summing-up speech on the role and tasks of the trade unions at the Second All-Russia Congress of Miners, his pamphlet, *Once Again on the Trade Unions, the Current Situation and the Mistakes of Trotsky and Bukharin*, his "Speech Delivered at the Fourth All-Russia Congress of Garment Workers", and others. These works substantiate the forms and methods of the Party's work among the masses in the new conditions of transition to the peace-time effort of economic recovery, and define the role and tasks of the trade unions as a school of communism in socialist construction. In his uncompromising struggle against the Workers' Opposition, Democratic Centralists and Left Communists, who tried to erode the Party and undermine the dictatorship of the proletariat and the Party's leading role in the Soviets and trade unions, Lenin directed his main blow at the Trotskyites as the core of the anti-Party groupings.

A considerable section of the volume consists of reports, speeches and draft resolutions at the Tenth Party Congress. Among them are the report and summing-up speech on the political work of the Central Committee of the R.C.P.(B.); speech on the trade unions; report and summing-up speech

on the tax in kind; "Preliminary Draft Resolution of the
Tenth Congress of the R.C.P. on Party Unity"; "Preliminary Draft Resolution of the Tenth Congress of the R.C.P.
on the Syndicalist and Anarchist Deviation in Our Party";
report and summing-up speech on Party unity and the
anarcho-syndicalist deviation, etc. These works characterise Lenin's struggle for the Party's unity, the consolidation
of the alliance between the working class and the peasantry
on the new economic basis, and the strengthening of the
dictatorship of the proletariat.

The volume includes Lenin's well-known pamphlet,
*The Tax in Kind (The Significance of the New Policy and
Its Conditions)*, in which he gave an all-round substantiation
of the New Economic Policy as a special policy of the
proletarian state securing the possibility of laying the
foundation of a socialist economy, and as a way for the
successful construction of socialism. This question is also
dealt with in other works appearing in this volume, including "Report on the Tax in Kind Delivered at a Meeting of
Secretaries and Responsible Representatives of R.C.P.(B.)
Cells of Moscow and Moscow Gubernia", report and summing-up speech on the tax in kind at the Tenth All-Russia
Conference of the R.C.P.(B.), and recorded speeches.

There are many works showing Lenin's direction of
national economic planning and organisation. Among them
are "Integrated Economic Plan", draft Instructions of the
Council of Labour and Defence to Local Soviet Bodies,
"Speech on Local Economic Bodies Delivered at a Sitting
of the All-Russia Central Executive Committee", "Speech
Delivered at the Third All-Russia Food Conference", and
others.

A number of speeches and documents in the volume
show Lenin's activity in building up the state apparatus,
and in training and drawing the broad mass of working
people into government. They are: "Instructions of the
Central Committee to Communists Working in the People's
Commissariat for Education", "The Work of the People's
Commissariat for Education", "Speech Delivered at an
Enlarged Conference of Moscow Metalworkers", "Speech
at a Plenary Meeting of the Moscow Soviet of Workers'
and Peasants' Deputies", Speech Delivered at the All-

Russia Congress of Transport Workers", "To the Petrograd City Conference of Non-Party Workers", and others.

The volume contains Lenin's theses, reports and speeches at the Third Congress of the Communist International: theses for a report on the tactics of the R.C.P. at the Third Congress of the Communist International; speech on the Italian question, speech in defence of the tactics of the Communist International, and report on the tactics of the R.C.P.(B.). These documents define the tasks of the Communist Parties and their methods of winning over the working people.

Nine items in this volume are included in the *Collected Works* for the first time. They are: "Rough Draft of Theses Concerning the Peasants", "Preliminary Draft Resolution on Improving the Condition of Workers and Needy Peasants", speech and proposal on the fuel question at the Tenth Congress of the R.C.P.(B.), report on concessions at a meeting of the Communist group of the All-Russia Central Council of Trade Unions, "Letter on Oil Concessions", and "To the Trade Union Committee and All Workers of the First State Motor Works". "Draft Resolution on Questions of the New Economic Policy" is also published in full for the first time. All these works deal with the rehabilitation and development of the national economy and improvement of the working people's living standards.

Another document published here for the first time is the decree of the Council of People's Commissars "Concerning the Conditions Ensuring the Research Work of Academician I. P. Pavlov and His Associates". This decree shows the concern of the Communist Party and the Soviet Government for the development of Soviet science.

V. I. LENIN
May 1921

THE TRADE UNIONS, THE PRESENT SITUATION AND TROTSKY'S MISTAKES[1]

SPEECH DELIVERED AT A JOINT MEETING
OF COMMUNIST DELEGATES
TO THE EIGHTH CONGRESS OF SOVIETS, COMMUNIST MEMBERS
OF THE ALL-RUSSIA CENTRAL COUNCIL OF TRADE UNIONS
AND COMMUNIST MEMBERS OF THE MOSCOW CITY COUNCIL
OF TRADE UNIONS
DECEMBER 30, 1920

Comrades, I must first of all apologise for departing from the rules of procedure, for anyone wishing to take part in the debate should have heard the report, the second report and the speeches. I am so unwell, unfortunately, that I have been unable to do this. But I was able yesterday to read the principal printed documents and to prepare my remarks. This departure from the rules will naturally cause you some inconvenience; not having heard the other speeches, I may go over old ground and leave out what should be dealt with. But I had no choice.

My principal material is Comrade Trotsky's pamphlet, *The Role and Tasks of the Trade Unions*. When I compare it with the theses he submitted to the Central Committee, and go over it very carefully, I am amazed at the number of theoretical mistakes and glaring blunders it contains. How could anyone starting a big Party discussion on this question produce such a sorry excuse for a carefully thought out statement? Let me go over the main points which, I think, contain the original fundamental theoretical errors.

Trade unions are not just historically necessary; they are historically inevitable as an organisation of the industrial proletariat, and, under the dictatorship of the proletariat, embrace nearly the whole of it. This is basic, but Comrade Trotsky keeps forgetting it; he neither appreciates it nor makes it his point of departure, all this while dealing with "The Role and Tasks of the Trade Unions", a subject of infinite compass.

It follows from what I have said that the trade unions have an extremely important part to play at every step of the dictatorship of the proletariat. But what is their part? I find that it is a most unusual one, as soon as I delve into this question, which is one of the most fundamental theoretically. On the one hand, the trade unions, which take in all industrial workers, are an organisation of the ruling, dominant, governing class, which has now set up a dictatorship and is exercising coercion through the state. But it is not a state organisation; nor is it one designed for coercion, but for education. It is an organisation designed to draw in and to train; it is, in fact, a school: a school of administration, a school of economic management, a school of communism. It is a very unusual type of school, because there are no teachers or pupils; this is an extremely unusual combination of what has necessarily come down to us from capitalism, and what comes from the ranks of the advanced revolutionary detachments, which you might call the revolutionary vanguard of the proletariat. To talk about the role of the trade unions without taking these truths into account is to fall straight into a number of errors.

Within the system of the dictatorship of the proletariat, the trade unions stand, if I may say so, between the Party and the government. In the transition to socialism the dictatorship of the proletariat is inevitable, but it is not exercised by an organisation which takes in all industrial workers. Why not? The answer is given in the theses of the Second Congress of the Communist International on the role of political parties in general. I will not go into this here. What happens is that the Party, shall we say, absorbs the vanguard of the proletariat, and this vanguard exercises the dictatorship of the proletariat. The dictatorship cannot be exercised or the functions of government performed without a foundation such as the trade unions. These functions, however, have to be performed through the medium of special institutions which are also of a new type, namely, the Soviets. What are the practical conclusions to be drawn from this peculiar situation? They are, on the one hand, that the trade unions are a *link* between the vanguard and the masses, and by their daily work bring conviction to the masses, the masses of the class which alone is capable of taking us from capitalism to communism. On the other hand, the trade unions are a "reservoir" of the state power. This is what the trade unions are in the period of transition from capitalism to communism. In general, this transition cannot be achieved without the leadership of that class which is the only class capitalism has trained for large-scale production and which alone is divorced from the interests of the petty proprietor. But the dictatorship of the proletariat cannot be exercised through an organisation embracing the whole of that class, because in all capitalist countries (and not only over here, in one of the most backward) the proletariat is still so divided, so degraded, and so corrupted in parts (by imperialism in some countries) that an organisation taking in the whole proletariat cannot directly exercise proletarian dictatorship. It can be exercised only by a vanguard that has absorbed the revolutionary energy of the class. The whole is like an arrangement of cogwheels. Such is the basic mechanism of the dictatorship of the proletariat, and of the essentials of transition from capitalism to communism From this alone it is evident that there is something fundamentally wrong in principle when Comrade Trotsky points, in his first thesis, to "ideological confusion", and speaks of a crisis as existing specifically and particularly in the trade unions. If we are to speak of a crisis, we can do so only after analysing the political situation. It is Trotsky who is in "ideological confusion", because in this key question of the trade unions' role, from the standpoint of transition from capitalism to communism, he has lost sight of the fact that we have here a complex arrangement of cogwheels which cannot be a simple one; for the dictatorship of the proletariat cannot be exercised by a mass proletarian organisation. It cannot work without a number of "transmission belts" running from the vanguard to the mass of the advanced class, and from the latter to the mass of the working people. In Russia, this mass is a peasant one. There is no such mass anywhere else, but even in the most advanced countries there is a non-proletarian, or a not entirely proletarian, mass. That is in itself enough to produce ideological confusion. But it's no use Trotsky's pinning it on others.

When I consider the role of the trade unions in production, I find that Trotsky's basic mistake lies in his always dealing with it "in principle", as a matter of "general principle". All his theses are based on "general principle", an approach which is in itself fundamentally wrong, quite apart from the fact that the Ninth Party Congress said enough and more than enough about the trade unions' role in production,[2] and quite apart from the fact that in his own theses Trotsky quotes the perfectly clear statements of Lozovsky and Tomsky, who were to be his "whipping boys" and an excuse for an exercise in polemics. It turns out that there is, after all, no clash of principle, and the choice of Tomsky and Lozovsky, who wrote what Trotsky himself quotes, was an unfortunate one indeed. However hard we may look, we shall not find here any serious divergence of principle. In general, Comrade Trotsky's great mistake, his mistake of principle, lies in the fact that by raising the question of "principle" at this time he is dragging back the Party and the Soviet power. We have, thank heaven, done with principles and have gone on to practical business. We chatted about principles—rather more than we should have—at the Smolny. Today, three years later, we have decrees on all points of the production problem, and on many of its components; but such is the sad fate of our decrees: they are signed, and then we ourselves forget about them and fail to carry them out. Meanwhile, arguments about principles and differences of principle are invented. I shall later on quote a decree dealing with the trade unions' role in production, a decree all of us, including myself, I confess, have forgotten.

The actual differences, apart from those I have listed, really have nothing to do with general principles. I have had to enumerate my "differences" with Comrade Trotsky because, with such a broad theme as "The Role and Tasks of the Trade Unions", he has, I am quite sure, made a number of mistakes bearing on the very essence of the dictatorship of the proletariat. But, this apart, one may well ask, why is it that we cannot work together, as we so badly need to do? It is because of our different *approach* to the mass, the different way of winning it over and *keeping in touch* with it. That is the whole point. And this makes the trade union a very peculiar institution, which is set up under capitalism, which inevitably exists in the transition from capitalism to communism, and whose future is a question mark. The time when the trade unions are actually called into question is a long way off: it will be up to our grandchildren to discuss that. What matters now is how to approach the mass, to establish contact with it and win it over, and how to get the intricate transmission system working (how to run the dictatorship of the proletariat). Note that when I speak of the intricate transmission system I do not mean the machinery of the Soviets. What it may have in the way of intricacy of transmission comes under a special head. I have only been considering, in principle and in the abstract, class relations in capitalist society, which consists of a proletariat, a non-proletarian mass of working people, a petty bourgeoisie and a bourgeoisie. This alone yields an extremely complicated transmission system owing to what has been created by capitalism, quite apart from any red-tape in the Soviet administrative machinery. And that is the main point to be considered in analysing the difficulties of the trade unions' "task". Let me say this again: the actual differences do not lie where Comrade Trotsky sees them but in the question of how to approach the mass, win it over, and keep in touch with it. I must say that had we made a detailed, even if small-scale, study of our own experience and practices, we should have managed to avoid the hundreds of quite unnecessary "differences" and errors of principle in which Comrade Trotsky's pamphlet abounds. Some of his theses, for instance, polemicise against "Soviet trade-unionism". As if we hadn't enough trouble already, a new bogey has been invented. Who do you think it is? Comrade Ryazanov, of all people. I have known him for twenty odd years. You have known him less than that, but equally as well by his work. You are very well aware that assessing slogans is not one of his virtues,· which he undoubtedly has. Shall we then produce theses to show that "Soviet trade-unionism" is just something that Comrade Ryazanov happened to say with little relevance? Is that being serious? If it is, we shall end up with having "Soviet trade-unionism", "Soviet anti-peace-signing", and what not!

A Soviet "ism" could be invented on every single point.
(*Ryazanov*: "Soviet anti-Brestism.") Exactly, "Soviet anti-
Brestism".

While betraying this lack of thoughtfulness, Comrade
Trotsky falls into error himself. He seems to say that in
a workers' state it is not the business of the trade unions
to stand up for the material and spiritual interests of the
working class. That is a mistake. Comrade Trotsky speaks
of a "workers' state". May I say that this is an abstraction.
It was natural for us to write about a workers' state in
1917; but it is now a patent error to say: "Since this is a
workers' state without any bourgeoisie, against whom then
is the working class to be protected, and for what purpose?"
The whole point is that it is not quite a workers' state.
That is where Comrade Trotsky makes one of his main mistakes. We have got down from general principles to practical discussion and decrees, and here we are being dragged
back and prevented from tackling the business at hand.
This will not do. For one thing, ours is not actually a
workers' state but a workers' and peasants' state. And
a lot depends on that. (*Bukharin*: "What kind of state?
A workers' and peasants' state?") Comrade Bukharin back
there may well shout "What kind of state? A workers' and
peasants' state?" I shall not stop to answer him. Anyone
who has a mind to should recall the recent Congress of
Soviets,[3] and that will be answer enough.

But that is not all. Our Party Programme—a document
which the author of the *ABC of Communism* knows
very well—shows that ours is a workers' state *with a bureaucratic twist to it*. We have had to mark it with this dismal,
shall I say, tag. There you have the reality of the transition. Well, is it right to say that in a state that has taken
this shape in practice the trade unions have nothing to
protect, or that we can do without them in protecting the
material and spiritual interests of the massively organised
proletariat? No, this reasoning is theoretically quite wrong.
It takes us into the sphere of abstraction or an ideal we
shall achieve in 15 or 20 years' time, and I am not so sure
that we shall have achieved it even by then. What we
actually have before us is a reality of which we have a
good deal of knowledge, provided, that is, we keep our

heads, and do not let ourselves be carried away by intellectualist talk or abstract reasoning, or by what may appear to be "theory" but is in fact error and misapprehension of the peculiarities of transition. We now have a state under which it is the business of the massively organised proletariat to protect itself, while we, for our part, must use these workers' organisations to protect the workers from their state, and to get them to protect our state. Both forms of protection are achieved through the peculiar interweaving of our state measures and our agreeing or "coalescing" with our trade unions.

I shall have more to say about this coalescing later on. But the word itself shows that it is a mistake to conjure up an enemy in the shape of "Soviet trade-unionism", for "coalescing" implies the existence of *distinct* things that *have yet to be* coalesced: "coalescing" implies the need to be able to use measures of the state power to protect the material and spiritual interests of the massively organised proletariat *from* that very same state power. When the coalescing has produced *coalescence* and *integration*, we shall meet in congress for a business-like discussion of actual experience, instead of "disagreements" on principle or theoretical reasoning in the abstract. There is an equally lame attempt to find differences of principle with Comrades Tomsky and Lozovsky, whom Comrade Trotsky treats as trade union "bureaucrats"—I shall later on say which side in this controversy tends to be bureaucratic. We all know that while Comrade Ryazanov may love a slogan, and must have one which is all but an expression of principle, it is not one of Comrade Tomsky's many vices. I think, therefore, that it would be going a bit too far to challenge Comrade Tomsky to a battle of principles on this score (as Comrade Trotsky has done). I am positively astonished at this. One would have thought that we had grown up since the days when we all sinned a great deal in the way of factional, theoretical and various other disagreements— although we naturally did some good as well. It is time we stopped inventing and blowing up differences of principle and got down to practical work. I never knew that Tomsky was eminently a theoretician or that he claimed to be one; it may be one of his failings, but that is something else

again. Tomsky, who has been working very smoothly
with the trade union movement, must in his position
provide a reflection of this complex transition—whether he
should do so consciously or unconsciously is quite another
matter and I am not saying that he has always done it
consciously—so that if something is hurting the mass, and
they do not know what it is, and he does not know what it
is (*applause, laughter*) but raises a howl, I say that is not
a failing but should be put down to his credit. I am quite
sure that Tomsky has many partial theoretical mistakes.
And if we all sat down to a table and started thoughtfully
writing resolutions or theses, we should correct them all;
we might not even bother to do that because production
work is more interesting than the rectifying of minute
theoretical disagreements.

I come now to "industrial democracy", shall I say,
for Bukharin's benefit. We all know that everyone has his
weak points, that even big men have little weak spots,
and this also goes for Bukharin. He seems to be incapable
of resisting any little word with a flourish to it. He seemed
to derive an almost sensuous pleasure from writing the resolution on industrial democracy at the Central Committee
Plenum on December 7. But the closer I look at this
"industrial democracy", the more clearly I see that it is half-
baked and theoretically false. It is nothing but a hodgepodge. With this as an example, let me say once again,
at a Party meeting at least: "Comrade N. I. Bukharin, the
Republic, theory and you yourself will benefit from less
verbal extravagance." (*Applause.*) Industry is indispensable. Democracy is a category proper only to the political
sphere. There can be no objection to the use of this word
in speeches or articles. An article takes up and clearly
expresses one relationship and no more. But it is quite
strange to hear you trying to turn this into a thesis, and
to see you wanting to coin it into a slogan, uniting the
"ayes" and the "nays"; it is strange to hear you say, like
Trotsky, that the Party will have "to choose between two
trends". I shall deal separately with whether the Party
must do any "choosing" and who is to blame for putting
the Party in this position of having to "choose". Things
being what they are, we say: "At any rate, see that you

choose fewer slogans, like 'industrial democracy', which contain nothing but confusion and are theoretically wrong." Both Trotsky and Bukharin failed to think out this term theoretically and ended up in confusion. "Industrial democracy" suggests things well beyond the circle of ideas with which they were carried away. They wanted to lay greater emphasis and focus attention on industry. It is one thing to emphasise something in an article or speech; it is quite another to frame it into a thesis and ask the Party to choose, and so I say: cast your vote against it, because it is confusion. Industry is indispensable, democracy is not. Industrial democracy breeds some utterly false ideas. The idea of one-man management was advocated only a little while ago. We must not make a mess of things and confuse people: how do you expect them to know when you want democracy, when one-man management, and when dictatorship. But on no account must we renounce dictatorship either—I hear Bukharin behind me growling: "Quite right." (*Laughter. Applause.*)

But to go on. Since September we have been talking about switching from the principle of priority to that of equalisation, and we have said as much in the resolution of the all-Party conference, which was approved by the Central Committee.[4] The question is not an easy one, because we find that we have to combine equalisation with priority, which are incompatible. But after all we do have some knowledge of Marxism and have learned how and when opposites can and must be combined; and what is most important is that in the three and a half years of our revolution we have actually combined opposites again and again.

The question obviously requires thoughtfulness and circumspection. After all, we did discuss these questions of principle at those deplorable plenary meetings of the Central Committee*—which yielded the groups of seven and eight, and Comrade Bukharin's celebrated "buffer group"[6]—and we did establish that there was no easy tran-

---

*The reference is to the November and December plenary meetings of the Central Committee in 1920. For the text of their resolutions see *Pravda* No. 255 of November 13, and No. 281 of December 14, and also *Izvestia of the C.C., R.C.P.*[5] No. 26 of December 20.

sition from the priority principle to that of equalisation.
We shall have to put in a bit of effort to implement the
decision of the September Conference. After all, these opposite terms can be combined either into a cacophony or
a symphony. Priority implies preference for one industry
out of a group of vital industries because of its greater
urgency. What does such preference entail? How great can
it be? This is a difficult question, and I must say that it
will take more than zeal to solve it; it may even take more
than a heroic effort on the part of a man who is possibly
endowed with many excellent qualities and who will do
wonders on the right job; this is a very peculiar matter and
calls for the correct approach. And so if we are to raise this
question of priority and equalisation we must first of all
give it some careful thought, but that is just what we fail
to find in Comrade Trotsky's work; the further he goes in
revising his original theses, the more mistakes he makes.
Here is what we find in his latest theses:

"The equalisation line should be pursued in the sphere of *consumption*, that is, the conditions of the working people's existence as
individuals. In the sphere of *production*, the principle of priority
will long remain decisive for us"... (thesis 41, p. 31 of Trotsky's
pamphlet).

This is a real theoretical muddle. It is all wrong. Priority is preference, but it is nothing without preference
in consumption. If all the preference I get is a couple of
ounces of bread a day I am not likely to be very happy.
The preference part of priority implies preference in consumption as well. Otherwise, priority is a pipe dream,
a fleeting cloud, and we are, after all, materialists. The
workers are also materialists; if you say shock work, they
say, let's have the bread, and the clothes, and the beef.
That is the view we now take, and have always taken, in
discussing these questions time without number with
reference to various concrete matters in the Council of
Defence,[7] when one would say: "I'm doing shock work",
and would clamour for boots, and another: "I get the boots,
otherwise your shock workers won't hold out, and all your
priority will fizzle out."

We find, therefore, that in the theses the approach to
equalisation and priority is basically wrong. What is more,

it is a retreat from what has actually been achieved and tested in practice. We can't have that; it will lead to no good.

Then there is the question of "coalescing". The best thing to do about "coalescing" right now is to keep quiet. Speech is silver, but silence is golden. Why so? It is because we have got down to coalescing in practice; there is not a single large gubernia economic council, no major department of the Supreme Economic Council, the People's Commissariat for Communications, etc., where something is not being coalesced *in practice*. But are the results all they should be? Ay, there's the rub. Look at the way coalescence has *actually* been carried out, and what it has produced. There are countless decrees introducing coalescence in the various institutions. But we have yet to make a business-like study of our own practical experience; we have yet to go into the actual results of all this; we have yet to discover what a certain type of coalescence has produced in a particular industry, what happened when member X of the gubernia trade union council held post Y in the gubernia economic council, how many months he was at it, etc. What we have not failed to do is to invent a disagreement on coalescence as a principle, and make a mistake in the process, but then we have always been quick at that sort of thing; but we were not up to the mark when it came to analysing and verifying our own experience. When we have congresses of Soviets with committees not only on the application of the better-farming law in the various agricultural areas but also on coalescence and its results in the Saratov Gubernia flour-milling industry, the Petrograd metal industry, the Donbas coal industry, etc., and when these committees, having mustered the facts, declare: "We have made a study of so and so", then I shall say: "Now we have got down to business, we have finally grown up." But could anything be more erroneous and deplorable than the fact that we are being presented with "theses" splitting hairs over the principle of coalescence, after we have been at it for three years? We have taken the path of coalescence, and I am sure it was the right thing to do, but we have not yet made an adequate study of the results of our experience. That is why keeping quiet is the only common sense tactics on the question of coalescence.

A study must be made of practical experience. I have signed decrees and resolutions containing instructions on practical coalescence, and no theory is half so important as practice. That is why when I hear: "Let's discuss 'coalescence'", I say: "Let's analyse what we have done." There is no doubt that we have made many mistakes. It may well be that a great part of our decrees need amending. I accept that, for I am not in the least enamoured of decrees. But in that case let us have some practical proposals as to what actually has to be altered. That would be a business-like approach. That would not be a waste of time. That would not lead to bureaucratic projecteering. But I find that that is exactly what's wrong with Trotsky's "Practical Conclusions", Part VI of his pamphlet. He says that from one-third to one-half of the members of the All-Russia Central Council of Trade Unions and the Presidium of the Supreme Economic Council should serve on both bodies, and from one-half to two-thirds, on the collegiums, etc. Why so? No special reason, just "rule of thumb". It is true, of course, that rule of thumb is frequently used to lay down similar proportions in our decrees, but then why is it inevitable in decrees? I hold no brief for all decrees as such and have no intention of making them appear better than they actually are. Quite often rule of thumb is used in them to fix such purely arbitrary proportions as one-half or one-third of the total number of members, etc. When a decree says that, it means: try doing it this way, and later on we shall assess the results of your "tryout". We shall later sort out the results. After sorting them out, we shall move on. We are working on coalescence and we expect to improve it because we are becoming more efficient and practical-minded.

But I seem to have lapsed into "production propaganda". That can't be helped. It is a question that needs dealing with in any discussion of the role of the trade unions in production.

My next question will therefore be that of production propaganda. This again is a practical matter and we approach it accordingly. Government agencies have already been set up to conduct production propaganda. I can't tell whether they are good or bad; they have to be tested and there's no need for any "theses" on this subject at all.

If we take a general view of the part trade unions have to play in industry, we need not, in this question of democracy, go beyond the usual democratic practices. Nothing will come of such tricky phrases as "industrial democracy", for they are all wrong. That is the first point. The second is production propaganda. The agencies are there. Trotsky's theses deal with production propaganda. That is quite useless, because in this case theses are old hat. We do not know as yet whether the agencies are good or bad. But we can tell after testing them in action. Let us do some studying and polling. Assuming, let us say, that a congress has 10 committees with 10 men on each, let us ask: "You have been dealing with production propaganda, haven't you? What are the results?" Having made a study of this, we should reward those who have done especially well, and discard what has proved unsuccessful. We do have some practical experience; it may not be much but it is there; yet we are being dragged away from it and back to these "theses on principles". This looks more like a "reactionary" movement than "trade unionism".

There is then the third point, that of bonuses. Here is the role and task of the trade unions in production: distribution of bonuses *in kind*. A start on it has been made. Things have been set in motion. Five hundred thousand poods of grain had been allocated for the purpose, and one hundred and seventy thousand has been distributed. How well and how correctly, I cannot tell. The Council of People's Commissars was told that they were not making a good job of this distribution, which turned out to be an additional wage rather than a bonus. This was pointed out by officials of the trade unions and the People's Commissariat for Labour. We appointed a commission to look into the matter but that has not yet been done. One hundred and seventy thousand poods of grain has been given away, but this needs to be done in such a way as to reward those who display the heroism, the zeal, the talent, and the dedication of the thrifty manager, in a word, all the qualities that Trotsky extols. But the task now is not to extol this in theses but to provide the bread and the beef. Wouldn't it be better, for instance, to deprive one category of workers of their beef and give it as a bonus to workers designated as "shock" workers? We do not renounce that kind of priority. That is a priority we need. Let us take a closer look at our practices in the application of priority.

The fourth point is disciplinary courts. I hope Comrade Bukharin will not take offence if I say that without disciplinary courts the role of the trade unions in industry, "industrial democracy", is a mere trifle. But the fact is that there is nothing at all about this in your theses. "Great grief!" is therefore the only thing that can be said about Trotsky's theses and Bukharin's attitude, from the standpoint of principle, theory and practice.

I am confirmed in this conclusion when I say to myself: yours is not a Marxist approach to the question. This quite apart from the fact that there are a number of theoretical mistakes in the theses. It is not a Marxist approach to the evaluation of the "role and tasks of the trade unions", because such a broad subject cannot be tackled without giving thought to the peculiar political aspects of the present situation. After all, Comrade Bukharin and I did say in the resolution of the Ninth Congress of the R.C.P. on trade unions that politics is the most concentrated expression of economics.

If we analysed the current political situation, we might say that we were going through a transition period within a transition period. The whole of the dictatorship of the proletariat is a transition period, but we now have, you might say, a heap of new transition periods: the demobilisation of the army, the end of the war, the possibility of having a much longer breathing space in peace than before, and a more solid transition from the war front to the labour front. This—and this alone—is causing a change in the attitude of the proletarian class to the peasant class. What kind of change is it? Now this calls for a close examination, but nothing of the sort follows from your theses. Until we have taken this close look, we must learn to wait. The people are overweary, considerable stocks that had to be used for certain priority industries have been so used;

the proletariat's attitude to the peasantry is undergoing a change. The war weariness is terrible, and the needs have increased, but production has increased insufficiently or not at all. On the other hand, as I said in my report to the Eighth Congress of Soviets, our application of coercion was correct and successful whenever we had been able to back it up from the start with persuasion. I must say that Trotsky and Bukharin have entirely failed to take account of this very important consideration.

Have we laid a sufficiently broad and solid base of persuasion for all these new production tasks? No, indeed, we have barely started doing it. We have not yet made the masses a party to them. Now I ask you, can the masses tackle these new assignments right away? No, they cannot, because while there is now no need for special propaganda on the question of, say, whether Wrangel the landowner should be overthrown or whether any sacrifices should be spared for the purpose, we have just started to work on this question of the role of the trade unions in production, and I mean the business aspect of the matter and not the question of "principle", the reasoning about "Soviet trade-unionism" and such like trifles; we have just set up the agency for production propaganda, but we have as yet no experience. We have introduced the payment of bonuses in kind, but we lack the experience. We have set up the disciplinary courts, but we are not yet aware of the results. Still, from the political standpoint it is the preparedness of the masses that is crucial. Has the question been prepared, studied, weighed, and considered from this angle? No, far from it. And that is a basic, deep-going and dangerous political mistake, because if ever there was need to act according to the rule of measuring your cloth seven times before cutting it once, it is in this question. We find instead that the cutting has been started in earnest without a single measure having been taken. We are told that "the Party must choose between two trends", but the false slogan of "industrial democracy" was invented without a single measuring.

We must try to understand the meaning of this slogan, especially in the present political situation, when the masses are confronted with bureaucratic practices in visual form, and when we have the question itself on the agenda. Comrade Trotsky says in his theses that on the question of workers' democracy it remains for the Congress to "enter it unanimously in the record". That is not correct. There is more to it than an entry in the record; an entry in the record fixes what has been fully weighed and measured, whereas the question of industrial democracy is far from having been fully weighed, tried and tested. Just think how the masses may interpret this slogan of "industrial democracy".

"We, the rank and file who work among the masses, say that there is need for new blood, that things must be corrected and the bureaucrats ousted, and here you are beating about the bush, talking about getting on with production and displaying democracy in achieving success in production; we refuse to get on with production under such a bureaucratic set-up of central and other boards, we want a different one." You have not given the masses a chance to discuss things, to see the point, and to think it over; you have not allowed the Party to gain fresh experience but are already acting in haste, overdoing it, and producing formulas which are theoretically false. Just think how this mistake will be further amplified by unduly zealous functionaries! A political leader is responsible not only for the quality of his leadership but also for the acts of those he leads. He may now and again be unaware of what they are about, he may often wish they had not done something, but the responsibility still falls on him.

I now come to the November 9 and December 7 plenary meetings of the Central Committee, which gave expression to all these mistakes in action, rather than in logical categories, premises and theoretical reasoning. This threw the Central Committee into confusion; it is the first time this has happened in our Party's history, in time of revolution, and it is dangerous. The crux was that there was a division, there was the "buffer" group of Bukharin, Preobrazhensky and Serebryakov, which did the most harm and created the most confusion.

You will recall the story of Glavpolitput[8] and Tsektran.[9] The resolution of the Ninth Congress of the R.C.P. in April 1920 said that Glavpolitput was being set up as a "temporary" institution, and that conditions should be brought back to normal *"as soon as possible"*. In September you read, "Return to normal conditions".* The plenary meeting was held in November (November 9), and Trotsky came up with his theses and ideas about trade-unionism. However fine some of his points about production propaganda may be, he should have been told that all this was neither here nor there, quite beside the mark, and a step backward; it is something the C.C. should not be dealing with at present. Bukharin says: "It is very good." It may be very good, but that is no answer to the question. After a heated debate, a resolution is adopted by 10 to 4 saying in a polite and comradely way that Tsektran has itself "already got down to . . . strengthening and developing methods of proletarian democracy within the union". It adds that Tsektran must "take an active part in the general work of the All-Russia Central Council of Trade Unions, being incorporated in it on an equal footing with other trade union bodies".

What is the gist of the Central Committee's decision? It is obviously this: "Comrades of Tsektran! You must do more than go through the motions of carrying out Congress and C.C. decisions, you must actually do so to help all trade unions by your work, wipe out every trace of red-tape, favouritism, arrogance, the we-are-better-than-you attitude, and boasts of being richer and getting more aid."

We then get down to brass tacks. A commission is set up, and the names of its members are published. Trotsky walks out, refuses to serve on the commission, and disrupts its work. What are his reasons? There is only one. Lutovinov is apt to play at opposition. That is true, and that also goes for Osinsky. Frankly speaking, it is not a pleasant

* See *Izvestia of the C.C.*, *R.C.P.* No. 26, p. 2, the Resolution of the September Plenum of the C.C., Paragraph 3, which said: "The C.C. further believes that there has been a great improvement in the grave situation in the transport workers' unions, which produced Glavpolitput. and Politvod,[10] as temporary levers for assisting and organising the work. Therefore, incorporation of these organisations in the union, as union agencies being adapted to and absorbed by the union apparatus, can and must now proceed."

game. But do you call that a reason? Osinsky was making
an excellent job of the seed campaign. The thing to do was
to work with him, in spite of his "opposition campaign",
for this business of disrupting the work of a commission
is bureaucratic, un-Soviet, un-socialist, incorrect and
politically harmful. Such methods are doubly incorrect
and politically harmful at a time when there is need to
separate the wheat from the chaff within the "opposition".
When Osinsky conducts an "opposition campaign", I tell
him: "This is a harmful campaign", but it is a pleasure
to see him conduct the seed campaign. I shall not deny
that, like Ishchenko and Shlyapnikov, Lutovinov is making
a mistake in his "opposition campaign", but that is no reason
to disrupt the work of a commission.

What did the commission in fact signify? It signified
transition to practical work from intellectualist talk
about sterile disagreements. What the commission was due
to discuss and deal with was production propaganda,
bonuses, and disciplinary courts. It was then that Comrade
Bukharin, the head of the "buffer group", together with
Preobrazhensky and Serebryakov, seeing the Central Committee dangerously divided, set out to create a buffer, one
that I find difficult to describe in parliamentary terms.
If I could draw cartoons as well as Comrade Bukharin
does, I would depict him as a man pouring a bucket of
kerosene on the flames, and give the following caption:
"Buffer kerosene". Comrade Bukharin wanted to create
something, and his intentions were no doubt most sincere
and entirely in the "buffer" spirit. But the buffer failed to
materialise; the upshot was that he failed to take account
of the political situation and, what is more, made some
theoretical mistakes.

Should all such disputes have been brought up for broad
discussion? Was it worth going into these trifles? Was
it worth wasting the few precious weeks before a Party
congress? We could have used the time to analyse and study
the question of bonuses, disciplinary courts and coalescence.
Those are the questions we could have given a practical
solution to in the C.C. commission. If Comrade Bukharin
wished to create a buffer, instead of giving a display of
barking up the wrong tree, he should have demanded and

insisted that Comrade Trotsky remained on the commission. If he had said and done that, we should have been on the right track, with the commission looking into the practical aspects of such things as one-man management, democracy, appointees, etc.

But to go on. By December (the December 7 Plenary Meeting), we were already faced with this flare-up of the watermen, which intensified the conflict, and as a result there were now eight votes in the Central Committee to our seven. Comrade Bukharin, in an effort to bring about a "reconciliation" through the use of his "buffer", hastily wrote the "theoretical" part of the December plenum's resolution, but with the commission a shambles, nothing, of course, could come of it.

Where did Glavpolitput and Tsektran err? Certainly not in their use of coercion; that goes to their credit. Their mistake was that they failed to switch to normal trade union work at the right time and without conflict, as the Ninth Congress of the R.C.P. required; they failed to adapt themselves to the trade unions and help them by meeting them on an equal footing. Heroism, zeal, etc., are the positive side of military experience; red-tape and arrogance are the negative side of the experience of the worst military types. Trotsky's theses, whatever his intentions, do not tend to play up the best, but the worst in military experience. It must be borne in mind that a political leader is responsible not only for his own policy but also for the acts of those he leads.

The last thing I want to tell you about—something I called myself a fool for yesterday—is that I had altogether overlooked Comrade Rudzutak's theses. His weak point is that he does not speak in ringing tones; he is not an impressive or eloquent speaker. He is liable to be overlooked. Unable to attend the meetings yesterday, I went through my material and found a printed leaflet issued for the Fifth All-Russia Trade Union Conference, which was held from November 2 to 6, 1920.[11] It is called: *The Tasks of the Trade Unions in Production.* Let me read it to you, it is not long.

FIFTH ALL-RUSSIA TRADE UNION CONFERENCE

The tasks of the trade unions in production

(THESES OF COMRADE RUDZUTAK'S REPORT)

1. Immediately after the October Revolution, the trade unions proved to be *almost the only* bodies which, while exercising workers' *control*, were able and bound to undertake the work of organising and *managing production*. In that early period of the Soviet power, no state apparatus for the management of the national economy had yet been set up, while sabotage on the part of factory owners and senior technicians brought the working class squarely up against the task of safeguarding industry and getting the whole of the country's economic apparatus back into normal running order.

2. In the subsequent period of the Supreme Economic Council's work, when a considerable part of it consisted in liquidating private enterprises and organising state management to run them, *the trade unions carried on this work jointly and side by side with the state* economic management *agencies*.

This *parallel set-up* was explained and justified by the weakness of the state agencies; historically it was vindicated by the establishment of full contact between the trade unions and the economic management agencies.

3. *The centre of gravity in the management of industry* and the drafting of a production programme *shifted to these agencies* as a result of their administration, the gradual spread of their control over production and management and the co-ordination of the several parts. In view of this, the work of the trade unions in organising production was reduced to *participation in forming the collegiums* of chief administrations, central boards, and factory managements.

4. At the present time, we are once again squarely faced with the question of establishing the closest possible ties between the economic agencies of the Soviet Republic and the trade unions, for the best use must be made of every working individual, and the whole mass of producers must be induced to take a conscious part in production, for the state apparatus of economic management, gradually gaining in size and complexity, has been transformed into a huge bureaucratic machine which is out of all proportion to the scale of industry, and is inevitably impelling the trade unions to take direct part in organising production not only through its men in the economic agencies but also as an organised whole.

5. While the Supreme Economic Council's point of departure in drawing up an overall production programme is *the availability of the material elements of production* (raw materials, fuel, the state of machinery, etc.), the trade unions must look at it *from the standpoint of organising labour* for the tasks of production and its best use. Therefore, the overall *production programme, in whole and in part, must be drawn up with the participation of the trade unions* in order to combine the use of the material resources of production and manpower in the best possible way.

6. Only if the whole mass of those engaged in production *consciously take a hand* in establishing real labour discipline, fighting deserters from the labour front, etc., can these tasks be fulfilled. *Bureaucratic methods and orders* will not do; it must be brought home to each participant in production that his production tasks are appropriate and important; that each must take a hand not only in fulfilling his assignments, but also play an intelligent part in correcting any technical and organisational defects in the sphere of production.

The tasks of the trade unions in this sphere are tremendous. They must teach *their members in each shop* and in each factory to *react to and take account of all defects in the use of manpower arising from improper handling* of technical means or unsatisfactory management. *The sum total of the experience gained by separate* enterprises and industry as a whole must be used to combat red-tape, bureaucratic practices and carelessness.

7. In order to lay special emphasis on the importance of these production tasks, they must be organisationally worked into current operations. As the *economic departments* of the trade unions, which are being set up in pursuance of the decision of the Third All-Russia Congress, extend their activity, they must gradually explain and define the nature of all trade union work. Thus, in the present social conditions, when all of production is geared to the satisfaction of the working people's needs, *wage rates and bonuses must be closely tied in with and must depend on the extent to which the production plan is fulfilled.* Bonuses in kind and partial payment of wages in kind must be gradually transformed into a *system of workers' supply* which depends on the level of labour productivity.

8. Trade union work on these lines would, on the one hand, put an end to the existence of *parallel bodies (political departments, etc.)* and, on the other, restore the close ties between the masses and the economic management agencies.

9. After the Third Congress, the trade unions largely failed to carry out their programme for participation in economic construction, owing, first, to the *military conditions*, and second, to their *organisational weakness* and isolation from the administrative and practical work of the economic bodies.

10. In view of this, the trade unions should set themselves the following immediate practical tasks: a) the most active participation in solving production and management problems; b) direct participation, with the respective economic agencies, *in setting up competent* administrative bodies; c) careful consideration of the various *types of management bodies*, and their influence on production; d) unfailing participation in working out and laying down economic *plans* and production programmes; e) *organisation of labour* in accordance with the economic priorities; f) development of an extensive organisation for production *agitation and propaganda*.

11. The economic departments of the *trade unions* and of their organisations must be actually transformed into powerful and expeditious levers for the trade unions' systematic participation in organising production.

12. In the matter of providing workers with steady material supplies, the trade unions must shift their *influence onto the distributive bodies of the Commissariat for Food*, both local and central, taking a practical and business-like part and exercising *control* in all the distributive bodies, and paying special attention to the activity of central and gubernia *workers' supply commissions*.

13. In view of the fact that the narrow departmental interests of some chief administrations, central boards, etc., have plunged the so-called "priority" into a state of utter confusion, the trade unions must everywhere uphold the real order of economic priorities and review the existing system so as to determine them in accordance with the actual importance of the various industries and the availability of material resources in the country.

14. Special attention must be given to the so-called model group of factories to help them set an example through the organisation of efficient management, labour discipline and trade union activities.

15. In labour organisation, apart from the introduction of a harmonious wage-rate system and the overhaul of output rates, the trade unions should take a firm hand in fighting the various *forms of labour desertion* (absenteeism, lateness, etc.). The disciplinary courts, which have not received due attention until now, must be turned into a real means of combating breaches of proletarian labour discipline.

16. The economic departments must be entrusted with the fulfilment of these tasks and also the drafting of a practical plan for production propaganda and a number of measures to improve the economic condition of the workers. It is necessary, therefore, to authorise the economic department of the All-Russia Central Council of Trade Unions to call a special *All-Russia Conference of Economic Departments* in the near future to discuss the practical problems of economic construction in connection with the work of state economic agencies.

I hope you see now why I called myself names. There you have a platform, and it is very much better than the one Comrade Trotsky wrote after a great deal of thinking, and the one Comrade Bukharin wrote (the December 7 Plenum resolution) without any thinking at all. All of us members of the Central Committee who have been out of touch with the trade union movement for many years would profit from Comrade Rudzutak's experience, and this also goes for Comrade Trotsky and Comrade Bukharin. The trade unions have adopted this platform.

We all entirely forgot about the disciplinary courts, but "industrial democracy", without bonuses in kind or disciplinary courts, is nothing but empty talk,

I make a comparison between Rudzutak's theses and those submitted by Trotsky to the Central Committee. At the end of thesis 5, I read:

"... a reorganisation of the unions must be started right away, that is, a selection of functionaries must be above all made from precisely that angle"....

There you have an example of the real bureaucratic approach: Trotsky and Krestinsky selecting the trade union "functionaries"!

Let me say this once again: here you have an explanation of Tsektran's mistake. It was not wrong to use pressure; that goes to its credit. It made the mistake of failing to cope with the general tasks of all the trade unions, of failing to act itself and to help all the trade unions to employ the disciplinary comrades' courts more correctly, swiftly and successfully. When I read about the disciplinary courts in Comrade Rudzutak's theses it occurred to me that there might be a decree on this matter. And in fact there was. It is the *Regulations* Governing Workers' Disciplinary Comrades' Courts, issued on November 14, 1919 (*Collection of Statutes* No. 537).

The trade unions have the key role in these courts. I don't know how good these courts are, how well they function, and whether they always function. A study of our own practical experience would be a great deal more useful than anything Comrades Trotsky and Bukharin have written.

Let me end by summing up everything there is on the question. I must say that it was a great mistake to put up these disagreements for broad Party discussion and the Party Congress. It was a political mistake. We should have had a business-like discussion in the commission, and only there, and would have in that case moved forward; as it is we are sliding back, and shall keep sliding back to abstract theoretical propositions for several weeks, instead of dealing with the problem in a business-like manner. Personally, I am sick and tired of it, and quite apart from my illness, it would give me great pleasure to get away from it all. I am prepared to seek refuge anywhere.

The net result is that there are a number of theoretical

mistakes in Trotsky's and Bukharin's theses: they contain a number of things that are wrong in principle. Politically, the whole approach to the matter is utterly tactless. Comrade Trotsky's "theses" are politically harmful. The sum and substance of his policy is bureaucratic harassment of the trade unions. Our Party Congress will, I am sure, condemn and reject it. (*Prolonged, stormy applause.*)

Published in pamphlet form
in 1921

Published according to the pamphlet text collated with the verbatim report edited by Lenin

THE PARTY CRISIS

The pre-Congress discussion is in full swing. Minor differences and disagreements have grown into big ones, which always happens when someone persists in a minor mistake and balks at its correction, or when those who are making a big mistake seize on the minor mistake of one or more persons.

That is how disagreements and splits always grow. That is how we "grew up" from minor disagreements to syndicalism, which means a complete break with communism and an inevitable split in the Party if it is not healthy and strong enough to purge itself of the malaise.

We must have the courage to face the bitter truth. The Party is sick. The Party is down with the fever. The whole point is whether the malaise has affected only the "feverish upper ranks", and perhaps only those in Moscow, or the whole organism. And if the latter is the case, is it capable of healing itself completely within the next few weeks, before the Party Congress and at the Party Congress, making a relapse impossible, or will the malaise linger and become dangerous?

What is it that needs to be done for a rapid and certain cure? *All* members of the Party must make a calm and painstaking *study* of 1) the essence of the disagreements and 2) the development of the Party struggle. A study must be made of both, because the essence of the disagreements is revealed, clarified and specified (and very often transformed as well) in the *course of the struggle*, which, passing through its various stages, always shows, at every stage, a *different* line-up and number of combatants, *different* positions in the struggle, etc. A *study* must be made of both, and a demand made for the most exact, printed documents that can be thoroughly verified. Only a hopeless idiot will believe oral statements. If *no* documents are available, there must be an examination of witnesses on *both* or several sides and the grilling must take place in the presence of witnesses.

Let me outline the essence of the disagreements and the successive stages in the struggle, as I see them.

Stage one. The Fifth All-Russia Trade Union Conference, November 2-6. The battle is joined. Trotsky and Tomsky are the only Central Committee "combatants". Trotsky lets drop a "catchy phrase" about "shaking up" the trade unions. Tomsky argues very heatedly. The majority of the Central Committee members are on the fence. The serious mistake they (and I above all) made was that we "overlooked" Rudzutak's theses, *The Tasks of the Trade Unions in Production*, adopted by the Fifth Conference. That is the *most* important document in the *whole* of the controversy.

Stage two. The Central Committee Plenum of November 9. Trotsky submits his "draft theses", *The Trade Unions and Their Future Role*, advocating the "shake-up" policy, *camouflaged* or adorned with talk of a "severe crisis" gripping the trade unions, and their new tasks and methods. Tomsky, strongly supported by Lenin, considers that in view of Tsektran's irregularities and bureaucratic excesses it is the "shake-up" that is the crux of the whole controversy. In the course of it, Lenin makes a number of obviously exaggerated and therefore mistaken "attacks", which produces the need for a "buffer group", and this is made up of ten members of the Central Committee (the group includes Bukharin and Zinoviev, but neither Trotsky nor Lenin). It resolves "not to put the disagreements up for broad discussion", and, *cancelling Lenin's report* (to the trade unions), appoints Zinoviev as the rapporteur and instructs him to "present a business-like and non-controversial report".

Trotsky's theses are rejected. Lenin's theses are adopted. In its final form, the resolution is adopted by ten votes to four (Trotsky, Andreyev, Krestinsky and Rykov). And this resolution advocates "sound forms of the militarisation of labour", condemns "the degeneration of centralism and militarised forms of work into bureaucratic practices, petty tyranny, red-tape", etc. Tsektran is instructed to "take a more active part in the general work of the All-Russia Central Council of Trade Unions, being incorporated in it on an equal footing with other trade union bodies".

The Central Committee sets up a trade union commission and elects Comrade Trotsky to it. He refuses to work on the commission, magnifying by this step *alone* his original mistake, which subsequently leads to factionalism. Without that step, his mistake (in submitting incorrect theses) remained a very minor one, such as every member of the Central Committee, without exception, has had occasion to make.

Stage three. The conflict between the water transport workers and Tsektran in December. The Central Committee Plenary Meeting of December 7. It is no longer Trotsky and Lenin, but Trotsky and Zinoviev who are the chief "combatants". As chairman of the trade union commission, Zinoviev inquires into the December dispute between the water transport workers and Tsektran. The Central Committee Plenary Meeting of December 7. Zinoviev makes a practical proposal for an immediate change in the composition of Tsektran. This is opposed by a majority of the Central Committee. Rykov goes over to Zinoviev's side. Bukharin's resolution—the substantive part of which is three-quarters in favour of the water transport workers, while the preamble, rejecting the proposal to "reconstruct" the trade unions "from above" (§ 3), approves of the celebrated "industrial democracy" (§ 5)—is adopted. Our group of Central Committee members is in the minority, being opposed to Bukharin's resolution chiefly because we consider the "buffer" a paper one; for Trotsky's non-participation in the trade union commission's work actually implies a continuation of the struggle and its transfer outside the Central Committee. We propose that the Party Congress be convened on February 6, 1921. That is adopted. The postponement to March 6 was agreed to later, on the demand of the outlying areas.

Stage four. The Eighth Congress of Soviets. On December 25, Trotsky issues his "platform pamphlet", *The Role and Tasks of the Trade Unions.* From the standpoint of formal democracy, Trotsky had an uncontested right to issue his platform, for on December 24 the Central Committee had permitted free discussion. From the standpoint of revolutionary interest, this was blowing up the mistake out of all proportion and *creating a faction* on a faulty platform. The pamphlet quotes from the Central Committee resolution of December 7 only that part which refers to "industrial democracy" but does *not* quote what was said against "reconstruction from above". The buffer created by Bukharin on December 7 with Trotsky's aid was wrecked by Trotsky on December 25. The pamphlet from beginning to end is shot through with the "shake-up" spirit. Apart from its intellectualist flourishes ("production atmosphere", "industrial democracy"), which are wrong in theory and in practice fall within the concept, ambit and tasks of production propaganda, it *fails* to indicate any "new" "tasks or methods" that were to gild or camouflage or justify the "shake-up".

Stage five. The discussion before thousands of responsible Party workers from all over Russia at the R.C.P. group of the Eighth Congress of Soviets on December 30. The controversy flares up to full blast. Zinoviev and Lenin on one side, Trotsky and Bukharin on the other. Bukharin wants to play the "buffer", but speaks only against Lenin and Zinoviev, and not a word against Trotsky. Bukharin reads out an excerpt from his theses (published on January 16), but *only* that part which says nothing about the rupture with communism and the switch to syndicalism. Shlyapnikov (on behalf of the Workers' Opposition[12]) reads out the syndicalist platform, which Trotsky had demolished beforehand (thesis 16 of his platform) and which (partly, perhaps, for that reason) no one is inclined to take seriously.

In my opinion, the climax of the whole discussion of December 30 was the reading of Comrade Rudzutak's theses. Indeed, Comrades Trotsky and Bukharin, far from being able to object to them, even invented the legend that the "best part" of the theses had been drawn up by *members of Tsektran*—Holtzmann, Andreyev and Lyubimov. And that is why Trotsky humorously and amiably twitted Lenin on his unsuccessful "diplomacy", by which, he said, Lenin had wanted to "call off or disrupt" the discussion, and find a "lightning conductor", "accidentally catching hold of Tsektran instead of the lightning conductor".

The legend was exploded that very day, December 30, by Rudzutak, who pointed out that Lyubimov "did not exist" on the All-Russia Central Council of Trade Unions, that in its presidium Holtzmann had voted against these theses, and that they had been drawn up by a commission consisting of Andreyev, Tsiperovich and himself.[13]

But let us for a moment assume that Comrades Trotsky and Bukharin's legend is true. Nothing so completely defeats them as such an assumption. For what is the conclusion if the "Tsektranites" had inserted their "new" ideas into Rudzutak's resolution, if Rudzutak had accepted them, if all the trade unions had adopted this resolution (November 2-6!), and if Bukharin and Trotsky have nothing to say against it?

It is that all of Trotsky's disagreements are artificial, that *neither* he *nor* the "Tsektranites" *have any* "new tasks or methods", and that everything practical and substantive had been said, adopted and *decided upon* by the trade unions, *even before the question was raised in the Central Committee.*

If anyone ought to be taken thoroughly to task and "shaken up", it is not the All-Russia Central Council of Trade Unions but the Central Committee of the R.C.P., for having "overlooked" Rudzutak's theses, a mistake which allowed an altogether empty discussion to flare up. There is nothing to *cover up* the mistake of the Tsektranites (which is not an excessive one but is, in essence, a very common one, consisting in some exaggeration of bureaucracy). What is more, it needs to be rectified, and not covered up, toned down or justified. That's all there is to it.

I summed up the substance of Rudzutak's theses on December 30 in four points: 1) Ordinary democracy (without any exaggerations, without denying the Central Committee's right of "appointment", etc., but also without any obstinate defence of the mistakes and excesses of certain "appointees", which need to be rectified); 2) Production propaganda (this includes all that is practical in clumsy, ridiculous, theoretically wrong "formulas" like "industrial democracy", "production atmosphere", etc.). We have

established a *Soviet institution*, the All-Russia Production
Propaganda Bureau. We must do everything to support it
and not spoil production work by *producing . . . bad theses*.
That's all there is to it; 3) Bonuses in kind and 4) Disciplinary comrades' courts. Without Points 3 and 4, all talk
about "the role and tasks in production", etc., is empty,
highbrow chatter; and it is these two points that are omitted
from Trotsky's "platform pamphlet". But they are in
Rudzutak's theses.

While dealing with the December 30 discussion, I must
correct another mistake of mine. I said: "Ours is not actually
a workers' state but a workers' and peasants' state."
Comrade Bukharin immediately exclaimed: "What kind of
a state?" In reply I referred him to the Eighth Congress of
Soviets, which had just closed. I went back to the report
of that discussion and found that I was wrong and Comrade
Bukharin was right. What I should have said is: "A workers'
state is an abstraction. What we actually have is a workers'
state, with this peculiarity, firstly, that it is not the working
class but the peasant population that predominates in the
country, and, secondly, that it is a workers' state with
bureaucratic distortions." Anyone who reads the whole
of my speech will see that this correction makes no
difference to my reasoning or conclusions.

Stage six. The Petrograd organisation issues an "Appeal
to the Party" against Trotsky's platform, and the Moscow Committee issues a counter-statement (*Pravda*,
January 13[14]).

This is a transition from the struggle between factions,
formed from above, to the intervention of lower organisations.
It is a big step towards recovery. Curiously enough, the
Moscow Committee noticed the "dangerous" side of the
Petrograd organisation's issuing a platform, but refused to
notice the *dangerous side* of Comrade Trotsky's forming a
faction on December 25! Some wags have said this is "buffer"
(one-eyed) blindness.

Stage seven. The trade union commission concludes its
work and issues a platform (a pamphlet, entitled *Draft
Decision of the Tenth Congress of the R.C.P. on the Role
and Tasks of the Trade Unions*,[15] dated January 14 and
signed by nine members of the Central Committee—

Zinoviev, Stalin, Tomsky, Rudzutak, Kalinin, Kamenev, Petrovsky, Artyom and Lenin, and also by Lozovsky, a member of the trade union commission; Comrades Shlyapnikov and Lutovinov seem to have "fled" to the Workers' Opposition). It was published in *Pravda* on January 18, with the following additional signatures: Schmidt, Tsiperovich and Milyutin.

On January 16, *Pravda* carries the Bukharin platform (signed: "On behalf of a group of comrades, Bukharin, Larin, Preobrazhensky, Serebryakov, Sokolnikov, Yakovleva") and the Sapronov platform (signed: "A group of comrades standing for democratic centralism", Bubnov, Boguslavsky, Kamensky, Maximovsky, Osinsky, Rafail, Sapronov).[16] The enlarged meeting of the Moscow Committee on January 17 was addressed by spokesmen for these platforms, and also by the "Ignatovites"[17] (theses published in *Pravda* on January 19 and signed by Ignatov, Orekhov, Korzinov, Kuranova, Burovtsev, Maslov).*

What we find here is, on the one hand, increased solidarity (for the platform of the nine Central Committee members is in complete accord with the decision of the Fifth All-Russia Conference of Trade Unions); and, on the other, confusion and disintegration, with Bukharin and Co.'s theses being an all-time low in *ideological* disintegration. We have here one of those "turns" which in the old days Marxists used to call "not so much historical as hysterical". Thesis 17 says: "At the present time, these nominations must be made *mandatory*" (that is, the trade unions' nominations to the respective "chief administrations and central boards").

This is a clean break with communism and a transition to syndicalism. It is, in essence, a repetition of Shlyapnikov's "unionise the state" slogan, and means transferring the Supreme Economic Council apparatus

---

* Incidentally, the Party should demand that every "platform" be issued with the full signatures of all the comrades responsible for it. This demand is met by the "Ignatovites" and the "Sapronovites" but not by the "Trotskyites", the "Bukharinites" and the "Shlyapnikovites", who refer to anonymous comrades allegedly responsible for their platforms.

piecemeal to the respective trade unions. To say, "I propose *mandatory* nominations", is exactly the same as
saying, "I appoint".

Communism says: The Communist Party, the vanguard
of the proletariat, leads the non-Party workers' masses,
educating, preparing, teaching and training the masses
("school" of communism)—first the workers and then the
peasants—to enable them eventually to concentrate in their
hands the administration of the whole national economy.

Syndicalism hands over to the mass of non-Party workers, who are compartmentalised in the industries, the
management of their industries ("the chief administrations
and central boards"), thereby making the Party superfluous,
and failing to carry on a sustained campaign either in
training the masses or in *actually* concentrating in *their*
hands the management *of the whole national economy*.

The Programme of the R.C.P. says: "The trade unions *should
eventually arrive*" (which means that they are not yet there or
even on the way) "at a *de facto* concentration in their hands"
(in *their*, that is, the hands of the trade unions, that is,
the hands of the fully organised *masses*; anyone will see
how far we have still to go even to the very first approaches
to this *de. facto* concentration) . . . concentration of what?
"of the whole administration of the whole national economy,
as a single economic entity" (hence, not branches of industry,
or even industry as a whole, but industry *plus* agriculture,
etc. Are we anywhere near to actually concentrating the
management of agriculture in the hands of the trade unions?).
The R.C.P. Programme then speaks of the "ties" between
the "central state administration" and the "broad masses
of toilers", and of the "*participation* of the trade unions
in running the economy".

Why have a Party, if industrial management is to be
appointed ("mandatory nomination") by the trade unions
nine-tenths of whose members are non-Party workers?
Bukharin has talked himself into a logical, theoretical and
practical implication of a split in the Party, or, rather, a
breakaway of the syndicalists from the Party.

Trotsky, who had been "chief" in the struggle, has now
been "outstripped" and entirely "eclipsed" by Bukharin,
who has thrown the struggle into an altogether new balance

by talking himself into a mistake that is much more
serious than all of Trotsky's put together.

How could Bukharin talk himself into a break with
communism? We know how soft Comrade Bukharin is; it
is one of the qualities which endears him to people, who
cannot help liking him. We know that he has been ribbed
for being as "soft as wax". It turns out that any "unprincipled" person, any "demagogue" can leave any mark he
likes on this "soft wax". The sharp words in quotation
marks were used by Comrade Kamenev, during the January
17 discussion, and he had a perfect right to do so. But, of
course, neither Kamenev nor anyone else would dream of
attributing or reducing it all to unprincipled *demagogy*.

On the contrary, there is an objective logic in factional
struggles which inevitably leads even the best of men—if
they persist in their mistaken attitude—into a state which
differs little if at all from unprincipled demagogy. That
is the lesson of the entire history of factional wars (for
example, the alliance of the Vperyodists and the Mensheviks
against the Bolsheviks[18]). That is why we must make a
study not only of the nature of the disagreements in the
abstract, but also of their concrete development and change
at the various stages of the struggle. This development
was summed up in the January 17 discussion.[19] Neither
the "shake-up" nor the "new production tasks" can any
longer be advocated (because all the efficient and sensible
ideas went into Rudzutak's theses). The alternative then
is to find what Lassalle called "the physical strength of
mind" (and character) to admit the mistake, rectify it and
turn over this page of the history of the R.C.P., or—to
cling to the remaining allies, no matter who they are, and
"ignore" the principles altogether. There remain only the
adherents of "democracy" *ad nauseam*. And Bukharin is
sliding down towards them and syndicalism.

While we are slowly absorbing what was sound in the
"democratic" Workers' Opposition, Bukharin has to cling
to what is *unsound*. On January 17, Comrade Bumazhny,
a prominent Tsektranite, or Trotskyite, expressed his
readiness to accept Bukharin's syndicalist proposals. The
"Sapronovites" have gone so far as to insist in the same
thesis (3) on a "profound crisis." and a "bureaucratic necrosis"

of the trade unions, while proposing, as being "absolutely" necessary, the "extension of the trade unions' *rights* in production" . . . probably because of their "bureaucratic necrosis"? Can this group be taken seriously? They had heard the talk about the *role* of the trade unions in production, and wishing to outshout the others, blurted out: "extension of rights" on the occasion of "bureaucratic necrosis". You need read no more than the first few lines of their "practical" proposals: "The presidium of the Supreme Economic Council shall be nominated by the All-Russia Central Council of Trade Unions and confirmed by the All-Russia Central Executive Committee." And what is their *democratic* position in "principle"? Listen to this (thesis 2): "They [Zinoviev and Trotsky]* in fact express two trends within the same group of *ex-militarisers of the economy.*"

Taken seriously, this is Menshevism and Socialist-Revolutionarism at their worst. But Sapronov, Osinsky and Co. should not be taken seriously, when, before every Party congress ("every blessed time on this very same spot"), these, I believe, superlative workers have a sort of paroxysmal seizure and try to outshout the others (the "champion shouter" faction) and solemnly make a hash of things. The "Ignatovites" try to keep up with the "Sapronovites". It is, of course, quite permissible (specially before a congress) for various groups to form blocs (and also to go vote chasing). But this should be done within the framework of communism (and not syndicalism) and in such a way as to avoid being ridiculous. Who is the highest bidder? Promisers of more "rights" to non-Party people, unite on the occasion of the congress of the Russian Communist Party! . . .

Our platform up to now has been: Do not defend but rectify the bureaucratic excesses. The fight against bureaucracy is a long and arduous one. Excesses can and must be rectified at once. It is not those who point out harmful excesses and strive to rectify them but those who resist rectification that undermine the prestige of the military workers and appointees. Such were the excesses of certain

---

* Interpolations in square brackets (within passages quoted by Lenin) have been introduced by Lenin, unless otherwise indicated.— *Ed.*

Tsektranites who, however, will continue to be (and have been) valuable workers. There is no need to harass the trade unions by inventing disagreements with them, when they themselves have decided upon and accepted all that is new, business-like and practical in the tasks of the trade unions in production. On this basis, let us vigorously work together for practical results.

We have now added to our platform the following: We must combat the ideological discord and the *unsound* elements of the opposition who talk themselves into repudiating all "militarisation of industry", and not only the "appointments method", which has been the prevailing one up to now, but all "appointments", that is, in the last analysis, repudiating the *Party*'s leading role in relation to the non-Party masses. We must combat the syndicalist deviation, which will kill the Party unless it is entirely cured of it.

The Entente* capitalists will surely try to take advantage of our Party's malaise to mount another invasion, and the Socialist-Revolutionaries, to hatch plots and rebellions. We need have no fear of this because we shall all unite as one man, without being afraid to admit the malaise, but recognising that it demands from all of us a greater discipline, tenacity and firmness at every post. By the time the Tenth Congress of the R.C.P. meets in March, and after the Congress, the Party will not be weaker, but stronger.

January 19, 1921

Pravda No. 13, January 21, 1921
     Signed: *N. Lenin*

Published according to
the *Pravda* text
collated with the text
of the pamphlet: N. Lenin,
Party Crisis, 1921

---

* *Entente* or the "Allies" —Britain, France, the U.S.A., Japan and other countries that took part in the intervention against Soviet Russia. It should not be confused with *Entente cordiale*, the alliance of France and Great Britain and, later, tsarist Russia.—*Tr.*

THE SECOND ALL-RUSSIA CONGRESS OF MINERS[20]

1

REPORT ON THE ROLE AND TASKS OF THE TRADE UNIONS DELIVERED ON JANUARY 23 AT A MEETING OF THE COMMUNIST GROUP OF THE CONGRESS

The morbid character of the question of the role and tasks of the trade unions is due to the fact that it took the form of a factional struggle much too soon. This vast, boundless question should not have been taken up in such haste, as it was done here, and I put the chief blame on Comrade Trotsky for all this fumbling haste and precipitation. All of us have had occasion to submit inadequately prepared theses to the Central Committee and this is bound to go on because all our work is being done in a rush. This is not a big mistake, for all of us have had to act in haste. Taken by itself, it is a common mistake and is unavoidable because of the extremely difficult objective conditions. All the more reason, therefore, to treat factional, controversial issues with the utmost caution; for in such matters even not very hot-headed persons—something, I'm afraid, I cannot say about my opponent—may all too easily fall into this error. To illustrate my point, and to proceed at once to the heart of the matter, let me read you the chief of Trotsky's theses.

In his pamphlet, towards the end of thesis No. 12, he writes:

"We observe the fact that as economic tasks move into the foreground, many trade unionists take an ever more aggressive and uncompromising stand against the prospect of 'coalescence' and the practical conclusions that follow from it. Among them we find Comrades Tomsky and Lozovsky.

"What is more, many trade unionists, balking at the new tasks and methods, tend to cultivate in their midst a spirit of corporative exclusiveness and hostility for the new men who are being drawn into the given branch of the economy, thereby actually fostering the survivals of craft-unionism among the organised workers."

I could quote many similar passages from Trotsky's pamphlet. I ask, by way of factional statement: Is it becoming for such an influential person, such a prominent leader, to attack his Party comrades in this way? I am sure that 99 per cent of the comrades, excepting those involved in the quarrel, will say that this should not be done.

I could well understand such a statement if Comrades Tomsky and Lozovsky were guilty, or could be suspected of being guilty, of, say, having flatly refused to sign the Brest Peace Treaty, or of having flatly opposed the war. The revolutionary interest is higher than formal democracy. But it is fundamentally wrong to approach the subject in such haste at the present moment. It won't do at all. This point says that many trade unionists tend to cultivate in their midst a spirit of hostility and exclusiveness. What does that mean? What sort of talk is this? Is it the right kind of language? Is it the right approach? I had earlier said that I might succeed in acting as a "buffer" and staying out of the discussion, because it is harmful to fight with Trotsky—it does the Republic, the Party, and all of us a lot of harm—but when this pamphlet came out, I felt I had to speak up.

Trotsky writes that "many trade unionists tend to cultivate a spirit of hostility for the new men". How so? If that is true, those who are doing so should be named. Since this is not done, it is merely a shake-up, a bureaucratic approach to the business. Even if there is a spirit of hostility for the new men, one should not say a thing like that. Trotsky accuses Lozovsky and Tomsky of bureaucratic practices. I would say the reverse is true. It is no use reading any further because the approach has spoiled everything; he has poured a spoonful of tar into the honey, and no matter how much honey he may add now, the whole is already spoiled. '

Whose fault is it that many trade unionists tend to cultivate a spirit of hostility for the new men? Of course, a bufferite or a Tsektranite will say it is the trade unionists'.

The fact is that in this case idle fancy and invention have accumulated like the snowdrifts in the storm outside. But, comrades, we must sort things out and get at the substance. And it is that a spirit of hostility has been aroused

among the masses by a number of tactless actions. My
opponent asserts that certain people have been cultivating
a spirit of hostility. This shows that the question is seen
in the wrong light. We must sort things out. The All-Russia
Conference was held in November, and that is where the
"shake-up" catchword was launched. Trotsky was wrong in
uttering it. Politically it is clear that such an approach
will cause a split and bring down the dictatorship of the
proletariat.

We must understand that trade unions are not government
departments, like People's Commissariats, but comprise the
whole organised proletariat; that they are a special type
of institution and cannot be approached in this way. And
when there arose this question of a wrong approach, latent
with the danger of a split, I said: "Don't talk about any
broad discussion for the time being; go to the commission
and examine the matter carefully over there." But the
comrades said: "No, we can't do that; it is a violation of
democracy." Comrade Bukharin went so far as to talk about
the "sacred slogan of workers' democracy". Those are his
very words. When I read that I nearly crossed myself.
(*Laughter.*) I insist that a mistake always has a modest
beginning and then grows up. Disagreements always start
from small things. A slight cut is commonplace, but if it
festers, it may result in a fatal illness. And this thing here
is a festering wound. In November, there was talk about
a shake-up; by December, it had become a big mistake.

The December Plenary Meeting of the Central Committee
was against us. The majority sided with Trotsky and carried
Trotsky and Bukharin's resolution, which you must have
read. But even the C.C. members who did not sympathise
with us had to admit that the water transport workers had
more right on their side than Tsektran. That is a fact. When
I ask what Tsektran's fault was, the answer is not that
they had brought pressure to bear—that goes to their credit
—but that they had allowed bureaucratic excesses.

But once you have realised that you had allowed excesses
you ought to rectify them, instead of arguing against rectification. That is all there is to it. It will take decades to
overcome the evils of bureaucracy. It is a very difficult
struggle, and anyone who says we can rid ourselves of bureau-

cratic practices overnight by adopting anti-bureaucratic platforms is nothing but a quack with a bent for fine words. Bureaucratic excesses must be rectified right away. We must detect and rectify them without calling bad good, or black white. The workers and peasants realise that they have still to learn the art of government, but they are also very well aware that there are bureaucratic excesses, and it is a double fault to refuse to correct them. This must be done in good time, as the water transport workers have pointed out, and not only when your attention is called to it.

Even the best workers make mistakes. There are excellent workers in Tsektran, and we shall appoint them, and correct their bureaucratic excesses. Comrade Trotsky says that Comrades Tomsky and Lozovsky—trade unionists both— are guilty of cultivating in their midst a spirit of hostility for the new men. But this is monstrous. Only someone in the lunatic fringe can say a thing like that.

This haste leads to arguments, platforms and accusations, and eventually creates the impression that everything is rotten.

You know when people fall out it only takes them a couple of days to start abusing each other's relatives down to the tenth generation. You ask: "What are you quarrelling over?" "Oh, his aunt was this, and his grandfather was that." "I don't mean now; how did the whole thing start?" It turns out that in the course of two days a heap of disagreements has piled up.

Tsektran has allowed excesses in a number of cases, and these were harmful and unnecessary bureaucratic excesses. People are liable to allow excesses everywhere. There are departments with a staff of 30,000 in Moscow alone. That is no joke. There's something to be corrected, there's a wall to be scaled. There must be no fear, no thought of causing offence or dissension. To start a factional struggle and accuse Tomsky of cultivating among the masses a spirit of hostility for the Tsektranites is utterly to distort the facts, absolutely to spoil all the work, and entirely to damage all relations with the trade unions. But the trade unions embrace the whole proletariat. If this thing is persisted in and voted on by platforms, it will lead to the downfall of the Soviet power.

If the Party falls out with the trade unions, the fault lies with the Party, and this spells certain doom for the Soviet power. We have no other mainstay but the millions of proletarians, who may not be class conscious, are often ignorant, backward and illiterate, but who, being proletarians, follow their own Party. For twenty years they have regarded this Party as their own. Next comes a class which is not ours, which may side with us, if we are wise and if we pursue a correct policy within our own class. We have now reached the supreme moment of our revolution: we have roused the proletarian masses and the masses of poor peasants in the rural areas to give us their conscious support. No revolution has ever done this before. There is no class that can overthrow us: the majority of the proletarians and the rural poor are behind us. Nothing can ruin us but our own mistakes. This "but" is the whole point. If we cause a split, for which we are to blame, everything will collapse because the trade unions are not only an official institution, but also the source of all our power. They are the class which the economics of capitalism has converted into the economic amalgamator, and which through its industry brings together millions of scattered peasants. That is why one proletarian has more strength than 200 peasants.

That is just why Trotsky's whole approach is wrong. I could have analysed any one of his theses, but it would take me hours, and you would all be bored to death. Every thesis reveals the same thoroughly wrong approach: "Many trade unionists tend to cultivate a spirit of hostility." There is a spirit of hostility for us among the trade union rank and file because of our mistakes, and the bureaucratic practices up on top, including myself, because it was I who appointed Glavpolitput. What is to be done? Are things to be set right? We must correct Tsektran's excesses, once we realise that we are a solid workers' party, with a firm footing, and a head on its shoulders. We are not renouncing either the method of appointment, or the dictatorship. This will not be tolerated by workers with a twenty years' schooling in Russia. If we condone this mistake, we shall surely be brought down. It is a mistake, and that is the root of the matter.

Trotsky says Lozovsky and Tomsky are balking at the new tasks. To prove this will put a new face on the matter. What are the new tasks?

Here we are told: "production atmosphere", "industrial democracy" and "role in production". I said, at the very outset, in the December 30 discussion, that that was nothing but words, which the workers did not understand, and that it was all part of the task of production propaganda. We are not renouncing the dictatorship, or one-man management; these remain, I will support them, but I refuse to defend excesses and stupidity. "Production atmosphere" is a funny phrase that will make the workers laugh. Saying it more simply and clearly is all part of production propaganda. But a special institution has been set up for the purpose.

About enhancing the role of the trade unions in production, I replied on December 30 and in the press, and said that we have Comrade Rudzutak's resolution, which was adopted at the Conference on November 5. Comrades Trotsky and Bukharin said that Tsektran had drafted this resolution. Although this has been refuted, let me ask: if they had drafted it, who, in that case, is kicking? The trade unions adopted it and Tsektran drafted it. Well and good. There's no point, therefore, in quarrelling like children and raising factional disagreements. Has Comrade Trotsky brought up any new tasks? No, he hasn't. The fact is that his new points are all worse than the old ones. Comrade Trotsky is campaigning to get the Party to condemn those who are balking at new tasks, and Tomsky and Lozovsky have been named as the greatest sinners.

Rudzutak's resolution is couched in clearer and simpler language, and has nothing in it like "production atmosphere" or "industrial democracy". It says clearly that every trade union member must be aware of the vital necessity of increasing productivity in the country. It is put in simple and intelligible language. All this is stated better than in Trotsky's theses, and more fully, because bonuses in kind and disciplinary courts have been added. Without the latter, all this talk of getting the transport system going and improving things is humbug. Let us set up commissions and disciplinary courts. In this matter Tsektran has allowed excesses. We propose calling a spade a spade: it is no use covering up excesses with new tasks; they must be corrected. We have no intention of renouncing coercion. No sober-minded worker would go so far as to say that we could now dispense with coercion, or that we could dissolve the trade unions, or let them have the whole of industry. I can imagine Comrade Shlyapnikov blurting out a thing like that.

In the whole of his speech there is one excellent passage on the experience of the Sormovo Works, where, he said, absenteeism was reduced by 30 per cent. This is said to be true. But I am a suspicious sort, I suggest that a commission be sent there to investigate and make a comparison of Nizhni-Novgorod and Petrograd. There is no need to have a meeting about this: it can all be done in commission. Trotsky says that there is an attempt to prevent coalescence, but that is nonsense. He says we must go forward. Indeed, if the engine is good; but if it isn't, we must put it into reverse. The Party will benefit from this, because we must study experience.

Production is at a standstill, but some people have been busy producing bad theses. This question requires study and experience. You are trade unionists and miners who are doing their job. Now since you have taken up this question, you must inquire, demand figures, verify them over and over again—don't take any statements for granted—and when you have done that, let us know the result. If it is good, then go on; if it is bad, go back. This means work, not talk. All this should have been done at Party meetings.

At the Eighth Congress of Soviets, I said that we ought to have less politics. When I said that I thought we would have no more political mistakes, but here we are, three years after the Soviet revolution, talking about syndicalism. This is a shame. If I had been told six months ago that I would be writing about syndicalism, I would have said that I preferred to write about the Donbas. Now we are being distracted, and the Party is being dragged back. A small mistake is growing into a big one. That is where Comrade Shlyapnikov comes in. Point 16 of Comrade Trotsky's theses gives a correct definition of Shlyapnikov's mistake.

In an effort to act the buffer, Bukharin clutched at Shlyapnikov, but it would have been better for him to clutch at a straw. He promises the unions mandatory nominations, which means they are to have the final say in appointments. But that is exactly what Shlyapnikov is saying. Marxists have been combating syndicalism all over the world. We have been fighting in the Party for over twenty years, and we have given the workers visual proof that the Party is a special kind of thing which needs forward-looking men prepared for sacrifice; that it does make mistakes, but corrects them; that it guides and selects men who know the way and the obstacles before us. It does not deceive the workers. It never makes promises that cannot be kept. And if you skip the trade unions you will make a hash of everything we have achieved over the past three years. Comrade Bukharin, with whom I discussed this mistake, said: "Comrade Lenin, you are picking on us."

I take mandatory nominations to mean that they will be made under the direction of the Party's Central Committee. But in that case, what are the rights we are giving them? There will then be no chance of having a bloc. The workers and the peasants are two distinct classes. Let us talk about vesting the rights in the trade unions when electricity has spread over the whole country—if we manage to achieve this in twenty years it will be incredibly quick work, for it cannot be done quickly. To talk about it before then will be deceiving the workers. The dictatorship of the proletariat is the most stable thing in the world because it has won confidence by its deeds, and because the Party took great care to prevent diffusion.

What does that mean?

Does every worker know how to run the state? People working in the practical sphere know that this is not true, that millions of our organised workers are going through what we always said the trade unions were, namely, a school of communism and administration. When they have attended this school for a number of years they will have learned to administer, but the going is slow. We have not even abolished illiteracy. We know that workers in touch with peasants are liable to fall for non-proletarian slogans. How many of the workers have been engaged in government? A few thousand throughout Russia and no more. If we say that it is not the Party but the trade unions that put up

the candidates and administrate, it may sound very
democratic and might help us to catch a few votes, but
not for long. It will be fatal for the dictatorship of the
proletariat.

Read the decision of the Second Congress of the Comintern.[21] Its resolutions and decisions have gone round the
world. The recent Socialist Congress in France revealed
that we have won a majority in a country where chauvinism is most virulent; we have split the Party and ejected
the corrupt leaders, and we did this in opposition to the
syndicalists.[22] And all the best workers and leaders there
have adopted our theory. Even syndicalists—revolutionary
syndicalists—are siding with us all over the world. I myself
have met American syndicalists who, after a visit to this
country, say: "Indeed, you cannot lead the proletariat
without a Party." You all know that this is a fact. And
it is quite improper for the proletariat to rush into the
arms of syndicalism and talk about mandatory nominations
to "all-Russia producers' congresses". This is dangerous
and jeopardizes the Party's guiding role. Only a very small
percentage of the workers in the country are now organised.
The majority of the peasants will follow the Party because
its policy is correct, and because, during the Brest peace
ordeal, it was capable of making temporary sacrifices and
retreats, which was the right thing to do. Are we to throw
all this away? Was it all a windfall? No, it was all won
by the Party in decades of hard work. Everybody believes
the word of the Bolsheviks, who have had twenty years
of Party training.

To govern you need an army of steeled revolutionary
Communists. We have it, and it is called the Party. All
this syndicalist nonsense about mandatory nominations of
producers must go into the wastepaper basket. To proceed
on those lines would mean thrusting the Party aside and
making the dictatorship of the proletariat in Russia impossible. This is the view I believe it to be my Party duty to
put to you. It is, in my opinion, enunciated in the form
of practical propositions in the platform called *Draft
Decision of the Tenth Congress of the R.C.P.* and signed by
Lenin, Zinoviev, Tomsky, Rudzutak, Kalinin, Kamenev,
Lozovsky, Petrovsky, Sergeyev and Stalin. Lozovsky, who

is not a member of the Central Committee, was included because he was on the trade union commission from which Shlyapnikov and Lutovinov, unfortunately, resigned. It is up to the workers to decide whether Shlyapnikov was right in resigning, and he will be censured, if he was wrong. I am convinced that all class-conscious workers will accept this platform and that the present disagreements in our Party will be confined to fever at the top. I am sure the workers will put them right, remain at their posts, maintain Party discipline and join in an efficient but careful drive to increase production and secure full victory for our cause. (*Prolonged applause.*)

Published in the *Bulleten Vtorogo vserossiiskogo syezda gornorabochikh (Bulletin of the Second All-Russia Congress of Miners)* No. 1, January 25, 1921

Published according to the *Bulleten* text

2

SPEECH CLOSING THE DISCUSSION DELIVERED AT A MEETING OF THE COMMUNIST GROUP OF THE CONGRESS JANUARY 24

Comrades, I should like to begin by speaking about who is trying to intimidate whom, and about Comrade Shlyapnikov, who has tried hard to scare us. Everyone here said Lenin was trying to raise the bogey of syndicalism. This is ridiculous because the very idea of using syndicalism as a bogey is ridiculous. I think we ought to start with our programmes, by reading the Programme of the Communist Party to see what it says. Comrades Trotsky and Shlyapnikov referred to the same passage which happens to be its Paragraph 5. Let me read it to you in full:

"5. The organisational apparatus of socialised industry should rely chiefly on the trade unions, which must to an ever increasing degree divest themselves of the narrow craft-union spirit and become large industrial associations, embracing the majority, and eventually all of the workers in the given branch of industry."

Comrade Shlyapnikov quoted this passage in his speech. But, if the figures were correct, those who were managing the organisations constituted 60 per cent, and these consisted of workers. Furthermore, when reference is made to the Programme, this should be done properly, bearing in mind that Party members know it thoroughly, and do not confine themselves to reading one extract, as Trotsky and Shlyapnikov have done. Comrades, there is much history to show that the workers cannot organise otherwise than by industries. That is why the idea of industrial unionism has been adopted all over the world. That is for the time being, of course. There is talk about the need to cast off the narrow craft-union spirit. I ask you, has this been done to, say, a tenth? Of course, not, is the sincere answer. Why forget this?

Who is it who says to the unions: "You have not yet divested yourselves of the narrow craft-union spirit, and must get on with it"? It is the R.C.P. which does this in its Programme. Read it. To depart from this is to abandon the Programme for syndicalism. Despite the hints at Lenin's "intimidation", the Programme is still there. You depart from it by quoting the first part and forgetting the second. In which direction? Towards syndicalism. Let me read further:

"The trade unions being, on the strength of the laws of the Soviet Republic and established practice, participants in all the local and central organs of industrial management, should eventually arrive at a *de facto* concentration in their hands of the whole administration of the whole national economy, as a single economic entity."

Everyone makes references to this paragraph. What does it say? Something that is absolutely indisputable: "should eventually arrive." It does not say that they are arriving. It does not contain the exaggeration which, once made, reduces the whole to an absurdity. It says, "should eventually arrive". Arrive where? At a *de facto* concentration and administration. When are you due to arrive at this point? This calls for education, and it must be so organised as to teach everyone the art of administration. Now can you say, with a clear conscience, that the trade unions are able to fill any number of executive posts with suitable men at any time? After all, it is not six million, but sixty thousand or, say, a hundred thousand men that you need to fill all the executive posts. Can they nominate this number? No, they cannot—not yet—as anyone will say who is not chasing after formulas and theses and is not misled by the loudest voices. Years of educational work lie ahead for the Party, ranging from the abolition of illiteracy to the whole round of Party work in the trade unions. An enormous amount of work must be done in the trade unions to achieve this properly. This is exactly what it says: "should eventually arrive at a *de facto* concentration in their hands of the whole administration of the whole national economy". It does not say branches of industry, as Trotsky does in his theses. One of his first theses quotes the Programme correctly, but another one says: organisation of industry. I'm afraid that is no way to quote. When you are

writing some theses and you want to quote the Programme,
you must read it to the end. Anyone who takes the trouble
to read this Paragraph 5 right through and give it ten
minutes' thought will see that Shlyapnikov has departed
from the Programme, and that Trotsky has leaped over it.
Let's read Paragraph 5 to the end:

"The trade unions, ensuring in this way indissoluble ties between
the central state administration, the national economy and the broad
masses of working people, should draw the latter into direct economic
management on the widest possible scale. At the same time, the
participation of the trade unions in economic management and their
activity in drawing the broad masses into this work are the principal
means of combating the bureaucratisation of the economic apparatus
of the Soviet power and making possible the establishment of truly
popular control over the results of production."

You find that you must first achieve *de facto* concentration. But what are you ensuring now? First, there are the
ties within the central state administration. This is a huge
machine. You have not yet taught us to master it. And so,
you must ensure ties between the central state administration—that's one; national economy—that's two; and the
masses—that's three. Have we got those ties? Are the trade
unions capable of administration? Anybody over thirty
years of age with some little practical experience of Soviet
organisation will laugh at this. Read the following:

"At the same time, the participation of the trade unions in economic management and their activity in drawing the broad masses
into this work are the principal means of combating the bureaucratisation of the economic apparatus of the Soviet power and making
possible the establishment of truly popular control over the results
of production."

First, there is need to create ties between the central
state organisations. We have no intention of concealing
this malaise, and our Programme says: ensure ties with
the masses, and ensure the participation of the trade unions
in economic management. There are no loud words in this.
When you have done that in such a way as to reduce
absenteeism by, say, 3 per cent—let alone 30—we shall say:
you have done a fine job. Our present Programme says:
". . . the participation of the trade unions in economic
management and their activity in drawing the broad masses
into this work . . . ." It does not contain a single promise

or a single loud word; nor does it say anything about
your doing the electing. It does not resort to demagogy,
but says that there is an ignorant, backward mass, that there
are trade unions, which are so strong that they are leading
the whole of the peasantry, and which themselves follow the
lead of the Party, with a twenty-year schooling in the fight
against tsarism. No country has gone through what Russia
has, and that is the secret of our strength. Why is this
regarded as a miracle? Because in a peasant country, only the
trade unions can provide the economic bonds to unite millions of scattered farms, if this mass of six million has faith
in its Party, and continues to follow it as it had hitherto.
That is the secret of our strength, and the way it works
is a political question. How can a minority govern a huge
peasant country, and why are we so composed? After our
three years' experience, there is no external or internal
force that can break us. Provided we do not make any extra-
stupid mistakes leading to splits, we shall retain our positions; otherwise everything will go to the dogs. That is
why, when Comrade Shlyapnikov says in his platform:

"The All-Russia Congress of Producers shall elect a body to
administer the whole national economy,"

I say: read the whole of Paragraph 5 of our Programme,
which I have read out to you, and you will see that there
is no attempt at intimidation either on Lenin's or anyone
else's part.

Shlyapnikov concluded his speech by saying: "We must
eliminate bureaucratic methods in government and the
national economy." I say this is demagogy. We have had this
question of bureaucratic practices on the agenda since last
July. After the Ninth Congress of the R.C.P. last July,
Preobrazhensky also asked: Are we not suffering from
bureaucratic excesses? Watch out! In August, the Central
Committee endorsed Zinoviev's letter: Combat the evils
of bureaucracy. The Party Conference met in September,
and endorsed it. So, after all, it was not Lenin who invented
some new path, as Trotsky says, but the Party which said:
"Watch out: there's a new malaise." Preobrazhensky raised
this question in July; we had Zinoviev's letter in August;
there was the Party Conference in September and we had a

long report on bureaucratic practices at the Congress of
Soviets in December. The malaise is there. In our 1919
Programme we wrote that bureaucratic practices existed.
Whoever comes out and demands a stop to bureaucratic
practices is a demagogue. When you are called upon to
"put a stop to bureaucratic practices", it is demagogy. It
is nonsense. We shall be fighting the evils of bureaucracy
for many years to come, and whoever thinks otherwise is
playing demagogue and cheating, because overcoming the
evils of bureaucracy requires hundreds of measures, wholesale literacy, culture and participation in the activity of
the Workers' and Peasants' Inspection.[23] Shlyapnikov has
been People's Commissar for Labour and People's Commissar
for Trade and Industry. Has *he* put a stop to bureaucratic
practices? Kiselyov has been on the Central Board of
the Textile Industry. Has *he* put a stop to the evils of
bureaucracy?

Let me say this once again: We shall have grown up
when all our congresses resolve themselves into sections and
marshal the facts about coalescence among the millers and
the Donbas miners. But writing a string of useless platforms
shows up our poor economic leadership. I repeat that nothing can break us, neither external nor internal forces, if
we do not lead things up to a split. I say that Tsektran is
more than a bludgeon, but exaggerating this has led up to a
split. Anyone can be guilty of an excess of bureaucratic
practices, and the Central Committee is aware of it, and is
responsible for it. In this respect, Comrade Trotsky's mistake lies in that he drew up his theses in the wrong spirit.
They are all couched in terms of a shake-up, and they have
all led to a split in the union. It is not a matter of giving
Trotsky bad marks—we are not schoolchildren and have
no use for marks—but we must say that his theses are wrong
in content and must therefore be rejected.

Published in the *Bulleten*
Vtorogo vserossiishogo syezda
*gornorabochikh (Bulletin of the Second
All-Russia Congress of Miners)* No. 2,
January 26, 1921

Published according
to the *Bulleten* text

CONCERNING THE CONDITIONS ENSURING THE RESEARCH WORK OF ACADEMICIAN I. P. PAVLOV AND HIS ASSOCIATES

DECREE OF THE COUNCIL OF PEOPLE'S COMMISSARS

In view of Academician I. P. Pavlov's outstanding scientific services, which are of tremendous importance to the working people of the world, the Council of People's Commissars decrees:

1. To set up, on the strength of the Petrograd Soviet's proposal, a special commission with broad powers, consisting of Comrade M. Gorky, chief of Petrograd's institutions of higher learning, Comrade Kristi, and member of the collegium of the Petrograd Soviet's Administrative Department, Comrade Kaplun, whose task is to create, as soon as possible, the best conditions to ensure the research work of Comrade Pavlov and his associates.

2. To authorise the State Publishers to print, in the best printing-house, a de luxe edition of the scientific work prepared by Academician Pavlov, summing up the results of his research over the past twenty years, leaving to Academician I. P. Pavlov the right of property in this work in Russia and abroad.

3. To authorise the Workers' Supply Commission to issue to Academician Pavlov and his wife a special ration equal in caloricity to two academic rations.

4. To authorise the Petrograd Soviet to assure Professor Pavlov and his wife of the use for life of the flat they now occupy, and to furnish it and Academician Pavlov's laboratory with every possible facility.

Chairman of the Council of People's Commissars

V. Ulyanov (Lenin)

Moscow, the Kremlin,
January 24, 1921

Published in the newspaper
Izvestia No. 30,
February 11, 1921

Published according
to the original
signed by *Lenin*

ONCE AGAIN ON THE TRADE UNIONS, THE CURRENT SITUATION AND THE MISTAKES OF TROTSKY AND BUKHARIN[24]

The Party discussion and the factional struggle, which is of a type that occurs before a congress—before and in connection with the impending elections to the Tenth Congress of the R.C.P.—are waxing hot. The first factional pronouncement, namely, the one made by Comrade Trotsky on behalf of "a number of responsible workers" in his "platform pamphlet" (*The Role and Tasks of the Trade Unions*, with a preface dated December 25, 1920), was followed by a sharp pronouncement (the reader will see from what follows that it was deservedly sharp) by the Petrograd organisation of the R.C.P. ("Appeal to the Party", published in *Petrogradskaya Pravda*[25] on January 6, 1921, and in the Party's Central Organ, the Moscow *Pravda*, on January 13, 1921). The Moscow Committee then came out against the Petrograd organisation (in the same issue of *Pravda*). Then appeared a verbatim report, published by the bureau of the R.C.P. group of the All-Russia Central Council of Trade Unions, of the discussion that took place on December 30, 1920, at a very large and important Party meeting, namely, that of the R.C.P. group at the Eighth Congress of Soviets. It is entitled *The Role of the Trade Unions in Production* (with a preface dated January 6, 1921). This, of course, is by no means all of the discussion material. Party meetings to discuss these issues are being held almost everywhere. On December 30, 1920, I spoke at a meeting in conditions in which, as I put it then, I "departed from the rules of procedure", i.e., in conditions in which I could

not take part in the discussion or hear the preceding and
subsequent speakers. I shall now try to make amends and
express myself in a more "orderly" fashion.

THE DANGER OF FACTIONAL
PRONOUNCEMENTS TO THE PARTY

Is Comrade Trotsky's pamphlet *The Role and Tasks of
the Trade Unions* a factional pronouncement? Irrespective
of its content, is there any danger to the Party in a pronouncement of this kind? Attempts to hush up this question
are a particularly favourite exercise with the members of
the Moscow Committee (with the exception of Comrade
Trotsky, of course), who see the factionalism of the Petrograd comrades, and with Comrade Bukharin, who, however,
felt obliged, on December 30, 1920, to make the following
statement on behalf of the "buffer group":

"... when a train seems to be heading for a crash, a buffer is not
a bad thing at all" (report of the December 30, 1920 discussion, p. 45).

So there is some danger of a crash. Can we conceive of
intelligent members of the Party being indifferent to the
question of how, where and when this danger arose?

Trotsky's pamphlet opens with the statement that "it
is the fruit of collective work", that "a number of responsible workers, particularly trade unionists (members of the
Presidium of the All-Russia Central Council of Trade
Unions, the Central Committee of the Metalworkers' Union,
Tsektran and others)" took part in compiling it, and that
it is a "platform pamphlet". At the end of thesis 4 we read
that "the forthcoming Party Congress will have to *choose*
[Trotsky's italics] between the two trends within the trade
union movement".

If this is not the formation of a faction by a member
of the Central Committee, if this does not mean "heading
for a crash", then let Comrade Bukharin, or anyone of his
fellow-thinkers, explain to the Party any other possible
meaning of the words "factionalism", and the Party
"seems to be heading for a crash". Who can be more
purblind than men wishing to play the "buffer" and *closing
their eyes* to *such* a "danger of a crash"?

Just imagine: after the Central Committee had spent

two plenary meetings (November 9 and December 7) in an unprecedentedly long, detailed and heated discussion of Comrade Trotsky's original draft theses and of the entire trade union policy that he advocates for the Party, one member of the Central Committee, *one out of nineteen*, forms a group outside the Central Committee and presents its "collective work" as a "platform", inviting the Party Congress "to choose between *two* trends"! This, incidentally, quite apart from the fact that Comrade Trotsky's announcement of two and only two trends on December 25, 1920, despite Bukharin's coming out as a "buffer" on November 9, is a glaring exposure of the Bukharin group's true role as abettors of the worst and most harmful sort of factionalism. But I ask any Party member: Don't you find this attack and insistence upon "choosing" between two trends in the trade union movement rather sudden? What is there for us to do but stare in astonishment at the fact that after three years of the proletarian dictatorship even one Party member can be found to "attack" the two trends issue *in this way*?

Nor is that all. Look at the factional attacks in which this pamphlet abounds. In the very first thesis we find a threatening "gesture" at "certain workers in the trade union movement" who are thrown "back to trade-unionism, pure and simple, which the Party repudiated in principle long ago" (evidently the Party is represented by only one member of the Central Committee's nineteen). Thesis 8 grandiloquently condemns "the craft conservatism prevalent among the top trade union functionaries" (note the truly bureaucratic concentration of attention on the "top"!). Thesis 11 opens with the astonishingly tactful, conclusive and business-like (what is the most polite word for it?) "hint" that the "majority of the trade unionists . . . give only formal, that is, *verbal*, recognition" to the resolutions of the Party's Ninth Congress.

We find that we have some very authoritative judges before us who say the *majority* (!) of the trade unionists give only *verbal* recognition to the Party's decisions.

Thesis 12 reads:

"... many trade unionists take an ever more aggressive and uncompromising stand against the prospect of 'coalescence'.... Among them we find Comrades Tomsky and Lozovsky.

"What is more, many trade unionists, balking at the new tasks and methods, tend to cultivate in their midst a spirit of corporative exclusiveness and hostility for the new men who are being drawn into the given branch of the economy, thereby actually fostering the survivals of craft-unionism among the organised workers."

Let the reader go over these arguments carefully and ponder them. They simply abound in "gems". Firstly, the pronouncement must be assessed from the standpoint of factionalism! Imagine what Trotsky would have said, and how he would have said it, if Tomsky had published a platform accusing Trotsky and "many" military workers of cultivating the spirit of bureaucracy, fostering the survivals of savagery, etc. What is the "role" of Bukharin, Preobrazhensky, Serebryakov and the others who fail to see—positively fail to note, utterly fail to note—the aggressiveness and factionalism of all *this*, and refuse to see how much more factional it is than the pronouncement of the Petrograd comrades?

Secondly, take a closer look at the approach to the subject: many trade unionists "tend to cultivate in their midst a spirit" .... This is an out-and-out bureaucratic approach. The whole point, you see, is not the level of development and living conditions of the masses in their millions, but the "spirit" which Tomsky and Lozovsky tend to cultivate "in their midst".

Thirdly, Comrade Trotsky has unwittingly revealed the *essence* of the whole controversy which he and the Bukharin and Co. "buffer" have been evading and camouflaging with such care.

What is the point at issue? Is it the fact that many trade unionists are balking at the new tasks and methods and tend to cultivate in their midst a spirit of hostility for the new officials?

Or is it that the masses of organised workers are legitimately protesting and inevitably showing readiness to throw out the new officials who refuse to rectify the useless and harmful excesses of bureaucracy?

Is it that someone has refused to understand the "new tasks and methods"?

Or is it that someone is making a clumsy attempt to cover up his defence of certain useless and harmful excesses of bureaucracy with a lot of talk about new tasks and methods?

It is this *essence* of the dispute that the reader should bear in mind.

FORMAL DEMOCRACY AND THE REVOLUTIONARY INTEREST

"Workers' democracy is free from fetishes", Comrade Trotsky writes in his theses, which are the "fruit of collective work". "Its sole consideration is the revolutionary interest" (thesis 23).

Comrade Trotsky's theses have landed him in a mess. That part of them which is correct is not new and, what is more, turns *against* him. That which is new is all wrong.

I have written out Comrade Trotsky's correct propositions. They turn against him not only on the point in thesis 23 (Glavpolitput) but on the others as well.

Under the rules of formal democracy, Trotsky *had a right* to come out with a factional platform even against the whole of the Central Committee. That is indisputable. What is also indisputable is that the Central Committee had endorsed this formal right by its decision on freedom of discussion adopted on December 24, 1920. Bukharin, the buffer, recognises this formal right for Trotsky, but not for the Petrograd organisation, probably because on December 30, 1920, he talked himself into "the sacred slogan of workers' democracy" (verbatim report, p. 45). . . .

Well, and what about the revolutionary interest?

Will any serious-minded person who is not blinded by the factional egotism of "Tsektran" or of the "buffer" faction, will anyone in his right mind say that *such* a pronouncement on the trade union issue by *such* a prominent leader as Trotsky does promote *the revolutionary interest*?

Can it be denied that, even if Trotsky's "new tasks and methods" were as sound as they are in fact unsound (of which later), his very approach would be damaging to himself, the Party, the trade union movement, the training of millions of trade union members and the Republic?

It looks as if the kind Bukharin and his group call themselves a "buffer" because they have firmly decided *not to think* about the obligations this title imposes upon them.

THE POLITICAL DANGER OF SPLITS
IN THE TRADE UNION MOVEMENT

Everyone knows that big disagreements sometimes grow out of minute differences, which may at first appear to be altogether insignificant. A slight cut or scratch, of the kind everyone has had scores of in the course of his life, may become very dangerous and even fatal *if* it festers and *if* blood poisoning sets in. This may happen in any kind of conflict, even a purely personal one. This also happens in politics.

Any difference, even an insignificant one, may become politically dangerous if it has a chance to grow into a split, and I mean the kind of split that will shake and destroy the whole political edifice, or lead, to use Comrade Bukharin's simile, to a crash.

Clearly, in a country under the dictatorship of the proletariat, a split in the ranks of the proletariat, or between the proletarian party and the mass of the proletariat, is not just dangerous; it is extremely dangerous, especially when the proletariat constitutes a small minority of the population. And splits in the trade union movement (which, as I tried hard to emphasise in my speech on December 30, 1920, is a movement of the almost completely organised proletariat) mean precisely splits in the mass of the proletariat.

That is why, when the whole thing started at the Fifth All-Russia Conference of Trade Unions on November 2-6, 1920 (and that is exactly where it did start), and when right after the Conference—no, I am mistaken, *during* that Conference—Comrade Tomsky appeared before the Political Bureau in high dudgeon and, fully supported by Comrade Rudzutak, the most even-tempered of men, began to relate that at the Conference Comrade Trotsky had talked about "shaking up" the trade unions and that he, Tomsky, had opposed this—when that happened, I decided there and then that policy (i.e., the Party's trade union policy) lay at the root of the controversy, and that Comrade Trotsky, with his "shake-up" policy against Comrade Tomsky, was entirely in the wrong. For, *even if the "shake-up" policy were partly justified* by the "new tasks and methods" (Trotsky's thesis 12), it cannot be tolerated at the present time, and in the present situation, because it threatens a split.

It now seems to Comrade Trotsky that it is "an utter travesty" to ascribe the "shake-up-from-above" policy to him (L. Trotsky, "A Reply to the Petrograd Comrades", *Pravda* No. 9, January 15, 1921). But "shake-up" is a real "catchword", not only in the sense that after being uttered by Comrade Trotsky at the Fifth All-Russia Conference of Trade Unions it has, you might say, "caught on" throughout the Party and the trade unions. Unfortunately, it remains true even today in the much more profound sense that it alone epitomises *the whole spirit, the whole trend* of the platform pamphlet entitled *The Role and Tasks of the Trade Unions.* Comrade Trotsky's platform pamphlet is shot through with the spirit of the "shake-up-from-above" policy. Just recall the accusation made against Comrade Tomsky, or "many trade unionists", that they "tend to cultivate in their midst a spirit of hostility for the new men"!

But whereas the Fifth All-Russia Conference of Trade Unions (November 2-6, 1920) only saw the makings of the atmosphere fraught with splits, the split within Tsektran became a fact in early December 1920.

This event is basic and essential to an understanding of the political essence of our controversies; and Comrades Trotsky and Bukharin are mistaken if they think hushing it up will help matters. A hush-up in this case does not produce a "buffer" effect but rouses passions; for the question has not only been placed on the agenda by developments, but has been emphasised by Comrade Trotsky in his platform pamphlet. It is this pamphlet that repeatedly, in the passages I have quoted, particularly in thesis 12, raises the question of whether the essence of the matter is that "many trade unionists tend to cultivate in their midst a spirit of hostility for the new men", or that the "hostility" of the *masses* is legitimate in view of certain useless and harmful excesses of bureaucracy, for example, in Tsektran.

The issue was bluntly and properly stated by Comrade Zinoviev in his very first speech on December 30, 1920, when he said that it was "Comrade Trotsky's immoderate adherents" who had brought about a split. Perhaps that is why Comrade Bukharin abusively described Comrade Zinoviev's speech as "a lot of hot air"? But every Party member who reads the verbatim report of the December 30, 1920

discussion will see that that is not true. He will find that
it is Comrade Zinoviev who quotes and operates with the
facts, and that it is Trotsky and Bukharin who indulge
most in intellectualist verbosity minus the facts.

When Comrade Zinoviev said, "Tsektran stands on feet
of clay and has already split into three parts", Comrade
Sosnovsky interrupted and said:

"That is something you have encouraged" (verbatim
report, p. 15).

Now this is a serious charge. If it were proved, there
would, of course, be no place on the Central Committee,
in the R.C.P., or in the trade unions of our Republic for
those who were guilty of *encouraging a split* even in one of
the trade unions. Happily, this serious charge was advanced
in a thoughtless manner by a comrade who, I regret
to say, has now and again been "carried away" by thoughtless polemics before this. Comrade Sosnovsky has even
managed to insert "a fly in the ointment" of his otherwise
excellent articles, say, on production propaganda, and this
has tended to negate all its pluses. Some people (like Comrade Bukharin) are so happily constituted that they are
incapable of injecting venom into their attacks even when
the fight is bitterest; others, less happily constituted, are
liable to do so, and do this all too often. Comrade Sosnovsky would do well to watch his step in this respect, and
perhaps even ask his friends to help out.

But, some will say, the charge is there, even if it has
been made in a thoughtless, unfortunate and patently
"factional" form. In a serious matter, the badly worded
truth is preferable to the hush-up.

That the matter is serious is beyond doubt, for, let me
say this again, the *crux* of the issue lies in this area to a
greater extent than is generally suspected. Fortunately,
we are in possession of sufficiently objective and conclusive
facts to provide an answer *in substance* to Comrade Sosnovsky's point.

First of all, there is on the same page of the verbatim
report Comrade Zinoviev's statement denying Comrade
Sosnovsky's allegation and making precise references to
conclusive facts. Comrade Zinoviev showed that Comrade
Trotsky's accusation (made obviously, let me add, in an

outburst of factional zeal) was quite a different one from
Comrade Sosnovsky's; Comrade Trotsky's accusation was
that Comrade Zinoviev's *speech at the September All-Russia
Conference of the R.C.P.* had helped to bring about or had
brought about the split. (This charge, let me say in parenthesis, is quite untenable, if only because Zinoviev's September speech was approved in substance by the Central
Committee and the Party, and there has been no formal
protest against it since.)

Comrade Zinoviev replied that at the Central Committee
meeting Comrade Rudzutak had used the minutes to prove
that "*long before* any of my [Zinoviev's] speeches and the
All-Russia Conference the question [concerning certain
unwarranted and harmful excesses of bureaucracy in Tsek-
tran] had been examined in Siberia, on the Volga, in the
North and in the South".

That is an absolutely precise and clear-cut statement
of fact. It was made by Comrade Zinoviev in his first speech
before thousands of the most responsible Party members,
and his facts were *not* refuted either by Comrade Trotsky,
who spoke *twice later*, or by Comrade Bukharin, who *also
spoke later.*

Secondly, the December 7, 1920 *resolution of the Central
Committee's Plenary Meeting concerning the dispute between
the Communists working in water transport and the Communist group at the Tsektran Conference*, given in the same
verbatim report, was an even more definite and official
refutation of Comrade Sosnovsky's charges. The part of
the resolution dealing with Tsektran says:

"In connection with the dispute between Tsektran and the water
transport workers, the Central Committee resolves: 1) To set up a
Water Transport Section within the amalgamated Tsektran; 2) To
convene a congress of railwaymen and water transport workers in
February to hold normal elections to a new Tsektran; 3) To authorise
the old Tsektran to function until then; 4) To abolish Glavpolitvod
and Glavpolitput immediately and to transfer all their funds and
resources to the trade union on normal democratic lines."

This shows that the water transport workers, far from
being censured, are deemed to be *right* in every essential.
Yet *none* of the C.C. members who had signed the common
platform of January 14, 1921 (except Kamenev) voted for

the resolution. (The platform referred to is the *Role and Tasks of the Trade Unions. Draft Decision of the Tenth Congress of the R.C.P.*, submitted to the Central Committee by a group of members of the Central Committee and the trade union commission. Among those who signed it was Lozovsky, a member of the trade union commission but not of the Central Committee. The others were Tomsky, Kalinin, Rudzutak, Zinoviev, Stalin, Lenin, Kamenev, Petrovsky and Artyom Sergeyev.)

This resolution was carried *against* the C.C. members listed above, that is, against our group, for we would have voted against allowing the old Tsektran to continue temporarily. Because we were sure to win, Trotsky was forced to vote for Bukharin's resolution, as otherwise our resolution would have been carried. Comrade Rykov, who had been *for* Trotsky in November, took part in the trade union commission's examination of the dispute between Tsektran and the water transport workers in December, and saw that the latter were right.

To sum up: the December 7 majority in the Central Committee consisted of Comrades Trotsky, Bukharin, Preobrazhensky, Serebryakov and other C.C. members who are above suspicion of being biased *against* Tsektran. Yet the substance of their resolution did not censure the water transport workers but Tsektran, which they just stopped short of dissolving there and then. This proves Sosnovsky's charge to be quite groundless.

There is one other point to be dealt with, if we are to leave no room for ambiguity. What were these "certain unwarranted and harmful excesses of bureaucracy" to which I have repeatedly referred? Isn't *this* last charge unsupported or exaggerated?

Once again it was Comrade Zinoviev who, in his very first speech on December 30, 1920, provided the answer which was as precise as one could wish. He quoted from Comrade Zoff's water transport circular of May 3, 1920: "Committee treadmill abolished."[26] Comrade Zinoviev was quite right in saying this was a fundamental error. It exemplified the unwarranted and harmful excesses of bureaucracy and the "appointments system". But he said there and then that some appointees were "not half as experienced or as tried" as Comrade Zoff. I have heard Comrade Zoff referred to in the Central Committee as a most valuable worker, and this is fully borne out by my own observations in the Council of Defence. It has not entered anyone's mind either to make scapegoats of such comrades or to undermine their authority (as Comrade Trotsky suggests, without the least justification, on page 25 of his report). Their authority is not being undermined by those who try to correct the "appointees'" mistakes, but by those who would defend them even when they are wrong.

We see, therefore, that the danger of splits within the trade union movement was not imaginary but real. And we find that the actual disagreements really boiled down to a demand that certain unwarranted and harmful excesses of bureaucracy, and the appointments system should not be justified or defended, but corrected. That is all there is to it.

DISAGREEMENTS ON PRINCIPLE

There being deep and basic disagreements on principle— we may well be asked—do they not serve as vindication for the sharpest and most factional pronouncements? Is it possible to vindicate such a thing as a split, provided there is need to drive home some entirely new idea?

I believe it is, provided of course the disagreements are truly very deep and there is no other way to rectify a wrong trend in the policy of the Party or of the working class.

But the whole point is that there are no such disagreements. Comrade Trotsky has tried to point them out, and failed. A tentative or conciliatory approach had been possible—and necessary—*before* the publication of his pamphlet (December 25) ("such an approach is ruled out even in the case of disagreements and vague new tasks"); but *after* its publication we had to say: Comrade Trotsky is essentially wrong on all his new points.

This is most evident from a comparison of his theses with Rudzutak's which were adopted by the Fifth All-Russia Conference of Trade Unions (November 2-6). I quoted the latter in my December 30 speech and in the January 21 issue of *Pravda*. They are fuller and more correct than

Trotsky's, and wherever the latter differs from Rudzutak, he is wrong.

Take this famous "industrial democracy", which Comrade Bukharin hastened to insert in the Central Committee's resolution of December 7. It would, of course, be ridiculous to quibble about this ill-conceived brainchild ("tricky flourishes"), if it merely occurred in an article or speech. But, after all, it was Trotsky and Bukharin who put themselves into the ridiculous position by *insisting in their theses* on this very term, which is the one feature that distinguishes their "platforms" from Rudzutak's theses adopted by the trade unions.

The term is theoretically wrong. In the final analysis, every kind of democracy, as political superstructure in general (which must exist until classes have been abolished and a classless society established), serves production and is ultimately determined by the relations of production in a given society. It is, therefore, meaningless to single out "industrial democracy", for this leads to confusion, and the result is a dummy. That is the first point.

The second is that if you look at Bukharin's own explanation given in the resolution of the C.C. Plenary Meeting on December 7, which he drafted, you will find that he says: "Accordingly, the methods of workers' democracy must be those of industrial democracy, which means. . . ." Note the "which means"! The fact is that Bukharin opens his appeal to the masses with such an outlandish term that he must *give a gloss on* it. This, I think, is *undemocratic* from the democratic standpoint. You must write for the masses without using terms that require a glossary. This is bad from the "production" standpoint because time is wasted in explaining unnecessary terms. "Which means," he says, "that nomination and seconding of candidates, elections, etc., must proceed with an eye not only to their political staunchness, but also business efficiency, administrative experience, leadership, and proved concern for the working people's material and spiritual interests."

The reasoning there is obviously artificial and incorrect. For one thing, democracy is more than "nomination and seconding of candidates, elections, etc." Then, again, not all elections should be held with an eye to political

staunchness and business efficiency. Comrade Trotsky notwithstanding, an organisation of many millions must have a
certain percentage of canvassers and bureaucrats (we shall
not be able to make do without good bureaucrats for many
years to come). But we do not speak of "canvassing" or
"bureaucratic" democracy.

The third point is that it is wrong to consider only the
elected, the organisers, the administrators, etc. After all,
they constitute a minority of outstanding men. It is the
mass, the rank and file that we must consider. Rudzutak
has it in simpler, more intelligible and theoretically more
correct terms (thesis 6):

"... it must be brought home to each participant in production
that his production tasks are appropriate and important; that each
must not only take a hand in fulfilling his assignments, but also play
an intelligent part in correcting any technical and organisational
defects in the sphere of production."

The fourth point is that "industrial democracy" is a
term that lends itself to misinterpretation. It may be read
as a repudiation of dictatorship and individual authority.
It may be read as a suspension of ordinary democracy or
a pretext for evading it. Both readings are harmful, and
cannot be avoided without long special commentaries.

Rudzutak's plain statement of the same ideas is more
correct and more handy. This is indirectly confirmed by
Trotsky's parallel of "war democracy" which he draws with
his own term in an article, "Industrial Democracy", in
Pravda of January 11, and which fails to refute that his
term is inaccurate and inconvenient (for he side-steps the
whole issue and fails to compare his theses with Rudzutak's). Happily, as far as I can recall, we have never had
any factional controversy over that kind of term.

Trotsky's "production atmosphere" is even wider of the
mark, and Zinoviev had good reason to laugh at it. This
made Trotsky very angry, and he came out with this
argument: "We once had a war atmosphere. . . . We must now
have a production atmosphere and not only on the surface
but deep down in the workers' mass. This must be as
intense and practical an interest in production as was earlier
displayed in the fronts. . . ." Well, there you are: the message must be carried "deep down into the workers' mass"

in the language of Rudzutak's theses, because "production atmosphere" will only earn you a smile or a shrug. Comrade Trotsky's "production atmosphere" has essentially the same meaning as production propaganda, but such expressions must be avoided when production propaganda is addressed to the workers at large. The term is an example of how *not* to carry it on among the masses.

POLITICS AND ECONOMICS.
DIALECTICS AND ECLECTICISM

It is strange that we should have to return to such elementary questions, but we are unfortunately forced to do so by Trotsky and Bukharin. They have both reproached me for "switching" the issue, or for taking a "political" approach, while theirs is an "economic" one. Bukharin even put that in his theses and tried to "rise above" either side, as if to say that he was combining the two.

This is a glaring theoretical error. I said again in my speech that politics is a concentrated expression of economics, because I had earlier heard my "political" approach rebuked in a manner which is inconsistent and inadmissible for a Marxist. Politics must take precedence over economics. To argue otherwise is to forget the ABC of Marxism.

Am I wrong in my political appraisal? If you think so, say it and prove it. But you forget the ABC of Marxism when you say (or imply) that the political approach is equivalent to the "economic", and that you can take "the one and the other".

What the political approach means, in other words, is that the wrong attitude to the trade unions will ruin the Soviet power and topple the dictatorship of the proletariat. (In a peasant country like Russia, the Soviet power would surely go down in the event of a split between the trade unions and a Party in the wrong.) This proposition can (and must) be tested in substance, which means looking into the rights and wrongs of the approach and taking a decision. To say: I "appreciate" your political approach, "*but*" it is only a political one and we "*also* need an economic one", is tantamount to saying: I "appreciate" your point that in taking that particular step you are liable to break your neck, *but* you must also take into consideration that it is better to be clothed and well-fed than to go naked and hungry.

Bukharin's insistence on combining the political *and* the economic approach has landed him in theoretical *eclecticism*.

Trotsky and Bukharin make as though they are concerned for the growth of production whereas we have nothing but formal democracy in mind. This picture is wrong, because the *only* formulation of the issue (which the Marxist standpoint *allows*) is: without a correct political approach to the matter the given class will be unable to stay on top, *and, consequently*, will be incapable of solving *its production problem* either.

Let us take a concrete example. Zinoviev says: "By carrying things to a split within the trade unions, you are making a political mistake. I spoke and wrote about the growth of production back in January 1920, citing the construction of the public baths as an example." Trotsky replies: "What a thing to boast of: a pamphlet with the public baths as an example (p. 29), 'and not a single word' about the tasks of the trade unions" (p. 22).

This is wrong. The example of the public baths is worth, you will pardon the pun, a dozen "production atmospheres", with a handful of "industrial democracies" thrown in. It tells the masses, the whole bulk of them, what the trade unions are to do, and does this in plain and intelligible terms, whereas all these "production atmospheres" and "democracies" are so much murk blurring the vision of the workers' masses, and *dimming* their understanding.

Comrade Trotsky also rebuked me for not "saying a word" (p. 66) about "the role that has to be played—and is being played—by the levers known as the trade union apparatus".

I beg to differ, Comrade Trotsky. By reading out Rudzutak's theses *in toto* and endorsing them, I made a statement on the question that was *fuller, plainer, clearer and more correct* than all your theses, your report or co-report, and speech in reply to the debate. I insist that bonuses in kind and disciplinary comrades' courts mean a great deal more to economic development, industrial management, and wider trade union participation in production than the absolutely abstract (and therefore empty) talk about "industrial democracy", "coalescence", etc.

Behind the effort to present the "production" standpoint (Trotsky) or to overcome a one-sided political approach and combine it with an economic approach (Bukharin) we find:

1) Neglect of Marxism, as expressed in the theoretically incorrect, eclectic definition of the relation between politics and economics;

2) Defence or camouflage of the political mistake expressed in the shake-up policy, which runs through the *whole* of Trotsky's platform pamphlet, and which, unless it is admitted and corrected, *leads* to the collapse of the dictatorship of the proletariat;

3) A step back in purely economic and production matters, and the question of how to increase production; it is, in fact, a step back from Rudzutak's *practical* theses, with their concrete, vital and urgent tasks (develop production propaganda; learn proper distribution of bonuses in kind and correct use of coercion through disciplinary comrades' courts), to the highbrow, abstract, "empty" and theoretically incorrect general *theses* which *ignore* all that is most practical and business-like.

That is where Zinoviev and myself, on the one hand, and Trotsky and Bukharin, on the other, actually stand on this question of politics and economics.

I could not help smiling, therefore, when I read Comrade Trotsky's objection in his speech of December 30: "In his summing-up at the Eighth Congress of Soviets of the debate on the situation, Comrade Lenin said we ought to have less politics and more economics, but when he got to the trade union question he laid emphasis on the political aspect of the matter" (p. 65). Comrade Trotsky thought these words were "very much to the point". Actually, however, they reveal a terrible confusion of ideas, a truly hopeless "ideological confusion". Of course, I have always said, and will continue to say, that we need more economics and less politics, but if we are to have this we must clearly be rid of political dangers *and political mistakes*. Comrade Trotsky's political mistakes, aggravated by Comrade Bukharin, *distract* our Party's attention from economic tasks and "production" worK, and, *unfortunately, make us waste time* on correcting them and arguing it out with the syndicalist deviation (which leads to the collapse of the dictatorship of the proletariat), objecting to the incorrect approach to the trade union movement (which leads to the collapse of the Soviet power), and debating general "theses", instead of having a practical and business-like "economic" discussion as to whether it was the Saratov millers, the Donbas miners, the Petrograd metalworkers or some other group that had the best results in coalescing, distributing bonuses in kind, and organising comrades' courts, on the basis of Rudzutak's theses, adopted by the Fifth All-Russia Trade Union Conference on November 2-6.

Let us now consider what good there is in a "broad discussion". Once again we find political mistakes distracting attention from economic tasks. I was against this "broad" discussion, and I believed, and still do, that it was a mistake--a political mistake--on Comrade Trotsky's part to disrupt the work of the trade union commission, which ought to have held a business-like discussion. I believe Bukharin's buffer group made the political mistake of misunderstanding the tasks of the buffer (in which case they had once again substituted eclecticism for dialectics), for from the "buffer" standpoint they should have vigorously opposed any broad discussion and demanded that the matter should be taken up by the trade union commission. Here is what came of this.

On December 30, Bukharin went so far as to say that "we have proclaimed the new and sacred slogan of workers' democracy, which means that questions are no longer to be discussed in the board-room within the corporation or at small meetings but are to be placed before big meetings. I insist that by taking the trade union issue before such a large meeting as this one we are not taking a step backward but forward" (p. 45). And this man has accused Zinoviev of spouting "hot air" and overdoing the democracy! I say that he himself has given us a lot of hot air and has shown some unexampled bungling; he has completely failed to understand that formal democracy must be subordinate to the revolutionary interest.

Trotsky is in the same boat. His charge is that "Lenin

wants at all costs to disrupt or shelve the discussion of the matter in essence" (p. 65). He declares: "My reasons for refusing to serve on the commission were clearly stated in the Central Committee: until such time as I am permitted, on a par with all other comrades, to air these questions fully in the Party press, I do not expect any good to come of any cloistered examination of these matters, and, consequently, of work on the commission" (p. 69).

What is the result? Less than a month has passed since Trotsky started his "broad discussion" on December 25, and you will be hard put to find one responsible Party worker in a hundred who is not fed up with the discussion and has not realised its futility (to say no worse). For Trotsky has made the Party waste time on a discussion of words and bad theses, and has ridiculed as "cloistered" the *business-like* economic discussion in the commission, which was to have studied and verified practical experience and projected its lessons for *progress* in real "production" work, in place of the *regress* from vibrant activity to scholastic exercises in all sorts of "production atmospheres".

Take this famous "coalescence". My advice on December 30 was that we should keep mum on this point, because we had *not studied* our own practical experience, and without that any discussion was bound to degenerate into "hot air" and draw off the Party's forces *from* economic work. I said it was bureaucratic projecteering for Trotsky to propose in his theses that from one-third to one-half and from one-half to two-thirds of the economic councils should consist of trade unionists.

For this I was upbraided by Bukharin who, I see from p. 49 of the report, made a point of proving to me at length and in great detail that "when people meet to discuss something, they should not act as deaf-mutes" (*sic*). Trotsky was also angry and exclaimed:

"Will every one of you please make a note that on this particular date Comrade Lenin described this as a bureaucratic evil. I take the liberty to predict that within a few months we shall have accepted for our guidance and consideration that the All-Russia Central Council of Trade Unions and the Supreme Economic Council, the Central Committee of the Metalworkers' Union and the Metals Department, etc., are to have from one-third to one-half of their members in common" (p. 68).

'When I read that I asked Comrade Milyutin (Deputy
Chairman of the Supreme Economic Council) to let me have
the available *printed* reports on coalescence. I said to myself: why not make a small start on the *study of our practical
experience*; it's so dull engaging in "general Party talk"
(Bukharin's expression, p. 47, which has every chance of
becoming a catchword like "shake-up") to no useful purpose,
without the facts, and inventing disagreements, definitions
and "industrial democracies".

Comrade Milyutin sent me several books, including *The
Report of the Supreme Economic Council to the Eighth All-
Russia Congress of Soviets* (Moscow, 1920; preface dated
December 19, 1920). On its p. 14 is a table showing workers' participation in administrative bodies. Here is the
table (covering only part of the gubernia economic councils
and factories):

Administrative body	Total members	Workers		Specialists		Office workers and others	
		Number	Per cent	Number	Per cent	Number	Per cent
Presidium of Supreme Economic Council and gubernia economic councils . . .	187	107	57.2	22	11.8	58	31.0
Collegiums of chief administrations, departments, central boards and head offices	140	72	51.4	31	22.2	37	26.4
Corporate and one-man managements of factories	1,143	726	63.5	398	34.8	19	1.7
Total . .	1,470	905	61.6	451	30.7	114	7.7

It will be seen that 61.6 per cent, that is, closer to two-
thirds than to one-half, of the staff of administrative bodies
now consists of workers. And this *already proves* that what
Trotsky wrote on this matter in his theses was an exercise
in bureaucratic projecteering. To talk, argue and write

platforms about "one-third to one-half" and "one-half to two-thirds" is the most useless sort of "general Party talk", which diverts time, attention and resources from *production* work. It is empty politicking. All this while, a great deal of good could have been done in the commission, where men of experience would have refused to write any theses without a study of the facts, say, by polling a dozen or so "common functionaries" (out of the thousand), by comparing their impressions and conclusions with objective statistical data, and by making an attempt to obtain practical guidance for the future: that being our experience, do we go straight on, or do we make some change in our course, methods and approach, and how; or do we call a halt, for the good of the cause, and check things over and over again, make a few changes here and there, and so on and so forth.

Comrades, a real "executive" (let me also have a go at "production propaganda") is well aware that even in the most advanced countries, the capitalists and their executives take years—sometimes ten and more—to study and test their own (and others') practical experience, making innumerable starts and corrections to tailor a system of management, select senior and junior executives, etc., fit for their particular business. That was the rule under capitalism, which throughout the civilised world based its business practices on *the experience and habits of centuries*. We who are breaking new ground must put in a long, persistent and patient effort to retrain men and change the old habits which have come down to us from capitalism, but this can only be done little by little. Trotsky's approach is quite wrong. In his December 30 speech he exclaimed: "Do or do not our workers, Party and trade union functionaries have any production training? Yes or no? I say: No" (p. 29). This is a ridiculous approach. It is like asking whether a division has enough felt boots: Yes or no?

It is safe to say that even ten years from now we shall have to admit that all our Party and trade union functionaries do not have enough production training, in much the same way as the workers of the Military Department, the trade unions and the Party will not have had enough military experience. But we have made a *start* on production training by having about a thousand workers, and trade union members and delegates take part in management and run factories, head offices and other bodies higher up the scale. The basic principle underlying "production training"—which is the training of *our own selves*, of the old underground workers and professional journalists—is that we should start a painstaking and detailed study of our own practical experience, and teach others to do so, according to the rule: Look before you leap. The fundamental and absolute rule behind "production training" is systematic, circumspect, practical and business-like verification of what this one thousand have done, and even more efficient and careful correction of their work, taking a step forward only when there is ample proof of the usefulness of a given method, system of management, proportion, selection of men, etc. And it is this rule that Comrade Trotsky has broken by his theses and approach. All his theses, his entire platform pamphlet, are so wrong that they have diverted the Party's attention and resources from practical "production" work to a lot of empty talk.

DIALECTICS AND ECLECTICISM.
"SCHOOL" AND "APPARATUS"

Among Comrade Bukharin's many excellent traits are his theoretical ability and keen interest in getting at the theoretical roots of every question. That is a very valuable trait because you cannot have a proper understanding of any mistake, let alone a political one, unless you dig down to its theoretical roots among the basic premises of the one who makes it.

Responding to this urge, Comrade Bukharin tended to shift the controversy into the theoretical sphere, beginning from December 30, if not earlier.

In his speech on that day he said: "That neither the political nor the economic factor can be ignored is, I believe, absolutely incontrovertible—and that is the theoretical essence of what is here known as the 'buffer group' or its ideology" (p. 47).

The gist of his theoretical mistake in this case is substitution of eclecticism for the dialectical interplay of politics and economics (which we find in Marxism). His theoretical attitude is: "on the one hand, and on the other", "the one and the other". That is eclecticism. Dialectics requires an all-round consideration of relationships in their concrete development but not a patchwork of bits and pieces. I have shown this to be so on the example of politics and economics.

That of the "buffer" has gone to reinforce the point. You need a buffer, and it is useful when the Party train is heading for a crash. No question about that at all. Bukharin has built up his "buffer" problem eclectically, by collecting odd pieces from Zinoviev and Trotsky. As a "buffer", Bukharin should have decided for himself just where, when and how each individual or group had made their mistake, whether it was a theoretical mistake, one of political tact, factional pronouncement, or exaggeration, etc. He should have done that and gone *hammer and tongs at every* such mistake. But he has failed to understand his task of "buffer", and here is good proof of it.

The Communist group of Tsektran's Petrograd Bureau (the C.C. of the Railwaymen's and Water Transport Workers' Union), an organisation sympathising with Trotsky, has stated its opinion that, "on the main issue of the trade unions' role in production, Comrades Trotsky and Bukharin hold views which are variations of one and the same standpoint". It has issued Comrade Bukharin's report in Petrograd on January 3, 1921, in pamphlet form (N. Bukharin, *The Tasks of the Trade Unions*, Petrograd, 1921). It says:

"Comrade Trotsky's original formulation was that the trade union leadership should be removed and suitable comrades found to take their place, etc. He had earlier advocated a 'shake-up', but he has now abandoned the idea, and it is therefore quite absurd to use it as an argument against him" (p. 5).

I will let pass the numerous factual inaccuracies in this statement. (Trotsky used the term "shake-up" at the Fifth All-Russia Conference of Trade Unions, November 2 6. He mentions "selection of leadership" in Paragraph 5 of his theses which he submitted to the Central Committee on

November 8, and which, incidentally, some of his supporters have published as a leaflet. The whole of Trotsky's pamphlet, *The Role and Tasks of the Trade Unions*, December 25, reveals the same kind of mentality, the same spirit as I have pointed out before. When and how he "abandoned" this attitude remains a mystery.) I am now dealing with a different matter. When the "buffer" is an eclectic, he passes over some mistakes and brings up others; he says nothing of them in Moscow on December 30, 1920, when addressing thousands of R.C.P. functionaries from all over Russia; but he brings them up in Petrograd on January 3, 1921. When the "buffer" is a dialectician, he directs the full brunt of his attack at every mistake he sees on either side, or on all sides. And that is something Bukharin does not do. He does not even try to examine Trotsky's pamphlet in the light of the "shake-up" policy. *He simply says nothing about it.* No wonder his buffer performance has made everyone laugh.

To proceed. In that same Petrograd speech he says (p. 7):

"Comrade Trotsky's mistake is insufficient support for the school-of-communism idea."

During the December 30 discussion, Bukharin reasoned as follows:

"Comrade Zinoviev has said that the trade unions are a school of communism, and Trotsky has said that they are a technical and administrative apparatus for industrial management. I see no logical grounds for proof that either proposition is wrong; both, and a combination of both, are right" (p. 48).

Bukharin and his "group" or "faction" make the same point in their thesis 6: "On the one hand, they [the trade unions] are a school of communism . . . and on the other, they are—increasingly—a component part of the economic apparatus and of state administration in general" (*Pravda*, January 16).

That is where we find Comrade Bukharin's fundamental theoretical mistake, which is substitution of eclecticism (especially popular with the authors of diverse "fashionable" and reactionary philosophical systems) for Marxist dialectics.

When Comrade Bukharin speaks of "logical" grounds, his whole reasoning shows that he takes—unconsciously, perhaps—the standpoint of formal or scholastic logic, and not of dialectical or Marxist logic. Let me explain this by taking the simple example which Comrade Bukharin himself gives. In the December 30 discussion he said:

"Comrades, many of you may find that the current controversy suggests something like this: two men come in and invite each other to define the tumbler on the lectern. One says: 'It is a glass cylinder, and a curse on anyone who says different.' The other one says: 'A tumbler is a drinking vessel, and a curse on anyone who says different'" (p. 46).

The reader will see that Bukharin's example was meant to give me a popular explanation of the harm of one-track thinking. I accept it with gratitude, and in the one-good-turn-deserves-another spirit offer a popular explanation of the difference between dialectics and eclecticism.

A tumbler is assuredly both a glass cylinder and a drinking vessel. But there are more than these two properties, qualities or facets to it; there are an infinite number of them, an infinite number of "mediacies" and inter-relationships with the rest of the world. A tumbler is a heavy object which can be used as a missile; it can serve as a paperweight, a receptacle for a captive butterfly, or a valuable object with an artistic engraving or design, and this has nothing at all to do with whether or not it can be used for drinking, is made of glass, is cylindrical or not quite, and so on and so forth.

Moreover, if I needed a tumbler just now for drinking, it would not in the least matter how cylindrical it was, and whether it was actually made of glass; what would matter though would be whether it had any holes in the bottom, or anything that would cut my lips when I drank, etc. But if I did not need a tumbler for drinking but for a purpose that could be served by any glass cylinder, a tumbler with a cracked bottom or without one at all would do just as well, etc.

Formal logic, which is as far as schools go (and should go, with suitable abridgements for the lower forms), deals with formal definitions, draws on what is most common, or glaring, and stops there. When two or more different definitions are taken and combined at random (a glass cylinder and a drinking vessel), the result is an eclectic definition which is indicative of different facets of the object, and nothing more.

Dialectical logic demands that we should go further. Firstly, if we are to have a true knowledge of an object we must look at and examine all its facets, its connections and "mediacies". That is something we cannot ever hope to achieve completely, but the rule of comprehensiveness is a safeguard against mistakes and rigidity. Secondly, dialectical logic requires that an object should be taken in development, in change, in "self-movement" (as Hegel sometimes puts it). This is not immediately obvious in respect of such an object as a tumbler, but it, too, is in flux, and this holds especially true for its purpose, use and *connection* with the surrounding world. Thirdly, a full "definition" of an object must include the whole of human experience, both as a criterion of truth and a practical indicator of its connection with human wants. Fourthly, dialectical logic holds that "truth is always concrete, never abstract", as the late Plekhanov liked to say after Hegel. (Let me add in parenthesis for the benefit of young Party members that you *cannot* hope to become a *real*, intelligent Communist without making a study—and I mean *study* — of all of Plekhanov's philosophical writings, because nothing better has been written on Marxism anywhere in the world.*)

I have not, of course, run through the whole notion of dialectical logic, but what I have said will do for the present. I think we can return from the tumbler to the trade unions and Trotsky's platform.

"A school, on the one hand, and an apparatus on the other", says Bukharin, and writes as much in his theses. Trotsky's mistake is "insufficient support for the school-

---

* By the way, it would be a good thing, first, if the current edition of Plekhanov's works contained a special volume or volumes of all his philosophical articles, with detailed indexes, etc., to be included in a series of standard textbooks on communism; secondly, I think the workers' state must·demand that professors of philosophy should have a knowledge of Plekhanov's exposition of Marxist philosophy and ability to impart it to their students. But all that is a digression from "propaganda" to "administration".

of-communism idea"; Zinoviev errs by being lukewarm on the apparatus "factor".

Why is Bukharin's reasoning no more than inert and empty eclecticism? It is because he does not even try to make an independent analysis, from his own standpoint, either of the whole course of the current controversy (as Marxism, *that is*, dialectical logic, unconditionally demands) or of the whole approach to the question, the whole presentation—the whole trend of the presentation, if you will— of the question at the present time and in these concrete circumstances. You do not see Bukharin doing that at all! His approach is one of pure abstraction: he makes no attempt at concrete study, and takes bits and pieces from Zinoviev and Trotsky. That is eclecticism.

Here is another example to clarify the picture. I know next to nothing about the insurgents and revolutionaries of South China (apart from the two or three articles by Sun Yat-sen, and a few books and newspaper articles I read many years ago). Since there are these uprisings, it is not too far-fetched to assume a controversy going on between Chinese No. 1, who says that the insurrection is the product of a most acute nation-wide class struggle, and Chinese No. 2, who says that insurrection is an art. That is all I need to know in order to write theses *à la* Bukharin: "On the one hand, . . . on the other hand". The one has failed to reckon with the art "factor", and the other, with the "acuteness factor", etc. Because no *concrete* study is made of *this particular* controversy, question, approach, etc., the result is a dead and empty eclecticism.

On the one hand, the trade unions are a school, and on the other, an apparatus; but they also happen to be an organisation of working people, an almost exclusive organisation of industrial workers, an organisation by industry, etc.* Bukharin does not make any analysis for himself, nor does he produce a shred of evidence to prove why it is that we should consider the first two "facets" of the question

* Incidentally, here again Trotsky makes a mistake. He thinks that an industrial union is designed to control industry. That is wrong. When you say that a union is an industrial one you mean that it admits to membership workers in one industry, which is inevitable at the present level of technology and culture (in Russia and elsewhere).

or object, instead of the third, the fourth, the fifth, etc.
That is why his group's theses are an eclectic soap bubble.
His presentation of the "school-apparatus" relationship is
fundamentally eclectic and wrong.

The only way to view this question in the right light
is to descend from empty abstractions to the concrete, that
is, the present issue. Whether you take it in the form it
assumed at the Fifth All-Russia Conference of Trade Unions,
or as it was presented and *slanted* by Trotsky himself in his
platform pamphlet of December 25, you will find that his
whole approach is quite wrong and that he has gone off at
à tangent. He has failed to understand that the trade unions
can and must be viewed as a school both when raising the
question of "Soviet trade-unionism", and when speaking
of production propaganda in general, and even when considering "coalescence" and trade union participation in
industrial management, *as Trotsky does*. On this last point,
as it is presented in Trotsky's platform pamphlet, the
mistake lies in his failure to grasp that the trade unions
are a *school of technical and administrative management
of production*. In the context of the controversy, you cannot say: "a school, on the one hand, and something else
on the other"; given Trotsky's approach, *the trade unions,
whichever way you look at them, are a school*. They are a
school of unity, solidarity, management and administration,
where you learn how to protect your interests. Instead of
making an effort to comprehend and correct Comrade Trotsky's fundamental mistake, Comrade Bukharin has produced
a funny little amendment: "On the one hand, and on the
other."

Let us go deeper into the question. Let us see what the
present trade unions are, as an "apparatus" of industrial
management. We have seen from the incomplete returns
that about 900 workers—trade union members and delegates
—are engaged in industrial management. If you multiply
this number by 10 or even by 100—if it helps to clarify
your fundamental mistake let us assume this incredible
speed of "advance" in the immediate future—you still
have an insignificant proportion of those directly engaged
in *management*, as compared with the mass of six million
trade union members. This makes it even clearer that it

is quite wrong to look to the "leading stratum", and talk about the trade unions' role in production and industrial management, as Trotsky does, forgetting that 98:5 per cent (6 million minus 90,000 equals 5,910,000 or 98.5 per cent of the total) *are learning, and will have to continue to do so for a long time to come.* Don't say school *and* management, say *school of management.*

In his December 30 argument against Zinoviev, whom he accused, quite groundlessly and incorrectly, of denying the "appointments system", that is, the Central Committee's right and duty to make appointments, Comrade Trotsky inadvertently drew the following telltale comparison:

"Zinoviev tends to overdo the propaganda angle on every practical matter, forgetting that it is not only a source of material for agitation, but also a problem requiring an administrative solution" (p. 27).

Before I explain in detail the *potential* administrative approach to the issue, let me say that Comrade Trotsky's fundamental mistake is that he treats (rather, maltreats) *the questions* he himself had brought up in his platform pamphlet as *administrative* ones, whereas *they* could be and ought to be viewed *only from the propaganda angle.*

In effect, what are Trotsky's good points? One undoubtedly good and useful point is his *production propaganda*, but that is not in his theses, but in his *speeches*, specially when he forgets about his unfortunate polemics with the allegedly "conservative" wing of the trade-unionists. He would undoubtedly have done (and I believe he will do) a great deal of good in the trade union commission's practical business, as speaker and writer, and as a member of the All-Russia Production Propaganda Bureau. His platform theses were a mistake, for through them, like a scarlet thread, runs the administrative approach to the "crisis" and the "two trends" within the trade unions, the interpretation of the R.C.P. Programme, "Soviet trade-unionism", "production training" and "coalescence". I have listed all the main points of Trotsky's "platform" and they all happen to be topics which, considering the material at Trotsky's disposal, can be correctly approached at the present time only from the propaganda angle.

The state is a sphere of coercion. It would be madness

to renounce coercion, especially in the epoch of the dictatorship of the proletariat, so that the administrative approach
and "steerage" are indispensable. The Party is the leader,
the vanguard of the proletariat, which rules directly.
It is not coercion but expulsion from the Party that is
the specific means of influence and the means of purging
and steeling the vanguard. The trade unions are a reservoir
of the state power, a school of communism and a school
of management. The specific and cardinal thing in this
sphere is *not* administration but the *"ties" "between* the
central state administration" (and, of course, the local
as well), "the national economy and the *broad masses* of
the working people" (see Party Programme, economic
section, § 5, dealing with the trade unions).

The whole of Trotsky's platform pamphlet betrays an
incorrect approach to the problem and a misunderstanding
of this relationship.

Let us assume that Trotsky had taken a different approach
to this famous question of "coalescence" in connection
with the other topics of his platform, and that his pamphlet
was entirely devoted to a detailed investigation of, say,
90 of the 900 cases of "coalescence" where trade union
officials and members concurrently held elective trade
union posts and Supreme Economic Council posts in industrial management. Let us say these 90 cases had been
analysed together with the returns of a selective statistical
survey, the reports of inspectors and instructors of Rabkrin
and the People's Commissariats concerned: let us say they
had been analysed in the light of the data supplied by the
administrative bodies, the results of the work, the headway
in production, etc. That would have been a correct administrative approach, and would have fully vindicated the "shake-up"
line, which implies concentrating attention on removals,
transfers, appointments and the immediate demands to
be made on the "leading stratum". When Bukharin said
in his January 3 speech, published by the Tsektran people
in Petrograd, that Trotsky had at first wanted a "shake-up"
but had now abandoned the idea, he made another one of
his eclectical mistakes, which is ridiculous from the practical
standpoint and theoretically inadmissible for a Marxist.
He takes the question in the abstract, being unable (or

unwilling) to get down to brass tacks. So long as we, the Party's Central Committee and the whole Party, continue to run things, that is, govern, we shall never—we cannot—dispense with the "shake-up", that is, removals, transfers, appointments, dismissals, etc. But Trotsky's platform pamphlet deals with something else, and does not raise the "question of practical business" at all. It is not this but the *"trends* within the trade union movement" (Trotsky's thesis 4, end) that was being debated by Zinoviev and Trotsky, Bukharin and myself, and in fact the whole Party.

This is essentially a political question. Because of the substance of the case—this concrete, particular "case"—it is impossible to correct Trotsky's mistake by means of eclectic little amendments and addenda, as Bukharin has been trying to do, being moved undoubtedly by the most humane sentiments and intentions.

There is only one answer.

First, there must be a correct solution of the political question of the "trends within the trade union movement", the relationship between classes, between politics and economics, the specific role of the state, the Party, the trade unions, as "school" and apparatus, etc.

Second, once the correct political decision has been adopted, a diversified nation-wide production propaganda campaign must be carried through, or, rather, systematically carried forward with persistence and patience over a long term, under the sponsorship and direction of a state agency. It should be conducted in such a way as to cover the same ground over and over again.

Third, the "questions of practical business" must not be confused with trend issues which properly belong to the sphere of "general Party talk" and broad discussions; they must be dealt with as practical matters in the working commissions, with a hearing of witnesses and a study of memoranda, reports and statistics. And any necessary "shake-up" must be carried out only on that basis and in those circumstances: only under a decision of the competent Soviet or Party organ, or of both.

Trotsky and Bukharin have produced a hodgepodge of political mistakes in approach, breaks in the middle of the transmission belts, and unwarranted and futile attacks on "administrative steerage". It is now clear where the "theoretical" source of the mistake lies, since Bukharin has taken up that aspect of it with his example of the tumbler. His theoretical—in this case, gnosiological—mistake lies in his substitution of eclecticism for dialectics. His eclectic approach has confused him and has landed him in syndicalism. Trotsky's mistake is one-track thinking, compulsiveness, exaggeration and obstinacy. His platform says that a tumbler is a drinking vessel, but this particular tumbler happens to have no bottom.

CONCLUSION

It remains for me to go over a few more points which must be dealt with to prevent misunderstanding.

Thesis 6 of Trotsky's platform quotes Paragraph 5 of the economic section of the R.C.P. Programme, which deals with the trade unions. Two pages later, his thesis 8 says: "Having lost the old basis of their existence, the class economic struggle, the trade unions..." (that is wrong, and is a hasty exaggeration: the trade unions no longer have to face the *class* economic struggle but the *non-class* "economic struggle", which means combating bureaucratic distortions of the Soviet apparatus, safeguarding the working people's material and spiritual interests in ways and means inaccessible to this apparatus, etc. This is a struggle they will unfortunately have to face for many more years to come). "The trade unions," says Trotsky, "have, for various reasons, not yet succeeded in mustering the necessary forces and working out the necessary methods enabling them to solve the new task, that of *organising production*" (Trotsky's italics, p. 9, thesis 8), "set before them by the proletarian revolution and formulated in our Programme."

That is yet another hasty exaggeration which is pregnant with grave error. The Programme does not contain any such formulation nor does it set the trade unions the task of "organising production". Let us go over the propositions in the Party's Programme as they unfold in the text:

(1) "The organisational apparatus" (but not the others) "of socialised industry should rely chiefly" (but not exclusively) "on the trade unions." (2) "They must to an ever

increasing degree divest themselves of the narrow craft-union spirit" (how? under the leadership of the Party and through the proletariat's educational and other influence on the non-proletarian mass of working people) "and become large industrial associations, embracing the majority, and eventually all of the workers in the given industry."

That is the first part of the section of the Party Programme dealing with the trade unions. You will have noted that it starts by laying down very "*strict* conditions" demanding a long sustained effort for what is to follow. And what follows is this:

"The trade unions being, on the strength of the laws of the Soviet Republic and established practice, participants" (note the cautious statement: participants only) "in all the local and central organs of industrial management, should eventually arrive at a *de facto* concentration in their hands of the whole administration of the whole national economy, as a single economic entity" (note this: should arrive at a *de facto* concentration of management not of branches of industry and not of industry as a whole, but of the whole national economy, and moreover, as an economic entity. In economic terms, this condition may be considered fulfilled only when the petty producers both in industry and agriculture account for less than one-half of the population and the national economy). "The trade unions ensuring in this way" (the way which helps to realise all the conditions listed earlier) "indissoluble ties between the central state administration, the national economy and the broad masses of working people, should draw the latter" (that is, the masses, the majority of the population) "into direct economic management on the widest possible scale. At the same time, the participation of the trade unions in economic management and their activity in drawing the broad masses into this work are the principal means of combating the bureaucratisation of the economic apparatus of the Soviet power and making possible the establishment of truly popular control over the results of production."

There again, in that last sentence, we find a very cautious phrase: "participation in economic management"; and another reference to the recruitment of the broad masses as the chief (but not the only) means of combating bureaucratic practices; finally, we find a highly cautious statement: "*making possible*" the establishment of "*popular*"—that is, workers' and peasants', and not just purely proletarian—"*control*".

It is obviously wrong to boil this down to the Party Programme "formulating" the trade unions' task as "organisation of production". And if you insist on this error, and write it into your platform theses, you will get nothing but an anti-communist, syndicalist deviation.

Incidentally, Comrade Trotsky says in his theses that "over the last period we have not made any headway towards the goal set forth in the Programme but have in fact retreated from it" (p. 7, thesis 6). That statement is unsupported, and, I think, wrong. It is no proof to say, as Trotsky did in the discussions, that the trade unions "themselves" admit this. That is not the last resort, as far as the Party is concerned, and, generally speaking, the proof lies only in a serious and objective study of a great number of facts. Moreover, even if such proof were forthcoming, there would remain this question: Why have we retreated? Is it because "many trade-unionists" are "balking at the new tasks and methods", as Trotsky believes, or because "we have not yet succeeded in mustering the necessary forces and working out the necessary methods" to cut short and correct certain unwarranted and harmful excesses of bureaucracy?

Which brings me to Bukharin's rebuke of December 30 (repeated by Trotsky yesterday, January 24, during our discussion in the Communist group of the Second Miners' Congress) that we have "dropped the line laid down by the Ninth Party Congress" (p. 46 of the report on the December 30 discussion). He alleged that at that Congress I had defended the militarisation of labour and had jeered at references to democracy, all of which I now "repudiate". In his reply to the debate on December 30, Comrade Trotsky added this barb: "Lenin takes account of the fact that . . . there is a grouping of opposition-minded comrades within the trade unions" (p. 65); that I view it from the "diplomatic angle" (p. 69), and that there is "manoeuvring inside the Party groups" (p. 70), etc. Putting such a complexion on the case is, of course, highly flattering for Trotsky, and worse than unflattering for me. But let us look at the facts.

In that same discussion on December 30, Trotsky and Krestinsky established the fact that "as long ago as July (1920), Comrade Preobrazhensky had proposed to the Central Committee that we should switch to a new track in respect of the internal life of our workers' organisations" (p. 25). In August, Comrade Zinoviev drafted a letter, and the Central Committee approved a *C.C. letter* on combating red-tape and extending democracy. In September, the question was brought up at a Party conference whose decisions were endorsed by the Central Committee. In December, the question of combating red-tape was laid before the Eighth Congress of Soviets. Consequently, the whole Central Committee, the whole Party and the whole workers' and peasants' Republic had recognised that the question of the bureaucracy and ways of combating its evils was high on the agenda. Does any "repudiation" of the Ninth Congress of the R.C.P. follow from all this? Of course, not. The decisions on the militarisation of labour, etc., are incontestable, and there is no need for me at all to withdraw any of my jibes at the references to democracy by those who challenged these decisions. What does follow is that we shall be extending democracy in the workers' organisations, without turning it into a fetish; that we shall redouble our attention to the struggle against bureaucratic practices; and that we shall take special care to rectify any unwarranted and harmful excesses of bureaucracy, no matter who points them out.

One final remark on the minor question of priority and equalisation. I said during the December 30 discussion that Trotsky's formulation of thesis 41 on this point was theoretically wrong, because it implied priority in production and equalisation in consumption. I replied that priority implied preference and that that was nothing unless you also had it in consumption. Comrade Trotsky reproached me for "extraordinary forgetfulness" and "intimidation" (pp. 67 and 68), and I am surprised to find that he has not accused me also of manoeuvring, diplomatic moves, etc. He has made "concessions" to my equalitarian line, but I have attacked him.

Actually, however, anyone who takes an interest in
Party affairs, can turn to indisputable Party documents:
the November resolution of the C.C. Plenum, point
4, and Trotsky's platform pamphlet, thesis 41. However
"forgetful" I may be, and however excellent Comrade
Trotsky's memory, it is still a fact that thesis 41 contains
a theoretical error, which the C.C. resolution of November
9 does not. The resolution says: "While recognising the
necessity of keeping to the principle of priority in carrying
out the economic plan, the Central Committee, in complete
solidarity with the decisions of the last All-Russia Conference
(September), deems it necessary to effect a gradual but
steady transition to equality in the status of various groups
of workers and their respective trade unions, all the while
building up the organisation on the scale of the union as
a whole." That is clearly aimed against Tsektran, and it
is quite impossible to put any other construction on the exact
meaning of the resolution. Priority is here to stay.
Preference is still to be given to enterprises, trade unions,
trusts and departments on the priority list (in regard to
fulfilment of the economic plan), but at the same time, the
"equalitarian line"—which was supported not by "Comrade
Lenin alone", but was approved *by the Party Conference and
the Central Committee, that is, the entire Party*—makes this
clear-cut demand: get on with the gradual but steady
transition to equalisation. That Tsektran failed to carry
out this C.C. resolution (November) is evident from the
Central Committee's December resolution (on Trotsky and
Bukharin's motion), which contains another reminder of
the "principles of ordinary democracy". The theoretical
error in thesis 41 is that it says: equalisation in consumption,
priority in production. That is an economic absurdity
because it implies a gap between production and consumption. I did not say—and could never have said—anything
of the sort. If you don't need a factory, close it down. Close
down all the factories that are not absolutely essential,
and give preference to those that are. Give preference to,
say, transport. Most certainly. But the preference must
not be overdone, as it was in Tsektran's case, which was
why the *Party* (and not just Lenin) issued this directive:
get on with the gradual but steady *transition* to equality.

And Trotsky has no one but himself to blame for having come out—after the November Plenary Meeting, which gave a clear-cut and theoretically correct solution—with a factional pamphlet on "the two trends" and proposed a formulation in his thesis 41 which is wrong in economic terms.

Today, January 25, it is exactly one month since Comrade Trotsky's factional statement. It is now patent that this pronouncement, inappropriate in form and wrong in essence, has diverted the Party from its practical economic and production effort into rectifying political and theoretical mistakes. But, it's an ill wind, as the old saying goes.

Rumour has it that some terrible things have been said about the disagreements on the Central Committee. Mensheviks and Socialist-Revolutionaries undoubtedly shelter (and have sheltered) behind the opposition, and it is they who are spreading the rumours, incredibly malicious formulations, and inventions of all sorts to malign the Party, put vile interpretations on its decisions, aggravate conflicts and ruin its work. That is a political trick used by the bourgeoisie, including the petty-bourgeois democrats, the Mensheviks and the Socialist-Revolutionaries, who, for very obvious reasons, hate—and cannot help hating—the Bolsheviks' guts. Every intelligent member of the Party is familiar with this political trick, and knows its worth.

Because of the disagreements on the Central Committee, it had to appeal to the Party, and the discussions that followed clearly revealed the essence and scope of these disagreements. That killed the rumours and the slander. The Party learns its lessons and is tempered in the struggle against factionalism, a new malaise (it is new in the sense that after the October Revolution we had forgotten all about it). Actually, it is an old malaise, with relapses apparently bound to occur over the next few years, but with an easier cure now well in sight.

The Party is learning not to blow up its disagreements. Let me quote at this point Comrade Trotsky's correct remark about Comrade Tomsky: "I have always said

—even when the polemic against Comrade Tomsky was at its bitterest—that it is quite clear to me that only men with his experience and authority ought to be our trade union leaders. I told this to the Party group of the Fifth Conference of the Trade Unions, and repeated it at the Zimin theatre a few days ago. Ideological struggle within the Party does not mean mutual ostracism but mutual influence"[27] (p. 34 of the report on the December 30 discussion). The Party will naturally apply this correct approach to Comrade Trotsky himself.

During the discussion it was Comrade Shlyapnikov and his group, the so-called Workers' Opposition, who showed the most pronounced syndicalist trend. This being an obvious deviation from communism and the Party, we shall have to reckon with it, talk it over, and make a special propaganda effort to explain the error of these views and the danger of making such mistakes. Comrade Bukharin, who actually coined the syndicalist phrase "mandatory nominations" (by trade unions to management bodies) tries to vindicate himself in today's issue of *Pravda*, but I'm afraid his line of defence is highly ineffective and quite wrong. He wants us to know, you see, that he deals with the role of the Party in his other points. I should think so! If it were otherwise it would have been more than just a *mistake*, requiring correction and allowing some slight rectification: it would have been withdrawal from the Party. When you say "mandatory nominations" but neglect to add, there and then, that they are *not* mandatory for the Party, you have a syndicalist deviation, and that is *in*compatible with communism and the Party Programme. If you add: "mandatory but *not* for the Party" you are giving the non-Party workers a false sense of having some increase in their rights, whereas in fact there will be no change at all. The longer Comrade Bukharin persists in his deviation from communism—a deviation that is wrong theoretically and deceptive politically—the more deplorable will be the fruits of his obstinacy. You cannot maintain an untenable proposition. The Party does not object to the extension of the rights of the non-Party workers in general, but a little reflection will show what can and what cannot be done in this respect.

In the discussion by the Communist group of the Second All-Russia Miners' Congress, Shlyapnikov's platform was defeated despite the backing it got from Comrade Kiselyov, who commands special prestige in that union: our platform won 137 votes, Shlyapnikov's, 62, and Trotsky's, 8. The syndicalist malaise must and will be cured.

In this one month, Petrograd, Moscow and a number of provincial towns have shown that the Party responded to the discussion and has rejected Comrade Trotsky's wrong line by an overwhelming majority. While there may have been some vacillation "at the top" and "in the provinces", in the committees and in the offices, the rank-and-file membership—the mass of Party workers—came out solidly against this wrong line.

Comrade Kamenev informed me of Comrade Trotsky's announcement, during the discussion in the Zamoskvorechye District of Moscow on January 23, that he was withdrawing his platform and joining up with the Bukharin group on a new platform. Unfortunately, I heard nothing of this from Comrade Trotsky either on January 23 or 24, when he spoke against me in the Communist group of the Miners' Congress. I don't know whether this is due to another change in Comrade Trotsky's platform and intentions, or to some other reason. In any case, his January 23 announcement shows that the Party, without so much as mustering all its forces, and with only Petrograd, Moscow and a minority of the provincial towns going on record, has corrected Comrade Trotsky's mistake promptly and with determination.

The Party's enemies had rejoiced too soon. They have not been able—and will never be able—to take advantage of some of the inevitable disagreements within the Party to inflict harm on it and on the dictatorship of the proletariat in Russia.

January 25, 1921

Published as a pamphlet
in January 1921
by the Press Department
of the Moscow Soviet
of Workers',
Peasants' and Red Army Deputies

Published according
to the pamphlet text
collated with the manuscript

SPEECH DELIVERED
AT AN ENLARGED CONFERENCE
OF MOSCOW METALWORKERS
FEBRUARY 4, 1921[28]

I regret that I am unable to participate in the work of your Conference and that I must confine myself to a brief statement of my views.

From the speeches the comrades have delivered here I gather that you want to know all about the sowing campaign. Very many people think that there is something tricky about the Soviet government's policy towards the peasants. Our policy in this sphere is one that we are always ready to reveal to the masses. The fundamental problem of the Soviet power is that our own victories have not yet been followed by victories in other countries. If you give our Constitution a careful reading, you will see that we have not made any fantastic promises, but insist on the need for dictatorship, because the whole bourgeois world is against us.

We are told: the peasants' condition is not the same as that of the workers, there is some trick in this. But it is one that we have openly proclaimed.

Anyone who has stopped to think of the relation of forces between ourselves and the bourgeoisie knows that they are stronger; yet, for three years, they have been unable to crush us. That is not a miracle; we do not believe in miracles. The simple truth is that they cannot unite, and are quarrelling over the division of the spoils. Most of the oppressed countries are colonies, and a minority live on their labour, but atop a volcano.

They are stronger, but the movement is growing over there as well. The capitalists have a stronger military force, but they have had a set-back, and we say: the worst is over, but the enemy will make further attempts. Of the Europeans who have visited us none has claimed that his country could have avoided the rags and the queues; and they all agree that, after six years of war, even Britain would have been in a similar state.

We must do our best to establish proper relations between the workers and the peasants. The peasants are another class. We shall have socialism when there are no classes, when all the means of production belong to the working people. We still have classes, it will take many, many years to abolish them, and only a quack will promise to do it overnight. The peasants prefer to go it alone, each one on his own farm, and with his own stock of corn. This gives them power over everybody. An armed enemy is lying in wait for us, and if we are to prevent him from overthrowing us, we must establish proper relations between the workers and the peasants.

If you take the workers and the peasants, you will find that the latter are more numerous. The capitalists claim to have a democracy under which workers and peasants enjoy equal rights. So long as the peasants follow the bourgeoisie and the workers are isolated, they will be defeated. If we forget that, the capitalists will beat us. We have not promised equality, and we have not got it. There can be no equality so long as one has plenty of corn and the other has none.

The capitalists realised that you can share out the land, but not the factories. We have a dictatorship of the proletariat, a term that scares the peasants, but it is the only means of uniting them and making them follow the lead of the workers. We believe this is the correct solution, and the working class will succeed in uniting the peasantry. Only then will the road be open to further advance towards the abolition of classes.

What is the policy of the American capitalists? They are doling out land, and the peasants follow them and are lulled by their talk of equality. Either you are duped in this fashion, or you see through it, unite with the workers and drive out the capitalists.

This is our policy, and you will find it in our Constitution. I was told here that we ought to review the sowing

campaign plans. I know that this spring the peasants are
having it very bad. For the workers, the worst is over.
We have not promised equality to anyone: if you want to
be with the workers, come with us, come over to the socialist
side; if not, go over to the Whites. We never promised
a liberal regime; the one we have has helped us to escape
the bondage of the landowners and capitalists. During
these three years the workers starved and froze, and took
over the idle factories. But they also got the power. Even
the peasants in the fertile areas came to see the difference
between the workers' rule and Denikin's, and they have
made their choice. Our victory over Denikin was not a
miracle; it was due to the fact that even the rich peasants
realised what the Constituent Assembly had come to; this
drove home the point that the proof of the pudding was
in the eating.

The peasants realised that the more territory the Whites
seized, the more peasants would be drafted into the army,
and as soon as enough of them had been collected in the
army, they overthrew Denikin.

We do not promise a land flowing with milk and honey.
But over there you are promised equality, and get saddled
with a landowner. That is why we won.

We are told we ought to review our plans for the sowing
campaign. I say: nobody has suffered as much as the workers.
During this period, the peasants received land and could
obtain corn. This winter the peasants are in desperate
straits and their discontent is understandable.

Let us review the relations between the workers and
the peasants. We have said that the workers have made
incredible sacrifices. This year the peasants are in a terrible
plight, and we know it. We are not opposed to reviewing
these relations. What is the main goal of the sowing campaign? It is to sow all the land, otherwise we are surely
doomed. Do you know how much grain has been taken
from the peasants this year? About three hundred million
poods. What would the working class have done without
it? Even so it starved. We know that the conditions of
the peasants are hard, but there is no other way out of
the situation. We have completely suspended the surplus
grain appropriation system in thirteen gubernias. Last

year we supplied eight million poods of seed grain, and after the harvest we got back six million poods. Now we have supplied approximately fifteen million. To cancel the sowing campaign would be like jumping out of a fifth storey window. We cannot promise the peasants to relieve them of want at a stroke; to do that our factories would have to multiply their output a hundredfold.

If we did not give the workers even the short ration they are now getting, industry would have ground down to a stop.

It is true that for three years the workers got nothing at all. But there is no cure-all.

The working class has been exhausted by these three years, and this spring will be a very hard one for the peasants. But you help us with the sowing campaign—to sow all the fields—then we shall manage to overcome our difficulties.

In Hungary, the peasants failed to help the Hungarian workers and fell under the power of the landowners.

There is the alternative before you. What is the way out of this difficult situation? It is to concentrate efforts on the sowing campaign, point out the mistakes, and make corrections; otherwise there is no way out of the difficulties.

First published
in full in 1927

Published according
to a typewritten copy
of the minutes

SPEECH DELIVERED
AT THE FOURTH ALL-RUSSIA
CONGRESS OF GARMENT WORKERS
FEBRUARY 6, 1921[29]

Comrades, it gives me great pleasure to greet your Congress on behalf of the Central Committee of our Party and of the Council of People's Commissars. What gives me even greater pleasure is your unanimous decision of yesterday, following the happy reconciliation and successful resolution of the conflict and the friction among you, which required such strenuous efforts from all, and some from our Party as well. I am sure, comrades, that this slight clash and its successful settlement will be an earnest that in your future work, as members of the union and of the Party, you will be able to solve all the numerous difficulties and problems that still lie ahead of us.

Comrades, speaking of the position of our Republic in general—of the internal and external position of the Soviet power—the greatest difficulties that confronted us were, of course, those of our external positions. The greatest difficulties of the entire proletarian revolution in Russia arose from our having had to take the initiative in the socialist revolution due to the course of the imperialist war and the preceding development of the first revolution in 1905; this imposed unprecedented difficulties on us, and on our country. You all know, of course—I think that in your branch of industry this is more evident to you than to the workers of other industries—you all know to what extent capital is an international force, to what extent all the big capitalist enterprises, factories, shops, etc., all over the world are linked up together; this makes it obvious that in substance capital cannot be completely defeated in one country. It is an international force, and in order to rout it the workers must also make a concerted effort on an international scale. Ever since 1917, when we fought the bourgeois-republican governments in Russia, and ever since the power of the Soviets was established at the end of 1917, we have been telling the workers again and again that the cardinal task, and the fundamental condition of our victory is to spread the revolution to, at least, a few of the most advanced countries. And our main difficulties over the past four years have been due to the fact that the West European capitalists managed to bring the war to an end and stave off revolution.

We in Russia had particularly striking evidence of the extremely precarious position of the bourgeoisie during the imperialist war. We also heard that in all other countries it was the end of the war that marked the intensification of the political crisis, for then the people were armed and it was an opportune moment for the proletariat to have done with the capitalists at one stroke. For a number of reasons the West European workers failed to do this, and for nearly four years now we have had to defend our positions single-handed.

As a consequence, the difficulties that fell to the lot of the Soviet Republic of Russia were without number, because the military forces of the capitalists of the whole world (vastly superior to our own, of course) did all they possibly could to help our landowners. We know full well of the incredible hardships and privations the working class of Russia has had to bear, but if we are emerging today from more than three years of successfully repulsing their military invasions and overcoming their obstructions, we have a perfect right to say without any exaggeration that the worst of our difficulties are behind us. If in spite of their overwhelming military superiority, the capitalists of the world have failed to crush this weak and backward country in the course of three years, it was only because we I ave had the dictatorship of the proletariat and enjoyed the massive sympathy of the working people all over the world, we can safely say, in every country without exception. And if the capitalists of the whole world have failed in

their attempt to crush Soviet Russia, which was not a hard
task for them because of their enormous military superiority,
we can say, I repeat, that in the international sphere,
the greatest danger-point of the whole Soviet revolution is
past, the worst difficulties are over.

The danger is still there, of course; the negotiations
for final peace are still dragging on and there are signs
that a rather difficult period in these negotiations is setting
in, for the French imperialists, in particular, are pressing
on with their efforts to push Poland into another war,
and are spreading all sorts of false rumours about Soviet
Russia not wanting peace.

Actually, we have done everything to prove that we do;
we signed the provisional terms several months ago, and
they were such that everyone was surprised by our spirit of
compromise. We are not going back on any point of these
terms, but we shall certainly refuse to be soaked under
the pretext of a division of the property which under tsarism
had belonged to the Polish and to the Russian people, which
at the time both groaned under the yoke of tsarism. That
is something we cannot have. We accept a fair division
of the property, which is to be regarded as common, and
a part of the railway property, and consider as indisputable
the need to restore to the Polish people all objects of cultural
value to which they attach especial importance, and which
had been stolen and carried off to Russia in the days of
the tsar. We have always anticipated that difficult problems
would arise in the settlement of this matter; but if under
the pressure of the French imperialists the Poles want to
create a conflict and sabotage peace at all costs, there is
nothing we can do about it. If there is to be peace, good
will must be shown on both sides, whether in the case of
a very serious conflict within a separate alliance or between
two states. If the Poles once again yield to the pressure of
the French imperialists, then, I repeat, the effort to conclude peace may be frustrated. You are well aware, of
course, what new difficulties will confront us if the French
imperialists succeed in sabotaging this peace; and we all
know from a number of sources and reports that attempts
are being made and enormous efforts are being exerted to
this end, and that the foreign capitalists are spending

millions upon millions to organise another invasion of
Soviet Russia in the spring. We now have over three years'
experience of the way these invasions are organised. We
know that unless they have the aid of a neighbouring state,
the foreign capitalists cannot hope to organise anything
like a serious expedition, and the millions they have been
handing out to the various groups headed by Savinkov,
or to the group of Socialist-Revolutionaries who are publishing their newspaper in Prague[30] and sometimes speak in
the name of the Constituent Assembly, these millions
will go down the drain, and they will have nothing to show
for it but a lot of spoiled newsprint and wasted ink in
various printing offices in Prague.

But there are countries like Rumania, which has not
tried to fight Russia, and Poland, which is ruled by an
exploiting class and a military clique of adventurers. We
know that they cannot muster large forces against us, but
we also know that what we prize most is peace and an opportunity to devote all our efforts to restoring our economy.
So we must be extremely careful. We have the right to tell
ourselves that the worst difficulties in international politics
are behind us, but it would be extremely thoughtless to
shut our eyes to the possibility of fresh attempts. Of course,
now that we have eliminated the Wrangel front, and Rumania had not risked war when the odds were on her side, it
is hardly likely that she will risk it now; but we must not
forget that the ruling classes in Rumania and Poland are
in a position which may be said to be bordering on the desperate. Both countries have been sold to foreign capitalists
lock, stock, and barrel. Both are up to their ears in debt,
and have no means of paying up. Their bankruptcy is
inevitable. The revolutionary movement of the workers and
peasants is growing steadily. Bourgeois governments in
such straits have been known to rush headlong into the
craziest adventures, for which there was no other explanation but their desperate and hopeless situation. That
is why we must still reckon with the possibility of fresh
attempts at armed invasion.

Our conviction that these attempts will be frustrated,
and that the position of the capitalist powers all over the
world is, generally speaking, precarious, springs chiefly

from the mounting economic crisis in all countries, and
the growth of the communist working-class movement.
In Europe, the revolution has not been following the same
lines as ours. As I have said, the workers and peasants of
the West European countries, who were in arms when the
war ended, failed to strike in a swift revolution that would
have been the least painful. The imperialist war, however,
had so shaken the position of these states that not only
has the economic crisis there not yet run its course, but
there are signs that in every country without exception,
even in the richest and most advanced, it will become even
more acute next spring. Capital is an international evil,
and just because of this all countries find themselves so
grappled to each other that when some go down they tend
to drag down the rest.

The rich countries have naturally waxed richer: during
the war their capitalists piled up huge profits. But in the
overwhelming majority of the European countries, trade
has been dislocated and disrupted owing to the complete
devastation not only of Russia, but even of Germany, and
owing to the depression and the currency depreciation.
The richest countries are suffocating, being unable to sell
their industrial goods because of the depreciating currency,
unemployment is growing to incredible proportions everywhere, and an unprecedented economic crisis is looming
all over the world.

Meanwhile, the working class—which its capitalists had
bribed by giving sizable hand-outs from their profits to
the upper strata of the working class to entice it away
from the revolution—is recovering from its blindness after
the three-and-a-half-year war against Soviet Russia, while
the communist movement is growing steadily and taking
on depth not only in the parties, but also in the trade unions
all over the world, although not as fast as we should like.
The ruling classes all over the world are particularly apprehensive of the changes that are taking place in the trade
union movement. In Europe, they are not afraid of the
prospect of facing a party that could lead the revolutionary
proletariat, as was the case in the Russian revolution, when
in the course of a few months, no, weeks, the Party was
transformed from an illegal one into one commanding

nation-wide forces, and backed by millions of people. Europe has not had such a party for years. But every capitalist sees the trade unions, and knows that they unite millions of workers and that the machinery of capitalism is bound to break down, unless the capitalists control them through the leaders who call themselves socialists but pursue the policy of the capitalists. This they know, feel and sense. The most telltale fact, for instance, was that in Germany the whole bourgeois press and the whole press of the social-traitors meeting in the Second International and calling themselves socialists, but loyally serving the capitalists, was whipped into a frenzy not so much because of Zinoviev's visit to Germany, as of that of the Russian trade unionists, for no one has stirred up the German trade unions to such an extent as they did on their first short visit to that country. This savage fury of the German bourgeois press and all the Communist-hating capitalists shows how precarious their position is. An international, world-wide struggle has flared up for influence with the trade unions, with millions of members in all civilised countries, for on them depends this inner work, which is not always readily perceptible. The inexorable growth of the economic crisis is deciding the fate of the capitalist countries.

The attempted coup[31] by the German monarchist party was thwarted by the resistance of the German trade unions, when the workers who had followed Scheidemann and the murderers of Liebknecht and Luxemburg rose and crushed the military forces. As the economic crisis gains momentum, we find the same thing happening in Great Britain, and to a large extent in America as well. That is why it is the international situation that gives us most hope and conviction that the internal situation in the capitalist countries tends to sap all of their strength, and that our international position, which was difficult yesterday and remains such today, despite our great successes, will undoubtedly improve, and that we shall be able to devote all our efforts to solving our internal tasks. I shall not enlarge on these tasks, because all of you who are engaged in industry are more familiar with the tasks of construction than I am, and it would be superfluous for me to deal with them at length.

I heard the final remark made by the preceding speaker, and I join him in saying that every member must now concentrate most attention on the practical tasks of production and economic construction now before us. The trade unions now unite nearly all the industrial workers; they unite the class that has borne the brunt of the burden of the past three years. In Russia, the working class is exercising its dictatorship; it is the ruling class in a country where workers are in a minority. But it is precisely because the working class is ruling the country and because the workers had borne the brunt of capitalist exploitation, that it is assured of the sympathy and massive support of the working peasantry and all those who do not live on the labour of others. This explains what is a sealed book not only to the capitalists but also to the socialists who have remained enemies of the Third International, and what they take to be a trick on the part of our government. They cannot understand how the working class could fight on for three years, against enormous odds, and beat them. But the majority of the peasants must support the working class because the workers have come to power for the first time in history, and because power has been taken by the class that had been most exploited. They have realised that the working class is right, and have withdrawn their support from the bourgeoisie, which, by the way, they regard as a term of abuse. I met a peasant who complained about present conditions and was obviously not in sympathy with the Soviet government's food policy, and certain other issues. The poor peasants of his district had called him a "bourgeois", and he felt this to be an affront. "I refuse to be called by such a disgraceful name," he said. And there is a world of meaning in the fact that this term has come to be regarded as an odious one by the peasants— even the well-to-do middle peasants who have worked with their own hands, who know what it takes to earn a living, and who have been exploited by landowners and capitalists (and that is something they have all experienced). It is the basis of our propaganda and agitation, and the influence exercised by the working class through the state. It is this support of the peasant masses that the working class is assured of in spite of the resistance of the rich and profiteering crowd. And that is why our trade unions are not only associations of working people, not only the builders of our economy—that is their main task—but also a political force building a new state without landowners and capitalists. Although a minority, they can and will build a new communist society, because we are assured of the support of the millions upon millions of those who have always lived by their own labour. In greeting your Congress, I want to say that I am quite sure that we shall succeed in our tasks despite all the difficulties confronting us. (*Prolonged applause.*)

First published in 1922
in the book:
*Chetvyorty vserossiiski syezd rabochikh
shveinoi promyshlennosti.
Stenograficheski otchot
(The Fourth All-Russia Congress
of Garment Workers,
February 1-6, 1921.
Verbatim Report)*
Petrograd

Published according
to the text of the book

INSTRUCTIONS OF THE CENTRAL COMMITTEE TO COMMUNISTS WORKING IN THE PEOPLE'S COMMISSARIAT FOR EDUCATION

1. Unreservedly adhering to the position defined by the Programme of the R.C.P. in regard to polytechnical education (see, in particular, §§ 1 and 8 of the section dealing with education), the Party must regard the lowering of the age for general and polytechnical education from seventeen to fifteen as only a practical expedient necessitated by the country's poverty and ruin caused by the wars imposed upon us by the Entente.

Vocational training for persons of fifteen years of age and upwards "in conjunction with . . . general polytechnical education" (§ 8 mentioned above) is absolutely compulsory all over the country, wherever there is the slightest opportunity to introduce it.

2. The main failing of the People's Commissariat for Education is its lack of practical efficiency, inadequate attention to the recording and verification of practical experience, lack of systematic application of its lessons, and prevalence of general arguments and abstract slogans. The People's Commissar and the Collegium must concentrate on combating these defects.

3. The enlistment of specialists, i.e., of teachers with theoretical and long practical experience, and of persons having such experience in technical (including agronomic) vocational training for work at the centre, is improperly organised in the People's Commissariat for Education in general, and in Glavprofobr,* in particular.

---

* The Chief Administration for Vocational Training under the People's Commissariat for Education.—*Tr.*

The registration of such workers, the study of their experience, the verification of the results of their work, and their systematic enlistment for responsible posts in local, and specially central, work must be organised immediately. Not a single serious measure should be carried out without canvassing the opinion of these specialists and obtaining their continued co-operation.

It goes without saying that the enlistment of specialists must be carried out under these two indispensable conditions: first, specialists who are not Communists must work under the control of Communists; secondly, Communists alone must determine the content of the curricula, in so far as this concerns general educational subjects, and particularly philosophy, the social sciences and communist education.

4. Curricula for the main types of educational establishments and for courses, lectures, readings, colloquia and practice periods must be drawn up and endorsed by the Collegium and the People's Commissar.

5. The Standard Labour School Department, and, in particular, Glavprofobr, must devote greater attention to the wider and more systematic enlistment of all suitable technical and agronomic forces for the promotion of technical vocational and polytechnical education and to the utilisation for that purpose of every tolerably well-organised industrial and agricultural enterprise (state farm, agricultural experimental station, well-organised farm, etc., electric power stations, etc.).

To avoid disruption of normal operations, the forms and the order in which economic enterprises and establishments are to be used for polytechnical education are to be determined by agreement with the economic agencies concerned.

6. Clear, concise and practical forms of reporting must be devised to make it possible to estimate the scale and verify the results of the work. The organisation of this work in the People's Commissariat for Education is highly unsatisfactory.

7. The distribution of newspapers, pamphlets, magazines and books to libraries and reading-rooms in schools and elsewhere is also highly unsatisfactory. The result is that

newspapers and books reach only a small section of Soviet office workers and extremely few factory workers and peasants. This whole system must be reorganised from top to bottom.

Pravda No. 25, February 5, 1921
Published according
to the manuscript

THE WORK OF THE PEOPLE'S COMMISSARIAT FOR EDUCATION

Pravda No. 25 of February 5 carried "*Instructions* of the Central Committee of the R.C.P. to Communists Working in the People's Commissariat for Education (in connection with the reorganisation of the Commissariat)".

Unfortunately, there are three misprints in Point 1 distorting the meaning: the text said "political" instead of "polytechnical" education.

I should like to draw our comrades' attention to these instructions and to call for an exchange of opinion on some of the more important points.

A five-day Party Conference on educational questions was held in December 1920. It was attended by 134 delegates with voice and vote, and 29 with voice. A report of its proceedings is given in a *Supplement to the Bulletin of the Eighth Congress of Soviets on the Party Conference on Education* (published by the All-Russia Central Executive Committee, January 10, 1921). The resolutions of the Conference, the report of the proceedings, all the articles published in the above-mentioned *Supplement*—except for the introductory article by Comrade Lunacharsky and the article by Comrade Grinko—reveal a wrong approach to polytechnical education. They suffer from the very defect on combating which the Central Committee in its instructions urges the People's Commissar and the Collegium to concentrate their attention, namely, too many general arguments and abstract slogans.

The question of polytechnical education has in the main been settled by our Party Programme in its paragraphs 1 and 8 of the section dealing with the people's education. It is these paragraphs that are dealt with in the Central Committee's Instructions. Paragraph 1 deals with *polytechnical education* up to the age of seventeen; and Paragraph 8 speaks of "the extensive development of vocational training for persons of the age of seventeen and upwards *in conjunction with general polytechnical education*".

Thus, the Party Programme puts the question squarely. The arguments about *"polytechnical or monotechnical* education" (the words I have put in quotes and italics, monstrously absurd though they are, are the very words that we find on page 4 of the *Supplement*) are fundamentally wrong and downright impermissible for a Communist; they betray ignorance of the Programme and an idle inclination for abstract slogans. While we are *temporarily* compelled to lower the age (for passing from general polytechnical education to polytechnical vocational training) from seventeen to fifteen, the *"Party must regard"* this lowering of the age "as only" (point 1 of the Central Committee's Instructions) a practical expedient necessitated by the *"country's poverty and ruin"*.

General arguments with futile efforts to "substantiate" this lowering are claptrap. Let us stop this game of general arguments and "theorising"! Attention must be concentrated on the "recording and verification of *practical* experience" and the "systematic *application of its lessons"*.

We may have very few competent people with knowledge and *practical* pedagogical experience but we do have some. We suffer from our inability to find them, install them in the proper executive posts, and join them in *studying* the practical experience of Soviet state development. Now this is precisely what the Party Conference in December 1920 failed to do, and if this was not done at a conference of 163—one hundred and sixty-three!—educational workers, it is quite evident that there must be a general, fundamental flaw in the organisation of this work, which made it necessary for the Party's Central Committee to issue special instructions.

In the Commissariat for Education there are two—just two—comrades who have special assignments. These are the People's Commissar, Comrade Lunacharsky, who exercises general direction, and Deputy Commissar, Comrade Pokrovsky, who directs affairs, firstly, as Deputy People's Commissar, and secondly, as official adviser (and director) on scientific matters and questions of Marxism in general. The whole Party knows both Comrade Lunacharsky and Comrade Pokrovsky very well and has no doubt, of course, that in this respect both are, in their way, "specialists" in the People's Commissariat for Education. None of the other workers of the Commissariat can afford to *specialise* in this way: their "speciality" must lie in skilfully organising the enlistment of expert teachers, in organising their work properly, and in systematically applying the lessons of practical experience. The Central Committee's instructions refer to this in points 2, 3 and 5.

The Party workers' conference should have heard reports by specialists—teachers with some ten years' practical experience—who could have told us what is being done and has been done in the various spheres, say, vocational training, how we are coping with it in our Soviet organisation, what has been achieved, illustrated with examples (which could surely be found, even if in small number), what were the main defects, and how these could be removed, stated in concrete terms.

The Party workers' conference made *no* such record of *practical* experience, and heard no teachers on their application of this experience; but fatuous efforts were made to produce "general arguments" and appraise "abstract slogans". The whole Party, all the workers of the People's Commissariat for Education, must realise this defect and correct it in a common effort. Local workers should exchange experience and help the Party to give publicity to the exemplary gubernias, uyezds, districts, schools, or expert teachers who have achieved good results in a relatively narrow, local or special field. Taking as a basis the achievements that have stood the test of practice, we must press on and, after proper verification, apply this local experience on a nation-wide scale, promoting talented, or simply capable, teachers to more responsible posts, giving them a wider sphere of activity, etc.

The touchstone of a Communist's work in education (and educational institutions) should be his efforts in organising the enlistment of specialists, his ability to find them, utilise their knowledge, secure the co-operation of expert teachers with the Communist leadership, and verify what and how much *is being done*. He must show ability to make progress—even if very slowly and on a very small scale—so long as it is achieved in *practical* matters, on the basis of *practical* experience. But we shall not move forward if the People's Commissariat for Education continues to be full of people who pretend to provide "Communist leadership" while there is a vacuum in the practical sphere, a shortage, or total lack, of practical specialists, inability to promote them, hear what they have to say and take account of their experience. The Communist leader must prove his claim to leadership by *recruiting* a growing number of experienced teachers to help him, and by showing his *ability* to help *them* in their work, to promote *them*, and take account of and bring out *their* experience.

In *this* sense the invariable slogan must be: *less* "leadership", more practical work, that is to say, fewer general arguments and more facts, and I mean verified facts, showing where, when and what progress we are making or whether we are marking time, or retreating. The Communist who is a real leader will correct the curricula drawn up by the experienced teachers, compile a good textbook and achieve *practical*, even if slight, improvements in the content of the work of a *score, a hundred, or a thousand* expert teachers. But there is not much use in the Communist who *talks* about "leadership", *but is incapable* of enlisting any specialists for practical work, getting them to achieve practical results in *their* work, and utilising the practical experience gained by hundreds upon hundreds of teachers.

That this is the main flaw in the work of the People's Commissariat for Education is evident from a paging through the fine booklet, *The People's Commissariat for Education. October 1917-October 1920. Brief Report*. Comrade Lunacharsky admits this when he refers in the preface (p. 5) to the "obvious lack of the practical approach". But much more effort will be needed to drive this home to all the Communists in the People's Commissariat for Education and make them practise these truths. This booklet shows that our knowledge of the facts is poor, very poor indeed; we do not know how to collect them; we are unable to judge how many questions we ought to raise and the number of answers we can expect to get (taking into consideration our level of culture, our customs, and our means of communication). We don't know how to collect evidence of practical experience and sum it up. We indulge in empty "general arguments and abstract slogans", but do not know how to utilise the services of competent teachers, in general, and of competent engineers and agronomists for technical education, in particular; we don't know how to utilise factories, state farms, tolerably well-organised enterprises and electric power stations for the purpose of polytechnical education.

In spite of these defects, the Soviet Republic is making progress in public education; there is no doubt about that. There is a mighty urge for light and knowledge "down below", that is to say, among the mass of working people whom capitalism had been hypocritically cheating out of an education and depriving of it by open violence. We can be proud that we are promoting and fostering this urge. But it would be a real crime to ignore the defects in our work, and the fact that we have not yet learned properly to *organise* the state apparatus of education.

Take also the distribution of newspapers and books, the question dealt with in the last point of the Central Committee's Instructions, point 7.

The Council of People's Commissars issued its decree on "The Centralisation of Libraries" (p. 439, *Collection of Statutes*, 1920, No. 87) on November 3, 1920, providing for the creation of *a single network of libraries of the R.S.F.S.R.*

Here are some of the data I have been able to obtain on the question from Comrade Malkin of the Central Periodicals Administration, and from Comrade Modestov of the Library Section of the Moscow Department of Education. In 38 gubernias, 305 uyezds, the number of libraries in central Soviet Russia (excluding Siberia and North Caucasus) was as follows:

Central	libraries	. . . .	342
District, urban	"	. . . .	521
Volost	"	. . . .	4,474
Travelling	"	. . . .	1,661
Village reading-rooms	. . . .		14,739
Miscellaneous ("rural, juvenile, reference, libraries of various institutions and organisations")	. . . .		12,203

Total	. . . .	33,940

Comrade Modestov believes, on the basis of his experience, that about three-quarters of this number actually exist, while the rest are only listed as such. For Moscow Gubernia, the Central Periodicals Administration gives the figure of 1,223 libraries, while Comrade Modestov's figure is 1,018; of these 204 are in the city proper and 814 in the gubernia, not counting the trade union libraries (probably about 16) and the army libraries (about 125).

As far as can be judged from a comparison of the different gubernias, these figures are not very reliable—let us hope the actual figure does not turn out to be under 75 per cent! In Vyatka Gubernia, for example, there are 1,703 village reading-rooms, in Vladimir Gubernia—37, in Petrograd Gubernia—98, in Ivanovo-Voznesensk Gubernia—75, etc. Of the "miscellaneous" libraries there are 36 in Petrograd Gubernia, 378 in Voronezh Gubernia, 525 in Ufa Gubernia, 31 in Pskov Gubernia, etc.

These figures seem to show that the thirst for knowledge among the mass of workers and peasants is tremendous, and that the striving for education and the establishment of libraries is mighty and "popular" in the real sense of the word. But we are still very short of ability in organising, regulating, shaping and properly satisfying this popular urge. Much remains to be done in creating a real *integrated network* of libraries.

How are we distributing the newspapers and books? According to the Administration's 1920 figures for eleven months, we distributed 401 million copies of newspapers and 14 million books. Here are the figures for three newspapers (January 12, 1921), compiled by the Periodicals Section of the Central Administration for the Distribution of Books.[32]

	Izvestia	Pravda	Bednota
Branches of the Central Periodicals Administration	191,000	139,000	183,000
Military Bureau for the Supply of Literature and Newspapers to Divisional Dispatch Offices. . .	50,000	40,000	85,000
Railway organisations, Railway Dept., Central Periodicals Administration and Agitation Centres	30,000	25,000	16,000
Offices and Organisations in the City of Moscow	65,000	35,000	8,000
Commandant of the City of Moscow	8,000	7,000	6,000
Passenger trains	1,000	1,000	1,000
Public Reading Stands and Files	5,000	3,000	1,000
Total . . .	350,000	250,000	300,000

The figure for public reading stands, i.e., the really massive distribution, is astonishingly small, as against the enormous figures for the "establishments", etc., in the capital, evidently the papers grabbed and bureaucratically utilised by "Soviet bureaucrats", both military and civilian.

Here are a few more figures taken from the reports of the local branches of the Central Periodicals Administration. In September 1920, its Voronezh Gubernia branch received newspapers twelve times (that is to say, there were no papers on eighteen of the thirty days in September). Those received were distributed as follows: *Izvestia* (to branches of the C.P.A.): uyezd—4,986 copies (4,020; 4,310)*; district—7,216 (5,860; 10,064); volost—3,370 (3,200; 4,285); Party organisations—447 (569; 3,880); Soviet establishments—1,765 (1,641; 509)—note that Soviet establishments received nearly three times as many copies of *Pravda* as Party organisations! Then follow: Agitation and Educational Department of the Military Commissariat—5,532 (5,793; 12,332); agitation centres—352 (400; 593); village reading-rooms—*nil*. Subscribers—7,167 (3,080; 764). Thus, "subscribers" (actually, of course, "Soviet bureaucrats") received a fat slice. Public reading stands—460 (508; 500). Total: 32,517 (25,104; 37,237).

---

* First figure—*Pravda*, second, *Bednota*.

In November 1920, Ufa Gubernia received 25 consign-
ments, that is to say, there was no delivery on five days
only. Distribution: Party organisations—113 (1,572; 153);
Soviet establishments—2,763 (1,296; 1,267); Agitation and
Educational Department of the Military Commissariat—
687 (470; 6,500); Volost Executive Committees—903 (308;
3,511); village reading-rooms—36 (*Pravda*—8, eight copies!
—2,538); subscribers—*nil*; "various uyezd organisations"—
1,044 (219; 991). Total: 5,841 (4,069; 15,429).

Lastly, the report of the branch in Pustoshensk Volost,
Sudogoda Uyezd, Vladimir Gubernia for December 1920.
Party organisations—1 (1; 2); Soviet offices—2 (1; 3);
Agitation and Educational Department of the Military
Commissariat—2 (1; 2); Volost Executive Committees—2
(1; 3); post and telegraph offices—1 (1; 1); Urshelsky Works
Committee—1 (1; 2); District Department of Social Main-
tenance—1 (0; 3). Total: 10 (6; 16).

What is the conclusion to be drawn from these fragmen-
tary data? I believe it is what our Party Programme says,
namely: "Only the first steps in the transition from capitalism to communism are being taken ... at the present time."

Under capitalism, a newspaper is a capitalist enterprise,
a means of enrichment, a medium of information and enter-
tainment for the rich, and an instrument for duping and
cheating the mass of working people. We have smashed this
instrument of profit-making and deceit. We *have begun*
to convert the newspapers into an instrument for educating
the masses and for teaching them to live and run their
economy *without* the landowners and capitalists. But we
are only at the start of the road. Not much has been done
during the last three years or so. A great deal remains to
be done: the road ahead is very long indeed. Let us
have less political fireworks, fewer general arguments and
abstract slogans from inexperienced Communists who fail
to understand their tasks; let us have more production
propaganda and, above all, more efficient and capable
application of practical experience to fit the development
of the masses.

We have abolished newspaper subscriptions (I have no
data on the distribution of books; there the situation is
probably even worse). This is a step from capitalism to

communism. But capitalism cannot be killed at one stroke; it rears its head in the form of "Soviet bureaucrats" grabbing the newspapers on various pretexts—they must be grabbing a great number, though we cannot say just how many. There must be a sustained drive in this field against the Soviet bureaucrats, who must be "rapped over the knuckles" for grabbing books and newspapers. Their share— and they themselves—must be steadily reduced. Unfortunately, we are unable to slash their number down to one-tenth, or one-hundredth—it would be a fraud to promise this at our present level of culture, but we can and must whittle it down. No real Communist will fail to do this.

We must see to it that books and newspapers are, as a rule, distributed gratis *only* to the libraries and reading-rooms, which provide a proper reading service for the whole country and the whole mass of workers, soldiers and peasants. This will accelerate, intensify and make more effective the people's eager quest for knowledge. That is when education will advance by leaps and bounds.

Here is some simple arithmetic by way of illustration: there are 350,000 copies of *Izvestia* and 250,000 copies of *Pravda* for the whole of Russia. We are poor. We have no newsprint. The workers are short of fuel, food, clothes and footwear. The machines are worn out. The buildings are falling apart. Let us assume that we actually have for the country as a whole—that is some 10,000 odd volosts— 50,000 libraries and reading-rooms. This would give no less than three for each volost, and certainly one for each factory and military unit. Let us further assume that we have not only learned to take "the first step from capitalism to communism", but also the second and the third. Let us assume that we have learned to distribute three copies of newspapers to every library and reading-room, of which, say, two go on the "public reading stands" (assuming that we have taken the fourth step from capitalism to communism, I make the bold assumption that instead of pasting newspapers on walls in the barbarous way which spoils them, we fix them with wooden pegs—we have no metal tacks, and there will be a shortage of metal even at the "fourth step"!— to a smooth board for convenient reading and to keep the papers from spoiling). And so, two copies each for 50,000

libraries and reading-rooms for "pasting up" and one copy
to be kept in reserve. Let us also assume that we have
learned to allow the Soviet bureaucrats, the pampered
"grandees" of the Soviet Republic, a *moderate* number of
newspapers for them to waste, let us say, no more than a
few thousand copies.

On these bold assumptions the country will have a much
better service with 160,000, or, say, 175,000 copies. The
papers will be there for everyone to read the news (if the
"travelling libraries" which, in my opinion, Comrade
F. Dobler so successfully defended in *Pravda* just the other
day, are properly organised[33]). All this needs is 350,000
copies of two newspapers. Today, there are 600,000 copies,
a large part of which is being grabbed by the "Soviet bureaucrats", wasted as "cigarette paper", etc., simply through
the habits acquired under capitalism. This would give us
a saving of 250,000 copies, or, despite our extreme poverty,
a saving equal to *two* dailies with a circulation of 125,000
each. Each of these could carry to the people every day
serious and valuable literary material and the best modern
and classical fiction, and textbooks on general educational
subjects, agriculture and industry. Long before the war,
the French bourgeoisie learned to make money by publishing popular fiction, not at 3.50 francs a volume for the
gentry, but at 10 centimes (i.e., 35 times as cheap, 4 kopeks
at the pre-war rate) in the form of a proletarian newspaper; why, in that case, can't we do the same—at the
second step from capitalism to communism. Why can't
we do the same thing and learn, within a year, even in our
present state of poverty, to give the people two copies of a
newspaper through each of the 50,000 libraries and reading-
rooms, all the necessary textbooks and world classics,
and books on modern science and engineering.

We shall learn to do this, I am sure.

February 7, 1921

Pravda No. 28, February 9, 1921   Published according
Signed: *N. Lenin*   to the *Pravda* text

ROUGH DRAFT
OF THESES CONCERNING THE PEASANTS[34]

1. Satisfy the wish of the non-Party peasants for the substitution of a tax in kind for the surplus appropriation system (the confiscation of surplus grain stocks).

2. Reduce the size of this tax as compared with last year's appropriation rate.

3. Approve the principle of making the tax commensurate with the farmer's effort, reducing the rate for those making the greater effort.

4. Give the farmer more leeway in using his after-tax surpluses in local trade, provided his tax is promptly paid up in full.

Written on February 8, 1921
First published in 1932

Published according
to the manuscript

LETTER ON OIL CONCESSIONS

To Members of the Political Bureau
and Comrade Rykov,

Stalin,
Bukharin,
Kamenev,
Krestinsky,
Rykov

We are in receipt of replies to the Political Bureau's query concerning oil concessions both from Krasin (and Bogdatyan) and Chairman of Glavneft* Dosser and his four experts.

In connection with the report, *The State of the Oil Industry by the End of 1920* (Baku, 1920), I am sending these replies on to Comrade Stalin, and request all members of the Political Bureau to ring him up to obtain all this material and read it in good time. (All you have to do with regard to the printed report is to read through what I have marked off with a blue pencil on the pages listed on the cover, that is, on the page before the text.)

This material needs to be read urgently, because it is desirable to have a Political Bureau decision (8.00 p.m. Monday, February 14).

The material gives ample proof that:

(a) disaster is *imminent*;

(b) everything must be done to lease out the concessions in Baku (that is, find the concessionaires);

(c) the Glavneft Chairman is extremely stupid. Stupidity in such high quarters is a menace.

These three points summed up:

(a) Disaster is looming. This point is driven home *by the Glavneft experts*. The fool Dosser tries to *mi-*

---

* Chief Oil Industry Administration.—*Tr.*

nimise the danger in his "memo". That is the height of stupidity. The opinions of *all* the Glavneft *experts* should be read and compared with Dosser's toned-down conclusion.

(b) Dosser formulates his conclusion as follows: "There is doubtful benefit in inviting a concessionaire." It looks as though he has, like the truly well-intentioned fool that he is, scared his experts into believing that an anti-concession stand is the only decent one to take for a "Soviet" citizen. That's a really "good turn" he has done us!

In the practical plane, the reports of the Glavneft experts (which are business-like and are strictly borne out by the "end of 1920" printed report) clarify *the kind of terms* we should lay down for the concessionaire.

It is, of course, "doubtful" whether a concessionaire can be found on these terms. But no politician in his right mind would consult Dosser or the experts on that.

It is up to us to make every effort to find such concessionaires.

If we don't, so much the worse for us.

If we fail to make an all-out effort to find a concessionaire, we shall find ourselves bankrupt.

The working out of the terms must be speeded up.

An immediate start must be made in fighting a highly dangerous prejudice which could easily carry a section of the workers and which must be debunked at any cost. It is this "idea": "We don't want to work for the capitalists", or its variant, "We don't want to work for the capitalists when workers nearby are not doing it".

The harm of it (refuted by the R.C.P. Programme and Marxism in general) is evident from this rough calculation, which epitomises the conclusion given in the experts' reports.

We are extracting $100a$ of oil.

Output is dropping.

Flooding threatens disaster.

If we get a concessionaire, who will help to extract $100a+100b$ of oil, and if we have to pay him $98b$ for this, our output will rise, instead of dropping, even if ever so slowly ($100a+2b$).

Here is the question: are the workers who give the concessionaire 98b out of the 100b working for "the capitalists"
or for the Soviet power?

There is no difficulty about the answer.

Please go over the enclosed material and reports urgently,
to allow us to take a decision as soon as possible. There
is extreme danger in any delay.

February 12, 1921

Lenin

First published in 1945   Published according
in *Lenin Miscellany XXXV*   to the manuscript

INTEGRATED ECONOMIC PLAN

What is being said and written on this subject leaves a very painful impression. Take L. Kritsman's articles in *Ekonomicheskaya Zhizn*[35] (I—December 14, 1920; II—December 23; III—February 9; IV—February 16; and V—February 20). There is nothing there but empty talk and word-spinning, a refusal to consider and look into what has been done in this field. Five long articles of reflection on how to approach the study of facts and data, instead of any actual examination of them.

Take Milyutin's theses (*Ekonomicheskaya Zhizn*, February 19), or Larin's (ibid., February 20); listen to the speeches of "responsible" comrades: they all have the same basic defects as Kritsman's articles. They all reveal the dullest sort of scholasticism, including a lot of twaddle about the law of concatenation, etc. It is a scholasticism that ranges from the literary to the bureaucratic, to the exclusion of all practical effort.

But what is even worse is the highbrow bureaucratic disdain for the vital work that has been done and that needs to be continued. Again and again there is the emptiest "drawing up of theses" and a concoction of plans and slogans, in place of painstaking and thoughtful study of our own practical experience.

The only serious work on the subject is the *Plan for the Electrification of the R.S.F.S.R.*, the report of GOELRO (the State Commission for the Electrification of Russia) to the Eighth Congress of Soviets, published in December 1920 and distributed at the Congress. It outlines an integrated economic plan which has been worked out—only as a rough approximation, of course—by the best brains in the Republic on the instructions of its highest bodies. We have to make a very modest start in fighting the complacency born of the ignorance of the grandees, and the intellectualist conceit of the Communist literati, by telling the story of this book, and describing its content and significance.

More than a year ago—February 2-7, 1920—the All-Russia Central Executive Committee met in session and adopted a resolution on electrification which says:

"Along with the most immediate, vital and urgent tasks in organising transport, coping with the fuel and food crises, fighting epidemics, and forming disciplined labour armies, Soviet Russia now has, for the first time, an opportunity of starting on more balanced economic development, and working out a nation-wide state economic plan on scientific lines and consistently implementing it. In view of the prime importance of electrification ... mindful of the importance of electrification for industry, agriculture and transport, ... and so on and so forth ..., the Committee resolves: to authorise the Supreme Economic Council to work out, in conjunction with the People's Commissariat for Agriculture, a project for the construction of a system of electric power stations...."

This seems to be clear enough, doesn't it? "A nation-wide state economic plan on scientific lines": is it possible to misread these words in the decision adopted by our highest authority? If the literati and the grandees, who boast of their communism before the "experts", are ignorant of this decision it remains for us to remind them that ignorance of our laws is no argument.

In pursuance of the All-Russia C.E.C. resolution, the Presidium of the Supreme Economic Council, on February 21, 1920, confirmed the Electrification Commission set up under the Electricity Department, after which the Council of Defence endorsed the statute on GOELRO, whose composition the Supreme Economic Council was instructed to determine and confirm by agreement with the People's Commissariat for Agriculture. On April 24, 1920, GOELRO issued its *Bulletin* No. 1,[36] containing a detailed programme of works and a list of the responsible persons, scientists, engineers, agronomists and statisticians on the several subcommissions to direct operations in the various areas, together with the specific assignments each had undertaken. The list of persons and their assignments runs to ten printed pages of *Bulletin* No. 1. The best talent available to the Supreme Economic Council, the People's Commissariat for Agriculture and the People's Commissariat for Communications has been recruited.

The GOELRO effort has produced this voluminous—and first-class—scientific publication. Over 180 specialists worked on it. There are more than 200 items on the list of works they have submitted to GOELRO. We find, first, a summary of these works (the first part of the volume, running to over 200 pages): a) electrification and a state economic plan; followed by b) fuel supply (with a detailed "fuel budget" for the R.S.F.S.R. *over the next ten years*, with an estimate of the manpower required); c) water power; d) agriculture; e) transport; and f) industry.

The plan ranges over about ten years and gives an indication of the number of workers and capacities (in 1,000 hp). Of course, it is only a rough draft, with possible errors, and a "rough approximation", but it is a real scientific plan. We have precise calculations by experts for every major item, and every industry. To give a small example, we have their calculations for the output of leather, footwear at two pairs a head (300 million pairs), etc. As a result, we have a material and a financial (gold rubles) balance-sheet for electrification (about 370 million working days, so many barrels of cement, so many bricks, poods of iron, copper, and other things; turbine generator capacities, etc.). It envisages ("at a very rough estimate") an 80 per cent increase in manufacturing, and 80-100 per cent, in extracting industry over the next ten years. The gold balance deficit (+ 11,000 million — 17,000 million leaves a total deficit of about 6,000 million) "can be covered by means of concessions and credit operations".

It gives the site of the first 20 steam and 10 water power district electric stations, and a detailed description of the economic importance of each.

The general summary is followed, in the same volume, by a list of works for each area (with a separate paging): Northern, Central Industrial (both of which are especially well set out in precise detail based on a wealth of scientific data), Southern, Volga, Urals, Caucasian (the Caucasus is taken as a whole in anticipation of an economic agreement between its various republics), Western Siberia and Turkestan. For each of the areas, electric power capacities are projected beyond the first units; this is followed by the "GOELRO Programme *A*", that is, the plan for the use of *existing* electric power stations on the most rational and economic lines. Here is another small example: it is estimated that a grid of the Petrograd stations (Northern Area) could yield the following economy (p. 69): up to one-half of the capacities could be diverted to the logging areas of the North, such as Murmansk and Archangel, etc. The resulting increase in the output and export of timber could yield *"up to 500 million rubles' worth of foreign exchange a year in the immediate period ahead"*.

"Annual receipts from the sale of our northern timber could very well equal our gold reserves over the next few years" (ibid., p. 70), provided, of course, we stop talking about plans and start studying and *applying* the plan already worked out by our scientists.

Let me add that we have an embryonic calendar programme for a number of other items (though not for all, of course). This is more than a general plan: it is an estimate for each year, from 1921 to 1930, of the number of stations that can be run in, and the proportions to which the existing ones can be enlarged, provided again we start doing what I have just said, which is not easy in view of the ways of our intellectualist literati and bureaucratic grandees.

A look at Germany will bring out the dimensions and value of GOELRO's effort. Over there, the scientist Ballod produced a similar work: he compiled a scientific plan for the socialist reconstruction of the whole national economy of Germany.[37] But his being a capitalist country, the plan never got off the ground. It remains a lone-wolf effort, and an exercise in literary composition. With us over here it was a state assignment, mobilising hundreds of specialists and producing an integrated economic plan on scientific lines within 10 months (and not two, of course, as we had originally planned). We have every right to be proud of this work, and it remains for us to *understand how* it should be used. What we now have to contend with is failure to understand *this fact*.

The resolution of the Eighth Congress of Soviets says:

"The Congress ... *approves the work of the Supreme Economic Council*, etc., especially that of GOELRO *in drawing up the plan for the electrification of Russia* ·... regards this plan *as the first step in a great economic endeavour*, authorises the All-Russia Central Executive Committee, etc., *to put the finishing touches to the plan and to endorse it*, at the very earliest date. . . . It authorises the adoption of all measures for *the most extensive popularisation* of this plan.... A study of this plan must be an item in the curricula of *all educational establishments of the Republic, without exception*",[38] etc.

The bureaucratic and intellectualist defects of our apparatus, especially of its top drawer, are most glaringly revealed by the attitude to this resolution taken by some people in Moscow and their efforts to twist it, to the extent of ignoring it altogether. Instead of advertising the plan, the literati produce theses and empty disquisitions on how to start working out a plan. The grandees, in purely bureaucratic fashion, lay stress on the need to "approve" the plan, by which they do not mean concrete assignments (the dates for the construction of the various installations, the purchase of various items abroad, etc.) but some muddled idea, such as working out a *new* plan. The misunderstanding this produces is monstrous, and there is talk of partially restoring the old before getting on with the new. Electrification, it is said, is something of an "electrofiction". Why not gasification, we are asked; GOELRO, they also say, is full of bourgeois specialists, with only a handful of Communists; GOELRO should provide the cadre of experts, instead of staffing the general planning commission, and so forth.

The danger lies in this discord, for it betrays an inability to work, and the prevalence of intellectualist and bureaucratic complacency, to the exclusion of all real effort. The conceited ignoramus is betrayed by his jibes at the "fantastic" plan, his questions about gasification, etc. The nerve of their trying, offhand, to pick holes in something it took an army of first-class specialists to produce! Isn't it a shame to try to shrug it off with trite little jokes, and to put on airs about one's right "to withhold approval"?

It is time we learned to put a value on science and got

rid of the "communist" conceit of the dabbler and the bureaucrat; it is time we learned to work systematically, making use of our own experience and practice.

Of course, "plans" naturally give rise to endless argument and discussion, but when the task is to get down to the study of the only scientific plan before us, we should not allow ourselves to engage in general statements and debates about underlying "principles". We should get down to correcting it on the strength of *practical* experience and a more detailed study. Of course, the grandees always retain the right to "give or withhold approval". A sober view of this right, and a reasonable reading of the resolution of the Eighth Congress concerning the approval of the plan, which it endorsed and handed down to us for the broadest popularisation, show that approval must be taken to mean the placing of a series of orders and the issue of a set of instructions, such as the items to be purchased, the building to be started, the materials to be collected and forwarded, etc. Upon the other hand, "approval" from the bureaucratic standpoint means arbitrary acts on the part of the grandees, the red-tape runaround, the commissions-of-inquiry game, and the strictly bureaucratic foul-up of anything that is going.

Let us look at the matter from yet another angle. There is a special need to tie in the scientific plan for electrification with existing short-term plans and their actual implementation. That this must be done is naturally beyond doubt. But how is it to be done? To find out, the economists, the literati, and the statisticians should stop their twaddle about the plan in general, and get on with a detailed study of the implementation of our plans, our mistakes in this practical business, and ways of correcting them. Otherwise we shall have to grope our way long. Over and above such a study of our practical experience, there remains the very small matter of administrative technique. Of planning commissions we have more than enough. Take two men from the department under Ivan Ivanovich and integrate them with one from the department under Pavel Pavlovich, or vice versa. Link them up with a subcommission of the general planning commission. All of which boils down to administrative technique. Various combinations should be tried out, and the best selected. That is elementary.

The whole point is that we have yet to learn the art of approach, and stop substituting intellectualist and bureaucratic projecteering for vibrant effort. We have, and have had, short-term food and fuel plans, and there are glaring mistakes in both. That is unquestionable. But the efficient economist, instead of penning empty theses, will get down to a study of the facts and figures, and analyse our own practical experience. He will pin-point the mistakes and suggest a remedy. This kind of study will suggest to the efficient administrator the transfers, alterations of records, recasting of the machinery, etc., to be proposed or put through. You don't find us doing anything of the sort.

The main flaw is in the wrong approach to the relationships between the Communists and the specialists, the administrators and the scientists and writers. There is no doubt at all that some aspects of the integrated economic plan, as of any other undertaking, call for the administrative approach or for decisions by Communists alone. Let me add that new aspects of that kind can always come to the fore. That, however, is the purely abstract way of looking at it. Right now, our communist writers and administrators are taking quite the wrong approach, because they have failed to realise that in this case we should be learning all we can from the bourgeois specialists and scientists, and cutting out the administrative game. GOELRO's is the only integrated economic plan we can hope to have just now. It should be amplified, elaborated, corrected and applied in the light of well scrutinised practical experience. The opposite view boils down to the purely "pseudo-radical conceit, which in actual fact is nothing but ignorance", as our Party Programme puts it.[39] Ignorance and conceit are equally betrayed by the view that we can have another general planning commission in the R.S.F.S.R. in addition to GOELRO, which, of course, is not to deny that some advantage may be gained from partial and business-like changes in its membership. It is only on this basis—by continuing what has been started—that we can hope to make any serious improvements in the general economic

plan; any other course will involve us in an administrative
game, or high-handed action, to put it bluntly. The task
of the Communists inside GOELRO is to issue fewer orders,
rather, to refrain from issuing any at all, and to be very
tactful in their dealings with the scientists and technicians (the R.C.P. Programme says: "Most of them inevitably
have strong bourgeois habits and take the bourgeois view
of things "). The task is to learn from them and to help
them to broaden their world-view on the basis of achievements in their particular field, always bearing in mind
that the engineer's way to communism is *different* from that
of the underground propagandist and the writer; he is guided
along *by the evidence of his own science*, so that the agrono-
mist, the forestry expert, etc., each have *their own path* to
tread towards communism. The Communist who has failed
to prove his ability to bring together and guide the work
of specialists in a spirit of modesty, going to the heart of
the matter and studying it in detail, is a potential menace.
We have many such Communists among us, and I would
gladly swap dozens of them for one conscientious qualified
bourgeois specialist.

There are two ways in which Communists outside
GOELRO can help to establish and implement the integrated economic plan. Those of them who are economists,
statisticians or writers should start by making a study of
our own practical experience, and suggest corrections and
improvements only after such a detailed study of the facts.
Research is the business of the scientist, and once again,
because we are no longer dealing with general principles,
but with practical experience, we find that we can obtain
much more benefit from a "specialist in science and technology", even if a bourgeois one, than from the conceited
Communist who is prepared, at a moment's notice, to write
"theses", issue "slogans" and produce meaningless abstractions. What we need is more factual knowledge and
fewer debates on ostensible communist principles.

Upon the other hand, the Communist administrator's
prime duty is to see that he is not carried away by the
issuing of orders. He must learn to start by looking at the
achievements of science, insisting on a verification of the
facts, and locating and studying the mistakes (through

reports, articles in the press, meetings, etc.), before proceeding with any corrections. We need more practical studies of our mistakes, in place of the Tit Titych[49] type of tactics ("I might give my approval, if I feel like it").

Men's vices, it has long been known, are for the most part bound up with their virtues. This, in fact, applies to many leading Communists. For decades, we had been working for the great cause, preaching the overthrow of the bourgeoisie, teaching men to mistrust the bourgeois specialists, to expose them, deprive them of power and crush their resistance. That is a historic cause of world-wide significance. But it needs only a slight exaggeration to prove the old adage that there is only one step from the sublime to the ridiculous. Now that we have convinced Russia, now that we have wrested Russia from the exploiters and given her to the working people, now that we have crushed the exploiters, we must learn to run the country. This calls for modesty and respect for the efficient "specialists in science and technology", and a business-like and careful analysis of our numerous *practical* mistakes, and their gradual but steady correction. Let us have less of this intellectualist and bureaucratic complacency, and a deeper scrutiny of the practical experience being gained in the centre and in the localities, and of the available achievements of science.

February 21, 1921

Pravda No. 39, February 22, 1921
Signed: *N. Lenin*

Published according to
the *Pravda* text
collated with the proofs
containing Lenin's corrections

GREETINGS
TO THE FIFTH ALL-UKRAINE CONGRESS
OF SOVIETS[41]

Comrades, I send my heartfelt greetings to the Fifth All-Ukraine Congress of Soviets. I am sure that the alliance between the poor peasants and Ukrainian workers will strengthen Soviet Ukraine and consolidate the Ukrainian Republic, despite the enemy's traps and machinations.

I have asked Comrade Petrovsky to convey my regret at being unable to accept your invitation to attend the Congress. Nevertheless, I hope to be able to visit Soviet Ukraine in the near future. I wish the Congress success in consolidating the power of the workers and peasants and in restoring the national economy.

Yours, *Lenin*

Kommunist (Kharkov) No. 45.
February 27, 1921

Published according
to the *Kommunist* text

SPEECH AT A PLENARY MEETING
OF THE MOSCOW SOVIET OF WORKERS'
AND PEASANTS' DEPUTIES
FEBRUARY 28, 1921[42]

(*Prolonged applause.*) Before going on to the domestic
situation—a subject which, quite naturally, arouses great
interest and much concern—let me run over the salient
international developments. To be brief, I shall deal with
only three. The first is our conference with Turkish delegates which has opened here in Moscow.[43] This is an especially welcome fact, because there had been many obstacles
to direct negotiations with the Turkish Government delegation, and now that there is an opportunity of reaching
an understanding here in Moscow, we feel sure that a firm
foundation will be laid for closer relations and friendship.
Of course, this will not be achieved through diplomatic
machinations (in which, we are not afraid to admit, our
adversaries have the edge on us), but through the fact that
over the past few years both nations have had to endure
untold suffering at the hands of the imperialist powers.
A previous speaker referred to the harm of isolation from
the imperialist countries. But when a wolf attacks a sheep,
there is hardly any point in advising the sheep to avoid
isolation from the wolf. (*Laughter, applause.*) Up to now,
the Eastern peoples may have been like sheep before the
imperialist wolf, but Soviet Russia was the first to show
that, despite her unparalleled military weakness, it is
not so easy for the wolf to get his claws and teeth into her.
This example has proved to be catching for many nations,
regardless of whether or not they sympathise with the
"Bolshevik rumour-mongers". We are a popular topic all
over the world, and, in relation to Turkey, have even been

described as malicious rumour-mongers. Of course, we have so far been unable to do anything in this sphere, but the Turkish workers and peasants have demonstrated that the resistance on the part of modern nations to plunder is a thing that has to be reckoned with: Turkey herself resisted plunder by the imperialist governments with such vigour that even the strongest of them have had to keep their hands off her. That is what makes us regard the current negotiations with the Turkish Government as a very great achievement. We have no hidden motives. We know that these negotiations will proceed within a very modest framework, but they are important because the workers and peasants of all countries are drawing steadily closer together, despite all the formidable obstructions. This is something we should bear in mind when assessing our present difficulties.

The second thing worth recalling in connection with the international situation is the state of the peace talks in Riga.[44] You know that in order to conclude a peace with any degree of stability we have been making the greatest possible concessions to all the states formerly within the Russian Empire. This is very natural because national oppression is one of the main factors which arouses hatred for the imperialists and unites the peoples against them, and few states in the world have sinned as much in this respect as the old Russian Empire and the bourgeois republic of Kerensky, the Mensheviks and Socialist-Revolutionaries in alliance with the bourgeoisie. That is why it is in respect of these nations that we have shown the greatest willingness to make concessions and readiness to accept such peace terms, for which some Socialist-Revolutionaries have virtually called us Tolstoyans. We don't care, because we have to show the greatest willingness to compromise with these nations, to dispel the age-old suspicions generated by the old oppression, and to lay the foundation for a union of workers and peasants of various nations which once suffered together at the hands of tsarism and the Russian landowners, and now suffer at the hands of imperialism. In respect of Poland, this policy has been largely frustrated by the Russian whiteguards, Socialist-Revolutionaries and Mensheviks, who enjoy "freedom of the press", "freedom of speech" and other wonderful "freedoms", alongside the extraordinary freedom of the French and other capitalists to buy up a larger part of Poland, where they are at liberty to spread their propaganda in an effort to push Poland into a war against us. The capitalists are now doing their utmost to disrupt the peace that has been concluded. One of the reasons why we cannot demobilise our army, as we should like to do, is that we must reckon with the possibility of war on a much larger scale than some people imagine. Those who say that we need not put so much into defence are wrong, because our enemies are resorting to all sorts of machinations and intrigues to break up the final peace with Poland, the provisional terms of which have already been signed. These negotiations have lately been dragging on, and although a few weeks ago things had come to such a pass that there was reason to fear a serious crisis, we recently decided to make some further concessions, not because we thought they were warranted, but because we considered it necessary to thwart the intrigues of the Russian whiteguards, Socialist-Revolutionaries and Mensheviks in Warsaw, and of the Entente imperialists, who are making the greatest efforts to prevent peace. It has not yet been signed, but let me say that we have every reason to be optimistic: it will be signed in the near future, and we shall succeed in thwarting the intrigues against its conclusion. Although this is only guesswork on my part, I believe the prospect will gladden us all. But let us not count our chickens before they are hatched. That is why we shall not slacken or weaken our military effort however slightly, but we shall not be afraid to make a few more concessions to bourgeois Poland, so as to wrest the workers and peasants of Poland from the Entente and prove to them that the workers' and peasants' government does not deal in national strife. We shall defend this peace even at the price of considerable sacrifice.

The third international question is the events in the Caucasus. There have been large-scale developments there recently, and although we do not yet know the details their implication is that we are on the brink of a major war. We were, of course, disturbed at the clash between Armenia and Georgia, for these events turned the Armenian-Georgian war into an insurrection, with a section of the Russian troops taking part. The upshot of all this was that, for the time being, the tables have been turned on the Armenian bourgeoisie, which had been scheming against us, so that, according to the latest but still unconfirmed reports, Soviet power has been established in Tiflis. (*Applause.*) We know that the insurrection began in the neutral zone of Armenia, which lies between Georgia and Armenia, and which Georgia had occupied with the consent of the Entente imperialists. When the Mensheviks, particularly the Georgian Mensheviks, speak of the harm of isolation from the Western powers, they usually mean the reliance on the Entente imperialists, who are stronger than anyone else. But some whiteguards tend to forget that the advanced capitalists are more deceitful than anyone else, and say to themselves: can Armenia, the Armenian peasants, etc., or the ravaged Soviet Republic be compared to the united imperialist powers of the world? Let us turn to the advanced capitalists for they are the civilised forces of the world. That is how the Georgian Mensheviks seek to justify their unseemly defence of the capitalists, and they had control of the only railway line, the Armenian peasants' food supply line.

No one will have the patience to read all the telegrams, statements and protests we exchanged with Georgia on this question. If we had had a peace treaty with Georgia, our policy would have been to procrastinate as long as possible. You must understand, however, that the Armenian peasants did not view the treaty question in that light, and things culminated in the terrible insurrection which broke out in early February and spread with astonishing rapidity, involving not only Armenians, but also Georgians. There has been hardly any news from over there, but our assumptions have been borne out by the latest available report. We know perfectly well that the Georgian bourgeoisie and the Georgian Mensheviks do not rely for support on their working people, but on their capitalists, who are only looking for a pretext to start hostilities. Upon the other hand, we have had our stake on the working people for three years and we shall continue to have it on them to the last even in this backward and oppressed country.

With all our circumspection and all our efforts to strength-
en the Red Army, we shall ultimately do everything
possible to put out the flames in the Caucasus. We shall
demonstrate in the East what we have been able to demonstrate in the West: when Soviet power is in, national
oppression is out. On this, in the final analysis, depends
the outcome of the struggle, and because of their superior
numbers the workers and peasants will ultimately prove to
be stronger than the capitalists.

Let me now turn from foreign policy to home affairs.
I have been unable, unfortunately, to hear the whole of
Comrade Bryukhanov's report. He has given you the facts
in detail and I need not go over that again. I want to deal
with the main thing, which may possibly show us the causes
of our terrible crisis. We shall have to set ourselves a task
and find a way to solve it. There is a path, we have found
it, but we are not yet strong enough to follow it with the
persistence and the regularity demanded by the difficult
post-war conditions. We are in every respect poverty-
stricken, and yet we are no more destitute than the workers
of Vienna. They and their children are starving and dying,
but they have not the main thing that we have: they have
no hope. They are dying, crushed by capitalism; they are
in a position where they have to endure sacrifices, but not
as we do. We make sacrifices for the war which we have
declared on the whole capitalist world. That is the difference between the position of the workers of Petrograd
and Moscow and that of the workers of Vienna. Now, in
the spring, our hardships due to the food shortage have once
again become more acute, after the improvement earlier
on. The fact is that we had miscalculated. When the plan
for surplus-food appropriation was drawn up, we thought
we could improve on our success. The people had gone
hungry for so long that their condition had to be improved
at all costs. It was essential not only to help, but to improve
things. We had failed to see that if we improved things
then, we should be hard pressed later on, and it was due
to this mistake that we now face a food crisis. We have
made the same mistake elsewhere: in the Polish war, and
in fuel. The procurement of food and fuel—coal, oil, firewood—are all different types of work, but in all three we

have made identical mistakes. At the time of the severest
hardships, we overestimated our resources and failed to take
stock of them properly. We failed to realise that we were
using up our resources all at once, we failed to estimate
our reserves, and we put nothing by for a rainy day. This
is, generally speaking, a good rule of thumb that any
peasant follows in his simple, everyday economy. But there
we were, acting on a nation-wide scale as if we gave no
thought to the reserves so long as we had enough for today,
so that when we were finally faced with and brought up short
by this question of reserves we were quite unable to put
anything by for a rainy day.

During the Polish war we had a vigorous, daring Red
Army, but we advanced too far—to the very gates of
Warsaw, and then had to roll back, almost to Minsk. The
same thing has happened with the food supply. True enough,
we emerged from the war as victors. In 1920, we offered
the Polish landowners and bourgeoisie peace on terms
more advantageous to them than the present terms. They
were taught a lesson, and the whole world was taught a
lesson, which nobody had previously bargained for. When
we speak about our position we tell the truth; if anything,
we tend to exaggerate the negative side. In April 1920,
we said: transport is falling to pieces, there is no food.
We said this frankly in our newspapers and spoke about
it openly at mass meetings in the best halls of Moscow and
Petrograd. The spies of Europe rushed to cable the news,
and over there some people rubbed their hands in glee and
said: "Get on with the job, you Poles: you see how badly
things are going with them, we shall soon crush them."
But we were telling the truth, sometimes tending to exaggerate the negative side. Let the workers and peasants know
that our difficulties are not over. And when the Polish
army, with French, British and other military advisers
and arms and money, went into battle, it was defeated.
And now, when we say that our affairs are in poor shape,
when our ambassadors report that the whole of the bourgeois
press is saying "The Soviet power is doomed", when even
Chernov has said that it will undoubtedly fall, we say:
"You can shout your heads off, that's what freedom of
the press on capitalist money is for, you have as much of

this freedom as you want, but we are still not in the least afraid to speak the bitter truth." Indeed, the situation this spring has worsened again, and our papers are full of admissions of this bad situation. But we say to the foreign capitalists, the Mensheviks, the S.R.s, the Savinkovites,[45] or whatever else they are called: just you try to cash in on this and you will find yourselves in a far deeper hole. (*Applause*.) It is obviously a difficult transition from our state of utter destitution in 1918-19, when it was very hard to think about a year's reserve or allocation, and when all we could do was to look one or two weeks ahead and say "we'll see" about the third one. It is obviously difficult to change over from this situation to that of 1920, when we saw that our army was bigger than that of the Poles, when we had twice as much grain as the previous year, when we had fuel, and when there was one and a half times more Donets and Siberian coal. We were unable to distribute this on a nation-wide scale. You must remember that annual estimates require a special approach and special conditions. We knew that the spring would be worse than the autumn, but how much worse, we could not know. It is not a matter of figures or distribution but a matter of the degree to which the workers and peasants have starved, and the extent of the sacrifice they are still able to make for the common cause of all workers and peasants. Who can estimate this? Some may point out this error—it is an error, and we make no effort to conceal the fact, just as we did not conceal it in the case of the Polish war—but let those who blame us for it—and justly so—give us an estimate for projecting the national amount to be set aside from the first six months' grain reserves, so as to leave something in stock for the six months after that. No such estimates have been made. We first tried to work out some in 1920 and miscalculated. In certain respects, a revolution is a miracle. If we had been told in 1917 that we would hold out in three years of war against the whole world, that, as a result of the war, two million Russian landowners, capitalists and their children would find themselves abroad, and that we would turn out to be the victors, no one of us would have believed it. A miracle took place because the workers and peasants rose against the attack of the

landowners and capitalists in such force that even powerful
capitalism was in danger. But just because of the miracle
we lost the habit of taking the long view of things. That
is why all of us now have to limp along. The forthcoming
Party Congress is to be called earlier, because we need to
sum up this new experience in earnest. The defence of the
workers' and peasants' power was achieved by a miracle,
not a divine miracle—it was not something that fell from
the skies—but a miracle in the sense that, no matter how
oppressed, humiliated, ruined and exhausted the workers
and peasants were, precisely because the revolution went
along with the workers, it mustered very much more strength
than any rich, enlightened and advanced state could have
mustered. But this will not work in economics, where—
perhaps the word is not altogether appropriate—you need
"thrift". We have not yet learned to practise "thrift".
We must bear in mind that we have defeated the bourgeoisie, but that they are still with us and so the struggle goes
on. And spreading panic is one of their ways of fighting us.
We must not forget that they are past masters at it. They
have their newspapers, although not printed ones, but
splendidly distributed, and they are doing much more than
making mountains out of molehills. But under no circumstances must we succumb to panic. The situation has been
aggravated because we have made mistakes in every field
of work. Let us not be afraid of these mistakes, let us not
be afraid to admit them; let us not indulge in mutual recrim-
ination; but if we are to make use of all our resources and
put in the greatest effort in every field, we must know how
to reckon. Reckoning will give us control of the whole
Republic, for proper reckoning alone will give us an estimate
of the large amounts of available grain and fuel. The bread
ration will be short for a lusty appetite, but the amount
cannot be increased all at once. There will be a shortage
only if we do not lay in stocks, but we shall have enough
if we make a correct estimate and give to the most needy,
and take from those who have large surpluses rather than
from those who, over the last three years, may have given
away their last crust. Have the peasants of the Ukraine
and Siberia seen the point of this reckoning? Not yet,
I'm afraid. Their present and past grain surpluses have

never been matched in central Russia, nor have they ever experienced such a plight. The peasants of the Ukraine, Siberia and Northern Caucasus have never known such destitution and hunger as the peasants of Moscow and Petrograd gubernias (who received far less than the Ukrainian peasants) have endured for three years. Their surpluses usually ran to hundreds of poods, and they were accustomed to receive goods at once for that kind of surplus. There is nowhere to obtain the goods from, now that the factories are at a standstill. To set them going once again will take time and preparation, and workers. Our tremendous sacrifices are not made in a state of desperation, but in a fight that wins one victory after another. This is a distinction that makes all the difference.

That is the main point that I wished to make here, not in terms of the exact figures given by the comrade responsible for food supplies and by the comrade responsible for fuel, but in terms of economics and politics, to help understand how our recent mistakes differ from earlier ones, and while they are different they still have this in common, that we have tried to jump two rungs when we only had the possibility of climbing one. Nevertheless, we are now at a higher stage. That is good. This year we shall have a much better fuel balance than last year. And let me give you one final fact in regard to the food supply: the Deputy Commander-in-Chief of the republican forces in Siberia has cabled that communications have been restored and that seven train-loads of grain are on their way to Moscow. At one time there were disturbances and kulak revolts. Of course, it is possible to joke about rumour-mongers, but it is necessary to appreciate that after all we have learned a thing or two in the course of the class struggle. We know that the tsarist government called us rumour-mongers, but when we speak of the Socialist-Revolutionary and Menshevik rumour-mongers, we are speaking of another class, of people who support the bourgeoisie and who take advantage of every difficulty to issue leaflets and say: "Look, 300 poods of grain surpluses are being confiscated from you; you give everything away, and get nothing in return but coloured bits of paper." Don't we know these rumour-mongers! What is their class? No matter what they call themselves, Socialist-Revolutionaries, lovers of liberty, of people's power, constituent assemblies, and so on, they are the same old landowners. We have heard all they have to say and have learned to understand their true meaning. These revolts indicate that there are people among the peasants who do not wish to reconcile themselves either to surplus food requisitioning or to the tax. Someone here has mentioned the tax. Much of what he said was common sense, but he should have added that before we said anything about it from this platform, the newspaper *Pravda*, which is the Central Organ of the Russian Communist Party, carried tax proposals signed not only by casual contributors but by staff correspondents.[46] When the non-Party peasant says to us: "Make your calculations conform to the needs of the small peasant; he needs confidence; I shall give so much and then I shall look to my own affairs," we say: "Yes, that is business-like, that is common sense and is in keeping with local conditions." So long as we have no machines, so long as the peasant himself has no wish to change over from small-scale to large-scale farming, we are inclined to take this idea into account and we shall place this question before the Party Congress due to be held in a week's time, sort it out and take a decision satisfactory to the non-Party peasant and to the mass of the people. In our apparatus there is, of course, much that is imperfect and inexcusable, because a great deal, a very, very great deal of the bureaucratic practices has seeped in. But weren't there the same kind of mistakes and imperfections in our Red Army? We could not rid ourselves of them right away, but thanks to the help of the workers and peasants, the Army was, nevertheless, victorious. What took place in the Red Army is bound to happen in another form in all spheres, and we shall be cured of these bureaucratic distortions—condemned on every hand because they are evidence of our mistakes and misfortunes—by persistent work, not succumbing to panic and not turning a blind eye to those who, taking advantage of these mistakes, are trying to repeat the Kolchak and Denikin affairs. Any amount of scandalous practices in the way of the pilfering of coal is taking place in the Ukraine, while here we are suffering from a great shortage. Over there they have had 120 governments, and the rich peasants have been corrupted. They cannot understand that there is a workers' and peasants' government and that, if it confiscates grain, it does so in order to ease the position of the workers and peasants. Until we are able to achieve full clarity on all these questions in that area, we shall continue to receive news of disturbances, banditry and revolts. This is inevitable because we have inherited from capitalism a peasant who is isolated and cannot help being ignorant and full of resentment, and it will take us years to re-educate him. We see this every spring, and we shall continue to see it every spring for some time to come.

The south-eastern railways are quite another matter. This year we have mainly existed on the resources supplied us by Siberia and the Northern Caucasus. Here is a five-day report. It says 8 cars were sent in every day from February 1; the second five-day report gives the figure of 32 cars; the third, 60; the fourth, 109; but we should be receiving 200 cars a day, and only in the last five days, from February 20 to 24, have we been getting 120 cars a day. That is three train-loads. Today Comrade Fomin reports that during the past two days we have received four train-loads. As one comrade has said, the position in the Donets Basin is that there is no grain because there is no coal, and there is no coal because there is no grain. This vicious circle must be broken at some point by the energy, pressure and heroism of the working people, so that all the wheels start turning. We are beginning to emerge from the enormous difficulties that we have experienced in this respect. A ray of light has appeared. I do not at all wish, comrades, to lull you with promises and I have no intention of announcing that this difficult period has ended. Nothing of the sort! There are signs of improvement, but the period remains incredibly difficult, and, in comparison with last autumn, it need not have been as difficult as it is now, despite the fact that we are cut off from Western Europe. In order not to be cut off, we have had to accept the idea of granting concessions: here's your 500 per cent profit, and let's have more grain, paraffin oil, etc. We are prepared to grant concessions, and will grant them. This will mean a new struggle, because we are not going to give them 500 per cent,

or perhaps even more, without bargaining, and to switch
to this struggle is equivalent to switching all our trains
onto new rails.

For this it is essential to convince the capitalists that
they cannot butt in on us with a war. We have decisively
accepted the policy of concessions. You know that we have
had many arguments with the peasants and workers about
this, you know that the workers have said: "Have we got
rid of our own bourgeoisie only to let the foreigners in?"
We have explained to them that we cannot switch all at
once from scarcity to abundance, and in order to ease this
transition, in order to obtain the necessary amount of
grain and textiles, we must be able to make every necessary
sacrifice. Let the capitalists benefit from their own greed,
so long as we are able to improve the position of the workers
and peasants. It is no easy thing, however, to get this concession business going. We published a decree about this
in November, but so far not a single concession has been
granted. Of course, this is due to the influence of the whiteguard and Menshevik press. Russian newspapers are now
published in every country in the world, and in all of them
the Mensheviks are clamouring against any concessions
and saying that in Moscow things are not going well, that
the Soviet power is about to collapse, and that the capitalists should not believe the Bolsheviks and should have
nothing to do with them. But we shall not abandon the
fight: we have defeated the capitalists, but we have not
destroyed them; they have now moved on to Warsaw,
which once used to be the centre of the struggle against
the Russian autocracy, and is now the rallying point of
the whiteguards against Soviet Russia. We shall fight them
everywhere, both on the foreign and on the home front.

I have here a telegram from Comrade Zinoviev in Petrograd which says that, in connection with the arrests there,
a leaflet found in the possession of one of those detained
makes it clear that he is a spy of foreign capitalists. There
is another leaflet, headed *To the Faithful*, which is also
counter-revolutionary in content. Further, Comrade Zinoviev informs us that Menshevik leaflets posted up in Petrograd call for strikes, and over here in Moscow this has been
blown up into a rumour about some kind of demonstration.

In actual fact, one Communist was killed by an agent pro-
vocateur, and he is the only victim of these unhappy days.
When Denikin was at Orel, the whiteguard papers said he
was advancing at almost 100 versts an hour. These papers
will not surprise us. We take a sober view of things. We must
rally closer, comrades. Otherwise, what are we to do? Try
another Kerensky or Kolchak "coalition" government?
Kolchak, let us say, is no longer with us, but another might
take his place. There are any number of Russian generals,
quite enough for a large army. We must speak frankly and
have no fear of the newspapers being published in all the
cities of the world. These are all trifles, and we shall not keep
silent about our difficult position because of them. But we
shall say this: comrades, we are carrying on this difficult
and bloody struggle, and if at the moment they cannot
attack us with guns, they attack us with lies and slander,
taking advantage of every instance of need and poverty in
order to help our enemies. I repeat, all of this we have
experienced and survived. We have lived through far
greater difficulties; we know this enemy extremely well,
and we shall defeat him this spring; we shall defeat him
by working more successfully, and by calculating more
carefully. (*Applause.*)

Pravda No. 46,
March 2, 1921

Published according
to the *Pravda* text
collated with the
verbatim report

LETTER TO G. K. ORJONIKIDZE

March 2, 1921

Sergo Orjonikidze

Please convey to the Georgian Communists, and in particular to all members of the Georgian Revolutionary Committee, my warm greetings to Soviet Georgia. My special request to them is to inform me whether or not we are in complete agreement on the following three questions: •

First, immediate arming of the workers and poor peasants and formation of a strong Georgian Red Army.

Second, there is need for a special policy of concessions with regard to the Georgian intelligentsia and small merchants. It should be realised that it is not only imprudent to nationalise them, but that there is even need for certain sacrifices in order to improve their position and enable them to continue their small trade.

Third, it is of tremendous importance to devise an acceptable compromise for a bloc with Jordania or similar Georgian Mensheviks, who before the uprising had not been absolutely opposed to the idea of Soviet power in Georgia on certain terms.

Please bear in mind that Georgia's domestic and international positions both require that her Communists should avoid any mechanical copying of the Russian pattern. They must skilfully work out their own flexible tactics, based on bigger concessions to all the petty-bourgeois elements.

Please reply,
Lenin

Pravda Gruzii No. 5,
March 6, 1921

Published according
to the manuscript

INTERNATIONAL WORKING WOMEN'S DAY

The gist of Bolshevism and the Russian October Revolution is getting into politics the very people who were most oppressed under capitalism. They were downtrodden, cheated and robbed by the capitalists, both under the monarchy and in the bourgeois-democratic republics. So long as the land and the factories were privately owned this oppression and deceit and the plunder of the people's labour by the capitalists were inevitable.

The essence of Bolshevism and the Soviet power is to expose the falsehood and mummery of bourgeois democracy, to abolish the private ownership of land and the factories and concentrate all state power in the hands of the working and exploited masses. They, these masses, get hold of politics, that is, of the business of building the new society. This is no easy task: the masses are downtrodden and oppressed by capitalism, but there is no other way—and there can be no other way—out of the wage-slavery and bondage of capitalism.

But you cannot draw the masses into politics without drawing in the women as well. For under capitalism the female half of the human race is doubly oppressed. The working woman and the peasant woman are oppressed by capital, but over and above that, even in the most democratic of the bourgeois republics, they remain, firstly, deprived of some rights because the law does not give them equality with men; and secondly—and this is the main thing—they remain in "household bondage", they continue to be "household slaves", for they are overburdened with the drudgery of the most squalid, backbreaking and stultifying toil in the kitchen and the family household.

No party or revolution in the world has ever dreamed of striking so deep at the roots of the oppression and inequality of women as the Soviet, Bolshevik revolution is doing. Over here, in Soviet Russia, no trace is left of any inequality between men and women under the law. The Soviet power has eliminated all there was of the especially disgusting, base and hypocritical inequality in the laws on marriage and the family and inequality in respect of children.

This is only the first step in the liberation of woman. But none of the bourgeois republics, including the most democratic, has dared to take even this first step. The reason is awe of "sacrosanct private property".

The second and most important step is the abolition of the private ownership of land and the factories. This and this alone opens up the way towards a complete and actual emancipation of woman, her liberation from "household bondage" through transition from petty individual housekeeping to large-scale socialised domestic services.

This transition is a difficult one, because it involves the remoulding of the most deep-rooted, inveterate, hide-bound and rigid "order" (indecency and barbarity would be nearer the truth). But the transition has been started, the thing has been set in motion, we have taken the new path.

And so on this international working women's day countless meetings of working women in all countries of the world will send greetings to Soviet Russia, which has been the first to tackle this unparalleled and incredibly hard but great task, a task that is universally great and truly liberatory. There will be bracing calls not to lose heart in face of the fierce and frequently savage bourgeois reaction. The "freer" or "more democratic" a bourgeois country is, the wilder the rampage of its gang of capitalists against the workers' revolution, an example of this being the democratic republic of the United States of North America. But the mass of workers have already awakened. The dormant, somnolent and inert masses in America, Europe and even in backward Asia were finally roused by the imperialist war.

The ice has been broken in every corner of the world.

Nothing can stop the tide of the peoples' liberation from the imperialist yoke and the liberation of working men and women from the yoke of capital. This cause is being carried forward by tens and hundreds of millions of working men and women in town and countryside. That is why this cause of labour's freedom from the yoke of capital will triumph all over the world.

March 4, 1921

Published on March 8, 1921,
in a Supplement to *Pravda* No. 51
Signed: *N. Lenin*

Published according
to the Supplement text

TENTH CONGRESS
OF THE R.C.P.(B.)[47]

MARCH 8-16, 1921

First published in full in 1921 in the book: *Desiaty syezd rossiiskoi hommunisticheskoi partii. Stenograficheshi otchot (The Tenth Congress of the R.C.P. Verbatim Report, March 8-16, 1921,* Moscow

Published according to the text of the book collated with the verbatim report

1
SPEECH AT THE OPENING OF THE CONGRESS
MARCH 8

(*Prolonged applause.*) Comrades, allow me to declare the Tenth Congress of the Russian Communist Party open. We have passed through a very eventful year both in international and in our own internal history. To begin with the international situation, let me say that this is the first time we have met in conditions in which the Communist International has ceased to be a mere slogan and has really been converted into a mighty organisation with foundations —real foundations—in the major advanced capitalist countries. What had only been a set of resolutions at the Second Congress of the Communist International[48] has been successfully implemented during the past year and has found expression, confirmation and consolidation in such countries as Germany, France and Italy. It is enough to name these three countries to show that the Communist International, since its Second Congress in Moscow last summer, has become part and parcel of the working-class movement in all the major advanced countries of Europe— more than that, it has become the chief factor in international politics. This is such a great achievement, comrades, that however difficult and severe the various trials ahead of us—and we cannot and must not lose sight of them— no one can deprive us of it!

Furthermore, comrades, this is the first congress that is meeting without any hostile troops, supported by the capitalists and imperialists of the world, on the territory of the Soviet Republic. The Red Army's victories over the past year have enabled us to open a Party Congress in such conditions for the first time. Three and a half years of

unparalleled struggle, and the last of the hostile armies
has been driven from our territory—that is our achievement!
Of course, that has not won us everything, not by a long
shot; nor have we won all that we have to—real freedom
from imperialist invasion and intervention. On the contrary,
their warfare against us has taken a form that is less military but is in some respects more severe and more dangerous.
The transition from war to peace—which we hailed at the
last Party Congress[49] and in the light of which we have
tried to organise our work—is still far from completed.
Our Party is still confronted with incredibly difficult
tasks, not only in respect of the economic plan—where
we have made quite a few mistakes—or the basis of economic construction, but also the basis of relations between
the classes remaining in our society, in this Soviet Republic.
These relations have undergone a change, and this—you
will all agree—should be one of the chief questions for you
to examine and decide here.

Comrades, we have passed through an exceptional year,
we have allowed ourselves the luxury of discussions and
disputes within the Party.[50] This was an amazing luxury
for a Party shouldering unprecedented responsibilities and
surrounded by mighty and powerful enemies uniting the
whole capitalist world.

I do not know how you will assess that fact now. Was
it fully compatible with our resources, both material and
spiritual? It is up to you to appraise this. At all events,
however, I must say that the slogan, task and aim which
we should set ourselves at this Congress and which we must
accomplish at all costs, is to emerge from the discussions
and disputes stronger than before. (*Applause.*) You, comrades, cannot fail to be aware that all our enemies—and
their name is legion—in all their innumerable press organs
abroad repeat, elaborate and multiply the same wild rumour
that our bourgeois and petty-bourgeois enemies spread here
inside the Soviet Republic, namely: discussion means disputes; disputes mean discord; discord means that the
Communists have become weak; press hard, seize the opportunity, take advantage of their weakening! This has become
the slogan of the hostile world. We must not forget this
for a moment. Our task now is to show that, to whatever

extent we have allowed ourselves this luxury in the past, whether rightly or wrongly, we must emerge from this situation in such a way that, having properly examined the extraordinary abundance of platforms, shades, slight shades and almost slight shades of opinion, that have been formulated and discussed, we at our Party Congress could say to ourselves: at all events, whatever form the discussion has taken up to now, however much we have argued among ourselves—and we are confronted with so many enemies— the task of the dictatorship of the proletariat in a peasant country is so vast and difficult that formal cohesion is far from enough. (Your presence here at the Congress is a sign that we have that much.) Our efforts should be more united and harmonious than ever before; there should not be the slightest trace of factionalism—whatever its manifestations in the past. That we must not have on any account. That is the only condition on which we shall accomplish the immense tasks that confront us. I am sure that I express the intention and firm resolve of all of you when I say: at all events, the end of this Congress must find our Party stronger, more harmonious, and more sincerely united than ever before. (*Applause.*)

2

REPORT ON THE POLITICAL WORK
OF THE CENTRAL COMMITTEE OF THE R.C.P.(B.)
MARCH 8

Comrades, the question of the Central Committee's political work, as you are, of course, aware, is so closely bound up with the whole work of the Party and Soviet institutions, and with the whole course of the revolution, that in my view, at any rate, there can be no question of a report in the full sense of the word. Accordingly, I take it to be my task to try to single out some of the more important events which, I think, represent the cardinal points of our work and of Soviet policy over the past year, which are most typical of what we have gone through and which provide most food for thought concerning the reasons for the course taken by the revolution, the significance of our mistakes— and these have been many—and the lessons for the future. For no matter how natural it is to report on the events of the past year, no matter how essential it is for the Central Committee, and no matter how interesting such a report in itself may be for the Party, the tasks of the current and forthcoming struggle are so urgent, difficult and grave, and press so hard upon us that all our attention is unwittingly concentrated on how to draw the appropriate conclusions from past experience and how best to solve present and future problems on which all our attention is focused.

Of all the key problems of our work in the past year, which chiefly hold our attention and with which, in my opinion, our mistakes are mainly connected, the most important is the transition from war to peace. All, or possibly most of you, will recall that we have attempted this transition several times during the past three and a half years, without once having completed it; and apparently we shall not accomplish it this time either because international capitalism is too vitally interested in preventing it. I recall that in April 1918, i.e., three years ago, I had occasion to speak to the All-Russia Central Executive Committee about our tasks, which at the time were formulated as if the Civil War had in the main come to an end, when in actual fact it had only just begun. You will all recall that at the previous Party Congress we based all our plans on the transition to peaceful construction, having assumed that the enormous concessions then made to Poland[51] would assure us of peace. As early as April, however, the Polish bourgeoisie, which, with the imperialists of the capitalist countries, interpreted our peaceful stand as a sign of weakness, started an offensive for which they paid dearly: they got a peace that was much worse. But we were unable to switch to peaceful construction and had once again to concentrate on the war with Poland and subsequently on wiping out Wrangel. That is what determined the substance of our work in the year under review. Once again all our work turned on military problems.

Then followed the transition from war to peace when the last enemy soldier was finally driven from the territory of the R.S.F.S.R.

This transition involved upheavals which we had certainly never foreseen. That is undoubtedly one of the main causes of all our mistakes in policy during the period under review, from which we are now suffering. We now realise that some of the tasks we had grossly underrated were posed by the demobilisation of the army, which had to be created in a country that had suffered unparalleled strains and stresses, and that had gone through several years of imperialist war. Its demobilisation put a terrible strain on our transport facilities, and this was intensified by the famine due to the crop failure and the fuel shortage, which largely brought the railways to a standstill. That is largely the source of the series of crises—economic, social and political—that hit us. At the end of last year I had occasion to point out that one of the main difficulties of the coming spring would be that connected with the demobilisation of the army. I also pointed this out at the big discussion on December 30, which many of you may have attended. I must say that at the time we had scarcely any idea of the scale of these

difficulties. We had not yet seen the extent of the possible
technical difficulties; but then neither had we realised the
extent to which the demobilisation would intensify all the
misfortunes which befell the Soviet Republic, exhausted
as it was by the old imperialist war and the new civil war.
To some extent it would be right to say that the demobilisation brings out these difficulties to an even greater degree.
For a number of years, the country had been dedicated to
the solution of war tasks and had given its all to solve them.
It had ungrudgingly sacrificed all it had, its meagre reserves and resources, and only at the end of the war were
we able to see the full extent of that devastation and poverty which now condemn us to the simple healing of wounds
for a long time to come. But even to this we cannot devote
ourselves entirely. The technical difficulties of army demobilisation show a good part of the depth of that devastation
which inevitably breeds, apart from other things, a whole
series of economic and social crises. The war had habituated
us—hundreds of thousands of men, the whole country—
to war-time tasks, and when a great part of the army, having
solved these military tasks, finds very much worse conditions and incredible hardships in the countryside, without
any opportunity—because of this and the general crisis—
to apply its labour, the result is something midway between
war and peace. We find that it is a situation in which
we cannot very well speak of peace. For it is the demobilisation—the end of the Civil War—that makes it impossible for us to concentrate on peaceful construction, because
it brings about a continuation of the war, but in a new form.
We find ourselves involved in a new kind of war, a new form
of war, which is summed up in the word "banditism"—
when tens and hundreds of thousands of demobilised soldiers, who are accustomed to the toils of war and regard
it almost as their only trade, return, impoverished and
ruined, and are unable to find work.

Failure to reckon with the scale of the difficulties connected with the demobilisation was undoubtedly a mistake
on the part of the Central Committee. It must, of course,
be said that we had nothing to go on, for the Civil War
was so arduous an effort that there was only one guiding
principle: everything for victory on the Civil War front,

and nothing else. It was only by observing this principle, and by the Red Army's unparalleled efforts in the struggle against Kolchak, Yudenich and others, that we could hope to achieve victory over the imperialists who had invaded Soviet Russia.

From this crucial fact, which determined a whole series of mistakes and intensified the crisis, I should like to turn to the question of how a whole number of even more profound discrepancies, erroneous calculations or plans were brought to light in the work of the Party and the struggle of the entire proletariat. These were not only mistakes in planning, but in determining the balance of forces between our class and those classes in collaboration with which, and frequently in struggle against which, it had to decide the fate of the Republic. With this as a starting-point, let us turn to the results of the past, to our political experience, and to what the Central Committee, as the policy-making body, must understand and try to explain to the whole Party. These questions range from the course of our war with Poland to food and fuel. Our offensive, our too swift advance almost as far as Warsaw, was undoubtedly a mistake. I shall not now analyse whether it was a strategic or a political error, as this would take me too far afield. Let us leave it to future historians, for those of us who have to keep beating off the enemy in hard struggle have no time to indulge in historical research. At any rate, the mistake is there, and it was due to the fact that we had overestimated the superiority of our forces. It would be too difficult to decide now to what extent this superiority of forces depended on the economic conditions, and on the fact that the war with Poland aroused patriotic feelings even among the petty-bourgeois elements, who were by no means proletarians or sympathisers with communism, by no means giving unconditional support to the dictatorship of the proletariat; sometimes, in fact, they did not support it at all. But the fact remains that we had made a definite mistake in the war with Poland.

We find a similar mistake in food. With regard to surplus food appropriation and its fulfilment there can be no doubt that the year under review was more favourable than the previous one. This year the amount of grain collected is over 250 million poods. By February 1, the figure was estimated at 235 million poods, as against the 210 million poods for the whole of the previous year; that is to say, more was collected in a much shorter period than for the whole of the previous year. It turned out, however, that of these 235 millions collected by February 1, we had used up 155 million poods within the first six months, that is, an average of 25 million or even more poods a month. Of course, we must on the whole admit that we were unable to space out our reserves properly, even when they were better than last year's. We failed to see the full danger of the crisis approaching with the spring, and succumbed to the natural desire to increase the starving workers' ration. Of course, it must be said that there again we had no basis for our estimates. All capitalist countries, in spite of the anarchy and chaos intrinsic to capitalism, have as a basis for their economic planning, the experience of many decades which they can compare, for they have the same economic system differing only in details. From this comparison it is possible to deduce a genuinely scientific law, a certain regularity and uniformity. We cannot have and have not had anything of the kind, and it was quite natural that when at the end of the war the possibility finally arose to give the starving population a little more, we were unable all at once to establish the correct proportion. We should have obviously limited the increase in the ration, so as to create a certain reserve fund for a rainy day, which was due to come in the spring, and which has now arrived. That we failed to do. Once again it is a mistake typical of all our work, a mistake which shows that the transition from war to peace confronted us with a whole number of difficulties and problems, and we had neither the experience, the training, nor the requisite material to overcome them, and this worsened, intensified and aggravated the crisis to an extraordinary extent.

We undoubtedly had something similar in fuel. It is crucial to economic construction. The output estimates and proper distribution of fuel had, of course, to be the basis for the entire transition from war to peace—to economic construction—which was discussed at the previous Party Congress and which has been the main concern and the focal point of all our policy during the year under review. There can be no question of overcoming our difficulties or reha- bilitating our industry without it. In this respect, we are clearly in a better position now than we were last year. We used to be cut off from the coal and oil districts, but we got the coal and oil after the Red Army's victories. In any case, our fuel resources have increased. We know that the fuel resources with which we entered upon the year under review were greater than before. Accordingly, we made the mistake of immediately permitting such a wide distribution of fuel that these resources were exhausted and we were faced with a fuel crisis before we had put everything in proper working order. You will hear special reports on all these problems, and I cannot even give you any approximate figures. But in any case, bearing in mind the experience of the past, we must say that this mistake was due to a wrong understanding of the state of affairs and the rapid pace of transition from war to peace. It turned out that the tran- sition could only be made at a much slower pace than we had imagined. The lesson driven home to us over the past year is that the preparations had to be longer, and the pace slower. It is a lesson that the whole Party will need par- ticularly to learn in order to determine our main tasks for the year ahead, if we are to avoid similar mistakes in the future.

I must add that the crop failure aggravated these mistakes and especially the resultant crises. I have pointed out that the food effort during the year under review gave us very much better food reserves, but that too was one of the main sources of the crises, because the crop failure had led to an acute feed shortage, a great loss of cattle and widespread ruin among the peasants, so that these grain procurements fell mainly in places where the grain surplus was not very large. There are far greater surpluses in various outlying areas of the Republic, in Siberia and in the Northern Cau- casus, but it is there that the Soviet power was less stable, the Soviet government apparatus least efficient, and trans- portation from over there was very difficult. That is why it turned out that we collected the increased food reserves from the gubernias with the poorer crops and this went to intensify the crisis in the peasant economy considerably.

Here again we clearly see that our estimates were not as accurate as they should have been. But then we were in such a tight corner that we had no choice. A country which, after a devastating imperialist war, survived such a thing as a long civil war, could not, of course, exist without giving the front everything it had. And, once ruined, what could it do but take the peasants' surpluses, even without compensating them by any other means. We had to do this to save the country, the army, and the workers' and peasants' government. We said to the peasants: "Of course, you are lending your grain to the workers' and peasants' state, but unless you do, you cannot expect to save the country from the landowners and the capitalists." We could do nothing else in the circumstances forced upon us by the imperialists and the capitalists through their war. We had no choice. But these circumstances led to such a weakening of the peasant economy after the long war that the crop failure was due also to the smaller sown area, worsening equipment, lower crop yields, shortage of hands, etc. The crop failure was disastrous, but the collection of surplus grain, which was rather better than we had expected, was accompanied by an aggravation of the crisis that may bring us still greater difficulties and calamities in the months to come. We must carefully reckon with this fact when analysing our political experience of the past year, and the political tasks we set ourselves for the year ahead. The year under review has left the following year with the same urgent problems.

I shall now deal with another point from a totally different sphere—the trade union discussion, which has taken up so much of the Party's time. I mentioned it earlier on today, and could naturally only venture the cautious remark that I thought many of you would consider this discussion as being too great a luxury. I must add, for my part, that I think it was quite an impermissible luxury, and we certainly made a mistake when we allowed it, for we had failed to realise that we were pushing into the forefront a question which for objective reasons cannot be there. We allowed ourselves to indulge in this luxury, failing to realise how much attention we distracted from the vital and threatening question before us, namely, this question of the crisis

What are the actual results of this discussion, which has been going on for so many months and which must have bored most of you? You will hear special reports on it, but I should like to draw your attention to one aspect of the matter. It is that in this case the saying, "Every cloud has a silver lining", has been undoubtedly justified.

Unfortunately, there was rather a lot of cloud, and very little silver lining. (*Laughter.*) Still, the silver lining was there, for although we lost a great deal of time and diverted the attention of our Party comrades from the urgent tasks of the struggle against the petty-bourgeois elements surrounding us, we did learn to discern certain relationships which we had not seen before. The good thing was that the Party was bound to learn something from this struggle. Although we all knew that, being the ruling party, we had inevitably to merge the Party and government leadership—they are merged and will remain so—the Party nevertheless learned a certain lesson in this discussion which cannot be ignored. Some platforms mostly got the votes of the "top" section of the Party. Some platforms which were sometimes called "the platforms of the Workers' Opposition", and sometimes by other names, clearly proved to be an expression of a syndicalist deviation. That is not just my personal opinion, but that of the vast majority of those present. (*Voices*: "That's right.")

In this discussion, the Party proved itself to have matured to such an extent that, aware of a certain wavering of the "top" section and hearing the leadership say: "We cannot agree—sort us out," it mobilised rapidly for this task and the vast majority of the more important Party organisations quickly responded: "We do have an opinion, and we shall let you know it."

During the discussion we got a number of platforms. There were so many of them that, although in view of my position I should have read them all, I confess I had not. (*Laughter.*) I do not know whether all those present had found the time to read them, but, in any case, I must say that this syndicalist, and to a certain degree even semi-anarchist, deviation, which has crystallised, gives food for thought. For several months we allowed ourselves to wallow in the luxury of studying shades of opinion.

Meanwhile, the demobilisation of the army was producing
banditry and aggravating the economic crisis. The discussion
should have helped us to understand that our Party, with
at least half a million members and possibly even more,
has become, first, a mass party, and, second, the government party, and that as a mass party it reflects something
of what is taking place outside its ranks. It is extremely
important to understand this.

There would be nothing to fear from a slight syndicalist or semi-anarchist deviation; the Party would have
swiftly and decisively become aware of it, and would have
set about correcting it. But it is no time to argue about
theoretical deviations when one of them is bound up with
the tremendous preponderance of peasants in the country,
when their dissatisfaction with the proletarian dictatorship is mounting, when the crisis in peasant farming is
coming to a head, and when the demobilisation of the peasant army is setting loose hundreds and thousands of broken
men who have nothing to do, whose only accustomed occupation is war and who breed banditry. At the Congress,
we must make it quite clear that we cannot have arguments
about deviations and that we must put a stop to that. The
Party Congress can and must do this; it must draw the
appropriate lesson, and add it to the Central Committee's
political report, consolidate and confirm it, and make it
a Party law and duty. The atmosphere of the controversy
is becoming extremely dangerous and constitutes a direct
threat to the dictatorship of the proletariat.

A few months ago, when I had occasion to meet and argue
with some comrades in a discussion and said, "Beware,
this constitutes a threat to working-class rule and the dictatorship of the proletariat," they replied, "This is intimidation, you are terrorising us." On several occasions I have
had to hear my remarks being labelled in this manner, and
accusations of intimidation thrown about, and I replied that
it would be absurd for me to try to intimidate old revolutionaries who had gone through all sorts of ordeals. But
when you see the difficulties the demobilisation is producing
you can no longer say it was an attempt at intimidation,
or even an unavoidable exaggeration in the heat of the
controversy; it was, in fact, an absolutely exact indication

of what we now have, and of our need for unity, discipline and restraint. We need all this not only because otherwise a proletarian party cannot work harmoniously, but because the spring has brought and will bring even more difficult conditions in which we cannot function without maximum unity. These two main lessons, I think, we shall still be able to learn from the discussion. I think it necessary to say, therefore, that whilst we did indulge in luxury and presented the world with a remarkable example of a party, engaged in a most desperate struggle, permitting itself the luxury of devoting unprecedented attention to the detailed elucidation of separate points of platforms—all this in face of a crop failure, a crisis, ruin and demobilisation— we shall now draw from these lessons a political conclusion —not just a conclusion pointing to some mistake, but a political conclusion—concerning the relations between classes, between the working class and the peasants. These relations are not what we had believed them to be. They demand much greater unity and concentration of forces on the part of the proletariat, and under the dictatorship of the proletariat they are a far greater danger than all the Denikins, Kolchaks and Yudeniches put together. It would be fatal to be deluded on this score! The difficulties stemming from the petty-bourgeois element are enormous, and if they are to be overcome, we must have great unity, and I don't mean just a semblance of unity. We must all pull together with a single will, for in a peasant country only the will of the mass of proletarians will enable the proletariat to accomplish the great tasks of its leadership and dictatorship.

Assistance is on its way from the West-European countries but it is not coming quickly enough. Still it is coming and growing.

I pointed out this morning that one of the most important factors of the period under review, one closely related to the work of the Central Committee, is the organisation of the Second Congress of the Comintern. Of course, compared with last year, the world revolution has made considerable headway. Of course, the Communist International, which at the time of last year's Congress existed only in the form of proclamations, has now begun to function as an independent party in each country, and not merely as an advanced party —communism has become central to the working-class movement as a whole. In Germany, France and Italy the Communist International has become not only the centre of the working-class movement, but also the focus of political life in these countries. Any German or French newspaper you picked up last autumn contained abuse of Moscow and the Bolsheviks, who were called all sorts of names; in fact, the Bolsheviks and the 21 conditions for admission to the Third International[52] were made the central issue of their entire political life. That is an achievement no one can take away from us! It shows how the world revolution is growing and how it is paralleled by the aggravation of the economic crisis in Europe. But in any case, it would be madness on our part to assume that help will shortly arrive from Europe in the shape of a strong proletarian revolution, and I am sure no one here is making such an assumption. In these last three years, we have learned to understand that placing our stake on the world revolution does not mean relying on a definite date, and that the accelerating pace of development may or may not lead to a revolution in the spring. Therefore, we must be able to bring our work in line with the class balance here and elsewhere, so as to be able to maintain the dictatorship of the proletariat for a long time, and, however gradually, to remedy all our numerous misfortunes and crises. This is the only correct and sober approach.

I shall now turn to an item concerning the work of the Central Committee during the present year which is closely related to the tasks facing us. It is the question of our foreign relations.

Prior to the Ninth Party Congress, our attention and all our endeavours were aimed at switching from our relations of war with the capitalist countries to relations of peace and trade. For that purpose we undertook all sorts of diplomatic moves and bested men who were undoubtedly skilled diplomats. When, for instance, the representatives of America or of the League of Nations[53] proposed that we halt hostilities against Denikin and Kolchak on certain stated terms, they thought we would land in difficulties. In actual fact, it was they who landed in difficulties and we who scored a great diplomatic victory. They were made to look silly, they had to withdraw their terms, and this was subsequently exposed in all the diplomatic writings and press of the world. But we cannot rest content with a diplomatic victory. We need more than that: we need genuine trade relations. However, only this year has there been some development in trade relations. There is the question of trade relations with Britain, which has been central since the summer of last year. In this connection, the war with Poland was a considerable setback for us. Britain was ready to sign a trade agreement. The British bourgeoisie wanted it, but court circles in Britain were against it and hampered it, and the war with Poland delayed it. It so happens that the matter has not been settled yet.

Today's papers, I think, say that Krasin has told the press in London that he expects the trade agreement to be signed shortly.[54] I do not know whether these hopes are fully justified. I cannot be certain that it will actually take place, but for my part I must say that we in the Central Committee have devoted a great deal of attention to this question and considered it correct for us to compromise in order to achieve a trade agreement with Britain. Not only because we could obtain more from Britain than from other countries—she is, in this respect, not as advanced as, say, Germany or America. She is a colonial power, with too great a stake in Asian politics, and is sometimes too sensitive to the successes of the Soviet power in certain countries lying near her colonies. That is why our relations with Britain are especially tenuous. This tenuousness arises from such an objective tangle of causes that no amount of skill on the part of the Soviet diplomatists will help. But we need a trade treaty with Britain owing to the possibility opening up for a treaty with America, whose industrial capacity is so much greater.

The concession issue is bound up with this. We devoted far more attention to it last year than before. A decree of the Council of People's Commissars issued on November 23 set out the concession question in a form most acceptable to foreign capitalists. When certain misinterpretations or insufficient understanding of this problem arose in Party circles, a number of meetings of senior Party workers were held to discuss it. On the whole, there was not a great deal of disagreement, although we did hear of many protests from workers and peasants. They said: "We got rid of our own capitalists, and now they want to call in some foreign capitalists." Of course, the Central Committee had no statistics at its disposal to decide to what extent these protests were due to ignorance, or expressed the hopes of the kulak or outright capitalist section of the non-Party people who believe they have a legitimate right to be capitalists in Russia, and not like the foreign capitalists who are invited in without any power, but with real power. Indeed, it is most unlikely that statistics on such factors are available anywhere in the world. But this decree was, at any rate, a step towards establishing relations with a view to granting concessions. I must add that in practice—and this is something we must never forget—we have not secured a single concession. The point at issue is whether we should try to get them at all costs. Whether we get them or not does not depend on our arguments or decisions, but on international capital. On February 1 of this year, the Council of People's Commissars took another decision on the concessions. Its first clause says: "To approve in principle the granting of oil concessions in Grozny and Baku and at other working oilfields and to open negotiations which should be pressed forward."

There was some difference of opinion on this point. Some comrades thought it was wrong to grant concessions in Grozny and Baku, as this would arouse opposition among the workers. The majority on the Central Committee, including myself, took the view that there were possibly no grounds for the complaints.

The majority on the Central Committee and I myself took the view that it was essential to grant these concessions, and we shall ask you to back it up with your authority. It is vital to have such an alliance with the state trusts of the advanced countries because our economic crisis is so deep that we cannot, on our own, rehabilitate our ruined economy without machinery and technical aid from abroad. Getting the equipment out here is not enough. We could grant concessions to the biggest imperialist trusts on a wider basis: say, a quarter of Baku, a quarter of Grozny, and a quarter of our best forest reserves, so as to assure ourselves of an essential basis by the installation of the most modern machinery; on the other hand, in return for this we shall be getting badly needed machinery for the remaining part. In this way we shall be able to close a part—say, a quarter or a half—of the gap between us and the modern, advanced trusts of other countries. No one, with anything like a sober view of the present situation, will doubt that unless we do this we shall be in a very difficult position indeed, and shall be unable to overtake them without a superhuman effort. Negotiations with some of the largest world trusts have already begun. Naturally, for their part they are not simply doing us a good turn: they are in it only for the fantastic profits. Modern capitalism—as a non-belligerent diplomat would put it—is a robber, a ring. It is not the old capitalism of pre-war days: because of its monopoly of the world market its profit margins run to hundreds of per cents. Of course, this will exact a high price, but there is no other way out because the world revolution is marking time. There is no other way for us to raise our technology to the modern level. And if one of the crises were to give a sharp spur to the world revolution, and if it were to arrive before the concession terms ran out, our concession obligations would turn out to be less onerous than they appear on paper.

On February 1, 1921, the Council of People's Commissars decided to purchase 18,500,000 poods of coal abroad, for our fuel crisis was already in evidence. It had already become clear by then that we would have to expend our gold reserves not only on the purchase of machinery. In the latter case, our coal output would have increased, for we would have boosted our production if, instead of coal, we had bought machines abroad to develop our coal industry, but the crisis was so acute that we had to opt for the worse economic step and spend our money on the coal we could have produced at home. We shall have to make further compromises to buy consumer goods for the peasants and workers.

I should now like to deal with the Kronstadt events.[55] I have not yet received the latest news from Kronstadt, but I have no doubt that this mutiny, which very quickly revealed to us the familiar figures of whiteguard generals, will be put down within the next few days, if not hours.

There can be no doubt about this. But it is essential that we make a thorough appraisal of the political and economic lessons of this event.

What does it mean? It was an attempt to seize political power from the Bolsheviks by a motley crowd or alliance of ill-assorted elements, apparently just to the right of the Bolsheviks, or perhaps even to their "left"—you can't really tell, so amorphous is the combination of political groupings that has tried to take power in Kronstadt. You all know, undoubtedly, that at the same time whiteguard generals were very active over there. There is ample proof of this. A fortnight before the Kronstadt events, the Paris newspapers reported a mutiny at Kronstadt. It is quite clear that it is the work of Socialist-Revolutionaries and white-guard émigrés, and at the same time the movement was reduced to a petty-bourgeois counter-revolution and petty-bourgeois anarchism. That is something quite new. This circumstance, in the context of all the crises, must be given careful political consideration and must be very thoroughly analysed. There is evidence here of the activity of petty-bourgeois anarchist elements with their slogans of unrestricted trade and invariable hostility to the dictatorship of the proletariat. This mood has had a wide influence on the proletariat. It has had an effect on factories in Moscow and a number of provincial centres. This petty-bourgeois counter-revolution is undoubtedly more dangerous than Denikin, Yudenich and Kolchak put together, because ours is a country where the proletariat is in a minority, where peasant property has gone to ruin and where, in addition, the demobilisation has set loose vast numbers of potentially mutinous elements. No matter how big or small the initial, shall I say, shift in power, which the Kronstadt sailors and workers put forward—they wanted to correct the Bolsheviks in regard to restrictions in trade—and this looks like a small shift, which leaves the same slogans of "Soviet power" with ever so slight a change or correction. Yet, in actual fact the whiteguards only used the non-Party elements as a stepping stone to get in. This is politically inevitable. We saw the petty-bourgeois, anarchist elements in the Russian revolution, and we have been fighting them for decades. We have seen them in action since February

1917, during the great revolution, and their parties' attempts to prove that their programme differed little from that of the Bolsheviks, but that only their methods in carrying it through were different. We know this not only from the experience of the October Revolution, but also of the outlying regions and various areas within the former Russian Empire where the Soviet power was temporarily replaced by other regimes. Let us recall the Democratic Committee in Samara.[56] They all came in demanding equality, freedom, and a constituent assembly, and every time they proved to be nothing but a conduit for whiteguard rule. Because the Soviet power is being shaken by the economic situation, we must consider all this experience and draw the theoretical conclusions a Marxist cannot escape. The experience of the whole of Europe shows the practical results of trying to sit between two stools. That is why in this context we must say that political friction, in this case, is a great danger. We must take a hard look at this petty-bourgeois counter-revolution with its calls for freedom to trade. Unrestricted trade—even if it is not as bound up initially with the whiteguards as Kronstadt was—is still only the thin end of the wedge for the whiteguard element, a victory for capital and its complete restoration. We must, I repeat, have a keen sense of this political danger.

It shows what I said in dealing with our platforms discussion: in face of this danger we must understand that we must do more than put an end to Party disputes as a matter of form—we shall do that, of course. We need to remember that we must take a much more serious approach to this question.

We have to understand that, with the peasant economy in the grip of a crisis, we can survive only by appealing to the peasants to help town and countryside. We must bear in mind that the bourgeoisie is trying to pit the peasants against the workers; that behind a façade of workers' slogans it is trying to incite the petty-bourgeois anarchist elements against the workers. This, if successful, will lead directly to the overthrow of the dictatorship of the proletariat and, consequently, to the restoration of capitalism and of the old landowner and capitalist regime. The political danger here is obvious. A number of revolutions have clearly gone

that way; we have always been mindful of this possibility
and have warned against it. This undoubtedly demands
of the ruling party of Communists, and of the leading revolutionary elements of the proletariat a different attitude
to the one we have time and again displayed over the past
year. It is a danger that undoubtedly calls for much greater
unity and discipline; it undoubtedly requires that we should
all pull harder together. Otherwise we shall not cope with
the dangers that have fallen to our lot.

Then there are the economic problems. What is the meaning of the unrestricted trade demanded by the petty-bourgeois
elements? It is that in the proletariat's relations with the
small farmers there are difficult problems and tasks we
have yet to solve. I am speaking of the victorious proletariat's relations with the small proprietors when the proletarian revolution unfolds in a country where the proletariat
is in a minority, and the petty bourgeoisie, in a majority.
In such a country the proletariat's role is to direct the
transition of these small proprietors to socialised and collective work. Theoretically this is beyond dispute. We have
dealt with this transition in a number of legislative acts,
but we know that it does not turn on legislative acts, but
on practical implementation, which, we also know, can
be guaranteed when you have a very powerful, large-scale
industry capable of providing the petty producer with such
benefits that he will see its advantages in practice.

That is how Marxists and all socialists who have given
thought to the social revolution and its tasks have always
regarded the question in theory. But Russia's most pronounced characteristic of which I have spoken is that we have,
on the one hand, not only a minority, but a considerable
minority of proletarians, and, on the other, a vast majority
of peasants. And the conditions in which we have had to
defend the revolution made the solution of our problems
incredibly difficult. We have not been able to show all
the advantages of large-scale production, for it lies in ruins,
and is dragging out a miserable existence. It can only be
rehabilitated by demanding sacrifices from these very same
small farmers. To get industry on its feet you need
fuel; if you need fuel, you must rely on firewood; and if
you rely on firewood, you must look to the peasant and

his horse. In conditions of crisis, the fodder shortage and the loss of cattle, the peasant must give his produce on credit to the Soviet power for the sake of a large-scale industry which has not yet given him a thing. That is the economic situation which gives rise to enormous difficulties and demands a deeper analysis of the conditions of transition from war to peace. We cannot run a war-time economy otherwise than by telling the peasants: "You must make loans to the workers' and peasants' state to help it pull through." When concentrating on economic rehabilitation, we must understand that we have before us a small farmer, a small proprietor and producer who will work for the market until the rehabilitation and triumph of large-scale production. But rehabilitation on the old basis is impossible; it will take years, at least a decade, and possibly longer, in view of the havoc. Until then we shall have to deal, for many long years, with the small producer as such, and the unrestricted trade slogan will be inevitable. It is dangerous, not because it covers up the aspirations of the whiteguards and Mensheviks, but because it may become widespread in spite of the peasants' hatred for the whiteguards. It is apt to spread because it conforms to the economic conditions of the small producer's existence. It is out of such considerations that the Central Committee adopted its decision to start a discussion on the substitution of a tax for surplus food appropriation and today placed this question squarely before the Congress, a motion which today's resolution approves.[57] The tax and appropriation problem had been brought up in our legislation a long time ago, back in late 1918. The tax law was dated October 30, 1918. The law on a tax in kind on the farmer was enacted, but never became operative. A number of instructions were issued in the few months after its promulgation, but it was never applied. On the other hand, the confiscation of surpluses from the peasants was a measure with which we were saddled by the imperative conditions of war-time, but which no longer applies to anything like the peace-time conditions of the peasant's economy. He needs the assurance that, while he has to give away a certain amount, he will have so much left to sell locally.

The whole of our economy and its various branches were

affected throughout by war-time conditions. With this in mind, our task was to collect a definite quantity of food, regardless of what it did to the national turnover. As we turn from problems of war to those of peace, we take a different view of the tax in kind: we see it not only from the standpoint of meeting the needs of the state, but also those of the small farms. We must try to understand the economic forms of the petty farmer's indignation against the proletariat which has been in evidence and which is being aggravated in the current crisis. We must try to do our utmost in this respect for it is a matter of vital importance. We must allow the peasant to have a certain amount of leeway in local trade, and supplant the surplus food appropriation by a tax, to give the small farmer a chance to plan his production and determine its scale in accordance with the tax. We know quite well, of course, that in our conditions this is a very difficult thing to do. The sown area, the crop yield, and the farm implements have all been reduced, the surpluses have undoubtedly decreased, and in very many cases have disappeared altogether. These circumstances must be regarded as a fact. The peasant will have to go hungry for a while in order to save the towns and factories from famine. That is something quite understandable on a country-wide scale, but we do not expect the poverty-stricken lone-wolf farmer to understand it. And we know that we shall not be able to do without coercion, on which the impoverished peasants are very touchy. Nor must we imagine that this measure will rid us of the crisis. But we do regard it as our task to make the maximum concessions, to give the small producer the best conditions to come into his own. Up to now, we have been adapting ourselves to the tasks of war; we must now adapt ourselves to the conditions of peace. The Central Committee is faced with this task—the task of switching to the tax in kind in conditions of proletarian power, and it is closely bound up with the question of concessions. You will be having a special discussion on this problem, and it requires your special consideration. By granting concessions, the proletarian power can secure an agreement with advanced capitalist states. On it depends our industrial growth, without which we cannot hope to advance towards communism.

On the other hand, in this period of transition in a country where the peasants predominate, we must manage to go over to measures giving economic security to the peasants, and do the most we can to ease their economic condition. Until we have remoulded the peasant, until large-scale machinery has recast him, we must assure him of the possibility of running his economy without restrictions. We are now in a transitional phase, and our revolution is surrounded by capitalist countries. As long as we are in this phase, we are forced to seek highly complex forms of relationships. Oppressed by war, we were unable to concentrate on how to establish economic relations between the proletarian state power, with an incredibly devastated large-scale industry, and the small farmers, and how to find forms of coexistence with them, who, as long as they remain small farmers, cannot exist without their small economy having some system of exchange. I believe this to be the Soviet Government's most important question in the sphere of economics and politics at the present time. I believe that it sums up the political results of our work, now that the war period has ended and we have begun, in the year under review, to make the transition to peace.

This transition is bound up with such difficulties and has so clearly delineated this petty-bourgeois element, that we must take a sober view of it. We view this series of events in terms of the class struggle, and we have never doubted that the relations between the proletariat and the petty bourgeoisie are a difficult problem, demanding complex measures or, to be more accurate, a whole system of complex, transitional measures, to ensure the victory of the proletarian power. The fact that we issued our tax in kind decree at the end of 1918 proves that the Communists were aware of this problem, but were unable to solve it because of the war. With the Civil War on, we had to adopt war-time measures. But it would be a very great mistake indeed if we drew the conclusion that these are the only measures and relations possible. That would surely lead to the collapse of the Soviet power and the dictatorship of the proletariat. When the transition to peace takes place in a period of economic crisis, it should be borne in mind that it is easier to build up a proletarian state in a country with large-

scale production than in one with a predominantly small-
scale production. This problem has to be approached in a
whole number of ways, and we do not close our eyes to these
difficulties, or forget that the proletariat is one thing, and
the small-scale producer, another. We have not forgotten
that there are different classes, that petty-bourgeois, anarchist counter-revolution is a political step to whiteguard rule.
We must face this squarely, with an awareness that this
needs, on the one hand, maximum unity, restraint and
discipline within the proletarian party, and on the other,
a series of economic measures which we have not been able
to carry out so far because of the war. We must recognise
the need to grant concessions, and purchase machinery and
equipment to satisfy agriculture, so as to exchange them
for grain and re-establish relations between the proletariat
and the peasants which will enable it to exist in peace-
time conditions. I trust that we shall return to this problem, and I repeat that, in my view, we are dealing here
with an important matter, and that the past year, which
must be characterised as a period of transition from war to
peace, confronts us with some extremely difficult problems.

Let me say a few words in conclusion about combating
bureaucratic practices, the question which has taken up
so much of our time. It came up before the Central Committee last summer; in August the Central Committee sent
a circular to all organisations, and the matter was put
before a Party conference in September. Finally, at the
December Congress of Soviets, it was dealt with on a wider
scale.[58] We do have a bureaucratic ulcer; it has been
diagnosed and has to be treated in earnest. Of course, in the
discussion that we have had some platforms dealt with the
problem quite frivolously, to say the least, and, by and
large, from a petty-bourgeois viewpoint. There is no doubt
that some discontent and stirrings have recently been in
evidence among non-Party workers. Non-Party meetings
in Moscow have clearly turned "democracy" and "freedom"
into slogans leading up to the overthrow of the Soviet power.
Many, or, at any rate, some representatives of the Workers'
Opposition have battled against this petty-bourgeois, counter-
revolutionary evil, and have said: "We shall unite against
this." And in actual fact they have been able to display

the maximum unity. I cannot tell whether all the supporters of the Workers' Opposition group and other groups
with semi-syndicalist platforms are like them. We need
to learn more about this at the Congress, we need to understand that the struggle against the evils of bureaucracy is
absolutely indispensable, and that it is just as intricate
as the fight against the petty-bourgeois element. The
bureaucratic practices of our state system have become such
a serious malaise that they are dealt with in our Party
Programme, because they are connected with this petty-
bourgeois element, which is widely dispersed. This malaise
can only be cured by the working people's unity and their
ability not only to welcome the decrees of the Workers'
and Peasants' Inspection (have you seen many decrees
that have not been welcomed?) but to exercise their right
through the Inspection, something you don't find either
in the villages, the towns, or even the capital cities. Those
who shout loudest against the evils of bureaucracy very
frequently do not know how to exercise this right. Very
great attention needs to be paid to this fact.

In this area, we often see those who battle against this
evil, possibly with a sincere desire to help the proletarian
party, the proletarian dictatorship and the proletarian
movement, actually helping the petty-bourgeois, anarchist
element, which on more than one occasion during the
revolution has shown itself to be the most dangerous enemy
of the proletarian dictatorship. And now—and this is the
main conclusion and lesson of the past year—it has once
again shown itself to be the most dangerous enemy, which
is most likely to have followers and supporters in a country
like ours, to change the mood of the broad masses and to
affect even a section of the non-Party workers. That is when
the proletarian state finds itself in a very difficult position.
Unless we understand this, learn our lesson, and make this
Congress a turning-point both in economic policy and in
the sense of maximum unity of the proletariat, we shall
have to apply to ourselves the unfortunate saying: we have
forgotten nothing of what—small and trifling at times—
deserves to be forgotten, and have learned nothing of the
serious things this year of the revolution should have
taught us. I hope that will not be the case! (Stormy applause.)

3

SUMMING-UP SPEECH
ON THE REPORT OF THE C.C. OF THE R.C.P.(B.)
MARCH 9

(*Prolonged applause.*) Comrades, one would have expected the criticism, remarks, additions and amendments,
etc., elicited by the report on the political activity of the
Central Committee to concentrate on political work and
political mistakes, and to give political advice.

Unfortunately, when you take a closer look at the debate
and go over the main points made in it, you cannot help
asking yourself: Was it not because the speeches were so
strangely vapid, and almost all the speakers were
from the Workers' Opposition, that the Congress folded
up its debate so quickly? Indeed, just what has been said
of the Central Committee's political work and current
political tasks? Most of the speakers said they belonged to
the Workers' Opposition. This is no trifling title. And it is
no trifling matter to form an opposition in such a Party and
at such a moment!

Comrade Kollontai, for example, said bluntly: "Lenin's
report evaded Kronstadt." When I heard that I didn't know
what to say. Everyone present at this Congress knows perfectly well—newspaper reports will naturally not be as explicit
as the speeches here are—that my report tied in everything
—from beginning to end—with the lessons of Kronstadt.
If anything, I deserve to be reproached for devoting the
greater part of my report to the lessons that flow from the
Kronstadt events, and the smaller part to past mistakes,
political facts and crucial points in our work, which, in
my opinion, determine our political tasks and help us to
avoid such mistakes in the future.

What did we hear of the lessons of Kronstadt?

When people come forward in the name of an opposition,
which they call a "workers'" opposition, and say that the

Central Committee has failed to steer the Party's policy properly, we must tell them that we need pointers indicating what was wrong on the main questions, and ways of rectifying it. Unfortunately, we heard absolutely nothing, not a word or sound, about the present situation and its lessons. No one even touched upon the conclusion that I drew. It may be wrong, but the whole point of making reports at congresses is precisely to rectify what is wrong. The political conclusion to be drawn from the present situation is that the Party must be united and any opposition prevented. The economic conclusion is that we must not rest content with what has been achieved in the policy of reaching an agreement between the working class and the peasantry; we must seek new ways and put them to the test. I was quite specific about what we needed to do. Perhaps I was wrong, but nobody said a word about that. One of the speakers, I think it was Ryazanov, reproached me only for having suddenly sprung the tax on the Congress, before the ground had been prepared for it by discussion. That is not true. The surprising thing is that responsible comrades can make such statements at a Party Congress. The tax discussion was started in *Pravda* a few weeks ago. If the comrades who are fond of the game of opposition and like to complain that we are not providing an opportunity for broad discussion did not choose to take part in it, they have no one to blame but themselves. We are connected with *Pravda*'s editorial board not only through Comrade Bukharin's being a member of the Central Committee, but also through the Central Committee discussions of all the most important subjects and lines of policy. Otherwise there can be no political work. The Central Committee submitted the tax question for discussion. Articles were published in *Pravda*. Nobody replied to them. Those who refrained from replying showed that they did not wish to go into the matter. When, at a meeting of the Moscow Soviet—after these articles had been published—somebody, I do not remember whether it was a non-Party man or a Menshevik, got up and began to talk about the tax, I said: You don't seem to know what's being said in *Pravda*. It was more natural to say that sort of thing to a non-Party man than to a member of the Party. It was no accident that the discussion was started in *Pravda*; and we shall have to deal with it here. The criticism has been altogether unbusiness-like. The question was put up for discussion, and the critics should have taken part in it; because they had failed to do so, their criticism is groundless. The same may be said of the political question. I repeat: all my attention was concentrated on drawing the correct conclusion from recent events.

We are passing through a period of grave danger: as I have said the petty-bourgeois counter-revolution is a greater danger than Denikin. The comrades did not deny this. The peculiar feature of this counter-revolution is that it is petty-bourgeois and anarchistic. I insist that there is a connection between its ideas and slogans and those of the Workers' Opposition. There was no response to this from any of the speakers, although most of them belonged to the Workers' Opposition. And yet, the Workers' Opposition pamphlet, which Comrade Kollontai published for the Congress, serves to confirm my assertion better than anything else. And I suppose I shall have to deal chiefly with this pamphlet to explain why the counter-revolution, to which I have referred, is assuming an anarchist, petty-bourgeois form, why it is so vast and dangerous, and why the speakers from the Workers' Opposition have failed entirely to realise the danger.

But before replying to them I want to say a word or two, before I forget, on another subject, namely Osinsky. This comrade, who has written a great deal and has brought out his own platform, gets up and criticises the Central Committee's report. We could have expected him to criticise our principal measures, and this would have been very valuable for us. Instead, he said that we had "thrown out" Sapronov, which showed that our calls for unity were at variance with our deeds; and he made a point of stressing that two members of the Workers' Opposition had been elected to the Presidium. I am surprised that an extremely prominent Party worker and writer, who occupies a responsible post, can talk about such trifles, which are of tenth-rate importance! Osinsky has the knack of seeing political trickery in everything. He sees it also in the fact that two seats on the Presidium were given to the Workers' Opposition.

At a Party meeting in Moscow I called attention to the rise of the Workers' Opposition, and I regret that I must do so again now, at the Party Congress. It had revealed itself in October and November by bringing in the two-room system, and the formation of factions.

We have repeatedly said, and I have, in particular, that our task is to separate the wheat from the chaff in the Workers' Opposition, because it has spread to some extent, and has damaged our work in Moscow. There was no difference of opinion in the Central Committee on that score. There was evidence of damage to our work, the start of factionalism and a split in November, during the two-room conference[59]—when some met here and others down at the other end of the floor, and when I had my share of the trouble, for I had to act as errand-boy and shuttle between the rooms.

Back in September, during the Party Conference,[60] we regarded it as our task to separate the wheat from the chaff for the group could not be regarded as consisting entirely of good stuff. When we hear complaints about inadequate democracy, we say: it is absolutely true. Indeed, it is not being practised sufficiently. We need assistance and advice in this matter. We need real democracy, and not just talk. We even accept those who call themselves the Workers' Opposition, or something worse, although I think that for members of the Communist Party no name can be worse or more disreputable. But even if they had adopted a much worse title, we say to ourselves: since this is a malaise that has affected a section of the workers we must pay the closest attention to it. And we should be given credit for the very thing that Comrade Osinsky has accused us of, though why he should have done so, I don't know.

I now come to the Workers' Opposition. You have admitted that you are in opposition. You have come to the Party Congress with Comrade Kollontai's pamphlet which is entitled *The Workers' Opposition*. When you sent in the final proofs, you knew about the Kronstadt events and the rising petty-bourgeois counter-revolution. And it is at a time like this that you come here, calling yourselves a Workers' Opposition. You don't seem to realise the responsibility you are undertaking, and the way you are disrupting our

7*

unity! What is your object? We will question you and put
you through a test right here.

Comrade Osinsky used this expression in a polemical
sense; he seemed to think that we were guilty of some
mistake or misdemeanour. Like Ryazanov, he saw political
trickery in our policy towards the Workers' Opposition.
It is not political trickery; it is the policy the Central
Committee has been pursuing, and will continue to pursue.
Since unhealthy trends and groups have arisen, let us more
than redouble our attention to them.

If there is anything at all sound in that opposition, we
must make every effort to sift it from the rest. We cannot
combat the evils of bureaucracy effectively, or practise
democracy consistently because we lack the strength and
are weak. We must enlist those who can help us in this
matter, and expose and sift out those who produce such
pamphlets on the pretext of helping us.

This task of sifting is being facilitated at the Party Congress. Representatives of the ailing group have been elected
to the Presidium and these "poor", "wronged", and "ban-
ished" people will no longer dare to complain and wail.
There's the rostrum, up on it, and let's have your answer!
You have spoken more than anyone else. Now let us see what
you have in store for us, with this looming danger, which,
you admit, is a greater one than Denikin! What have you
come up with? What is the nature of your criticism? We
must have this test now, and I think it will be the final
one. We have had enough of that sort of thing! The Party
will not be trifled with in this way! Whoever comes to the
Congress with such a pamphlet is trifling with the Party.
You can't play that kind of game when hundreds of thousands of demoralised veterans are playing havoc with our
economy—the Party will not stand for such treatment.
You can't behave that way. You must realise that, and
put a stop to it!

After these preliminary remarks about the election to
the Presidium and the character of the Workers' Opposition
I want to draw your attention to Comrade Kollontai's
pamphlet. It really deserves your attention, for it sums
up the activity this opposition has been carrying on for
several months, or the disintegration it has caused. It was

said here, by a comrade from Samara, I think, that I had stuck the label of syndicalism on the Workers' Opposition, in an "administrative" fashion. The reference is altogether misplaced, and we must investigate which of the questions calls for an administrative solution. Comrade Milonov tried to score with a terrifying catchword, but it fell flat. He said that I stuck on a label in "administrative" fashion. I have said before that at our meetings Comrade Shlyapnikov and others have accused me of "intimidating" people with the word "syndicalism". When this was mentioned at one of our discussions, at the Miners' Congress, I think, I replied to Comrade Shlyapnikov: "Do you hope to take in any grown-ups?" After all, Comrade Shlyapnikov and I have known each other for many, many years, ever since the period of our underground work and emigration—how can he say that I am trying to intimidate anyone by characterising certain deviations? And when I say that the stand of the Workers' Opposition is wrong, and that it is syndicalism—what has administrating got to do with it?! And why does Comrade Kollontai write that I have been bandying the word "syndicalism" about in frivolous fashion? She ought to produce some proof before saying anything like that. I am prepared to allow that my proof is wrong, and that Comrade Kollontai's statement is weightier—I am prepared to believe that. But we must have some little proof—not in the form of words about intimidating or administrating (which, unfortunately, my official duties compel me to engage in a great deal), but in the form of a definite reply, refuting my accusation that the Workers' Opposition is a deviation towards syndicalism.

I made it before the whole Party, with a full sense of responsibility, and it was printed in a pamphlet in 250,000 copies, and everyone has read it. Evidently, all the comrades have prepared for this Congress, and they should know that the syndicalist deviation is an anarchist deviation, and that the Workers' Opposition, which is hiding behind the backs of the proletariat, is a petty-bourgeois, anarchist element.

That it has been penetrating into the broad masses is evident and the Party Congress has thrown light on this fact. That this element has become active is proved by

Comrade Kollontai's pamphlet and Comrade Shlyapnikov's theses. And this time you can't get away with talk about being a true proletarian, as Comrade Shlyapnikov is in the habit of doing.

Comrade Kollontai starts her pamphlet with the following: "The opposition," we read on page one, "consists of the advanced section of the class-organised proletarians, who are Communists." A delegate from Siberia told the Miners' Congress[61] that over there they had discussed the same questions as were being discussed in Moscow, and Comrade Kollontai mentions this in her pamphlet:

"'We had no idea that there were disagreements and discussions in Moscow about the role of the trade unions,' a delegate from Siberia told the Miners' Congress, 'but we were set astir by the same questions that you are faced with over here.'"

Further:

"The Workers' Opposition has the backing of the proletarian masses, or, to be more precise: it is the class-welded, class-conscious and class-consistent section of our industrial proletariat."

Well, thank heaven, we now know that Comrade Kollontai and Comrade Shlyapnikov are "class-welded" and "class-conscious". But, comrades, when you say and write such things you must have some sense of proportion! Comrade Kollontai writes on page 25, and this is one of the main points of the Workers' Opposition theses, the following:

"The organisation of the management of the national economy is the function of an All-Russia Congress of Producers organised in trade and industrial unions, which shall elect a central body to run the whole of the national economy of the Republic."

That is the very thesis of the Workers' Opposition that I have quoted in every case in the discussion and in the press. I must say that after reading it I did not trouble to read the rest, as that would have been a waste of time; for that thesis made it quite clear that these people had reached the limit, and that theirs is a petty-bourgeois, anarchist element. Now, in the light of the Kronstadt events, that thesis sounds queerer than ever.

At the Second Congress of the Comintern last summer,

I pointed to the significance of the resolution on the role of the Communist Party. It is a resolution uniting the Communist workers and the Communist Parties of the world. It explains everything. Does that mean that we are fencing off the Party from the whole of the working class, which is definitely exercising a dictatorship? That is what certain "Leftists" and very many syndicalists think, and the idea is now widespread. It is the product of petty-bourgeois ideology. The theses of the Workers' Opposition fly in the face of the decision of the Second Congress of the Comintern on the Communist Party's role in operating the dictatorship of the proletariat. It is syndicalism because—consider this carefully—our proletariat has been largely declassed; the terrible crises and the closing down of the factories have compelled people to flee from starvation. The workers have simply abandoned their factories; they have had to settle down in the country and have ceased to be workers. Are we not aware of the fact that the unprecedented crises, the Civil War, the disruption of proper relations between town and country and the cessation of grain deliveries have given rise to a trade in small articles made at the big factories—such as cigarette lighters—which are exchanged for cereals, because the workers are starving, and no grain is being delivered? Have we not seen this happen in the Ukraine, or in Russia? That is the economic source of the proletariat's declassing and the inevitable rise of petty-bourgeois, anarchist trends.

The experience of all our hardships tells us how desperately hard it is to combat them. After two and a half years of the Soviet power we came out in the Communist International and told the world that the dictatorship of the proletariat would not work except through the Communist Party. At the time, the anarchists and syndicalists furiously attacked us and said: "You see, this is what they think —a Communist Party is needed to operate the proletarian dictatorship."[62] But we said this before the whole Communist International. After all this, you have these "class-conscious and class-welded" people coming and telling us that "the organisation of the management of the national economy is the function of an All-Russia Congress of Producers" (Comrade Kollontai's pamphlet). What is this "All-

Russia Congress of Producers"? Are we going to waste more time on that sort of opposition in the Party? I think we have had enough of this discussion! All the arguments about freedom of speech and freedom to criticise, of which the pamphlet is full and which run through all the speeches of the Workers' Opposition, constitute nine-tenths of the meaning of these speeches, which have no particular meaning at all. They are all words of the same order. After all, comrades, we ought to discuss not only words, but also their meaning. You can't fool us with words like "freedom to criticise". When we were told that there were symptoms of a malaise in the Party, we said that this deserved our redoubled attention: the malaise is undoubtedly there, let us help to cure it; but tell us how you intend to go about it. We have spent quite a lot of time in discussion, and I must say that the point is now being driven farther home with "rifles" than with the opposition's theses. Comrades, this is no time to have an opposition. Either you're on this side, or on the other, but then your weapon must be a gun, and not an opposition. This follows from the objective situation, and you mustn't blame us for it. Comrades, let's not have an opposition just now! I think the Party Congress will have to draw the conclusion that the opposition's time has run out and that the lid's on it. We want no more oppositions! (*Applause.*)

This group has long been free to criticise. And now, at this Party Congress, we ask: What are the results and the content of your criticism? What have you taught the Party by your criticism? We are prepared to enlist the services of those of you who stand closest to the masses, the really class-welded and class-mature masses. If Comrade Osinsky regards this as political trickery he will be isolated, for the rest will regard it as a real help to Party members. We must really help those who live with the workers' masses, who have intimate knowledge of them, who have experience and can advise the Central Committee. Let them call themselves what they like—it makes no difference—as long as they help in the work, as long as they help us, instead of playing at opposition and insisting on having groups and factions at all costs. But if they continue this game of opposition, the Party will have to expel them.

And when on this very same page of her pamphlet Comrade Kollontai writes in bold type about "lack of confidence in the working class", the idea is that they are a real "workers'" opposition. There is an even more striking expression of this idea on page 36:

"The Workers' Opposition cannot, and must not, make any concessions. This does not mean calling for a split.... No, its aim is different Even in the event of defeat at the Congress, it must remain within the Party and firmly defend its point of view, step by step, saving the Party and straightening out its line."

"Even in the event of defeat at the Congress"—my word, what foresight! (*Laughter.*) You will pardon me if I take the liberty of saying, on my own behalf, that I am sure that is something the Party Congress will certainly not permit! (*Applause.*) Everyone has the right to straighten out the Party's line, and you have had every opportunity of doing so.

The condition has been laid down at the Party Congress that there must not be the slightest suspicion that we want to expel anybody. We welcome every assistance in getting democracy working, but when the people are exhausted it will take more than talk to do it. Everyone who wants to help is to be welcomed; but when they say that they will "make no concessions" and will make efforts to save the Party, while remaining in it, we say: yes, if you are allowed to stay! (*Applause.*)

In this case, we have no right to leave any room for ambiguity. We certainly need help in combating bureaucracy, safeguarding democracy, and extending contacts with the truly working-class masses. We can and must make "concessions" in this respect. And though they keep saying that they will not make any concessions, we shall repeat: We will. That's not making concessions but helping the workers' Party. In this way, we shall win over all the sound and proletarian elements in the Workers' Opposition to the side of the Party, leaving outside the "class-conscious" authors of syndicalist speeches. (*Applause.*) This has been done in Moscow. The Moscow Gubernia Conference last November ended up in two rooms: some met in one, others, in another. That was the eve of a split. The last Moscow Conference said, "We will take from the Workers'

Opposition those we want, and not those they want", because we need the assistance of men who are connected with the masses of workers and who can teach us how to combat the evils of bureaucracy in practice. This is a difficult task. I think the Party Congress should take note of the Muscovites' experience and stage a test, not only on this point, but on all the points of the agenda. As a result, the people who declare that they "will make no concessions" must be told: "But the Party will." We must all pull together. By means of this policy we shall sift the sound elements from the unsound in the Workers' Opposition, and the Party will be strengthened.

Just think: it was said here that production should be run by an "All-Russia Congress of Producers". I find myself groping for words to describe this nonsense, but am reassured by the fact that all the Party workers present here are also Soviet functionaries who have been doing their work for the revolution for one, two or three years. It is not worth criticising that sort of thing in their presence. When they hear such tedious speeches they close the discussion, because it is frivolous to speak of an "All-Russia Congress of Producers" running the national economy. A proposal of that kind could be made in a country where the political power has been taken but no start has been made on the work. We have made a start. And it is a curious fact that on page 33 of this pamphlet we find the following:

"The Workers' Opposition is not so ignorant as to disregard the great role of technique and of technically trained forces.... It has no intention to set up its organs of administration of the national economy elected by the Producers' Congress and then to dissolve the economic councils, chief administrations and central boards. No, the idea is quite different: it is to subordinate these necessary, technically valuable centres of administration to its guidance, assign theoretical tasks to them and use them in the same way as the factory owners once used the services of technical experts."

In other words, Comrade Kollontai and Comrade Shlyapnikov, and their "class-welded" followers, are to subordinate to their necessary guidance the economic councils, chief administrations and central boards—all the Rykovs, Nogins and other "nonentities"—and assign to them theoretical tasks! Comrades, are we to take that seriously? If you have had any "theoretical tasks", why had you not assigned them before? Why did we proclaim freedom of discussion? It was not merely to engage in verbal exchanges. During the war we used to say: "This is not the time for criticism: Wrangel is out there. We correct our mistakes by beating Wrangel." After the war, we hear shouts of "We want freedom of discussion!" When we ask, "Tell us our mistakes!", we are told, "The economic councils and chief administrations must not be dissolved; they must be assigned theoretical tasks." Comrade Kiselyov, as a representative of the "class-welded" Workers' Opposition, was left in an insignificant minority at the Miners' Congress, but, when he was head of the Chief Administration of the Textile Industry, why did he not teach us how to combat the evils of bureaucracy? Why did not Comrade Shlyapnikov, when he was a People's Commissar, and Comrade Kollontai, when she too was a People's Commissar, why did they not teach us how to combat the evils of bureaucracy? We know that we have a touch of bureaucracy, and we, who have to deal with this bureaucratic machine at first hand, suffer as a result. You sign a paper—but how is it applied in practice? How do you check up on it, when the bureaucratic machine is so enormous? If you know how to make it smaller, dear comrades, please share your knowledge with us! You have a desire to argue, but you give us nothing apart from general statements. Instead, you indulge in demagogy pure and simple. For it is sheer demagogy to say: "The specialists are ill-treating the workers; the workers are leading a life of penal servitude in a toilers' republic."

Comrades, I entreat you all to read this pamphlet. You could not find a better argument against the Workers' Opposition than Comrade Kollontai's pamphlet, *The Workers' Opposition*. You will see that this is really no way to approach the question. We all admit that bureaucratic practices are a vexed question, and as much is stated in our Party Programme. It is very easy to criticise the chief administrations and economic councils, but your kind of criticism leads the masses of non-Party workers to think they should be dissolved. The Socialist-Revolutionaries seize upon this Some Ukrainian comrades have told me that Left Socialist-Revolutionaries, at their conference,[63] formulated their proposals in exactly the same way. And what about the Kronstadt resolutions[64]? You have not all read them? We will show them to you: they say the same thing. I emphasised the danger of Kronstadt because it lies precisely in the fact that the change demanded was apparently very slight: "The Bolsheviks must go . . . we will correct the regime a little." That is what the Kronstadt rebels are demanding. But what actually happened was that Savinkov arrived in Revel, the Paris newspapers reported the events a fortnight before they actually occurred, and a whiteguard general appeared on the scene. That is what actually happened. All revolutions have gone that way. That is why we are saying: Since we are faced with that sort of thing, we must unite, and, as I said in my first speech, counter it with rifles, no matter how innocent it may appear to be. To this the Workers' Opposition does not reply, but says: "We shall not dissolve the economic councils but 'subordinate them to our guidance'." The "All-Russia Congress of Producers" is to subordinate to its guidance the Economic Council's 71 chief administrations. I ask you: is that a joke? Can we take them seriously? This is the petty-bourgeois, anarchist element not only among the masses of the workers, but also in our own Party; and that is something we cannot tolerate in any circumstances. We have allowed ourselves a luxury: we gave these people the opportunity to express their opinions in the greatest possible detail and have heard their side of it several times. When I had occasion to debate with Comrades Trotsky and Kiselyov at the Second Miners' Congress, two points of view were definitely revealed. The Workers' Opposition said: "Lenin and Trotsky will unite." Trotsky came out and said: "Those who fail to understand that it is necessary to unite are against the Party; of course we will unite, because we are men of the Party." I supported him. Of course, Comrade Trotsky and I differed; and when more or less equal groups appear within the Central Committee, the Party will pass judgement, and in a way that will make us unite in accordance with the Party's will and instructions. Those are the statements Comrade Trotsky and I made at the Miners' Congress, and repeat here; but the Workers'

Opposition says: "We will make no concessions, but we will remain in the Party." No, that trick won't work! (*Applause.*) I repeat that in combating the evils of bureaucracy we welcome the assistance of every worker, whatever he may call himself, if he is sincere in his desire to help. This help is highly desirable if sincere. In this sense we will make "concessions" (I take the word in quotation marks). No matter how provocative the statements against us, we shall make "concessions" because we know how hard the going is. We cannot dissolve the economic councils and chief administrations. It is absolutely untrue to say that we have no confidence in the working class and that we are keeping the workers out of the governing bodies. We are on the look-out for every worker who is at all fit for managerial work; we are glad to have him and give him a trial. If the Party has no confidence in the working class and does not allow workers to occupy responsible posts, it ought to be ousted! Go on, be logical and say it! I have said that that is not true: we are on our last legs for want of men and we are prepared to take any assistance, with both hands, from any efficient man, especially if he is a worker. But we have no men of this type, and this creates the ground for anarchy. We must keep up the fight against the evils of bureaucracy —and it demands hundreds of thousands of men.

Our Programme formulates the task of combating the evils of bureaucracy as one of extremely long duration. The wider the dispersal of the peasantry, the more inevitable are bureaucratic practices at the centre.

It is easy to write things like this: "There is something rotten in our Party." You know what weakening the Soviet apparatus means when there are two million Russian émigrés abroad. They were driven out by the Civil War. They have gratified us by holding their meetings in Berlin, Paris, London, and all the other capitals but ours. They support this element that is called the small producer, the petty-bourgeois element.

We shall do everything that can be done to eliminate bureaucratic practices by promoting workers from below, and we shall accept every piece of practical advice on this matter. Even if we give this the inappropriate name of "concessions", as some here have done, there is no doubt that, despite this pamphlet, 99 per cent of the Congress will say, "In spite of this we will make 'concessions' and win over all that is sound." Take your place by the side of the workers and teach us how to combat the evils of bureaucracy, if you know how to do it better than we do; but don't talk as Shlyapnikov has done. That is not the sort of thing that one can brush aside. I shall not deal with the theoretical part of his speech because Kollontai said the same thing. I shall deal with the facts he quoted. He said that potatoes were rotting, and asked why Tsyurupa was not being prosecuted.

But I ask: Why is Shlyapnikov not prosecuted for making such statements? Are we seriously discussing discipline and unity in an organised Party, or are we at a meeting of the Kronstadt type? For his is a Kronstadt, anarchist type of statement, to which the response is a gun. We organised members of the Party, have come here to rectify our mistakes. If Shlyapnikov thinks that Tsyurupa ought to be prosecuted, why had he not, as an organised member of the Party, lodged a complaint with the Control Commission? When we were setting up the Control Commission, we said: The Central Committee is swamped with administrative work. Let us elect people who enjoy the confidence of the workers, who will not have so much administrative work and will be able to examine complaints on behalf of the Central Committee. This created a means of developing criticism and rectifying mistakes. If Tsyurupa was so wrong why was not a complaint lodged with the Control Commission? Instead, Shlyapnikov comes to the Congress, the most responsible assembly of the Party and the Republic, and starts hurling accusations about rotting potatoes, and asking why Tsyurupa is not being prosecuted. But I ask, doesn't the Defence Department make any mistakes? Are not battles lost and waggons and supplies abandoned? Shall we then prosecute the military workers? Comrade Shlyapnikov comes here and hurls accusations which he himself does not believe, and which he cannot prove. Potatoes are rotting. Of course, many mistakes will be made, for our machinery wants adjustment, and our transport is not running smoothly. But when instead of a rectification of our mistakes such accusations are hurled at random, and when, in addition—as several comrades here have noted—there is an undertone of malice in this question of why Tsyurupa is not being prosecuted, then I say: Why not prosecute us, the Central Committee? We think that such talk is demagogy. Either proceedings should be started against Tsyurupa and us, or against Shlyapnikov; but no work can be done in such a spirit. When Party comrades talk as Shlyapnikov has done here—and he always talks like that at other meetings—and Comrade Kollontai's pamphlet says the same thing, although she mentions no names, we say: We cannot go on like this, for it is the kind of demagogy that the Makhno anarchists and the Kronstadt elements jump at. We are both members of the Party, and both of us are standing before this most responsible tribunal. If Tsyurupa has committed an unlawful act and we, the Central Committee, have condoned it, then why not come out with a definite charge, instead of throwing about words that will be caught up here, in Moscow, tomorrow, and immediately carried by the grapevine telegraph to the bourgeoisie. To-morrow all the gossips in the Soviet offices will be rubbing their hands in glee and repeating your words with delight. If Tsyurupa is the kind of man Shlyapnikov accuses him of being, and if, as he demands, he ought to be prosecuted, then I say that we must seriously ponder over his words; such accusations are not lightly made. Those who make accusations of this sort should be either removed from the Party or told: We are putting you on this potato job; you go to such and such a gubernia and let's see whether you have less rotting potatoes than in the gubernias under Tsyurupa's charge.

4

PRELIMINARY DRAFT RESOLUTION ON IMPROVING THE CONDITION OF WORKERS AND NEEDY PEASANTS

The exhaustion caused by the privation and the calamities and havoc of the seven-year war, and the overstrain due to the virtually superhuman exertions on the part of the working class of Russia over the past three and a half years, have now been so aggravated that they demand urgent measures on the part of the Soviet power.

The Tenth Congress of the R.C.P. accordingly demands that the whole Party and all Party and Soviet establishments should redouble their attention to this question and immediately work out measures to improve the condition of the workers and ease their hardships at all costs.

The Congress approves of the decision taken by the Central Committee and the Soviet Government to release a part of the gold reserve for the purchase of consumer goods for the workers, and demands an extension of this measure and an immediate amendment, with that end in view, of our import plan.

The Congress authorises the Central Committee to set up a special Central Commission to implement urgent measures to improve the condition of the workers, which should be organised in such a way as to work in close contact with, on the one hand, the Central Committee of the R.C.P. and the All-Russia Central Council of Trade Unions, and, on the other, with the Council of People's Commissars and the Council of Labour and Defence, for the swiftest implementation of the measures to be adopted, and to allow the workers themselves to exercise control over the implementation of these measures. The Commission must set up subcommissions in the Commissariats which are in the best position right away to assign a part of their machinery and resources to help improve the condition of the workers (People's Commissariats for Foreign Trade, Food, Defence, and Health, the Government Buildings Committee, etc.). Subcommissions are especially needed in the gubernias where industrial workers are chiefly concentrated. The Congress entrusts the Central Committee and Party workers of the Commissariats concerned to work out an ordinance governing the operation of these commissions without delay.

In view of the acute hardships inflicted on the peasantry by the crop failure—in very many cases aggravated by the demobilisation of the army—the Tenth Congress authorises the Central Committee to take, through the Council of People's Commissars and the All-Russia Central Executive Committee, measures similar to those outlined above to improve the condition of needy peasants, without confining itself to the commission earlier set up for that purpose by the All-Russia Central Executive Committee.

Published according
to the manuscript

5

SPEECH ON THE TRADE UNIONS
MARCH 14

Comrades, Comrade Trotsky was particularly polite in his polemics with me today and reproached me for being, or said that I was, extremely cautious. I thank him for the compliment, but regret that I cannot return it. On the contrary, I must speak of my incautious friend, so as to express my attitude to the mistake which has caused me to waste so much time, and which is now making us continue the debate on the trade union question, instead of dealing with more urgent matters. Comrade Trotsky had his final say in the discussion on the trade union question in *Pravda* of January 29, 1921. In his article, "There Are Disagreements, But Why Confuse Things?", he accused me of being responsible for this confusion by asking who started it all. The accusation recoils on Trotsky, for he is trying to shift the blame. The whole of his article was based on the claim that he had raised the question of the role of the trade unions in production, and that this is the subject that ought to have been discussed. This is not true; it is not this that has caused the disagreements, and made them painful. And however tedious it may be after the discussion to have to repeat it again and again—true, I took part in it for only one month—I must restate that that was not the starting-point; it started with the "shake-up" slogan that was proclaimed at the Fifth All-Russia Conference of Trade Unions on November 2-6.[65] Already at that time it was realised by everyone who had not overlooked Rudzutak's resolution—and among those were the members of the Central Committee, including myself—that no disagreements could be found on the role of the trade unions in production. But the three-

month discussion revealed them. They existed, and they
were a political mistake. During a discussion at the Bolshoi Theatre, Comrade Trotsky accused me before responsible Party workers of disrupting the discussion.[66] I take
that as a compliment: I did try to disrupt the discussion
in the form it was being conducted, because with a severe
spring ahead of us such pronouncements were harmful.
Only the blind could have failed to see that.

Comrade Trotsky now laughs at my asking who started it
all, and is surprised that I should reproach him for refusing
to serve on the commission. I did it because this is very
important, Comrade Trotsky, very important, indeed; your
refusal to serve on the trade union commission was a violation of Central Committee discipline. And when Trotsky
talks about it, the result is not a controversy, but a shake-
up of the Party, and a generation of bitter feeling; it leads
to extremes—Comrade Trotsky used the expression "diabolical rage". I recall an expression used by Comrade Holtzmann—I will not quote it because the word "diabolical"
calls to mind something fiendish, whereas Holtzmann reminds
one of something angelic. There is nothing "diabolical"
about it, but we must not forget that both sides go to
extremes, and, what is much more monstrous, some of the
nicest comrades have gone to extremes. But when Comrade
Trotsky's authority was added to this, and when in a public speech on December 25 he said that the Congress must
choose between two trends, such words are unpardonable!
They constitute the political mistake over which we are
fighting. And it is naïve for people to try to be witty about
two-room conferences. I should like to see the wag who
says that Congress delegates are forbidden to confer to prevent their votes from being split. That would be too much
of an exaggeration. It was Comrade Trotsky and Tsektran's
political mistake to raise the "shake-up" question and to do
it in an entirely wrong way. That was a political mistake,
and it is yet to be rectified. As regards transport, we have
a resolution.[67]

What we are discussing is the trade union movement, and
the relationship between the vanguard of the working class
and the proletariat. There is nothing discreditable in our
dismissing anybody from a high post. This casts no reflec-

tion upon anybody. If you have made a mistake the Congress will recognise it as such and will restore mutual relations and mutual confidence between the vanguard of the working class and the workers' mass. That is the meaning of the "Platform of Ten".[68] It is of no importance that there are things in it that can be substituted, and that this is emphasised by Trotsky and enlarged upon by Ryazanov. Someone said in a speech that there is no evidence of Lenin's having taken a hand in the platform or of his having taken any part in drafting it. I say to this: If I had a hand, by writing or phoning, in everything I sign, I would have gone mad long ago. I say that in order to establish mutual relations and mutual confidence between the vanguard of the working class and the workers' mass, it was necessary, if Tsektran had made a mistake—and anyone can make a mistake—to rectify it. But it is a source of political danger to defend the mistake. We would have been faced with political bankruptcy if we had not done everything we could to turn the attitudes expressed here by Kutuzov to the service of democracy. Persuasion must come before coercion. We must make every effort to persuade people before applying coercion. We were not able to carry conviction to the broad masses, and disturbed the correct relationship between them and the vanguard.

When people like Kutuzov devote part of a business-like speech to pointing out the scandalous bureaucratic practices in our machinery we say: That is true, our state is one with bureaucratic distortions. And we invite the non-Party workers to join us in fighting them. I must say here that we should enlist comrades like Kutuzov for this work and promote them. That is the lesson of our experience.

As for the syndicalist deviation—it is ridiculous. That is all we have to say to Shlyapnikov, who maintained that the "All-Russia Congress of Producers", a demand set down in black and white in their platform and confirmed by Kollontai, can be upheld by a reference to Engels. Engels speaks of a communist society which will have no classes, and will consist only of producers.[69] Do we now have classes? Yes, we do. Do we have a class struggle? Yes, and a most furious one! To come in the midst of this furious class struggle and talk about an "All-Russia Congress of Producers"—

isn't that a syndicalist deviation which must be emphatically and irrevocably condemned? We saw that in this platform hurly-burly even Bukharin was tripped up by the one-third nomination proposal. Comrades, in the history of the Party we must not forget such waverings.

And now, since the Workers' Opposition has defended democracy, and has made some sound demands, we shall do our utmost to mend our fences with it; and the Congress as such should make a definite selection. You say that we are not doing enough to combat the evils of bureaucracy—come and help us, come closer and help us in the fight; but it is not a Marxist, not a communist notion to propose an "All-Russia Congress of Producers". The Workers' Opposition, with Ryazanov's help, is putting a false construction on our Programme which says: "The trade unions *should eventually* arrive at a *de facto* concentration in their hands of the whole administration of the whole national economy, as a single economic entity."[70] Exaggerating, as he always does, Shlyapnikov thinks that it will take us twenty-five centuries. . . . The Programme says: the trade unions "should eventually arrive", and when a Congress says that this has been done, the demand will have been carried out.

Comrades, if the Congress now declares before the proletariat of the whole of Russia and of the whole world that it regards the proposals of the Workers' Opposition as a syndicalist semi-deviation, I am sure that all the truly proletarian and sound elements in the opposition will follow us and help us to regain the confidence of the masses, which has been shaken by Tsektran's slight mistake. I am sure that we shall strengthen and rally our ranks in a common effort and march forward together to the hard struggle that lies ahead. And marching forward unanimously, with firmness and resolution, we shall win out. (*Applause.*)

6

REPORT ON THE SUBSTITUTION
OF A TAX IN KIND FOR THE SURPLUS-
GRAIN APPROPRIATION SYSTEM
MARCH 15

Comrades, the question of substituting a tax for surplus-grain appropriation is primarily and mainly a political question, for it is essentially a question of the attitude of the working class to the peasantry. We are raising it because we must subject the relations of these two main classes, whose struggle or agreement determines the fate of our revolution as a whole, to a new or, I should perhaps say, a more careful and correct re-examination and some revision. There is no need for me to dwell in detail on the reasons for it. You all know very well of course what totality of causes, especially those due to the extreme want arising out of the war, ruin, demobilisation, and the disastrous crop failure—you know about the totality of circumstances that has made the condition of the peasantry especially precarious and critical and was bound to increase its swing from the proletariat to the bourgeoisie.

A word or two on the theoretical significance of, or the theoretical approach to, this issue. There is no doubt that in a country where the overwhelming majority of the population consists of small agricultural producers, a socialist revolution can be carried out only through the implementation of a whole series of special transitional measures which would be superfluous in highly developed capitalist countries where wage-workers in industry and agriculture make up the vast majority. Highly developed capitalist countries have a class of agricultural wage-workers that has taken shape over many decades. Only such a class can socially, economically, and politically support a direct transition to socialism. Only in countries where this class is sufficiently developed is it possible to pass directly from capitalism to socialism, without any special country-wide transitional measures. We have stressed in a good many written works, in all our public utterances, and all our statements in the press, that this is not the case in Russia, for here industrial workers are a minority and petty farmers are the vast majority. In such a country, the socialist revolution can triumph only on two conditions. First, if it is given timely support by a socialist revolution in one or several advanced countries. As you know, we have done very much indeed in comparison with the past to bring about this condition, but far from enough to make it a reality.

The second condition is agreement between the proletariat, which is exercising its dictatorship, that is, holds state power, and the majority of the peasant population. Agreement is a very broad concept which includes a whole series of measures and transitions. I must say at this point that our propaganda and agitation must be open and above-board. We must condemn most resolutely those who regard politics as a series of cheap little tricks, frequently bordering on deception. Their mistakes have to be corrected. You can't fool a class. We have done very much in the past three years to raise the political consciousness of the masses. They have been learning most from the sharp struggles. In keeping with our world outlook, the revolutionary experience we have accumulated over the decades, and the lessons of our revolution, we must state the issues plainly—the interests of these two classes differ, the small farmer does not want the same thing as the worker.

We know that so long as there is no revolution in other countries, only agreement with the peasantry can save the socialist revolution in Russia. And that is how it must be stated, frankly, at all meetings and in the entire press. We know that this agreement between the working class and the peasantry is not solid—to put it mildly, without entering the word "mildly" in the minutes—but, speaking plainly it is very much worse. Under no circumstances must we try to hide anything; we must plainly state that the peasantry is dissatisfied with the form of our relations, that it does not want relations of this type and will not continue to live as it has hitherto. This is unquestionable. The peasantry has expressed its will in this respect definitely enough. It is the will of the vast masses of the working population. We must reckon with this, and we are sober enough politicians to say frankly: let us re-examine our policy in regard to the peasantry. The state of affairs that has prevailed so far cannot be continued any longer.

We must say to the peasants: "If you want to turn back, if you want to restore private property and unrestricted trade in their entirety, it will certainly and inevitably mean falling under the rule of the landowners and the capitalists. This has been proved by a number of examples from history and examples of revolutions. The briefest examination of the ABC of communism and political economy will prove that this is inevitable. Let us then look into the matter. Is it or is it not in the interest of the peasantry to part ways with the proletariat only to slip back—and let the country slip back—to the rule of the capitalists and landowners? Consider this, and let us consider it together."

We believe that if the matter is given proper consideration, the conclusion will be in our favour, in spite of the admittedly deep gulf between the economic interests of the proletariat and the small farmer.

Difficult as our position is in regard to resources, the needs of the middle peasantry must be satisfied. There are far more middle peasants now than before, the antagonisms have been smoothed out, the land has been distributed for use far more equally, the kulak's position has been undermined and he has been in considerable measure expropriated —in Russia more than in the Ukraine, and less in Siberia. On the whole, however, statistics show quite definitely that there has been a levelling out, an equalisation, in the village, that is, the old sharp division into kulaks and cropless peasants has disappeared. Everything has become more equable, the peasantry in general has acquired the status of the middle peasant.

Can we satisfy this middle peasantry as such, with its economic peculiarities and economic roots? Any Communist who thought the economic basis, the economic roots, of small farming could be reshaped in three years was, of course, a dreamer. We need not conceal the fact that there were a good many such dreamers among us. Nor is there anything particularly bad in this. How could one start a socialist revolution in a country like ours without dreamers? Practice has, of course, shown the tremendous role all kinds of experiments and undertakings can play in the sphere of collective agriculture. But it has also afforded instances of these experiments as such playing a negative role, when people, with the best of intentions and desires, went to the countryside to set up communes but did not know how to run them because they had no experience in collective endeavour. The experience of these collective farms merely provided examples of how not to run farms: the peasants around either laughed or jeered.

You know perfectly well how many cases there have been of this kind. I repeat that this is not surprising, for it will take generations to remould the small farmer, and recast his mentality and habits. The only way to solve this problem of the small farmer—to improve, so to speak, his mentality—is through the material basis, technical equipment, the extensive use of tractors and other farm machinery and electrification on a mass scale. This would remake the small farmer fundamentally and with tremendous speed. If I say this will take generations, it does not mean centuries. But you know perfectly well that to obtain tractors and other machinery and to electrify this vast country is a matter that may take decades in any case. Such is the objective situation.

We must try to satisfy the demands of the peasants who are dissatisfied and disgruntled, and legitimately so, and who cannot be otherwise. We must say to them: "Yes, this cannot go on any longer." How is the peasant to be satisfied and what does satisfying him mean? Where is the answer? Naturally it lies in the demands of the peasantry. We know these demands. But we must verify them and examine all that we know of the farmer's economic demands from the standpoint of economic science. If we go into this, we shall see at once that it will take essentially two things to satisfy the small farmer. The first is a certain freedom of exchange, freedom for the small private proprietor, and the second is the need to obtain commodities and products. What indeed would free exchange amount to if there was nothing to exchange, and freedom of trade, if there was nothing to trade with! It would all remain on paper, and classes cannot be satisfied with scraps of paper, they want the goods. These two conditions must be clearly understood. The second—how to get commodities and whether we shall be able to obtain them—we shall discuss later. It is the first condition—free exchange—that we must deal with now.

What is free exchange? It is unrestricted trade, and that means turning back towards capitalism. Free exchange and freedom of trade mean circulation of commodities between petty proprietors. All of us who have studied at least the elements of Marxism know that this exchange and freedom of trade inevitably lead to a division of commodity producers into owners of capital and owners of labour-power, a division into capitalists and wage-workers, i.e., a revival of capitalist wage-slavery, which does not fall from the sky but springs the world over precisely from the agricultural commodity economy. This we know perfectly well in theory, and anyone in Russia who has observed the small farmer's life and the conditions under which he farms must have seen this.

How then can the Communist Party recognise freedom to trade and accept it? Does not the proposition contain irreconcilable contradictions? The answer is that the practical solution of the problem naturally presents exceedingly great difficulties. I can foresee, and I know from the talks I have had with some comrades, that the preliminary draft on replacing surplus-grain appropriation by a tax—it has been handed out to you—gives rise to legitimate and inevitable questions, mostly as regards permitting exchange of goods within the framework of local economic turnover. This is set forth at the end of Point 8. What does it mean, what limits are there to this exchange, how is it all to be implemented? Anyone who expects to get the answer at this Congress will be disappointed. We shall find the answer in our legislation; it is our task to lay down the principle to be followed and provide the slogan. Our Party is the government party and the decision the Party Congress passes will be obligatory for the entire Republic: it is now up to us to decide the question in principle. We must do this and inform the peasantry of our decision, for the sowing season is almost at hand. Further we must muster our whole administrative apparatus, all our theoretical forces and all our practical experience, in order to see how it can be done. Can it be done at all, theoretically speaking: can freedom of trade, freedom of capitalist enterprise for the small farmer, be restored to a certain extent without undermining the political power of the proletariat? Can it be done? Yes, it can, for everything hinges on the extent. If we were able to obtain even a small quantity of goods and hold them in the hands of the state—the proletariat exercising political power—and if we could release these goods into circulation, we, as the state, would add economic power to our political power. Release of these goods into circulation would stimulate small farming, which is in a terrible state and cannot develop owing to the grievous war conditions and the economic chaos. The small farmer, so long as he remains small, needs a spur, an incentive that accords with his economic basis, i.e., the individual small farm. Here you cannot avoid local free exchange. If this turnover gives the state, in exchange for manufactured goods, a certain minimum amount of grain to cover urban and industrial requirements, economic circulation will be revived, with state power remaining in the hands of the proletariat and growing stronger. The peasants want to be shown in practice that the worker who controls the mills and factories—industry—is capable of organising exchange with the peasantry. And, on the other hand, the vastness of our agricultural country with its poor transport system, boundless expanses, varying climate, diverse farming conditions, etc., makes a certain freedom of exchange between local agriculture and local industry, on a local scale, inevitable. In this respect, we are very much to blame for having gone too far; we overdid the nationalisation of industry and trade, clamping down on local exchange of commodities. Was that a mistake? It certainly was.

In this respect we have made many patent mistakes, and it would be a great crime not to see it, and not to realise that we have failed to keep within bounds, and have not known where to stop. There has, of course, also been the factor of necessity—until now we have been living in the conditions of a savage war that imposed an unprecedented burden on us and left us no choice but to take war-time measures in the economic sphere as well. It was a miracle that the ruined country withstood this war, yet the miracle did not come from heaven, but grew out of the economic interests of the working class and the peasantry, whose mass enthusiasm created the miracle that defeated the landowners and capitalists. But at the same time it is an unquestionable fact that we went further than was theoretically and politically necessary, and this should not be concealed in our agitation and propaganda. We can allow free local exchange to an appreciable extent, without destroying, but actually strengthening the political power of the proletariat. How this is to be done, practice will show. I only wish to prove to you that theoretically it is conceivable. The proletariat, wielding state power, can, if it has any reserves at all, put them into circulation and thereby satisfy the middle peasant to a certain extent— on the basis of local economic exchange.

Now a few words about local economic exchange. First of all, the co-operatives. They are now in an extreme state of decline, but we naturally need them as a vehicle of local economic exchange. Our Programme stresses that the co-operatives left over from capitalism are the best distribution network and must be preserved. That is what the Programme says. Have we lived up to this? To a very slight extent, if at all, again partly because we have made mistakes, partly because of the war-time necessity. The co-operatives brought to the fore the more business-like, economically more advanced elements, thereby bringing out the Mensheviks and Socialist-Revolutionaries in the political sphere. This is a law of chemistry—you can't do anything about it! (*Laughter.*) The Mensheviks and Socialist-Revolutionaries are people who either consciously or unconsciously work to restore capitalism and help the Yudeniches. This too is a law. We must fight them. And if there is to be a fight, it must be done the military way; we had to defend ourselves, and we did. But do we have to perpetuate the present situation? No, we do not. It would be a mistake to tie our hands in this way. Because of this I submit a resolution on the question of the co-operatives; it is very brief and I shall read it to you:

"Whereas the resolution of the Ninth Congress of the R.C.P. on the co-operatives is based entirely on the principle of surplus-grain appropriation, which is now superseded by a tax in kind, the Tenth Congress of the R.C.P. resolves:

"That the said resolution be rescinded.

"The Congress instructs the Central Committee to draw up and carry out through Party and Soviet channels decisions to improve and develop the structure and activity of the co-operatives in conformity with the Programme of the R.C.P. and with a view to substituting the tax in kind for the surplus-grain appropriation system."[71]

You will say that this is rather vague. Yes, it is, and should necessarily be so to some extent. Why necessarily? Because if we are to be absolutely definite, we must know exactly what we are going to do over the year ahead. Who knows that? No one.

But the resolution of the Ninth Congress ties our hands by calling for "subordination to the Commissariat for Food". This is a fine institution, but it would be an obvious political mistake to subordinate the co-operatives to it and to no other, and to tie our hands at a time when we are reviewing our attitude to the small farmers. We must instruct the newly elected Central Committee to elaborate and carry out definite measures and changes, and to check up on every step we take forward or back—to what extent we must act, how to uphold our political interests, how much relaxation there must be to make things easier, how to check up on the results of our experience. Theoretically speaking, in this respect we are facing a number of transitional stages, or transitional measures. One thing is clear: the resolution of the Ninth Congress assumed that we would be advancing in a straight line, but it turned out, as has happened again and again throughout the history of revolutions, that the movement took a zigzag course. To tie one's hands with such a resolution would be a political mistake. Annulling it, we say that we must be guided by our Programme, which stresses the importance of the co-operative machinery.

As we annul the resolution, we say: work with a view to replacing surplus-grain appropriation by a tax. But when are we to do this? Not before the harvest, that is, in a few months' time. Will it be done the same way everywhere? In no circumstances. It would be the height of stupidity to apply the same pattern to central Russia, the Ukraine, and Siberia. I propose that this fundamental idea of unrestricted local exchange be formulated as a decision of this Congress.[72] I presume that following this decision the Central Committee will without fail send out a letter within the next few days and will point out—doing it better than I can do here (we shall find the best writers to polish up the style)—that there are to be no radical changes, no undue haste, or snap decisions, and that things should be done so as to give maximum satisfaction to the middle peasantry, without damaging the interests of the proletariat. Try one thing and another, study things in practice, through experience, then share your experience with us, and let us know what you have managed to do, and we shall set up a special commission or even several commissions to consider the experience that has been accumulated. I think we should issue a special invitation to Comrade Preobrazhensky, the author of *Paper Money in the Epoch of the Proletarian Dictatorship*. This is a highly important question, for money circulation is a splendid test of the state of commodity circulation in the country; when it is unsatisfactory, money is not worth the paper it is printed on. In order to proceed on the basis of experience, we must check and recheck the measures we have adopted.

We shall be asked where the goods are to come from, for unrestricted trade requires goods, and the peasants are shrewd people and very good at scoffing. Can we obtain any goods now? Today we can, for our international economic position has greatly improved. We are waging a fight against the international capitalists, who, when they were first confronted by this Republic, called us "brigands and crocodiles" (I was told by an English artiste[73] that she had heard these very words spoken by one of the most influential politicians). Crocodiles are despicable. That was the verdict of international capital. It was the verdict of a class enemy and quite correct from his point of view. However, the correctness of such conclusions has to be verified in practice. If you are world capital —a world power—and you use words like "crocodile" and have all the technical means at your disposal, why not try and shoot it! Capital did shoot—and got the worst of it. It was then that the capitalists, who are forced to reckon with political and economic realities, declared: "We must trade." This is one of our greatest victories. Let me tell you that we now have two offers of a loan to the amount of nearly one hundred million gold rubles. We have gold, but you can't sell gold, because you can't eat it. Everybody has been reduced to a state of impoverishment, currency relations between all the capitalist countries are incredibly chaotic as a result of the war. Moreover, you need a merchant marine to communicate with Europe, and we have none. It is in hostile hands. We have concluded no treaty with France; she considers that we are her debtors and, consequently, that every ship we have is hers. They have a navy and we have none. In these circumstances we have so far been in a position to make use of our gold on a limited and ridiculously insignificant scale. Now we have two offers from capitalist bankers to float a loan of one hundred million. Of course, they will charge us an exorbitant rate of interest. Still it is their first offer of this kind; so far they have said: "I'll shoot you and take everything for nothing." Now, being unable to shoot us, they are ready to trade with us. Trade agreements with America and Britain can now be said to be almost in the bag; the same applies to concessions. Yesterday I received another letter from Mr. Vanderlip, who is here and who, besides numerous complaints, sets forth a whole series of plans concerning concessions and a loan. He represents the shrewdest type of finance capitalist connected with the Western States of the U.S.A., those that are more hostile to Japan. So it is economically possible for us to obtain goods. How we shall manage to do it is another question, but a certain possibility is there.

I repeat, the type of economic relations which on top looks like a bloc with foreign capitalism makes it possible for the proletarian state power to arrange for free exchange with the peasantry below. I know—and I have had occasion to say this before—that this has evoked some sneers. There is a whole intellectual-bureaucratic stratum in Moscow, which is trying to shape "public opinion". "See what communism has come to!" these people sneer. "It's like a man

on crutches and face all bandaged up—nothing but a
picture puzzle." I have heard enough of gibes of this kind—
they are either bureaucratic or just irresponsible. Russia
emerged from the war in a state that can most of all be
likened to that of a man beaten to within an inch of his life; the
beating had gone on for seven years, and it's a mercy she can
hobble about on crutches! That is the situation we are in!
To think that we can get out of this state without crutches
is to understand nothing! So long as there is no revolution
in other countries, it would take us decades to extricate
ourselves, and in these circumstances we cannot grudge
hundreds of millions' or even thousands of millions' worth
of our immense wealth, our rich raw material sources, in
order to obtain help from the major capitalists. Later we shall
recover it all and to spare. The rule of the proletariat cannot
be maintained in a country laid waste as no country has
ever been before—a country where the vast majority are
peasants who are equally ruined—without the help of
capital, for which, of course, exorbitant interest will be
extorted. This we must understand. Hence, the choice is
between economic relations of this type and nothing at all.
He who puts the question otherwise understands absolutely
nothing in practical economics and is side-stepping the issue
by resorting to gibes. We must recognise the fact that the
masses are utterly worn-out and exhausted. What can you
expect after seven years of war in this country, if the more
advanced countries still feel the effects of four years of war?!

In this backward country, the workers, who have made
unprecedented sacrifices, and the mass of the peasants are
in a state of utter exhaustion after seven years of war. This
condition borders on complete loss of working capacity.
What is needed now is an economic breathing space. We had
hoped to use our gold reserve to obtain some means of production. It would be best of all to make our own machines,
but even if we bought them, we would thereby build up
our industry. To do this, however, you must have a worker
and a peasant who can work; yet in most cases they are in
no condition for it, they are exhausted, worn-out. They
must be assisted, and contrary to our old Programme the
gold reserve must be used for consumer goods. That Programme was theoretically correct, but practically unsound.

I shall pass on to you some information I have here from Comrade Lezhava. It shows that several hundred thousand poods of various items of food have already been bought in Lithuania, Finland, and Latvia and are being shipped in with the utmost speed. Today we have learned that a deal has been concluded in London for the purchase of 18,500,000 poods of coal, which we decided to buy in order to revive the industry of Petrograd and the textile industry. If we obtain goods for the peasant, it will, of course, be a violation of the Programme, an irregularity, but we must have a respite, for the people are exhausted to a point where they are not able to work.

I must say a few words about the individual exchange of commodities. When we speak of free exchange, we mean individual exchange of commodities, which in turn means encouraging the kulaks. What are we to do? We must not close our eyes to the fact that the switch from the appropriation of surpluses to the tax will mean more kulaks under the new system. They will appear where they could not appear before. This must not be combated by prohibitive measures but by association under state auspices and by government measures from above. If you can give the peasant machines you will help him grow, and when you provide machines or electric power, tens or hundreds of thousands of small kulaks will be wiped out. Until you can supply all that, you must provide a certain quantity of goods. If you have the goods, you have the power; to preclude, deny or renounce any such possibility means making all exchange unfeasible and not satisfying the middle peasant, who will be impossible to get along with. A greater proportion of peasants in Russia have become middle peasants, and there is no reason to fear exchange on an individual basis. Everyone can give something in exchange to the state: one, his grain surplus; another, his garden produce; a third, his labour. Basically the situation is this: we must satisfy the middle peasantry economically and go over to free exchange; otherwise it will be impossible—economically impossible—in view of the delay in the world revolution, to preserve the rule of the proletariat in Russia. We must clearly realise this and not be afraid to say it. In the draft decision to substitute a tax in kind for the surplus appropriation system (the text has been handed out to you) you will find many discrepancies, even contradictions, and that is why we have added these words at the end: "The Congress, approving in substance [this is a rather loose word covering a great deal of ground] the propositions submitted by the Central Committee to substitute a tax in kind for surplus-grain appropriation, instructs the Central Committee of the Party to co-ordinate these propositions with the utmost dispatch." We know that they have not been co-ordinated, for we had no time to do so. We did not go into the details. The ways of levying the tax in practice will be worked out in detail and the tax implemented by a law issued by the All-Russia Central Executive Committee and the Council of People's Commissars. The procedure outlined is this: if you adopt the draft today, it will be given the force of a decision at the very first session of the All-Russia Central Executive Committee, which will not issue a law either, but modified regulations; the Council of People's Commissars and the Council of Labour and Defence will later make them into a law, and, what is still more important, issue practical instructions. It is important that people in the localities should understand the significance of this and help us.

Why must we replace surplus appropriation by a tax? Surplus appropriation implied confiscation of all surpluses and establishment of a compulsory state monopoly. We could not do otherwise, for our need was extreme. Theoretically speaking, state monopoly is not necessarily the best system from the standpoint of the interests of socialism. A system of taxation and free exchange can be employed as a transitional measure in a peasant country possessing an industry—if this industry is running—and if there is a certain quantity of goods available.

The exchange is an incentive, a spur to the peasant. The proprietor can and will surely make an effort in his own interest when he knows that all his surplus produce will not be taken away from him and that he will only have to pay a tax, which should whenever possible be fixed in advance. The basic thing is to give the small farmer an incentive and a spur to till the soil. We must adapt our state economy to the economy of the middle peasant, which we have not managed to remake in three years, and will not be able to remake in another ten.

The state had to face definite responsibilities in the sphere of food. Because of this the appropriation quotas were increased last year. The tax must be smaller. The exact figures have not been defined, nor can they be defined. Popov's booklet, *Grain Production of the Soviet and Federated Republics*, gives the exact data issued by our Central Statistical Board and shows why agricultural production has fallen off.

If there is a crop failure, surpluses cannot be collected because there will be none. They would have to be taken out of the peasants' mouths. If there is a crop, everybody will go moderately hungry and the state will be saved, or it will perish, unless we take from people who do not eat their fill as it is. This is what we must make clear in our propaganda among the peasants. A fair harvest will mean a surplus of up to five hundred million poods. This will cover consumption and yield a certain reserve. The important thing is to give the peasants an economic incentive. The small proprietor must be told: "It is your job as a proprietor to produce, and the state will take a minimum tax."

My time is nearly up, I must close; I repeat: we cannot issue a law now. The trouble with our resolution is that it is not sufficiently legislative—laws are not written at Party congresses. Hence we propose that the resolution submitted by the C.C. be adopted as a basis and that the C.C. be instructed to co-ordinate the various propositions contained in it. We shall print the text of the resolution and Party officials in the various localities will try to co-ordinate and correct it. It cannot be co-ordinated from beginning to end; this is an insoluble problem, for life is too varied. To find the transitional measures is a very difficult task. If we are unable to do this quickly and directly, we must not lose heart, for we shall win through in the end. No peasant with the slightest glimmer of political consciousness will fail to understand that we, as the government, represent the working class and all those working people with whom the labouring peasants (and they make up nine-tenths of the total) can agree, that any turn back will mean a return to the old, tsarist government.

The experience of Kronstadt proves this. There they do not want either the whiteguards or our government—and there is no other—and as a result they find themselves in a situation which speaks best of all in our favour and against any new government.

We are now in a position to come to an agreement with the peasants, and this must be done in practice, skilfully, efficiently, and flexibly. We are familiar with the apparatus of the Commissariat for Food and know that it is one of the best we have. We see that it is better than that of the others and we must preserve it. Administrative machinery, however, must be subordinated to politics. The splendid apparatus of the Commissariat for Food will be useless if we cannot establish proper relations with the peasants, for otherwise this splendid apparatus will be serving Denikin and Kolchak, and not our own class. Since resolute change, flexibility and skilful transition have become politically necessary, the leaders must realise it. A strong apparatus must be suitable for any manoeuvre, but struggle is inevitable when its strength makes it unwieldy and hampers change. All efforts must, therefore, be turned to achieving our aim: the complete subordination of the apparatus to politics. Politics are relations between classes, and that will decide the fate of our Republic. The stronger the apparatus, as an auxiliary, the better and more suitable it is for manoeuvring. If it cannot manoeuvre, it is of no use to us.

I ask you to bear in mind this basic fact—it will take several months to work out the details and interpretations. The chief thing to bear in mind at the moment is that we must let the whole world know, by wireless this very night, of our decision; we must announce that this Congress of the government party is, in the main, replacing the surplus appropriation system by a tax and is giving the small farmer certain incentives to expand his farm and plant more; that by embarking on this course the Congress is correcting the system of relations between the proletariat and the peasantry and expresses its conviction that in this way these relations will be made durable. (*Stormy applause.*)

7

SUMMING-UP SPEECH ON THE TAX IN KIND
MARCH 15

Comrades, I think I can confine myself to a few fairly brief remarks. First of all, the question of the Siberian food supply workers. Yaroslavsky and Danishevsky have asked me to make the following statement. Drozhzhin has been put on trial to prove that he is not guilty. I can hear sceptical remarks, but at all events it must be said that this course is correct. We hear a lot of scandal and gossip, and this is the proper way of proving them to be false. Then again, a number of food supply workers in Tyumen have been shot for flogging, torture, rape and other crimes. Consequently, in no circumstances can this be connected with food supply work, but should be regarded as criminal outrages calling for harsher penalties than usual, in view of the conditions in which the food supply work is proceeding. From this aspect, therefore, the measures adopted were correct.

I should now like to start by saying a few words about the question of the co-operatives. Comrade Tsyurupa's report—as we all heard him say here—was not a co-report presenting a point of view opposite to that of the chief rapporteur. The Central Committee's decision to substitute a tax for the surplus-grain appropriation system was adopted with such obvious unanimity—and what is most important, we saw at once, even before the Congress opened, that various comrades in the localities had arrived at the same conclusions independently of this decision, on the basis of their own practical experience—that it is essentially impossible to doubt that as a measure it is proper and necessary. In his report, Comrade Tsyurupa added a few suggestions and warnings on a number of questions, but he did not propose a different policy.

The only departure from this general line in his report was made on the question of the co-operatives. He opposed my draft resolution, but I'm afraid his arguments do not carry conviction. We can hardly determine just now how relations in local free economic exchange will develop, and how the fund is to be handled—through co-operative societies or the restoration of small private trade. This question must certainly be examined, and in this respect we must make a careful study of local experience; that, of course, is something we all agree upon. I think, however, that the co-operative societies still present certain advantages. In so far as, politically—I have already pointed this out—they serve as centres for the organisation, centralisation and amalgamation of elements politically hostile to us and are in effect pursuing a Kolchak and Denikin policy, the co-operatives are only another form of small economy and small trade. Every emergence of the kulaks and the development of petty-bourgeois relations evidently give rise to corresponding political parties, which had been developing in Russia for decades, and with which we are quite familiar. The choice before us is not whether or not to allow these parties to grow—they are inevitably engendered by petty-bourgeois economic relations. The only choice before us, and a limited one at that, is between the forms of concentration and co-ordination of these parties' activities. It cannot possibly be proved that the co-operatives are worse in this respect. On the contrary, the Communists will have somewhat greater opportunities to exert systematic influence and control over the co-operatives.

The resolution on the co-operatives passed by the Ninth Congress was strongly defended here by Comrade Tsyurupa, and strongly opposed by Comrade Milyutin.

Incidentally, Comrade Tsyurupa said that I had been a witness to the struggle over the question of co-operatives before it was settled by the Congress. I must corroborate this. Indeed, there was a struggle, and the resolution adopted by the Ninth Congress put a stop to it by ensuring greater predominance, or it would be more exact to say complete predominance, for the Food Supply Department.

But it would, undoubtedly, be politically wrong, on these grounds, to forego greater freedom of action and freedom of choice of political measures in respect of the co-operatives. In my capacity of, say, Chairman of the Council of People's Commissars, I find it much more unpleasant to have to watch this petty strife, and even bickering, at scores of meetings, than to have the backing of a Congress resolution, which is binding on all and which puts a stop to this struggle. But we must not be swayed by such conveniences, but must look to the interests of a definite economic policy. You have all seen here, and the large number of notes—a great pile of notes—that I have received confirm it even more strikingly, that in this concrete question a vast number of difficulties of detail arise in the course of changing our policy. That is the whole point. And there is no doubt whatever that we shall be unable to solve them at one stroke. If we allow the resolution on the co-operatives adopted by the Ninth Congress to remain in force we shall have our hands tied. We shall put ourselves in a position where, being entirely subordinate to the Congress and bound to pursue its policy, we shall be unable to depart from the letter of this resolution. The resolution repeatedly refers to the surplus-grain appropriation system, but we are substituting a tax for it.

We have no idea how much latitude we shall leave to economic exchange.

That we must allow some is beyond doubt, and we must take account of and verify the economic conditions for it. That is why, of course, if we rescind the resolution of the Ninth Congress we shall be back where the question, which seems to have been closed to some extent, becomes an open one again. This is absolutely inevitable. To evade it would mean basically to prejudice the economic policy relations which we have outlined and which are, undoubtedly, more acceptable to the peasants.

There is evidently no difference of opinion at this Congress, or among Communists in general, as to whether the switch from appropriation to a tax is a more acceptable economic policy for the peasants. And we have a number of statements to this effect from non-Party peasants as well. This has been definitely established, and it alone suggests that we ought to have the change. Let me, therefore, read you the resolution on the co-operatives again:

"Whereas the resolution of the Ninth Congress of the R.C.P. on the co-operatives is based entirely on the principle of surplus-grain appropriation, which is now superseded by a tax in kind, the Tenth Congress of the R.C.P. resolves:

"That the said resolution be rescinded.

"The Congress instructs the Central Committee to draw up and carry out through Party and Soviet channels decisions to improve and develop the structure and activity of the co-operatives in conformity with the Programme of the R.C.P. and with a view to substituting the tax in kind for the surplus-grain appropriation system."

On behalf of the Central Committee, I shall ask the Congress to adopt the first resolution—the preliminary draft on substituting a tax for the surplus-grain appropriation system—to adopt it as a basis and instruct the Central Committee of the Party to co-ordinate the proposals, make the final draft and submit it to the All-Russia Central Executive Committee; and also the second resolution on the co-operatives.

I now come to the remarks made here. I must say that the questions I have received in writing are so numerous, there is such a heap of them, that not only am I unable to enumerate the subjects they touch upon, but I am compelled to give up the effort to classify them all in a suitable way for discussion here. I regret to say that I am compelled to abandon this task, but I will keep these notes as material for any future discussion of the subject.

Perhaps it will be possible to utilise them in greater detail in the press, or, at all events, to collect and classify them and then compile a detailed and really full summary for the benefit of the comrades economists, executives and political leaders who will be directly engaged in the task of drafting the law substituting the tax for surplus appropriation. At present, I can only select the two main trends and say a few words about the two main objections or remarks about the two main types or groups of questions raised in these notes.

The first deals with technical questions: these are numerous and detailed references to the difficulties and the many problems that will arise in carrying out these measures. I pointed out in my report that this was absolutely inevitable and that it is quite impossible at present to determine at once how we shall proceed to solve these difficulties.

The second deals with general principles of economic policy. Many, I should say most, of the speakers, and these written questions, all pointed to the inevitable increase in the strength of the petty bourgeoisie, the bourgeoisie and capitalism. A number of comrades wrote in their notes: "This is throwing open the door for the development of a bourgeoisie, small industry and capitalist relationships." In answer to this, comrades, I must say, repeating something of what I said in my report: There is no doubt whatever that the transition from capitalism to socialism is conceivable in different forms, depending upon whether big capitalist or small production relationships predominate in the country. And I must say on this score that criticism was expressed of certain conclusions drawn from my speech on the relation between state capitalism and free small-scale exchange; but no one has criticised my propositions, nor were they criticised in any of the notes I have received (I have read most of them, and they run to several dozen). Direct transition to communism would have been possible if ours was a country with a predominantly—or, say, highly developed—large-scale industry, and a high level of large-scale production in agriculture, otherwise the transition to communism is economically impossible. Comrade Milyutin said that we had a harmonious system, and that our laws represented, as he put it, to a certain extent, a harmonious system for such a transition, which, however, did not take account of the necessity of having to make a number of concessions to the petty bourgeoisie. But having said that, Comrade Milyutin drew a different conclusion from mine. The harmonious system that has been created was dictated by war and not by economic requirements, considerations or conditions. There was no other way out in the conditions of the unexampled ruin in which we found ourselves, when after a big war we were obliged to endure a number of civil wars. We must state quite definitely that in pursuing our policy, we may have made mistakes and gone to extremes in a number of cases. But in the war-time

conditions then prevailing, the policy was in the main a
correct one. We had no alternative but to resort to wholesale
and instant monopoly, including the confiscation of all surplus stocks, even without compensation. That was the only
way we could tackle the task. That was not a harmonious
economic system; it was not a measure called forth by
economic conditions, but one largely dictated to us by war
conditions. The main economic consideration now is to
increase the quantity of products. Our principal productive
forces, the peasants and workers, are in such a state of
impoverishment, ruin, weariness and exhaustion that for
a time we must subordinate everything to this main consideration—increasing the quantity of products at all costs.

Some ask: What connection is there between the
substitution of a tax for the surplus-grain appropriation
system and the sowing campaign now in progress? In their
notes, the comrades strive to expose a number of contradictions. I think that, in the main, there is economic
consistency here, and not contradiction. The sowing campaign is based on a number of measures directed towards
taking the utmost possible advantage of all economic
opportunities to increase the sown area. For this purpose,
we must redistribute the seed, store it properly and transport it. But scanty as our seed stocks are, we are unable
to transport them; very often we are compelled to resort
to various forms of mutual aid to reduce the area left
unsown to a minimum and to eliminate it altogether, in
spite of the appalling shortage of implements. That is out
of the question in a number of gubernias. If the non-Party
peasants, who in very many cases have themselves demanded
the switch to the tax—for it gives them an incentive to
develop their farms on the present economic basis—are
definitely told by the state authorities before the spring
campaign that this measure has been decided upon and
will be applied—does that run counter to the general policy
of the sowing campaign? No, it does not; it is a measure
that introduces an element of encouragement. I know that
it will be said that this is a very small element of encouragement. But that is not the point. It would, of course, be
something much more real, if we could immediately show
the peasants dozens of ships on their way from Britain with

goods to be exchanged for the grain they collect in the coming harvest. But it would be ridiculous to attempt to deceive people who have practical knowledge of the state of our commerce. We know that ships loaded with coal and a small quantity of foodstuffs are leaving Britain; we have the information from Comrade Krasin. We know that pending the conclusion of a trade agreement, which has not been signed yet, semi-legal commerce is being carried on with individual merchants whom the bourgeois government cannot, of course, prohibit from trading with us. It is a difficult task to break through the economic blockade, and, of course, we cannot make any great promises. At all events, we are doing all we can, and we are altering the imports plan accordingly.

From the standpoint of the small proprietor, the small farmer, the tax, which is to be smaller than surplus appropriation, will be more definite and will enable him to sow more, and assure him of the opportunity of using his surplus to improve his farm. From his standpoint, it is a policy of rendering the utmost assistance to the industrious farmer, and this is being emphasised in the sowing campaign. In the last analysis, all the objections can be reduced to the following: Who will gain most by this—the petty bourgeoisie, which is economically hostile to communism, or large-scale industry, which is the basis of the transition to socialism and—in the light of the state of the productive forces, that is, the touchstone of social development—is the basis of socialist economic organisation, for it unites the advanced industrial workers, the class which is exercising the dictatorship of the proletariat?

Several speakers tried to prove or draw the economic deduction that the petty bourgeoisie—handicraft commodity production—will undoubtedly gain most; and they urged this particularly on the grounds that as a result of our granting concessions, large-scale industry will cease to be socialist. I think there is fundamental economic error in these arguments. Even if it could be definitely proved that small industry will gain most, relatively, or even, say, absolutely, it would not, either theoretically or practically, disprove the correctness of the steps we are taking. The fact is that there is no other basis for the economic consolidation of our work of building socialism. Let us assume—purely for the sake of example and illustration—that small industry has a value of 100 (100 million work units, or 100 units of any other kind, it makes no difference) and large-scale industry, 200. Let us assume that on a capitalist basis small industry increases to 175, while large-scale industry remains at 200. We are assuming stagnation in large-scale industry and an enormous development of small industry. I think that even this worst assumption that I have made would represent an undoubted gain for us because at present, as this year's experience has shown, as our fuel and transport conditions indicate, and as the food distribution—which Comrade Milyutin very opportunely reminded us of—is showing, we are barely holding on.

Speakers here have asked, and I have received written questions to the same effect: "How will you retain the workers' state, if capitalism develops in the rural areas?" This peril—the development of small production and of the petty bourgeoisie in the rural areas—is an extremely serious one.

I now come to concessions. They signify a bloc with capitalism in the advanced countries. We must be clear in our minds about the nature of concessions. They signify an economic alliance, a bloc, a contract with advanced finance capital in the advanced countries, a contract that will give us a slight increase in products, but will also result in an increase in the products of the concessionaires. If we give the latter ore or timber, they will take the lion's share and leave us a small share. But it is so important for us to increase the quantity of products at our command that even a small share will be an enormous gain for us. Even a slight improvement in the condition of the urban workers, which will be guaranteed in the concessions agreement, and will not present the slightest difficulty to foreign capital, will be a gain and will serve to strengthen our large-scale industry. And this, as a result of its economic influence, will serve to improve the condition of the proletariat, the class which is wielding political power.

There is no ground to fear that small-scale agriculture and small industry will grow to dimensions that may prove dangerous for our large-scale industry. There must be certain signs for the rise of industry.

If we have a bad harvest (I have already mentioned Popov's pamphlet), and our resources are as scanty as they were last year, an abatement of the crisis and development of small industry are out of the question: capitalist rela- tions can be restored only if agricultural industry yields a surplus. That is possible, and this is very important, for it represents a material gain for us. The question of whether small or large-scale production will gain more will be determined by the extent to which we succeed in co-ordinating and combining the utilisation of our funds and the development of the market, which we shall achieve by means of concessions agreements with capitalism; and this will result in an increase in agricultural production for us. The result will depend upon which side makes the best use of these resources. I think that if the working class, which controls the most important branches of large- scale industry, concentrates on the key ones, it will gain more than small industry, even if the latter does have a relatively faster growth. The situation in our textile industry was such that at the end of 1920 there were obvious signs of an improvement, but there was a shortage of fuel. Otherwise we should have obtained about 800 million arshins* of cloth, and would have had materials of our own manufacture to exchange for farm products.

Owing to the fuel crisis, however, there has been an enormous drop in production. Although we have succeeded in purchasing coal abroad, and ships with this cargo will arrive in a week or two, we have nevertheless lost several weeks or even months.

Every improvement in the state of large-scale production and the possibility of starting some large factories will strengthen the position of the proletariat to such an extent that there will be no need to fear the petty-bourgeois ele- ment, even if it is growing. We must not be afraid of the growth of the petty bourgeoisie and small capital. What we must fear is protracted starvation, want and food shortage, which create the danger that the proletariat will

---

* Arshin is equal to 28 inches.—*Tr.*

be utterly exhausted and will give way to petty-bourgeois vacillation and despair. This is a much more terrible prospect. If output is increased the development of the petty bourgeoisie will not cause great harm, for the increased output will stimulate the development of large-scale industry. Hence, we must encourage small farming. It is our duty to do all we can to encourage small farming. The tax is one of the modest measures to be taken in this direction, but it is a measure that will undoubtedly provide such encouragement, and we certainly ought to adopt it. (*Applause.*)

1

First page of Lenin's "Preliminary Draft Resolution
of the Tenth Congress of the R.C.P.
on Party Unity". March 1921

Reduced

8

PRELIMINARY DRAFT RESOLUTION
OF THE TENTH CONGRESS OF THE R.C.P.
ON PARTY UNITY

1. The Congress calls the attention of all members of
the Party to the fact that the unity and cohesion of the
ranks of the Party, the guarantee of complete mutual confidence among Party members and genuine team-work that
really embodies the unanimity of will of the vanguard of
the proletariat, are particularly essential at the present
time, when a number of circumstances are increasing the
vacillation among the petty-bourgeois population of the
country.

2. Notwithstanding this, even before the general Party
discussion on the trade unions, certain signs of factionalism
had been apparent in the Party—the formation of groups
with separate platforms, striving to a certain degree to
segregate and create their own group discipline. Such symptoms of factionalism were manifested, for example, at a
Party conference in Moscow (November 1920) and at a Party
conference in Kharkov,[74] by the so-called Workers'
Opposition group, and partly by the so-called Democratic
Centralism group.

All class-conscious workers must clearly realise that
factionalism of any kind is harmful and impermissible,
for no matter how members of individual groups may
desire to safeguard Party unity, factionalism in practice
inevitably leads to the weakening of team-work and to
intensified and repeated attempts by the enemies of the
governing Party, who have wormed their way into it, to
widen the cleavage and to use it for counter-revolutionary
purposes.

The way the enemies of the proletariat take advantage
of every deviation from a thoroughly consistent commu-

nist line was perhaps most strikingly shown in the case of
the Kronstadt mutiny, when the bourgeois counter-
revolutionaries and whiteguards in all countries of the world
immediately expressed their readiness to accept the slogans
of the Soviet system, if only they might thereby secure the
overthrow of the dictatorship of the proletariat in Russia,
and when the Socialist-Revolutionaries and the bourgeois
counter-revolutionaries in general resorted in Kronstadt to
slogans calling for an insurrection against the Soviet
Government of Russia ostensibly in the interest of the Soviet
power. These facts fully prove that the whiteguards strive,
and are able, to disguise themselves as Communists, and
even as the most Left-wing Communists, solely for the purpose of weakening and destroying the bulwark of the proletarian revolution in Russia. Menshevik leaflets distributed
in Petrograd on the eve of the Kronstadt mutiny likewise
show how the Mensheviks took advantage of the disagreements and certain rudiments of factionalism in the Russian
Communist Party actually in order to egg on and support
the Kronstadt mutineers, the Socialist-Revolutionaries and
the whiteguards, while claiming to be opponents of mutiny
and supporters of the Soviet power, only with supposedly
slight modifications.

3. In this question, propaganda should consist, on the
one hand, in a comprehensive explanation of the harmful-
ness and danger of factionalism from the standpoint of
Party unity and of achieving unanimity of will among
the vanguard of the proletariat as the fundamental condition for the success of the dictatorship of the proletariat;
and, on the other hand, in an explanation of the peculiar
features of the latest tactical devices of the enemies of the
Soviet power. These enemies, having realised the hopeless-
ness of counter-revolution under an openly whiteguard
flag, are now doing their utmost to utilise the disagreements
within the Russian Communist Party and to further the
counter-revolution in one way or another by transferring
power to a political group which is outwardly closest to
recognition of the Soviet power.

Propaganda must also teach the lessons of preceding
revolutions, in which the counter-revolution made a point
of supporting the opposition to the extreme revolutionary

party which stood closest to the latter, in order to undermine and overthrow the revolutionary dictatorship and thus pave the way for the subsequent complete victory of the counter-revolution, of the capitalists and landowners.

4. In the practical struggle against factionalism, every organisation of the Party must take strict measures to prevent all factional actions. Criticism of the Party's short-comings, which is absolutely necessary, must be conducted in such a way that every practical proposal shall be sub-mitted immediately, without any delay, in the most precise form possible, for consideration and decision to the leading local and central bodies of the Party. Moreover, every critic must see to it that the form of his criticism takes account of the position of the Party, surrounded as it is by a ring of enemies, and that the content of his criticism is such that, by directly participating in Soviet and Party work, he can test the rectification of the errors of the Party or of individual Party members in practice. Analyses of the Party's general line, estimates of its practical expe-rience, check-ups of the fulfilment of its decisions, studies of methods of rectifying errors, etc., must under no cir-cumstances be submitted for preliminary discussion to groups formed on the basis of "platforms", etc., but must in all cases be submitted for discussion directly to all the members of the Party. For this purpose, the Congress orders a more regular publication of *Diskussionny Listok*[75] and special symposiums to promote unceasing efforts to ensure that criticism shall be concentrated on essentials and shall not assume a form capable of assisting the class enemies of the proletariat.

5. Rejecting in principle the deviation towards syndical-ism and anarchism, which is examined in a special reso-lution,[76] and instructing the Central Committee to secure the complete elimination of all factionalism, the Congress at the same time declares that every practical proposal concerning questions to which the so-called Workers' Oppo-sition group, for example, has devoted special attention, such as purging the Party of non-proletarian and unreliable elements, combating bureaucratic practices, developing democracy and workers' initiative, etc., must be examined with the greatest care and tested in practice. The Party

must know that we have not taken all the necessary measures in regard to these questions because of various obstacles, but that, while ruthlessly rejecting impractical and factional pseudo-criticism, the Party will unceasingly continue—trying out new methods—to fight with all the means at its disposal against the evils of bureaucracy, for the extension of democracy and initiative, for detecting, exposing and expelling from the Party elements that have wormed their way into its ranks, etc.

6. The Congress, therefore, hereby declares dissolved and orders the immediate dissolution of all groups without exception formed on the basis of one platform or another (such as the Workers' Opposition group, the Democratic Centralism group, etc.). Non-observance of this decision of the Congress shall entail unconditional and instant expulsion from the Party.

7. In order to ensure strict discipline within the Party and in all Soviet work and to secure the maximum unanimity in eliminating all factionalism, the Congress authorises the Central Committee, in cases of breach of discipline or of a revival or toleration of factionalism, to apply all Party penalties, including expulsion, and in regard to members of the Central Committee, reduction to the status of alternate members and, as an extreme measure, expulsion from the Party. A necessary condition for the application of such an extreme measure to members of the Central Committee, alternate members of the Central Committee and members of the Control Commission is the convocation of a Plenary Meeting of the Central Committee, to which all alternate members of the Central Committee and all members of the Control Commission shall be invited. If such a general assembly of the most responsible leaders of the Party deems it necessary by a two-thirds majority to reduce a member of the Central Committee to the status of alternate member, or to expel him from the Party, this measure shall be put into effect immediately.[77]

Published according
to the manuscript

9

PRELIMINARY DRAFT RESOLUTION
OF THE TENTH CONGRESS OF THE R.C.P.
ON THE SYNDICALIST AND ANARCHIST DEVIATION
IN OUR PARTY

1. A syndicalist and anarchist deviation has been definitely revealed in our Party in the past few months. It calls for the most resolute measures of ideological struggle and also for purging the Party and restoring its health.

2. The said deviation is due partly to the influx into the Party of former Mensheviks, and also of workers and peasants who have not yet fully assimilated the communist world outlook. Mainly, however, this deviation is due to the influence exercised upon the proletariat and on the Russian Communist Party by the petty-bourgeois element, which is exceptionally strong in our country, and which inevitably engenders vacillation towards anarchism, particularly at a time when the condition of the masses has greatly deteriorated as a consequence of the crop failure and the devastating effects of war, and when the demobilisation of the army numbering millions sets loose hundreds and hundreds of thousands of peasants and workers unable immediately to find regular means of livelihood.

3. The most theoretically complete and clearly defined expression of this deviation (*or:* one of the most complete, etc., expressions of this deviation) is the theses and other literary productions of the so-called Workers' Opposition group. Sufficiently illustrative of this is, for example, the following thesis propounded by this group: "The organisation of the management of the national economy is the function of an All-Russia Congress of Producers organised in industrial unions which shall elect a central body to run the whole of the national economy of the Republic."

The ideas at the bottom of this and numerous similar statements are radically wrong in theory, and represent a complete break with Marxism and communism, with the practical experience of all semi-proletarian revolutions and of the present proletarian revolution.

First, the concept "producer" combines proletarians with semi-proletarians and small commodity producers, thus radically departing from the fundamental concept of the class struggle and from the fundamental demand that a precise distinction be drawn between classes.

Secondly, the bidding for or flirtation with the non-Party masses, which is expressed in the above-quoted thesis, is an equally radical departure from Marxism.

Marxism teaches—and this tenet has not only been formally endorsed by the whole of the Communist International in the decisions of the Second (1920) Congress of the Comintern on the role of the political party of the proletariat, but has also been confirmed in practice by our revolution—that only the political party of the working class, i.e., the Communist Party, is capable of uniting, training and organising a vanguard of the proletariat and of the whole mass of the working people that alone will be capable of withstanding the inevitable petty-bourgeois vacillations of this mass and the inevitable traditions and relapses of narrow craft unionism or craft prejudices among the proletariat, and of guiding all the united activities of the whole of the proletariat, i.e., of leading it politically, and through it, the whole mass of the working people. Without this the dictatorship of the proletariat is impossible.

The wrong understanding of the role of the Communist Party in its relation to the non-Party proletariat, and in the relation of the first and second factors to the whole mass of working people, is a radical theoretical departure from communism and a deviation towards syndicalism and anarchism, and this deviation permeates all the views of the Workers' Opposition group.

4. The Tenth Congress of the Russian Communist Party declares that it also regards as radically wrong all attempts on the part of the said group and of other persons to defend their fallacious views by referring to Paragraph 5 of the economic section of the Programme of the Russian Com-

munist Party, which deals with the role of the trade unions. This paragraph says that "the trade unions should eventually arrive at a *de facto* concentration in their hands of the whole administration of the whole national economy, as a single economic entity" and that they will "ensure in this way indissoluble ties between the central state administration, the national economy and the broad masses of working people", "drawing" these masses "into direct economic management".

This paragraph in the Programme of the Russian Communist Party also says that a prerequisite for the state at which the trade unions "should eventually arrive" is the process whereby they increasingly "divest themselves of the narrow craft-union spirit" and embrace the majority "and eventually all" of the working people.

Lastly, this paragraph in the Programme of the Russian Communist Party emphasises that "on the strength of the laws of the R.S F.S.R., and established practice, the trade unions participate in all the local and central organs of industrial management".

Instead of studying the practical experience of participation in administration, and instead of developing this experience further, strictly in conformity with successes achieved and mistakes rectified, the syndicalists and anarchists advance as an immediate slogan "congresses or a congress of producers" "to elect" the organs of economic management. Thus, the leading, educational and organising role of the Party in relation to the trade unions of the proletariat, and of the latter to the semi-petty-bourgeois and even wholly petty-bourgeois masses of working people, is completely evaded and eliminated, and instead of continuing and correcting the practical work of building new forms of economy already begun by the Soviet state, we get petty-bourgeois-anarchist disruption of this work, which can only lead to the triumph of the bourgeois counter-revolution.

5. In addition to the theoretical fallacies and a radically wrong attitude towards the practical experience of economic organisation already begun by the Soviet government, the Congress of the Russian Communist Party discerns in the views of this and similar groups and persons a gross

political mistake and a direct political danger to the very existence of the dictatorship of the proletariat.

In a country like Russia, the overwhelming preponderance of the petty-bourgeois element and the devastation, impoverishment, epidemics, crop failures, extreme want and hardship inevitably resulting from the war, engender particularly sharp vacillations in the temper of the petty-bourgeois and semi-proletarian masses. First they incline towards a strengthening of the alliance between these masses and the proletariat, and then towards bourgeois restoration. The experience of all revolutions in the eighteenth, nineteenth, and twentieth centuries shows most clearly and convincingly that the only possible result of these vacillations—if the unity, strength and influence of the revolutionary vanguard of the proletariat is weakened in the slightest degree—will be the restoration of the power and property of the capitalists and landowners.

Hence, the views of the Workers' Opposition and of like-minded elements are not only wrong in theory, but are an expression of petty-bourgeois and anarchist wavering in practice, and actually weaken the consistency of the leading line of the Communist Party and help the class enemies of the proletarian revolution.

6. In view of all this, the Congress of the R.C.P., emphatically rejecting the said ideas, as being expressive of a syndicalist and anarchist deviation, deems it necessary:

First, to wage an unswerving and systematic struggle against these ideas;

Secondly, to recognise the propaganda of these ideas as being incompatible with membership of the R.C.P.

Instructing the C.C. of the Party strictly to enforce these decisions, the Congress at the same time points out that special publications, symposiums, etc., can and should provide space for a most comprehensive exchange of opinion between Party members on all the questions herein indicated.

Published according
to the manuscript

10

REPORT ON PARTY UNITY
AND THE ANARCHO-SYNDICALIST DEVIATION
MARCH 16[78]

Comrades, I do not think there is any need to say a great
deal on this question because the subjects on which an
official pronouncement must now be made on behalf of the
Party Congress, that is, on behalf of the whole Party, were
touched upon in all the questions discussed at the Congress.
The resolution "On Unity" largely contains a characterisa-
tion of the political situation. You must have all read the
printed text of this resolution that has been distributed.
Point 7, which introduces an exceptional measure, namely,
the right to expel a member from the Central Committee
by a two-thirds majority of a general meeting of members
of the C.C., alternate members and members of the Central
Control Commission, is not for publication. This measure
was repeatedly discussed at private conferences at which
representatives of all shades expressed their opinions. Let
us hope, comrades, that it will not be necessary to apply
this point; but it is necessary to have it, in view of the
new situation, when we are on the eve of a new and fairly
sharp turn, and want to abolish all traces of separatism.

Let me now deal with the resolution on syndicalist and
anarchist deviations. It is the question touched upon in
point 4 of the Congress agenda. The definition of our attitude to certain trends, or deviations in thinking, is the
pivot of the whole resolution. By saying "deviations", we
emphasise that we do not as yet regard them as something
that has crystallised and is absolutely and fully defined,
but merely as the beginning of a political trend of which the
Party must give its appraisal. Point 3 of the resolution on
the syndicalist and anarchist deviation, copies of which you

all probably have, evidently contains a misprint (judging by the remarks, it has been noticed). It should read: "illustrative of this is, for example, the following thesis of the Workers' Opposition: 'The organisation of the management of the national economy is the function of an All-Russia Congress of Producers organised in industrial unions which shall elect a central body to run the whole of the national economy of the Republic.'" We have repeatedly discussed this point during the Congress, at restricted conferences as well as at the open general sessions of the Congress. I think we have already made it clear that it is quite impossible to defend this point on the plea that Engels had spoken of an association of producers, because it is quite obvious, and an exact quotation of the appropriate passage will prove, that Engels was referring to a classless communist society. That is something we all take for granted. Once society is rid of classes, only the producers remain, without any division into workers and peasants. And we know perfectly well from all the works of Marx and Engels that they drew a very clear distinction between the period in which classes still exist and that in which they no longer do. Marx and Engels used to ridicule the idea that classes could disappear before communism, and said that communism alone meant their abolition.[79]

The position is that we are the first to raise the question of abolishing classes in the practical plane, and that two main classes remain in this peasant country—the working class and the peasantry. Alongside of them, however, are whole groups left over from capitalism.

Our Programme definitely says that we are taking the first steps and shall have a number of transitional stages. But in the practical work of Soviet administration and in the whole history of the revolution we have constantly had graphic illustrations of the fact that it is wrong to give theoretical definitions of the kind the opposition has given in this case. We know perfectly well that classes have remained in our country and will remain for a long time to come; and that in a country with a predominantly peasant population they are bound to remain for many, many years. It will take us at least ten years to organise large-scale industry to produce a reserve and secure control of agriculture. This is the shortest period even if the technical conditions are exceptionally favourable. But we know that our conditions are terribly unfavourable. We have a plan for building up Russia on the basis of modern large-scale industry: it is the electrification plan drawn up by our scientists. The shortest period provided for in that plan is ten years, and this is based on the assumption that conditions will be something like normal. But we know perfectly well that we do not have such conditions and it goes without saying that ten years is an extremely short period for us. We have reached the very core of the question: the situation is such that classes hostile to the proletariat will remain, so that in practice we cannot now create that which Engels spoke about. There will be a dictatorship of the proletariat. Then will come the classless society.

Marx and Engels sharply challenged those who tended to forget class distinctions and spoke about producers, the people, or working people in general. Anyone who has read Marx and Engels will recall that in all their works they ridicule those who talk about producers, the people, working people in general. There are no working people or workers in general; there are either small proprietors who own the means of production, and whose mentality and habits are capitalistic—and they cannot be anything else—or wage-workers with an altogether different cast of mind, wage-workers in large-scale industry, who stand in antagonistic contradiction to the capitalists and are ranged in struggle against them.

We have approached this question after three years of struggle, with experience in the exercise of the political power of the proletariat, and knowledge of the enormous difficulties existing in the relationships between classes, which are still there, and with remnants of the bourgeoisie filling the cracks and crevices of our social fabric, and holding office in Soviet institutions. In the circumstances the appearance of a platform containing the theses I have read to you is a clear and obvious syndicalist-anarchist deviation. That is no exaggeration: I have carefully weighed my words. A deviation is not yet a full-blown trend. A deviation is something that can be rectified. People have somewhat strayed or are beginning to stray from the path,

but can still be put right. That, in my opinion, is what the
Russian word *uklon* means. It emphasises that there is
nothing final in it as yet, and that the matter can be easily
rectified; it shows a desire to sound a warning and to raise
the question on principle in all its scope. If anyone has a
better word to express this idea, let us have it, by all means.
I hope we shall not start arguing over words. We are essentially examining this thesis as the main one, so as not
to go chasing after a mass of similar ideas, of which the
Workers' Opposition group has a great many. We will leave
our writers, and the leaders of this trend to go into the matter, for at the end of the resolution we make a point of saying
that special publications and symposiums can and should
give space to a more comprehensive exchange of opinion
between Party members on all the questions indicated. We
cannot now afford to put off the question. We are a party
fighting in acute difficulties. We must say to ourselves:
if our unity is to be more solid, we must condemn a definite
deviation. Since it has come to light, it should be brought
out and discussed. If a comprehensive discussion is necessary, let us have it, by all means; we have the men to give
chapter and verse on every point, and if we find it relevant
and necessary, we shall raise this question internationally
as well, for you all know and have just heard the delegate
of the Communist International say in his report that there
is a certain Leftist deviation in the ranks of the international revolutionary working-class movement. The deviation
we are discussing is identical with the anarchist deviation
of the German Communist Workers' Party, the fight against
which was clearly revealed at the last Congress of the Communist International.[80] Some of the terms used there to
qualify it were stronger than "deviation". You know that
this is an international question. That is why it would be
wrong to have done with it by saying, "Let's have no more
discussions. Full stop." But a theoretical discussion is one
thing, and the Party's political line—a political struggle—
is another. We are not a debating society. Of course, we are
able to publish symposiums and special publications and
will continue to do so but our first duty is to carry on the
fight against great odds, and that needs unity. If we are to
have proposals, like organising an "All-Russia Congress

of Producers", introduced into the political discussion and struggle, we shall be unable to march forward united and in step. That is not the policy we have projected over the next few years. It is a policy that would disrupt the Party's team-work, for it is wrong not only in theory, but also in its incorrect definition of the relations between classes— the crucial element which was specified in the resolution of the Second Congress of the Communist International,[81] and without which there is no Marxism. The situation today is such that the non-Party element is yielding to the petty-bourgeois vacillations which are inevitable in Russia's present economic condition. We must remember that in some respects the internal situation presents a greater danger than Denikin and Yudenich; and our unity must not be formal but must go deep down below the surface. If we are to create this unity, a resolution like the one proposed is indispensable.

The next very important thing in my opinion is Point 4 of this resolution, which gives an interpretation of our Programme. It is an authentic interpretation, that is, the author's interpretation. Its author is the Congress, and that is why it must give its interpretation in order to put a stop to all this wavering, and to the tricks that are some-times being played with our Programme, as if what it says about the trade unions is what some people would like it to say. You have heard Comrade Ryazanov's criticism of the Programme—let us thank the critic for his theo-retical researches. You have heard Comrade Shlyapnikov's criticism. That is something we must not ignore. I think that here, in this resolution, we have exactly what we need just now. We must say on behalf of the Congress, which endorses the Programme and which is the Party's supreme organ: here is what we understand the Programme to mean. This, I repeat, does not cut short theoretical discussion. Proposals to amend the Programme may be made; no one has suggested that this should be prohibited. We do not think that our Programme is so perfect as not to require any modification whatever; but just now we have no formal proposals, nor have we allocated any time for the exami-nation of this question. If we read the Programme carefully we shall find the following: "The trade unions . . . should

eventually arrive at a *de facto* concentration", etc. The
words, "should eventually arrive at a *de facto* concentration", should be underlined. And a few lines above that we
read: "On the strength of the laws . . . the trade unions
participate in all the local and central organs of industrial
management." We know that it took decades to build up
capitalist industry, with the assistance of all the advanced
countries of the world. Are we so childish as to think that
we can complete this process so quickly at this time of dire
distress and impoverishment, in a country with a mass of
peasants, with workers in a minority, and a proletarian vanguard bleeding and in a state of prostration? We have not
even laid the main foundation, we have only begun to give
an experimental definition of industrial management with
the participation of the trade unions. We know that want
is the principal obstacle. It is not true to say that we are
not enlisting the masses; on the contrary, we give sincere
support to anyone among the mass of workers with the
least sign of talent, or ability. All we need is for the conditions to ease off ever so little. We need a year or two, at
least, of relief from famine. This is an insignificant period
of time in terms of history but in our conditions it is a long
one. A year or two of relief from famine, with regular supplies of fuel to keep the factories running, and we shall
receive a hundred times more assistance from the working
class, and far more talent will arise from its ranks than
we now have. No one has or can have any doubts about
this. The assistance is not forthcoming at present, but not
because we do not want it. In fact, we are doing all we can
to get it. No one can say that the government, the trade
unions, or the Party's Central Committee have missed a
single opportunity to do so. But we know that the want
in the country is desperate, that there is hunger and poverty
everywhere, and that this very often leads to passivity.
Let us not be afraid to call a spade a spade: it is these calamities and evils that are hindering the rise of mass energy.
In such a situation, when the statistics tell us that 60 per
cent of the members of management boards are workers,
it is quite impossible to try to interpret the words in the
Programme—"The trade unions ... should eventually arrive
at a *de facto* concentration", etc.—*à la* Shlyapnikov.

An authentic interpretation of the Programme will enable us to combine the necessary tactical solidarity and unity with the necessary freedom of discussion, and this is emphasised at the end of the resolution. What does it say in essence? Point 6 reads:

"In view of all this, the Congress of the R.C.P., emphatically rejecting the said ideas, as being expressive of a syndicalist and anarchist deviation, deems it necessary, first, to wage an unswerving and systematic struggle against these ideas; secondly, to recognise the propaganda of these ideas as being incompatible with membership of the R.C.P.

"Instructing the C.C. of the Party strictly to enforce these decisions, the Congress at the same time points out that special publications, symposiums, etc., can and should provide space for a most comprehensive exchange of opinion between Party members on all the questions herein indicated."

Do you not see—you all who are agitators and propagandists in one way or another—the difference between the propaganda of ideas within political parties engaged in struggle, and the exchange of opinion in special publications and symposiums? I am sure that everyone who takes the trouble to understand this resolution will see the difference. And we hope that the representatives of this deviation whom we are taking into the Central Committee will treat the decisions of the Party Congress as every class-conscious disciplined Party member does. We hope that with their assistance we, in the Central Committee, shall look into this matter, without creating a special situation. We shall investigate and decide what it is that is going on in the Party—whether it is the propaganda of ideas within a political party engaged in struggle, or the exchange of opinion in special publications and symposiums. There is the opportunity for anyone interested in a meticulous study of quotations from Engels. We have theoreticians who can always give the Party useful advice. That is necessary. We shall publish two or three big collections—that is useful and absolutely necessary. But is this anything like the propaganda of ideas, or a conflict of platforms? How can these two things be confused? They will not be confused by anyone who desires to understand our political situation.

Do not hinder our political work, especially in a difficult situation, but go on with your scientific research.
We shall be very happy to see Comrade Shlyapnikov supplement his recent book on his experiences in the underground
revolutionary struggle with a second volume written in his
spare time over the next few months and analysing the
concept of "producer". But the present resolution will serve
as our landmark. We opened the widest and freest discussion. The platform of the Workers' Opposition was published in the central organ of the Party in 250,000 copies.
We have weighed it up from all sides, we have elected
delegates on its basis, and finally we have convened this
Congress, which, summing up the political discussion, says:
"The deviation has come to light, we shall not play hide-
and-seek, but shall say openly: a deviation is a deviation
and must be straightened out. We shall straighten it out,
and the discussion will be a theoretical one."

That is why I renew and support the proposal that we
adopt both these resolutions, consolidate the unity of the
Party, and give a correct definition to what should be dealt
with by Party meetings, and what individuals—Marxists,
Communists who want to help the Party by looking into
theoretical questions—are free to study in their spare time.
(*Applause.*)

11

SUMMING-UP SPEECH ON PARTY UNITY
AND THE ANARCHO-SYNDICALIST DEVIATION
MARCH 16

Comrades, we have heard some incredibly harsh expressions here, and the harshest, I think, was the accusation that our resolution is slanderous. But some harsh expressions tend to expose themselves. You have the resolution. You know that we took two representatives of the Workers' Opposition into the Central Committee and that we used the term "deviation". I emphasise the meaning of this term. Neither Shlyapnikov nor Medvedyev proposed any other. The theses we have criticised here have been criticised by the representatives of all shades of opinion. After this, how can one talk of slander? If we had ascribed to someone something which is not true there would have been some sense in this harsh expression. As it is, it is simply a sign of irritation. That is not a serious objection!

I now come to the points that have been mentioned here. It has been stated that the Democratic Centralism group was given unfair treatment. You have followed the development of the agreement between groups and the exchange of opinion on the question of the election to the Central Committee brought up by the representatives of the Democratic Centralism group. You know that ever since the private conference that was attended by the whole of the Workers' Opposition group and a number of very prominent comrades, representatives of all shades, I, for one, have publicly urged that it would be desirable to have representatives of the Workers' Opposition and Democratic Centralism groups on the Central Committee. No one opposed this at the conference, which was attended by all the comrades of the Workers' Opposition and representatives of all shades. It is quite clear that the election of a representative of the Democratic Centralism group as an alternate and not as

a full member of the Central Committee was the result of
a lengthy exchange of opinion, and an agreement arrived
at among the groups. It is captious to regard this as a sign
of mistrust in or unfairness to the Democratic Centralism
group. We in the Central Committee have done everything
to emphasise our desire to be fair. This is a fact that cannot
be obliterated. It is cavilling to draw the conclusion that
someone has been unfairly treated. Or take the argument
of a comrade from the Democratic Centralism group that
Point 7 of the resolution was superfluous because the Central
Committee already had that right. We propose that Point
7 be withheld from publication because we hope it will
not be necessary to apply it; it is an extreme measure. But
when the comrade from the Democratic Centralism group
says: "The Rules give you this right",[82] he shows that he
does not know the Rules, and is ignorant of the principles
of centralism and democratic centralism. No democracy
or centralism would ever tolerate a Central Committee
elected at a Congress having the right to expel its members.
(*A voice*: "Bypassing the Party.") Particularly bypassing the
Party. The Congress elects the Central Committee, thereby
expressing its supreme confidence and vesting leadership
in those whom it elects. And our Party has never allowed
the Central Committee to have such a right in relation to
its members. This is an extreme measure that is being
adopted specially, in view of the dangerous situation.
A special meeting is called: the Central Committee, plus
the alternate members, plus the Control Commission, all
having the same right of vote. Our Rules make no provision
for such a body or plenum of 47 persons; and never has
anything like it been practised. Hence, I repeat that the
comrades of the Democratic Centralism group know neither
the Rules, nor the principles of centralism or democratic
centralism. It is an extreme measure. I hope we shall not
have to apply it. It merely shows that the Party will resort
to what you have heard about in the event of disagreements
which in one aspect verge on a split. We are not children,
we have gone through some hard times, we have seen splits
and have survived them; we know what a trial they are, and
are not afraid of giving the danger its proper name.

Have we had at previous congresses, even amidst the

sharpest disagreements, situations which, in one aspect, verged on a split? No, we have not. Do we have such a situation now? Yes, we do. This point has been made repeatedly. Now, I think, these are disagreements we can combat.

It has also been said that unity is not created by such resolutions; that according to the resolution criticism must be expressed only through the medium of the gubernia committee; that lack of confidence has been expressed in the comrades of the Workers' Opposition and that this has hampered their presence on the Central Committee. But all of this is not true either. I explained from the very outset why we had chosen the word "deviation". If you don't like the word, accept the resolution as a basis and send it up to the Presidium for possible modification. If we find a milder term I would propose that it be substituted for the word "deviation", and also that other parts be modified. We shall not object to that. We cannot discuss such details here, of course. Hand in the resolution to the Presidium for editing and toning down. It is certainly impossible to couch it in stronger terms—I agree with that. But it is not true to say that the resolution means inciting one section of the Party against another.

I do not know the composition of the Workers' Opposition group in Samara, I have not been there; but I am sure that if any member of the Central Committee or delegate to the Congress of whatever shade of opinion—except the Workers' Opposition—were to set out to prove at a meeting of the Samara organisation that there is no incitement in the resolution, but a call for unity and for winning over the majority of the members of the Workers' Opposition, he would certainly succeed. When people here use the term "incitement" they forget about Point 5 of the resolution on unity, which notes the services of the Workers' Opposition. Are these not set down alongside each other? On the one hand, there is the "guilty of a deviation", and on the other, Point 5 says: "The Congress at the same time declares that every practical proposal concerning questions to which the so-called Workers' Opposition group, for example, has devoted special attention, such as purging the Party of non-proletarian and unreliable elements, combating bureaucratic practices, developing democracy and workers' initiative, etc., must be examined with the greatest care", etc. Is that incitement? It is a recognition of services. We say: On the one hand, in the discussion, you have shown a deviation which is politically dangerous, and even Comrade Medvedyev's resolution[83] admits this, although his wording is different. And then we go on to say: As for combating bureaucratic practices, we agree that we are not yet doing all that can be done. That is recognition of services and not incitement!

When a comrade from the Workers' Opposition is taken into the Central Committee, it is an expression of comradely confidence. And after this, anyone attending a meeting not inflamed with factional strife will hear it say that there is no incitement in this, and that it is an expression of comradely confidence. As for the extreme measure, it is a matter for the future: we are not resorting to it now, and are expressing our comradely confidence. If you think that we are wrong in theory, we can issue dozens of special publications on the subject. And if there are any young comrades, in the Samara organisation, for example, who have anything new to say on this question, then let's have it, Comrades Samarians! We shall publish a few of your articles. Everyone will see the difference between speeches at a Congress and words being bandied outside it. If you examine the precise text of the resolution you will find a theoretical definition of principle, which is not offensive in the least. Alongside of it is recognition of services in combating bureaucratic practices, a request for assistance and, what is more, inclusion of the representatives of this group in the Central Committee, which is the Party's greatest expression of confidence. Therefore, comrades, I move that both resolutions be adopted, by a roll-call vote, and then sent on to the Presidium for revision and modification of the formulations. As Comrade Shlyapnikov is a member of the Presidium, perhaps he will find a more appropriate substitute for the word "deviation".

As regards the notices of resignation, I move we adopt the following resolution: "The Congress calls upon all members of the dissolved Workers' Opposition group to submit to Party discipline, binding them to remain at their posts, and rejects Comrade Shlyapnikov's and all other resignations."[84]

12

REMARKS ON RYAZANOV'S AMENDMENT
TO THE RESOLUTION
ON PARTY UNITY
MARCH 16[85]

I think that, regrettable as it may be, Comrade Ryazanov's suggestion is impracticable. We cannot deprive the Party and the members of the Central Committee of the right to appeal to the Party in the event of disagreement on fundamental issues. I cannot imagine how we can do such a thing! The present Congress cannot in any way bind the elections to the next Congress. Supposing we are faced with a question like, say, the conclusion of the Brest peace? Can you guarantee that no such question will arise? No, you cannot. In the circumstances, the elections may have to be based on platforms. (*Ryazanov*: "On one question?") Certainly. But your resolution says: No elections according to platforms. I do not think we have the power to prohibit this. If we are united by our resolution on unity, and, of course, the development of the revolution, there will be no repetition of elections according to platforms. The lesson we have learned at this Congress will not be forgotten. But if the circumstances should give rise to fundamental disagreements, can we prohibit them from being brought before the judgement of the whole Party? No, we cannot! This is an excessive desire, which is impracticable, and I move that we reject it.

13

SPEECH ON THE FUEL QUESTION
MARCH 16

Allow me to take the floor to refer the fuel question to a commission. The fuel crisis is undoubtedly one of the—if not the—most important issue in all our economic development. But I ask myself: shall we be able to reach a final decision on such an important question on the basis of the report and co-report—the one setting forth the view of the Presidium of the Supreme Economic Council, which is to be given by Comrade Rykov, and the other, criticising that policy, Comrade Larin's standpoint—without referring it to a commission and studying documents which explain the essence of the matter and help to find out whether the whole depends on flaws in the machinery, scandalous practices and crimes, or the weakness of the peasant economy and the peasant horse, without which the supply of firewood is impossible? I ask myself: can we adopt a decision without a commission? And I say that we cannot. It would therefore be much better for us to elect an enlarged commission consisting mostly of comrades from the provinces, who are familiar with the fuel, and specifically the firewood, business, who have more than a book knowledge of it, and have actually had experience in the line. The commission would hear not only the rapporteurs but would summon a number of persons and see that the statements made by the rapporteur and co-rapporteur are documented. It will then report to the Central Committee, which will, on that basis, have to adopt a number of crucial decisions in that sphere. This procedure will yield much more productive and useful results than discussions at the Congress which could make us waste a whole day and eventually lead us up to no further than reference of the question to a commission.

14

PROPOSAL ON THE FUEL QUESTION
MARCH 16

I move that we instruct the Central Timber Board immediately to confer with delegates to the Congress who have practical experience in the work of fuel and firewood enterprises, with the view of working out right away urgent measures, especially in floating.

15

SPEECH IN CLOSING THE CONGRESS
MARCH 16

Comrades, we have concluded the work of the Party Congress, which has been meeting at an extremely important moment for the fate of our revolution. The Civil War, coming in the wake of so many years of imperialist war, has so torn and dislocated this country, that its revival is taking place in incredibly difficult conditions. Hence, we should not be surprised that there is a resurgence of the elements of disintegration and decay and of petty-bourgeois and anarchistic elements. One of the fundamental conditions for this is the extreme and unprecedented intensification of want and despair that has now gripped tens and hundreds of thousands, and possibly even larger numbers, of people who see no way out of this disastrous situation. But we know, comrades, that this country has had it even worse. Without shutting our eyes to the danger, or entertaining any sort of false optimism, we say frankly to ourselves and our comrades that the danger is great, but we have great trust in the solidarity of the vanguard of the proletariat. We know that no other force but the class-conscious proletariat can unite the millions of scattered small farmers, many of whom are suffering incredible hardships; no other force can unite them economically and politically against the exploiters. We are convinced that this force has emerged from the experience of the struggle— the gruelling experience of the revolution—sufficiently steeled to withstand all severe trials and the difficulties that lie ahead.

Comrades, apart from the decisions we have adopted on these lines, there is the exceptionally important decision our Congress has adopted on relations with the peasantry.

In it we make a most sober appraisal of the relations between classes, and are not afraid openly to admit that this is a most difficult task, namely, that of establishing proper relations between the proletariat and the predominating peasantry while normal relations are unfeasible. You can call relations normal only when the proletariat has control of large-scale industry and its products and fully satisfies the needs of the peasantry and, providing them with the means of subsistence, so alleviates their condition that there is a tangible and obvious improvement over the capitalist system. That is the only way to create a basis for a normally functioning socialist society. We cannot do this at present because of the crushing ruin, want, impoverishment and despair. But to help to rid ourselves of this accursed legacy we are reacting in a definite way to the relations established during the disastrous war. We will not conceal the fact that the peasantry have some very deep grounds for dissatisfaction. We shall explain the situation more fully, and tell them that we shall do all we can to improve it and pay more heed to the small proprietor's living conditions.

We must do everything to alleviate his condition, to give more to the small farmer, and assure him of greater security in private farming. We are not afraid of the anti-communist trend this measure is bound to produce.

Comrades, we have now been working for several years to lay, for the first time in history, the foundations of a socialist society and a proletarian state, and it is in the spirit of sober appraisal of these relations that we have expressed our full readiness to reconsider this policy and even to modify it. I think that the results of our Congress in this respect will be all the more successful because we have been solidly united on this fundamental question from the very outset. There was need for unanimity in the solution of two fundamental questions, and we have had no disagreements on the relations between the vanguard of the proletariat and its mass, and the relations between the proletariat and the peasantry. In spite of the very difficult political conditions, we have been more united in our decisions on these points than ever before.

Permit me now to deal with two points, which I ask not

to be entered into the minutes. The first is the question of concessions in Baku and Grozny. It was dealt with only in passing at this Congress. I was unable to attend that session, but I have been told that some comrades have their doubts or have been left with a sense of dissatisfaction. I don't think there are any grounds for this. The Central Committee thrashed out this question of granting concessions in Grozny and Baku. Several special commissions were set up and special reports from the departments concerned were called for. There was some disagreement, several votes were taken, but after the last one not a single member or group in the Central Committee wished to exercise their incontestable right to appeal to the Congress. The new Central Committee will, I think, have full formal and actual right to decide this big question on the strength of a Congress decision. Unless we grant concessions, we cannot hope to obtain the assistance of well-equipped modern capitalist industry. And unless we utilise the latter, we shall be unable to lay a proper foundation for our own large-scale production in such industries as oil, which is of exceptional importance for the whole of the world economy. We have not yet concluded a single concession agreement, but we shall do all we can to do so. Have you read in the newspapers about the opening of the Baku-Tiflis oil pipeline? There will soon be news of a similar pipeline to Batum. This will give us an outlet to the world market. We have to improve our economic position, and the technical equipment of our Republic, and give our workers more food and goods. Everything that helps to ease things in this respect is of tremendous value to us. That is why we are not afraid of leasing parts of Grozny and Baku. By leasing out one-fourth of Grozny and one-fourth of Baku, we shall be able—if we succeed—to raise the rest of them to the modern technical level of advanced capitalism. There is no other way for us to do this at present. Those who know the state of our economy will understand this. But once we have a base, even if it costs us hundreds of millions of gold rubles, we shall do everything to develop the rest.

The second question that I ask not to be published is the Presidium's special decision concerning the manner of reporting. You know that at this Congress we have repeatedly had to work in an atmosphere of excessive tension and a larger number of delegates were kept away from the sittings of the Congress than has usually been the case. We must, therefore, be more calm and thoughtful in drawing up a plan of how the reports are to be made in the localities, and we must be guided by a definite decision. Let me read you a comrade's draft of the Presidium's instructions to the delegates returning home (*reads*).[86] I have summed it up, and I think these few lines are sufficient to cause every delegate to ponder over the question and in his report to exercise the necessary caution, taking care not to exaggerate the danger of the situation or allow himself or those around him to panic, whatever the circumstances.

Now that world capitalism has started its incredibly frenzied, hysterical campaign against us, it would be particularly inappropriate for us to panic, and there is no reason to do so. Yesterday, by arrangement with Comrade Chicherin, I received a summary of the news on this question, and I think you will find it instructive. It is a summary of the news on the slander campaign about the situation in Russia. The comrade who made the summary writes: "Never before has the West-European press indulged in such an orgy of lies or engaged in the mass production of fantastic inventions about Soviet Russia as in the last fortnight. Since the beginning of March, the whole of the West-European press has been daily pouring out torrents of fantastic reports about insurrections in Russia; a counter-revolutionary victory; Lenin and Trotsky's flight to the Crimea; the white flag over the Kremlin; barricades in Petrograd and Moscow and their streets running with blood; hordes of workers converging on Moscow from the hills to overthrow the Soviet government; Budyonny's defection to the rebels; a counter-revolutionary victory in a number of Russian towns, a succession of names adding up to virtually all the gubernia capitals of Russia. The scope and method of the campaign betray it as a far-reaching plan adopted by all the leading governments. On March 2, the British Foreign Office announced through the *Press Association* that it regarded these reports as improbable, but immediately thereafter issued its own bulletin about a rising in Petrograd, a bombardment of Petrograd by the Kronstadt fleet, and fighting in the streets of Moscow.

On March 2, all the British newspapers published cabled reports about uprisings in Petrograd and Moscow: Lenin and Trotsky have fled to the Crimea; 14,000 workers in Moscow are demanding a constituent assembly; the Moscow arsenal and the Moscow-Kursk railway station are in the hands of the insurgent workers; in Petrograd, Vasilyevsky Ostrov is entirely in the hands of the insurgents.

Let me quote a few of the radio broadcasts and cables received on the following days: on March 3, Klyshko cabled from London that *Reuter* had picked up some absurd rumours about a rising in Petrograd and was assiduously circulating them.

March 6. The Berlin correspondent Mayson cables to New York that workers from America are playing an important part in the Petrograd revolution, and that Chicherin has radioed an order to General Hanecki to close the frontier to émigrés from America.

March 6. Zinoviev has fled to Oranienbaum; Red artillery is shelling the working-class quarter in Moscow; Petrograd is beleaguered (cable from Wiegand).

March 7. Klyshko cables that according to reports from Revel, barricades have been erected in the streets of Moscow; the newspapers carry reports from Helsingfors that anti-Bolshevik troops have taken Chernigov.

March 7. Petrograd and Moscow are in the hands of the insurgents; insurrection in Odessa; Semyonov advancing in Siberia at the head of 25,000 Cossacks; a Revolutionary Committee in Petrograd is in control of the fortifications and the fleet (reported by the Poldhu wireless station in England).

Nauen, March 7. The factory quarter in Petrograd is in revolt; an anti-Bolshevik insurrection has broken out in Volhynia.

Paris, March 7. Petrograd in the hands of a Revolutionary Committee; *Le Matin*[87] quotes reports from London saying the white flag is flying over the Kremlin.

Paris, March 8. The rebels have captured Krasnaya Gorka; Red Army regiments have mutinied in Pskov Gubernia; the Bolsheviks are sending Bashkirs against Petrograd.

March 10. Klyshko cables: the newspapers are asking whether Petrograd has fallen or not. According to reports from Helsingfors three-quarters of Petrograd is in the hands of the insurgents. Trotsky, or according to other reports, Zinoviev is in command of operations and has his headquarters in Tosna, or else in the Peter and Paul Fortress. According to other reports, Brusilov has been appointed Commander-in-Chief. Reports from Riga say that Petrograd, except for the railway stations, was captured on the 9th; the Red Army has retreated to Gatchina; strikers in Petrograd have raised the slogan: "Down with the Soviets and the Communists." The British War Office states that it is not yet known whether or not the Kronstadt rebels have joined up with the Petrograd rebels but, according to information at its disposal, Zinoviev is in the Peter and Paul Fortress, where he is in command of the Soviet troops.

Of a vast number of fabrications in this period I am taking only a few samples: Saratov has become an independent anti-Bolshevik republic (Nauen, March 11). Fierce anti-Communist riots in towns along the Volga (same source). Fighting between Byelorussian detachments and the Red Army in Minsk Gubernia (same source).

Paris, March 15. *Le Matin* reports that large numbers of Kuban and Don Cossacks are in revolt.

Nauen reported on March 14 that Budyonny's cavalry has joined up with the rebels near Orel. At various times insurrections were reported in Pskov, Odessa and other towns.

Krasin cabled on March 9 that the Washington correspondent of *The Times* said the Soviet regime was on its last legs and America was therefore deferring establishment of relations with the border states. Reports at various times quoted American banking circles as saying that in the circumstances trade with Russia would be a gamble.

The New York correspondent of *The Daily Chronicle* reported as early as March 4 that business circles and the Republican Party in America considered trade relations with Russia at the present time to be a gamble.

This campaign of lies is being undoubtedly conducted not only with an eye to America, but also to the Turkish delegation in London, and the plebiscite in Silesia.

Comrades, the picture is absolutely clear. The world press syndicate—over there they have a free press, which means that 99 per cent of the press is in the pay of the financial magnates, who have command of hundreds of millions of rubles—has launched a world-wide campaign on behalf of the imperialists with the prime object of disrupting the negotiations for a trade agreement with Britain, which Krasin has initiated, and the forthcoming trade agreement with America, which, as I have stated, we have been negotiating here, and reference to which was made at this Congress. This shows that the enemies around us, no longer able to wage their war of intervention, are now pinning their hopes on a rebellion. And the Kronstadt events revealed their connection with the international bourgeoisie. Moreover, we see that what they fear most, from the practical angle of international capital, is the resumption of proper trade relations. But they will fail in their attempts to disrupt them. There are some big businessmen here in Moscow, and they have stopped believing these false rumours. They have told us that a group of citizens in America has used an original method of propaganda in favour of Soviet Russia.

It has collected the diverse press reports about Russia over the past few months—about the flight of Lenin and Trotsky, about Trotsky shooting Lenin, and vice versa—and has published them in a pamphlet. You couldn't find a better way of popularising the Soviet power. Day after day they collected reports of the assassination of Lenin and Trotsky and showed how many times each had been shot or killed; such reports were repeated month after month. Finally, all these reports were collected in a pamphlet and published. The American bourgeois press has got a bad name for itself. That is the enemy whom two million Russian émigrés, landowners and capitalists, are serving; this is the army of the bourgeoisie confronting us. Let them try to disrupt trade relations and belittle the practical achievements of the Soviet power. We know that they will fail. And the reports of the international press, which controls hundreds of thousands of newspapers and supplies news to the whole world, show once again how we are surrounded by enemies and how much weaker they are as compared with last year.

That, comrades, is what we must understand. I think that the majority of the delegates present here have realised just how far we can let our disagreements go. It was naturally impossible to keep within these bounds during the struggle at the Congress. Men who have just emerged from the heat of battle cannot be expected to see these limits all at once. But we must have no doubts in our own mind when we look at our Party as the nucleus of the world revolution, and at the campaign which the world syndicate of states is now waging against us. Let them wage their campaign. We have sized it up, and we have exactly sized up our own disagreements. We know that by closing our ranks at this Congress we shall emerge from our disagreements solidly united, with the Party much stronger and marching with ever greater resolution towards international victories! (*Stormy applause.*)

SPEECH DELIVERED
AT THE ALL-RUSSIA CONGRESS
OF TRANSPORT WORKERS
MARCH 27, 1921[88]

Comrades, may I thank you all for your greetings and ask you to accept my greetings to your Congress. (*Stormy applause.*) Allow me to digress before dealing with the subject that directly concerns the work and tasks of this Congress and what the Soviet state expects of it.

As I was coming in through your hall just now, I saw a placard with this inscription: "The reign of the workers and peasants will last for ever." When I read this odd placard, which, it is true, was not up in the usual place, but stood in a corner—perhaps it had occurred to someone that it was not very apt and he had moved it out of the way— when I read this strange placard, I thought to myself: there you have some of the fundamental and elementary things we are still confused about. Indeed, if the reign of the workers and peasants would last for ever, we should never have socialism, for it implies the abolition of classes; and as long as there are workers and peasants, there will be different classes and, therefore, no full socialism. And as I pondered over the fact that three and a half years after the October Revolution we still have such odd placards (even if they are shifted out of the way) it occurred to me that there may still be great misunderstanding of the most common slogans in popular use. Take one of our most popular slogans which we all variously repeat: we all sing about our present fight being the last and decisive one. But I am afraid that if we were to ask a large section of the Communists against whom they are now waging this last battle (not the last one, of course, that's putting it on a bit thick, but one of the last and crucial ones) I am afraid only a few would give the right answer showing a clear understanding against what, or whom, we are now waging one of our last and decisive battles. It also seems to me that, in view of the political events which have caught the attention of the broad masses of workers and peasants, we ought once again to ascertain, or, at any rate, try to ascertain, against whom we are waging one of our last and crucial battles this spring, at this very moment. Let me go over this point.

To sort it out we should, I think, start by reviewing as precisely and as soberly as possible, the opposed forces on whose struggle hinges the fate of the Soviet power, and, generally speaking, the course and development of the proletarian revolution, which is a revolution for the over-throw of the capitalists in Russia and elsewhere. What are these forces? How are they grouped against one another? How are they deployed at present? Any marked aggravation of the political situation, every new turn in the political events, even if it is not considerable, should always cause every thinking worker and peasant to ask himself: "What are the forces involved? How are they grouped?" And only when we are able to estimate these forces correctly and quite soberly, irrespective of our sympathies and desires, shall we be able to draw the proper conclusions concerning our policy in general, and our immediate tasks in particular. Let me, therefore, give you a brief description of these forces.

There are basically three such forces. Take first the proletariat, the force that is closest to us. It is the first force, the first discrete class. You all know this very well, living in the very midst of it. What is its condition now? In the Soviet Republic it is the class that took power three and a half years ago, that has, since then, been exercising its domination—dictatorship—and has suffered and endured exhaustion, want and privation more than any other class. To the working class, to the proletariat, this period, during the greater part of which the Soviet state was engaged in a relentless civil war against the whole capitalist world, brought calamities, privation, sacrifice and intense want on a scale unparalleled in world history. A strange thing happened. The class that took political power did so in the knowledge that it was doing so alone.

That is intrinsic to the concept of the dictatorship of the proletariat. It has meaning only when one class knows that it is taking political power alone, and does not deceive others or itself with talk about "popular government by popular consent through universal suffrage". You all know that there are very many—far too many—people who love to hold forth on that subject, but, at any rate, you will not find them among proletarians, because they have realised that theirs is a dictatorship of the proletariat, and they say as much in their Constitution, the fundamental law of the Republic. This class was well aware that it was taking power alone, under extremely difficult conditions. It has exercised its political power as any dictatorship does, that is, with grim determination. In these three and a half years, it has suffered distress, want, starvation and a worsening of economic positions such as no other class in history has suffered. It is not surprising that as a result of its superhuman effort it is uncommonly weary, exhausted and strained.

How was a single class able to exercise its power in the teeth of the resistance and attacks of the world bourgeoisie, in a country where the proletariat is numerically so much smaller than the rest of the population? How was it able to do that in a backward country artificially cut off by armed force from countries with a more numerous, class-conscious, disciplined and organised proletariat? How could it hold on for three and a half years? What was its mainstay? We know that it was the mass of the peasants, at home. About this second force more in a moment, after we finish our examination of the first. I have said that never has its suffering been so great and acute as in this epoch of its dictatorship; and you all know it, having observed the life of your mates in the factories, railway depots, and workshops. Never before has the country been so weary and worn out. Where did this class get the moral strength to bear these privations? Clearly it had to draw on some source for the moral strength to overcome these material privations. As you know, the question of moral strength and support is a vague one; you can give any reading to moral strength. To avoid the danger of reading anything vague or fantastic into "moral strength", I ask myself:

Is there a precise definition of that which gave the proletariat the moral strength to bear the unprecedented material privations connected with its political rule? I think this will give us a precise answer. Ask yourself: Could the Soviet Republic have borne its trials over three and a half years, and withstood the onslaught of the whiteguards supported by the capitalists of the world, if it had had to face backward instead of advanced countries? You have only to put the question to see the obvious answer.

You know that for three and a half years the wealthiest powers of the world fought against us. The armed forces that were ranged against us and that supported Kolchak, Yudenich, Denikin and Wrangel—you all know this very well, for you all fought in the war—were immensely and clearly superior to our forces. You know perfectly well that these states are still very much stronger than we are. How is it, then, that they set out to vanquish the Soviet power, and failed? How did this happen? We have an exact answer: the proletariat of all the capitalist countries was on our side. Even when it was patently under the influence of the Mensheviks and Socialist-Revolutionaries—in the European countries they go by another name—it refused to support the fight against us. Eventually, the leaders were compelled to yield to the masses, and the workers disrupted the war. It was not we who won, for our armed forces were insignificant; the victory was won because the powers could not hurl the whole of their armed force against us. The course of a war depends on the workers of the advanced countries to such an extent that it cannot be waged against their will, and their passive and semi-passive resistance eventually disrupted the war against us. This incontrovertible fact gives the exact answer to the question as to the source on which the Russian proletariat drew for moral strength to hold out for three and a half years and win. The moral strength of the Russian worker lay in his knowledge and awareness of the tangible assistance and support which the proletariat of all the advanced countries of Europe was giving him in this struggle. The direction which the working-class movement in these countries is taking is indicated by this most important recent event: the split in the Socialist parties of Britain, France, Italy, and other countries (both vanquished and victors) which differ in cultural and economic development. The main development of the year in all countries has been the formation of Communist Parties, with the support of all that is most advanced in the working class, on the ruins of the Socialist and Social-Democratic parties—which in Russia are called Menshevik and Socialist-Revolutionary. And, of course, there can be no doubt that if we had been attacked by backward countries, without mighty proletarian masses, and not by advanced countries, we would have been unable to hold out for three and a half months, let alone three and a half years. Would our proletariat have had the moral strength if it had not relied on the sympathy of the workers of the advanced countries, who supported us in spite of the lies about the Soviet power circulated by the imperialists in millions of copies, and in spite of the efforts of the "labour leaders"—the Mensheviks and Socialist-Revolutionaries— who could have been expected to, and did, hamper the workers' struggle for us? With this support, our proletariat—numerically weak and tormented by poverty and privation—won out because it had the moral strength.

That is the first force.

The second is that which stands between developed capital and the proletariat. It is the petty bourgeoisie, the small proprietors, which in Russia constitute the overwhelming majority of the population—the peasantry. They are mainly small proprietors and small farmers. Nine-tenths of them are that way, and can be nothing else. They do not take part in the acute struggle daily waged by capital and labour. They have not been schooled; their economic and political conditions do not bring them together, but rather tend to separate, alienating them from each other, and transforming them into millions of lone-wolf small proprietors. Such are the facts and you are all perfectly well aware of them. It will take collectives, collective farms and communes years to change this. Thanks to the revolutionary energy and devotion of the proletarian dictatorship, this force was able to dispose of its enemies on the right—the landowner class—to sweep them right out and abolish their rule more swiftly than has ever been done before. But the more quickly it abolished the rule of the landowners,

the more quickly it turned to its farming on the nation-
alised land, the more resolutely it settled accounts with
the small minority of kulaks, the sooner it itself became
transformed into small proprietors. You know that there
has been a levelling-off in the Russian countryside in this
period. The number of peasants with large areas under
crop and without any at all has decreased, while the number of medium farms has increased. The countryside has
become more petty bourgeois. This is an independent class,
which, once the landowners and capitalists are expelled
and eliminated, is the only class capable of opposing the
proletariat. That is why it is absurd to write on placards
that the reign of the workers and peasants will last for
ever.

You know the political mood of this force. It is a vacillating force. We saw this to be true during our revolution
all over the country. There were some local features in
Russia proper, Siberia and the Ukraine, but the result
was the same everywhere: it is a vacillating force. For
a long time it was in the leading strings of the Socialist-
Revolutionaries and Mensheviks, with the aid of Kerensky,
in the Kolchak period, under the Constituent Assembly
in Samara, when the Menshevik Maisky was a Minister
of Kolchak or of one of his predecessors, etc. This force
wavered between the leadership of the proletariat and
that of the bourgeoisie. Why didn't it lead itself? After
all, it is the overwhelming majority. The fact is that the
economic conditions of these masses are such that they are
unable to organise and unite by their own efforts. This is
clear to anyone who is not misled by empty talk about
"universal suffrage", a constituent assembly and such like
"democracy" which has served to dupe the people in all
countries for hundreds of years and which the Socialist-
Revolutionaries and Mensheviks in our own country played
up for hundreds of weeks but fell through "on this very
spot every blessed time". (*Applause.*) We know from our
own experience—and revolutions all over the world confirm
it if we take the modern epoch of, say, a hundred and
fifty years—that the result has always been the same everywhere: the petty bourgeoisie in general, and the peasants
in particular, have failed in all their attempts to realise

their strength, and to direct economics and politics their own way. They have had to follow the leadership either of the proletariat, or the capitalists—there is no middle way open to them. Anyone who thinks of a middle way is an empty dreamer. There is much politics, economics, and history to prove it. The teachings of Marx show that once the small proprietors become owners of the means of production and land, exchange between them necessarily gives rise to capital, and simultaneously to the antagonisms between capital and labour. The struggle between capital and the proletariat is inevitable; it is a law manifesting itself all over the world. This must be accepted by anyone who refuses to fool himself.

These fundamental economic facts explain why this force cannot manifest itself through its own efforts, and why it has always failed in all its attempts to do so in the history of all revolutions. Whenever the proletariat was unable to lead the revolution, this force always followed the leadership of the bourgeoisie. That was the case in all revolutions. The Russians, of course, are of the same clay, and if they choose to pretend they are not, they will only look ridiculous. History metes out the same treatment to all. We, in particular, saw the truth of this under the rule of Kerensky. At that time, the government had the support of very many more political leaders than the Bolsheviks have. They were clever, educated men, with vast experience in politics and state administration. If we were to count all the officials who sabotaged us, but who did not make it their business to sabotage the Kerensky government, which relied on the Mensheviks and Socialist-Revolutionaries, we would find that they made up an overwhelming majority. Still that government collapsed. That shows that there were factors which offset the enormous preponderance of intellectual and educated forces accustomed to administering the state, an art they had acquired decades before they actually took over. Events ran the same course, with some modifications, in the Ukraine, the Don and the Kuban regions, and the result was exactly the same. That could not have been a coincidence. Such is the economic and political law governing the second force: hence, either the leadership of the proletariat—a hard road, but one which can help it to escape the rule of the landowners and capitalists—or the leadership of the capitalists, as it does in the advanced democratic republics, and even in America, where the free distribution of land (every settler was allotted sixty dessiatines* free of charge— better conditions can hardly be imagined!) has not yet entirely stopped, and where this has led to the complete domination of capital.

That is the second force.

Over here it is wavering, and is particularly weary. It has had to bear the burdens of the revolution, and in the past few years fresh burdens have been thrust upon it: a year of crop failure, surplus-grain appropriations, with cattle dying off because of the fodder shortage, etc. In the circumstances, it is not surprising that this second force— the masses of the peasantry—should give way to despair. They could not think of improving their condition although three and a half years have passed since the landowners were driven out, yet the improvement is becoming an urgent necessity. The dispersing army fails to find proper employment for its labour-power, and so this petty-bourgeois force is being transformed into an anarchic element, whose restiveness is an expression of its demands.

You are all familiar with the third force: the landowners and capitalists. It is no longer conspicuous in this country. But one crucial event, one critical lesson of the past few weeks—the Kronstadt events—was like a flash of lightning which threw more of a glare upon reality than anything else.

There is now no country in Europe without some whiteguard elements. Russian émigrés in Europe have been estimated to total about seven hundred thousand. These are fugitive capitalists and the mass of office workers who could not adapt themselves to Soviet rule. We see nothing of this third force, it has emigrated, but it lives and operates in alliance with the capitalists of the world, who are assisting it as they assisted Kolchak, Yudenich and Wrangel, with money and in other ways, because they have their international bonds. We all remember these people. You must have noticed the abundance of extracts from the

---

* about 160 acres.—*Tr.*

whiteguard press in our newspapers over the last few days, explaining the events in Kronstadt. In the last few days, they have been described by Burtsev, who puts out a newspaper in Paris, and have been appraised by Milyukov—you must have all read this. Why have our newspapers devoted so much attention to it? Was it right to do so? It was, because we must have a clear view of our enemy. Abroad, they are not so conspicuous, but you will find that they have not moved very far away, just a few thousand versts at most; and having moved that far, have taken cover. They are alive and kicking, and lying in wait. That is why we must keep a close watch on them, especially because they are more than just refugees. Indeed, they are the agents of world capital, who work with it hand in glove.

You must have noticed that these extracts from the whiteguard newspapers published abroad appeared side by side with extracts from British and French newspapers. They are one chorus, one orchestra. It is true that such orchestras are not conducted by a man with a score. International capital uses less conspicuous means than a conductor's baton, but that it is one orchestra should be clear from any one of these extracts. They have admitted that if the slogan becomes "Soviet power without the Bolsheviks" they will all accept it. Milyukov explains this with particular clarity. He has made a close study of history, and has had a refresher course in Russian history at first hand. He has supplemented his twenty years of book learning with twenty months of personal experience. He says he is prepared to accept the "Soviet power without the Bolsheviks" slogan. He cannot see from over there in Paris whether this is to be a slight shift to the right or to the left, towards the anarchists. From over there, he cannot see what is going on in Kronstadt, but asks the monarchists not to rush and spoil things by shouting about it. He declares that even if the shift is to be to the left, he is prepared to back the Soviet power against the Bolsheviks.

This is what Milyukov says, and it is absolutely right. When he says that the Kronstadt events reveal an urge to set up a Soviet regime without the Bolsheviks, he shows that he has learned something from Russian history and from the landowners and capitalists. It is a demand for a slight shift to the right, with a little bit of unrestricted trade, and a little bit of a constituent assembly—listen to any Menshevik, and you will hear it all, perhaps even without leaving this hall. If the slogan of the Kronstadt events is a slight deviation to the left—Soviet power with the anarchists, begotten by distress, war, the demobilisation of the army—why is Milyukov in favour of it? Because he knows that a deviation leads either to the proletarian dictatorship or to the capitalists.

Political power cannot exist in any other way. Although we are not waging our last battle but one of the last and decisive battles, the only correct answer to the question "Against whom shall we wage one of the decisive battles today?" is: "Against petty-bourgeois anarchy at home." (*Applause*.) As for the landowners and capitalists, we beat them in the first campaign, but only in the first one: the second is to be waged on an international scale. Modern capitalism cannot fight against us, even if it were a hundred times stronger, because over there, in the advanced countries, the workers disrupted its war yesterday and will disrupt it even more effectively today, because over there the consequences of the war are beginning to tell more and more. We have defeated the petty-bourgeois element at home, but it will make itself felt again. And that is taken into account by the landowners and the capitalists, particularly the clever ones, like Milyukov, who has told the monarchists: "Sit still, keep quiet, otherwise you will only strengthen the Soviet power." This has been proved by the general course of the revolutions in which the toilers, with temporary peasant support, set up short-lived dictatorships but had no consolidated power, so that after a brief period everything tended to slip back. This happened because the peasants, the toilers, the small proprietors, can have no policy of their own and must retreat after a period of vacillation. That was the case in the Great French Revolution, and, on a smaller scale, in all revolutions. And, of course, everyone has learned this lesson. Our whiteguards crossed the frontier, rode off a distance of three days' journey, and, backed and supported by West-European capital, are lying in wait and watching. Such is the situation. It makes clear the tasks and duties of the proletariat.

Weariness and exhaustion produce a certain mood, and sometimes lead to desperation. As usual, this tends to breed anarchism among the revolutionary elements. That was the case in all capitalist countries, and that is what is taking place in our own country. The petty-bourgeois element is in the grip of a crisis because it has had it hard over the past few years; not as hard as the proletariat had it in 1919, but hard, nevertheless. The peasantry had to save the state by accepting the surplus-grain appropriations without remuneration, but it can no longer stand the strain. That is why there is confusion and vacillation in its midst, and this is being taken into account by the capitalist enemy, who says: "All it needs is a little push, and it will start snowballing." That is the meaning of the Kronstadt events in the light of the alignment of class forces in the whole of Russia and on the international scale. That is the meaning of one of our last and crucial battles, for we have not beaten this petty-bourgeois-anarchist element, and the immediate fate of the revolution now depends on whether or not we succeed in doing so. If we do not, we shall slide down as the French Revolution did. This is inevitable, and we must not let ourselves be misled by phrases and excuses. We must do all we can to alleviate the position of these masses and safeguard the proletarian leadership. If we do this, the growing movement of the communist revolution in Europe will be further reinforced. What has not yet taken place there today, may well take place tomorrow, or the day after tomorrow, but in world history such periods, as between today and tomorrow, mean no less than a few years.

That is my answer to the question as to what we are now fighting for, in one of our last and crucial battles. That is my reading of recent events and the significance of the class struggle in Russia. It is now clear why it has become so acute and why we find it so hard to see that the chief enemy is not Yudenich, Kolchak or Denikin, but our own conditions.

I can now go on to the concluding part of my speech (which is already too long), namely, the state of railway and water transport, and the tasks of the Railway and Water Transport Workers Congress. I think that what

I have had to describe here is very intimately bound up with these tasks. There is hardly another section of the proletariat which comes so closely into contact with industry and agriculture in its everyday economic activity as the railway and water transport workers. You must supply the cities with food, and revive the rural areas by carrying the manufactured goods to them. That is clear to everyone, but it is much clearer to railway and water transport workers, because that is their everyday work. And from this, I think, follow the exceptionally important tasks and the responsibility now falling to the railway and water transport workers.

You all know that your Congress has been meeting just after some friction between the upper and the lower echelons of the union. When this question was brought up at the last Party Congress, decisions were adopted to reconcile them by subordinating the upper echelons to the lower, by rectifying the upper echelons' mistakes, which I think were of a minor nature but needed rectifying. You know that the Party Congress rectified these mistakes, that the Congress closed on a note of greater solidarity and unity in the ranks of the Communist Party than before. That is the legitimate, necessary and only correct reply that the vanguard, i.e., the leading section of the proletariat, can give to the movement of the petty-bourgeois-anarchist element. If we class-conscious workers realise the danger of this movement, if we rally our forces, work much more harmoniously and show a great deal more of solidarity, we shall multiply our forces. After our victory over the military attack, we shall conquer the vacillations and wavering of this element that is disturbing the whole of our everyday life and for that reason is, I repeat, dangerous. The decisions of the Party Congress, which rectified what was called to its attention, signify a great step forward in increasing the solidarity and unity of the proletarian army. Your Congress must do the same thing and implement the decisions of the Party Congress.

I repeat: the fate of the revolution depends more immediately upon the work of this section of the proletariat than upon any other. We must restore the exchange between agriculture and industry, and we need a material basis to do so. What is it? It is railway and water transport. That is why it is your duty to dedicate yourselves to your work and this applies not only to those of you who are members of the Communist Party, and are therefore conscious vehicles of the proletarian dictatorship, but also to those of you who do not belong to the Party, but represent a transport workers trade union with a million, or a million and a half, members. All of you, learning the lessons of our revolution and of all preceding revolutions, must understand the full gravity of the present situation. If you do not allow yourselves to be blinded by all sorts of slogans, such as "Freedom", "Constituent Assembly", "Free Soviets"—it is so easy to switch labels that even Milyukov has turned up as a supporter of the Soviets of a Kronstadt republic—if you do not close your eyes to the alignment of class forces, you will acquire a sound and firm basis for all your political conclusions. You will then see that we are passing through a period of crisis in which it depends on us whether the proletarian revolution continues to march to victory as surely as before, or whether the vacillations and waverings lead to the victory of the whiteguards, which will not alleviate the situation, but will set Russia back from the revolution for many decades. The only conclusion that you, representatives of railway and water transport workers, can and should draw is—let's have much more proletarian solidarity and discipline. Comrades, we must achieve this at all costs, and win. (*Stormy applause.*)

Pravda Nos. 67 and 68,   Published according
March 29 and 30, 1921   to the *Pravda* text

TO THE TRADE UNION COMMITTEE
AND ALL WORKERS
OF THE FIRST STATE MOTOR WORKS[89]

Dear comrades,

Comrade Smirnov, Chairman of your Trade Union Committee, has informed me of the production of motors and has invited me to attend the ceremony on April 7.

Please accept my congratulations, comrades, on the success of your efforts and the anniversary of the courses for mechanics. With all my heart, I wish you vigorous pursuit of your work, in which you are sure to score further successes. They are of especial significance from the standpoint of the whole mass of workers and peasants, because the development of motor production in Russia, with her abundant oil resources, holds out the possibility of organising the supply of peasant farms with efficient and low-cost machines. You must do all you can to make motor manufacture an even greater success.

With best wishes and communist greetings,

Lenin

Written on April 7, 1921

First published in *Pravda*
No. 21, January 21, 1940

Published according
to the manuscript

REPORT ON THE TAX IN KIND
DELIVERED AT A MEETING OF SECRETARIES AND RESPONSIBLE REPRESENTATIVES OF R.C.P.(B.) CELLS OF MOSCOW AND MOSCOW GUBERNIA
APRIL 9, 1921[90]

Comrades, one hears the most varied and highly confusing opinions on the question of the tax in kind and the change in our food policy, and also on the Soviet government's economic policy. Permit me, by arrangement with Comrade Kamenev, to share our subjects in such a way that he will give a detailed outline of the laws which have just been issued. This will be all the more appropriate for he chaired the commission which was appointed by the Party's Central Committee and later endorsed by the Council of People's Commissars, and which drew up all the recent laws at a number of conferences with representatives of the departments concerned. The last of these laws was issued yesterday, and we saw it in the newspapers this morning. There is no doubt that each of these laws raises a number of practical questions, and it will take some work to familiarise all the local Party and Soviet workers with them and to devise the proper methods of applying them in the localities.

I should like to draw your attention to their general significance, or the principle behind them. How are we to explain the fact that the Soviet government and the dictatorship of the proletariat are about to accept some freedom of trade? To what extent can unrestricted trade and individual enterprise be permitted side by side with the socialist economy? To what extent can we permit such a revival of capitalism, which may seem to be inevitable with a free market, however restricted? What has called

forth this change? What is its real meaning, character
and significance? And how should members of the Communist Party understand it? How is it to be explained, and
what are the limits of its practical application? This,
approximately, is the task I have set myself.

The first question is: what has called forth this change,
which many think to be too drastic and not sufficiently
justified?

The fundamental and principal reason for the change is
the extraordinarily acute crisis of peasant farming, and
its very difficult condition, which has proved to be much
harder by the spring of 1921 than could have been expected.
On the other hand, its consequences have affected the
restoration of our transport system and of our industry.
I should like to point out that most mistakes on the question
of substituting the tax in kind for the surplus-grain appropriation system, and on the significance of the change, are
made because there is no effort to analyse the nature of
the change and its implications. Here is a picture of peasant
farming by the spring of 1921: an extremely severe crisis
caused by the war-time ruin and aggravated by a disastrous
crop failure and the resultant fodder shortage (for the
failure also affected the hay crop) and loss of cattle; and
the weakening of the productive forces of peasant farming,
which in many places was doomed to utter ruin. And here
we come to this question: what is the connection between
this terribly acute crisis of peasant farming and the Soviet
government's abolition of the surplus-grain appropriation
system? I say that if we are to understand this measure we
must ask ourselves: what is the transition we are making?

In the event of a workers' revolution in a country with
a predominantly peasant population, with the factories,
works and railways taken over by the working class, what,
in essence, should be the economic relations between the
working class and the peasantry? They should obviously be
the following: the workers producing in the factories and
works, which now belong to them, all that is necessary
for the country—and that means also for the peasants,
who constitute the majority of the population—should
transport all these things on their railroads and river vessels
and deliver them to the peasants, in return for the surplus

agricultural produce. This is absolutely obvious and hardly requires detailed explanation althouh it is constantly forgotten in the tax discussions. But it should be borne in mind, because if we are to explain the significance of the tax in kind, which is only a transitional measure, we must have a clear understanding of what we want to achieve. What I have said makes it clear that we do not want the peasants' products to be delivered to the workers' state as appropriations of surplus grain, or a tax. We want them in exchange for all the goods the peasants need delivered to them by our transport system. We must have such an arrangement. It is a basis for the economy of a country which has adopted socialism. If peasant farming is to develop, we must also assure its transition to the next stage which must inevitably be one of gradual amalgamation of the small, isolated peasant farms—the least profitable and most backward—into large-scale collective farms. That is how socialists have always visualised it, and that is exactly how our own Communist Party sees it. I repeat, the greatest source of error and confusion is in appraising the tax in kind without making allowance for the specific features of the transitional measures which we must take, if we are to attain the goals which we can and must reach.

What, then, is the tax in kind? It is a measure in which we see something of the past and something of the future. A tax is something the state takes from the population without compensation. If it is fixed at approximately one-half of last year's rate of surplus-grain appropriations it alone will not suffice for the workers' state to maintain its Red Army, the whole of industry, and the whole of the non-agricultural population, and to develop production and relations with foreign countries, whose assistance in the way of machinery and equipment we need. On the one hand, the workers' state wants to rely on the tax at approximately one-half the surplus-grain appropriations rate, and on the other, on the exchange of manufactured goods for the surplus products of peasant farming. Hence, the tax contains a moiety of the old appropriation system and a moiety of that which is the only correct system, namely, the exchange of the manufactures of big socialist factories for the products of peasant farming through the medium

of food supply organisations of the working-class state
and workers' and peasants' co-operative societies.

Why are we compelled to resort to a measure of which
a moiety belongs to the past and a moiety only is put on
proper lines? After all, we are not at all sure that we shall
be able to put it on proper lines at once, or that it will be
at all considerable. Why are we compelled to resort to
such a half-measure? Why must we rely on such measures
in our food and economic policy? What is it that makes it
imperative? Everyone knows, of course, that it is not the
Soviet government's preference for some particular policy.
It is the grinding need and the desperate situation. You
know that for several years after the victory of the workers' revolution in Russia, after the imperialist war, we had
to endure a civil war, and it is now no exaggeration to
say that Russia suffered more than any other country involved in the imperialist war, including those which had
suffered because it was fought on their territory. For after
four years of imperialist war we endured three years of
civil war, which brought more havoc and industrial dislocation than any external war, because it was fought in
the very heart of the country. This terrible devastation is
the main reason why initially during the war—particularly
when the Civil War cut us off from grain areas, like Siberia,
the Caucasus and the whole of the Ukraine, and from our
supplies of coal and oil, and reduced our possibilities of
obtaining other types of fuel—we could hold out—in a
besieged fortress—only through the surplus-grain appropriation system, that is, by taking from the peasant whatever
surplus produce was available, and sometimes even a part
of his necessaries, in order to keep the army in fighting
trim and to prevent industry from going to pieces altogether. During the Civil War, this problem was one of
extraordinary difficulty, and was declared insoluble by all
the other parties. Take the Mensheviks and Socialist-
Revolutionaries, i.e., the parties of the petty bourgeoisie
and the kulaks. At the most acute moments of the Civil
War they did the most shouting about the Bolsheviks'
having undertaken a crazy task, and the impossibility of
holding out when all the powers were assisting the whiteguards. Indeed, the problem was one of exceptional diffi-

culty, and called for a supreme effort. It was successfully
solved only because of what, you might say, was the superhuman sacrifices on the part of the working class and the
peasantry. The working class never suffered such malnutri-
tion, such starvation, as it did in the first years of its dictatorship. This naturally left as the only alternative the
appropriation system, which meant taking from the peasant
all of his surplus and a part of his necessaries. He was
told: "You, too, will have to go hungry for a while, but
together we shall save our cause and drive off Denikin and
Wrangel." That was the only conceivable solution.

This was not an economic system or an economic plan for
a policy, adopted from a number of possible choices. That
was not the case at all. We could not think of restoring
industry without ensuring a minimum of food and fuel.
Appropriation of surpluses without remuneration—because
you can't call paper currency remuneration—was the only
answer to the task we set ourselves to preserve the remnants
of industry, to keep the workers from dispersing altogether,
and to maintain the army. We had no other way out.
That is what we are discarding, and I have already told
you what we are adopting. The tax is to help us make the
transition. If it were possible to restore our industry faster,
then perhaps, with a better harvest, we could make an
earlier transition to the exchange of manufactured goods
for agricultural products.

Many of you may remember that the question of switching efforts to the economic front was raised at the Ninth
Party Congress. At the time, all attention was focused on
it. We thought that we had finished with the war: after
all, we did offer bourgeois Poland incredibly favourable
peace terms. But the peace was disrupted, and there followed the Polish war and its sequel—Wrangel, etc. The
period between the Ninth and the Tenth congresses was
almost entirely a period of war. You know that we signed
a final peace treaty with the Poles only very recently;
and a few days ago we signed a peace agreement with
the Turks, which alone will rid us of interminable wars in
the Caucasus. We have only now concluded a trade agreement with Britain, which is of world-wide significance.
Only now has Britain been compelled to enter into

commercial relations with us. America, for example, still
refuses to do so. This will give you an idea of how hard
it was for us to extricate ourselves from the war. Had we
been able to realise the anticipations of the Ninth Congress
right away, we would, of course, have been able to provide
a much larger quantity of goods.

Today I had a visit from Comrade Korolyov of
Ivanovo-Voznesensk, our most industrial, proletarian, Red
gubernia. He gave me some facts and figures. In the first
year only six factories were in operation, and not one of
them ran for a month without stoppages. Industry was
grinding down to a standstill. During the past year, 22
factories were started for the first time, some running for
several months, others up to half a year, without stoppages. The planned target was set at 150 million arshins,
and according to the latest figures they produced 117
million arshins, getting only half the fuel they had been
allocated. That is how production plans were disrupted,
not only in Ivanovo-Voznesensk, but all over Russia. This
was due to a large extent to the decline of peasant farming, to loss of cattle, and the impossibility of transporting
a sufficient quantity of firewood to the railway stations
and river wharves, all of which gave Ivanovo-Voznesensk
less firewood, less peat, and less oil than it should have
had. The miracle is that, with only half the fuel they should
have got, they turned out 117 million arshins of the planned
150 million. They increased the productivity of labour and
transferred the workers to the best factories, obtaining a
high percentage of output. Here is a pretty good example,
on our own doorstep, illustrating our position. The Ninth
Congress fixed the textile target output at over 600 million
arshins, but we produced less than one-third of this because
even Ivanovo-Voznesensk Gubernia, which proved to be
the best, made only 117 million arshins. Picture to yourselves Russia's millions and these 117 million arshins of
cotton goods! This is poverty! The rehabilitation of industry lagged on such a scale that by the spring of 1921 it
seemed to be quite hopeless. We had to have a huge army,
and it was built up to several millions. Because of the
dislocation of transport, it was very hard to demobilise it
quickly in the winter. We did it only by a supreme effort.

That was the situation we faced. Was there any other way out but to cut food appropriations to the limit, taking 240 million poods of grain instead of 423 million? That is the least we must collect with a medium harvest, if we are to get by. If we are to have more, we must give peasant farming an opportunity to revive. This requires some measures, and the best one, of course, would be to restore large-scale industry. The best and the only economically correct measure would be to increase industrial output and give the peasant more of the things he needs, not only cotton goods for the farmer and his family, but also badly needed machines and implements, even if they are of the simplest kind. But the metal industry was in the same state as the textile industry. That was the situation we faced. We failed to restore industry after the Ninth Congress because we were hit by a year of war, fuel shortage, lack of transport facilities, and the prostration of peasant farming. What can be done to give the utmost assistance to peasant farming? Only a reduction of food appropriations and their conversion into a tax of 240 million poods, given a medium harvest, and even less, if the harvest is bad. The peasant must be sure that after paying a certain amount, fixed at the minimum level, he will be absolutely free to grow as much as he can and use the rest of his products to get what he needs and improve his farm not only with the help of industry, which would be the best and most rational way, but would take more resources than we now command. The tax is fixed at the minimum, and its enforcement in the localities will stimulate small industry, for we cannot set large-scale industry to rights as soon as we should like. This has been proved by the Ivanovo-Voznesensk programme, which yielded the largest portion of what we had planned for. We must wait another year until fuel stocks are large enough to ensure the operation of all the factories. We shall be lucky to do it in a year, or even two. Can we assure the peasant of supplies? We can, if the harvest turns out to be a good one.

When the question of the tax in kind was being decided at the Party Congress the delegates were given a pamphlet by Comrade Popov, Director of our Central Statistical Board, on grain output in Russia. An enlarged edition will be

published within a few days, and all of you should read it.
It gives an idea of grain production, with the figures
calculated from the returns of our census, which gave us the
exact figures of the population and an estimate of the size
of farms. It says that with a yield of 40 poods per dessiatine,
peasant farming on Soviet Russia's present area could
provide 500 million poods of surplus grain that would
cover the 350 million poods required by the urban population and leave us a fund for foreign trade and the improvement of peasant farming. The harvest was so bad that the
yield was no more than an average of twenty-eight poods
per dessiatine. This produced a deficit. If we accept the
statisticians' figure of requirements at eighteen poods per
head, we must subtract three poods per head and oblige
every peasant to go on short rations in order to keep the
army and the industrial workers on half-rations. In that
situation, we could do nothing but reduce the surplus
appropriations to a minimum and convert them into a tax.
We must concentrate on improving small peasant farming.
We had no cotton goods, machines or other goods produced
by large factories to give the peasant farmers, but it is a
problem requiring urgent solution, and we have to solve it
with the aid of small industry. We should have some results
from the new measure this very first year.

Now, why is peasant farming the focus? Because it alone
can give us the food and the fuel we need. If the working
class, as the ruling class exercising its dictatorship, wants
to run the economy properly, it must say: the crisis of
peasant farming is the weakest spot. It must be remedied,
and another start made on the revival of large-scale industry, so that in Ivanovo-Voznesensk district, for instance,
all 70 factories—and not just 22—are running again. These
large factories will then satisfy national demand, and the
working class will deliver the goods to the peasants in
exchange for farm produce, instead of taking it in the form
of a tax. That is the transition we are making, and the
price is short rations all round, if we are to save those who
alone can keep what is left of industry and the railways
going, and the army in the field to fight off the whiteguards.

Our grain appropriations were maligned by the Mensheviks, who said that the Soviet power had given the

population nothing but grain appropriations, want and destruction. They gloated over the fact that after the partial restoration of peace, after the end of the Civil War, the swift rehabilitation of our industry had proved to be impossible. But even the richest countries will take years to get their industry going full blast again. Even a rich country like France will take a long time to revive her industry, and she did not suffer as much from the war as we did, because only a small part of her territory was devastated. The astonishing thing is that in the first year of a partial peace we were able to start 22 factories out of 70 in Ivanovo-Voznesensk, and to produce 117 million arshins of cotton goods out of an anticipated 150 million. The grain appropriations had once been inevitable, but now we have had to change our food policy: we have had to switch from the surplus appropriation system to the tax. This will undoubtedly improve the peasant's condition, and give him an assurance and a sense of certainty that he will be free to exchange all his available grain surplus at least for local handicraft wares. This explains why the Soviet government must conduct an economic policy on these lines.

Now, in conclusion, let me explain how this policy can be reconciled with the communist standpoint and how it has come about that the communist Soviet power is promoting a free market. Is it good from the standpoint of communism? To answer this question we must make a careful examination of the changes that have taken place in peasant farming. First, we witnessed the assault of the whole of the peasantry on the rule of the landowners, who were fought both by the poor peasants and the kulaks, although, of course, their motives were different: the kulaks wanted to take the land away from the landowners to develop their own farms. That was when it became clear that the kulaks and the poor peasants had divergent interests and aims. In the Ukraine, this divergence of interests is still much more in evidence than it is over here. The poor peasants could derive very little direct benefit from the transfer of land from the landowners to themselves, because they had neither the materials nor the implements. We find the poor peasants organising to prevent the kulaks from seizing the land taken away from the landowners. The Soviet government helped the Poor Peasants' Committees that sprang up in Russia and in the Ukraine.[91] As a result, the middle peasants have become the predominant element in the rural areas. We know this from statistics, and everyone who lives in the country knows it from his own observations. The extremes of kulak and poor have been rounded off, and the majority of the population have come closer to the status of the middle peasant. If we want to raise the productivity of our peasant farming we must reckon chiefly with the middle peasant. The Communist Party has had to shape its policy accordingly.

Since the middle peasants now predominate in the rural areas, we must help them to improve their farming; moreover, we must make the same demands on them as we do on the workers. The principal question discussed at the last Party Congress was that of food propaganda: concentrate on the economic front; raise the productivity of labour and increase output! No progress is possible unless these tasks are fulfilled. If we say this to the worker, we must say as much to the peasant, but will demand in return that, after paying the tax, he should enlarge his farm, in the knowledge that no more will be exacted from him and that he will be free to use the whole of his surplus to develop his farm. Consequently, the change in policy in respect of the peasants is due to the change in their status. There are more middle peasants in the make-up of the rural areas and we must reckon with this, if we are to boost the productive forces.

Let me also remind you of the arguments I had with the "Left Communist" group in 1918, after the conclusion of the Brest-Litovsk peace.[92] Those who were in the Party at the time will remember that some Communists feared that the conclusion of the Brest Peace would disrupt all communist policy. In the course of the argument with these comrades I said, among other things: State capitalism is nothing to fear in Russia; it would be a step forward. That sounded very strange: How could state capitalism be a step forward in a Soviet socialist republic? I replied: Take a close look at the actual economic relations in Russia. We find at least five different economic systems, or structures, which, from bottom to top, are: first, the patriarchal economy, when the peasant farms produce only for their own needs, or are in a nomadic or semi-nomadic state, and we happen to have any number of these; second, small commodity production, when goods are sold on the market; third, capitalist production, the emergence of capitalists, small private capital; fourth, state capitalism, and fifth, socialism. And if we do take a close look we shall find all these relations in Russia's economic system even today. In no circumstances must we forget what we have occasion to see very often, namely, the socialist attitude of workers at state factories, who collect fuel, raw materials and food, or try to arrange a proper distribution of manufactured goods among the peasants and to deliver them with their own transport facilities. That is socialism. But alongside is small enterprise, which very often exists independently of it. Why can it do so? Because large-scale industry is not back on its feet, and socialist factories are getting perhaps only one-tenth of what they should be getting. In consequence, small enterprise remains independent of the socialist factories. The incredible havoc, the shortage of fuel, raw materials and transport facilities allow small enterprise to exist separately from socialism. I ask you: What is state capitalism in these circumstances? It is the amalgamation of small-scale production. Capital amalgamates small enterprises and grows out of them. It is no use closing our eyes to this fact. Of course, a free market means a growth of capitalism; there's no getting away from the fact. And anyone who tries to do so will be deluding himself. Capitalism will emerge wherever there is small enterprise and free exchange. But are we to be afraid of it, if we have control of the factories, transport and foreign trade? Let me repeat what I said then: I believe it to be incontrovertible that we need have no fear of this capitalism. Concessions are that kind of capitalism.

We have been trying hard to conclude concession agreements, but, unfortunately, have not yet concluded a single one. Nevertheless, we are nearer to them now than we were several months ago, when we last discussed concessions. What are concessions from the standpoint of economic relations? They are state capitalism. The Soviet government concludes an agreement with a capitalist. Under it, the latter is provided with certain things: raw materials, mines, oilfields, minerals, or, as was the case in one of the last proposals, even a special factory (the ball-bearing project of a Swedish enterprise). The socialist state gives the capitalist its means of production such as factories, mines and materials. The capitalist operates as a contractor leasing socialist means of production, making a profit on his capital and delivering a part of his output to the socialist state.

Why is it that we badly need such an arrangement? Because it gives us, all at once, a greater volume of goods which we need but cannot produce ourselves. That is how we get state capitalism. Should it scare us? No, it should not, because it is up to us to determine the extent of the concessions. Take oil concessions. They will give us millions of poods of paraffin oil right away, and that is more than we produce ourselves. This is to our advantage, because in exchange for the paraffin oil—and not paper money—the peasant will give us his grain surplus, and we shall immediately be able to improve the situation in the whole country. That is why the capitalism that is bound to grow out of a free market holds no terrors for us. It will be the result of growing trade, the exchange of manufactured goods, even if produced by small industry, for agricultural produce.

Today's law tells you that workers in some industries are to be issued a certain part of the articles manufactured in their factories in the form of a bonus in kind which they can exchange for grain. For example, provided they satisfy the requirements of the state, textile workers will receive a part of the textile goods they manufacture and will be able to exchange them for grain. This must be done to improve the condition of the workers and of the peasants as soon as possible. We cannot do this on a nation-wide scale, but it must be done at all costs. That is why we do not shut our eyes to the fact that a free market entails some development of capitalism, and we say: This capitalism will be under the control and surveillance of the state. We need have no fear of it because the workers' state has taken possession of the factories and railways. It will help to stimulate the economic exchange of peasant produce for the manufactures of neighbouring craftsmen, who will satisfy some, if not all, of the peasants' requirements in manufactured goods. The peasant economy will improve, and that is something we need to do desperately. Let small industry grow to some extent and let state capitalism develop—the Soviet power need have no fear of that. We must face the facts squarely and call a spade a spade, but we must also control and determine the limits of this development.

Concessions are nothing to be afraid of. There is nothing terrible about giving the concessionaires a few factories and retaining the bulk in our own hands. Of course, it would be absurd for the Soviet power to hand out the bulk of its property in the form of concessions. That would not be concessions, but a return to capitalism. There is nothing to fear in concessions so long as we retain possession of all the state enterprises and weigh up exactly and strictly the concessions we grant, and the terms and scale on which we grant them. Growing capitalism will be under control and supervision, while political power will remain in the hands of the working class and of the workers' state. The capital which will exist in the form of concessions and the capital which will inevitably grow through the medium of the co-operatives and a free market, have no terrors for us. We must try to develop and improve the condition of the peasantry, and make a great effort to have this benefit the working class. We shall be able to do all that can be done to improve peasant farming and develop local trade more quickly with concessions than without them, while planning our national economy for a much faster rehabilitation of large-scale socialist industry. We shall be able to do this more quickly with the help of a rested and recuperated peasant economy than with the absolutely poverty-stricken peasant farming we have had up to now.

That is what I have to say on the communist appreciation of this policy, on why it was necessary, and why, if properly applied, it will bring improvement immediately, or, at all events, more quickly than if it had not been applied.

Pravda Nos. 81, 82 and 83,   Published according
   April 15, 16 and 17, 1921   to the *Pravda* text

MESSAGE OF GREETINGS
TO THE CONFERENCE OF REPRESENTATIVES
OF WOMEN'S DEPARTMENTS
OF THE PEOPLES OF SOVIET REGIONS
AND REPUBLICS IN THE EAST[93]

I deeply regret that I am unable to attend your conference because of the pressure of work. Please accept my heartfelt greetings and best wishes of success in your work, particularly in preparing for the forthcoming First All-Russia Non-Party Congress of Women of the East, which, correctly prepared and conducted, must greatly help *the cause of awakening the women of the East and uniting them organisationally.*

Lenin

Pravda No. 77, April 10, 1921

Published according to the *Pravda* text collated with the original signed by Lenin

REPORT ON CONCESSIONS
AT A MEETING OF THE COMMUNIST GROUP
OF THE ALL-RUSSIA CENTRAL COUNCIL
OF TRADE UNIONS
APRIL 11, 1921[94]

Comrades, the concessions question has, rather unex-
pectedly, brought out some differences among us, for it
appeared to have been finally settled in principle as long
ago as the autumn of last year, and when the Council of
People's Commissars issued its concessions decree on November 23, there was no sign of protest, or of any disagreement, in Party circles, among the responsible workers, at
any rate. You are, of course, aware that the Party Congress
had to take a special decision confirming the concessions
decree and specifically extending it to cover any concessions in Baku and Grozny.[95] This had to be done at the Party
Congress to prevent any vacillation on policy in the Central
Committee, whose division on this very question has to
some extent proved to be quite out of line with earlier groupings, but which is largely connected with Baku. Some
Baku comrades resented the idea that Baku too—or, perhaps,
specifically—is to have concessions, and that it is desirable to
lease out a major part of its oilfields. Their arguments were
highly diverse, and ranged from references to their own
"exploration", which could be done without any foreigners,
to assertions that the old workers, who spent a lifetime
fighting the capitalists, refuse to be saddled with their yoke
once again, etc.

I am not going to say offhand how much of these arguments was based on general principles and how much on
Baku "patriotism" and localism. Let me say for my part
that I have opposed this view most vigorously in the belief
that if we do not manage to conduct a concessions policy
and attract foreign capital to our concessions, we can hardly

consider any serious practical measures to improve our economic position. We cannot seriously entertain the idea of an immediate improvement of the economic situation, unless we operate a policy of concessions, unless we discard our prejudices, our local patriotism, discard to some extent our craft patriotism, and to some extent the idea that we can do our own "exploring". We must be prepared for inconveniences, hardships and sacrifices; we must be ready to break our habits and possibly our addictions as well, for the sole purpose of working a marked change and improvement in the economic state of the key industries. This must be done at all costs.

The Party Congress concentrated on the policy in respect of the peasants and on the tax in kind, which has, in general, a high legislative priority and is, in particular, central to the Party's political efforts. In the context of both these issues, we have become aware that we are unable to boost productivity in large-scale industry as swiftly as the satisfaction of peasant needs demands, without the makeshifts of unrestricted trade and free production. These are the two crutches we must now use to move on, for, otherwise, as everyone in his right mind will see, we shall be unable to keep abreast of developments. After all, the situation is worsening, if only because the floating this spring has been largely hampered by various factors, chiefly the weather. There is a looming fuel crisis. The spring also holds out the threat of another crop failure, again because of the weather; this is liable to create a fodder shortage, which may, in its turn, still further reduce the fuel supply. If on top of this we happen to have a drought, the crisis threatens to be truly exceptional. We must understand that in these conditions what the Programme says—chiefly about the great need to increase the food supply—is not intended for admiration or for a show of great love for various resolutions (which the Communists have been doing with great zeal), but as a call to increase the quantity of foodstuffs at any cost. That is something we cannot do without the help of foreign capital. This should be plain to everyone who takes a realistic view of things. That is why the concessions question became important enough to be dealt with by the Party Congress.

After a short debate, the Council of People's Commissars adopted the basic principles of concessions agreements.[96] I shall now read them and underscore those which are of especial importance or have given rise to disagreements. We cannot seriously entertain the idea of economic development unless all members of the Party, specially the leaders of the trade union movement, that is, of the organised masses of the proletariat—its organised majority—understand the present situation and draw the appropriate conclusions. I shall read out the basic principles of the concessions agreement one by one, as they were adopted by the Council of People's Commissars. Let me add that we have not yet concluded a single concessions agreement. We have already given expression to our disagreements of principle—we are past masters at that sort of thing—but have not yet secured any concessions. I suppose this will make some people happy, which is unfortunate, because if we fail to attract capital to our concessions, we shall merely prove that we are poor businessmen. But then, of course, the Communists can always have a field day with resolutions, filling up all the stocks of paper that we have. Here is Point One:

"1. The concessionaire shall improve the condition of the workers employed at the concession enterprises (as compared with that of other workers employed at similar enterprises in the area) up to the average standard abroad."

We have inserted this basic provision in the agreement to bring out the gist of the matter at once for our Communists and chiefs of economic agencies. What is the most important aspect of any concession? It is, of course, an increase in the quantity of goods. That is self-evident. But what is also highly—if not much more—important is that we can secure an immediate improvement in the condition of the workers employed at the oil concession enterprises. These provisions of the concession agreement were adopted after several discussions, in particular, on the basis of the talks the plenipotentiaries of the R.S.F.S.R., specifically Comrade Krasin, have had with some of the financial magnates of modern imperialism. Let me say—and you are of course all aware of this—that the great majority of our Communists have a book knowledge of capitalism and finance capital; they may even have written a pamphlet or two on the subject, but 99 per cent of them don't know how to do business with financial magnates and, I'm afraid, will never learn.

In that respect, Comrade Krasin has had some exceptional experience, for he has made a study of the practices and organisation of industry in Germany and Russia. We informed him of these terms, and he replied that they were, on the whole, acceptable. The concessionaire is above all duty bound to improve the condition of the workers. This very point was discussed by Krasin in his exploratory talks with an oil king, and the West-European capitalists were quite clear on the point that, the condition of the workers being what it is, it was absolutely impossible to expect greater productivity. The proviso that the concessionaire must improve the workers' condition is not a humanitarian but a purely business proposition. Point Two:

"2. Account shall be taken of the lower productivity of the Russian worker and provision made for the possibility of a revision of the Russian worker's rate of labour productivity, depending on the improvement of his living conditions."

We had to make this reservation to prevent a one-sided reading of the clause. All these provisions are rules and directives for any representatives of the Soviet power who may have to deal with the concessions, and are the basis on which the agreements are to be worked out. We have drafts of an oil agreement, an agreement on ball-bearing plants, a draft timber concession, and an agreement on Kamchatka, which is being aired for a long time but is not being implemented for various reasons. Point Two was required to prevent a literal reading of Point One. We must consider the fact that labour productivity will not rise until the workers' condition improves. Refusal to consider this would be so unbusiness-like that the capitalist would not even bother to negotiate. Point Three:

"3. It shall be the duty of the concessionaire to supply the workers employed at the concession enterprises with the necessary means of subsistence from abroad, selling them to the workers at no higher than cost price plus a certain percentage for overhead expenses."

There was a proposal to set the figure at 10 per cent, but it was discarded in the final discussion. The important

thing here is that we stipulate the supply of the means of
subsistence for the workers from abroad. We know that
with the present state of peasant farming and the fuel
problem we shall be unable, within the next few years, to
effect a radical improvement in the workers' condition, and,
consequently, to increase labour productivity. It is, therefore, necessary for the concessionaire to include in the
agreement a provision covering the supply of all the means
of consumption from abroad, something he can easily do,
and we already have the tentative consent of some capitalist sharks on this point. The concessionaires will accept
these terms because they are extremely anxious to obtain
the tremendously valuable raw materials. For them the
supply of raw materials is a prime necessity. Whether these
priority enterprises will be employing 10,000, 20,000 or
30,000 workers, the concessionaires will have no trouble in
obtaining the necessaries for the workers, considering the
ties between modern syndicates and trusts, for very few
capitalists today are not syndicated and trustified, and all
large enterprises are based on monopoly, instead of the free
market; consequently, they can always block supplies of
raw materials and foodstuffs for other capitalists and obtain
all they require under all manner of provisional agreements.
These syndicates operate with hundreds of millions of
dollars. They will have vast stocks of food at their disposal,
and will, consequently, be able to obtain foodstuffs and
other necessaries for several tens of thousands of workers,
and transport them to Russia.

They will not find it an economic problem at all. They
will regard these enterprises as being on the priority list—
they will make a profit of 100, if not 1,000, per cent—and
supply them with food. I repeat, that will be no economic
problem for them at all. We must put at the heart of our
concessions policy the task of improving the condition
of the workers at the enterprises of the first category, and
then at the rest. Here is Point Four:

"4. It shall also be the duty of the concessionaire, in the
event of a request on the part of the R.S.F.S.R. Government,
to import another 50-100 per cent over and above the supplies he brings in for the workers employed at the concession enterprises, handing it over to the R.S.F.S.R. Govern-

ment in return for a payment of similar size (cost plus a certain percentage for overhead expenses). The R.S.F.S.R. Government shall have the right to meet this payment with a part of the product extracted by the concessionaire (that is, to deduct it from its own share)."

This stipulation was also accepted by the financial magnates in the exploratory talks because they put the concession enterprises on the priority list.

They will be in a position to monopolise the marketing of the oil which they can obtain from us, and this is why they can supply foodstuffs not only to the workers employed at their enterprises but also a certain percentage over and above that. A comparison of this clause with Point One shows that the pivot of our concessions policy is improvement of the condition of the workers, initially of those employed at the concession enterprises, and then, to a somewhat lesser extent, of the other workers as well, with some of the consumer goods being obtained from abroad. Even if we had the wherewithal to pay for them, we ourselves are not in a position to purchase them in the international market. You may have the currency, say, gold, but you must bear in mind that there is no free market, for it is all, or nearly all, controlled by the syndicates, cartels and trusts, which are ruled by their imperialist profits. They will supply consumer goods only to workers of their own enterprises, and not for those of others, because the old capitalism—meaning the free market—is no longer there. That shows the essence of our concessions policy in the context of the present conditions of finance capital and the behemoth struggle between the trusts. The concessions policy is an alliance concluded by one side against another, and so long as we are not strong enough, we must play off their hostile rivalry, so as to hold out until the victory of the international revolution. They can assure the workers of their maintenance because it is no trouble at all for a large modern enterprise to supply an extra 20,000 or 30,000 workers. This would allow us to meet the expenditure with raw materials, say, oil. If we were able to pay for this additional quantity of necessaries for the workers with an additional quantity of timber or ore—our chief resources—we should be in a position to start by

improving the condition of the workers employed at the
concession enterprises and use what is left to improve,
to a lesser extent, the condition of other workers. Point
Five:

"5. It shall be the duty of the concessionaire to abide
by the laws of the R.S.F.S.R., in particular, those relating
to working conditions, terms of payment, etc.; and enter
into agreements with the trade unions (in the event of the
concessionaire's demand we are prepared to add that under
such agreements both parties shall be bound by the average
norm of American or West-European workers)."

This reservation is being made to remove any fears the
capitalists may have in respect of our trade unions. We say
that agreements must be entered into with our trade unions
because their participation is stipulated by all the relevant
laws—all essential laws stipulate the participation of trade
unions which enjoy statutory status in accordance with
socialist principles. The well-informed capitalist is aware
that the trade unions are guided by Communist groups
and, through them, by the Party, and he would be highly
suspicious if we told him that he would have to enter into
agreements with our trade unions, because he would be
apprehensive of all sorts of absurdities on the part of these
Communists, and would, in consequence, make the most
incredible demands. Such fears are quite natural from the
capitalist standpoint. That is why we must say that we
favour a business agreement—otherwise there is nothing to
discuss. That is why we say we are prepared to make that
addendum. We are prepared to accept, for ourselves and our
trade unions, a norm equal to the average American or West-
European labour norm. Otherwise, I repeat, there can be
no question at all of any agreement adapted to capitalist
relations. Point Six:

"6. It shall be the duty of the concessionaire strictly
to observe the scientific and technical regulations in
conformity with Russian and foreign legislation (details to
be stated in each agreement)."

This point is to be elaborated in the agreement in particular detail. The oil agreement, for instance, contains
10 clauses setting forth and describing detailed scientific
regulations. Inability to attend to the proper scientific

exploitation of labour-power, as of the land, is the hallmark of capitalist economic operations. Scientific and technical regulations are a way of overcoming it. Incorrect or insufficiently correct working of oilfields is known to result in their flooding. It is clearly very important for us to obtain the technical equipment. You will recall that *The Plan for the Electrification of Russia* estimated just how much of that equipment we needed. I do not remember the exact figure, but the overall expenditures for electrification were estimated at 17,000 million gold rubles, with the priority projects taking about a decade to fulfil. We expect to cover up to 11,000 million from our own resources—gold and exports—which leaves 6,000 million outstanding. The authors of the plan say that we shall either have to borrow or lease. The deficit has to be made good. The plan was worked out for the whole Republic by the best brains and provides for a balanced development of all branches of industry. The chief problem is fuel and its most economic, rational and efficient use in the key industries. We should be unable to solve it if we did not have any concessions or credit facilities. These conditions may suddenly turn out to be non-existent, and that at the most welcome moment, say, after a large strike, like the one now on in Britain, or the one which was recently defeated in Germany.[97] But a successful strike and a successful revolution will come in the wake of an unsuccessful one, and we shall then find ourselves with socialist, instead of capitalist, relations.

Stoppages in oil extraction may prove to be disastrous. The capitalists have failed to reach Baku's 1905 rate. It turns out that the danger of flooding is also reckoned with abroad, for instance, in California and Rumania. Insufficient pump-off of water results in ever greater flooding.

There are detailed regulations on this score in Russian and foreign legislation. When dealing with this matter in Baku, we sought the opinion of our experts on Rumanian and Californian legislation. If we are to safeguard our oil resources, we must see that the scientific and technical regulations are observed. If we are to lease, say, a tract of forest we must see that the lumbering is done in a proper manner. If it should be an oil lease, we must stipulate measures to prevent flooding. In each case, there must be observance of scientific and technical regulations and rational exploitation. Where are the regulations to come from? They are to be taken from Russian and foreign legislation, and this will allay any suspicions that they are our own invention, in which case no capitalist will bother to negotiate with us. We intend to take what there is in Russian and foreign legislation. If we take the best of what there is in Russian and any foreign legislation, we shall have a basis to guarantee the standards attained by the leading capitalists. These are well-known business standards borrowed from capitalist practice, and not a Communist flight of fancy which the capitalists fear most of all. We guarantee that none of the terms, aspects or clauses of our concession agreement will go beyond the framework of capitalist legislation. We must never lose sight of this key proposition. We must take capitalist relationships as a basis to show that the capitalists will find these terms acceptable and profitable, but we, for our part, must turn them to good advantage. Otherwise, it is a waste of time to talk about concessions. But to return to what is recognised in capitalist legislation. Advanced capitalism is known to be superior to our own industry in technical organisation and improvements. For that reason, we are not confining ourselves to Russian legislation, and in the case of oil we have started to borrow from Russian, Rumanian and Californian legislation. We are entitled to take any law, which will dispel any suspicions of arbitrariness or whim. That will be easily understood by the modern advanced capitalist and financial magnate, in fact, finance capital as a whole, for our terms and standards will conform to those prevalent abroad, and we are proposing them with an eye to the business practices of capitalism. In this case, we are not indulging in any flights of fancy, but are setting ourselves the practical goal of improving our industry and raising it to the levels of modern advanced capitalism. Anyone who has an idea of the state of our industry will see that this will be a tremendous improvement. If we were to do this even in respect of a certain section of our industry, say, one-tenth of it, we should still be taking a great step forward, which would be feasible for them, and highly desirable for us. Point Seven:

"7. A rule similar to that set forth in Point Four shall also apply to the equipment imported by the concessionaire from abroad."

Point Four says that the concessionaire shall be bound, in the event the clause is written into the agreement, to import a certain quantity of goods for sale, against a special payment, over and above what he imports for his own operations. If the capitalist should import improved types of bores and tools for himself, we shall be entitled to demand that he import, say, an extra 25 per cent for us, over and above the bores he imports for himself, the payment arrangements to be the same as those specified in Point Four, that is, cost plus a definite percentage for overhead expenses.

The future is very bright, but we should never confuse our activity in these two planes: on the one hand, there is the agitation which brings nearer this future, and on the other, the ability now to adapt ourselves to and exist in the capitalist encirclement. If we fail to do that we might find ourselves in the position of one who has had his chance but was not alert enough to act in time. We must manage, by taking advantage of the peculiarities of the capitalist world and the capitalist avidity for raw materials, to derive all the benefits that would help us to consolidate our economic positions among the capitalists, strange as that may sound. The task seems to be an odd one: How can a socialist republic improve its positions with capitalist support? We had an instance of this during the war. We did not win the war because we were stronger, but because, while being weaker, we played off the enmity between the capitalist states. Either we now succeed in playing off the rivalry between the trusts, or we shall find ourselves unadapted to capitalist conditions and unable to exist in the capitalist encirclement. Point Eight:

"8. A special clause in each agreement shall regulate the question of payment to the workers employed at the concession enterprises of wages in foreign currency, special coupons, Soviet currency, etc."

You see that in this case we are prepared to accept payment in any currency, whether foreign or Soviet, or in coupons, and show goodwill by being prepared to consider any of the businessmen's proposals. Of the concrete proposals there is the one Vanderlip made to our representatives. He said: "I should like to pay the workers an average wage of, say, a dollar and a half a day. On my concession territory I would set up stores carrying all the goods the workers may need, and these will be available to those who receive special coupons; these coupons will be issued only to workers who are employed at my concession enterprises." Whether things work out as he says, remains to be seen, but we find this acceptable in principle. A great many difficulties naturally arise. It is, of course, no easy task to harmonise a concession geared to capitalist production with the Soviet standpoint, and every effort of that kind is, as I have said, a continuation of the struggle between capitalism and socialism. This struggle has assumed new forms, but it remains a struggle nonetheless. Every concessionaire remains a capitalist, and he will try to trip up the Soviet power, while we, for our part, must try to make use of his rapacity. We say: "We shall not grudge him even 150 per cent in profits, provided the condition of our workers is improved." That is the pivot of the struggle. In this sphere, of course, you need to be even more skilled than in struggling for the conclusion of a peace treaty. The capitalist powers behind the scenes take part in the struggle for the conclusion of any peace treaty. There was a foreign power pulling the strings behind each of the countries with whom we have signed a peace treaty—Latvia, Finland and Poland. We had to conclude these treaties in such a way that, on the one hand, they allowed the bourgeois republics to exist, and on the other, they secured advantages for the Soviet power from the standpoint of world diplomacy. Every peace treaty with a capitalist power is a record of certain war clauses. In much the same way, each clause of a concession agreement records some aspect of a war, and we should organise things in such a way as to safeguard our own interests in that war. This can be done because the capitalist will be receiving big profits from the concession enterprise, while we shall be obtaining some improvement in the condition of our workers, and some increase in the quantity of goods from our share in the output. If the wages should be paid in foreign currency, this will give rise to a number

of complex problems: how is this currency to be exchanged
for Soviet currency? how are we to fight speculation? etc.
We have accepted the idea that we have an answer to all
these problems, and need not fear any of them. This point
tells the capitalists that they are free to invent anything
they like. It makes no difference to us whether you bring
in the goods and sell them for special coupons, on special
terms, or only upon presentation of special certificates
issued personally to workers employed at the concession.
We shall manage to adapt ourselves to any terms in such
a way as to fight the capitalists on these terms and secure
a certain improvement in the condition of our workers.
This is the task we have set ourselves. We can't tell how it
will be resolved in a concession agreement, for we can't
very well offer the same terms of payment in some place like
Kamchatka as over here or in Baku. If the concession should
be located in the Donets Basin, the forms of payment cannot
conceivably be the same as for one in the far North. We
are not holding down the capitalists to some specific form
of payment. Every clause of the agreement will contain an
element of struggle between capitalists and socialists. We
are not afraid of this struggle, and are sure that we shall
manage to derive every possible benefit from the concessions. Point Nine:

"9. The concessionaire shall be free to make his own
terms of employment, living conditions and remuneration
with foreign skilled workers and employees.

"The trade unions shall not have the right to demand
application of Russian pay rates or of Russian rules of
employment to that category of workers."

We believed Point Nine to be absolutely indispensable
because it would be quite absurd to expect the capitalists to
trust the Communists. This is cleary stated both from the
standpoint of principle and especially from the businessman's
standpoint. For if we insisted on trade union endorsement of
these terms of employment, if we told the capitalists that we
accepted any foreign technician or specialist but only within
the framework of the Labour Code of the R.S.F.S.R., it would
be too much to expect any of the latter to accept, and the
demand would be a mere formality. It could be said that the
government says one thing and the trade unions another,

because they are two distinct bodies, thereby leaving a legal loophole. But this was not written for lawyers but for Communists, and it was done on the basis of the decisions of the Tenth Party Congress on how to conduct the concessions policy. All of our writings, to which people in Europe have access, say that the concessions policy is being directed by the Communist Party, which is the ruling party. This has been rendered into all foreign languages, and there is no catch in it. We would not be in a position to consider any concessions policy at all, if we, being the political leadership, failed to say that in this case we were unable and unwilling to make use of our influence with the trade unions. There is no sense in teaching communism to the capitalists. We are fine Communists, but we are not going to usher in the communist order through concessions. After all, a concession is an agreement with a capitalist power. We would surely have committed to a lunatic asylum any Communist who decided to go and conclude a treaty with a capitalist power on the basis of communist principles. We would tell him that he was a fine Communist in his way but a complete flop as a diplomatist in a capitalist country. The Communist who tried to demonstrate his communism in respect of the concessions policy in an agreement would be just as near to being committed to a lunatic asylum. What you need to have is a good idea of capitalist trade, and if you haven't got it, you're no good. Either don't go in for concessions at all, or make an effort to understand that we must try to use these capitalist conditions in our own interest, by allowing the foreign technicians and workers complete freedom. That we shall not insist on any restrictions in this sphere goes without saying.

Section Three of Point Nine, which follows, does contain a restriction:

"The proportion of foreign workers and employees to Russians, both in total and within the several categories, shall be agreed upon by the parties in concluding each concession agreement separately."

We cannot, of course, object to the importation of foreign workers into areas which we are unable to supply with Russian workers, as, for instance, in the Kamchatka timber industry. In the case of, say, the mining industry, where there is a lack of drinking water or foodstuffs, and where the capitalists would wish to build, we shall also allow them to bring in the greater part. On the other hand, where Russian workers are available, we stipulate a proportion to give our workers a chance, a) to learn, and b) to improve their condition. After all, we do want our workers to benefit from an improvement of our enterprises according to the last word in capitalist technology. The capitalists have not raised any objections in principle to any of these provisions. And here is Point Ten, the last one:

"10. The concessionaire may, by agreement with the government organs of the R.S.F.S.R., be granted the right to invite highly skilled specialists from among Russian citizens, the terms of employment being agreed with central government bodies in each case."

Plainly, we cannot guarantee full scope in this respect, as we can in respect of foreign technicians and workers. In the latter case, we refrain from interfering, and they are left entirely within the framework of capitalist relations. We promise no such scope for our specialists and technicians, for we cannot have our best men working at the concession enterprises. We have no desire to shut off all access for them to that area, but there must be supervision over the performance of the agreement from above and from below. The workers, members of the Communist Party, who will be employed at these enterprises, must supervise the performance of the terms of the agreement, both in respect of their technical training and observance of our laws. There were no objections in principle on this point in the exploratory talks with some of the magnates of modern capitalism.

All these points have been confirmed by the Council of People's Commissars, and I hope they give you a clear picture of the concessions policy we intend to conduct.

Each concession will undoubtedly be a new kind of war— an economic war—the fight carried into another plane. This calls for adaptation, but one that is in line with the Party Congress. If we are to attain our goal, we must have a respite and must be prepared to make sacrifices and endure hardships. Our goal is: in the capitalist encirclement

to make use of the greed of the capitalists for profit and the
rivalry between the trusts, so as to create conditions for
the existence of the socialist republic, which cannot exist
without having ties with the rest of the world, and must, in
the present circumstances, adjust its existence to capitalist relations. There is the question of actual terms. For
oil agreements, they are as follows: from one-quarter to
one-third of the whole of Grozny and of the whole of Baku.
We have worked out our share of the output: we shall be
retaining from 30 to 40 per cent of the oil extracted. We
have inserted a commitment to increase output within a
certain period to, say, 100 million, and another commitment to extend the oil pipeline from Grozny and Petrovsk
to Moscow. Whether we shall have to make any extra pay-
ments is to be stipulated in each agreement. But we should
be quite clear on the type of agreement concluded in these
conditions. The important thing, from the trade union
standpoint, is for the Party leadership to see the specific
features of this policy and set themselves the task of securing
such concessions at any cost, in pursuance of the decisions
of the Party Congress, in the context of tasks facing the
socialist system in the capitalist encirclement. Every
concession will be a gain and an immediate improvement
in the condition of a section of the workers and peasants.
The latter will stand to gain because each concession will
mean the production of additional goods, which we are
unable to produce ourselves, and which we shall be exchanging for their products, instead of taking them through a tax.

This is a very difficult operation, especially for the organs of the Soviet power. With this point as pivotal we
must set about to secure concessions, overriding the prejudices, inertia, ingrained customs, and the inconvenience
of some workers having a bigger pay packet than the others.
We could invent any number of excuses, in the way of
objections and inconveniences, to frustrate any practical
improvement, and that is what the foreign capitalists are
really banking on. I know of no other point that has drawn
so many objections from the most intelligent writers in the
Russian whiteguard press, the men the Kronstadt events
proved to be head and shoulders above Martov and Chernov.
They are very well aware that if we fail to improve the

condition of our workers and peasants because of our prejudices, we shall multiply our difficulties and altogether
undermine the prestige of the Soviet power. You know that
we must have that improvement at all costs. We shall not
grudge the foreign capitalist even a 2,000 per cent profit,
provided we improve the condition of the workers and
peasants. It is imperative that we do it.

First published in 1932

Published according
to the verbatim report

TO THE COMRADES COMMUNISTS
OF AZERBAIJAN, GEORGIA,
ARMENIA, DAGHESTAN, AND THE MOUNTAINEER
REPUBLIC

I send my warmest greetings to the Soviet Republics of the Caucasus, and should like to express the hope that their close alliance will serve as a model of national peace, unprecedented under the bourgeoisie and impossible under the capitalist system.

But important as national peace among the workers and peasants of the Caucasian nationalities is, the maintenance and development of the Soviet power, as the transition to socialism, are even more important. The task is difficult, but fully feasible. The most important thing for its successful fulfilment is that the Communists of the Transcaucasus should be fully alive to the *singularity* of their position, and of the position of their Republics, as distinct from the position and conditions of the R.S.F.S.R.; that they should appreciate the need to refrain from copying our tactics, but thoughtfully vary them in adaptation to the differing concrete conditions.

The Soviet Republic of Russia had no outside political or military assistance. On the contrary, for years and years it fought the Entente military invasions and blockade.

The Soviet Republics of the Caucasus have had political and some military assistance from the R.S.F.S.R. This alone has made a vast difference.

Second, there is now no cause to fear any Entente invasion or military assistance to the Georgian, Azerbaijan, Armenian, Daghestan and mountaineer whiteguards. The Entente "burnt their fingers" in Russia and that will probably compel them to be more cautious for some time.

Third, the Caucasian Republics have an even more pronounced peasant character than, Russia.

Fourth, Russia has been, and to a considerable extent still is, economically isolated from the advanced capitalist countries. The Caucasus is in a position to start trading and "living together" with the capitalist West sooner and with greater ease.

These are not all the differences, but they are sufficient to demonstrate the need for different tactics.

You will need to practise more moderation and caution, and show more readiness to make concessions to the petty bourgeoisie, the intelligentsia, and particularly the peasantry. You must make the swiftest, most intense and all possible economic use of the capitalist West through a policy of concessions and trade. Oil, manganese, coal (Tkvarcheli mines) and copper are some of your immense mineral resources. You have every possibility to develop an extensive policy of concessions and trade with foreign countries.

This must be done on a wide scale, with firmness, skill and circumspection, and it must be utilised to the utmost for improving the condition of the workers and peasants, and for enlisting the intelligentsia in the work of economic construction. Through trade with Italy, America and other countries, you must exert every effort to develop the productive forces of your rich land, your water resources and irrigation which is especially important as a means of advancing agriculture and livestock farming.

What the Republics of the Caucasus can and must do, as distinct from the R.S.F.S.R., is to effect a slower, more cautious and more systematic transition to socialism. That is what you must understand, and what you must be able to carry out, as distinct from our own tactics.

We fought to make the first breach in the wall of world capitalism. The breach has been made. We have maintained our positions in a fierce and superhuman war against the Whites, the Socialist-Revolutionaries and the Mensheviks, who were supported by the Entente countries, their blockade and military assistance.

You, Comrades Communists of the Caucasus, have no need to force a breach. You must take advantage of the favourable international situation in 1921, and learn to build the new with greater caution and more method. In 1921, Europe and the world are not what they were in 1917 and 1918.

Do not copy our tactics, but analyse the reasons for their peculiar features, the conditions that gave rise to them, and their results; go beyond the letter, and apply the spirit, the essence and the lessons of the 1917-21 experience. You must make trade with the capitalist countries your economic foundation right away. The cost should be no object even if it means letting them have tens of millions' worth of valuable minerals.

You must make immediate efforts to improve the condition of the peasants and start on extensive electrification and irrigation projects. What you need most is irrigation, for more than anything else it will revive the area and regenerate it, bury the past and make the transition to socialism more certain.

I hope you will pardon my slipshod style: I have had to write the letter at very short notice, so as to send it along with Comrade Myasnikov. Once again I send my best greetings and wishes to the workers and peasants of the Soviet Republics of the Caucasus.

N. Lenin

Moscow, April 14, 1921

Pravda Gruzii No. 55,   Published according
      May 8, 1921   to the newspaper text

TO THE PETROGRAD CITY CONFERENCE OF NON-PARTY WORKERS[98]

Comrades, I very much regret that I have been unable to go to Petrograd at your invitation. I send heartfelt greetings to the non-Party conference, and I welcome your work. The assistance of the non-Party masses and co-operation with them is of especial importance today, when the bourgeoisie of the world is conducting an incredible campaign of lies against Soviet Russia, in an effort to prevent us from concluding any trade agreements with foreign countries. The Kronstadt events have brought home to the workers and peasants the fact that any shift of power in Russia tends to favour the whiteguards; no wonder Milyukov and all intelligent leaders of the bourgeoisie welcomed the Kronstadt "Soviets without the Bolsheviks" slogan.

In conveying my greetings to the non-Party conference, I should like to wish you every success in your work, and ask you to pay special attention to the present need—in fact a constant need—of drawing more non-Party workers and peasants into economic construction. A regional economic centre has been set up in Petrograd. Let us intensify our effort. Local functionaries are being vested with broader powers and should show more initiative. The non-Party people should set to work, and let us have more and more men.

Greetings,
Lenin

Written on April 14, 1921
Published in 1921

Published according
to the manuscript
Written on April 14, 1921
Published in 1921

Published according to the manuscript

PLAN OF THE PAMPHLET
THE TAX IN KIND[99]

I
Etwa*:

1. General significance of the tax.
   ⌐ Retreat? Advance? (to commodity exchange).
   │ Is it another "Brest"?
   │ *Transition from surplus-grain appropriation (appropriation of surplus stocks) to commodity exchange.*
   └ "War" Communism versus *proper* economic relations.

2. The tax and unrestricted trade.
   ⌐ The tax and unrestricted trade.
   │ ⌠ Unrestricted trade *versus* the economic base ("local trade") of small-scale economy.
   │ ⟨   "   "   versus the political power of the proletariat.
   │ ⌡   "   "   versus concessions.
   └ Scope and conditions for a free market.

3. The middle peasant. (Levelling up.)
   ⌐ Is it a stake on the kulak?
   │ or the *middle peasant*.
   │ Levelling up.
   │ The industrious peasant.
   └ Greater output.

4. Methods of transition to socialist agriculture.
   ⌐ the small peasant
   │ collective farms
   └ *electrification*.
   ⌐5.⌐ Co-operatives.

* Approximately.—*Ed.*

6.] The struggle against the evils of bureaucracy (its economic roots).

7. [*The international situation and internal relations.*

8. Party and political crises (1920-21).

|Mensheviks+Socialist-Revolutionaries+anarchists
|(Kronstadt).

9. |*"Agreement"* with the peasantry? or *dictatorship*?

10. |Non-Party conferences.

II

Plan of Pamphlet:

To convey the meaning more precisely:

The substitution of a tax for the appropriation system in view of the general tasks and conditions of the present political situation.

h
a
r
d
!

The substitution of a tax for the appropriation system in view of the specific conditions of the present political situation.

The substitution of a tax for surplus-grain appropriation and agreement with the peasantry (or the tasks of a workers' government in a peasant country) and the tasks of the working class in respect of the peasantry.

The substitution of a tax for the appropriation system, its significance in principle: from "War" Communism to a *proper* socialist foundation.

The economic *essence* and foundation of socialism is neither appropriation nor tax, but exchange of the products of large-scale ("socialised") industry for peasant produce.

The appropriation system is not an "ideal", but a sad and bitter necessity. The opposite view is a dangerous mistake.

The appropriation system and the "apparatus". We should have perished long ago but for the "apparatus". Unless we wage a systematic and persevering struggle to improve it we shall perish before we manage to lay the foundation of socialism.

The alliance of the workers and peasants = α and ω of the Soviet power. "Necessary and adequate" condition for its stability.

This alliance against Denikin & Co. is *not the same* as the alliance (the same one) in *economic* organisation.

> The first = bourgeois revolution.
> The second = socialist revolution.

Transition from war to construction.

Ninth Congress 1920 (cf. April 1918) versus Tenth Congress (March 1921).

Switch from appropriation to regular commodity exchange.

The tax is in principle compatible with a free market in grain and other products.

Formal democracy versus the reality of class relations over the tax and other similar questions.

Coercion + persuasion (in appropriation)—in the tax— in "commodity exchange".

How much "free trade" is there to be? *After* paying the tax.

Scope for experiment, practice. Small trade	Tasks of local officials. Tasks of local authorities.

Type of economic relations or the economic system *before* the proletarian revolution in a number of major countries = concentration at the top

unrestricted peasant trade at the bottom . . .

a species of *state* capitalism (cf. April 1918).

"Stake" on the middle peasant? On the kulak? Restoration of bourgeois relationships?

Levelling up of the rural areas

"the poor peasants"
{
were given an equalitarian redistribution
" " landowners' land
" " opportunity to take from the kulaks
" " extraordinary assistance by the state.

The *pivot and touchstone* will now be (is) an increase in products (cf. Programme of the R.C.P.).[100] *Inde**: the "stake" on the middle peasant in agriculture.

The industrious peasant as the "central figure" of our economic revival.

Individual commodity exchange.

Role of the collective farms: many stupid things have been done. Prosecution for failure to implement the law *and incompetence* (three years).
Is socialism to fear the "individualism" of the peasant and his "free trade"? No.

Electrification: the yardstick. A long-range plan, but a *plan* and (ergo) a criterion. (Every plan is a yardstick, a criterion, a beacon, a landmark, etc.)

If we have electrification within 10 to 20 years, there is nothing to fear from the individualism of the small farmer and *his* unrestricted trade in local exchange. *If* we have no electrification, a return to capitalism is inevitable *in any case.*

The international situation is now favourable: a new equilibrium.

Their disintegration, our consolidation.	Entente versus Germany. America versus Japan (and Great Britain). America versus Europe. The imperialist world versus "Asia". (1/7) (4/7) $(0.250 \times 7 = 1.75)$ (a thousand million out of 1.750)[101]

Ten or twenty years of regular relations with the peasantry and victory is assured on a world scale (even if there is delay in the proletarian revolutions, which are maturing); otherwise 20-40 years of tormenting whiteguard terror.

---

* Hence.—*Ed.*

11*

*Aut-aut. Tertium non datur.**

NB:

"Agreement" with the peasantry? Constituent Assembly (overt or covert), voting, change of Constitution,Socialist-Revolutionaries and Mensheviks + anarchists.	*Co-operatives.* Their economic and political (Mensheviks and Socialist - Revolutionaries) aspects.	Ambiguity of the notion of "agreement", particularly versus "dictatorship".

Experience and lessons of Kronstadt (new feature in the political history of the Soviet power).	Uncompromising struggle against Mensheviks, Socialist-Revolutionaries, anarchists.

*Quid est "politica"?***
(1) the vanguard of the proletariat and *its* mass.
(2) the proletariat and the *peasantry.*
(3) the proletariat (and the peasantry) and the *bourgeoisie.*

NB:

Weariness, exhaustion, despair. . . . Lack of strength. . . . "Respite" . . . *evils of bureaucracy (Gegenstück**** of peasantry).	among working class *and* among the peasants.	"Top section" worn out, promotion of new people from "lower ranks"= (α) young people; (β) non-Party people.

NB NB:

Anarchism and the "Marxist" struggle against it. "Despair"?|

The pace is not what it should be (in war-time and peace-time construction).

---

* Either or There is no third road.—*Ed.*
** What is "politics"?—*Ed.*
*** Counterpart.—*Ed.*

In April 1918 and in April 1920, we imagined transition from the war to peace-time construction to be a simple one on the same lines of *policy*.

The transition is a complex one: relations with the peasantry are different, the pace is different, the situation is different.

Demobilisation of the army.

Banditry. (Devastation. Seven years of war.)

Either a whiteguard reign of terror, or the *dictatorship* of the proletariat, its (relaxing) leadership.

What is so *terrible* about the word "dictatorship"?

NB:

The non-Party peasant as a yardstick, a criterion, a counsellor—and a political slogan (=Socialist-Revolutionaries and Mensheviks). Vote? Overthrow the government? Or seek accord *with it*?

Non-Party conferences are *not* an absolute political weapon of the Mensheviks and Socialist-Revolutionaries + anarchists. *Caveant consules!* *

It is a well-tried trick of conventional bourgeois party politics and bourgeois parliamentarism to try to *"catch one"* through concessions. But we reject the *very basis* of bourgeois parliamentarism, and "conventional (bourgeois) party politics"!!

NB

NB: NB:

"The economic foundations for the withering away of the state" (*The State and Revolution*): *in this case* we also have the "economic *foundations*" for the *withering away* of bureaucracy, the top section and lower ranks, inequality (cf. "First Steps from Capitalism to Communism"). *The economic basis of socialism is not yet there*. What is this basis? *It is commodity exchange with the peasantry*!!

NB

Combating the evils of bureaucracy.

NB

* Let the consuls beware!—*Ed.*

NB

+*Note*. Significance of the political crisis in spring (Feb.-March) 1921 ("transitions") and Party crisis (Nov. or Sept. 1920-March 1921). Adapt the Party's top section to its mass or vice versa? The Party to the masses (proletariat+then the peasantry) or vice versa.

III

State capitalism not terrible but *desirable*.

Learning from state capitalism.

Examples:
1) Concessions.
2) Co-operatives.
3) Commission agents.
4) Leases.

Unorganised capitalism

"Elemental" *c'est le mot* 1794 versus 1921.

All *within proper limits* and on *definite* terms.
What are these limits?
Experience will show.
$\frac{1}{4}$ etwa.
"Trade" mainly and primarily. }

Combating profiteering. *Quid est?*

Tax in kind and trade.

instructions to food supply workers:
$100+100=200\%$
$?\Sigma 100+25$
$60+60$

These (3 and 4) forms are weak, because we are *weak and stupid*. Cf. bureaucratic practices. . . .

Free market α) to develop the productive forces of peasant farming β) to develop small industry γ) to combat the evils of bureaucracy.

Limits? Terms?
Practice will show.
Food supply worker: collect 100%

$$100+100=200$$

$$\text{Etwa:} \begin{cases} 100+ \ 25=125 \\ 60+ \ 60=120 \end{cases}$$

Combating profiteering?
Quid est?

Political aspect:
Petty-bourgeois element will overthrow (May 5, 1918).
"Example" of the French Revolution, cf. November 10,
1918
Anti-Kautsky
Pessimism or optimism?
Calculation of forces. Sober approach and fervent dedication.

IV

Conclusion Etwa:

Transition to politics.
Economics in the spring of 1921 transformed into
politics: "Kronstadt".

Role of Socialist-Revolutionaries+Mensheviks (Dan,
Rozhkov & Co., Martov & Co.). A "slight shift", to the
right or the left, makes no difference.

Milyukov is more intelligent than Chernov and Martov:
it is not so difficult to be more intelligent than these
conceited fools, phrase-mongers and knights of the petty-
bourgeois doctrine (1789-1848-1920).
   Their place is in prison and not at a *non-Party* conference.
1794 versus 1921.
   Vacillation of the "elements". (*Quid est* elements)
and firmness.
   Selection and
   promotion of men.

Pessimism or optimism? A most sober appraisal of the evil and the difficulties.

Dedication in the struggle. $\Sigma\Sigma =$

Summary:

1) "Trade". *Quid est?*
2) Small industry. Where are the raw materials?
3) Exchange.
4) Capitalism.
5) State capitalism.
6) Local initiative.
7) Mensheviks and Socialist-Revolutionaries+non-Party people.

Written in late March-
early April 1921

Published according
to the manuscript

THE TAX IN KIND

(THE SIGNIFICANCE OF THE NEW POLICY AND ITS CONDITIONS)[102]

IN LIEU OF INTRODUCTION

The question of the tax in kind is at present attracting very great attention and is giving rise to much discussion and argument. This is quite natural, because in present conditions it is indeed one of the principal questions of policy.

The discussion is somewhat disordered, a fault to which, for very obvious reasons, we must all plead guilty. All the more useful would it be, therefore, to try to approach the question, not from its "topical" aspect, but from the aspect of general principle. In other words, to examine the general, fundamental background of the picture on which we are now tracing the pattern of definite practical measures of present-day policy.

In order to make this attempt I will take the liberty of quoting a long passage from my pamphlet, *The Chief Task of Our Day. "Left-Wing" Childishness and the Petty-Bourgeois Mentality.* It was published by the Petrograd Soviet of Workers' and Soldiers' Deputies in 1918 and contains, first, a newspaper article, dated March 11, 1918, on the Brest Peace, and, second, my polemic against the then existing group of Left Communists, dated May 5, 1918. The polemic is now superfluous and I omit it, leaving what appertains to the discussion on "state capitalism" and the main elements of our present-day economy, which is transitional from capitalism to socialism.

Here is what I wrote at the time:

THE PRESENT-DAY ECONOMY OF RUSSIA
(EXTRACT FROM THE 1918 PAMPHLET)

State capitalism would be a step forward as compared with the present state of affairs in our Soviet Republic. If in approximately six months' time state capitalism became established in our Republic, this would be a great success and a sure guarantee that within a year socialism will have gained a permanently firm hold and will have become invincible in this country.

I can imagine with what noble indignation some people will recoil from these words. . . . What! The transition to state *capitalism* in the Soviet Socialist Republic would be a step forward? . . . Isn't this the betrayal of socialism?

We must deal with this point in greater detail.

Firstly, we must examine the nature of the *transition* from capitalism to socialism that gives us the right and the grounds to call our country a Socialist Republic of Soviets.

Secondly, we must expose the error of those who fail to see the petty-bourgeois economic conditions and the petty-bourgeois element as the *principal* enemy of socialism in our country.

Thirdly, we must fully understand the economic implications of the distinction between the *Soviet* state and the bourgeois state.

Let us examine these three points.

No one, I think, in studying the question of the economic system of Russia, has denied its transitional character. Nor, I think, has any Communist denied that the term Soviet Socialist Republic implies the determination of the Soviet power to achieve the transition to socialism, and not that the existing economic system is recognised as a socialist order.

But what does the word "transition" mean? Does it not mean, as applied to an economy, that the present system contains elements, particles, fragments of both capitalism and socialism? Everyone will admit that it does. But not all who admit this take the trouble to consider what elements actually constitute the various socio-economic structures that exist in Russia at the present time. And this is the crux of the question.

Let us enumerate these elements:

(1) patriarchal, i.e., to a considerable extent natural, peasant farming;

(2) small commodity production (this includes the majority of those peasants who sell their grain);

(3) private capitalism;

(4) state capitalism;

(5) socialism.

Russia is so vast and so varied that all these different types of socio-economic structures are intermingled. This is what constitutes the specific feature of the situation.

The question arises: What elements predominate? Clearly, in a small-peasant country, the petty-bourgeois element predominates and it must predominate, for the great majority—those working the land—are small commodity producers. The shell of state capitalism (grain monopoly, state-controlled entrepreneurs and traders, bourgeois co-operators) is pierced now in one place, now in another by *profiteers*, the chief object of profiteering being *grain*.

It is in this field that the main struggle is being waged. Between what elements is this struggle being waged if we are to speak in terms of economic categories such as "state capitalism"? Between the fourth and fifth in the order in which I have just enumerated them? Of course not. It is not state capitalism that is at war with socialism, but the petty bourgeoisie plus private capitalism fighting together against state capitalism and socialism. The petty bourgeoisie oppose *every kind* of state interference, accounting and control, whether it be state-capitalist or state-socialist. This is an unquestionable fact of reality whose misunderstanding lies at the root of many economic mistakes. The profiteer, the commercial racketeer, the disrupter of monopoly—these are our principal "internal" enemies, the enemies of the economic measures of the Soviet power. A hundred and twenty-five years ago it might have been excusable for the French petty bourgeoisie, the most ardent and sincere revolutionaries, to try to crush the profiteer by executing a few of the "chosen" and by making thunderous declarations. Today, however, the purely French approach to the question assumed by some Left Socialist-Revolutionaries can arouse nothing but disgust and revulsion in every politically conscious revolutionary. We know perfectly well that the economic basis of profiteering is both the small proprietors, who are exceptionally widespread in Russia, and private capitalism, of which every petty bourgeois is an agent. We know that the million tentacles of this petty-bourgeois octopus now and again encircle various sections of the workers, that instead of state monopoly, profiteering forces its way into every pore of our social and economic organism.

Those who fail to see this show by their blindness that they·are slaves of petty-bourgeois prejudices. . . .

The petty bourgeoisie have money put away, the few thousands that they made during the war by "honest" and especially by dishonest means. They are the characteristic economic type, that is, the basis of profiteering and private capitalism. Money is a certificate entitling the possessor to receive social wealth; and a vast section of small proprietors, numbering millions, cling to this certificate and conceal it from the "state". They do not believe in socialism or communism, and "mark time" until the proletarian storm blows over. Either we subordinate the petty bourgeoisie to our control and accounting (we can do this if we organise the poor, that is, the majority of the population or semi-proletarians, round the politically conscious proletarian vanguard), or they will overthrow our workers' power as surely and as inevitably as the revolution was overthrown by the Napoleons and the Cavaignacs who sprang from this very soil of petty proprietorship. That is how the question stands. That is the only view we can take of the matter. . . .

The petty bourgeois who hoards his thousands is an enemy of state capitalism. He wants to employ these thousands just for himself, against the poor, in opposition to any kind of state control. And the sum total of these thousands, amounting to many thousands of millions, forms the base for profiteering, which undermines our socialist construction. Let us assume that a certain number of workers produce in a few days values equal to 1,000. Let us then assume that 200 of this total vanishes owing to petty profiteering, various kinds of embezzlement and the evasion by the small **proprietors of Soviet decrees and regulations.** Every

politically conscious worker will say that if better order and
organisation could be obtained at the price of 300 out of
the 1,000 he would willingly give 300 instead of 200, for
it will be quite easy under the Soviet power to reduce
this "tribute" later on to, say, 100 or 50, once order and
organisation are established and the petty-bourgeois
disruption of state monopoly is completely overcome.

This simple illustration in figures, which I have
deliberately simplified to the utmost in order to make it
absolutely clear, explains the present correlation of state
capitalism and socialism. The workers hold state power
and have every legal opportunity of "taking" the whole
thousand, without giving up a single kopek, except for
socialist purposes. This legal opportunity, which rests upon
the actual transition of power to the workers, is an element
of socialism. But in many ways, the small-proprietary and
private-capitalist element undermines this legal position,
drags in profiteering and hinders the execution of Soviet
decrees. State capitalism would be a gigantic step forward
even if we paid *more* than we are paying at present (I took
the numerical example deliberately to bring this out more
sharply), because it is worth paying for "tuition", because it
is useful for the workers, because victory over disorder,
economic ruin and laxity is the most important thing,
because the continuation of the anarchy of small ownership
is the greatest, the most serious danger, and it will *certainly*
be our ruin (unless we overcome it), whereas not only will
the payment of a heavier tribute to state capitalism not
ruin us, it will lead us to socialism by the surest road.
When the working class has learned how to defend the state
system against the anarchy of small ownership, when it has
learned to organise large-scale production on a national
scale along state-capitalist lines, it will hold, if I may
use the expression, all the trump cards, and the consolidation of socialism will be assured.

In the first place *economically* state capitalism is immeasurably superior to our present economic system.

In the second place there is nothing terrible in it for
the Soviet power, for the Soviet state is a state in which the
power of the workers and the poor is assured. . . .

* * *

To make things even clearer, let us first of all take the most concrete example of state capitalism. Everybody knows what this example is. It is Germany. Here we have "the last word" in modern large-scale capitalist engineering and planned organisation, *subordinated to Junker-bourgeois imperialism*. Cross out the words in italics, and in place of the militarist, Junker, bourgeois, imperialist state put also a state, but of a different social type, of a different class content—a Soviet state, that is, a proletarian state, and you will have the sum total of the conditions necessary for socialism.

Socialism is inconceivable without large-scale capitalist engineering based on the latest discoveries of modern science. It is inconceivable without planned state organisation which keeps tens of millions of people to the strictest observance of a unified standard in production and distribution. We Marxists have always spoken of this, and it is not worth while wasting two seconds talking to people who do not understand even this (anarchists and a good half of the Left Socialist-Revolutionaries).

At the same time socialism is inconceivable unless the proletariat is the ruler of the state. This also is ABC. And history (which nobody, except Menshevik blockheads of the first order, ever expected to bring about "complete" socialism smoothly, gently, easily and simply) has taken such a peculiar course that it has given birth in 1918 to two unconnected halves of socialism existing side by side like two future chickens in the single shell of international imperialism. In 1918, Germany and Russia had become the most striking embodiment of the material realisation of the economic, the productive and the socio-economic conditions for socialism, on the one hand, and the political conditions, on the other.

A victorious proletarian revolution in Germany would immediately and very easily smash any shell of imperialism (which unfortunately is made of the best steel, and hence cannot be broken by the efforts of any chicken) and would bring about the victory of world socialism for certain, without any difficulty, or with only slight difficulty—if, of course, by "difficulty" we mean difficulty on a world-historical scale, and not in the parochial philistine sense.

While the revolution in Germany is still slow in "coming forth", our task is to *study* the state capitalism of the Germans, to *spare no effort* in copying it and not shrink from adopting dictatorial methods to hasten the copying of Western culture by barbarian Russia, without hesitating to use barbarous methods in fighting barbarism. If there are anarchists and Left Socialist-Revolutionaries (I recall offhand the speeches of Karelin and Ghe at the meeting of the Central Executive Committee) who indulge in Karelin-like reflections and say that it is unbecoming for us revolutionaries to "take lessons" from German imperialism, there is only one thing we can say in reply: the revolution that took these people seriously would perish irrevocably (and deservedly).

At present petty-bourgeois capitalism prevails in Russia, and it is *one and the same road* that leads from it to both large-scale state capitalism and to socialism, *through one and the same* intermediary station called "national accounting and control of production and distribution". Those who fail to understand this are committing an unpardonable mistake in economics. Either they do not know the facts of life, do not see what actually exists and are unable to look the truth in the face, or they confine themselves to abstractly comparing "socialism" with "capitalism" and fail to study the concrete forms and stages of the transition that is taking place in our country.

Let it be said in parenthesis that this is the very theoretical mistake which misled the best people in the *Novaya Zhizn* and *Vperyod*[103] camp. The worst and the mediocre of these, owing to their stupidity and spinelessness, tag along behind the bourgeoisie, of whom they stand in awe; the best of them have failed to understand that it was not without reason that the teachers of socialism spoke of a whole period of transition from capitalism to socialism and emphasised the "prolonged birth pangs" of the new society.[104] And this new society is again an abstraction which can come into being only by passing through a series of varied, imperfect and concrete attempts to create this or that socialist state.

It is because Russia cannot advance from the economic situation now existing here without traversing the ground *which is common* to state capitalism and to socialism (national accounting and control) that the attempt to frighten others as well as themselves with "evolution *towards* state capitalism" is utter theoretical nonsense. This is letting one's thoughts wander away from the true road of "evolution", and failing to understand what this road is. In practice, it is equivalent to *pulling us back* to small-proprietary capitalism.

In order to convince the reader that this is not the first time I have given this "high" appreciation of state capitalism and that I gave it *before* the Bolsheviks seized power, I take the liberty of quoting the following passage from my pamphlet, *The Impending Catastrophe and How To Combat It*, written in September 1917.

"Try to substitute for the Junker-capitalist state, for the landowner-capitalist state, a revolutionary-democratic state, i.e., a state which in a revolutionary way abolishes all privileges and does not fear to introduce the fullest democracy in a revolutionary way. You will find that, given a really revolutionary-democratic state, state-monopoly capitalism inevitably and unavoidably implies a step... towards socialism. . . .

"For socialism is merely the next step forward from state-capitalist monopoly. . . .

"State-monopoly capitalism is a complete material preparation for socialism, the threshold of socialism, a rung on the ladder of history between which and the rung called socialism there are no intermediate rungs" (pp. 27 and 28).

Please note that this was written when Kerensky was in power, that we are discussing *not* the dictatorship of the proletariat, *not* the socialist state, but the "revolutionary-democratic" state. Is it not clear that *the higher* we stand on this political ladder, *the more completely* we incorporate the socialist state and the dictatorship of the proletariat in the Soviets, *the less* ought we to fear "state capitalism"? Is it not clear that from the *material*, economic and productive point of view, we are not yet on the "threshold" of socialism? Is it not clear that we cannot pass through the door of socialism without crossing the "threshold" we have not yet reached? . . .

* * *

The following is also extremely instructive.

When we argued with Comrade Bukharin in the Central Executive Committee, he declared, among other things, that on the question of high salaries for specialists "they" were "to the right of Lenin", for in this case "they" saw no deviation from principle, bearing in mind Marx's words that under certain conditions it is more expedient for the working class to "buy out the whole lot of them"[105] (namely, the whole lot of capitalists, i.e., to *buy* from the bourgeoisie the land, factories, works and other means of production).

That is a very interesting statement. . . .

Let us consider Marx's idea carefully.

Marx was talking about the Britain of the seventies of the last century, about the culminating point in the development of pre-monopoly capitalism. At that time Britain was a country in which militarism and bureaucracy were less pronounced than in any other, a country in which there was the greatest possibility of a "peaceful" victory for socialism in the sense of the workers "buying out" the bourgeoisie. And Marx said that under certain conditions the workers would certainly not refuse to buy out the bourgeoisie. Marx did not commit himself, or the future leaders of the socialist revolution, to matters of form, to ways and means of bringing about the revolution. He understood perfectly well that a vast number of new problems would arise, that the whole situation would change in the course of the revolution, and that the situation would change radically and often in the course of the revolution.

Well, and what about Soviet Russia? Is it not clear that *after* the seizure of power by the proletariat and *after* the crushing of the exploiters' armed resistance and sabotage—*certain* conditions prevail which correspond to those which might have existed in Britain half a century ago had a peaceful transition to socialism begun there? The subordination of the capitalists to the workers in Britain would have been assured at that time owing to the following circumstances: (1) the absolute preponderance of workers, of proletarians, in the population owing to the absence of a peasantry (in Britain in the seventies there where signs that gave hope of an extremely rapid spread of socialism among agricultural labourers); (2) the excellent organisation of the proletariat in trade unions (Britain was at that time the leading country in the world in this respect); (3) the comparatively high level of culture of the proletariat, which had been trained by centuries of development of political liberty; (4) the old habit of the well-organised British capitalists of settling political and economic questions by compromise—at that time the British capitalists were better organised than the capitalists of any country in the world (this superiority has now passed to Germany). These were the circumstances which at the time gave rise to the idea that the *peaceful* subjugation of the British capitalists by the workers was possible.

In our country, at the present time, this subjugation is assured by certain premises of fundamental significance (the victory in October and the suppression, from October to February, of the capitalists' armed resistance and sabotage). But *instead of* the absolute preponderance of workers, of proletarians, in the population, and *instead of* a high degree of organisation among them, the important factor of victory in Russia was the support the proletarians received from the poor peasants and those who had experienced sudden ruin. Finally, we have neither a high degree of culture nor the habit of compromise. If these concrete conditions are carefully considered, it will become clear that we now can and ought to employ a *combination* of two methods. On the one hand, we must ruthlessly suppress the uncultured capitalists who refuse to have anything to do with "state capitalism" or to consider any form of compromise, and who continue by means of profiteering, by bribing the poor peasants, etc., to hinder the realisation of the measures taken by the Soviets. On the other hand, we must use the *method of compromise*, or of buying out the cultured capitalists who agree to "state capitalism", who are capable of putting it into practice and who are useful to the proletariat as intelligent and experienced organisers of the largest types of enterprises, which actually supply products to tens of millions of people.

Bukharin is an extremely well-read Marxist economist. He therefore remembered that Marx was profoundly right when he taught the workers the importance of preserving the organisation of large-scale production, precisely for the

purpose of facilitating the transition to socialism. Marx
taught that (as an exception, and Britain was then an
exception) the idea was conceivable of *paying the capitalists
well*, of buying them out, if the circumstances were such as
to compel the capitalists to submit peacefully and to come
over to socialism in a cultured and organised fashion,
provided they were paid well.

But Bukharin went astray because he did not go deep
enough into the specific features of the situation in Russia
at the present time—an exceptional situation when we,
the Russian proletariat, are *in advance* of any Britain or
any Germany as regards political system, as regards the
strength of the workers' political power, but are *behind*
the most backward West-European country as regards organising a good state capitalism, as regards our level of culture
and the degree of material and productive preparedness
for the "introduction" of socialism. Is it not clear that the
specific nature of the present situation creates the need for
a specific type of "buying out" operation which the workers must offer to the most cultured, the most talented, the
most capable organisers among the capitalists who are
ready to enter the service of the Soviet power and to help
honestly in organising "state" production on the largest
possible scale? Is it not clear that in this specific situation
we must make every effort to avoid two mistakes, both
of which are of a petty-bourgeois nature? On the one hand,
it would be a fatal mistake to declare that since there is
a discrepancy between our economic "forces" and our political strength, it "follows" that we should not have seized
power. Such an argument can be advanced only by a "man
in a muffler", who forgets that there will always be such a
"discrepancy", that it always exists in the development
of nature as well as in the development of society, that only
by a series of attempts—each of which, taken by itself, will
be one-sided and will suffer from certain inconsistencies—
will complete socialism be created by the revolutionary co-
operation of the proletarians of *all* countries.

On the other hand, it would be an obvious mistake to
give free rein to ranters and phrase-mongers who allow themselves to be carried away by the "dazzling" revolutionary
spirit, but who are incapable of sustained, thoughtful and

deliberate revolutionary work which takes into account the most difficult stages of transition.

Fortunately, the history of the development of revolutionary parties and of the struggle that Bolshevism waged against them has left us a heritage of sharply defined types, of which the Left Socialist-Revolutionaries and anarchists are striking examples of bad revolutionaries. They are now shouting hysterically, choking and shouting themselves hoarse, against the "compromise" of the "Right Bolsheviks". But they are incapable of understanding *what* is bad in "compromise", and *why* "compromise" has been justly condemned by history and the course of the revolution.

Compromise in Kerensky's time meant the surrender of power to the imperialist bourgeoisie, and the question of power is the fundamental question of every revolution. Compromise by a section of the Bolsheviks in October-November 1917 either meant that they feared the proletariat seizing power or wished to *share* power equally, not only with "unreliable fellow-travellers" like the Left Socialist-Revolutionaries, but also with enemies, with the Chernovists and the Mensheviks. The latter would inevitably have hindered us in fundamental matters, such as the dissolution of the Constituent Assembly, the ruthless suppression of the Bogayevskys, the universal setting up of the Soviet institutions, and in every act of confiscation.

Now power has been seized, retained and consolidated in the hands of a single party, the party of the proletariat, even without the "unreliable fellow-travellers". To speak of compromise at the present time when there is no question, and can be none, of sharing *power*, of renouncing the dictatorship of the proletariat over the bourgeoisie, is merely to repeat, parrot-fashion, words which have been learned by heart but not understood. To describe as "compromise" the fact that, having arrived at a situation when we can and must rule the country, we try to win over to our side, not grudging the cost, the most efficient people capitalism has trained and to take them into our service against small proprietary disintegration, reveals a total incapacity to think about the economic tasks of socialist construction.

TAX IN KIND, FREEDOM TO TRADE AND CONCESSIONS

In the arguments of 1918 quoted above there are a number of mistakes as regards the periods of time involved. These turned out to be longer than was anticipated at that time. That is not surprising. But the basic elements of our economy have remained the same. In a very large number of cases the peasant "poor" (proletarians and semi-proletarians) have become middle peasants. This has caused an increase in the small-proprietor, petty-bourgeois "element". The Civil War of 1918-20 aggravated the havoc in the country, retarded the restoration of its productive forces, and bled the proletariat more than any other class. To this was added the 1920 crop failure, the fodder shortage and the loss of cattle, which still further retarded the rehabilitation of transport and industry, because, among other things, it interfered with the employment of peasants' horses for carting wood, our main type of fuel.

As a result, the political situation in the spring of 1921 was such that immediate, very resolute and urgent measures had to be taken to improve the condition of the peasants and to increase their productive forces.

Why the peasants and not the workers?

Because you need grain and fuel to improve the condition of the workers. This is the biggest "hitch" at the present time, from the standpoint of the economy as a whole. For it is impossible to increase the production and collection of grain and the storage and delivery of fuel except by improving the condition of the peasantry, and raising their productive forces. We must start with the peasantry. Those who fail to understand this, and think this putting the peasantry in the forefront is "renunciation" of the dictatorship of the proletariat, or something like that, simply do not stop to think, and allow themselves to be swayed by the power of words. The dictatorship of the proletariat is the direction of policy by the proletariat. The proletariat, as the leading and ruling class, must be able to direct policy in such a way as to solve first the most urgent and "vexed" problem. The most urgent thing at the present time is to take measures that will immediately increase the productive forces of peasant farming. Only *in this way* will it be possible to improve the condition of the workers, strengthen the alliance between the workers and peasants, and consolidate the dictatorship of the proletariat. The proletarian or representative of the proletariat who *refused* to improve the condition of the workers *in this way* would *in fact* prove himself to be an accomplice of the whiteguards and the capitalists; to refuse to do it in this way means putting the craft interests of the workers above their class interests, and sacrificing the interests of the whole of the working class, its dictatorship, its alliance with the peasantry against the landowners and capitalists, and its leading role in the struggle for the emancipation of labour from the yoke of capital, for the sake of an immediate, short-term and partial advantage for the workers.

Thus, the first thing we need is immediate and serious measures to raise the productive forces of the peasantry.

This cannot be done without making important changes in our food policy. One such change was the replacement of the surplus appropriation system by the tax in kind, which implies a free market, at least in local economic exchange, after the tax has been paid.

What is the essence of this change?

Wrong ideas on this point are widespread. They are due mainly to the fact that no attempt is being made to study the meaning of the transition or to determine its implications, it being assumed that the change is from communism in general to the bourgeois system in general. To counteract this mistake, one has to refer to what was said in May 1918.

The tax in kind is one of the forms of transition from that peculiar War Communism, which was forced on us by extreme want, ruin and war, to regular socialist exchange of products. The latter, in its turn, is one of the forms of transition from socialism, with the peculiar features due to the predominantly small-peasant population, to communism.

Under this peculiar War Communism we actually took from the peasant all his surpluses—and sometimes even a part of his necessaries—to meet the requirements of the army and sustain the workers. Most of it we took on loan, for paper money. But for that, we would not have beaten the landowners and capitalists in a ruined small-peasant country. The fact that we did (in spite of the help our exploiters got from the most powerful countries of the world) shows not only the miracles of heroism the workers and peasants can perform in the struggle for their emancipation; it also shows that when the Mensheviks, Socialist-Revolutionaries and Kautsky and Co. *blamed* us for this War Communism they were acting as lackeys of the bourgeoisie. We deserve credit for it.

Just how much credit is a fact of equal importance. It was the war and the ruin that forced us into War Communism. It was not, and could not be, a policy that corresponded to the economic tasks of the proletariat. It was a makeshift. The correct policy of the proletariat exercising its dictatorship in a small-peasant country is to obtain grain in exchange for the manufactured goods the peasant needs. That is the only kind of food policy that corresponds to the tasks of the proletariat, and can strengthen the foundations of socialism and lead to its complete victory.

The tax in kind is a transition to this policy. We are still so ruined and crushed by the burden of war (which was on but yesterday and could break out anew tomorrow, owing to the rapacity and malice of the capitalists) that we cannot give the peasant manufactured goods in return for *all* the grain we need. Being aware of this, we are introducing the tax in kind, that is, we shall take the minimum of grain we require (for the army and the workers) in the form of a tax and obtain the rest in exchange for manufactured goods.

There is something else we must not forget. Our poverty and ruin are so great that we cannot restore large-scale socialist state industry *at one stroke*. This can be done with large stocks of grain and fuel in the big industrial centres, replacement of worn-out machinery, and so on. Experience has convinced us that this cannot be done at one stroke, and we know that after the ruinous imperialist war even the wealthiest and most advanced countries will be able to solve this problem only over a fairly long period of years. Hence, it is necessary, to a certain extent, to help to restore *small* industry, which does not demand of the state machines, large stocks of raw material, fuel and food, and which can immediately render some assistance to peasant farming and increase its productive forces right away.

What is to be the effect of all this?

It is the revival of the petty bourgeoisie and of capitalism on the basis of some freedom of trade (if only local). That much is certain and it is ridiculous to shut our eyes to it.

Is it necessary? Can it be justified? Is it not dangerous?

Many such questions are being asked, and most are merely evidence of simple-mindedness, to put it mildly.

Look at my May 1918 definition of the elements (constituent parts) of the various socio-economic structures in our economy. No one can deny the existence of all these five stages. (or constituent parts), of the five forms of economy—from the patriarchal, i.e., semi-barbarian, to the socialist system. That the small-peasant "structure", partly patriarchal, partly petty bourgeois, predominates in a small-peasant country is self-evident. It is an incontrovertible truth, elementary to political economy, which even the layman's everyday experience will confirm, that once you have exchange the small economy is bound to develop the petty-bourgeois-capitalist way.

What is the policy the socialist proletariat can pursue in the face of this economic reality? Is it to give the small peasant *all* he needs of the goods produced by large-scale socialist industries in exchange for his grain and raw materials? This would be the most desirable and "correct" policy—and we have started on it. But we cannot supply *all* the goods, very far from it; nor shall we be able to do so very soon—at all events not until we complete the first stage of the electrification of the whole country. What is to be done? One way is to try to prohibit entirely, to put the lock on all development of private, non-state exchange, i.e., trade, i.e., capitalism, which is inevitable with millions of small producers. But such a policy would be foolish and suicidal for the party that tried to apply it. It would be foolish because it is economically impossible. It would be suicidal because the party that tried to apply it would meet with inevitable disaster. Let us admit it: some Communists have sinned "in thought, word and deed" by adopting just *such* a policy. We shall try to rectify these mistakes, and this must be done without fail, otherwise things will come to a very sorry state.

The alternative (and this is the only sensible and the last *possible* policy) is not to try to prohibit or put the lock

on the development of capitalism, but to channel it into
state capitalism. This is economically possible, for state
capitalism exists—in varying form and degree—wherever there
are elements of unrestricted trade and capitalism in general.

Can the Soviet state and the dictatorship of the
proletariat be combined with state capitalism? Are they
compatible?

Of course they are. This is exactly what I argued in May
1918. I hope I had proved it then. I had also proved that
state capitalism is a step forward compared with the small-
proprietor (both small-patriarchal and petty-bourgeois)
element. Those who compare state capitalism only with
socialism commit a host of mistakes, for in the present
political and economic circumstances it is essential to compare state capitalism also with petty-bourgeois production.

The whole problem—in theoretical and practical terms—
is to find the correct methods of directing the development
of capitalism (which is to some extent and for some time
inevitable) into the channels of state capitalism, and to
determine how we are to hedge it about with conditions to
ensure its transformation into socialism in the near future.

In order to approach the solution of this problem we must
first of all picture to ourselves as distinctly as possible
what state capitalism will and can be in practice inside the
Soviet system and within the framework of the Soviet state.

Concessions are the simplest example of how the Soviet
government directs the development of capitalism into the
channels of state capitalism and "implants" state capitalism. We all agree now that concessions are necessary, but
have we all thought about the implications? What are
concessions under the Soviet system, viewed in the light of
the above-mentioned forms of economy and their inter-
relations? They are an agreement, an alliance, a bloc between
the Soviet, i.e., proletarian, state power and state capitalism
against the small-proprietor (patriarchal and petty-bourgeois) element. The concessionaire is a capitalist. He
conducts his business on capitalist lines, for profit, and is
willing to enter into an agreement with the proletarian
government in order to obtain superprofits or raw materials
which he cannot otherwise obtain, or can obtain only with
great difficulty. Soviet power gains by the development

of the productive forces, and by securing an increased quantity of goods immediately, or within a very short period. We have, say, a hundred oilfields, mines and forest tracts. We cannot develop all of them for we lack the machines, the food and the transport. This is also why we are doing next to nothing to develop the other territories. Owing to the insufficient development of the large enterprises the small-proprietor element is more pronounced in all its forms, and this is reflected in the deterioration of the surrounding (and later the whole of) peasant farming, the disruption of its productive forces, the decline in its confidence in the Soviet power, pilfering and widespread petty (the most dangerous) profiteering, etc. By "implanting" state capitalism in the form of concessions, the Soviet government strengthens large-scale production as against petty production, advanced production as against backward production, and machine production as against hand production. It also obtains a larger quantity of the products of large-scale industry (its share of the output), and strengthens state-regulated economic relations as against the anarchy of petty-bourgeois relations. The moderate and cautious application of the concessions policy will undoubtedly help us quickly to improve (to a modest extent) the state of industry and the condition of the workers and peasants. We shall, of course, have all this at the price of certain sacrifices and the surrender to the capitalist of many millions of poods of very valuable products. The scale and the conditions under which concessions cease to be a danger and are turned to our advantage depend on the relation of forces and are decided in the struggle, for concessions are also a form of struggle, and are a continuation of the class struggle in another form, and in no circumstances are they a substitution of class peace for class war. Practice will determine the methods of struggle.

Compared with other forms of state capitalism within the Soviet system, concessions are perhaps the most simple and clear-cut form of state capitalism. It involves a formal written agreement with the most civilised, advanced, West-European capitalism. We know exactly what our gains and our losses, our rights and obligations are. We know exactly the term for which the concession is granted. We know the

terms of redemption before the expiry of the agreement if it
provides for such redemption. We pay a certain "tribute" to
world capitalism; we "ransom" ourselves under certain
arrangements, thereby immediately stabilising the Soviet
power and improving our economic conditions. The whole
difficulty with concessions is giving the proper consideration and appraisal of all the circumstances when concluding
a concession agreement, and then seeing that it is fulfilled.
Difficulties there certainly are, and mistakes will probably
be inevitable at the outset. But these are minor difficulties compared with the other problems of the social
revolution and, in particular, with the difficulties arising
from other forms of developing, permitting and implanting
state capitalism.

The most important task that confronts all Party and
Soviet workers in connection with the introduction of the
tax in kind is to apply the principles of the "concessions"
policy (i.e., a policy that is similar to "concession" state
capitalism) to the other forms of capitalism –unrestricted
trade, local exchange, etc.

Take the co-operatives. It is not surprising that the tax
in kind decree immediately necessitated a revision of the
regulations governing the co-operatives and a certain extension of their "freedom" and rights. The co-operatives are
also a form of state capitalism, but a less simple one; its
outline is less distinct, it is more intricate and therefore
creates greater practical difficulties for the government.
The small commodity producers' co-operatives (and it is
these, and not the workers' co-operatives, that we are
discussing as the predominant and typical form in a small-
peasant country) inevitably give rise to petty-bourgeois,
capitalist relations, facilitate their development, push the
small capitalists into the foreground and benefit them most.
It cannot be otherwise, since the small proprietors predominate, and exchange is necessary and possible. In Russia's
present conditions, freedom and rights for the co-operative
societies mean freedom and rights for capitalism. It would
be stupid or criminal to close our eyes to this obvious truth.

But, unlike private capitalism, "co-operative" capitalism
under the Soviet system is a variety of state capitalism, and
as such it is advantageous and useful for us at the present

time—in certain measure, of course. Since the tax in kind
means the free sale of surplus grain (over and above that
taken in the form of the tax), we must exert every effort to
direct *this* development of capitalism—for a free market *is*
development of capitalism—into the channels of co-
operative capitalism. It resembles state capitalism in that
it facilitates accounting, control, supervision and the establishment of contractual relations between the state (in this
case the Soviet state) and the capitalist. Co-operative trade
is more advantageous and useful than private trade not only
for the above-mentioned reasons, but also because it
facilitates the association and organisation of millions of
people, and eventually of the entire population, and this in
its turn is an enormous gain from the standpoint of the
subsequent transition from state capitalism to socialism.

Let us make a comparison of concessions and co-
operatives as forms of state capitalism. Concessions are based
on large-scale machine industry; co-operatives are based on
small, handicraft, and partly even on patriarchal industry.
Each concession agreement affects one capitalist, firm,
syndicate, cartel or trust. Co-operative societies embrace
many thousands and even millions of small proprietors.
Concessions allow and even imply a definite agreement for a
specified period. Co-operative societies allow of neither.
It is much easier to repeal the law on the co-operatives
than to annul a concession agreement, but the annulment of
an agreement means a sudden rupture of the practical relations of economic alliance, or economic coexistence, with the
capitalist, whereas the repeal of the law on the co-operatives, or any law, for that matter, does not immediately
break off the practical coexistence of Soviet power and the
small capitalists, nor, in general, is it able to break off the
actual economic relations. It is easy to "keep an eye" on a
concessionaire but not on the co-operators. The transition
from concessions to socialism is a transition from one form
of large-scale production to another. The transition from
small-proprietor co-operatives to socialism is a transition
from small to large-scale production, i.e., it is more complicated, but, if successful, is capable of embracing wider
masses of the population, and pulling up the deeper and
more tenacious roots of the old, pre-socialist and even

pre-capitalist relations, which most stubbornly resist all
"innovations". The concessions policy, if successful, will
give us a few model—compared with our own—large enterprises built on the level of modern advanced capitalism.
After a few decades these enterprises will revert to us in
their entirety. The co-operative policy, if successful, will
result in raising the small economy and in facilitating its
transition, within an indefinite period, to large-scale
production on the basis of voluntary association.

Take a third form of state capitalism. The state enlists
the capitalist as a merchant and pays him a definite commission on the sale of state goods and on the purchase of
the produce of the small producer. A fourth form: the state
leases to the capitalist entrepreneur an industrial establishment, oilfields, forest tracts, land, etc., which belong to
the state, the lease being very similar to a concession
agreement. We make no mention of, we give no thought or
notice to, these two latter forms of state capitalism, not
because we are strong and clever but because we are weak
and foolish. We are afraid to look the "vulgar truth"
squarely in the face, and too often yield to "exalting
deception".[106] We keep repeating that "we" are passing
from capitalism to socialism, but do not bother to obtain a
distinct picture of the "we". To keep this picture clear we
must constantly have in mind the whole list—without any
exception—of the constituent parts of our national economy,
of all its diverse forms that I gave in my article of
May 5, 1918. "We", the vanguard, the advanced contingent
of the proletariat, are passing directly to socialism; but the
advanced contingent is only a small part of the whole of the
proletariat while the latter, in its turn, is only a small part
of the whole population. If "we" are successfully to solve
the problem of our immediate transition to socialism, we
must understand what *intermediary* paths, methods, means
and instruments are required for the transition from *pre-
capitalist* relations to socialism. That is the whole point.

Look at the map of the R.S.F.S.R. There is room for dozens
of large civilised states in those vast areas which lie to
the north of Vologda, the south-east of Rostov-on-Don
and Saratov, the south of Orenburg and Omsk, and the
north of Tomsk. They are a realm of patriarchalism,

and semi- and downright barbarism. And what about the peasant backwoods of the rest of Russia, where scores of versts of country track, or rather of trackless country, lie between the villages and the railways, i.e., the material link with the big cities, large-scale industry, capitalism and culture? Isn't that also an area of wholesale patriarchalism, Oblomovism[107] and semi-barbarism?

Is an immediate transition to socialism from the state of affairs predominating in Russia conceivable? Yes, it is, to a certain degree, but on one condition, the precise nature of which we now know thanks to a great piece of scientific work[108] that has been completed. It is electrification. If we construct scores of district electric power stations (we now know where and how these can and should be constructed), and transmit electric power to every village, if we obtain a sufficient number of electric motors and other machinery, we shall not need, or shall hardly need, any transition stages or intermediary links between patriarchalism and socialism. But we know perfectly well that it will take at least ten years only to complete the first stage of this "one" condition; this period can be conceivably reduced only if the proletarian revolution is victorious in such countries as Britain, Germany or the U.S.A.

Over the next few years we must learn to think of the intermediary links that can facilitate the transition from patriarchalism and small production to socialism. "We" continue saying now and again that "capitalism is a bane and socialism is a boon". But such an argument is wrong, because it fails to take into account the aggregate of the existing economic forms and singles out only two of them.

Capitalism is a bane compared with socialism. Capitalism is a boon compared with medievalism, small production, and the evils of bureaucracy which spring from the dispersal of the small producers. Inasmuch as we are as yet unable to pass directly from small production to socialism, some capitalism is inevitable as the elemental product of small production and exchange; so that we must utilise capitalism (particularly by directing it into the channels of state capitalism) as the intermediary link between small production and socialism, as a means, a path, and a method of increasing the productive forces.

Look at the economic aspect of the evils of bureaucracy. We see nothing of them on May 5, 1918. Six months after the October Revolution, with the old bureaucratic apparatus smashed from top to bottom, we feel none of its evils.

A year later, the Eighth Congress of the Russian Communist Party (March 18-23, 1919)[109] adopted a new Party Programme in which we spoke forthrightly of *"a partial revival of bureaucracy within the Soviet system"*—not fearing to admit the evil, but desiring to reveal, expose and pillory it and to stimulate thought, will, energy and action to combat it.

Two years later, in the spring of 1921, after the Eighth Congress of Soviets (December 1920), which discussed the evils of bureaucracy, and after the Tenth Congress of the Russian Communist Party (March 1921), which summed up the controversies closely connected with an analysis of these evils, we find *them* even more distinct and sinister. What are their economic roots? They are mostly of a dual character: on the one hand, a developed bourgeoisie needs a bureaucratic apparatus, primarily a military apparatus, and then a judiciary, etc., to use against the revolutionary movement of the workers (and partly of the peasants). That is something we have not got. Ours are class courts directed against the bourgeoisie. Ours is a class army directed against the bourgeoisie. The evils of bureaucracy are not in the army, but in the institutions serving it. In our country bureaucratic practices have different economic roots, namely, the atomised and scattered state of the small producer with his poverty, illiteracy, lack of culture, the absence of roads and *exchange* between agriculture and industry, the absence of connection and interaction between them. This is largely the result of the Civil War. We could not restore industry when we were blockaded, besieged on all sides, cut off from the whole world and later from the grain-bearing South, Siberia, and the coalfields. We could not afford to hesitate in introducing War Communism, or daring to go to the most desperate extremes: to save the workers' and peasants rule we had to suffer an existence of semi-starvation and worse than semi-starvation, but to hold on at all costs, in spite of unprecedented ruin and the absence of economic intercourse. We did not allow ourselves to be frightened, as the Socialist-Revolutionaries and Mensheviks did (who, in fact, followed the bourgeoisie largely because they were scared). But the factor that was crucial to victory in a blockaded country—a besieged fortress—revealed its negative side by the spring of 1921, just when the last of the whiteguard forces were finally driven from the territory of the R.S.F.S.R. In the besieged fortress, it was possible and imperative to "lock up" all exchange; with the masses displaying extraordinary heroism this could be borne for three years. After that, the ruin of the small producer increased, and the restoration of large-scale industry was further delayed, and postponed. Bureaucratic practices, as a legacy of the "siege" and the superstructure built over the isolated and downtrodden state of the small producer, fully revealed themselves.

We must learn to admit an evil fearlessly in order to combat it the more firmly, in order to start from scratch again and again; we shall have to do this many a time in every sphere of our activity, finish what was left undone and choose different approaches to the problem. In view of the obvious delay in the restoration of large-scale industry, the "locking up" of exchange between industry and agriculture has become intolerable. Consequently, we must concentrate on what we can do: restoring small industry, helping things from that end, propping up the side of the structure that has been half-demolished by the war and blockade. We must do everything possible to develop trade at all costs, without being afraid of capitalism, because the limits we have put to it (the expropriation of the landowners and of the bourgeoisie in the economy, the rule of the workers and peasants in politics) are sufficiently narrow and "moderate". This is the fundamental idea and economic significance of the tax in kind.

All Party and Soviet workers must concentrate their efforts and attention on generating the utmost local initiative in economic development—in the gubernias, still more in the uyezds, still more in the volosts and villages—for the special purpose of immediately improving peasant farming, even if by "small" means, on a small scale, helping it by developing small local industry. The integrated state economic plan demands that this should become the focus of concern and "priority" effort. Some improvement here, closest to the broadest and deepest "foundation", will permit of the speediest transition to a more vigorous and successful restoration of large-scale industry.

Hitherto the food supply worker has known only one fundamental instruction: collect 100 per cent of the grain appropriations. Now he has another instruction: collect 100 per cent of the tax in the shortest possible time and then collect another 100 per cent in exchange for the goods of large-scale *and small* industry. Those who collect 75 per cent of the tax and 75 per cent (of the second hundred) in exchange for the goods of large-scale and small industry will be doing more useful work of national importance than those who collect 100 per cent of the tax and 55 per cent (of the second hundred) by means of exchange. The task of the food supply worker now becomes more complicated. On the one hand, it is a fiscal task: collect the tax as quickly and as efficiently as possible. On the other hand, it is a general economic task: try to direct the co-operatives, assist small industry, develop local initiative in such a way as to increase the exchange between agriculture and industry and put it on a sound basis. Our bureaucratic practices prove that we are still doing a very bad job of it. We must not be afraid to admit that in this respect *we still have a great deal to learn from the capitalist.* We shall compare the practical experience of the various gubernias, uyezds, volosts and villages: in one place private capitalists, big and small, have achieved so much; those are their approximate profits. That is the tribute, the fee, we have to pay for the "schooling". We shall not mind paying for it if we learn a thing or two. That much has been achieved in a neighbouring locality through co-operation. Those are the profits of the co-operatives. And in a third place, that much has been achieved by purely state and communist methods (for the present, this third case will be a rare exception).

It should be the primary task of every regional economic centre and economic conference of the gubernia executive committees immediately to organise various experiments, or systems of "exchange" for the surplus stocks remaining after the tax in kind has been paid. In a few months' time practical results must be obtained for comparison and study.

Local or imported salt; paraffin oil from the nearest town; the handicraft wood-working industry; handicrafts using local raw materials and producing certain, perhaps not very important, but necessary and useful, articles for the peasants; "green coal" (the utilisation of small local water power resources for electrification), and so on and so forth—all this must be brought into play in order to stimulate exchange between industry and agriculture at all costs. Those who achieve the best results in this sphere, even by means of private capitalism, even without the co-operatives, or without directly transforming this capitalism into state capitalism, will do more for the cause of socialist construction in Russia than those who "ponder over" the purity of communism, draw up regulations, rules and instructions for state capitalism and the co-operatives, but do nothing practical to stimulate trade.

Isn't it paradoxical that private capital should be helping socialism?

Not at all. It is, indeed, an irrefutable economic fact. Since this is a small-peasant country with transport in an extreme state of dislocation, a country emerging from war and blockade under the political guidance of the proletariat—which controls the transport system and large-scale industry—it inevitably follows, first, that at the present moment local exchange acquires first-class significance, and, second, that there is a possibility of assisting socialism by means of private capitalism (not to speak of state capitalism).

Let's not quibble about words. We still have too much of that sort of thing. We must have more variety in practical experience and make a wider study of it. In certain circumstances, the exemplary organisation of local work, even on the smallest scale, is of far greater national importance than many branches of central state work. These are precisely the circumstances now prevailing in peasant farming in general, and in regard to the exchange of the surplus products of agriculture for industrial goods in particular. Exemplary organisation in this respect, even in a single volost, is of far greater national importance than the "exemplary" improvement of the central apparatus of any People's Commissariat; over the past three and a half years our central

apparatus has been built up to such an extent that it has
managed to acquire a certain amount of harmful routine;
we cannot improve it quickly to any extent, we do not know
how to do it. Assistance in the work of radically improving
it, securing an influx of fresh forces, combating
bureaucratic practices effectively and overcoming this
harmful routine must come from the localities and the
lower ranks, with the model organisation of a "complex", even
if on a small scale. I say "complex", meaning not just one
farm, one branch of industry, or one factory, but a *totality*
of economic relations, a *totality* of economic exchange,
even if only in a small locality.

Those of us who are doomed to remain at work in the
centre will continue the task of improving the apparatus
and purging it of bureaucratic evils, even if only on a
modest and immediately achievable scale. But the greatest
assistance in this task is coming, and will come, from the
localities. Generally speaking, as far as I can observe,
things are better in the localities than at the centre;
and this is understandable, for, naturally, the evils of
bureaucracy are concentrated at the centre. In this respect,
Moscow cannot but be the worst city, and in general the
worst "locality", in the Republic. In the localities we have
deviations from the average to the good and the bad sides,
the latter being less frequent than the former. The deviations towards the bad side are the abuses committed by
former government officials, landowners, bourgeois and other
scum who play up to the Communists and who sometimes
commit abominable outrages and acts of tyranny against
the peasantry. This calls for a terrorist purge, summary
trial and the firing squad. Let the Martovs, the Chernovs,
and non-Party philistines like them, beat their breasts
and exclaim: "I thank Thee, Lord, that I am not as
'these', and have never accepted terrorism." These simpletons "do not accept terrorism" because they choose to
be servile accomplices of the whiteguards in fooling the
workers and peasants. The Socialist-Revolutionaries and
Mensheviks "do not accept terrorism" because under the
flag of "socialism" they are fulfilling their function of
placing the masses *at the mercy of the whiteguard terrorism.*
This was proved by the Kerensky regime and the Kornilov

putsch in Russia, by the Kolchak regime in Siberia, and
by Menshevism in Georgia. It was proved by the heroes
of the Second International and of the "Two-and-a-Half"[116]
International in Finland, Hungary, Austria, Germany, Italy,
Britain, etc. Let the flunkey accomplices of whiteguard
terrorism wallow in their repudiation of all terrorism. We shall
speak the bitter and indubitable truth: in countries beset
by an unprecedented crisis, the collapse of old ties, and
the intensification of the class struggle after the imperialist
war of 1914-18—and that means all the countries of the
world—terrorism cannot be dispensed with, notwithstanding
the hypocrites and phrase-mongers. Either the whiteguard,
bourgeois terrorism of the American, British (Ireland),
Italian (the fascists), German, Hungarian and other
types, or Red, proletarian terrorism. There is no middle
course, no "third" course, nor can there be any.

The deviations towards the good side are the success
achieved in combating the evils of bureaucracy, the great
attention shown for the needs of the workers and peasants,
and the great care in developing the economy, raising the
productivity of labour and stimulating local exchange
between agriculture and industry. Although the good examples are more numerous than the bad ones, they are, nevertheless, rare. Still, they are there. Young, fresh communist
forces, steeled by civil war and privation, are coming
forward in all localities. We are still doing far too little
to promote these forces regularly from lower to higher posts.
This can and must be done more persistently, and on a
wider scale than at present. Some workers can and should be
transferred from work at the centre to local work. As leading men of uyezds, and of *volosts*, where they can organise
economic work *as a whole* on *exemplary* lines, they will
do far more good, and perform work of far greater *national*
importance, than by performing some function at the centre.
The exemplary organisation of the work will help to train
new workers and provide examples that other districts
could follow with relative ease. We at the centre shall be able
to do a great deal to encourage the other districts all over the
country to "follow" the good examples, and even make it
mandatory for them to do so.

By its very nature, the work of developing "exchange"

between agriculture and industry, the exchange of after-tax surpluses for the output of small, mainly handicraft, industry, calls for independent, competent and intelligent *local initiative*. That is why it is now extremely important from the national standpoint to organise the work in the uyezds and volosts on exemplary lines. In military affairs, during the last Polish war, for example, we were not afraid of departing from the bureaucratic hierarchy, "downgrading", or transferring members of the Revolutionary Military Council of the Republic to lower posts (while allowing them to retain their higher rank at the centre). Why not now transfer several members of the All-Russia Central Executive Committee. or members of collegiums, or other high-ranking comrades, to uyezd or even volost work? Surely, we have not become so "bureaucratised" as to "be ashamed" of that. And we shall find scores of workers in the central bodies who will be glad to accept. The economic development of the whole Republic will gain enormously; and the exemplary volosts, or uyezds, will play not only a great, but a positively crucial and historic role.

Incidentally, we should note as a small but significant circumstance the necessary change in our attitude to the problem of combating profiteering. We must foster "proper" trade, which is one that does not evade state control; it is to our advantage to develop it. But profiteering, in its politico-economic sense, *cannot* be distinguished from "proper" trade. Freedom to trade is capitalism; capitalism is profiteering. It would be ridiculous to ignore this.

What then should be done? Shall we declare profiteering to be no longer punishable?

No. We must revise and redraft all the laws on profiteering, and declare all *pilfering* and every direct or indirect, open or concealed *evasion of state control, supervision and accounting* to be a punishable offence (and in fact prosecuted with redoubled severity). It is by presenting the question in this way (the Council of People's Commissars has already started, that is to say, it has ordered that work be started, on the revision of the anti-profiteering laws) that we shall succeed in directing the rather inevitable but necessary development of capitalism into the channels of *state* capitalism.

POLITICAL SUMMARY AND DEDUCTIONS

I still have to deal, if briefly, with the political situation, and the way it has taken shape and changed in connection
with the economic developments outlined above.

I have already said that the fundamental features of
our economy in 1921 are the same as those in 1918. The
spring of 1921, mainly as a result of the crop failure and
the loss of cattle, brought a sharp deterioration in the condition of the peasantry, which was bad enough because of the
war and blockade. This resulted in political vacillations
which, generally speaking, express the very "nature" of
the small producer. Their most striking expression was the
Kronstadt mutiny.

The vacillation of the petty-bourgeois element was the
most characteristic feature of the Kronstadt events. There
was very little that was clear, definite and fully shaped.
We heard nebulous slogans about "freedom", "freedom to
trade", "emancipation", "Soviets without the Bolsheviks",
or new elections to the Soviets, or relief from "Party dictatorship", and so on and so forth. Both the Mensheviks
and the Socialist-Revolutionaries declared the Kronstadt
movement to be "their own". Victor Chernov sent a messen-
ger to Kronstadt. On the latter's proposal, the Menshevik
Valk, one of the Kronstadt leaders, voted for the *Constituent Assembly*. In a flash, with lightning speed, you might
say, the whiteguards mobilised all their forces *"for Kronstadt"*. Their military experts in Kronstadt, a number
of experts, and not Kozlovsky alone, drew up a plan for
a landing at Oranienbaum, which scared the vacillating
mass of Mensheviks, Socialist-Revolutionaries and non-
party elements. More than fifty Russian whiteguard newspapers published abroad conducted a rabid campaign
"for Kronstadt". The big banks, all the forces of finance
capital, collected funds to assist Kronstadt. That shrewd
leader of the bourgeoisie and the landowners, the Cadet
Milyukov, patiently explained to the simpleton Victor
Chernov directly (and to the Mensheviks Dan and Rozhkov,
who are in jail in Petrograd for their connection with
the Kronstadt events, indirectly)   that there is no
need to hurry with the Constituent Assembly, and that

Soviet power can and must be supported—*only without the Bolsheviks.*

Of course, it is easy to be cleverer than conceited simpletons like Chernov, the petty-bourgeois phrase-monger, or like Martov, the knight of philistine reformism doctored to pass for Marxism. Properly speaking, the point is not that Milyukov, as an individual, has more brains, but that, because of his class position, the party leader of the big bourgeoisie sees and understands the class essence and political interaction of things more clearly than the leaders of the petty bourgeoisie, the Chernovs and Martovs. For the bourgeoisie is really a class force which under capitalism, inevitably rules both under a monarchy and in the most democratic republic, and which also inevitably enjoys the support of the world bourgeoisie. But the petty bourgeoisie, i.e., all the heroes of the Second International and of the "Two-and-a-Half" International, cannot, by the very economic nature of things, be anything else than the expression of class impotence; hence the vacillation, phrase-mongering and helplessness. In 1789, the petty bourgeois could still be great revolutionaries. In 1848, they were ridiculous and pathetic. Their actual role in 1917-21 is that of abominable agents and out-and-out servitors of reaction, be their names Chernov, Martov, Kautsky, MacDonald, or what have you.

Martov showed himself to be nothing but a philistine Narcissus when he declared in his Berlin journal[111] that Kronstadt not only adopted Menshevik slogans but also proved that there could be an anti-Bolshevik movement which did not entirely serve the interests of the whiteguards, the capitalists and the landowners. He says in effect: "Let us shut our eyes to the fact that all the genuine whiteguards hailed the Kronstadt mutineers and collected funds in aid of Kronstadt through the banks!" Compared with the Chernovs and Martovs, Milyukov is right, for he is revealing the *true* tactics of the *real* whiteguard force, the force of the capitalists and landowners. He declares: "It does not matter whom we support, be they anarchists or any sort of Soviet government, *as long as* the Bolsheviks are overthrown, *as long as there is a shift in power*; it does not matter whether to the right or to the left, to the

Mensheviks or to the anarchists, as long as it is away from
the Bolsheviks. As for the rest—'we', the Milyukovs, 'we',
the capitalists and landowners, will do the rest 'ourselves';
we shall slap down the anarchist pygmies, the Chernovs
and the Martovs, as we did Chernov and Maisky in Siberia,
the Hungarian Chernovs and Martovs in Hungary, Kautsky
in Germany and the Friedrich Adlers and Co. in Vienna."
The real, hard-headed bourgeoisie have made fools of
hundreds of these philistine Narcissuses—whether Menshevik,
Socialist-Revolutionary or non-party—and have driven
them out scores of times in all revolutions in all countries.
History proves it. The facts bear it out. The Narcissuses
will talk; the Milyukovs and whiteguards will act.

Milyukov is absolutely right when he says, "If only
there is a power shift away from the Bolsheviks, no matter
whether it is a little to the right or to the left, the rest
will take care of itself." This is class truth, confirmed by
the history of revolutions in all countries, and by the
centuries of modern history since the Middle Ages. The scattered small producers, the peasants, are economically *and
politically* united either by the bourgeoisie (this has always
been—and will always be—the case under capitalism in
all countries, in all modern revolutions), or by the proletariat (that was the case in a rudimentary form for a very
short period at the peak of some of the greatest revolutions
in modern history; that has been the case in Russia in a
more developed form in 1917-21). Only the Narcissuses
will talk and dream about a "third" path, and a "third
force".

With enormous difficulty, and in the course of desperate
struggles, the Bolsheviks have trained a proletarian vanguard that is capable of governing; they have created and
successfully defended the dictatorship of the proletariat.
After the test of four years of practical experience, the
relation of class forces in Russia has become as clear as
day: the steeled and tempered vanguard of the only revolutionary class; the vacillating petty-bourgeois element;
and the Milyukovs, the capitalists and landowners, lying
in wait abroad and supported by the world bourgeoisie.
It is crystal-clear: only the latter are able to take advantage of any "shift of power", and will certainly do so.

In the 1918 pamphlet I quoted above, this point was put very clearly: "the principal enemy" is the "petty-bourgeois element". "Either we subordinate it to our control and accounting, or it will overthrow the workers' power as surely and as inevitably as the revolution was overthrown by the Napoleons and the Cavaignacs who sprang from this very soil of petty proprietorship. This is how the question stands. That is the only view we can take of the matter." (Excerpt from the pamphlet of May 5, 1918, cf. above.)

Our strength lies in complete clarity and the sober consideration of *all* the existing class magnitudes, both Russian and international; and in the inexhaustible energy, iron resolve and devotion in struggle that arise from this. We have many enemies, but they are disunited, or do not know their own minds (like all the petty bourgeoisie, all the Martovs and Chernovs, all the non-party elements and anarchists). But we are united—directly among ourselves and indirectly with the proletarians of all countries; we know just what we want. That is why we are invincible on a world scale, although this does not in the least preclude the possibility of defeat for individual proletarian revolutions for longer or shorter periods.

There is good reason for calling the petty-bourgeois element an element, for it is indeed something that is most amorphous, indefinite and unconscious. The petty-bourgeois Narcissuses imagine that "universal suffrage" abolishes the nature of the small producer under capitalism. As a matter of fact, it *helps* the bourgeoisie, through the church, the press, the teachers, the police, the militarists and a thousand and one forms of economic oppression, to *subordinate* the scattered small producers. Ruin, want and the hard conditions of life give rise to vacillation: one day for the bourgeoisie, the next, for the proletariat. Only the steeled proletarian vanguard is capable of withstanding and overcoming this vacillation.

The events of the spring of 1921 once again revealed the role of the Socialist-Revolutionaries and Mensheviks: they help the vacillating petty-bourgeois element to recoil from the Bolsheviks, to cause a "shift of power" in favour of the capitalists and landowners. *The Mensheviks and*

Socialist-Revolutionaries have now learned to don the "non-party" disguise. This has been fully proved. Only fools now fail to see this and understand that we must not allow ourselves to be fooled. Non-Party conferences are not a fetish. They are valuable if they help us to come closer to the impassive masses—the millions of working people still outside politics. They are harmful if they provide a platform for the Mensheviks and Socialist-Revolutionaries masquerading as "non-party" men. They are helping the mutinies, and the whiteguards. The place for Mensheviks and Socialist-Revolutionaries, avowed or in non-party guise, is not at a non-Party conference but in prison (or on foreign journals, side by side with the white-guards; we were glad to let Martov go abroad). We can and must find other methods of testing the mood of the masses and coming closer to them. We suggest that those who want to play the parliamentary, constituent assembly and non-Party conference game, should go abroad; over there, by Martov's side, they can try the charms of "democracy" and ask Wrangel's soldiers about them. We have no time for this "opposition" at "conferences" game. We are surrounded by the world bourgeoisie, who are watching for every sign of vacillation in order to bring back "their own men", and restore the landowners and the bourgeoisie. We will keep in prison the Mensheviks and Socialist-Revolutionaries, whether avowed or in "non-party" guise.

We shall employ every means to establish closer contacts with the masses of working people untouched by politics—except such means as give scope to the Mensheviks and Socialist-Revolutionaries, and the *vacillations that benefit Milyukov.* In particular, we shall zealously draw into Soviet work, primarily economic work, hundreds upon hundreds of non-Party people, real non-Party people from the masses, the rank and file of workers and peasants, and not those who have adopted non-party colours in order to crib Menshevik and Socialist-Revolutionary instructions which are so much to Milyukov's advantage. Hundreds and thousands of non-Party people are working for us, and scores occupy very important and responsible posts. We must pay more attention to the way they work. We must do more to promote and test thousands and thousands of rank-and-file workers, to try them out systematically and persistently, and appoint hundreds of them to higher posts, if experience shows that they can fill them.

Our Communists still do not have a sufficient understanding of their real duties of administration: they should not strive to do "everything themselves", running themselves down and failing to cope with everything, undertaking twenty jobs and finishing none. They should check up on the work of scores and hundreds of assistants, arrange to have their work checked up from below, i.e., by the real masses. They should *direct* the work and *learn* from those who have the knowledge (the specialists) and the experience in organising large-scale production (the capitalists). The intelligent Communist will not be afraid to learn from the military expert, although nine-tenths of the military experts are capable of treachery at every opportunity. The wise Communist will not be afraid to learn from a capitalist (whether a big capitalist concessionaire, a commission agent, or a petty capitalist co-operator, etc.), although the capitalist is no better than the military expert. Did we not learn to catch treacherous military experts in the Red Army, to bring out the honest and conscientious, and, on the whole, to utilise thousands and tens of thousands of military experts? We are learning to do the same thing (in an unconventional way) with engineers and teachers, although we are not doing it as well as we did it in the Red Army (there Denikin and Kolchak spurred us on, compelled us to learn more quickly, diligently and intelligently). We shall also learn to do it (again in an unconventional way) with the commission agents, with the buyers working for the state, the petty capitalist co-operators, the entrepreneur concessionaires, etc.

The condition of the masses of workers and peasants needs to be improved right away. And we shall achieve this by putting new forces, including non-Party forces, to useful work. The tax in kind, and a number of measures connected with it, will facilitate this; we shall thereby cut at the economic root of the small producer's inevitable vacillations. And we shall ruthlessly fight the political vacillations, which benefit no one but Milyukov. The waverers are many, we are few. The waverers are disunited, we are united. The waverers are not economically independent, the proletariat is. The waverers don't know their own minds: they want to do something very badly, but Milyukov won't let them. We know what we want.

And that is why we shall win.

CONCLUSION

To sum up.

The tax in kind is a transition from War Communism to a regular socialist exchange of products.

The extreme ruin rendered more acute by the crop failure in 1920 has made this transition urgently necessary owing to the fact that it was impossible to restore large-scale industry rapidly.

Hence, the first thing to do is to improve the condition of the peasants. The means are the tax in kind, the development of exchange between agriculture and industry, and the development of small industry.

Exchange is freedom of trade; it is capitalism. It is useful to us inasmuch as it will help us overcome the dispersal of the small producer, and to a certain degree combat the evils of bureaucracy; to what extent this can be done will be determined by practical experience. The proletarian power is in no danger, as long as the proletariat firmly holds power in its hands, and has full control of transport and large-scale industry.

The fight against profiteering must be transformed into a fight against stealing and the evasion of state supervision, accounting and control. By means of this control we shall direct the capitalism that is to a certain extent inevitable and necessary for us into the channels of state capitalism.

The development of local initiative and independent action in encouraging exchange between agriculture and industry must be given the fullest scope at all costs. The practical experience gained must be studied; and this experience must be made as varied as possible.

We must give assistance to small industry servicing peasant farming and helping to improve it. To some extent, this assistance may be given in the form of raw materials from the state stocks. It would be most criminal to leave these raw materials unprocessed.

We must not be afraid of Communists "learning" from bourgeois experts, including merchants, petty capitalist co-operators and capitalists, in the same way as we learned from the military experts, though in a different form. The results of the "learning" must be tested only by practical experience and by doing things better than the bourgeois experts at your side; try in every way to secure an improvement in agriculture and industry, and to develop exchange between them. Do not grudge them the "tuition" fee: none will be too high, provided we learn something.

Do everything to help the masses of working people, to come closer to them, and to promote from their ranks hundreds and thousands of non-Party people for the work of economic administration. As for the "non-party" people who are only Mensheviks and Socialist-Revolutionaries disguised in fashionable non-party attire *à la* Kronstadt, they should be kept safe in prison, or packed off to Berlin, to join Martov in freely enjoying all the charms of pure democracy and freely exchanging ideas with Chernov, Milyukov and the Georgian Mensheviks.

April 21, 1921

Published in pamphlet form
in May 1921

Published according
to the pamphlet text
collated with the manuscript

RECORDED SPEECHES[112]

1

THE TAX IN KIND

The surplus-food appropriation system has been replaced by a tax in kind. The All-Russia Central Executive Committee has issued a decree to that effect. In pursuance of this decree, the Council of People's Commissars has issued a law introducing the tax in kind.[113] It is now the duty of all Soviet institutions to inform the peasants of the law as broadly as possible and explain what it means.

Why was it necessary to substitute a tax in kind for the surplus-grain appropriation system? It is because the surplus appropriation system proved to be extremely inconvenient and onerous for the peasants, whose want and ruin were further aggravated by the 1920 crop failure. Furthermore, the fodder shortage led to greater loss of cattle; less firewood was transported from the forests; and there was a slowdown in the factories producing the goods to be exchanged for the peasants' grain. The workers' and peasants' government had to take steps immediately to alleviate the condition of the peasants.

The tax in kind amounts to only about one-half of the surplus-grain appropriation rate: grain, for example, will amount to 240 million poods instead of 423 million. Every peasant will know the exact amount of tax he has to pay beforehand, that is, in the spring. This will reduce the abuses in tax collection. It will be an incentive for the peasant to cultivate a larger area, to improve his farm, and try to raise yields.

This country has been devastated unbelievably first by the tsarist war, and then by the Civil War, that is, by the landowners' and capitalists' invasion against the Soviet power of workers and peasants. The national economy must be put on its feet at all costs. And the first thing to do is to restore, consolidate and improve peasant farming.

The tax in kind will help to improve peasant farming. The peasants will now set to work on their farms with greater confidence and with a will, and that is the main thing.

April 25, 1921   *N. Lenin*

First published in 1924   Published according
                                                    to the manuscript

2

CONCESSIONS AND THE DEVELOPMENT OF CAPITALISM

The Soviet government is inviting foreign capitalists to obtain concessions in Russia.

What is a concession? It is a contract between the government and a capitalist who undertakes to organise or improve production (for example, felling and floating timber, extracting coal, oil, ore, etc.) and to pay the government a share of the product obtained, keeping the rest as his profit.

Is it right for the Soviet government to invite foreign capitalists after expelling the Russian landowners and capitalists? Yes, it is, because, seeing that the workers' revolution in other countries is delayed, we have to make some sacrifices in order to achieve a rapid and even immediate improvement in the condition of the workers and peasants. The sacrifice is that over a number of years we shall be giving away to the capitalists tens of millions of poods of valuable products. The improvement in the condition of the workers and peasants is that we shall immediately obtain additional quantities of petroleum, paraffin oil, salt, coal, farming implements, and so forth. We have no right to forego the opportunity of immediately improving the condition of the workers and peasants, for our impoverishment makes it essential, and our sacrifices will not be fatal.

But is it not dangerous to invite the capitalists? Does it not imply a development of capitalism? Yes, it does imply a development of capitalism, but this is not dangerous, because power will still be in the hands of the workers and peasants, and the landowners and capitalists will not be getting back their property. A concession is something in the nature of a contract of lease. The capitalist becomes, for a specified period, the lessee of a certain part of state property under a contract, but he does not become the owner. The state remains the owner.

The Soviet government will see to it that the capitalist lessee abides by the terms of the contract, that the contract is to our advantage, and that, as a result, the condition of the workers and peasants is improved. On these terms the development of capitalism is not dangerous, and the workers and peasants stand to gain by obtaining a larger quantity of products.

April 25, 1921   *N. Lenin*

First published in 1924   Published according
                                                     to the manuscript

3

CONSUMERS' AND PRODUCERS' CO-OPERATIVE
SOCIETIES

Consumers' co-operative societies are associations of workers and peasants for the purpose of supplying and distributing the goods they need. Producers' co-operative societies are associations of small farmers or artisans for the purpose of producing and marketing products, whether agricultural (such as vegetables, dairy produce and the like) or non-agricultural (all sorts of manufactured goods, woodwork, ironware, leather goods, and so forth).

The substitution of the tax in kind for the surplus appropriation system will give the peasants grain surpluses which they will freely exchange for all sorts of manufactured goods.

Producers' co-operatives will help to develop small industry, which will supply the peasants with greater quantities of necessary goods. Most of these do not have to be transported by rail over long distances and do not need large factories for their manufacture. Everything must be done to foster and develop producers' co-operatives, and it is the duty of Party and Soviet workers to render them every assistance, for this will give the peasants immediate relief and improve their condition. At the present time, the revival and restoration of the national economy of the workers' and peasants' state depends most of all on the improvement of peasant life and farming.

There must also be support and development of consumers' co-operative societies, for they will ensure swift, regular and low-cost distribution of products. It remains for the Soviet authorities to supervise the activity of the co-operative societies to see that there are no fraudulent practices, no concealment from the government, no abuses. In no circumstances should they hamper the co-operative societies but should help and promote them in every way.

Written on April 25, 1921

First published in 1924

Published according to a
transcript from the record

TO COMRADE KRZHIZHANOVSKY
THE PRESIDIUM OF THE STATE PLANNING
COMMISSION

There is still hardly any evidence of the operation of an integrated state economic plan. The predominating tendency is to "revive" everything, all branches of the national economy indiscriminately, even all the enterprises that we have inherited from capitalism.

The State Planning Commission should organise its work in such a way as to have drawn up, at least by harvest time, the main principles of a state economic plan for the next year or two.

It should start with food, for this is the taproot of all our difficulties. An attempt must be made to draw up a national economic plan for three contingencies: a state reserve of (1) 200; (2) 250 and (3) 300 million poods of grain for the year (September 1, 1921 to September 1, 1922). Perhaps, if the difficulties of working out detailed calculations for the three contingencies prove too great, it would be more rational to confine ourselves to one detailed calculation based on the assumption that we obtain 250 million poods, with a surplus (300 minus 250) provided against a rainy day, and only approximate the details for the contingency of a complete shortage of grain (200 million poods) (so much to be bought from abread, so much to be "tightened up" in industry, transport, the army, etc.).

Assume that the state grain reserve amounts to so much; deduct a reserve for the contingency of war, interruptions in railway communication, etc.

Then comes fuel. The prospects ranging from so much to so much. Minimum and maximum amount of food required for this purpose. The possibility of increasing fuel supplies to such-and-such dimensions if the grain reserve is increased by so much.

Possibility of economising so much fuel by concentrating production in a few of the best factories. These calculations are essential. In this connection, estimate the possibilities of economising food by closing down unnecessary factories, or those not absolutely essential, and by transferring the workers (Where? Is such transfer feasible? If not—consider the minimum task of putting such workers on shorter rations).

Economising fuel by paying a bonus for saving it and by tighter supervision of consumption. Approximate estimate of such economy—if there are any data to base it on.

The army (as distinct from the navy, for which special calculations must be made for maximum reduction, verging on abolition, and reduction of expenditure). Basis of calculation—1.6 million by Sept. 1, 1921, and a provisional estimate for half the amount.

Soviet office staffs. Present size. Possibility of reducing by 25 or 50 per cent. Bonus for one-fourth (of present number of employees, those absolutely essential) for reducing the total number. This question of giving a bonus to the remaining fourth (or third, or half) for reducing the total number of mouths (and for reducing fuel consumption by, say, introducing a three-shift system and closing two out of three offices) must be examined with particular care in view of its exceptional importance.

Industry, divided into several groups with the smallest possible number of the main groups. Water and light. Minimum necessary to cover minimum requirements: (α) productive consumption, (β) individual consumption. Estimates for a definite number of main groups (the task of working out detailed calculations for the respective branches of industry, districts and towns may, perhaps, be assigned to special subcommissions, or special local agents, or to the gubérnia statistical bureaus, etc.)— calculate how many large factories all production can be concentrated in, and how many should be closed. Obviously, this extremely important question requires particularly careful study: firstly, purely statistical (data for 1920, and, if possible, also for 1918 and 1919; sometimes, in exceptional cases, pre-war statistics may be of auxiliary use); secondly, economic, which must solve the following special problem:

Is it possible to find for the redundant urban and industrial workers whom the state ought not to feed, and for whom other employment cannot be provided in the towns, temporary employment—for a year or two—in the grain districts on the understanding that they satisfy the needs of the surrounding farming population?

After industry, from which the building industry must be singled out, comes transport (perhaps this should be put before industry?), and electrification as a distinct item.

And so forth.

The estimates must be first drawn up at least in rough outline, as a first approximation; but they must be ready at an early date—within a month, or two, at the outside. They must give an overall picture of the total food and fuel expenditure for the year. This rough plan can afterwards be filled in, corrected, amended; but at this early date we must have the main plan for the year even if only in rough outline (or perhaps separate plans for each of the quarters, or thirds, of the year: Sept. 1, 1921 to Jan. 1, 1922; Jan. 1 to May 1, and May 1 to Sept. 1, 1922).

Nineteen-twenty must be taken as a basis for comparison throughout. Perhaps a number of estimates can and must be made on the basis of a comparative statistical and economic study of the data for 1920 and the "prospects" for 1921-22.

I request that the Presidium of the State Planning Commission inform me of the opinions on this letter of the majority and of its individual members, before submitting my proposal to the Plenum of the State Planning Commission.

Chairman of the Council of Labour and Defence,
V. Ulyanov (Lenin)

May 14, 1921

P.S. 1) Special attention must be paid to the industries producing articles that can be exchanged for grain, in order to obtain grain within the country. At all events these industries must be grouped separately so as to provide a definite answer to the question: In the event of a general shortage of grain, will it be possible, by setting aside a given quantity of food and fuel for certain branches of industry, or certain factories, to obtain a given quantity of goods which can be exchanged for a given quantity of grain? This provisional estimate must be drawn up beforehand, for application, in certain cases, after the harvest.

2) An attempt must be made to single out and count up: (a) the factories (and number of workers) that are absolutely essential for the state and (b) the factories—and number of workers—which are being kept running by tradition, routine, and the unwillingness of the workers to change their occupation and domicile, etc., and which should be closed down to rationalise production and concentrate industry in a few of the best factories operating in several shifts. Total number of factories and workers in each category. Estimate reduction of ration for second category as an incentive for closing these factories.

First published in 1923   Published according
                                           to the manuscript

INSTRUCTIONS
OF THE COUNCIL OF LABOUR AND DEFENCE
TO LOCAL SOVIET BODIES[114]

DRAFT

The primary task of the Soviet Republic is to restore the productive forces and revive agriculture, industry and transport. The ruin and impoverishment caused everywhere by the imperialist war are so vast that an economic crisis is raging throughout the world, and even in the advanced countries, which before the war were way ahead of Russia in their development and which suffered much less from the war than she did, economic rehabilitation is proceeding with enormous difficulty and will take many long years. This situation prevails even in many of the "victor" countries, despite the fact that they are allied with the richest capitalist powers and are exacting a fat tribute from the defeated, dependent and colonial countries.

Backward Russia, which in addition to the imperialist war endured more than three years of civil war, imposed upon the workers and peasants by the landowners and capitalists with the help of the world bourgeoisie, naturally finds the difficulties of economic rehabilitation so much more formidable. The heavy crop failure in 1920, the lack of fodder and the loss of cattle have had a disastrous effect on peasant farming.

In conformity with the law passed by the All-Russia Central Executive Committee, a tax in kind has been substituted for the surplus appropriation system. The farmer is free to exchange his surplus produce for various goods. The tax rates have been announced by order of the Council of People's Commissars. The tax amounts to approximately one-half of the produce obtained under the surplus appropriation system. The Council of People's Commissars has issued a new law on the co-operative societies giving them wider powers in view of the free exchange of surplus farm produce.

These laws have done a great deal for the immediate improvement of the condition of peasant farming and stimulation of peasant interest in enlarging the area under crop and improving methods of farming and livestock breeding. They have also done much to help revive and develop small local industry which can do without the procurement and transportation of large state stocks of food, raw materials and fuel.

Particularly great importance now attaches to independent local initiative in improving peasant farming, developing industry and establishing exchange between agriculture and industry. Great opportunities are being created for the application of new forces and fresh energy to the work of restoring the country's economy.

The Council of Labour and Defence, upon whom, in pursuance of the decision of the Eighth All-Russia Congress of Soviets, devolves the duty of co-ordinating and directing the activity of the People's Commissariats for the various sectors of the economy, insistently urges all local bodies to do their utmost to develop extensive activities for the all-round improvement of peasant farming and the revival of industry, in strict conformity with the new laws and in the light of the fundamental propositions and instructions given below.

We now have two main criteria of success in our work of economic development on a nation-wide scale. First, success in the speedy, full and, from the state point of view, proper collection of the tax in kind; and second— and this is particularly important—success in the exchange of manufactured goods for agricultural produce between industry and agriculture.

This is most vital, urgent and imperative. It will put all our efforts to the test and lay the foundations for implementing our great electrification plan, which will result in the restoration of our large-scale industry and transport to such proportions and on such a technical basis that we shall overcome starvation and poverty once and for all.

We must collect 100 per cent of the tax in kind, and, in addition, an equal quantity of food products through the

First page of Lenin's "Instructions of the Council of Labour and Defence to Local Soviet Bodies. Draft." May 1921

Reduced

free exchange of surplus farm produce for manufactured goods. Of course, this will not be achieved everywhere all at once, but it should be our short-term goal. We can achieve it in a very short time if we take the right view of the state of our economy and put our hearts into reviving it the right way. All local authorities and bodies in every gubernia, uyezd, regional centre and autonomous republic must join forces and co-ordinate their efforts to stimulate the exchange of surplus produce. Experience will show how far we can do this by increasing the output and delivery of goods made by the state in the big socialist factories. It will show how far we succeed in encouraging and developing small local industry, and what part will be played in this by the co-operative societies and the private traders, manufacturers and capitalists who are under state control. We must try out every method, giving the utmost scope to local initiative. The new task before us has never been tackled anywhere else before. We are trying to solve it in the conditions of post-war ruin, which prevent any precise estimation of our resources or of the effort we can expect of the workers and peasants, who have made such incredible sacrifices to defeat the landowners and capitalists. We must be bolder in widely applying a variety of methods and taking different approaches, giving rein to capital and private trade in varying degree, without being afraid to implant some capitalism, as long as we succeed in stimulating exchange at once and thereby revive agriculture and industry. We must ascertain the country's resources by practical experience, and determine the best way to improve the condition of the workers and peasants to enable us to proceed with the wider and more fundamental work of building up the economy and implementing the electrification plan.

The two main questions to which every Soviet official engaged in economic work must pay attention are: how much of their surplus farm produce, over and above the tax, have the peasants exchanged for the manufactures of small industry and private trade, and how much for manufactured goods provided by the state? These are the main lines to follow over the short haul in order to achieve the greatest results. They will provide the success indicators and enable us to decide on the subsequent tasks. Every aspect of

economic construction in general must be geared to these
two immediate tasks.

To attain this co-ordination, encourage local initiative,
enterprise and large-scale operations to the utmost, and
make sure that central bodies are guided by local experience
and local supervision, and vice versa, thereby eliminating
red tape and bureaucratic practices, the Council of Labour
and Defence has ordered (see text of the order) that:

first, regular economic conferences should be convened
in all districts for the purpose of co-ordinating the work
of the local departments of all the People's Commissariats
for the various sectors of the economy;

second, proper records of the local economic conferences
should be kept to facilitate the pooling of experience and
the organising of emulation, and mainly, to utilise the work of
the local organisations and its results as a means of checking
up on the methods and organisation of the central bodies.

The local economic conferences should be organised on
the lines of the C.L.D. (Council of Labour and Defence)
and their relationship with the local executive committees
should be similar to those between the C.L.D. and the
Council of People's Commissars. The C.L.D. functions as
a commission of the Council of People's Commissars. The
appointment of members of the Council of People's Commissars to the C.L.D. ensures the fullest co-ordination
of the work of both bodies, eliminates the possibility of
any friction between them, expedites matters and simplifies
procedures. Having no staff of its own, the C.L.D. utilises
that of various government departments, striving to sim-
plify their procedures and co-ordinate their operations.

Gubernia economic councils should stand in the same
relationship to the gubernia executive committees, and
that is the actual trend in practice. The C.L.D., in confirming the appointment of members and chairmen of regional
and territorial economic councils, strives to take account
of the experience of local workers and consults with them
on all its confirmations. The regional economic councils
must certainly strive, and will continue to strive, to co-
ordinate their work with that of the gubernia economic
councils, securing their fullest co-operation, keeping them
informed and stimulating their interest. This is hardly

the time to try to reduce these relationships to a set of regulations, for experience is still very short and any such attempt might result in a purely bureaucratic exercise. It is far more appropriate to allow practice to determine initially the most suitable form of relationship (the C.L.D. worked side by side with the Council of People's Commissars for about a year, virtually without a constitution). Let these forms be at first not absolutely stable: variety is desirable, useful and even necessary to enable us to make a more precise study and a fuller comparison of the various systems of relationships.

Uyezd and volost economic councils should be organised on the same lines, naturally with a lot of leeway in modifying the main type, that is, the executive committees may assume all the functions and duties of the economic conferences, convert their own "executive" or "economic" meetings into economic conferences, appoint (say, in the volosts and sometimes in the uyezds) special committees or even individuals to exercise all or some of the functions of the economic conferences, and so on and so forth. The *village committees* should be the bottom rung and should operate as the lower units of the C.L.D. in the rural districts. The Council of People's Commissars has already passed a law, issued in May 1921, which gives the village committees wider powers and defines their relationship with the village Soviets. The gubernia executive committees must draw up provisional regulations suitable for the given locality which, however, must not restrict, but give *the greatest possible scope* to "local" initiative in general, and that of the lowest units *in particular.*

In industrial uyezds and settlements, the district committees and factory committees, or the management boards of factories, should serve as the lower units of the C.L.D., depending on whether one or more branches of industry are being dealt with. In any case, *co-operation* with the uyezd executive committees, volost executive committees and village committees in directing *all* local economic life is absolutely essential in one form or another.

Furthermore, it is exceptionally important that local organisations should submit to the C.L.D. regular and precise information on their activity, for one of our main

evils is the inadequate study of practical experience, inadequate exchange of experience and mutual control—putting
orders from the centre to the test of local experience, and
subjecting local work to control by the centre. One of the
most important means of combating bureaucratic practices
and red tape should be to check the way the laws and orders
from the centre are carried out locally, and this requires
the printing of *public* reports, with *non-Party people* and people not working in the departments necessarily *taking a greater
hand. Nashe Khozyaistvo*, "the fortnightly journal of the Tver
Gubernia Economic Council" (No. 1, April 15, 1921; No. 2,
April 30, 1921), is evidence that the local need to study,
elucidate and publicise the results of our economic experience is being realised and satisfied the correct way. It
will not be possible, of course, to publish a journal in every
gubernia, not within the next few months, at any rate;
nor will it be possible everywhere to have a fortnightly
printing of 3,000 copies, as is the case in Tver. But every
gubernia, and every uyezd even, can—and should—compile a report on local economic activities once every two
months (or initially at longer intervals, by way of exception) and issue it in a printing of, say, 100 to 300 copies.
The paper and the printing facilities for such a small operation will surely be found everywhere, provided we realise
its urgency and importance, and see the necessity to satisfy
this need by taking the paper from many of the departments
which print a mass of useless and hardly urgent material.
The copy could be set up in small type and printed in two
columns (as the comrades in Tver are doing); the feasibility
and urgency of this will be quite clear if we realise the
simple truth that even a hundred copies, distributed one
to every gubernia library and all the major state libraries,
will provide a source of information for *the whole of Russia*,
which may perhaps be scanty but *sure*, and will serve as
a record of experience.

These reports must be published regularly, even if in
small printings, in order to maintain a proper record of
experience, and actually pool it, and enlist all the prominent and capable organisers among the non-Party people.
This is something we can and must do immediately.

When drawing up the reports, the questions put must

be answered as briefly and precisely as possible. The questions fall into four groups, the first being those especially prominent at the present time. They must be answered in every report with the maximum precision and in the greatest detail. That is particularly necessary because this group of questions is extremely vital and urgent for most uyezds at this very moment. Other questions will come to the fore for the smaller part of the uyezds and districts, that is, the purely industrial ones. The second group consists of questions which must also be answered in every report, but the answers can and should frequently be given in the form of brief summaries of reports already submitted to the government departments concerned. In all such cases, the reports to the C.L.D. must give: the dates on which the reports were sent off; the departments to which they were sent; and a brief summary of the reports in figures. The C.L.D. requires such reports for supervision over the various departments, as well as for the totals indicating the results in food supplies, fuel, industry, and so forth. The third group contains questions that need *not* be answered in every report. The answers to these questions must be given initially, that is, in the first report, but subsequent reports should add only the supplementary and new information as it accumulates. In many cases, there will be nothing to report at all on these questions every two months. The fourth group consists of miscellaneous, supplementary questions, which are not indicated in advance; they are not formulated by the centre but arise locally. This group must be compiled by the local bodies, and is not limited in any way. It goes without saying that questions pertaining to state secrets (army, or such as are connected with military operations, security, etc.) must be answered in special reports not for publication, but intended exclusively for the C.L.D. as confidential reports.

Here is a list of these questions:

FIRST GROUP OF QUESTIONS
1. COMMODITY EXCHANGE WITH THE PEASANTRY

At present, this question ranks first in importance and urgency. First, the state cannot carry on any economic development unless the army and the urban workers have

regular and adequate supplies of food; the exchange of
commodities must become the principal means of collecting foodstuffs. Secondly, commodity exchange is a test of
the relationship between industry and agriculture and the
foundation of all our work to create a fairly well regulated
monetary system. All economic councils and all economic
bodies must now concentrate on commodity exchange
(which also includes the exchange of manufactured goods,
for the manufactured goods made by socialist factories
and exchanged for the foodstuffs produced by the peasants
are not commodities in the politico-economic sense of the
word; at any rate, they are not only commodities, they
are no longer commodities, they are ceasing to be
commodities).

What preparations have been made for commodity
exchange? What has been done specifically to prepare for
it? By the Commissariat for Food? By the co-operative
societies? The number of co-operative shops available
for this purpose? Are there such shops in every volost?
In how many villages? Stock of goods for commodity
exchange? Prices on the "free" market? Surplus stocks of
grain and other farm produce? Is there any, and how much,
experience in commodity exchange? Totals and results?
What is being done to prevent the pilferage of goods stocks
earmarked for exchange, and of food stocks (a particularly
important point demanding investigation of *every case* of
pilferage)?

Salt and paraffin oil as articles for commodity exchange?
Textiles? Other goods? What items are needed most? What
are the chief peasant shortages? What can be supplied by
local, small, handicraft industry? Or by developing local
industry?

Facts and figures showing how commodity exchange is
organised and the results achieved are most important for
the conduct of the experiment on a country-wide scale.

Has the proper relationship been established between the
Commissariat for Food, the body controlling and supervis-
ing commodity exchange, and the co-operative societies,
the bodies carrying on commodity exchange? How does
this relationship operate in practice? In each locality?

What part does private trade play in commodity

exchange? To what extent is private trade developing, or developed? Number of private traders; their turnover in the major items, particularly foodstuffs?

2. THE STATE'S ATTITUDE TO THE CAPITALISTS

Commodity exchange and freedom of trade inevitably imply the appearance of capitalists and capitalist relationships. There is no reason to fear this. The workers' state has enough resources to keep *within the proper bounds* and control these relationships, which are useful and necessary in conditions of small-scale production. The thing to do at present is to make a close study of their dimensions and devise suitable methods (not restrictive, or rather, not prohibitive) of state control and accountancy.

To what extent is private trade developing as a result of the substitution of the tax for the surplus appropriation system? Can it be estimated or not? Is it only profiteering or regular trade as well? Is it registered, and if so, what are the results?

Private enterprise: have there been any offers from capitalists and entrepreneurs to lease enterprises or establishments, or commercial premises? Exact number of such offers and an analysis of them? How are the results of trading operations assessed (if only approximately)? Ditto as regards the accounts of leaseholders and commission agents, if any?

Have there been any offers from commission agents? To buy produce for the state on a commission basis? Or to market and distribute it? Or to organise industrial enterprises?

Handicraft industry: changes since the introduction of the tax in kind? Extent of development? Source of information?

3. ENCOURAGEMENT OF ENTERPRISE IN COMMODITY EXCHANGE, AND IN ECONOMIC DEVELOPMENT IN GENERAL

This question is closely bound up with the preceding one. The encouragement of initiative may often prove to have no connection with capitalist relationships. All economic councils and economic bodies in general should ask themselves: how is this to be encouraged? In view of the novelty of the task, it is scarcely possible to issue any definite instructions at present. The thing is to pay great attention to the question, encourage all initiative in economic matters, make a careful study of practical experience and let the country know what is being done.

When the small farmer pays his tax to the state and enters into commodity exchange with it (with the socialist factory) the economic situation created imperatively demands that the state, through its local bodies, should give all possible encouragement to enterprise and initiative. The exchange of the observations and experience of local bodies will enable us to collect material, and later on, perhaps, to supplement this general and inadequate formulation of the question with a number of examples and detailed instructions.

4. CO-ORDINATION OF THE ECONOMIC WORK OF VARIOUS DEPARTMENTS IN THE LOCAL ADMINISTRATIVE AREAS: VOLOSTS, UYEZDS AND GUBERNIAS

One of the great evils hindering our economic development is the absence of co-ordination in the work of the various local departments. Great attention must be devoted to this question. It is the function of the economic councils to eliminate this flaw and to stimulate the enterprise of local bodies. There must be a collection of practical examples to secure improvements and hold out the successful cases as a model for all. During the extreme food shortage, for instance, it was natural and inevitable that local bodies should be highly restricted in making decisions on the use of grain collected. As grain stocks increase, and under appropriate control, they must have a freer hand to do so. This can and should help to reduce red tape, cut down haulage of goods, encourage production and improve the condition of the workers and peasants. The food supply, small local industry, fuel, large-scale state industry, etc., are all bound up together, and their necessary division into "departments" for the purposes of state administration will cause harm unless constant efforts are made to co-ordinate them, remove friction, red tape, departmental narrow-mindedness and bureaucratic methods. The local bodies, which are closer to the mass of workers and peasants, have a better view of these defects, and it is therefore their business to devise methods of eliminating them by pooling their experience.

It is absolutely essential that definite, careful and detailed replies should be submitted to the following question: What has been done and how to co-ordinate the activity of the local state farms, timber committees, uyezd land departments, economic councils, and so forth?

How are officials penalised for satisfying local requirements to the detriment of the centre and in violation of orders from the centre? The names of those penalised? Is the number of such offences diminishing? Have the penalties been increased? If so, in what way?

5. IMPROVEMENT OF THE CONDITION OF THE WORKERS AND 6. DITTO OF THE PEASANTS

Every success achieved in economic development improves the condition of the workers and peasants. But, first, here again departmental narrow-mindedness and the lack of co-ordination are doing a great deal of harm. And, second, these questions must be brought up well to the fore to allow a careful observation of the results achieved in this sphere. What exactly has been achieved? In what way? Answers to these questions are essential.

Weariness and in some cases downright exhaustion as a result of the long years of war, first the imperialist war and then the Civil War, are so great that it is absolutely essential to make special efforts to improve the condition of the workers and peasants. Very far from everything is being done that could and should be done, even with our meagre resources. By no means all the departments and agencies are concentrating on it. It is therefore a matter of urgent necessity to collect and study local experience in this field. The reports should be compiled as precisely, fully and carefully as possible. If that is done, it will at once become evident which departments lag most and where. We shall then secure an improvement more quickly through a common effort.

7. INCREASING THE NUMBER OF GOVERNMENT OFFICIALS
IN ECONOMIC DEVELOPMENT

It is extremely important for us to enlarge this group of workers, but very little systematic effort is being made to do so. Under capitalism, the individual proprietors strove to obtain—secretly from one another, and tripping each other up—the services of good salesmen, managers and directors. It took them decades to do this, and only a few of the best firms achieved good results. Today, the workers' and peasants' state is the "proprietor", and it must select the best men for economic development; it must select the best administrators and organisers on the special and general, local and national scale, doing this *publicly*, in a methodical and systematic manner and on a broad scale. Now and again we still see traces of the initial period of the Soviet power—the period of fierce civil war and intense sabotage, traces of Communists isolating themselves in a narrow circle of rulers, being fearful or incapable of enlisting the services of sufficient numbers of non-Party people.

We must set to work quickly and energetically to correct this. A number of capable and honest non-Party people are coming to the fore from the ranks of the workers, peasants and intellectuals, and they should be promoted to more important positions in economic work, with the Communists continuing to exercise the necessary control and guidance. Conversely, we must have non-Party people controlling the Communists. For this purpose, groups of non-Party workers and peasants, whose honesty has been tested, should be invited to take part, on the one hand, in the Workers' and Peasants' Inspection, and on the other, in the informal verification and appraisal of work, quite apart from any official appointment.

In their reports to the C.L.D., the local bodies, particularly in the volosts, uyezds and districts, which have the best knowledge of the worker and peasant masses, should give *lists* of non-Party people who have proved their honesty at work, or who have simply become prominent at non-Party conferences, or who command universal respect in their factory, village, volost, etc., and should indicate their assignments in economic construction. By work is meant official position as well as *unofficial participation in control and verification*, regular attendance at informal conferences, etc.

There must be regular replies to these questions, for otherwise the socialist state will be unable to organise correctly the enlistment of the masses in the work of economic development. There are any number of honest and loyal workers. There are many of them among the non-Party people, but we do not know them. Only local reports can help us to find them and try them out in wider and gradually expanding fields of work, and cure the evil of isolation of Communist Party cells from the masses, an evil that is in evidence in many places.

8. METHODS AND RESULTS OF COMBATING BUREAUCRATIC PRACTICES AND RED TAPE

At first, most answers to this question will probably be very simple: methods—nil; results—nil. The decisions of the Eighth All-Russia Congress of Soviets have been read and forgotten.

But although the situation in this field is deplorable, we shall certainly not imitate those who give way to despair. We know that in Russia bureaucratic routine and red tape are mostly due to the low standard of culture and the consequences of the extreme ruin and impoverishment resulting from the war. This evil can be overcome only by strenuous and persistent effort over a long period of years. Therefore, we must not give way to despair, but make a new start every time, pick it up where it was abandoned, and try diverse ways of achieving our goal.

The reorganisation of the Workers' and Peasants' Inspection; enlistment of the services of non-Party people with and without this inspection; legal proceedings; reduction and careful selection of staffs; verification and co-ordination of the work of the various departments, and so on and so forth— all these measures, everything indicated in the decisions of the Eighth Congress of Soviets, all the measures and methods mentioned in the press must be systematically, steadily and repeatedly tried out, compared and studied.

The gubernia economic councils, and all the other bodies co-ordinating and directing economic development in the localities, must insist on the implementation of measures prescribed by the law and indicated by practical experience. Local experience must be pooled. Answers to this question must be sent in to the C.L.D., regardless of how hard it may be at first to teach people to give exact, full and timely answers. The C.L.D. will·see to it that this is done. It will undoubtedly produce good results, even if not as quickly as is expected by those who tend to reduce the "combating of red tape" to a mere phrase (or to a repetition of whiteguard, Socialist-Revolutionary and also Menshevik, gossip) instead of working hard to take definite steps.

SECOND GROUP OF QUESTIONS

9. REVIVAL OF AGRICULTURE: A) PEASANT FARMING; B) STATE FARMS; C) COMMUNES; D) ARTELS; E) CO-OPERATIVES; F) OTHER FORMS OF COLLECTIVE FARMING

The briefest summaries, giving the figures of the reports sent to the respective departments, with the date on which each report was sent.

More detailed information—not in every report, but periodically, every four or six months, and so forth—on the more important aspects of local farming, results of surveys, the major measures adopted, and their verified results.

Exact information must be given at least twice a year on the number of collective farms (all types, b-f), classified according to the degree of organisation—good, fair and unsatisfactory. A typical farm in each of the three groups must be described in detail at least twice a year, with exact data on size, location, production performance, its assistance to peasant farming, etc.

10. REVIVAL OF INDUSTRY: A) LARGE-SCALE INDUSTRY ENTIRELY CONTROLLED BY THE CENTRE; B) LARGE-SCALE INDUSTRY CONTROLLED WHOLLY OR PARTLY BY LOCAL BODIES; C) SMALL, HANDICRAFT, DOMESTIC, ETC., INDUSTRIES

The answers should be on the same lines as those for the preceding section. As regards category A, the local bodies, which have opportunities for making a close observation of the work of large national establishments, their influence on the neighbouring population, and the attitude of the population to them, must, in every report, give information on these establishments, the assistance given to them by local bodies, the results of this assistance, the assistance rendered to the local population by these establishments, their most urgent requirements, defects in their organisation, etc.

11. FUEL: A) FIREWOOD; B) COAL; C) OIL; D) SHALE; E) OTHER TYPES OF FUEL (WASTE FUEL, ETC.)

The same as for the two preceding questions: the briefest summaries, giving the figures of the reports sent to the respective departments and dates on which they were sent.

Detailed information on major points, on what is outside the scope of the department, on local co-ordination of work, etc.

Special attention must be paid to economising fuel. What measures are being taken? What are the results?

12. FOOD SUPPLIES

Summary of reports to the Commissariat for Food, following the same rules as above.

Market gardening and suburban farming (connected with industrial establishments). Results.

Local experience in organising school meals, the feeding of children, dining-rooms, public catering in general, etc.

Bi-monthly summaries in two figures are obligatory, that is, total number of persons receiving food, and total quantity of foodstuffs distributed.

In every large consuming centre (large or medium towns, military institutions in special settlements, etc.) we are feeding many extra people, former government officials who have crept into Soviet agencies, bourgeois lying low, profiteers, etc. There must be a determined drive to sift out these superfluous mouths who are breaking the fundamental law: He who does not work shall not eat. For this purpose, a responsible statistician must be appointed in all such places to study the returns of the census of August 28, 1920, and current statistical returns, and submit a signed report on the number of extra consumers every two months.

13. BUILDING INDUSTRY

Answers must be on the same lines as the preceding. Local initiative and self-reliance are particularly important in this sphere and must be given particularly wide scope. Detailed information on the major measures and results is obligatory.

14. MODEL AND HOPELESS ENTERPRISES AND ESTABLISHMENTS

A description of every enterprise, establishment and office connected with economic development and meriting the designation of model, or at least outstanding, or successful (in the event of there being none in the first two categories) is obligatory. Names of the members of the management boards of these establishments. Their methods. Results. Attitude of the workers and the population.

The same as regards hopeless and useless enterprises.

Of special importance is the question of closing down enterprises that are not absolutely essential (hopeless ones, such as might be closed down and their operations transferred to a smaller number of larger enterprises, etc.). Statistical summary of such superfluous establishments, their number and the order in which the Republic should gradually dispense with them.

15. IMPROVEMENT IN ECONOMIC WORK

Enumerate major and model cases of improvements introduced by inventors and workers of exceptional ability. Give names; enumerate experiments which the local bodies regard as important, and so forth.

16. BONUSES IN KIND

This is one of the most important factors in socialist development. The enlistment of labour is one of the most important and difficult problems of socialism.

Practical experience in this field must be systematically collected, recorded and studied.

Obligatory bi-monthly reports showing how many bonuses issued, what the bonuses consist of, what branch of industry (separately forestry and all other branches of work). A comparison of the results, output, with the number of bonuses in kind issued?

Have there been any cases of bonuses being converted into a wage reserve? Report each case separately.

Have bonuses been issued to conspicuously successful enterprises and individual workers? Give exact details of each case.

Investigate: can a local product be obtained (for export, or one particularly valuable for use in Russia) by increasing the bonuses in kind by a given quantity? This is highly important, because if this survey is properly conducted across the country we shall discover many valuable products which we could profitably export, even if we have to import a certain quantity of goods for the bonuses in kind.

17. THE TRADE UNIONS. THEIR PART IN PRODUCTION

The gubernia trade union councils and the uyezd trade union bodies must immediately appoint reporters and their deputies who must, on their own, and with the help of local statisticians, draw up bi-monthly reports on the subject.

As regards production propaganda, give exact facts and figures on lectures, meetings and demonstrations, with the names of organisers, etc.

But of even greater importance than production propaganda are the facts about the part the factory committees and the trade unions in general actually play in production. Forms of participation? Describe every typical case. Practical results. Compare establishments where the participation of the trade union in production is well, or fairly well, organised, with those where it is not.

The question of labour discipline is particularly important. Reports on the number of absentees are obligatory. Compare factories where labour discipline is bad with those where it is good.

Methods of improving labour discipline.

Comrades' disciplinary courts. How many, and when established? How many cases examined per month? Results?

18. STEALING

While some organisations are aware of this widespread evil and are fighting it, there are others which report that "in the department, office or factory in our charge, there is no stealing", "everything is in order".

Precise bi-monthly reports are obligatory. How many offices, establishments, and so forth, send in information? How many do not?

Brief summary of this information.

The measures taken to combat stealing.

Are managers, management boards, or factory committees called to account (for laxity in combating stealing)?

Are people searched? Are other methods of control employed; if so, what are they?

Is the new law on commodity exchange, and on the permission given the workers to retain part of their output for this purpose, having the effect of reducing stealing? Give precise details.

Local warehouses, that is, warehouses located in the given district, and belonging to the state or to the local authorities. Brief summary of the reports on these warehouses, giving the date on which each was sent.

Reports by the local authorities on state warehouses. Methods of protection. Stealing. Number of persons employed, etc.

19. PROFITEERING

Extent of this according to local information. Predominating type of profiteer. Workers? Peasants? Railway employees? Other Soviet employees? And so forth.

State of the railways and waterways.

Measures to combat profiteering and results obtained.

What records are being kept of profiteers and profiteering?

20. USE OF ARMY UNITS FOR LABOUR

Labour armies. Composition, numerical strength, and performance. Methods of accounting? Attitude of the local population?

Other forms of using army units—ditto universal military training units—for labour purposes.

Numerical strength of local army units—ditto local universal military training administration, and number of youths undergoing training in the units.

Concrete cases of employment of youths undergoing universal military training and Red Army men for definite forms of control work, sanitary inspection, help to the local population, various economic operations. Give a detailed description of each case, or if there are a number of cases give two typical ones: the most and the least successful.

21. LABOUR SERVICE AND LABOUR MOBILISATION

How are the local departments of the People's Commissariat for Labour organised? What are they doing?

Brief summaries of their reports sent to the People's Commissariat for Labour; give date on which each report was sent.

Describe, not less than once in four months, two typical cases of labour mobilisation; the most and the least successful.

Enumerate purposes for which labour service was enforced. Total figures of the number engaged and results of work done.

What part do the local departments of the Central Statistical Board play in organising labour service and labour mobilisation?

THIRD GROUP OF QUESTIONS

22. REGIONAL AND LOCAL ECONOMIC COUNCILS

When and how were the economic councils established in the localities at region, gubernia, uyezd and volost level? How is their work co-ordinated between themselves and with the village committees, the factory committees?

Economic councils of district Soviets in big towns. Their composition, work, how is the work organised, relations with the city Soviets?

Are there any district committees and district economic councils? Are they necessary? Is it necessary to set up the larger factory or industrial settlements, with their environs, as separate areas, and so forth?

23. GOSPLAN (THE STATE GENERAL PLANNING COMMISSION OF THE C.L.D.) AND ITS RELATIONSHIPS WITH LOCAL ECONOMIC BODIES

Are there any regional bodies of Gosplan? Or special representatives of the latter? Or groups of experts acting in such a capacity?

Is the work of the local bodies co-ordinated with Gosplan's? If so, how? Is such co-ordination necessary?

24. ELECTRIFICATION

Have the gubernia and uyezd libraries copies of the Plan for the Electrification of the R.S.F.S.R., which was submitted as a report to the Eighth Congress of Soviets? If so, how many copies? If not, it shows that the local delegates to the Eighth Congress of Soviets are dishonest and ought to be expelled from the Party and dismissed from their responsible posts, or else they are idlers who should be taught to do their duty by a term of imprisonment (at the Eighth Congress of Soviets, 1,500-2,000 copies were handed out for local libraries).

What measures have been taken to carry out the decision of the Eighth Congress of Soviets to conduct extensive propaganda of the electrification plan? How many articles on the subject have appeared in the local newspapers? How many lectures have been delivered? Number of persons attending these?

Have all local workers with theoretical or practical knowledge of electricity been mobilised for the purpose of delivering lectures on, or teaching, the subject? Number of such persons? How is their work being conducted? Are the local or nearest electric power stations utilised for lectures and purposes of instruction? Number of such stations?

How many educational establishments have included the electrification plan in their syllabus, in conformity with the decision of the Eighth Congress of Soviets?

Has anything practical been done towards carrying out this plan? Or any electrification work outside the plan? If so, what has been done?

Is there a local plan and schedule of work on electrification?

25. COMMODITY EXCHANGE WITH FOREIGN COUNTRIES

It is absolutely obligatory for all border areas to answer this question, but not only for them. Uyezds and gubernias adjacent to border areas also have opportunities for engaging in such commodity exchange and observing how it is organised. Furthermore, as indicated above (Point 16: Bonuses in Kind), localities even very remote from the border have opportunities to engage in commodity exchange with foreign countries.

State of the ports? Protection of the border? Volume and forms of trade? Brief summaries of the reports on this sent to the People's Commissariat for Foreign Trade, giving the date on which each report was sent.

Supervision of the work of the People's Commissariat for Foreign Trade by the local economic councils? Their opinions on practical organisation and results?

26. RAILWAY, WATER AND LOCAL TRANSPORT

Brief summaries of the reports sent to the appropriate department, giving date on which each report was sent.

State of affairs appraised from the local standpoint.

Defects in the transport system. Measures taken to improve it and their results?

The state of local transport facilities, and measures taken to improve them.

27. PRESS PUBLICITY FOR ECONOMIC WORK

Local publications and *Ekonomicheskaya Zhizn.* How is economic work treated in the press? Participation of non-Party people? Verification and appraisal of practical experience?

Circulation of local publications and of *Ekonomicheskaya Zhizn*? Are they available at the libraries and accessible to the public?

Publication of pamphlets and books on economic development. Give list of the publications issued.

Demand for foreign literature: to what extent is it satisfied? Are the publications of the Bureau of Foreign Science and Technology delivered? If so, what opinion is expressed about them? Other foreign publications in Russian and other languages?

FOURTH GROUP OF QUESTIONS

This group should include questions chosen at the discretion of and suggested by the local bodies themselves, and by individuals; moreover, these questions may have a direct or indirect, close or remote, connection with economic development.

———

These reports must be drawn up in co-operation with the members of the local staffs of the Central Statistical Board. Whether this is done by them, or any other persons, is up to the local economic council to decide, but the co-operation of the gubernia statistical bureau and uyezd statisticians is obligatory. Every report and every answer to a question, if written by different persons, must be signed by the author, giving his official position, if he holds one. Responsibility for the reports rests on the authors, and the local economic councils as a whole, and it shall be their duty to send in regular, punctual and truthful reports.

Wherever there is a shortage of local workers, courses of instruction in the compilation of reports must be organised under the supervision of statisticians and comrades, specially appointed for the purpose (from the Workers' and Peasants' Inspection, and other bodies). The names of the persons responsible for these courses and the schedule of instruction must be published.

May 21, 1921

Lenin

Published as a pamphlet in 1921   Published according
to the text of the pamphlet
collated with the manuscript

TENTH ALL-RUSSIA CONFERENCE OF THE R.C.P.(B.)[115]

MAY 26-28, 1921

Published in *Byulleten Vserossiiskoi Konferentsii R.K.P. (Bolshevikov)* (*Bulletin of the All-Russia Conference of the R.C.P. [B.]*) Nos. 1 and 2, May 27 and 28, 1921

Published according to the *Byulleten* text

1

SPEECH IN OPENING THE CONFERENCE
MAY 26

Comrades, permit me to declare the All-Russia Conference of the R.C.P. open.

You are aware, comrades, that this conference has been convened earlier than is prescribed by the Rules. Consequently, it is not an ordinary, or at least, not quite an ordinary conference. You are also aware that the main item on the agenda—the main question—that has compelled us to convene the conference before the planned date is that of economic policy—the tax in kind. It is central at the present time.

I propose that we proceed to elect the presidium of the conference.

———

2

REPORT ON THE TAX IN KIND
MAY 26

Comrades, I had occasion to discuss, for the benefit of the Party, the question of the tax in kind in a pamphlet with which, I suppose, the majority of you are familiar. That this question has been brought up for discussion at a Party conference came as a surprise to me, for I had not seen anything to indicate that this was called for. But very many of the comrades who have visited the localities, notably Comrade Osinsky upon his return from a tour of a number of gubernias, informed the Central Committee— and this was corroborated by several other comrades—that locally the policy which had taken shape in connection with the tax in kind remained largely unexplained and partly even misunderstood. In view of its exceptional importance, additional discussion at a Party conference seemed so necessary that it was decided to convene the conference earlier than scheduled. You are aware that we in the Central Committee have decided to divide the report on this point into four parts, to be given by four rapporteurs: Kamenev, on the work of the co-operatives; Milyutin, on small-scale industry; Comrade Svidersky, on the precise calculations and proposals of the People's Commissariat for Food, and the related organisational measures; the instructions and regulations on the tax system, partly approved, and partly to be approved shortly, by the Council of People's Commissars, are of especial importance in this connection. Finally, Comrade Khinchuk is to be the fourth rapporteur; he has been relieved of all his duties in the People's Commissariat for Food to allow him to concentrate entirely on the co-operatives, as Chairman of Tsentrosoyuz.*

---

* Central Council of Co-operative Societies.—*Tr.*

It has been decided, as the chief principle, that the commodity exchange in this case is to be handled by the People's Commissariat for Food, mostly and even chiefly, through Tsentrosoyuz and the co-operatives. These relations between the People's Commissariat for Food and Tsentrosoyuz should be formalised in an agreement, stating that all the goods available for exchange shall be handed over by the People's Commissariat for Food to Tsentrosoyuz. This makes the latter's role quite clear, and there is no need to go into it in detail. Thus, it has fallen to me to introduce the question of the general significance of this policy, and I should merely like to supplement what I have already said in the pamphlet. I have no direct information as to how this question is being presented in the localities or to the flaws, defects and unclarity that there prevail. I may have to elaborate certain points later on, when it becomes clearer from the questions that are raised at the conference, or from the subsequent debate, how the local officials and the Party are to be oriented.

As far as I can see, the misunderstandings and lack of clarity on the political tasks connected with the tax in kind and the New Economic Policy are perhaps due to the exaggeration of this or that aspect of the matter. But until we have organised this work on practical lines, these exaggerations are absolutely inevitable; and until we have carried out at least one food campaign on the new lines, it will hardly be possible at all to give any precise definition to the real limits for the application of this or that specific feature of this policy. I shall deal only in general outline with some of the contradictions which, as far as I could judge from several notes sent up at the meeting, have given rise to most misunderstanding. The tax in kind and the attendant changes in our policy are often interpreted as a sign of a drastic reversal of policy. It is not surprising that this interpretation is taken up and made most of by the whiteguard, particularly the Socialist-Revolutionary and Menshevik, press abroad. I do not know whether it is due to the operation of similar influences which have made themselves felt on the territory of the R.S.F.S.R., or to the acute discontent which was, and perhaps still is, evident in certain circles, owing to the extreme aggrava-

tion of the food situation, but this sort of perplexity may
have spread to some extent even in this country and created
what is largely a wrong conception of the significance of
the change that has been brought about and of the character
of the new policy.

Naturally, in view of the fact that the peasantry pre-
ponderates enormously among the population, the principal
task—of our policy in general, and of our economic policy
in particular—is to establish definite relations between the
working class and the peasantry. For the first time in modern
history we have a social system from which the exploiting
class has been eliminated but in which there are two
different classes—the working class and the peasantry. The
enormous preponderance of the peasantry could not but have
an effect on our economic policy, and our policy in general.
The principal problem that still confronts us—and will
inevitably confront us for many years to come—is that
of establishing proper relations between these two classes,
proper from the standpoint of abolishing classes. The enemies of the Soviet power discuss the formula of agreement
between the working class and the peasantry with such
frequency, and so very often use it against us, because it is
so vague. Agreement between the working class and the
peasantry may be taken to mean anything. Unless we assume
that, from the working-class standpoint, an agreement
is possible in principle, permissible, and correct only if it
supports the dictatorship of the working class and is one of
the measures aimed at the abolition of classes, then, of
course, it remains a formula on which all the enemies of the
Soviet power, all the enemies of the dictatorship, operate.
How is this agreement to be realised in the first period
of our revolution, i.e., the period which we can now
approximately consider as coming to a close? How was the
dictatorship of the proletariat maintained and consolidated
amidst the enormous preponderance of the peasant population? It is the Civil War that was the principal reason, the
principal motive force, and the principal determinant of
our agreement. Although, in many cases, the Civil War was
started with the whiteguards, the Socialist-Revolutionaries,
and the Mensheviks jointly participating in the alliance
against us, it invariably led to all the Socialist-Revolution-

ary Constituent Assembly and Menshevik elements finding themselves—either through a *coup d'état* or otherwise—driven into the background, which left the capitalist and landowner elements to head the whiteguard movement. That was the case under Kolchak and Denikin, and all the numerous smaller regimes and during campaigns against us. It was the principal factor that determined the form of the alliance between the proletariat and the peasantry. This circumstance multiplied our incredible difficulties, but upon the other hand, it spared us the necessity of racking our brains over how to apply the alliance formula, for it and the conditions of its realisation were both dictated by the circumstances of war, leaving us no choice whatsoever.

Only the working class could exercise the dictatorship in the form demanded by the Civil War and its conditions. The participation of the landowners in this war united the working class and the peasantry absolutely, unreservedly and irrevocably. In that respect there was no internal political wavering whatsoever. Amidst the gigantic difficulties that confronted us because Russia was cut off from her principal grain areas and food hardships had been aggravated to the extreme, we could not have carried out our food policy in practice without the appropriation of surplus grain. This meant taking not only the surplus stocks of grain, which would hardly have sufficed even if they had been properly distributed. I cannot here deal in detail with the irregularities which the system brought in its train. At all events, it served its main purpose—keeping industry going even when we were almost completely cut off from the grain districts. But this could have been at all satisfactory only in conditions of war. As soon as we had finally done away with the external enemy—and this became a fact only in 1921—another task confronted us, the task of establishing an *economic* alliance between the working class and the peasantry. It was only in the spring of 1921 that we actually got down to this task, and that was when the 1920 crop failure had worsened the condition of the peasantry to an incredible degree, and when we first witnessed some internal political wavering, which did not result from external enemy pressure, but from the relations between the working class and the peasantry. If we had had a very good, or at least a good, harvest in 1920, if the surplus appropriations had yielded 400 million out of the planned 420 million poods of grain, we would have been able to fulfil the greater part of our industrial programme and would have had a stock of manufactured urban goods to exchange for agricultural produce. But the opposite happened. A fuel crisis, even more acute than the food crisis, developed in some places and it was utterly impossible to satisfy the needs of the peasant farms in urban manufactures. Peasant farming was gripped by an incredibly acute crisis. Those were the circumstances that suggested that we could not possibly continue with the old food policy. We had to bring up the question of what economic basis we required immediately for the alliance between the working class and the peasantry as a stepping stone to further measures.

The stepping stone is to prepare the exchange of industrial goods for agricultural produce; to create a system under which the peasant would not have to surrender his produce otherwise than in exchange for urban and factory-made goods, but which would not subordinate him to any of the forms existing under the capitalist system. In view of the prevailing economic conditions, however, we could not even think about that. That is why we have adopted the transitional form I have spoken about, namely, to take produce in the form of a tax without giving any equivalent, and to obtain additional produce through the medium of exchange. But this requires an appropriate fund; ours is extremely small, and the possibility of augmenting it through foreign trade has arisen only this year, as a result of a number of agreements with capitalist countries. It is true that these are as yet a mere introduction, a foreword; no real trade has yet begun. There is continued sabotage and all sorts of attempts to disrupt these agreements by most or the greater part of the capitalist circles, and the most characteristic thing is that the Russian whiteguard press, including the Socialist-Revolutionary and Menshevik press, is hammering away at these agreements with more venom than at anything else. It is absolutely clear that the bourgeoisie is better prepared for the fight, that it is more developed than the proletariat, that its class-consciousness has been given a keener edge by all the "trouble" it has had to put up with, and that it is betraying an abnormal sensitiveness. A close look at the whiteguard press will show that it is hitting out at the very point that is the centre, the pivot, of our policy.

After the failure of the military invasion, which has quite obviously collapsed, although the struggle is still on, the whole of the whiteguard Russian press has set itself an unattainable aim: to tear up the trade agreements. The campaign which was started this spring on an extremely extensive scale, with the Socialist-Revolutionaries and Mensheviks in the forefront of the counter-revolutionary forces, had a definite aim—to tear up the economic agreements between Russia and the capitalist world by this spring; and to a considerable extent they succeeded in achieving their aim. It is true that we have concluded the principal agreements—their number is increasing—and we are overcoming the growing resistance to them. But there has been a very dangerous delay; for, without some assistance from abroad, rehabilitation of large-scale industry and restoration of regular exchange of commodities will either be impossible or will mean very dangerous delay. These are the conditions in which we are obliged to act, and these are the conditions which for the peasants have brought the question of restoring trade to the forefront. I shall not deal with the question of concessions, because it has been debated most at Party meetings, and has not lately given rise to any perplexity. The position is that we are continuing our assiduous offers of concessions, but the foreign capitalists have not yet received a single sizable concession, and we have not yet concluded any really serious concessions agreement. The whole difficulty lies in finding a way of enlisting West-European capital that has been tested in practice.

Theoretically, it is absolutely indisputable—and it seems to me that everyone's doubts on this score have been dispelled—theoretically, I say, it is absolutely clear that it would be to our advantage to pay off European capital with a few score or hundreds of millions, which we could give it in order to augment, in the shortest possible time, our stocks of equipment, materials, raw materials and machinery for the purpose of restoring our large-scale industry.

Large-scale industry is the one and only real basis upon which we can multiply our resources and build a socialist society. Without large factories, such as capitalism has created, without highly developed large-scale industry, socialism is impossible anywhere; still less is it possible in a peasant country, and we in Russia have a far more concrete knowledge of this than before; so that instead of speaking about restoring large-scale industry in some indefinite and abstract way, we now speak of the definite, precisely calculated and concrete plan of electrification. We have a precise plan projected by the best Russian specialists and scientists, a plan which gives us a definite picture of the resources, considering Russia's natural features, with which we can, must and will lay the basis of large-scale industry for our economy. Without it, no real socialist foundation for our economic life is possible. This remains absolutely indisputable, and if, in connection with the tax in kind, we have lately spoken about it in abstract terms, we must now say definitely that we must first of all restore large-scale industry. I myself have heard statements of this kind from several comrades, and all I could do in reply was, of course, to shrug my shoulders. It is absolutely ridiculous and absurd to assume that we could ever lose sight of this fundamental aim. The only question that arises here is: how could such doubts and perplexity arise in the minds of comrades, and how could they think that this key task, without which the material production basis of socialism is impossible, has been pushed into the background? These comrades must have misunderstood the relation between our state and small industry. Our main task is to restore large-scale industry, but in order to approach this task at all seriously and systematically we must restore small industry. Both this year, 1921, and last year, we had great gaps in our efforts to restore large-scale industry.

In the autumn and winter of 1920 we started several important branches of our large-scale industry, but we had to suspend them again. Why? Many factories were able to obtain enough manpower and sufficient supplies of raw materials; why then was work at these factories suspended? Because we were short of food and fuel. Without a state reserve of 400 million poods of grain (I take an approximate figure) backed up by regular monthly allotments, it is difficult to talk about any sort of regular economic development or of restoring large-scale industry. Without it we find that after having started work on restoring large-scale industry and continuing it for several months we have had to suspend it again. Most of the few factories that were started are now idle. Without fully assured and adequate food stocks the state cannot concentrate on systematically organising the rehabilitation of large-scale industry, organising it on a modest scale, perhaps, but in such a way as to keep it going continuously.

As regards fuel, until the Donbas is restored, and until we obtain a regular supply of oil, we shall have to continue to rely on timber, on firewood, which again means dependence on small-scale production.

That explains the mistake of those comrades who failed to understand why it is the peasant who must now be placed in the centre of things. Some workers say: the peasants are being favoured, but we get nothing. I have heard such talk, but I must say I think it is not very widespread, for such talk is dangerous, because it echoes the Socialist-Revolutionaries. It is an obvious political provocation; and is, besides, a survival of craft—not class—but craft-union prejudices of workers, when the working class regards itself a part of equitable capitalist society and fails to realise that it still stands on the old capitalist basis. These workers say, in fact: the peasant is being favoured, he has been relieved of surplus-grain appropriation, he is allowed to retain his grain surplus for the purpose of exchange; we workers at the bench want to have the same thing.

What is at the bottom of this point of view? It is, in essence, the old petty-bourgeois ideology: since the peasants are a component part of capitalist society, the working class also remains a component part of this society; hence, if the peasant trades, we too must trade. Here we undoubtedly see a revival of the old prejudices which grapple the worker to the old world. The Socialist-Revolutionaries and Mensheviks are the most ardent and, in fact, the only sincere, champions of the old capitalist world. You will find none among the hundreds, the thousands, and even the hundreds of thousands in all the other camps. But these rare specimens remain among the so-called pure democrats, whom the Socialist-Revolutionaries and Mensheviks represent. And the more persistently they advocate their views, the more dangerous is their influence over the working class. They are doubly dangerous when the working class has to go through periods of suspended production. The principal material basis for the development of proletarian class-consciousness is large-scale industry, where the worker sees the factories running, and daily feels the power that can really abolish classes.

When the workers lose their footing in this material production basis, some of them are beset by a sense of instability, uncertainty, despair and skepticism, and this has a definite effect when combined with outright provocations by our bourgeois democrats, i.e., the Socialist-Revolutionaries and Mensheviks. This produces a mentality which makes people, even in the ranks of the Communist Party, reason in this way: the peasants were given a handout; for the same reasons, and by the same methods, a handout should be given to the workers. We have had to yield to this mentality to some extent. The decree on bonuses to workers in the form of a part of the goods they produce is, of course, a concession to these sentiments, which have their roots in the past and are engendered by skepticism and despair. Within certain small limits, this concession was necessary. It has been made. But we must not for a moment forget that we have been making a concession that is necessary from no other standpoint but the economic one: the interests of the proletariat. Its basic and most vital interests are bound up with the rehabilitation of large-scale industry as a solid economic foundation. When that is done, it will consolidate its dictatorship, it will be sure to carry its dictatorship to success, in the teeth of all the political and military difficulties. Why, then, were we obliged to make a concession, and why would it be extremely dangerous to give it a wider interpretation than it deserves? It is only because temporary food and fuel difficulties compelled us to take this path.

What is the principal economic determinant of the policy when we say, "We must not base our relations with the peasants on surplus-grain appropriation but on a tax"? It is that under the surplus-grain appropriation system the small peasant farms have no proper economic basis and are doomed to remain dead for many years. Small farming cannot exist and develop, because the petty farmer loses interest in consolidating and developing his activity and in increasing his output, all of which leaves us without an economic basis. We have no other basis or source, and unless the state is able to accumulate large stocks of food it is no use thinking about the rehabilitation of large-scale industry. That is why we are first of all applying this policy which is changing our food relations.

We are conducting this policy so as to have a fund for the rehabilitation of large-scale industry; to relieve the working class from all interruption of work, which should not be experienced even by our large-scale industry, miserable though it is when compared with that of the advanced countries; to relieve the proletarian of the need to find the means of subsistence by resorting to the petty-bourgeois method of profiteering, which is not a proletarian method and threatens us with the gravest economic dangers. Owing to our present deplorable conditions, proletarians are obliged to earn a living by methods which are not proletarian and are not connected with large-scale industry. They are obliged to procure goods by petty-bourgeois profiteering methods, either by stealing, or by making them for themselves in a publicly-owned factory, in order to barter them for agricultural produce—and that is the main economic danger, jeopardising the existence of the Soviet system. The proletariat must now exercise its dictatorship in such a way as to have a sense of security as a class, with a firm footing. But the ground is slipping from under its feet. Instead of large, continuously running factories, the proletarian sees something quite different, and is compelled to enter the economic sphere as a profiteer, or as a small producer.

We must spare no sacrifice in this transitional period to save the proletariat from this. To ensure the continuous, if slow, rehabilitation of large-scale industry we must not hesitate to throw sops to the greedy foreign capitalists, because, from the standpoint of building socialism, it is at present to our advantage to overpay the foreign capitalists some hundreds of millions in order to obtain the machines and materials for the rehabilitation of large-scale industry, which will restore the economic basis of the proletariat, and will transform it into a steadfast proletariat, instead of one engaged in profiteering. The Mensheviks and Socialist-Revolutionaries have deafened us with their shouts that since the proletariat has been declassed, we ought to abandon the tasks of the dictatorship of the proletariat. They have been shouting that since 1917, and the surprising thing is that they have not grown tired of shouting it up to 1921. But when we hear these attacks we do not say that there has been no declassing, and that there are no flaws. What we say is that Russian and international realities are such that even though the proletariat has to go through a period when it is declassed, and has to suffer from these handicaps, it can nevertheless fulfil its task of winning and holding political power.

It would be absurd and ridiculous to deny that the fact that the proletariat is declassed is a handicap. By 1921, we realised that after the struggle against the external enemy, the main danger and the greatest evil confronting us was our inability to ensure the continuous operation of the few remaining large enterprises. This is the main thing. Without such an economic basis, the working class cannot firmly hold political power. In order to ensure the continued rehabilitation of large-scale industry we must organise the food supply in such a way as to collect and properly distribute a fund of, say, 400 million poods. It would be utterly impossible for us to collect it through the old surplus-grain appropriation system: 1920 and 1921 are proof of this. Now we see that we can nonetheless fulfil this extremely difficult task by means of the tax in kind. We cannot fulfil it with the old methods, and so we must try some new ones. It can be done by means of the tax in kind and by establishing proper relations with the peasant as a small producer. We have devoted considerable effort to prove this theoretically.

I think, judging by the Party press and by what is being said at meetings, that it has been fully proved theoretically that this task can be fulfilled if the proletariat retains possession of the transport system, the big factories, the economic basis as well as political power. We must give the peasant a fair amount of leeway as a small producer. Unless we revive peasant farming we shall not solve the food problem.

It is within this framework that we must deal with the question of developing small industry on the basis of unrestricted trade and free turnover. This free turnover is a means to establish economically stable relations between the working class and the peasantry. We now have more and more precise data on agricultural output. A pamphlet on grain output was distributed at the Party Congress; it was still in proofs when it was distributed to the delegates. Since then the material contained in it has been supplemented and circulated. The pamphlet in its final form has now been sent to the press, but it is not yet ready for the conference, and I am unable to say whether it will be ready before the conference comes to a close and the delegates disperse. We shall do all we can to get it out in time, but we cannot promise to do so.

This is a small part of our effort to determine, as precisely as possible, the position in regard to agricultural output, and the resources at our disposal.

Still, we can say that there is evidence that we are quite able to solve this economic problem, particularly this year, when the harvest prospects are not too bad, or not as bad as we anticipated in spring. This assures us of the possibility of accumulating an agricultural reserve that will enable us to devote ourselves entirely to the task of steadily, even if slowly, restoring our large-scale industry.

In order to solve the problem of accumulating food stocks for industry we must devise a form of relations with the peasant, the small proprietor, and there is no other form except that of the tax in kind; no one has come up with another form, and none can be imagined. But we must have a practical solution of this problem: we must arrange to have the tax collected in a proper manner, and not in the old way, when grain was taken two or three times, leaving the peasant in a worse plight than ever, inflicting the most suffering on the more industrious and destroying every possibility of establishing economically stable relations. The tax in kind, while also a levy on every peasant, must be collected in a different way. On the basis of the collected and published data we can say that the tax in kind will now bring about a crucial change, but whether it will cover everything is still, to some extent, an open question. Of one thing we can be quite certain, however, and it is that we must bring about an immediate improvement in the condition of the peasant.

The task that confronts the local workers is to collect the tax in kind in full, and do so in the shortest possible time. The difficulties are increased by the fact that the harvest promises to be an unusually early one this year, and if our preparations are based on the customary dates, we run the risk of being too late. That is why the early convocation of the Party conference was important and opportune. We must work more quickly than before to prepare the apparatus for collecting the tax in kind. The accumulation of a minimum state fund of 240 million poods of grain and the possibility of making the position of the peasant secure depend on the speed with which the tax in kind is collected. Delay in collecting it will cause a certain amount of inconvenience to the peasant. The tax will not be paid voluntarily, we shall not be able to dispense with coercion, for the levy imposes some restrictions on the peasant farm. If we drag out the process of collecting the tax, the peasant will be discontent and will say that he is not free to dispose of his surplus. If the freedom is to be such in practice, the tax must be collected quickly; the tax-collector must not hover over the peasant for long, and so the period between the harvesting and the collection of the tax in full must be reduced to a minimum.

That is one task. The other is to maximise the peasant's freedom of trade and the revival of small-scale industry, so as to allow some leeway to the capitalism that grows up on the basis of small private property and petty trade. We should not be afraid of it, for it is not dangerous to us in the least.

We need not fear it at all in view of the general economic and political situation that has now arisen, with the proletariat controlling all the sources of large-scale production, and denationalisation in any shape or form entirely out of the question. At a time when we are suffering most of all from a severe shortage of goods and utter impoverishment, it is ridiculous to fear the threat of capitalism based on small commercial agriculture. To fear it is to fail altogether to take account of the relation of forces in our economy. It means to fail to understand that the peasant economy, as a small-scale peasant economy, cannot be stable at all without some free exchange and the attendant capitalist relations.

This is what you must firmly impress on your minds, comrades. And our main task is to give a push to the comrades in all the localities, to give them the utmost scope for initiative, to stimulate them to display the utmost self-reliance and boldness. In this respect we are still suffering from the fear of doing things on a really wide scale. We have no more or less definitely tabulated local data showing from practical experience what the situation is in regard to local goods exchange and trade, what success has been achieved in restoring and developing small industry—which can alleviate the condition of the peasant right away, without the great effort of transporting large stocks of food and fuel to the industrial centres that large-scale industry entails. From the general economic standpoint, not enough is being done locally in this respect. We have no information on this from the localities, we do not know what the position is all over the Republic, we have no examples of really well-organised work; and my impression is that the Trade Union Congress and the Congress of the Supreme Economic Council[116] have none either.

Here again, the principal defect of these congresses is that we devote ourselves mainly to such threadbare things as theses, general programmes and arguments, instead of giving the participants a chance to swap local experience and say, on returning home: "Out of a thousand examples we heard one good one, and we shall follow it." Actually, we have not only one good example in a thousand, we have many more; but least of all do we see congress work arranged in this way.

I have no wish to forestall events, but I must say a word or two about collective supplies for the workers, i.e., about the proposal to substitute for the ration system a system under which certain factories that are actually in operation will be assured of a certain quantity of food in proportion to their output. The idea is an excellent one, but we have turned it into something semi-fantastic, without however doing any real preparatory work for it. We have no example as yet of any particular factory, even one employing a small number of workers, in a particular uyezd, having tried out this system and having secured such-and-such results. That is something we do not as yet have, and it is one of the greatest drawbacks in our work. We must keep repeating that instead of discussing general problems, which was all very well in 1918, i.e., in the long distant past, we must, in this 1921, discuss practical problems. By telling congresses first of all about the examples of well-organised work—there are quite enough of them—we would make it an obligation for the rest to strive to imitate the best that has been achieved in a few rare and exceptional localities. I have in mind the work of the Trade Union Congress, but it also applies to all work connected with the food problem.

Quite a lot has been done in some cases, in a few localities, to prepare for the collection of the tax in kind, the organisation of trade, etc., but we have not managed to study this experience; and the great task that confronts us now is to induce the vast majority of the localities to follow the example of the best. Our task now is to study practical experience and raise the backward and medium uyezds and volosts, the standard of which is absolutely unsatisfactory, to the level of the insignificant number of highly satisfactory ones. At our congresses we must shift our main attention from the study of general theses and programmes of meetings to the study of practical experience, to the study of the examples set by the satisfactory and highly satisfactory districts, and to raising the backward and medium ones, which predominate, to the level of these good ones, which may be few but are still there.

Those are the remarks to which I must confine myself. (*Applause.*)

3

SUMMING-UP SPEECH ON THE TAX IN KIND
MAY 27

Comrades, although many comrades from the provinces have expressed dissatisfaction with the reports and the debate, it seems to me that we have, at any rate, achieved one object—we have ascertained how the new policy is understood and applied locally. The conference could hardly have set itself any other aim than that of securing an exchange of opinion for the purpose of thoroughly assimilating this new policy and of unanimously proceeding to its proper application. This we have achieved. True, there has been some perplexity and even wavering, which, unfortunately, in some cases, went far beyond perplexity over practical questions and conjectures about whether the new policy was meant "seriously" or "not seriously", and for how long. What Comrade Vareikis said, for example, was really not communist at all, and in content smacked of Menshevism. I must say this quite bluntly. How could he keep asking: "Tell us, is the peasantry a class, or not a class?" Of course, it is a class. In that case, he says, it must have political concessions, or, if not that, then certain measures should be taken in that direction, which will resemble Zubatovism[117] just the same.

Reference was made here to the fact that Martov had put the case squarely, whereas Vareikis was adding: "To a certain extent", "to some degree", "partly". This caused incredible, monstrous confusion. It is the same sort of confusion that was displayed when we were being accused of employing force. Again we have to explain that when we speak of dictatorship we mean the employment of coercion. Every state implies employment of coercion; but the whole

difference lies in whether it is employed against the
exploited or against the exploiters. Is it employed against
the toiling and exploited class? The same applies to the
reference to Zubatovism. What was Zubatovism? It was
support for the oppressor class by means of small economic
concessions to the oppressed classes. That is why the
response at that time was: economic concessions will not help
you to induce the proletariat, the class that is fighting for
the emancipation of all the oppressed, to abandon the idea
of capturing political power and of destroying the system
of oppression. At present the proletariat holds power and
guides the state. It guides the peasantry. What does that
mean? It means, first, pursuing a course towards the abolition of classes, and not towards the small producer. If we
strayed from this bedrock course we should cease to be
socialists and would find ourselves in the camp of the petty
bourgeoisie, the Socialist-Revolutionaries and Mensheviks,
who are now the proletariat's most bitter enemies. Not
long ago Comrade Bukharin quoted in *Pravda* some
utterances of such a serious political thinker as Milyukov
(Chernov and Martov come nowhere near him), who argued
that only a socialist party could occupy the arena of political
struggle in Russia today. And since the "socialist" parties,
the Socialist-Revolutionaries and the Mensheviks, desire
to take the trouble of fighting the Bolsheviks, they "are
welcome to try". That is literally what Milyukov said,
and it proves that he is cleverer than Martov and Chernov,
simply because he is a representative of the big bourgeoisie (even if he personally had less brains than Chernov
and Martov). Milyukov is right. He takes a very sober
account of the stages of political development and says that
Socialist-Revolutionism and Menshevism are the necessary
stepping stones leading to a reversion to capitalism. The
bourgeoisie needs such stepping stones, and whoever does
not understand this is stupid.

From the standpoint of the interests of the bourgeoisie,
Milyukov is absolutely right. Since we, being the party of
the proletariat, are leading the peasantry, we must pursue
a course towards strengthening large-scale industry, and
must therefore be prepared to make economic concessions.
The proletariat led the peasantry, and did it in such a way

that during the Civil War the peasantry obtained more economic benefits than the proletariat. In Martov's terms, this is Zubatovism. Economic concessions have been made to the peasantry. These concessions were made to a section of the working people constituting the majority of the population. Is this policy wrong? No, it is the only correct one! And no matter what you say about Martov's catchwords, about it being impossible to deceive a class, I ask you nevertheless: where is our deception? We say that there are two paths to choose: one following Martov and Chernov—and through them to Milyukov—and the other following the Communists. As for us, we are fighting for the abolition of capitalism and the establishment of communism. Ours is a very hard road, and many are weary and lack faith. The peasants lack faith. But are we deceiving them? It is ridiculous to say that we are deceiving a class, and have lost our way amidst three pines, or even two, for the working class and the peasantry are only two classes. The proletariat leads the peasantry, which is a class that cannot be driven out as the landowners and capitalists were driven out and destroyed. We must remould it by prolonged and persistent effort, entailing great privation. It depends on us, the ruling party, how much of the suffering will fall to the lot of the proletariat and how much to that of the peasantry. How is this suffering to be shared? Is it to be on a basis of equality? Let Chernov and Martov say that. We say that we must be guided by the interests of the proletariat, that is, we must obtain safeguards against the restoration of capitalism and ensure the road to communism. Since the peasantry is now wearier and more exhausted, or rather it thinks that it is so, we make more concessions to it in order to obtain safeguards against the restoration of capitalism and to ensure the road to communism. That is the correct policy, and we are guided exclusively by class considerations. We tell the peasants frankly and honestly, without any deception: in order to hold the road to socialism, we are making a number of concessions to you, comrade peasants, but only within the stated limits and to the stated extent; and, of course, we ourselves shall be the judge of the limits and the extent. The concession itself is being made with an eye to distributing the burdens which, up to now, the proletariat has borne to a larger extent than the peasantry. During the three and a half years of the dictatorship of the proletariat, it has voluntarily borne more hardships than the peasantry. This is an absolutely obvious and incontrovertible truth. This is how the question stands in regard to the relations between the proletariat and the peasantry: either the peasantry comes to an agreement with us and we make economic concessions to it—or we fight. That is why all other arguments are but evidence of a terrible confusion. As a matter of fact, any other road leads to Milyukov, and the restoration of the landowners and capitalists. We say that we shall agree to make any concession within the limits of what will sustain and strengthen the power of the proletariat, which, in spite of all difficulties and obstacles, is unswervingly advancing towards the abolition of classes and towards communism.

The next point is that much of the criticism of Comrade Svidersky's speech was wrong. All the members of the opposition at once hurled themselves upon him with what might be called brilliant parliamentary speeches, Comrade Larin proving to be the most brilliant representative of the "parliamentary opposition". The Soviet system does not provide many opportunities for making parliamentary speeches; but nature asserts herself, and although we have no parliamentary institutions, the parliamentary manner survives. Concerning Comrade Svidersky they complained that he had proposed the introduction of a food supply inspectorate, and had even gone to the length of talking about a food dictatorship. Comrade Svidersky may have overstated his case, but he is right in substance. We distributed the reporters' roles in such a way that each played on a different instrument, as it were. The report on the question of exchange was made by the representative of Tsentrosoyuz, Comrade Khinchuk—the co-operator. As you are well aware, Tsentrosoyuz has concluded an agreement with the state. If some of the comrades have not read it, this only goes to show that they have not treated the material of the conference in a business-like way. Our state concludes an agreement with the representative of Tsentrosoyuz: the representative of the People's Commissariat for Food concludes an agreement with the representative of the co-operative societies, and co-operators abroad must reckon with our agreement. Under the agreement all goods are delivered to the co-operative societies, so that the co-operators may trade on our behalf—on behalf of the centralised state, the big factories, and the proletariat—but not on their own behalf. This is a major and most important condition, because there can be no other arrangement. Petrograd and Moscow are starving, while the well-fed gubernias, as Comrade Bryukhanov's figures show, have eaten twice as much, and sent us half as much as they should have. What do you say: in the circumstances, do we or do we not need a food dictatorship? I think we do; we need it very much, indeed, because there is any amount of this laxity all over the country. You must realise that we cannot do without coercion, and Tsentrosoyuz must do the distributing under our control.

We say to Tsentrosoyuz: you have traded well and we will give you a bonus in the form of a definite percentage. This is stipulated in the agreement, and we will encourage this commission-basis trading by every sort of bonus system. We will give a bonus for profitable trade; but we will demand that this trade is carried on for our benefit, for the benefit of the state, which has centralised large-scale industry, and which is governed by the proletariat. Does large-scale industry stand to gain? Who stands to gain?

How can you ensure food supplies without a tax? You cannot. We do not know whether the tax or the exchange will yield most, but we do know—and it is a fact—that we lack an adequate fund for exchange. At the present time, you cannot get what you need without an instrument of coercion. Never! This is obvious. And in this, Svidersky, as a representative of his line, is absolutely right. We have approved of the establishment of a food supply inspectorate, and the Presidium of the All-Russia Central Executive Committee will bring more pressure to bear on you because you know who ought to be appointed; that is your business; but once you make the appointment, see that the man does his job. Things being what they are, unless the state is assured of approximately 400 million poods of grain, it is no use talking about large-scale industry and socialist construction. Those who have not learned this in the course of the past three years are not worth arguing with. But in spite of our numerous mistakes, we have increased this fund. True, while increasing the fund in 1920, we blundered over distribution, but enormous progress was made nonetheless. We must approach the subject soberly and say that to collect the tax in kind we need an expeditious apparatus, and it is no use making liberal speeches and hinting that a food supply inspectorate is such a nasty thing.

I am not aware of the existence of a "communist" system under which you could expect to collect—without coercion —a tax from the peasantry constituting a majority of the population in the period of transition from capitalism to communism. If you want to sustain large-scale industry— the basis of the proletarian dictatorship—then you must want this apparatus to function. And this, naturally, demands centralism. Look at the figures. Unfortunately, few of you are sufficiently familiar with them. See how much the localities have kept for themselves, in spite of the orders from the centre. The comrades from Moscow and Petrograd have quoted figures here showing that the orders from the centre are not being fully carried out. It turns out that three reminders were given, and an equal number of censures. What else is there to do? There remains nothing but dismissal, arrest and so forth. (*A voice*: "How many such cases were there?") There were many cases of infringements, but few dismissals. That is what I wanted to say in defence of this line of policy.

The harvest this year will evidently be a fair one in many parts, and will set in earlier than we expected. Hence, we must make preparations beforehand, the situation now being such that we must swiftly collect the main fund. Consequently, it is absolutely wrong to take the approach that many did here.

As for Comrade Larin, his talents lie more in the sphere of parliamentary opposition and journalism than business efficiency. He is tireless in the drawing-up of projects. He mentioned that he had proposed a good plan as early as January 1920, but if we were to collect all of his projects and pick out the good ones, we would probably find that they add up to one in ten thousand.

On May 10, he submitted a scheme to the Central Committee's Political Bureau for a general introduction of a collective supply system. Its main principle is alluring, but when was it proposed? On May 10, 1921, when there was an absolute shortage of food in centres like Moscow and Petrograd, when these important centres of the Russian Republic were temporarily doomed to semi-starvation and even worse. It is ridiculous to propose a reshuffle of the food supply organisations at a time when men are on their last legs, and are overworking the trunk-lines to Siberia, the Caucasus and the Ukraine, in an effort to track down every trainload, every car almost. What the devil is the use of introducing a collective supply system at a time like that? The Political Bureau adopted the following resolution: "That the scheme proposed by Larin and the All-Russia Central Council of Trade Unions [the A.C.C.T.U., of course, hastened to put its signature to it] be rejected; that the author of the scheme be instructed to re-examine the question with greater care, in the light of the actual possibilities of obtaining supplies...." This principle was reiterated (in Chubar's and Holtzmann's theses, if you have read them) at the Trade Union Congress; Chubar had formulated the main parts of his theses in harmony with the policy of circumspection laid down by the Party's Central Committee. Holtzmann and Larin behaved according to the rule which Larin, half in jest, whispered in my ear at the end of the meeting of the Political Bureau. (I don't think I shall be committing an indiscretion if I relate this conversation.) When Larin saw that the resolution had been adopted he said to me: "You have given us your little finger, but we will take your hand." Then I said to myself—although I had known it before—now we know how to bargain with Larin. If he asks for a million rubles, offer him fifty kopeks. (*Laughter.*) During the debate, when Larin was asked for the facts, he quoted the example (which he said was "brilliant") of the construction of the Kizlyar-Staro-Terek railway. Although it has already been shown that there is nothing new in this example, that similar experiments have been made before, it is a sign of progress to hear definite examples and results of experience, instead of general arguments and countless theses. It would be disastrous if everyone began reading and discussing these theses, nine-tenths of which you cannot read to the end without a splitting headache.

It is not theses, but a record of local experience, that we need. Let us study this experience, instead of piling system upon system and drawing up laws on collective supplies when we lack even the minimum of real supplies. Practical work is going on in the localities. We were told: it is not right to reproach the localities for not sharing their experiences. The Central Committee was reproached here for not giving publicity to local experience. But we have none of it: our time is taken up entirely with decrees. The majority of us are immersed in this unpleasant work, and that is why we cannot see local experience. It is your business to bring it to us. Larin was right in quoting the fine example of the Kizlyar-Terek railway, for it was a piece of local experience. But even here he allowed his imagination to run away with him, and Chubar and Osinsky had to put him right. This is not the only example. He said that a worker received 28 pounds under the old system and four poods under the new system. I was doubtful about the figures and so I asked him: Where did you get that from? He replied that they had been certified by the Workers' and Peasants' Inspection. But we know that Larin is not only a parliamentary man, but also a cartoonist. First, he drew a cartoon satirising the Workers' and Peasants' Inspection. And now he says: four poods instead of 28 pounds—certified by the Workers' and Peasants' Inspection. First, he undermines confidence in the Workers' and Peasants' Inspection by relating anecdotes of that kind, and then presents the certificate of the Workers' and Peasants' Inspection as sole proof. Chubar and Osinsky say that this system has been repeatedly employed in the timber industry. The whole point is to compare the experience of one locality with that of another. The best part of Larin's statement was his description of the work on the Kizlyar-Terek railway. But what we need to know is whether things have not been done better in Tula or Tambov. The centre cannot tell you that, because we do not know. You should bring us this information from the localities, show us the facts, teach us, and we will all learn, and try to follow the best example.

The number of local centres, on the uyezd or district level, with such experience is two or three per thousand, possibly more, but surely two or three can be found. This experience must be thoroughly studied in a business-like fashion. We must carefully sift the evidence and verify the figures, and not rely merely on speeches by the opposition. If we do this, the centre will be able to learn.

I think the most important outcome of the debate has been the information we got on how the exchange of commodities was begun; the only thing lacking was the precise facts. Donbas comrades cabled to say: We have obtained 3,000 poods of wheat through exchange. This referred to a small district, but there were no details. I expected the comrades to come forward here and tell us what they gave in return, and through what organisation the exchange was made: the Commissariat for Food, a lessee, concessionaire or private entrepreneur? This we do not know; and yet it is far more important than our decrees. Decrees can be read, and it is hardly worth getting together to discuss them; but it is certainly worth while to come together to discuss how they obtained 3,000 poods of wheat in the Donbas, and whether the comrades in Volhynia or Tambov have not done better. Quite a good deal has been done locally. The comrades should come here and tell us the results of their practical experience over there. One will say: "I started doing so and so, but was hindered by the central organisation." Another will say: "I managed to bring the central organisation to heel." As for Tambov Gubernia, the comrade who delivered a parliamentary speech and thundered against the Commissariat for Food vaguely hinted that they had set up co-operative shops and agencies. The comrades had accepted this. Over there they have to put up with a number of additional difficulties; part of the area has not been sown, severe conditions generally, handicap upon handicap. Nevertheless, from what he said it is evident that exchange has begun and the co-operatives are functioning. Even pomade was mentioned. How much pomade did you take? And on what terms was it distributed? You must even trade in pomade; when you are trading you must reckon with the demand. If there is a demand for pomade, we must supply it. If we run things

properly we can restore large-scale industry even with the
aid of pomade. What we must calculate, though, is how
much of it we need to buy, or obtain, to be able to purchase
1,000 poods of grain. (*Voice*: What about icons; there's
a demand for icons.) As for icons, someone has just given
a reminder that the peasants are asking for icons. I think
that we should not follow the example of the capitalist
countries and put vodka and other intoxicants on the
market, because, profitable though they are, they will lead
us back to capitalism and not forward to communism; but
there is no such danger in pomade. (*Laughter.*) As for church
bells, we differ on that, and some comrades think that in
some places the bells will soon be voluntarily recast into
copper wire for electrification. Besides, there are so many of
them in Russia at the moment that they can hardly be used
by religious people for their original purpose, because the
need is no longer there. As regards Volhynia, it was
stated that there are places there where they give a pood
of grain for ten pounds of salt. But how was this trans-
acted? Did you have any agents? How did you trade? Who
looked after the goods? Who locked up the warehouses?
How much was stolen? That is the main thing but
nothing was said about it at all. Instead, we were told
that the Poles had given a pood of salt for a pood of grain.
In conversation with the comrade I said that if the Poles
offered a pood of salt for a pood of grain and the peasants
offered you a pood of grain for ten pounds of salt, then you
could have traded something for yourselves. What prevented
you from doing that? The centre, it was said. I'm sorry but
I simply cannot believe that the centre prevented you from
obtaining four poods of grain for a pood of Polish salt.
We could not have opposed a thing like that; I refuse to
believe it. The comrades complained that before, when
the army was there, everything had to be done through
the military authorities; but now that the army is no longer
there and there is no war, permission must be obtained
from the centre. A comrade said that now they had the
Southern Paper Trust and that they were fighting this Trust.
But when I asked to whom they had complained about
this organisation he answered that he did not know. But
this is very important.

They were unable to name the body to whom they had sent their complaint about the Southern Paper Trust. I do not know what this Paper Trust is. In all probability it is a body that suffers from the same bureaucratic distortion that all our Soviet organisations are afflicted with. The capitalists are still fighting us. We have compelled many of them to seek protection under Milyukov's wing abroad; but many thousands are still here, waging war against us according to all the rules of the art of bureaucracy. But how are you combating this, comrades? Do you think you can take this Paper Trust and all the rest of them with your bare hands? We did not fight Denikin with bare hands, but armed ourselves strongly, and organised an army. But here we have excellent officials, who consider that it is in the interests of their class to play dirty tricks on us, to hamper our work; they think that they are saving civilisation by helping to bring about the downfall of the Bolsheviks, and they know how to run an office a hundred times better than we do. There was nowhere for us to learn this business. We must fight them according to all the rules of the art and take proceedings against Party comrades who go about lodging complaints, or telling anecdotes about the dirty tricks that are being played in some office or other. They go about Moscow telling anecdotes about the bureaucratic tricks that are being played. But you, comrades, who are intelligent Communists, what have you done to combat this?—"I lodged a complaint."—Where did you file your complaint? It turns out that no complaint had been filed, whereas it should have been sent to the Council of People's Commissars and to the All-Russia Central Executive Committee; in other words, they should have exercised all their rights provided for by our Constitution. Of course, we may suffer a reverse here and there in this war. But has there ever been a war, even the most victorious, without any reverses? In this one reverses are also possible, but the fight must go on. Many of us, however, are not taking it seriously. Have you taken legal proceedings against those who are responsible for red tape? Has any people's court convicted anyone for making a worker or a peasant call at an office four or five times and finally sending him off with an answer which is formally correct, but is essentially sheer mockery? You are Communists, aren't you? Then why don't you set a trap for these bureaucratic gentlemen and then haul them before a people's court, and into prison, for this red tape? How many people have you put into prison for red tape? Everyone will say, of course, that it is a troublesome business. Someone may be offended. Many take this view, but do not find it too much trouble to complain and tell anecdotes. Very often one cannot tell the difference between these anecdotes and the slander published by the Mensheviks and Socialist-Revolutionaries in foreign journals. The Mensheviks write: "We have our own correspondents in all the Soviet offices in Moscow." (*Laughter.*) Quite often the anecdotes that are told here, and those with which the speeches of the parliamentary opposition are replete, appear in the Menshevik journals a few days later. But you should know where to draw the line; you must see the difference between a serious struggle and the telling of anecdotes. Of course, when people are tired, an anecdote told by a capable speaker may help to let off steam. Judging from my own observations this is so, and I have no objections from this point of view. But we need something more: we must study the methods used to catch the culprits, count up how many were caught and brought to trial, and sum up the results obtained. If we proceed on these lines we will win this war, although it takes far more skill than the Civil War.

I should like to say a word or two about Nikolayev Gubernia. The comrade from Nikolayev Gubernia gave us a number of valuable facts, but in most cases he gave no details. He said: "There is a demand for textiles and iron, but not for pomade." Others said, however, that there was no demand for textiles. The comrade came up against the profiteers, and being obliged to pursue the free market policy, he wants to know how to combat them. We cannot fight them in the old way; and to fight them in the new way we have mounted guards in the transport system, and a number of new decrees have been passed; but, of course, no quick results can be expected. But where is your local experience in this matter? A number of decrees have now been passed for the protection of the transport system, not against the profiteers, but against its "improper use". Special commissions, Extraordinary Three-Man Commissions have been set up by 'the Cheka and the Transport Cheka; the War Department and the People's Commissariat for Railways are also taking a hand. But what are the bodies functioning in your districts? How do they co-ordinate their work? What is being done about the complaints that the profiteers are getting the upper hand? How do they operate? This is what we ought to discuss. But comrades come here and complain: "The profiteers have got the upper hand." We have adopted the decrees. Perhaps they are no good, they must be put to the test, but how is this to be done? We test our decrees by publishing them. You know them; you come here to discuss them and tell us how they are applied. You must tell us: in such and such a place, such and such a Transport Three-Man Commission has done the following. In one place it was successful, in another it was not. Perhaps the speeches will not be as brilliant as those we heard about the food dictatorship; but unless we do this we shall never learn to make fewer mistakes in drafting decrees, and that is the main thing.

Let me deal in conclusion with the deductions which, I think, Comrade Osinsky has quite rightly drawn, and which sum up our activities. His deductions were three. First: "Seriously and for a long time". I think he is quite right. The policy is a long-term one and is being adopted in earnest. We must get this well into our heads and remember it, because, owing to the gossip habit, rumours are being spread that we are indulging in a policy of expedients, that is to say, political trickery, and that what is being done is only for the present day. That is not true. We are taking class relationships into account and have our eyes on what the proletariat must do to lead the peasantry in the direction of communism in spite of everything. Of course, we have to retreat; but we must take it very seriously and look at it from the standpoint of class forces. To regard it as a trick is to imitate the philistines, the petty bourgeoisie, who are alive and kicking not only outside the Communist Party. But I would not go along with Comrade Osinsky in his estimate of the period. He said "seriously and for a long

time" meant 25 years. I am not that pessimistic; I shall
refrain from estimating the period, but I think his figure
is a bit too pessimistic. We shall be lucky to project our
policy for some 5 or 10 years, because we usually fail to do
so even for 5 weeks.

We must promote enterprising non-Party workers. We
must reiterate over and over again that, after all is said and
done, meetings, congresses and conferences held by the
Communist Party and other organisations in Soviet Russia
must not be what they have been in the past, and still
are, that is to say, assemblies with speeches in the spirit
of parliamentary oppositions and the drawing up of resolutions. We have so many resolutions that nobody even
takes the trouble to file them, let alone read them. We
must devote our attention to business and not to resolutions.
Under the bourgeois system, business matters were managed
by private owners and not by state agencies; but now,
business matters are our common concern. These are the
politics that interest us most. Of course, we can denounce
the Mensheviks for the 999th time, they deserve it; but
after all is said and done, this is mere repetition, and
many of us have now been doing it these thirty years.
Most of us have had enough of it.

What is much more interesting is how, in this socialist
state, we are to exchange textiles, pomade and other things
for grain, and obtain an extra pood of flour in exchange
for Polish salt. Although it is not our custom, Party
meetings must take up the question of enterprise and
initiative. The whole capitalist world is starving. They
have an abundance of salt, pomades, and other things of
that sort, and if we apply the slogan of local exchange
properly and show initiative, we shall obtain extra poods
of grain.

Comrade Gusev has handed me a draft of the rules
and regulations for a Communist Producers' Co-operative
Society. Its substance is contained in Point 5, in which
the members of the society ask to be assured a "healthy,
hygienic ration". (*Laughter.*) A "healthy, hygienic ration"
is the goal of our whole food policy. We must collect 240
million poods of grain by means of the tax, and 160 million
through commodity exchange, making a total of 400

million poods, so that the peasants may feel that this system is economically stable.

The surplus-grain appropriation system could not be continued any longer. The policy had to be changed. In this respect, we are facing what is, perhaps, the most difficult period of our construction effort. If we were to compare the whole work of the Communist Party to a four-year course in the higher sciences, we could say that our present position is as follows: we are taking our examination to pass from the third course to the fourth; we have not yet passed the examination, but there is every sign that we shall. We can say that the first course lasted from the 1870s to 1903; it was the initial introductory period, ranging from Narodnaya Volya, Social-Democracy and the Second International to Bolshevism. That was the first course.

The second course lasted from 1903 to 1917, with a serious preparatory course for revolution, and the first essay in revolution in 1905. The third course lasted from 1917 to 1921, a period of four years, which in content was more important than the first forty years. This was a very practical test, when the proletariat came to power, but it was not yet the crucial test. Although in our anthem we sing: "The last fight let us face", I must say that, unfortunately, it was not the last fight, but one of the fights just before the last, to be absolutely exact. At present we are taking our examination to pass from the third course to the fourth. Taking Osinsky's example of years, I think we should allow ten, because we shall have to take an exam to pass from the third course to the fourth. After that we must do well in the fourth course and then we shall really be invincible. We can win on the economic front. If we are victorious in relation to the peasantry and collect a "healthy, hygienic ration" this year, we shall pass to the fourth course. After that, all the work of construction that we are planning will be more serious.

This is the task confronting us. That is why I take the liberty, once again, in conclusion to express the hope that, in spite of the difficulties, and all the old traditions which frown on the idea of discussing local questions of minor economics at congresses, conferences and fine parliamentary assemblies, we shall, nevertheless, say to ourselves: being Communists, we shall have to devote ourselves to these tasks. We must study the practical experience gained in economic work in the localities, where the decrees are being applied, where they are tested, where their defects should be rectified, where we must begin to do the things that are later summed up at our meetings. If we do that, our work of construction will make real and durable progress. (*Stormy applause.*)

4

DRAFT RESOLUTION ON QUESTIONS
OF THE NEW ECONOMIC POLICY

1. The fundamental political task of the moment is for all Party and Soviet workers to gain a complete understanding of the New Economic Policy and to implement it to the letter.

The Party regards this policy as being established for a long period of years, and demands that everyone should carry it out unconditionally with thoroughness and diligence.

2. Commodity exchange is brought to the fore as the principal lever of the New Economic Policy. It is impossible to establish a correct relationship between the proletariat and the peasantry, or an altogether stable form of economic alliance between these two classes in the period of transition from capitalism to socialism, without regular commodity exchange or the exchange of products between industry and agriculture.

The exchange of commodities, in particular, is required to stimulate the extension of the peasants' area under crop and improvement of peasant farming.

Local initiative and enterprise must be given all-round support and development at all costs.

Gubernias with the greatest grain surpluses must be placed on the priority list for commodity exchange.

3. Considering co-operatives to be the main apparatus for commodity exchange, the conference recognises as correct the policy of contracts between the agencies of the People's Commissariat for Food and the co-operative societies, and the transfer, under government control, by the former to the latter of commodity-exchange stocks to fulfil the assignments of the government;

the co-operatives to be given broad opportunities for procurement and all-round development of local industry and revival of economic life in general;

support for credit operations by the co-operatives;

anarchic commodity exchange (that is, exchange which eludes all control and state supervision) to be combated by concentration of exchange chiefly in the hands of the co-operatives, without, however, any restrictions on regular free market operations;

market analysis.

4. Support for small and medium (private and co-operative) enterprises, chiefly those not requiring supplies from state raw material, fuel and food reserves.

Permission to lease government enterprises to private persons, co-operatives, artels and associations. The right of local economic agencies to conclude such contracts without authorisation from superior agencies. Obligatory notification of the Council of Labour and Defence in each such case.

5. Review of (certain sections of) production programmes for large-scale industry towards increasing the manufacture of consumer goods and peasant household articles.

Extension of enterprise and initiative by each large establishment in the disposal of financial and material resources. Submission of a precise decree to that effect for approval by the Council of People's Commissars.

6. Development of the system of bonuses in kind and the establishment by way of experiment of a collective supply system.

Establishment of a more correct distribution of foodstuffs with the aim of increasing labour productivity.

7. The need to maintain and enlarge the apparatus for the full and expeditious collection of the tax in kind everywhere. Investment of food agencies with the necessary Party authority for that purpose. Maintenance and enhancement of the centralisation of the food apparatus.

8. To concentrate all the enumerated measures on the current year's practical and urgent task: collection of at least 400 million poods of grain stocks as a basis for the rehabilitation of large-scale industry and the implementation of the electrification plan.

9. To adopt in principle the draft Instructions of the C.L.D., authorising the All-Russia Central Executive Committee group to enact them into law.

To recognise the strict fulfilment of the Instructions in general and the recruitment and promotion of non-Party people for work, in particular, as the Party's unconditional and primary task.

10. To establish special responsibility on the part of central agencies for any hampering of local initiative and insufficient support of it. To authorise the All-Russia Central Executive Committee group to work out a corresponding decision and have it adopted at the very next session.

11. The conference authorises the Central Committee and all Party organisations to carry out a system of measures to intensify agitation and propaganda and effect the necessary transfer of Party cadres to ensure complete understanding and steady implementation of the enumerated tasks.

12. To set as the Party's most important task the careful and all-round publicising and study in the press and at trade union, Soviet, and Party meetings, conferences, congresses, etc., of the practical experience gained in economic development locally and at the centre.

First published in full, according to page proofs with Lenin's corrections

5

SPEECH IN CLOSING THE CONFERENCE
MAY 28

Comrades, I think that I can confine myself to a very short speech As you are aware, we convened this special conference mainly for the purpose of achieving complete understanding on economic policy between the centre and the localities, among Party and all Soviet workers. I think that the conference has fully achieved its object. Some speakers noted that Comrade Osinsky gave the correct expression to the feelings of very many, probably, the majority of local Party workers when he said that we must remove all doubt about the fact that the policy adopted by the Tenth Party Congress and subsequently reinforced by decrees and orders has unquestionably been accepted by the Party in earnest and for a long time. This is what the conference most emphatically expressed and amplified by a number of points. When the comrades return to their localities, not the slightest possibility of wrong interpretation will remain. Of course, in adopting a policy to be pursued over a number of years we do not for a moment forget that everything may be altered by the international revolution, its rate of development and the circumstances accompanying it. The current international situation is such that some sort of a temporary, unstable equilibrium, but equilibrium for all that, has been established; it is the kind of equilibrium under which the imperialist powers have been compelled to abandon their desire to hurl themselves at Soviet Russia, despite their hatred for her, because the disintegration of the capitalist world is steadily progressing, unity is steadily diminishing, while the onslaught of the forces of the oppressed colonies, which have a population of over a thousand million, is increasing from year to year, month to month, and even week to week. But we can make no conjectures on this score. We are now exercising our main influence on the international revolution through our economic policy. The working people of all countries without exception and without exaggeration are looking to the Soviet Russian Republic. This much has been achieved. The capitalists cannot hush up or conceal anything. That is why they so eagerly catch at our every economic mistake and weakness. The struggle in this field has now become global. Once we solve this problem, we shall have certainly and finally won on an international scale. That is why for us questions of economic development become of absolutely exceptional importance. On this front, we must achieve victory by a steady rise and progress which must be gradual and necessarily slow. I think that as a result of the work of our conference we shall certainly achieve this goal. (*Applause.*)

Published in *Pravda* No. 119,
June 2, 1921

Published according
to the *Pravda* text

SPEECH ON LOCAL ECONOMIC BODIES DELIVERED AT A SITTING OF THE ALL-RUSSIA CENTRAL EXECUTIVE COMMITTEE MAY 30, 1921[118]

Comrades, I have very little to add to what Comrade Osinsky has said, for he has already explained the preliminary draft of the Instructions, copies of which you have, and the main idea underlying it. As there are details in this matter which virtually determine the whole issue, it was decided not to limit its examination to the Council of Labour and Defence and the Council of People's Commissars, but to bring it before the Party conference, where the Instructions were approved in principle, and before the supreme legislative body—the Session of the All-Russia Central Executive Committee. Local workers must make a careful verification of the methods by which this law is to be implemented, and it may be necessary at first to lay down a number of supplementary rules.

Care must be taken that this measure is not, in any circumstances, converted into just another source of increased red tape. This would not be unlikely if we were to receive too many reports, or if the methods of compiling them did not guarantee that they could be checked. Comrades, we must give thought to the methods of compiling the reports, and you may find it appropriate to elect a special commission which, guided by the suggestions that will be made here and the instructions and directives you give it, will put the matter of the reports into final shape. We already have a fair amount of material on this question. Naturally, if reports are to be submitted, they must come not only from the various economic bodies, but also from the People's Commissariats, that is, including those which do not run branches of the economy but are nevertheless closely connected with economic work. One of the main objects of printing the reports is to bring them within reach of the non-Party masses, and of the population in general. We cannot use mass production methods and print these reports in large numbers, and so we must concentrate them in the libraries. That being the case, we must arrange for brief printed summaries of these reports, giving the gist of what is of most interest to the population. The technical facilities for this are available. Before coming here to speak I made inquiries of the representative of the Central Paper Board. He has sent me a precise report covering 339 uyezd centres, and showing that each of these has the printing facilities and the paper to print very brief reports. He has based his calculations on the assumption that the smallest of these uyezd centres would print 16 pages in octavo, once a month, of course. But once a month is too often. Whether you decide on once in two months, or in four, or perhaps even a longer period, will evidently be determined by the reports we get from the localities. He has assumed that there would be 1,000 copies, and has accordingly estimated that the required quantity of paper is now available. A thousand copies would enable us to supply these reports at least to every uyezd library and so bring them within the reach of all who are interested in them, particularly the masses of non-Party people. Of course, this will initially have to be an experiment; no one can guarantee that it will be successful at once, and that there will be no defects.

To conclude my brief supplementary remarks I should like to emphasise one other thing. One of the most important tasks confronting us at present is that of massive enlistment of non-Party people for this work, ensuring that apart from Party members and in any case officials of the department concerned, the largest possible number of non-Party people should have an interest in the work and be enlisted in it. It appeared to us that this could not be achieved in any way except by publishing the reports, at any rate, the more essential part of them. Some establishments send in extremely full reports. All the information that we have had on this question up to now shows that some local bodies are excellently organised. At all events, the work in the localities is constantly providing us with a great deal of very encouraging material. What we really lack is the ability to publicise the best examples—which are not many— and set them up as models which all should be obliged to emulate. Our press does not publicise these really exemplary local organisations which have practical experience. Printing these reports and bringing them within the reach of the broad masses of the population, by supplying copies to every library, if only on the uyezd level, should help— provided conferences of non-Party people are properly convened—to enlist far greater numbers in the economic drive. Any number of resolutions have been passed on this subject. In some places, something has been done, but taking the country as a whole, certainly far too little is being done. By this method, however, we shall improve the work of the establishments and make it possible for every local worker in every responsible economic post to provide the centre with signed reports containing precise and definite information on his practical experience, which could be used as a model. This seems to be what we lack most at the present time.

Let us leave it to practice to decide how these reports are subsequently to be summarised and studied, and utilised at conferences, congresses and by establishments. Considering the available experience of local workers, the main thing now is to approve this decree and put it to the test and be sure to obtain results by the forthcoming All-Russia Congress (some time next December) which would show just how this measure could be developed, improved, modified and enlarged on the basis of experience.

These are the brief supplementary remarks that I should like to confine myself to for the time being.

First published in full in
*I-IV sessii Vserossiiskogo
Tsentralnogo Ispolnitelnogo
Komiteta VIII sozyva.
Stenograficheski otchot
(I-IV Sessions of the Eighth
All-Russia
Central Executive Committee.
Verbatim Report)*
Moscow, 1922

Published according
to the text of the book

SPEECH DELIVERED AT THE THIRD
ALL-RUSSIA FOOD CONFERENCE
JUNE 16, 1921[119]

Comrades, first of all permit me to greet your conference on behalf of the Council of People's Commissars and of the Central Committee of the R.C.P.

Comrades, we all understand, of course, why such special attention should be paid to your conference, not only by those who are engaged in food supply work, but by all Soviet and Party workers, by the whole Party, and by all those who are at all seriously concerned about the fate of the Soviet Republic and its tasks. Your conference has met at a moment of exceptional importance, and for that reason it cannot possibly be regarded as an ordinary, or regular food conference, like any you have attended in the past, and will no doubt attend again in the future.

The exceptional importance of your present conference is due to two circumstances. The first is an unavoidable one—what we feared—the fact that for the second year our country is afflicted by a disaster that entails grave hardships. We do not know whether we are in for a long cycle of drought, as has been predicted these two years, but it is now clear that the grain and hay crop will fail in a large area of the country for the second year running, and the prospects are menacing. I will not say just now how large is the area which, according to the grain and hay crop reports, is affected by the drought; at all events, it is considerable. Whatever it is, the prospect is that in many gubernias there will be a large deficit in the tax in kind, and, moreover, the condition of the population in a number of gubernias will be desperate; so that, instead of collecting a certain quantity of surplus produce from these gubernias for the maintenance of the army, the working class and industry, the food supply workers will have to assist the starving in these gubernias. The unanticipated tasks which thus devolve upon you, as food supply workers, will make your work much more arduous. This is the first circumstance.

The second circumstance, which is not as unexpected, is the moment of change, the turning point that has been reached, in our whole food policy. This is the first food campaign to be launched since the radical change in our food policy. This is the first time we have met to sum up the experience of local food supply workers and to prepare for our forthcoming tasks since the Soviet government was obliged to change, not only its food policy but, in many respects, the very principles of its economic policy; since the extremely severe hardships the peasants suffered last year, and the impossibility, as it turned out, of rapidly restoring large-scale industry, compelled us to switch all our state work to new lines.

Reckoning with the gravity of the situation in the country and the impossibility of rapidly restoring large-scale industry, means making preparations to help small-peasant farming, at all costs, at any price, pull out of its critical position to a bearable one, and for this purpose to revive small, local industry, and adopt measures which, by at once placing small production on a sound basis, would open up opportunities for local trade, thereby enlarging the sphere for the investment of capital, and also switching to new lines the whole Soviet power—its very foundations, and its entire economic policy.

You are well aware of the effort it has cost us all, and you particularly, during the past three years to build up something like a stable food supply apparatus and to run it so that it might fulfil at least the most urgent and essential tasks. Hence, there is no need to tell you, who have been in the thick of all this, what it means quickly to reorganise all our work and switch it over to new lines; what it means to organise amidst so many unknowns, and, at the same time, to solve the problem of obtaining a larger quantity of food. You know all about it. Year after year, in spite of the terrible, unprecedented, sometimes superhuman difficulties created by the Civil War, our food policy has produced striking and tangible results, and the improvement has been far more rapid than in any other sphere of Soviet work. But you also know, of course, that although, as a result of the strenuous efforts of the food supply workers, we have succeeded in raising grain collections from 110 million poods in the first year to over 280 million poods, you know very well that this is not enough.

We are now, for the first time, entering on a big food supply campaign without any whiteguard troops or foreign armies on the territory of the R.S.F.S.R. But to this must be added some reservations: except for the intervention started by the Japanese in the Far Eastern Republic. Which shows again that in the very first year when we can say that, on the whole, we have done with the Civil War, it becomes evident that we are surrounded by the international bourgeoisie, whom the Red Army taught a harsh lesson, but who has not by any means abandoned the idea of resuming the attack, in open or undercover, systematic or sporadic form, at the very first opportunity. So even here we have no sure guarantee. But in addition to all this you know that the very transition from war to economic development, the transition about which we talked so long, and to which we devoted several Party conferences and congresses, this transition in itself, as a transition, created fresh difficulties of vast proportions because, with a dislocated state apparatus and transport a shambles, enormous difficulties arose from the very transition from the old, large army, ranged on the frontier in battle formation, to a peace-time army. The signs are that we have overcome most of these difficulties; nevertheless, as anyone familiar with the situation will agree, quite a number of difficulties still confront us.

That is why I say that this food conference is exceptionally important, that it must settle other questions besides those specifically connected with the food supply, that your attention and efforts on behalf of the Republic are required not only in your capacity of food supply workers, and men on whom the Soviet government has placed the crucial task of supplying the population with food. I say that this is not enough. You as Party workers must exert all your efforts to fulfil a number of tasks which so far exist only in the form of instructions and decisions adopted by the supreme organs of the Soviet power and by the Party. And you know perfectly well what a wide gap there is between general decisions, general instructions, and their practical application. You are aware that this entails enormous effort, which must be exerted in order to put these principles successfully into practice, to prevent them from remaining a dead letter, as, unfortunately, often happens in Soviet Russia.

I should like to remind you of the decision adopted by the last Party Conference, which dealt specifically with the question of the New Economic Policy.[120] The Party conference was called urgently for the purpose of convincing all comrades that this policy had been adopted, as was said at the conference, in earnest and for a long time and to prevent any wavering on that score in future, for there has been some wavering and uncertainty. The Party conference, as the supreme organ of the ruling, government Party, the leading authority of the working class, emphasised the importance of collecting the large food stock of 400 million poods. It laid emphasis on the point that the whole meaning of our food policy, permitting a large measure of unrestricted trade, boils down to building up a big food fund, as a large state reserve. Without it, neither the restoration of large-scale industry nor the restoration of the currency will be possible, and every socialist understands that unless large-scale industry—the only real basis—is restored, it is no use talking about socialist construction.

No country has been so devastated as ours. It had been more backward than other countries before the imperialist war, which brought it more ruin than it did to any other country, and in addition we had to endure the untold hardships of another three years of war against the bourgeoisie and the landowners. The vanquished countries with which Russia might be compared, countries like Serbia and Austria—where industry has been ruined to an extent equal to, and in some cases even greater than, that of Russia—are in desperate straits. Counting on the assistance of the bourgeoisie—for they did not rise against it—they are crushed by a double burden: starvation, ruin and impoverishment (as in our case), plus the realisation that their position is hopeless, that they had put their stake on the bourgeoisie and are perishing without any prospects of assistance. But, in spite of all our incredible difficulties, we see and clearly realise, and the mass of workers and peasants clearly realise —in spite of our incredible difficulties fresh forces are arising. Every difficulty brought to life fresh forces, created new sources of energy and indicated new paths. The work these forces have performed proves to us that, terribly slow though it is, we are making progress, that frightfully hard though it may be to overcome difficulties at times, we are nevertheless overcoming them. There is a growing realisation that economic relationships are being built upon entirely new lines, that great as its sufferings may be, the working class is, step by step, day after day, finding solutions for all problems without the aid of the capitalists, and is fighting them, and dislodging them from one position after another.

This, comrades, seems to me to be the sum and substance of the decisions adopted by the Party conference. And with this I want particularly to emphasise that the present conference is not only a conference of specialists, but of Party and Soviet workers upon whom will devolve the practical task of building, under extremely difficult conditions, the new forms of economic policy and the foundation of the whole Soviet edifice.

We shall have to build in two ways: by collecting the tax and by reviving commodity exchange. The tax has been fixed, on the assumption of an average harvest, at 240 million poods, which is inadequate even for a short ration for the army which we need, and for the absolutely essential industrial enterprises. It will be difficult to collect this amount in full, not only in view of the threatening crop failure, but under any circumstances.

I have not got the exact figures before me showing the changes in the percentages of fulfilment of our food supply plans and assignments according to districts during the three years that we have been carrying on food supply operations. But everyone knows that the machinery we have created by our joint efforts is running far more smoothly than that of a number of other People's Commissariats, and that our efficiency is steadily increasing. I also take it as an irrefutable fact that this year, when so much attention is being devoted to this work, we shall cope more fully with the tasks the Republic has set us. We must achieve, if not 100 per cent, then as near to that figure as possible; and we can achieve it, even amidst the difficulties created by the threatening failure of the harvest. The tax deficit may run to tens of millions of poods, but this may be balanced by the extra amount that is likely to be collected in areas where the harvest has been particularly good.

Comrades, the harvest absolutely refuses to reckon with the state of the food supply apparatus, and it has not given us the satisfaction of being particularly good where the food supply apparatus is particularly good. If we look at the chart indicating the harvest prospects we shall find that the areas of the R.S.F.S.R. and of neighbouring and fraternal republics where the harvest outlook is particularly good, or is above the average, are the very regions where the food supply apparatus is certainly not above the average, but even below it. Vigorous measures must be taken to transfer extra food supply workers to these areas, but we know too few people who are sufficiently trained and experienced to adapt themselves to the new areas quickly and get things moving at once. This is a matter that requires very close attention.

The main thing is commodity exchange, and it is this the Party conference put into the forefront and the last Party Congress decided. It is the question that is engaging most of the concern and attention of all those who are at the head of Soviet and Party work in Moscow. How well are we prepared for it? What has been actually done? What part of these plans has been carried out? You will be the first to have to answer these questions from first-hand experience. Your experience in this matter and its summing up will be of particular and vital importance.

This is a new field, and additional forces must be sent in. It demands that the food supply apparatus should be something more than it has been up to now—nothing but a more or less uniform and smoothly running machine for collecting a quantity of food products. No, here you will have to take account of the difference in the localities, in the goods demanded and the equivalents offered. You will not have to adjust yourselves to what the Soviet government wants, and to what the Soviet apparatus can carry out. No, you will have to adjust yourselves to the economic conditions of the small farmers, and will have to reckon with their satisfied and outstanding needs. You have fought the profiteers and have combated trade conducted in contravention of government orders. You will have to go on fighting them. But in order to engage in the exchange of commodities and avoid being beaten in the free market—which means being beaten by unrestricted trade—you must know it thoroughly, compete with it, fight it with its own weapons and beat it at its own game, but to be able to do that you must have a thorough knowledge of it.

The old bureaucratic methods are of no use; we need precise knowledge of commercial conditions and the ability to react quickly to every change. For this purpose, food products and articles for exchange must be rapidly transported from place to place over the vast territory of the R.S.F.S.R. The difficulties ahead of us are enormous. But this will be the basis of the whole of our New Economic Policy for the period until we fully restore large-scale industry. This may take at least ten years, during which time we must create such relations between the working class and the peasantry—the only classes that can serve as a base on which to build up our economy—and such an alliance between them as will economically satisfy both sides. It must be an alliance in which the small peasant will be reckoned with as a small peasant, until we are able to provide him with all the products of large-scale industry.

We must reckon with the small proprietor who sells his surplus products. We must also reckon with the need to improve the condition of the urban population—the workers. Unless we do this, we shall fail in our further work of construction that will so consolidate the transition to socialism that there will be no turning back. That is why commodity exchange is now the most important part of our economic policy. This is the task you, food supply workers, business managers and co-operators, will have to tackle.

This is what the Soviet government, the Party, and the whole Republic expect of you, for your attitude to this work and your successes will determine the success of what the Soviet Republic is now staking everything on in the work of socialist construction.

Comrades, I must say in conclusion that your conference has a special task before it: to consider a matter that was raised in the Political Bureau of the Party's Central Committee in May, and settled, after discussion on the Central Committee, at the All-Russia Congress of Trade Unions. It is to set to work, with due circumspection and very gradually, but immediately, to try out the system of collective supplies. The present system of food distribution has proved to be defective, and this cannot go on. The system of distributing food on the egalitarian principle has led to equalisation, which sometimes proves to be an obstacle to increasing output. The Republic must utilise the food surpluses it collects to maintain only what is needed for industry. We cannot maintain all our factories, nor is it necessary to do so: that would be wasteful management. We cannot restore the whole of large-scale industry, and so we must select and maintain only those factories which have the best equipment and promise a greater output.

Food supply workers cannot just go on thinking that their business boils down to collecting so many millions of poods and distributing them in certain fixed rations, on the present ration cards, say, and that there is the end of it. The immediate thing is to integrate the activity of all the economic People's Commissariats. The conscientious food supply worker must not only be interested in food supply work, but in all economic activity. More is expected of him now.

He cannot go on being only a food supply worker. He must be an economist appraising every step in the light of the work of all the economic People's Commissariats, and of all the results achieved by that work.

It is wrong to think that food distribution is only a matter of fairness. We must bear in mind that it is a method, an instrument, and a means of increasing output. State food supplies must be given only to those employees who are really needed, on the condition that productivity of labour is increased to the utmost. And if the distribution of food is to be used as a political instrument, then it must be used to reduce the number of those who are not absolutely needed and to encourage those who actually are. If the distribution of food is a political instrument for restoring our industry, then we must maintain the industrial enterprises which are really needed now, and certainly stop maintaining those we do not need now, and thus economise fuel and food. For a number of years we have been managing these things very badly. This must now be rectified.

Thus, you see that the closer you look into the matter the wider you find the tasks confronting your food conference. I hope, however, that none of you will be intimidated by the complexity of these tasks, and that, on the contrary, the unusual nature of your tasks as Soviet and Party workers will stimulate you to fresh efforts to fulfil them. Our past experience of the work of other People's Commissariats clearly proves the necessity of combining Soviet and Party work. Food supply workers have carried out a number of urgent tasks under extremely difficult conditions; and they did it successfully because in these cases the Soviet and Party bodies resorted to unconventional methods, urgent measures and shock-work campaign operations. I repeat that it is the fundamental basis of our economic policy that is the main subject of your food conference. It must engage all your attention.

In conclusion, permit me to express the conviction that our united efforts in the direction we have taken will lay a firm foundation for a successful economic policy that will create an alliance between the working class and the peasantry, the two main classes on which the Soviet power rests, the economic alliance which alone can guarantee the success of all our work of socialist construction. (*Stormy applause*.)

Pravda Nos. 133 and 134,
June 22 and 23, 1921

Published according
to the newspaper text

THIRD CONGRESS
OF THE COMMUNIST
INTERNATIONAL[121]

JUNE 22-JULY 12, 1921

First published in full as a pamphlet, *Tezisy doklada o taktike R.K.P. na III kongresse Kommunisticheskogo Internatsionala* (*Theses for a Report on the Tactics of the R.C.P. at the Third Congress of the Communist International*) in 1921; the speeches and the report in the book, *Treti vsemirny kongress Kommunisticheskogo Internatsionala. Stenograficheski otchot* (*Third World Congress of the Communist International. Verbatim Report*), Petrograd, 1922

The *Tezisy* are published according to the manuscript; the speech on the Italian question, the speech in defence of the tactics of the Communist International, and the report on the tactics of the R.C.P., according to the text of the book

15*

1

THESES FOR A REPORT ON THE TACTICS OF THE R.C.P.

1. THE INTERNATIONAL POSITION OF THE R.S.F.S.R.

The international position of the R.S.F.S.R. at present is distinguished by a certain equilibrium, which, although extremely unstable, has nevertheless given rise to a peculiar state of affairs in world politics.

This peculiarity is the following. On the one hand, the international bourgeoisie is filled with furious hatred of, and hostility towards, Soviet Russia, and is prepared at any moment to fling itself upon her in order to strangle her. On the other hand, all attempts at military intervention, which have cost the international bourgeoisie hundreds of millions of francs, ended in complete failure, in spite of the fact that the Soviet power was then weaker than it is now and that the Russian landowners and capitalists had whole armies on the territory of the R.S.F.S.R. Opposition to the war against Soviet Russia has grown considerably in all capitalist countries, adding fuel to the revolutionary movement of the proletariat and extending to very wide sections of the petty-bourgeois democrats. The conflict of interests between the various imperialist countries has become acute, and is growing more acute every day. The revolutionary movement among the hundreds of millions of oppressed peoples of the East is growing with remarkable vigour. The result of all these conditions is that international imperialism has proved unable to strangle Soviet Russia, although it is far stronger, and has been obliged for the time being to grant her recognition, or semi-recognition, and to conclude trade agreements with her.

The result is a state of equilibrium which, although highly unstable and precarious, enables the Socialist Republic to exist—not for long, of course—within the capitalist encirclement.

2. THE INTERNATIONAL ALIGNMENT OF CLASS FORCES

This state of affairs has given rise to the following international alignment of class forces.

The international bourgeoisie, deprived of the opportunity of waging open war against Soviet Russia, is waiting and watching for the moment when circumstances will permit it to resume the war.

The proletariat in all the advanced capitalist countries has already formed its vanguard, the Communist Parties, which are growing, making steady progress towards winning the majority of the proletariat in each country, and destroying the influence of the old trade union bureaucrats and of the upper stratum of the working class of America and Europe, which has been corrupted by imperialist privileges.

The petty-bourgeois democrats in the capitalist countries, whose foremost sections are represented by the Second and Two-and-a-Half Internationals, serve today as the mainstay of capitalism, since they retain an influence over the majority, or a considerable section, of the industrial and commercial workers and office employees who are afraid that if revolution breaks out they will lose the relative petty-bourgeois prosperity created by the privileges of imperialism. But the growing economic crisis is worsening the condition of broad sections of the people everywhere, and this, with the looming inevitability of new imperialist wars if capitalism is preserved, is steadily weakening this mainstay.

The masses of the working people in the colonial and semi-colonial countries, who constitute the overwhelming majority of the population of the globe, were roused to political life at the turn of the twentieth century, particularly by the revolutions in Russia, Turkey, Persia and China. The imperialist war of 1914-18 and the Soviet power in Russia are completing the process of converting these masses into an active factor in world politics and in the revolutionary

destruction of imperialism, although the educated philistines of Europe and America, including the leaders of the
Second and Two-and-a-Half Internationals, stubbornly
refuse to see this. British India is at the head of these
countries, and there revolution is maturing in proportion, on
the one hand, to the growth of the industrial and railway
proletariat, and, on the other, to the increase in the brutal
terrorism of the British, who with ever greater frequency
resort to massacres (Amritsar),[122] public floggings, etc.

3. THE ALIGNMENT OF CLASS FORCES IN RUSSIA

The internal political situation in Soviet Russia is determined by the fact that here, for the first time in history,
there have been, for a number of years, only two classes—
the proletariat, trained for decades by a very young, but
modern, large-scale machine industry, and the small
peasantry, who constitute the overwhelming majority of
the population.

In Russia, the big landowners and capitalists have not
vanished, but they have been subjected to total expropriation and crushed politically as a class, whose remnants are
hiding out among Soviet government employees. They have
preserved their class organisation abroad, as émigrés, numbering probably from 1,500,000 to 2,000,000 people, with
over 50 daily newspapers of all bourgeois and "socialist"
(i.e., petty-bourgeois) parties, the remnants of an army, and
numerous connections with the international bourgeoisie.
These émigrés are striving, with might and main, to destroy
the Soviet power and restore capitalism in Russia.

4. THE PROLETARIAT AND THE PEASANTRY IN RUSSIA

This being the internal situation in Russia, the main
task now confronting her proletariat, as the ruling class,
is properly to determine and carry out the measures that are
necessary to lead the peasantry, establish a firm alliance
with them and achieve the transition, in a series of gradual
stages, to large-scale, socialised, mechanised agriculture.
This is a particularly difficult task in Russia, both because
of her backwardness, and her extreme state of ruin as a

result of seven years of imperialist and civil war. But apart from these specific circumstances, this is one of the most difficult tasks of socialist construction that will confront all capitalist countries, with, perhaps, the sole exception of Britain. However, even in regard to Britain it must not be forgotten that, while the small-tenant farmers there constitute only a very small class, the percentage of workers and office employees who enjoy a petty-bourgeois standard of living is exceptionally high, due to the actual enslavement of hundreds of millions of people in Britain's colonial possessions.

Hence, from the standpoint of development of the world proletarian revolution as a single process, the epoch Russia is passing through is significant as a practical test and a verification of the policy of a proletariat in power towards the mass of the petty bourgeoisie.

5. THE MILITARY ALLIANCE BETWEEN THE PROLETARIAT AND THE PEASANTRY IN THE R.S.F.S.R.

The basis for proper relations between the proletariat and the peasantry in Soviet Russia was created in the period of 1917-21 when the invasion of the capitalists and landowners, supported by the whole world bourgeoisie and all the petty-bourgeois democratic parties (Socialist-Revolutionaries and Mensheviks), caused the proletariat and the peasantry to form, sign and seal a military alliance to defend the Soviet power. Civil war is the most intense form of class struggle, but the more intense it is, the more rapidly its flames consume all petty-bourgeois illusions and prejudices, and the more clearly experience proves even to the most backward strata of the peasantry that only the dictatorship of the proletariat can save it, and that the Socialist-Revolutionaries and Mensheviks are in fact merely the servants of the landowners and capitalists.

But while the military alliance between the proletariat and the peasantry was—and had perforce to be—the primary form of their firm alliance, it could not have been maintained even for a few weeks without an economic alliance between the two classes. The peasants received from the workers' state all the land and were given protection against the landowners and the kulaks; the workers have been receiving from the peasants loans of food supplies until large-scale industry is restored.

6. THE TRANSITION TO PROPER ECONOMIC RELATIONS BETWEEN THE PROLETARIAT AND THE PEASANTRY

The alliance between the small peasants and the proletariat can become a correct and stable one from the socialist standpoint only when the complete restoration of transport and large-scale industry enables the proletariat to give the peasants, in exchange for food, all the goods they need for their own use and for the improvement of their farms. With the country in ruins, this could not possibly be achieved at once. The surplus appropriation system was the best measure available to the insufficiently organised state to maintain itself in the incredibly arduous war against the landowners. The crop failure and the fodder shortage in 1920 particularly increased the hardships of the peasantry, already severe enough, and made the immediate transition to the tax in kind imperative.

The moderate tax in kind will bring about a big improvement in the condition of the peasantry at once, and will at the same time stimulate them to enlarge crop areas and improve farming methods.

The tax in kind signifies a transition from the requisition of all the peasants' surplus grain to regular socialist exchange of products between industry and agriculture.

7. THE CONDITIONS UNDER WHICH THE SOVIET GOVERNMENT CAN PERMIT CAPITALISM AND CONCESSIONS, AND THE SIGNIFICANCE THEREOF

Naturally, the tax in kind means freedom for the peasant to dispose of his after-tax surplus at his own discretion. Since the state cannot provide the peasant with goods from socialist factories in exchange for all his surplus, freedom to trade with this surplus necessarily means freedom for the development of capitalism.

Within the limits indicated, however, this is not at all dangerous for socialism as long as transport and large-scale industry remain in the hands of the proletariat. On the contrary, the development of capitalism, controlled and regulated by the proletarian state (i.e., "state" capitalism in *this* sense of the term), is advantageous and necessary in an extremely devastated and backward small-peasant country (within certain limits, of course), inasmuch as it is capable of hastening the *immediate* revival of peasant farming. This applies still more to concessions: without denationalising anything, the workers' state leases certain mines, forest tracts, oilfields, and so forth, to foreign capitalists in order to obtain from them extra equipment and machinery that will enable us to accelerate the restoration of Soviet large-scale industry.

The payment made to the concessionaires in the form of a share of the highly valuable products obtained is undoubtedly tribute, which the workers' state pays to the world bourgeoisie; without in any way glossing this over, we must clearly realise that we stand to gain by paying this tribute, so long as it accelerates the restoration of our large-scale industry and substantially improves the condition of the workers and peasants.

8. THE SUCCESS OF OUR FOOD POLICY

The food policy pursued by Soviet Russia in 1917-21 was undoubtedly very crude and imperfect, and gave rise to many abuses. A number of mistakes were made in its implementation. But as a whole, it was the only possible policy under the conditions prevailing at the time. And it did fulfil its historic mission: it saved the proletarian dictatorship in a ruined and backward country. There can be no doubt that it has gradually improved. In the first year that we had full power (August 1, 1918 to August 1, 1919) the state collected 110 million poods of grain; in the second year it collected 220 million poods, and in the third year—over 285 million poods.

Now, having acquired practical experience, we have set out, and expect, to collect 400 million poods (the tax in kind is expected to bring in 240 million poods). Only when it is actually in possession of an adequate stock of food will the workers' state be able to stand firmly on its own feet economically, secure the steady, if slow, restoration of large-scale industry, and create a proper financial system.

9. THE MATERIAL BASIS OF SOCIALISM AND THE PLAN FOR THE ELECTRIFICATION OF RUSSIA

A large-scale machine industry capable of reorganising agriculture is the only material basis that is possible for socialism. But we cannot confine ourselves to this general thesis. It must be made more concrete. Large-scale industry based on the latest achievements of technology and capable of reorganising agriculture implies the electrification of the whole country. We had to undertake the scientific work of drawing up such a plan for the electrification of the R.S.F.S.R. and we have accomplished it. With the co-operation of over two hundred of the best scientists, engineers and agronomists in Russia, this work has now been completed; it was published in a large volume and, as a whole, endorsed by the Eighth All-Russia Congress of Soviets in December 1920. Arrangements have now been made to convene an all-Russia congress of electrical engineers in August 1921 to examine this plan in detail, before it is given final government endorsement. The execution of the first part of the electrification scheme is estimated to take ten years, and will require about 370 million man-days.

In 1918, we had eight newly erected power stations (with a total capacity of 4,757 kw); in 1919, the figure rose to 36 (total capacity of 1,648 kw), and in 1920, it rose to 100 (total capacity of 8,699 kw).

Modest as this beginning is for our vast country, a start has been made, work has begun and is making steady progress. After the imperialist war, after a million prisoners of war in Germany had become familiar with modern up-to-date technique, after the stern but hardening experience of three years of civil war, the Russian peasant is a different man. With every passing month he sees more clearly and more vividly that only the guidance given by the proletariat is capable of leading the mass of small farmers out of capitalist slavery to socialism.

10. THE ROLE OF "PURE DEMOCRACY", THE SECOND AND TWO-AND-A-HALF INTERNATIONALS, THE SOCIALIST-REVOLUTIONARIES AND THE MENSHEVIKS AS THE ALLIES OF CAPITAL

The dictatorship of the proletariat does not signify a cessation of the class struggle, but its continuation in a new form and with new weapons. This dictatorship is essential as long as classes exist, as long as the bourgeoisie, overthrown in one country, intensifies tenfold its attacks on socialism on an international scale. In the transition period, the small farmer class is bound to experience certain vacillations. The difficulties of transition, and the influence of the bourgeoisie, inevitably cause the mood of this mass to change from time to time. Upon the proletariat, enfeebled and to a certain extent declassed by the destruction of the large-scale machine industry, which is its vital foundation, devolves the very difficult but paramount historic task of holding out in spite of these vacillations, and of carrying to victory its cause of emancipating labour from the yoke of capital.

The policy pursued by the petty-bourgeois democratic parties, i.e., the parties affiliated to the Second and Two-and-a-Half Internationals, represented in Russia by the S.R. (Socialist-Revolutionary) and Menshevik parties, is the political expression of the vacillations of the petty bourgeoisie. These parties now have their headquarters and newspapers abroad, and are actually in a bloc with the whole of the bourgeois counter-revolution and are serving it loyally.

The shrewd leaders of the Russian big bourgeoisie headed by Milyukov, the leader of the Cadet (Constitutional-Democratic) Party, have quite clearly, definitely and openly appraised this role of the petty-bourgeois democrats, i.e., the Socialist-Revolutionaries and Mensheviks. In connection with the Kronstadt mutiny, in which the Mensheviks, Socialist-Revolutionaries and whiteguards joined forces, Milyukov declared in favour of the "Soviets without the Bolsheviks" slogan. Elaborating on the idea, he wrote that the Socialist-Revolutionaries and Mensheviks "are welcome to try" (*Pravda* No. 64, 1921, quoted from the Paris *Posledniye Novosti*[123]), because upon them devolves the task of *first taking* power away from the Bolsheviks. Milyukov, the leader of the big bourgeoisie, has correctly appraised the lesson taught by all revolutions, namely, that the petty-bourgeois democrats are incapable of holding power, and always serve merely as a screen for the dictatorship of the bourgeoisie, and a stepping stone to its undivided power.

The proletarian revolution in Russia again and again confirms this lesson of 1789-94 and 1848-49, and also what Frederick Engels said in his letter to Bebel of December 11, 1884.

. . . "Pure democracy . . . when the moment of revolution comes, acquires a temporary importance . . . as the final sheet-anchor of the whole bourgeois and even feudal economy. . . . Thus between March and September 1848 the whole feudal-bureaucratic mass strengthened the liberals in order to hold down the revolutionary masses. . . . In any case our sole adversary on the day of the crisis and on the day after the crisis will be the whole of the reaction which will group around pure democracy, and this, I think, should not be lost sight of." (Published in Russian in *Kommunistichesky Trud*[124] No. 360, June 9, 1921, in an article by Comrade V. Adoratsky: "Marx and Engels on Democracy". In German, published in the book, Friedrich Engels, *Politisches Vermächtnis*, Internationale Jugend-Bibliothek, Nr. 12, Berlin, 1920, S. 19.)

N. Lenin

Moscow, Kremlin, June 13, 1921

2

SPEECH ON THE ITALIAN QUESTION
JUNE 28

Comrades, I should like to reply mainly to Comrade Lazzari. He said: "Quote concrete facts, not words." Excellent. But if we trace the development of the reformist-opportunist trend in Italy, what will that be, words or facts? In your speeches and in the whole of your policy you lose sight of the fact, which is so important for the socialist movement in Italy, that not only this trend, but an opportunist-reformist group has existed for quite a long time. I still very well remember the time when Bernstein started his opportunist propaganda, which ended in social-patriotism, in the treason and bankruptcy of the Second International. We have known Turati ever since, not only by name, but for his propaganda in the Italian party and in the Italian working-class movement, of which he has been a disrupter for the past twenty years. Lack of time prevents me from closely studying the material concerning the Italian party; but I think that one of the most important documents on this subject is a report, published in a bourgeois Italian newspaper—I don't remember which, *La Stampa*[125] or *Corriere della Sera*[126]—of the conference held by Turati and his friends in Reggio Emilia.[127] I compared that report with the one published in *Avanti!*[128] Is this not proof enough? After the Second Congress of the Communist International, we, in our controversy with Serrati and his friends, openly and definitely told them what, in our opinion, the situation was. We told them that the Italian party could not become a Communist Party as long as it tolerated people like Turati in its ranks.

What is this, political facts, or again just words? After the Second Congress of the Communist International we openly said to the Italian proletariat: "Don't unite with the reformists, with Turati." Serrati launched a series of articles in the Italian press in opposition to the Communist International and convened a special conference of reformists.[129] Was all this mere words? It was something more than a split: it was the creation of a new party. One must have been blind not to have seen this. This document is of decisive importance for this question. All those who attended the Reggio Emilia conference must be expelled from the party; they are Mensheviks—not Russian, but Italian Mensheviks. Lazzari said: "We know the Italian people's mentality." For my part I would not dare to make such an assertion about the Russian people, but that is not important. "Italian Socialists understand the spirit of the Italian people very well," said Lazzari. Perhaps they do, I will not argue about that. But they do not know Italian Menshevism, if the concrete facts and the persistent refusal to eradicate Menshevism is anything to go by. We are obliged to say that—deplorable though it may be—the resolution of our Executive Committee must be confirmed. A party which tolerates opportunists and reformists like Turati in its ranks cannot be affiliated to the Communist International.

"Why should we change the name of the party?" asks Comrade Lazzari. "The present one is quite satisfactory." But we cannot share this view. We know the history of the Second International, its fall and bankruptcy. Do we not know the history of the German party? And do we not know that the great misfortune of the working-class movement in Germany is that the break was not brought about before the war? This cost the lives of twenty thousand workers, whom the Scheidemannists and the Centrists betrayed to the German Government by their polemics with and complaints against the German Communists.[130]

And do we not now see the same thing in Italy? The Italian party was never a truly revolutionary party. Its great misfortune is that it did not break with the Mensheviks and reformists before the war, and that the latter continued to remain in the party. Comrade Lazzari says: "We fully recognise the necessity of a break with the reformists; our only disagreement is that we did not think it necessary to bring it about at the Leghorn Congress." But

the facts tell a different story. This is not the first time that
we are discussing Italian reformism. In arguing about this
with Serrati last year, we said: "You won't mind us asking
why the split in the Italian party cannot be brought about
immediately, why it must be postponed?" What did Serrati
say in reply to that? Nothing. And Comrade Lazzari, quoting an article by Frossard in which the latter said, "We
must be adroit and clever", evidently thinks that this is an
argument in his favour and against us. I think he is mistak-
en. On the contrary, it is an excellent argument in our
favour and against Comrade Lazzari. What will the Italian
workers say when you are obliged to explain your conduct
and your resignation? What will you tell them if they
declare our tactics to be clever and adroit compared with
the zigzags of the pseudo-Communist Left—the Left which
at times is not even simply Communist and more often
looks like anarchism?

What is the meaning of the tales told by Serrati and
his party about the Russians only wanting everyone to
imitate them? We want the very opposite. It takes more
than memorising communist resolutions and using revolutionary phrases on every possible occasion. That is not
enough, and we are opposed beforehand to Communists
who know this or that resolution by heart. The mark of
true communism is a break with opportunism. We shall be
quite frank and open with those Communists who subscribe
to this and, boldly, in the conviction that we are right,
will tell them: "Don't do anything stupid; be clever and
skilful." But we shall speak in this way only with Communists who have broken with the opportunists, something
that cannot yet be said about you. I repeat therefore: I
hope the Congress will confirm the resolution of the Executive Committee. Comrade Lazzari said: "We are in the
preparatory period." This is absolutely true. You are in the
preparatory period. The first stage of this period is a break
with the Mensheviks, similar to the one we brought about
with our Mensheviks in 1903. The sufferings the whole of
the German working class has had to endure during this
long and weary post-war period in the history of the German
revolution are due to the fact that the German party did
not break with the Mensheviks.

Comrade Lazzari said that the Italian party is passing through the preparatory period. This I fully accept. And the first stage is a definite, final, unambiguous and determined break with reformism. When that is brought about the masses will side solidly with communism. The second stage is by no means a repetition of revolutionary slogans. It will be the adoption of our wise and skilful decisions, which will always be such, and which will always say: fundamental revolutionary principles must be adapted to the specific conditions in the various countries.

The revolution in Italy will run a different course from that in Russia. It will start in a different way. How? Neither you nor we know. The Italian Communists are not always Communists to a sufficient degree. Did a single Communist show his mettle when the workers seized the factories in Italy?[131] No. At that time, there was as yet no communism in Italy; there was a certain amount of anarchism, but no Marxian communism. The latter has still to be created and the masses of the workers must be imbued with it by means of the experience of the revolutionary struggle. And the first step along this road is a final break with the Mensheviks, who for more than twenty years have been collaborating and working with the bourgeois government. It is quite probable that Modigliani, whom I was able to watch to some extent at the Zimmerwald and Kienthal conferences, is a sufficiently astute politician to keep out of the bourgeois government and to keep in the centre of the Socialist Party, where he can be far more useful to the bourgeoisie. But all the theories of Turati and his friends, all their propaganda and agitation, signify collaboration with the bourgeoisie. Is this not proved by the numerous quotations in Gennari's speech? Indeed, it is the united front which Turati has already prepared. That is why I must say to Comrade Lazzari: "Speeches like yours and like the one which Comrade Serrati made here do not help to prepare for the revolution, they disorganise it." (*Shouts*: "Bravo!" *Applause*.)

You had a considerable majority at Leghorn. You had 98,000 votes against 14,000 reformist and 58,000 communist votes. As the beginning of a purely communist movement in a country like Italy, with its well-known traditions, where the ground has not been sufficiently prepared for a split, this vote is a considerable achievement for the Communists.

This is a great victory and tangible proof of the fact that the working-class movement in Italy will develop faster than our movement developed in Russia, because, if you are familiar with the figures concerning our movement, you must know that in February 1917, after the fall of tsarism and during the bourgeois republic, we were still a minority compared with the Mensheviks. Such was the position after fifteen years of fierce fighting and splits. Our Right wing did not grow—and it was not so easy to prevent it from growing, as you seem to think when you speak of Russia in such a disparaging tone. Undoubtedly, development in Italy will proceed quite differently. After fifteen years of struggle against the Mensheviks, and after the fall of tsarism, we started work with a much smaller number of adherents. You have 58,000 communistically minded workers against 98,000 united Centrists who occupy an indefinite position. This is proof, this is a fact, which should certainly convince all those who refuse to close their eyes to the mass movement of the Italian workers. Nothing comes all at once. But it certainly proves that the mass of workers—not the old leaders, the bureaucrats, the professors, the journalists, but the class that is actually exploited, the vanguard of the exploited—supports us. And it proves what a great mistake you made at Leghorn. This is a fact. You controlled 98,000 votes, but you preferred to go with 14,000 reformists against 58,000 Communists. You should have gone with them even if they were not genuine Communists, even if they were only adherents of Bordiga—which is not true, for after the Second Congress Bordiga quite honestly declared that he had abandoned all anarchism and anti-parliamentarism. But what did you do? You chose to unite with 14,000 reformists and to break with 58,000 Communists. And this is the best proof that Serrati's policy has been disastrous for Italy. We never wanted Serrati in Italy to copy the Russian revolution. That would have been stupid. We are intelligent and flexible enough to avoid such stupidity. But Serrati has proved that his policy in Italy was wrong. Perhaps he should have manoeuvred. This is the expression that he repeated

most often when he was here last year. He said: "We know
how to manoeuvre, we do not want slavish imitation. That
would be idiocy. We must manoeuvre, so as to bring about
a separation from opportunism. You Russians do not know
how to do that. We Italians are more skilful at that sort
of thing. That remains to be seen." And what is it we saw?
Serrati executed a brilliant manoeuvre. He broke away from
58,000 Communists. And now these comrades come here and
say: "If you reject us the masses will be confused." No, comrades, you are mistaken. The masses of the workers in Italy
are confused now, and it will do them good if we tell them:
"Comrades, you must choose; Italian workers, you must
choose between the Communist International, which will
never call upon you slavishly to imitate the Russians,
and the Mensheviks, whom we have known for twenty years,
and whom we shall never tolerate as neighbours in a
genuinely revolutionary Communist International." That is
what we shall say to the Italian workers. There can be
no doubt about the result. The masses of workers will follow
us. (*Loud approval.*)

3

SPEECH IN DEFENCE OF THE TACTICS
OF THE COMMUNIST INTERNATIONAL
JULY 1

Comrades! I deeply regret that I must confine myself
to self-defence. (*Laughter.*) I say deeply regret, because after
acquainting myself with Comrade Terracini's speech and
the amendments introduced by three delegations, I should
very much like to take the offensive, for, properly speaking,
offensive operations are essential against the views defended
by Terracini and these three delegations.[132] If the Congress
is not going to wage a vigorous offensive against such
errors, against such "Leftist" stupidities, the whole movement is doomed. That is my deep conviction. But we are
organised and disciplined Marxists. We cannot be satisfied
with speeches against individual comrades. We Russians
are already sick and tired of these Leftist phrases. We are
men of organisation. In drawing up our plans, we must
proceed in an organised way and try to find the correct
line. It is, of course, no secret that our theses are a compromise. And why not? Among Communists, who have already
convened their Third Congress and have worked out definite
fundamental principles, compromises under certain conditions are necessary. Our theses, put forward by the Russian
delegation, were studied and prepared in the most careful
way and were the result of long arguments and meetings
with various delegations. They aim at establishing the basic
line of the Communist International and are especially
necessary now after we have not only formally condemned
the real Centrists but have expelled them from the Party.
Such are the facts. I have to stand up for these theses. Now,
when Terracini comes forward and says that we must
continue the fight against the Centrists, and goes on to tell

how it is intended to wage the fight, I say that if these amendments denote a definite trend, a relentless fight against this trend is essential, for otherwise there is no communism and no Communist International. I am surprised that the German Communist Workers' Party has not put its signature to these amendments. (*Laughter*.) Indeed, just listen to what Terracini is defending and what his amendments say. They begin in this way: "On page 1, column 1, line 19, the word 'majority' should be deleted." Majority! That is extremely dangerous! (*Laughter*.) Then further: instead of the words "'basic propositions', insert 'aims'". Basic propositions and aims are two different things; even the anarchists will agree with us about aims, because they too stand for the abolition of exploitation and class distinctions.

I have met and talked with few anarchists in my life, but all the same I have seen enough of them. I sometimes succeeded in reaching agreement with them about aims, but never as regards principles. Principles are not an aim, a programme, a tactic or a theory. Tactics and theory are not principles. How do we differ from the anarchists on principles? The principles of communism consist in the establishment of the dictatorship of the proletariat and in the use of state coercion in the transition period. Such are the principles of communism, but they are not its aim. And the comrades who have tabled this proposal have made a mistake.

Secondly, it is stated there: "the word 'majority' should be deleted." Read the whole passage:

"The Third Congress of the Communist International is setting out to review questions of tactics under conditions when in a whole number of countries the objective situation has become aggravated in a revolutionary sense, and when a whole number of communist mass parties have been organised, which, incidentally, in their actual revolutionary struggle have nowhere taken into their hands the virtual leadership of the majority of the working class."

And so, they want the word "majority" deleted. If we cannot agree on such simple things, then I do not understand how we can work together and lead the proletariat to victory. Then it is not at all surprising that we cannot reach agreement on the question of principles either. Show

me a party which has already won the majority of the
working class. Terracini did not even think of adducing
any example. Indeed, there is no such example.

And so, the word "aims" is to be put instead of "principles", and the word "majority" is to be deleted. No, thank
you! We shall not do it. Even the German party—one of
the best—does not have the majority of the working class
behind it. That is a fact. We, who face a most severe struggle, are not afraid to utter this truth, but here you have
three delegations who wish to begin with an untruth, for
if the Congress deletes the word "majority" it will show
that it wants an untruth. That is quite clear.

Then comes the following amendment: "On page 4,
column 1, line 10, the words 'Open Letter', etc., should
be deleted."[133] I have already heard one speech today in
which I found the same idea. But there it was quite natural.
It was the speech of Comrade Hempel, a member of the
German Communist Workers' Party. He said: "The 'Open
Letter' was an act of opportunism." To my deep regret
and shame, I have already heard such views privately. But
when, at the Congress, after such prolonged debate, the
"Open Letter" is declared opportunist—that is a shame
and a disgrace! And now Comrade Terracini comes forward
on behalf of the three delegations and wants to delete the
words "Open Letter". What is the good then of the fight
against the German Communist Workers' Party? The
"Open Letter" is a model political step. This is stated in
our theses and we must certainly stand by it. It is a model
because it is the first act of a practical method of winning
over the majority of the working class. In Europe, where
almost all the proletarians are organised, we must win the
majority of the working class and anyone who fails to understand this is lost to the communist movement; he will never
learn anything if he has failed to learn that much during
the three years of the great revolution.

Terracini says that we were victorious in Russia although
the Party was very small. He is dissatisfied with what is
said in the theses about Czechoslovakia. Here there are
27 amendments, and if I had a mind to criticise them I
should, like some orators, have to speak for not less than
three hours. . . . We have heard here that in Czechoslo-

vakia the Communist Party has 300,000-400,000 members, and that it is essential to win over the majority, to create an invincible force and continue enlisting fresh masses of workers. Terracini is already prepared to attack. He says: if there are already 400,000 workers in the party, why should we want more? Delete! (*Laughter.*) He is afraid of the word "masses" and wants to eradicate it. Comrade Terracini has understood very little of the Russian revolution. In Russia, we were a small party, but we had with us in addition the majority of the Soviets of Workers' and Peasants' Deputies throughout the country. (*Cries:* "Quite true!") Do you have anything of the sort? We had with us almost half the army, which then numbered at least ten million men. Do you really have the majority of the army behind you? Show me such a country! If these views of Comrade Terracini are shared by three other delegations, then something is wrong in the International! Then we must say: "Stop! There must be a decisive fight! Otherwise the Communist International is lost." (*Animation.*)

On the basis of my experience I must say, although I am taking up a defensive position (*laughter*), that the aim and the principle of my speech consist in defence of the resolution and theses proposed by our delegation. It would, of course, be pedantic to say that not a letter in them must be altered. I have had to read many resolutions and I am well aware that very good amendments could be introduced in every line of them. But that would be pedantry. If, nevertheless, I declare now that in a political sense not a single letter can be altered, it is because the amendments, as I see them, are of a quite definite political nature and because they lead us along a path that is harmful and dangerous to the Communist International. Therefore, I and all of us and the Russian delegation must insist that not a single letter in the theses is altered. We have not only condemned our Right-wing elements—we have expelled them. But if, like Terracini, people turn the fight against the Rightists into a sport, then we must say: "Stop! Otherwise the danger will become too grave!"

Terracini has defended the theory of an offensive struggle.[134] In this connection the notorious amendments propose a formula two or three pages long. There is no need for us

to read them. We know what they say. Terracini has stated
the issue quite clearly. He has defended the theory of an
offensive, pointing out "dynamic tendencies" and the
"transition from passivity to activity". We in Russia have
already had adequate political experience in the struggle
against the Centrists. As long as fifteen years ago, we were
waging a struggle against our opportunists and Centrists,
and also against the Mensheviks, and we were victorious
not only over the Mensheviks, but also over the semi-
anarchists.

If we had not done this, we would not have been able
to retain power in our hands for three and a half years,
or even for three and a half weeks, and we would not have
been able to convene communist congresses here. "Dynamic
tendencies", "transition from passivity to activity"—these
are all phrases the Left Socialist-Revolutionaries had used
against us. Now they are in prison, defending there the
"aims of communism" and thinking of the "transition from
passivity to activity". (*Laughter.*) The line of reasoning
followed in the proposed amendments is an impossible one,
because they contain no Marxism, no political experience, and
no reasoning. Have we in our theses elaborated a general
theory of the revolutionary offensive? Has Radek or anyone
of us committed such a stupidity? We have spoken of the
theory of an offensive in relation to a quite definite country
and at a quite definite period.

From our struggle against the Mensheviks we can quote
instances showing that even before the first revolution
there were some who doubted whether the revolutionary
party ought to conduct an offensive. If such doubts assailed
any Social-Democrat—as we all called ourselves at that
time—we took up the struggle against him and said that he
was an opportunist, that he did not understand anything
of Marxism and the dialectics of the revolutionary party.
Is it really possible for a party to dispute whether a revolutionary offensive is permissible in general? To find such
examples in this country one would have to go back some
fifteen years. If there are Centrists or disguised Centrists
who dispute the theory of the offensive, they should be
immediately expelled. That question cannot give rise to
disputes. But the fact that even now, after three years of the

Communist International, we are arguing about "dynamic tendencies", about the "transition from passivity to activity" —that is a shame and a disgrace.

We do not have any dispute about this with Comrade Radek, who drafted these theses jointly with us. Perhaps it was not quite correct to begin talking in Germany *about the theory* of the revolutionary offensive when an actual offensive had not been prepared. Nevertheless the March action was a great step forward in spite of the mistakes of its leaders. But this does not matter. Hundreds of thousands of workers fought heroically. However courageously the German Communist Workers' Party fought against the bourgeoisie, we must repeat what Comrade Radek said in a Russian article about Hölz. If anyone, even an anarchist, fights heroically against the bourgeoisie, that is, of course, a great thing; but it is a real step forward if hundreds of thousands fight against the vile provocation of the social-traitors and against the bourgeoisie.

It is very important to be critical of one's mistakes. We began with that. If anyone, after a struggle in which hundreds of thousands have taken part, comes out against this struggle and behaves like Levi, then he should be expelled. And that is what was done. But we must draw a lesson from this. Had we really prepared for an offensive? (*Radek*: "We had not even prepared for defence.") Indeed only newspaper articles talked of an offensive. This theory as applied to the March action in Germany in 1921 was incorrect—we have to admit that—but, in general, the theory of the revolutionary offensive is not at all false.

We were victorious in Russia, and with such ease, because we prepared for our revolution during the imperialist war. That was the first condition. Ten million workers and peasants in Russia were armed, and our slogan was: an immediate peace at all costs. We were victorious because the vast mass of the peasants were revolutionarily disposed against the big landowners. The Socialist-Revolutionaries, the adherents of the Second and the Two-and-a-Half Internationals, were a big peasant party in November 1917. They demanded revolutionary methods but, like true heroes of the Second and the Two-and-a-Half Internationals, lacked the courage to act in a revolutionary way. In August and September 1917 we said: "Theoretically we are fighting the Socialist-Revolutionaries as we did before, but practically we are ready to accept their programme because only we are able to put it into effect." We did just what we said. The peasantry, ill-disposed towards us in November 1917, after our victory, who sent a majority of Socialist-Revolutionaries into the Constituent Assembly, were won over by us, if not in the course of a few days—as I mistakenly expected and predicted—at any rate in the course of a few weeks. The difference was not great. Can you point out any country in Europe where you could win over the majority of the peasantry in the course of a few weeks? Italy perhaps? (*Laughter*.) If it is said that we were victorious in Russia in spite of not having a big party, that only proves that those who say it have not understood the Russian revolution and that they have absolutely no understanding of how to prepare for a revolution.

Our first step was to create a real Communist Party so as to know whom we were talking to and whom we could fully trust. The slogan of the First and Second congresses was "Down with the Centrists!" We cannot hope to master even the ABC of communism, unless all along the line and throughout the world we make short shrift of the Centrists and semi-Centrists, whom in Russia we call Mensheviks. Our first task is to create a genuinely revolutionary party and to break with the Mensheviks. But that is only a preparatory school. We are already convening the Third Congress, and Comrade Terracini keeps saying that the task of the preparatory school consists in hunting out, pursuing and exposing Centrists and semi-Centrists. No, thank you! We have already done this long enough. At the Second Congress we said that the Centrists are our enemies. But, we must go forward really. The second stage, after organising into a party, consists in learning to prepare for revolution. In many countries we have not even learned how to assume the leadership. We were victorious in Russia not only because the undisputed majority of the working class was on our side (during the elections in 1917 the overwhelming majority of the workers were with us against the Mensheviks), but also because half the army, immediately after our seizure of power, and nine-tenths of the peasants,

in the course of some weeks, came over to our side; we were
victorious because we adopted the agrarian programme of
the Socialist-Revolutionaries instead of our own, and put
it into effect. Our victory lay in the fact that we carried out
the Socialist-Revolutionary programme; that is why this
victory was so easy. Is it possible that you in the West
can have such illusions? It is ridiculous! Just compare
the concrete economic conditions, Comrade Terracini and
all of you who have signed the proposed amendments!
In spite of the fact that the majority so rapidly came to
be on our side, the difficulties confronting us after our
victory were very great. Nevertheless we won through
because we kept in mind not only our aims but also our
principles, and did not tolerate in our Party those who
kept silent about principles but talked of aims, "dynamic
tendencies" and the "transition from passivity to activity".
Perhaps we shall be blamed for preferring to keep such
gentlemen in prison. But dictatorship is impossible in any
other way. We must prepare for dictatorship, and this
consists in combating such phrases and such amendments.
(*Laughter.*) Throughout, our theses speak of the masses.
But, comrades, we need to understand what is meant by
masses. The German Communist Workers' Party, the Left-
wing comrades, misuse this word. But Comrade Terracini,
too, and all those who have signed these amendments, do
not know how the word "masses" should be read.

I have been speaking too long as it is; hence I wish to
say only a few words about the concept of "masses". It is
one that changes in accordance with the changes in the
nature of the struggle. At the beginning of the struggle it
took only a few thousand genuinely revolutionary workers
to warrant talk of the masses. If the party succeeds in
drawing into the struggle not only its own members, if it
also succeeds in arousing non-party people, it is well on the
way to winning the masses. During our revolutions there were
instances when several thousand workers represented the
masses. In the history of our movement, and of our struggle
against the Mensheviks, you will find many examples
where several thousand workers in a town were enough to
give a clearly mass character to the movement. You have
a mass when several thousand non-party workers, who

usually live a philistine life and drag out a miserable existence, and who have never heard anything about politics, begin to act in a revolutionary way. If the movement spreads and intensifies, it gradually develops into a real revolution. We saw this in 1905 and 1917 during three revolutions, and you too will have to go through all this. When the revolution has been sufficiently prepared, the concept "masses" becomes different: several thousand workers no longer constitute the masses. This word begins to denote something else. The concept of "masses" undergoes a change so that it implies the majority, and not simply a majority of the workers alone, but the majority of all the exploited. Any other kind of interpretation is impermissible for a revolutionary, and any other sense of the word becomes incomprehensible. It is possible that even a small party, the British or American party, for example, after it has thoroughly studied the course of political development and become acquainted with the life and customs of the nonparty masses, will at a favourable moment evoke a revolutionary movement (Comrade Radek has pointed to the miners strike as a good example[135]). You will have a mass movement if such a party comes forward with its slogans at such a moment and succeeds in getting millions of workers to follow it. I would not altogether deny that a revolution can be started by a very small party and brought to a victorious conclusion. But one must have a knowledge of the methods by which the masses can be won over. For this thoroughgoing preparation of revolution is essential. But here you have comrades coming forward with the assertion that we should immediately give up the demand for "big" masses. They must be challenged. Without thoroughgoing preparation you will not achieve victory in any country. Quite a small party is sufficient to lead the masses. At certain times there is no necessity for big organisations.

But to win, we must have the sympathy of the masses. An absolute majority is not always essential; but what is essential to win and retain power is not only the majority of the working class—I use the term "working class" in its West-European sense, i.e., in the sense of the industrial proletariat—but also the majority of the working and exploited rural population. Have you thought about this?

Do we find in Terracini's speech even a hint at this thought? He speaks only of "dynamic tendency" and the "transition from passivity to activity". Does he devote even a single word to the food question? And yet the workers demand their victuals, although they can put up with a great deal and go hungry, as we have seen to a certain extent in Russia. We must, therefore, win over to our side not only the majority of the working class, but also the majority of the working and exploited rural population. Have you prepared for this? Almost nowhere.

And so, I repeat: I must unreservedly defend our theses and I feel I am bound to do it. We not only condemned the Centrists but expelled them from the Party. Now we must deal with another aspect, which we also consider dangerous. We must tell the comrades the truth in the most polite form (and in our theses it is told in a kind and considerate way) so that no one feels insulted: we are confronted now by other, more important questions than that of attacks on the Centrists. We have had enough of this question. It has already become somewhat boring. Instead, the comrades ought to learn to wage a real revolutionary struggle. The German workers have already begun this. Hundreds of thousands of proletarians in that country have been fighting heroically. Anyone who opposes this struggle should be immediately expelled. But after that we must not engage in empty word-spinning but must immediately begin to learn, on the basis of the mistakes made, how to organise the struggle better. We must not conceal our mistakes from the enemy. Anyone who is afraid of this is no revolutionary. On the contrary, if we openly declare to the workers: "Yes, we have made mistakes", it will mean that they will not be repeated and we shall be able better to choose the moment. And if during the struggle itself the majority of the working people prove to be on our side—not only the majority of the workers, but the majority of all the exploited and oppressed—then we shall really be victorious. (*Prolonged, stormy applause.*)

4

REPORT ON THE TACTICS OF THE R.C.P.
JULY 5

Comrades, strictly speaking I was unable to prepare
properly for this report. All that I was able to prepare for
you in the way of systematic material was a translation
of my pamphlet on the tax in kind and the theses on the
tactics of the Russian Communist Party. To this I merely
want to add a few explanations and remarks.

I think that to explain our Party's tactics we must first
of all examine the *international situation*. We have already
had a detailed discussion of the economic position of capitalism internationally, and the Congress has adopted definite
resolutions on this subject.[136] I deal with this subject
in my theses very briefly, and only from the political standpoint. I leave aside the economic basis, but I think that in
discussing the international position of our Republic we
must, politically, take into account the fact that a certain
equilibrium has now undoubtedly set in between the forces
that have been waging an open, armed struggle against
each other for the supremacy of this or that leading class.
It is an equilibrium between bourgeois society, the international bourgeoisie as a whole, and Soviet Russia. It is, of
course, an equilibrium only in a limited sense. It is only
in respect to this military struggle, I say, that a certain
equilibrium has been brought about in the international
situation. It must be emphasised, of course, that this is
only a relative equilibrium, and a very unstable one. Much
inflammable material has accumulated in capitalist countries, as well as in those countries which up to now have
been regarded merely as the objects and not as the subjects
of history, i.e., the colonies and semi-colonies. It is quite
possible, therefore, that insurrections, great battles and

revolutions may break out there sooner or later, and very suddenly too. During the past few years we have witnessed the direct struggle waged by the international bourgeoisie against the first proletarian republic. This struggle has been at the centre of the world political situation, and it is there that a change has taken place. Inasmuch as the attempt of the international bourgeoisie to strangle our Republic has failed, an equilibrium has set in, and a very unstable one it is, of course.

We know perfectly well, of course, that the international bourgeoisie is at present much stronger than our Republic, and that it is only the peculiar combination of circumstances that is preventing it from continuing the war against us. For several weeks now, we have witnessed fresh attempts in the Far East to renew the invasion,[137] and there is not the slightest doubt that similar attempts will continue. Our Party has no doubts whatever on that score. The important thing for us is to establish that an unstable equilibrium does exist, and that we must take advantage of this respite, taking into consideration the characteristic features of the present situation, adapting our tactics to the specific features of this situation, and never forgetting that the necessity for armed struggle may arise again quite suddenly. Our task is still to organise and build up the Red Army. In connection with the food problem, too, we must continue to think first of all of our Red Army. We can adopt no other line in the present international situation, when we must still be prepared for fresh attacks and fresh attempts at invasion on the part of the international bourgeoisie. In regard to our practical policy, however, the fact that a certain equilibrium has been reached in the international situation has some significance, but only in the sense that we must admit that, although the revolutionary movement has made progress, the development of the international revolution this year has not proceeded along as straight a line as we had expected.

When we started the international revolution, we did so not because we were convinced that we could forestall its development, but because a number of circumstances compelled us to start it. We thought: either the international revolution comes to our assistance, and in that case our victory will be fully assured, or we shall do our modest revolutionary work in the conviction that even in the event of defeat we shall have served the cause of the revolution and that our experience will benefit other revolutions. It was clear to us that without the support of the international world revolution the victory of the proletarian revolution was impossible. Before the revolution, and even after it, we thought: either revolution breaks out in the other countries, in the capitalistically more developed countries, immediately, or at least very quickly, or we must perish. In spite of this conviction, we did all we possibly could to preserve the Soviet system under all circumstances, come what may, because we knew that we were not only working for ourselves, but also for the international revolution. We knew this, we repeatedly expressed this conviction before the October Revolution, immediately after it, and at the time we signed the Brest-Litovsk Peace Treaty. And, generally speaking, this was correct.

Actually, however, events did not proceed along as straight a line as we had expected. In the other big, capitalistically more developed countries the revolution has not broken out to this day. True, we can say with satisfaction that the revolution is developing all over the world, and it is only thanks to this that the international bourgeoisie is unable to strangle us, in spite of the fact that, militarily and economically, it is a hundred times stronger than we are. (*Applause.*)

In Paragraph 2 of the theses I examine the manner in which this situation arose, and the conclusions that must be drawn from it. Let me add that my final conclusion is the following: the development of the international revolution, which we predicted, is proceeding, but not along as straight a line as we had expected. It becomes clear at the first glance that after the conclusion of peace, bad as it was, it proved impossible to call forth revolution in other capitalist countries, although we know that the signs of revolution were very considerable and numerous, in fact, much more considerable and numerous than we thought at the time. Pamphlets are now beginning to appear which tell us that during the past few years and months these revolutionary symptoms in Europe have been much more serious than we had suspected. What, in that case, must we do now? We must now thoroughly prepare for revolution and make a deep study of its concrete development in the advanced capitalist countries. This is the first lesson we must draw from the international situation. As for our Russian Republic, we must take advantage of this brief respite in order to adapt our tactics to this zigzag line of history. This equilibrium is very important politically, because we clearly see that in many West-European countries, where the broad mass of the working class, and possibly the overwhelming majority of the population, are organised, the main bulwark of the bourgeoisie consists of the hostile working-class organisations affiliated to the Second and the Two-and-a-Half Internationals. I speak of this in Paragraph 2 of the theses, and I think that in this connection I need deal with only two points, which were discussed during the debate on the question of tactics. First, winning over the majority of the proletariat. The more organised the proletariat is in a capitalistically developed country, the greater thoroughness does history demand of us in preparing for revolution, and the more thoroughly must we win over the majority of the working class. Second, the main bulwark of capitalism in the industrially developed capitalist countries is the part of the working class that is organised in the Second and the Two-and-a-Half Internationals. But for the support of this section of the workers, these counter-revolutionary elements within the working class, the international bourgeoisie would be altogether unable to retain its position. (*Applause.*)

Here I would also like to emphasise the significance of *the movement in the colonies*. In this respect we see in all the old parties, in all the bourgeois and petty-bourgeois labour parties affiliated to the Second and the Two-and-a-Half Internationals, survivals of the old sentimental views: they insist on their profound sympathy for oppressed colonial and semi-colonial peoples. The movement in the colonial countries is still regarded as an insignificant national and totally peaceful movement. But this is not so. It has undergone great change since the beginning of the twentieth century: millions and hundreds of millions, in fact the overwhelming majority of the population of the globe, are

now coming forward as independent, active and revolutionary factors. It is perfectly clear that in the impending
decisive battles in the world revolution, the movement of
the majority of the population of the globe, initially directed towards national liberation, will turn against capitalism
and imperialism and will, perhaps, play a much more
revolutionary part than we expect. It is important to emphasise the fact that, for the first time in our International,
we have taken up the question of preparing for this struggle.
Of course, there are many more difficulties in this enormous
sphere than in any other, but at all events the movement
is advancing. And in spite of the fact that the masses
of toilers—the peasants in the colonial countries—are still
backward, they will play a very important revolutionary
part in the coming phases of the world revolution.
(*Animated approval.*)

As regards the internal political position of our Republic
I must start with a close examination of class relationships.
During the past few months changes have taken place in
this sphere, and we have witnessed the formation of new
organisations of the exploiting class directed against us.
The aim of socialism is to abolish classes. In the front ranks
of the exploiting class we find the big landowners and the
industrial capitalists. In regard to them, the work of
destruction is fairly easy; it can be completed within a few
months, and sometimes even a few weeks or days. We in
Russia have expropriated our exploiters, the big landowners
as well as the capitalists. They had no organisations of their
own during the war and operated merely as the appendages
of the military forces of the international bourgeoisie.
Now, after we have repulsed the attacks of the international
counter-revolution, organisations of the Russian bourgeoisie
and of all the Russian counter-revolutionary parties have
been formed abroad. The number of Russian émigrés scattered
in all foreign countries may be estimated at one and a
half to two millions. In nearly every country they publish
daily newspapers, and all the parties, landowner and petty-
bourgeois, not excluding the Socialist-Revolutionaries and
Mensheviks, have numerous ties with foreign bourgeois
elements, that is to say, they obtain enough money to run
their own press. We find the collaboration abroad of

absolutely all the political parties that formerly existed in Russia, and we see how the "free" Russian press abroad, from the Socialist-Revolutionary and Menshevik press to the most reactionary monarchist press, is championing the great landed interests. This, to a certain extent, facilitates our task, because we can more easily observe the forces of the enemy, his state of organisation, and the political trends in his camp. On the other hand, of course, it hinders our work, because these Russian counter-revolutionary émigrés use every means at their disposal to prepare for a fight against us. This fight again shows that, taken as a whole, the class instinct and class-consciousness of the ruling classes are still superior to those of the oppressed classes, notwithstanding the fact that the Russian revolution has done more than any previous revolution in this respect. In Russia, there is hardly a village in which the people, the oppressed, have not been roused. Nevertheless, if we take a cool look at the state of organisation and political clarity of views of the Russian counter-revolutionary émigrés, we shall find that the class-consciousness of the bourgeoisie is still superior to that of the exploited and the oppressed. These people make overy possible attempt and skilfully take advantage of every opportunity to attack Soviet Russia in one way or another, and to dismember it. It would be very instructive—and I think the foreign comrades will do that—systematically to watch the most important aspirations, the most important tactical moves, and the most important trends of this Russian counter-revolution. It operates chiefly abroad, and it will not be very difficult for the foreign comrades to watch it. In some respects, we ought to learn from this enemy. These counter-revolutionary émigrés are very well informed, they are excellently organised and are good strategists. And I think that a systematic comparison and study of the manner in which they are organised and take advantage of every opportunity may have a powerful propaganda effect upon the working class. This is not general theory, it is practical politics; here we can see what the enemy has learned. During the past few years, the Russian bourgeoisie has suffered a terrible defeat. There is an old saying that a beaten army learns a great deal. The beaten reactionary army has learned a great deal, and has learned it thoroughly. It is learning with great avidity, and has really made much headway. When we took power at one swoop, the Russian bourgeoisie was unorganised and politically undeveloped. Now, I think, its development is on a par with modern, West-European development. We must take this into account, we must improve our own organisation and methods, and we shall do our utmost to achieve this. It was relatively easy for us, and I think that it will be equally easy for other revolutions, to cope with these two exploiting classes.

But, in addition to this class of exploiters, there is in nearly all capitalist countries, with the exception, perhaps, of Britain, a class of small producers and small farmers. The main problem of the revolution now is how to fight these two classes. In order to be rid of them, we must adopt methods other than those employed against the big landowners and capitalists. We could simply expropriate and expel both of these classes, and that is what we did. But we cannot do the same thing with the remaining capitalist classes, the small producers and the petty bourgeoisie, which are found in all countries. In most capitalist countries, these classes constitute a very considerable minority, approximately from thirty to forty-five per cent of the population. Add to them the petty-bourgeois elements of the working class, and you get even more than fifty per cent. These cannot be expropriated or expelled; other methods of struggle must be adopted in their case. From the international standpoint, if we regard the international revolution as one process, the significance of the period into which we are now entering in Russia is, in essence, that we must now find a practical solution for the problem of the relations the proletariat should establish with this last capitalist class in Russia. All Marxists have a correct and ready solution for this problem in theory. But theory and practice are two different things, and the practical solution of this problem is by no means the same as the theoretical solution. We know definitely that we have made serious mistakes. From the international standpoint, it is a sign of great progress that we are now trying to determine the attitude the proletariat in power should adopt towards the last capitalist class—the rock-bottom of capitalism—small private property, the small producer. This problem now confronts us in a practical way. I think we shall solve it. At all events, the experiment we are making will be useful for future proletarian revolutions, and they will be able to make better technical preparations for solving it.

In my theses I tried to analyse *the problem of the relations between the proletariat and the peasantry.* For the first time in history there is a state with only two classes, the proletariat and the peasantry. The latter constitutes the overwhelming majority of the population. It is, of course, very backward. How do the relations between the peasantry and the proletariat, which holds political power, find practical expression in the development of the revolution? The first form is alliance, close alliance. This is a very difficult task, but at any rate it is economically and politically feasible.

How did we approach this problem practically? We concluded an alliance with the peasantry. We interpret this alliance in the following way: the proletariat emancipates the peasantry from the exploitation of the bourgeoisie, from its leadership and influence, and wins it over to its own side in order jointly to defeat the exploiters.

The Menshevik argument runs like this: the peasantry constitutes a majority; we are pure democrats, therefore, the majority should decide. But as the peasantry cannot operate on its own, this, in practice, means nothing more nor less than the restoration of capitalism. The slogan is the same: Alliance with the peasantry. When we say that, we mean strengthening and consolidating the proletariat. We have tried to give effect to this alliance between the proletariat and the peasantry, and the first stage was a military alliance. The three years of the Civil War created enormous difficulties, but in certain respects they facilitated our task. This may sound odd, but it is true. The war was not something new for the peasants; a war against the exploiters, against the big landowners, was something they quite understood. The overwhelming majority of the peasants were on our side. In spite of the enormous distances, and the fact that the overwhelming majority of our peasants are unable to read or write, they assimilated our propaganda very easily. This proves that the broad masses—and this applies also to the most advanced countries—learn faster from their own practical experience than from books. In Russia, moreover, learning from practical experience was facilitated for the peasantry by the fact that the country is so exceptionally large that in the same period different parts of it were passing through different stages of development.

In Siberia and in the Ukraine the counter-revolution was able to gain a temporary victory because there the bourgeoisie had the peasantry on its side, because the peasants were against us. The peasants frequently said, "We are Bolsheviks, but not Communists. We are for the Bolsheviks because they drove out the landowners; but we are not for the Communists because they are opposed to individual farming." And for a time, the counter-revolution managed to win out in Siberia and in the Ukraine because the bourgeoisie made headway in the struggle for influence over the peasantry. But it took only a very short time to open the peasants' eyes. They quickly acquired practical experience and soon said, "Yes, the Bolsheviks are rather unpleasant people, we don't like them, but still they are better than the whiteguards and the Constituent Assembly." "Constituent Assembly" is a term of abuse not only among the educated Communists, but also among the peasants. They know from practical experience that the Constituent Assembly and the whiteguards stand for the same thing, that the former is inevitably followed by the latter. The Mensheviks also resort to a military alliance with the peasantry, but they fail to understand that a military alliance alone is inadequate. There can be no military alliance without an economic alliance. It takes more than air to keep a man alive; our alliance with the peasantry could not possibly have lasted any length of time without the economic foundation, which was the basis of our victory in the war against our bourgeoisie. After all our bourgeoisie has united with the whole of the international bourgeoisie.

The basis of our economic alliance with the peasantry was, of course, very simple, and even crude. The peasant obtained from us all the land and support against the big landowners. In return for this, we were to obtain food. This alliance was something entirely new and did not rest on the ordinary relations between commodity producers and consumers. Our peasants had a much better understanding of this than the heroes of the Second and the Two-and-a-Half Internationals. They said to themselves, "These Bolsheviks are stern leaders, but after all they are our own people." Be that as it may, we created in this way the foundations of a new economic alliance. The peasants gave their produce to the Red Army and received from the latter assistance in protecting their possessions. This is always forgotten by the heroes of the Second International, who, like Otto Bauer, totally fail to understand the actual situation. We confess that the initial form of this alliance was very primitive and that we made very many mistakes. But we were obliged to act as quickly as possible, we had to organise supplies for the army at all costs. During the Civil War we were cut off from all the grain districts of Russia. We were in a terrible position, and it looks like a miracle that the Russian people and the working class were able to endure such suffering, want, and privation, sustained by nothing more than a deep urge for victory. (*Animated approval and applause.*)

When the Civil War came to an end, however, we faced a different problem. If the country had not been so laid waste after seven years of incessant war, it would, perhaps, have been possible to find an easier transition to the new form of alliance between the proletariat and the peasantry. But bad as conditions in the country were, they were still further aggravated by the crop failure, the fodder shortage, etc. In consequence, the sufferings of the peasants became unbearable. We had to show the broad masses of the peasants immediately that we were prepared to change our policy, without in any way deviating from our revolutionary path, so that they could say, "The Bolsheviks want to improve our intolerable condition immediately, and at all costs."

And so, *our economic policy was changed*; the tax in kind superseded the requisitions. This was not invented at one stroke. You will find a number of proposals in the Bolshevik press over a period of months, but no plan that really promised success. But this is not important. The important

thing is that we changed our economic policy, yielding to
exclusively practical considerations, and impelled by
necessity. A bad harvest, fodder shortage and lack of fuel—all,
of course, have a decisive influence on the economy as a
whole, including the peasant economy. If the peasantry
goes on strike, we get no firewood; and if we get no firewood,
the factories will have to idle. Thus, in the spring of 1921,
the economic crisis resulting from the terrible crop failure
and the fodder shortage assumed gigantic proportions. All
that was the aftermath of the three years of civil war.
We had to show the peasantry that we could and would
quickly change our policy in order immediately to alleviate
their distress. We have always said—and it was also said
at the Second Congress—that revolution demands sacrifices. Some comrades in their propaganda argue in the following way: we are prepared to stage a revolution, but it must
not be too severe. Unless I am mistaken, this thesis was
put forward by Comrade Smeral in his speech at the Congress
of the Communist Party of Czechoslovakia. I read about it
in the report published in the Reichenberg *Vorwärts*.[138]
There is evidently a Leftist wing there; hence this source
cannot be regarded as being quite impartial. At all events,
I must say that if Smeral did say that, he was wrong. Some
comrades who spoke after Smeral at this Congress said,
"Yes, we shall go along with Smeral because in this way
we shall avoid civil war." (*Laughter.*) If these reports are
true, I must say that such agitation is neither communistic
nor revolutionary. Naturally, every revolution entails enormous sacrifice on the part of the class making it. Revolution
differs from ordinary struggle in that ten and even a hundred
times more people take part in it. Hence every revolution
entails sacrifices not only for individuals, but for a whole
class. The dictatorship of the proletariat in Russia has
entailed for the ruling class—the proletariat—sacrifices,
want and privation unprecedented in history, and the case
will, in all probability, be the same in every other country.

The question arises: How are we to distribute this
burden of privation? We are the state power. We are able to
distribute the burden of privation to a certain extent, and
to impose it upon several classes, thereby relatively allevi-
ating the condition of certain strata of the population.

But what is to be our principle? Is it to be that of fairness, or of majority? No. We must act in a practical manner. We must distribute the burdens in such a way as to preserve the power of the proletariat. This is our only principle. In the beginning of the revolution the working class was compelled to suffer incredible want. Let me state that from year to year our food policy has been achieving increasing success. And the situation as a whole has undoubtedly improved. But the peasantry in Russia has certainly gained more from the revolution than the working class. There is no doubt about that at all. From the standpoint of theory, this shows, of course, that our revolution was to some degree a bourgeois revolution. When Kautsky used this as an argument against us, we laughed. Naturally, a revolution which does not expropriate the big landed estates, expel the big landowners or divide the land is only a bourgeois revolution and not a socialist one. But we were the only party to carry the bourgeois revolution to its conclusion and to facilitate the struggle for the socialist revolution. The Soviet power and the Soviet system are institutions of the socialist state. We have already established these institutions, but we have not yet solved the problem of economic relations between the peasantry and the proletariat. Much remains to be done, and the outcome of this struggle depends upon whether we solve this problem or not. Thus, the distribution of the burden of privation is one of the most difficult practical problems. On the whole, the condition of the peasants has improved, but dire suffering has fallen to the lot of the working class, precisely because it is exercising its dictatorship.

I have already said that in the spring of 1921 the most appalling want caused by the fodder shortage and the crop failure prevailed among the peasantry, which constitutes the majority of our population. We cannot possibly exist unless we have good relations with the peasant masses. Hence, our task was to render them immediate assistance. The condition of the working class is extremely hard. It is suffering horribly. Those who have more political understanding, however, realise that in the interest of the dictatorship of the working class we must make tremendous efforts to help the peasants at any price. The vanguard of the working class has realised this, but in that vanguard there are still people who cannot understand it, and who are too weary to understand it. They regarded it as a mistake and began to use the word "opportunism". They said, "The Bolsheviks are helping the peasants. The peasants, who are exploiting us, are getting everything they please, while the workers are starving." But is that opportunism? We are helping the peasants because without an alliance with them the political power of the proletariat is impossible, its preservation is inconceivable. It was this consideration of expediency and not that of fair distribution that was decisive for us. We are assisting the peasants because it is absolutely necessary to do so in order that we may retain political power. The supreme principle of the dictatorship is the maintenance of the alliance between the proletariat and the peasantry in order that the proletariat may retain its leading role and its political power.

The only means we found for this was the adoption of the tax in kind, which was the inevitable consequence of the struggle. This year, we shall introduce this tax for the first time. This principle has not yet been tried in practice. From the military alliance we must pass to an economic alliance, and, theoretically, the only basis for the latter is the introduction of the tax in kind. It provides the only theoretical possibility for laying a really solid economic foundation for socialist society. The socialised factory gives the peasant its manufactures and in return the peasant gives his grain. This is the only possible form of existence of socialist society, the only form of socialist development in a country in which the small peasants constitute the majority, or at all events a very considerable minority. The peasants will give one part of their produce in the form of tax and another either in exchange for the manufactures of socialist factories, or through the exchange of commodities.

This brings us to the most difficult problem. It goes without saying that the tax in kind means freedom to trade. After having paid the tax in kind, the peasant will have the right freely to exchange the remainder of his grain. This freedom of exchange implies freedom for capitalism. We say this openly and emphasise it. We do not conceal it in the least. Things would go very hard with us if we attempted to conceal it. Freedom to trade means freedom for capitalism, but it also means a new form of capitalism. It means that, to a certain extent, we are re-creating capitalism. We are doing this quite openly. It is state capitalism. But state capitalism in a society where power belongs to capital, and state capitalism in a proletarian state, are two different concepts. In a capitalist state, state capitalism means that it is recognised by the state and controlled by it for the benefit of the bourgeoisie, and to the detriment of the proletariat. In the proletarian state, the same thing is done for the benefit of the working class, for the purpose of withstanding the as yet strong bourgeoisie, and of fighting it. It goes without saying that we must grant concessions to the foreign bourgeoisie, to foreign capital. Without the slightest denationalisation, we shall lease mines, forests and oilfields to foreign capitalists, and receive in exchange manufactured goods, machinery, etc., and thus restore our own industry.

Of course, we did not all agree on the question of state capitalism at once. But we are very pleased to note in this connection that our peasantry has been developing, that it has fully realised the historical significance of the struggle we are waging at the present time. Ordinary peasants from the most remote districts have come to us and said: "What! We have expelled our capitalists, the capitalists who speak Russian, and now foreign capitalists are coming!" Does not this show that our peasants have developed? There is no need to explain to a worker who is versed in economics why this is necessary. We have been so ruined by seven years of war that it will take many years to restore our industry. We must pay for our backwardness and weakness, and for the lessons we are now learning and must learn. Those who want to learn must pay for the tuition. We must explain this to one and all, and if we prove it in practice, the vast masses of the peasants and workers will agree with us, because in this way their condition will be immediately improved, and because it will ensure the possibility of restoring our industry. What compels us to do this? We are not alone in the world. We exist in a system of capitalist states.[139] . . . On one side, there are the colonial countries, but they cannot help us yet. On the other side, there are the capitalist countries, but they are our enemies. The result is a certain equilibrium, a very poor one, it is true. Nevertheless, we must reckon with the fact. We must not shut our eyes to it if we want to exist. Either we score an immediate victory over the whole bourgeoisie, or we pay the tribute.

We admit quite openly, and do not conceal the fact, that concessions in the system of state capitalism mean paying tribute to capitalism. But we gain time, and gaining time means gaining everything, particularly in the period of equilibrium, when our foreign comrades are preparing thoroughly for their revolution. The more thorough their preparations, the more certain will the victory be. Meanwhile, however, we shall have to pay the tribute.

A few words about our food policy. Undoubtedly, it was a bad and primitive policy. But we can also point to some achievements. In this connection I must once again emphasise that the only possible economic foundation of socialism is large-scale machine industry. Whoever forgets this is no Communist. We must analyse this problem concretely. We cannot present problems in the way the theoreticians of the old school of socialism do. We must present them in a practical manner. What is modern large-scale industry? It is the electrification of the whole of Russia. Sweden, Germany and America have almost achieved this, although they are still bourgeois. A Swedish comrade told me that in Sweden a large part of industry and thirty per cent of agriculture are electrified. In Germany and America, which are even more developed capitalistically, we see the same thing on a larger scale. Large-scale machine industry is nothing more nor less than the electrification of the whole country. We have already appointed a special commission consisting of the country's best economists and engineers. It is true that nearly all of them are hostile to the Soviet power. All these specialists will come over to communism, but not our way, not by way of twenty years of underground work, during which we unceasingly studied and repeated over and over again the ABC of communism.

Nearly all the Soviet government bodies were in favour of inviting the specialists. The expert engineers will come to us when we give them practical proof that this will increase the country's productive forces. It is not enough to prove it to them in theory; we must prove it to them in practice, and we shall win these people over to our side if we present the problem differently, not from the standpoint of the theoretical propaganda of communism. We say: large-scale industry is the only means of saving the peasantry from want and starvation. Everyone agrees with this. But how can it be done? The restoration of industry on the old basis will entail too much labour and time. We must give industry a more modern form, i.e., we must adopt electrification. This will take much less time. We have already drawn up the plans for electrification. More than two hundred specialists—almost to a man opposed to the Soviet power—worked on it with keen interest, although they are not Communists. From the standpoint of technical science, however, they had to admit that this was the only correct way. Of course, we have a long way to go before the plan is achieved. The cautious specialists say that the first series of works will take at least ten years. Professor Ballod has estimated that it would take three to four years to electrify Germany. But for us even ten years is not enough. In my theses I quote actual figures to show you how little we have been able to do in this sphere up to now. The figures I quote are so modest that it immediately becomes clear that they are more of propaganda than scientific value. But we must begin with propaganda. The Russian peasants who fought in the world war and lived in Germany for several years learned how modern farming should be carried on in order to conquer famine. We must carry on extensive propaganda in this direction. Taken by themselves, these plans are not yet of great practical value, but their propaganda value is very great.

The peasants realise that something new must be created. They realise that this cannot be done by everybody working separately, but by the state working as a whole. The peasants who were prisoners of war in Germany found out what real cultural life is based on. Twelve thousand kilowatts is a very modest beginning. This may sound funny to the foreigner who is familiar with electrification in America, Germany or Sweden. But he laughs best who laughs last. It is, indeed, a modest beginning. But the peasants are beginning to understand that new work must be carried out on a grand scale, and that this work has already begun. Enormous difficulties will have to be overcome. We shall try to establish relations with the capitalist countries. We must not regret having to give the capitalists several hundred million kilogrammes of oil on condition that they help us to electrify our country.

And now, in conclusion, a few words about *"pure democracy"*. I will read you a passage from Engels's letter to Bebel of December 11, 1884. He wrote:

"Pure democracy... when the moment of revolution comes, acquires a temporary importance as the extreme bourgeois party, as which it already played itself off in Frankfort, and as the final sheet-anchor of the whole bourgeois and even feudal economy. . . . Thus between March and September 1848 the whole feudal-bureaucratic mass strengthened the liberals in order to hold down the revolutionary masses. . . . In any case our sole adversary on the day of the crisis and on the day after the crisis will be the *whole of the reaction which will group around pure democracy*, and this, I think, should not be lost sight of."

Our approach must differ from that of the theoreticians. The whole reactionary mass, not only bourgeois, but also feudal, groups itself around "pure democracy". The German comrades know better than anyone else what "pure democracy" means, for Kautsky and the other leaders of the Second and the Two-and-a-Half Internationals are defending this "pure democracy" from the wicked Bolsheviks. If we judge the Russian Socialist-Revolutionaries and Mensheviks, not by what they say, but by what they do, we shall find that they are nothing but representatives of petty-bourgeois "pure democracy". In the course of our revolution they have given us a classic example of what "pure democracy" means, and again during the recent crisis, in the days of the Kronstadt mutiny. There was serious unrest among the peasantry, and discontent was also rife among the workers. They were weary and exhausted. After all, there is a limit to human endurance. They had starved for three years, but you cannot go on starving for four or five years. Naturally, hunger has a tremendous influence on political activity. How did the Socialist-Revolutionaries and Mensheviks behave? They wavered all the time, thereby strengthening the bourgeoisie. The organisation of all the Russian parties abroad has revealed the present state of affairs. The shrewdest of the leaders of the Russian big bourgeoisie said to themselves: "We cannot achieve victory in Russia immediately. Hence our slogan must be: 'Soviets without the Bolsheviks.'" Milyukov, the leader of the Constitutional-Democrats, defended the Soviet power from the attacks of the Socialist-Revolutionaries. This sounds very strange; but such are the practical dialectics which we, in our revolution, have been studying in a peculiar way, from the practical experience of our struggle and of the struggle of our enemies. The Constitutional-Democrats defend "Soviets without the Bolsheviks" because they understand the position very well and hope that a section of the people will rise to the bait. That is what the clever Constitutional-Democrats say. Not all the Constitutional-Democrats are clever, of course, but some of them are, and these have learned something from the French Revolution. The present slogan is to fight the Bolsheviks, whatever the price, come what may. The whole of the bourgeoisie is now helping the Mensheviks and Socialist-Revolutionaries, who are now the vanguard of all reaction. In the spring we had a taste of the fruits of this counter-revolutionary co-operation.[140]

That is why we must continue our relentless struggle against these elements. Dictatorship is a state of intense war. That is just the state we are in. There is no military invasion at present; but we are isolated. On the other hand, however, we are not entirely isolated, since the whole international bourgeoisie is incapable of waging open war against us just now, because the whole working class, even though the majority is not yet communist, is sufficiently class-conscious to prevent intervention. The bourgeoisie is compelled to reckon with the temper of the masses even though they have not yet entirely sided with communism. That is why the bourgeoisie cannot now start an offensive against us, although one is never ruled out. Until the final issue is decided, this awful state of war will continue. And we say: "A la guerre comme à la guerre; we do not promise any freedom, or any democracy." We tell the peasants quite openly that they must choose between the rule of the bourgeoisie, and the rule of the Bolsheviks—in which case we shall make every possible concession within the limits of retaining power, and later we shall lead them to socialism. Everything else is deception and pure demagogy. Ruthless war must be declared against this deception and demagogy. Our point of view is: for the time being—big concessions and the greatest caution, precisely because a certain equilibrium has set in, precisely because we are weaker than our combined enemies, and because our economic basis is too weak and we need a stronger one.

That, comrades, is what I wanted to tell you about our tactics, the tactics of the Russian Communist Party. (*Prolonged applause.*)

IDEAS ABOUT A STATE ECONOMIC "PLAN"

The principal mistake we have all been making up to now is too much optimism; as a result, we succumbed to bureaucratic utopias. Only a very small part of our plans has been realised. Life, everyone, in fact, has laughed at our plans.

This must be radically altered.

Anticipate the worst. We already have some experience; it is slight, but practical.

Food supplies? Frumkin says: The ideal is 150 million poods from the tax + 50 million poods by means of exchange +40 million poods from the Ukraine = 240 million poods.

We must base our calculations on a *total of 200* million poods for the year.

What are we to do with this paltry, starvation figure? 200 : 12=16 2/3.

(α) Take a minimum for the army, i.e., calculate the rations for a minimum army.

(β) Include in the plan the economic work of the army on a modest, extremely modest scale.

1 *subbotnik**, 60 per cent of the army (participating).

1 out of 3 subbotniks 50 per cent participants (50 per cent of the army), etc.

(γ) For office employees—drastic reduction.

(δ) The workers.

Immediately draw up a list of the best *enterprises* (stress *enterprises*) by industries.

Close down $\frac{1}{2}$ to $\frac{4}{5}$ of those now running.

The rest to run in two shifts. Only those which have enough *fuel* and *bread*, even if the minimum quantity of grain is collected (200 million poods) and fuel (?) *for the whole year*.

Do this in *rough outline*, as a first approximation, immediately, in a month, no later.

Fuel, we have.

A People's Commissariat for Communications, we have.

---

* Voluntary work on week-ends without pay.—*Tr.*

There is no need to be exact about food; *take 200 million poods.*

Industry *according to branches* and *gubernias* (don't put it off until we get the figures for the "whole"), get this done with the utmost speed,

and, *the main thing,*

put 70 per cent of the members of the State Planning Commission to work *14 hours a day* (let science sweat a bit; we have given them good rations, now we must make them work).

Each one to be given the task of keeping *"general supervision"* (I think that is what it is called in the regulations of the State Planning Commission) over *definite* enterprises.

Take *700* as the number of large establishments, enterprises, depots (railway), state farms, etc., etc., that we must (and can, even at the worst: 200 million poods of grain in the course of the year) start and keep running from October 1, 1921 to October 1, 1922.

$700 : 35$ members of the State Planning Commission $= 20$.

Say 30 (not all the members of the State Planning Commission will be continuously engaged on current work).

Take the trouble to supervise *these 30 unremittingly.* You are responsible for this.

Over and above these, keep an eye on another 30-70, less important; don't keep them under constant observation, but *make inquiries* in passing, from time to time.

To supervise unremittingly means *answering* with your head for the rational consumption of fuel and grain, for the maximum stocking of the one and the other, for the maximum deliveries, for economising fuel (in industry, on the railways, etc.), for economising food (feed *only* good workers), for increasing productivity of labour, *etc.*

All the rest—lease or give to anybody you please, or close, or "abandon", forget about, until *a sound improvement* is achieved, which will enable us to operate confidently, not with 200 million poods of grain $+X$ million poods of fuel, but with *300* million poods of grain $+150$ per cent of X fuel.

These are my ideas about the State Planning Commission. *Think it over.* Let's discuss it.

July 4

Lenin

First published in 1924

Published according
to the manuscript

GREETINGS TO THE DELEGATE CONGRESS OF TSENTROSOYUZ[141]

I send my greetings to the assembly of Tsentrosoyuz delegates on behalf of the Council of People's Commissars and of the Central Committee of the R.C.P. I deeply regret that I cannot be present to express my views on the most complicated problems confronting the co-operative societies.

I have no doubt that the pooling of experience of the work already done will help you to solve these problems in harmony with the plan for the country's overall economic development. Success in the practical work that now lies ahead will depend largely on the establishment, through the medium of commodity exchange, of proper relations between urban industry and agriculture. It will depend on the ability of the co-operative societies, by steady and persistent effort, to clear the way for the development of commodity exchange and to take the lead in this field. It will depend on their ability to collect the scattered stocks of commodities and to secure the production of new ones. In the long run, the practical solution of these problems is the best way to achieve our aims, namely, to restore agriculture and, on that basis, to strengthen and develop large-scale industry.

These problems have been complicated very much by the crop failure, which has become apparent in a number of gubernias. In your work, you will have to devote special attention to this fresh disaster and keep its consequences in mind when tackling all current questions.

I am sure that, short as the experience of work under the new conditions may be, Soviet co-operative societies will succeed in closely linking up their work with the general task of overcoming the chaos in the country's economy, and will display the utmost energy in this fight.

Written on July 16, 1921

Published in *Pravda* No. 156,
        July 19, 1921

Published according
to the *Pravda* text

MESSAGE OF GREETINGS
TO THE FIRST INTERNATIONAL CONGRESS
OF REVOLUTIONARY TRADE
AND INDUSTRIAL UNIONS[142]

July 18

Comrade Rykov,
Please be so kind as to convey to the delegates of the International Congress of Trade Unions the following:
I thank them from the bottom of my heart for the invitation to the Congress sent through you. I deeply regret that I am unable to accept it because of ill-health, for on doctor's orders I have had to leave Moscow for a month's holiday.

Please convey to the delegates my greetings and heartfelt wishes for the success of the Congress. It is hard to find words to express the full importance of the International Congress of Trade Unions. The winning of trade unionists to the ideas of communism is making irresistible headway everywhere, in all countries, throughout the world. The process is sporadic, overcoming a thousand obstacles, but it is making irresistible progress. The International Congress of Trade Unions will quicken this movement. Communism will triumph in the trade unions. No power on earth can avert the collapse of capitalism and the victory of the working class over the bourgeoisie.

Warm greetings and confidence in the inevitable victory of communism.

N. Lenin

Published in 1921

Published according
to the manuscript

APPEAL
TO THE INTERNATIONAL PROLETARIAT[143]

Several gubernias in Russia have been hit by a famine whose proportions are apparently only slightly less than those of the 1891 calamity.

It is the painful aftermath of Russia's backwardness and of seven years of war, first, the imperialist, and then, the Civil War, which was forced upon the workers and peasants by the landowners and capitalists of all countries.

We need help. The Soviet Republic of workers and peasants expects this help from the working people, the industrial workers and the small farmers.

The mass of both the former and the latter are themselves oppressed by capitalism and imperialism everywhere, but we are convinced that they will respond to our appeal, despite their own hard condition caused by unemployment and the rising cost of living.

Those who have suffered from capitalist oppression all their lives will understand the position of the workers and peasants of Russia, they will grasp or, guided by the instinct of working and exploited people, will sense the need of helping the Soviet Republic, whose lot it was to be the first to undertake the hard but gratifying task of overthrowing capitalism. That is why the capitalists of all countries are revenging themselves upon the Soviet Republic; that is why they are planning a fresh campaign, intervention, and counter-revolutionary conspiracies against it.

All the greater, we trust, will be the vigour and the self-sacrifice with which the workers and the small labouring farmers of all countries will help us.

N. Lenin

August 2, 1921

Pravda No. 172, August 6, 1921

Published according to the *Pravda* text collated with the manuscript

APPEAL TO THE PEASANTS OF THE UKRAINE

This year, the Ukraine, west of the Dnieper, has had an excellent harvest. The workers and peasants in the famine-stricken Volga area, who are now suffering hardships only a little less severe than the dreadful calamity of 1891, look to the Ukrainian farmers for help. Help must come quickly. Help must be abundant. No farmer must refrain from sharing his surplus with the starving Volga peasants who have no seed with which to sow their fields.

Let every uyezd that is well supplied with grain send, say, two or three peasant delegates to the Volga to deliver the grain, and to see for themselves the terrible suffering, want and starvation, and tell their fellow-countrymen upon their return how urgently help is needed.

Chairman of the Council of People's
Commissars, *V. Ulyanov* (*Lenin*)

August 2, 1921

Pravda No. 172, August 6, 1921

Published according to
the *Pravda* text collated
with the manuscript

A LETTER TO G. MYASNIKOV[144]

August 5, 1921

Comrade Myasnikov,

I have only just managed to read *both* your articles. I am unaware of the nature of the speeches you made in the Perm (I think it was Perm) organisation and of your conflict with it. I can say nothing about that; it will be dealt with by the Organisation Bureau, which, I hear, has appointed a special commission.

My object is a different one: it is to appraise your articles as literary and political documents.

They are interesting documents.

Your main mistake is, I think, most clearly revealed in the article "Vexed Questions". And I consider it my duty to do all I can to try to convince you.

At the beginning of the article you make a correct application of dialectics. Indeed, whoever fails to understand the substitution of the slogan of "civil peace" for the slogan of "civil war" lays himself open to ridicule, if nothing worse. In this, you are right.

But precisely because you are right on this point, I am surprised that in drawing your conclusions, you should have forgotten the dialectics which you yourself had properly applied.

"Freedom of the press, from the monarchists to the anarchists, inclusively". . . . Very good! But just a minute: every Marxist and every worker who ponders over the four years' experience of our revolution will say, "Let's look into this—*what sort* of freedom of the press? What *for*? For *which class*?"

We do not believe in "absolutes". We laugh at "pure democracy".

The "freedom of the press" slogan became a great world slogan at the close of the Middle Ages and remained so up to the nineteenth century. Why? Because it expressed the ideas of the progressive bourgeoisie, i.e., its struggle against kings and priests, feudal lords and landowners.

No country in the world has done as much to liberate the masses from the influence of *priests* and *landowners* as the R.S.F.S.R. has done, and is doing. We have been performing *this* function of "freedom of the press" *better than anyone else* in the world.

All over the world, wherever there are capitalists, freedom of the press means freedom to *buy up* newspapers, to *buy* writers, to *bribe*, buy and fake "public opinion" for the *benefit of the bourgeoisie.*

This is a fact.

No one will ever be able to refute it.

And what about us?

Can anyone deny that the bourgeoisie in this country has been defeated, *but not destroyed*? That it *has gone into hiding*? Nobody can deny it.

Freedom of the press in the R.S.F.S.R., which is surrounded by the bourgeois enemies of the whole world, means freedom of *political organisation* for the bourgeoisie and its most loyal servants, the Mensheviks and Socialist-Revolutionaries.

This is an irrefutable fact.

The bourgeoisie (all over the world) is still very much stronger than we are. To place in its hands yet *another* weapon like freedom of political organisation (= freedom of the press, for the press is the core and foundation of political organisation) means facilitating the enemy's task, means helping the class enemy.

We have no wish to commit suicide, and therefore, we will not do this.

We clearly see this *fact*: "freedom of the press" means *in practice* that the international bourgeoisie will immediately buy up hundreds and thousands of Cadet, Socialist-Revolutionary and Menshevik writers, and will organise their propaganda and fight against us.

That is a fact. "They" are richer than we are and will buy a "force" ten times larger than we have, to fight us.

No, we will not do it; we will not help the international bourgeoisie.

How could you *descend* from a class appraisal—from the appraisal of the relations between *all* classes—to the sentimental, philistine appraisal? This is a mystery to me.

On the question: "civil peace or civil war", on the question of how *we* have won over, and *will continue* to "win over", the peasantry (to the side of the proletariat), on these two key world questions (= questions that affect the very *substance* of world politics), on these questions (which are dealt with in *both* your articles), you *were able* to take the Marxist standpoint, instead of the philistine, sentimental standpoint. You *did take account* of the relationships of *all* classes in a *practical*, sober way.

And suddenly you slide down into the abyss of sentimentalism!

"Outrage and abuses are rife in this country: freedom of the press will expose them."

That, as far as I can judge from your two articles, is where you slipped up. You have allowed yourself to *be depressed* by certain sad and deplorable *facts*, and lost the ability *soberly* to appraise the forces.

Freedom of the press will help *the force* of the world bourgeoisie. That is a fact. "Freedom of the press" *will not help to purge the Communist Party* in Russia of a number of its weaknesses, mistakes, misfortunes and maladies (it cannot be denied that there is a spate of these maladies), because this is *not* what the world bourgeoisie wants. But freedom of the press will be a weapon in the hands of *this world bourgeoisie*. It is not dead; it is alive. It is lurking nearby and watching. It has already *hired* Milyukov, to whom Chernov and Martov (partly because of their stupidity, and partly because of factional spleen against us; but mainly because of the objective logic of their petty-bourgeois-democratic position) are giving "faithful and loyal" service.

You took the wrong fork in the road.

You wanted to *cure* the Communist Party of its maladies and have snatched at *a drug* that will cause certain death—not at your hands, of course, but at the hands of the world bourgeoisie (+Milyukov+Chernov+Martov).

A LETTER TO G. MYASNIKOV
507

You forgot a minor point, a very tiny point, namely:
the world bourgeoisie and its "freedom" to buy up *for
itself* newspapers, and *centres of political organisation.*

No, we will not take this course. *Nine hundred* out of
every thousand *politically* conscious workers will refuse to
take this course.

We have many maladies. Mistakes (our *common* mistakes,
all of us have made mistakes, the Council of Labour and
Defence, the Council of People's Commissars and the
Central Committee) like those we made in distributing fuel
and *food* in the autumn and winter of 1920 (those were
enormous mistakes!) have greatly aggravated the maladies
springing from our situation.

Want and calamity abound.

They have been terribly *intensified* by the famine
of 1921.

It will cost us a supreme effort to extricate ourselves,
but we will get out, and have already begun to do so.

We will extricate ourselves, for, in the main, our policy
is a correct one, and takes into account *all* the class forces
on an *international* scale. We will extricate ourselves
because we do not try to make our position look better than
it is. We realise all the difficulties. We see *all* the maladies,
and are taking measures to cure them methodically, with
perseverance, and without giving way to panic.

You have allowed panic to get the better of you; panic
is a slope—once you stepped on it you slid down into a
position that looks very much as if you are forming a new
party, or are about to commit suicide.

You must not give way to panic.

Is there any isolation of the Communist Party cells
from the Party? There is. It is an evil, a misfortune, a
malaise.

It is there. It is a severe ailment.

We can see it.

It must be cured by proletarian and Party measures
and not by means of "freedom" (*for the bourgeoisie*).

Much of what you say about reviving the country's
economy, about mechanical ploughs, etc., about fighting
for "influence" over the peasantry, etc., is true and
useful.

Why not *bring this out* separately? We shall get together and work harmoniously in one party. The benefits will be great; *they will not come all at once*, but *very* slowly.

Revive the Soviets; secure the co-operation of non-Party people; let *non-Party* people verify the work of Party members: this is absolutely right. *No end* of work there, and it has hardly been started.

Why not amplify *this* in a *practical* way? In a pamphlet for the Congress?

Why not take that up?

Why be afraid of *spade* work (*denounce* abuses through the Central Control Commission, or the Party press, *Pravda*)? Misgivings about slow, difficult and arduous spade work cause people to give way to panic and to seek an "easy" way out: "freedom of the press" (*for the bourgeoisie*).

Why should you persist in your mistake—an obvious mistake—in your non-Party, *anti-proletarian* slogan of "freedom of the press"? Why not take up the less "brilliant" (scintillating with bourgeois brilliance) spade work of driving out abuses, combating them, and *helping* non-Party people in a practical and business-like way?

Have you ever brought up any *particular* abuse to the notice of the C.C., and suggested a definite *means* of eradicating it?

No, you have not.

Not a single time.

You saw a spate of misfortunes and maladies, gave way to despair and rushed into the arms of the enemy, the bourgeoisie ("freedom of the press" *for the bourgeoisie*). My advice is: do not give way to despair and panic.

We, and those who sympathise with us, the workers and peasants, still have an immense reservoir of strength. We still have plenty of health and vigour.

We are not doing enough to cure our ailments.

We are not doing a good job of practising the slogan: promote non-Party people, let non-Party people verify the work of Party members.

But we can, and will, do a hundred times more in this field than we are doing.

I hope that after thinking this over carefully you will not, out of false pride, persist in an obvious political mistake ("freedom of the press"), but, pulling yourself together and overcoming the panic, will get down to practical work: help to establish *ties* with non-Party people, and help non-Party people to *verify* the work of Party members.

There is no end of work in this field. Doing this work you can (and should) help to *cure* the disease, slowly but surely, instead of chasing after will-o'-the-wisps like "freedom of the press".

With communist greetings,
Lenin

Published in 1921

Published according
to the manuscript

TO COMRADE THOMAS BELL

Dear comrade,

I thank you very much for your letter, of August 7. I have read nothing concerning the English movement last months because of my illness and overwork.

It is extremely interesting what you communicate. Perhaps it is the *beginning* of the real proletarian mass movement in Great Britain *in the communist sense*. I am afraid we have till now in England few very feeble propagandist societies for communism (inclusive the British Communist Party[145]) but no really *mass* communist movement.

If the South Wales Miners' Federation has decided on July 24 to affiliate to the Third International by a majority of 120 to 63—perhaps it is the beginning of a new era. (How many miners there are in England? More than 500,000? How much in South Wales? 25,000? How many miners were *really* represented in Cardiff July 24, 1921?)

If these miners are not too small minority, if they fraternise with soldiers and begin a *real* "class war"—we must do all our possible to *develop* this movement and strengthen it.

Economic measures (like communal kitchens) are good but they are not much important *now*, *before* the victory of the proletarian revolution in England. *Now* the *political* struggle is the most important.

English capitalists are shrewd, clever, astute. They *will support* (directly or indirectly) communal kitchens *in order* to divert the attention *from political aims*.

What is important is (if I am not mistaken):

1) To create a very good, really proletarian, really mass *Communist Party* in this part of England, that is, such party which will *really* be the *leading* force in *all* labour

movement in this part of the country. (Apply the resolution on organisation and work of the Party adopted by the Third Congress to this part of your country.)

2) To start a daily paper of the working class, for the working class in this part of the country.

To start it not as a business (as usually newspapers are started in capitalist countries), not with big sum of money, not in ordinary and usual manner—but as an *economic and political* tool of the *masses* in their struggle.

Either the miners of this district are capable to pay *halfpenny* daily (for the beginning *weekly*, if you like) for their *own* daily (or weekly) newspaper (be it very small, it is not important)—*or there is no beginning of really communist mass movement in this part of your country.*

If the Communist Party of this district cannot collect a few pounds in order to publish *small leaflets* daily as a beginning of the really *proletarian* communist newspaper— if it is so, if *every* miner will not pay a penny for it, then there is *not serious*, not genuine affiliation to the Third International.

English Government will apply the shrewdest means in order to suppress every beginning of this kind. Therefore we must be (in the beginning) very prudent. The paper must be *not too revolutionary* in the beginning. If you will have three editors, at least one must be *non-communist*. (At least two genuine workers.) If nine-tenths of the workers do not buy this paper, if two-thirds $\left(\frac{120}{120+63} \right)$ do not pay special contributions (f. 1 penny *weekly*) for *their* paper— it will be no workers' newspaper.

I should be very glad to have few lines from you concerning this theme and beg to apologise for my bad English.

With communist greetings,

Lenin

Written on August 13, 1921

First published
in the *Workers' Weekly* No. 205,
January 21, 1927
The Russian translation appeared
in *Pravda* No 21,
January 27, 1927

A LETTER TO THE GERMAN COMMUNISTS

Dear comrades,

I had intended to state my view of the lessons of the Third Congress of the Communist International in a detailed article. Unfortunately, I have not yet been able to start on this work because of ill-health. The fact that a Congress of your Party, the United Communist Party of Germany (V.K.P.D.),[146] has been called for August 22, compels me to hasten with this letter, which I have to finish within a few hours, if I am not to be late in sending it to Germany.

So far as I can judge, the position of the Communist Party in Germany is a particularly difficult one. This is understandable.

Firstly, and mainly, from the end of 1918, the international position of Germany very quickly and sharply aggravated her internal revolutionary crisis and impelled the vanguard of the proletariat towards an immediate seizure of power. At the same time, the German and the entire international bourgeoisie, excellently armed and organised, and taught by the "Russian experience", hurled itself upon the revolutionary proletariat of Germany in a frenzy of hate. Tens of thousands of the best people of Germany— her revolutionary workers—were killed or tortured to death by the bourgeoisie, its heroes, Noske and Co., its servants, the Scheidemanns, etc., and by its indirect and "subtle" (and therefore particularly valuable) accomplices, the knights of the "Two-and-a-Half International", with their despicable spinelessness, vacillations, pedantry and philistinism. The armed capitalists set traps for the unarmed workers; they killed them wholesale, murdered their

leaders, ambushing them one by one, and making excellent use to this end of the counter-revolutionary howling
of both shades of Social-Democrats, the Scheidemannites
and the Kautskyites. When the crisis broke out, however,
the German workers lacked a genuine revolutionary party,
owing to the fact that the split was brought about too late,
and owing to the burden of the accursed tradition of "unity"
with capital's corrupt (the Scheidemanns, Legiens, Davids
and Co.) and spineless (the Kautskys, Hilferdings and
Co.) gang of lackeys. The heart of every honest and class-
conscious worker who accepted the Basle Manifesto of 1912[147]
at its face value and not as a "gesture" on the part of the
scoundrels of the "Second" and the "Two-and-a-Half"
grades, was filled with incredibly bitter hatred for the
opportunism of the old German Social-Democrats, and this
hatred—the greatest and most noble sentiment of the best
people among the oppressed and exploited masses—blinded
people and prevented them from keeping their heads and
working out a correct strategy with which to reply to the
excellent strategy of the Entente capitalists, who were
armed, organised and schooled by the "Russian experience",
and supported by France, Britain and America. This hatred
pushed them into premature insurrections.

That is why the development of the revolutionary working-
class movement in Germany has since the end of 1918
been treading a particularly hard and painful road. But it
has marched and is marching steadily forward. There is
the incontrovertible fact of the gradual swing to the left
among the masses of workers, the real majority of the
labouring and exploited people in Germany, both those
organised in the old, Menshevik trade unions (i.e., the
unions serving the bourgeoisie) and those entirely, or almost
entirely, unorganised. What the German proletariat must
and will do—and this is the guarantee of victory—is
keep their heads; systematically rectify the mistakes of
the past; steadily win over the mass of the workers both
inside and outside the trade unions; patiently build up a
strong and intelligent Communist Party capable of giving
real leadership to the masses at every turn of events; and
work out a strategy that is on a level with the best international strategy of the most advanced bourgeoisie, which

is "enlightened" by agelong experience in general, and the "Russian experience" in particular.

On the other hand, the difficult position of the Communist Party of Germany is aggravated at the present moment by the break-away of the not very good Communists on the left (the Communist Workers' Party of Germany, K.A.P.D.) and on the right (Paul Levi and his little magazine *Unser Weg* or *Sowjet*[148]).

Beginning with the Second Congress of the Communist International, the "Leftists" or "K.A.P.-ists" have received sufficient warning from us in the international arena. Until sufficiently strong, experienced and influential Communist Parties have been built, at least in the principal countries, the participation of semi-anarchist elements in our international congresses has to be tolerated, and is to some extent even useful. It is useful insofar as these elements serve as a clear "warning" to inexperienced Communists, and also insofar as they themselves are still capable of learning. All over the world, anarchism has been splitting up—not since yesterday, but since the beginning of the imperialist war of 1914-18—into two trends: one pro-Soviet, and the other anti-Soviet; one in favour of the dictatorship of the proletariat, and the other against it. We must allow this process of disintegration among the anarchists to go on and come to a head. Hardly anyone in Western Europe has experienced anything like a big revolution. There, the experience of great revolutions has been almost entirely forgotten, and the transition from the desire to be revolutionary and from talk (and resolutions) about revolution to real revolutionary work is very difficult, painful and slow.

It goes without saying, however, that the semi-anarchist elements can and should be tolerated only within certain limits. In Germany, we tolerated them for quite a long time. The Third Congress of the Communist International faced them with an ultimatum and fixed a definite time limit. If they have now voluntarily resigned from the Communist International, all the better. Firstly, they have saved us the trouble of expelling them. Secondly, it has now been demonstrated most conclusively and most graphically, and proved with precise facts to all vacillating workers, and all those who have been inclined towards anarchism because of their hatred for the opportunism of the old Social-Democrats, that the Communist International has been patient, that it has not expelled anarchists immediately and unconditionally, and that it has given them an attentive hearing and helped them to learn.

We must now pay less attention to the K.A.P.-ists. By polemising with them we merely give them publicity. They are too unintelligent; it is wrong to take them seriously; and it is not worth being angry with them. They have no influence among the masses, and will acquire none, unless we make mistakes. Let us leave this tiny trend to die a natural death; the workers themselves will realise that it is worthless. Let us propagate and implement, with greater effect, the organisational and tactical decisions of the Third Congress of the Communist International, instead of giving the K.A.P.-ists publicity by arguing with them. The infantile disorder of "Leftism" is passing and will pass away as the movement grows.

Similarly we are now needlessly helping Paul Levi, we are needlessly giving him publicity by polemising with him. That we should argue with him is exactly what he wants. Now, after the decisions of the Third Congress of the Communist International, we must forget about him and devote all our attention, all our efforts, to peaceful, practical and constructive work (without any squabbling, polemics, or bringing up of the quarrels of yesterday), in the spirit of the decisions of the Third Congress. It is my conviction that Comrade K. Radek's article, "The Third World Congress on the March Action, and Future Tactics" (in *Die Rote Fahne*,[149] the Central Organ of the United Communist Party of Germany, issues of July 14 and 15, 1921), sins quite considerably against this general and unanimously adopted decision of the Third Congress. This article, a copy of which was sent me by one of the Polish Communists, is quite unnecessarily—and in a way that positively harms our work—directed not only against Paul Levi (that would be very unimportant), but also against Clara Zetkin. And yet Clara Zetkin herself concluded a "peace treaty" in Moscow, during the Third Congress, with the C.C. (the "Centrale") of the United Communist Party of Germany, providing for joint, non-factional work! And we all approved of the treaty. In his misplaced polemical zeal, Comrade K. Radek has gone to the length of saying something positively untrue, attributing to Zetkin the idea of "putting off" (*verlegt*) "every general action by the Party" (*jede allgemeine Aktion der Partei*) "until the day when large masses rise" (*auf den Tag, wo die grossen Massen aufstehen werden*). It goes without saying that by such methods Comrade K. Radek is rendering Paul Levi the best service the latter could wish for. There is nothing Paul Levi wants so much as a controversy endlessly dragged out, with as many people involved in it as possible, and efforts to drive Zetkin away from the party by polemical breaches of the "peace treaty" which she herself concluded, and which was approved by the entire Communist International. Comrade K. Radek's article serves as an excellent example of how Paul Levi is assisted from the "Left".

Here I must explain to the German comrades why I defended Paul Levi so long at the Third Congress. Firstly, because I made Levi's acquaintance through Radek in Switzerland in 1915 or 1916. At that time Levi was already a Bolshevik. I cannot help entertaining a certain amount of distrust towards those who accepted Bolshevism *only after* its victory in Russia, and after it had scored a number of victories in the international arena. But, of course, this reason is relatively unimportant, for, after all, my personal knowledge of Paul Levi is very small. Incomparably more important was the second reason, namely, that *essentially* much of Levi's criticism of the March action in Germany in 1921 was *correct* (not, of course, when he said that the uprising was a "putsch"; that assertion of his was absurd).

It is true that Levi did all he possibly could, and much besides, to weaken and spoil his criticism, and make it difficult for himself and others to understand the *essence* of the matter, by bringing in a mass of details in which he was obviously wrong. Levi couched his criticism in an impermissible and harmful form. While urging others to pursue a cautious and well-considered strategy, Levi himself committed worse blunders than a schoolboy, by rushing into battle so prematurely, so unprepared, so absurdly and wildly that he was certain to lose any "battle" (spoiling or hampering his work for many years), although the "battle" could and should have been won. Levi behaved like an "anarchist intellectual" (if I am not mistaken, the German term is *Edelanarchist*), instead of behaving like an organised member of the proletarian Communist International. Levi committed a breach of discipline.

By this series of incredibly stupid blunders Levi made it difficult to concentrate attention on the essence of the matter. And the essence of the matter, i.e., the appraisal *and correction* of the innumerable mistakes made by the United Communist Party of Germany during the March action of 1921, has been and continues to be of enormous importance. In order to explain and correct these mistakes (which some people enshrined as gems of Marxist tactics) *it was necessary* to have been on the *Right* wing during the Third Congress of the Communist International. Otherwise the *line* of the Communist International would have been a *wrong* one.

I defended and had to defend Levi, insofar as I saw before me opponents of his who merely shouted about "Menshevism" and "Centrism" and refused to see the mistakes of the March action and the need to explain and correct them. These people made a caricature of revolutionary Marxism, and a pastime of the struggle against "Centrism". They might have done the greatest harm to the whole cause, for "no one in the world can compromise the revolutionary Marxists, if they do not compromise themselves".

I said to these people: Granted that Levi has become a Menshevik. As I have scant knowledge of him personally, I will not insist, if the point is proved to me. But it has not yet been proved. All that has been proved till now is that he *has lost his head*. It is childishly stupid to declare a man a Menshevik merely on these grounds. The training of experienced and influential party leaders is a long and difficult job. And without it the dictatorship of the proletariat, and its "unity of will", remain a phrase. In Russia, it took us fifteen years (1903-17) to produce a group of leaders—fifteen years of fighting Menshevism, fifteen years of tsarist persecution, fifteen years, which included the years of the first revolution (1905), a great and mighty revolution.

Yet we have had our sad cases, when even fine comrades have "lost their heads". If the West-European comrades imagine that they are insured against such "sad cases" it is sheer childishness, and we cannot but combat it.

Levi had to be expelled for breach of discipline. Tactics had to be determined *on the basis* of a most detailed explanation and correction of the mistakes made during the March 1921 action. If, *after* this, Levi wants to behave in the old way, he will show that his expulsion was justified; and the wavering or hesitant workers will be given all the more forceful and convincing proof of the absolute correctness of the Third Congress decisions concerning Paul Levi.

Having made a cautious approach at the Congress to the appraisal of Levi's mistakes, I can now say with all the more assurance that Levi has hastened to confirm the worst expectations. I have before me No. 6 of his magazine *Unser Weg* (of July 15, 1921). It is evident from the editorial note printed at the head of the magazine that the decisions of the Third Congress are known to Paul Levi. What is his reply to them? Menshevik catchwords such as "a great excommunication" (*grosser Bann*), "canon law" (*kanonisches Recht*), and that he will "quite freely" (*in vollständiger Freiheit*) "discuss" these decisions. What greater freedom can a man have if he has been freed of the title of party member and member of the Communist International! And please note that he expects party members to write for him, for Levi, anonymously!

First—he plays a dirty trick on the party, hits it in the back, and sabotages its work.

Then—he discusses the essence of the Congress decisions. That is magnificent.

But by doing this Levi puts paid to himself.

Paul Levi wants to continue the fight.

It will be a great strategic error to satisfy his desire. I would advise the German comrades to prohibit all controversy with Levi and his magazine in the columns of the daily party press. He must not be given publicity. He must not be allowed to divert the fighting party's attention from important matters to unimportant ones. In cases of extreme necessity, the controversy could be conducted in weekly or monthly magazines, or in pamphlets, and as far as possible care must be taken not to afford the K.A.P.-ists and Paul Levi the pleasure they feel when they are mentioned by name; reference should simply be made to "certain not very clever critics who at all costs want to regard themselves as Communists".

I am informed that at the last meeting of the enlarged C.C. (*Ausschuss*), even the Left-winger Friesland was compelled to launch a sharp attack on Maslow, who is playing at Leftism and wishes to exercise himself in "hunting Centrists". The unreasonableness (to put it mildly) of this Maslow's conduct was also revealed over here, in Moscow. Really, this Maslow and two or three of his supporters and confederates, who obviously do not wish to observe the "peace treaty" and have more zeal than sense, should be sent by the German party to Soviet Russia for a year or two. We would find useful work for them. We would make men of them. And the international and German movement would certainly gain thereby.

The German Communists must at all costs end the internal dissension, get rid of the quarrelsome elements on both sides, forget about Paul Levi and the K.A.P.-ists and get down to real work.

There is plenty to be done.

In my opinion, the tactical and organisational resolutions of the Third Congress of the Communist International mark a great step forward. Every effort must be exerted to really put both resolutions into effect. This is a difficult matter, but it can and should be done.

First, the Communists had to proclaim their principles to the world. That was done at the First Congress. It was the first step.

The second step was to give the Communist International organisational form and to draw up conditions for affiliation to it—conditions making for real separation from the Centrists, from the direct and indirect agents of the bourgeoisie within the working-class movement. That was done at the Second Congress.

At the Third Congress it was necessary to start practical, constructive work, to determine concretely, taking account of the practical experience of the communist struggle already begun, *exactly what* the line of further activity should be in respect of tactics and of organisation. We have taken this third step. We have an army of Communists all over the world. It is still poorly trained and poorly organised. It would be extremely harmful to forget this truth or be afraid of admitting it. Submitting ourselves to a most careful and rigorous test, and studying the experience of our own movement, we must train this army efficiently; we must organise it properly, and test it in all sorts of manoeuvres, all sorts of battles, in attack and in retreat. We cannot win without this long and hard schooling.

The "crux" of the situation in the international communist movement in the summer of 1921 was that some of the best and most influential sections of the Communist International did not quite properly understand this task; *they exaggerated* the "struggle against Centrism" *ever so slightly*; they *went ever so slightly beyond* the border line at which this struggle turns into a pastime and revolutionary Marxism begins to be compromised.

That was the "crux" of the Third Congress.

The exaggeration was a slight one; but the danger arising out of it was enormous. It was difficult to combat it, because the exaggerating was done by really the best and most loyal elements, without whom the formation of the Communist International would, perhaps, have been impossible. In the tactical amendments published in the newspaper *Moskau*[150] in German, French and English and signed by the German, Austrian and Italian delegations, this exaggeration was definitely revealed—the more so because these amendments were proposed to a draft resolution that was already final (following long and all-round preparatory work). The rejection of these amendments was a *straightening out* of the line of the Communist International; it was a victory over the danger of exaggeration.

Exaggeration, if not corrected, was sure to kill the Communist International. For "no one in the world can compromise the revolutionary Marxists, if they do not compromise themselves". No one in the world will be able to prevent the victory of the Communists over the Second and the Two-and-a-Half Internationals (and under the conditions prevailing in twentieth-century Western Europe and America, after the first imperialist war, this means victory over the bourgeoisie) *unless* the Communists prevent it themselves.

Exaggeration, however slight, means preventing victory.

Exaggeration of the struggle against Centrism means *saving* Centrism, means *strengthening* its position, its influence over the workers.

In the period between the Second and the Third Congresses, we learned to wage a victorious struggle against Centrism on an international scale. This is proved by the facts. We will continue to wage this struggle (expulsion of Levi and of Serrati's party) to the end.

We have, however, *not yet* learned, on an international scale, to combat wrong exaggerations in the struggle against Centrism. But we have become conscious of this defect, as has been proved by the course and outcome of the Third Congress. And precisely because we have become conscious of our defect *we will rid ourselves of it.*

And then we shall be invincible, because without support inside the proletariat (through the medium of the bourgeois agents of the Second and the Two-and-a-Half Internationals) the bourgeoisie in Western Europe and America *cannot* retain power.

More careful, more thorough preparation for fresh and more decisive battles, both defensive and offensive—that is the fundamental and principal thing in the decisions of the Third Congress.

"... Communism will become a mass force in Italy if the Italian Communist Party unceasingly and steadily fights the opportunist policy of Serratism and at the same time is able to maintain close contact with the proletarian masses in the trade unions, during strikes, during clashes with the counter-revolutionary fascist organisations; if it is able to merge the movements of all the working-class organisations and to transform the spontaneous outbreaks of the working class into carefully prepared battles...."

"The United Communist Party of Germany will be the better able to carry out mass action, the better it adapts its fighting slogans to the actual situation in future, the more thoroughly it studies the situation, and the more co-ordinated and disciplined the action it conducts...."

Such are the most pertinent passages of the tactical resolution of the Third Congress.

To win over the majority of the proletariat to our side—such is the "principal task" (the heading of Point 3 of the resolution on tactics).

Of course, we do not give the winning of the majority a formal interpretation, as do the knights of philistine "democracy" of the Two-and-a-Half International. When in Rome, in July 1921, the entire proletariat—the reformist proletariat of the trade unions and the Centrists of Serrati's party—*followed* the Communists against the fascists, that was *winning over the majority* of the working class to our side.

This was far, very far, from winning them decisively; it was doing so only partially, only momentarily, only locally. But it was winning over the majority, and that is possible even if, formally, the majority of the proletariat follow bourgeois leaders, or leaders who pursue a bourgeois policy (as do all the leaders of the Second and the Two-and-a-Half Internationals), or if the majority of the proletariat are wavering. This winning over is gaining ground steadily in every way throughout the world. Let us make more thorough and careful preparations for it; let us not allow a single serious opportunity to slip by when the bourgeoisie compels the proletariat to undertake a struggle; let us learn to correctly determine the moment when the *masses* of the proletariat *cannot but* rise together with us.

Then victory will be assured, no matter how severe some of the defeats and transitions in our great campaign may be.

Our tactical and strategic methods (if we take them on an international scale) still lag behind the excellent strategy of the bourgeoisie, which has learned from the example of Russia and will not let itself be "taken by surprise". But our forces are greater, immeasurably greater; we are learning tactics and strategy; we have advanced this "science" on the basis of the mistakes of the March 1921 action. We shall completely master this "science".

In the overwhelming majority of countries, our parties are still very far from being what real Communist Parties should be; they are far from being real vanguards of the genuinely revolutionary and only revolutionary class, with every single member taking part in the struggle, in the movement, in the everyday life of the masses. But we are aware of this defect, we brought it out most strikingly in the Third Congress resolution on the work of the Party. And we shall overcome this defect.

Comrades, German Communists, permit me to conclude by expressing the wish that your party congress on August 22 will with a firm hand put a stop once and for all to the trivial struggle against those who have broken away on the left and the right. Inner-party struggles must stop! Down with everyone who wants to drag them out, directly or indirectly. We know our tasks today much more clearly, concretely and thoroughly than we did yesterday; we are not afraid of pointing openly to our mistakes in order to rectify them. We shall now devote all the Party's efforts to improving its organisation, to enriching the quality and content of its work, to creating closer contact with the masses, and to working out increasingly correct and accurate working-class tactics and strategy.

With communist greetings,

N. Lenin

August 14, 1921

Published in 1921   Published according
                                                    to the manuscript

———

NOTES

[1] Lenin's first speech to Party activists in the discussion of the role and tasks of the trade unions in socialist construction was delivered at the Bolshoi Theatre on December 30, 1920.

Trotsky had started the discussion in the Communist group of the Fifth All-Russia Trade Union Conference on November 3 with his call "to tighten the screws of War Communism" as opposed to the Party's line to stimulate democratic activity in the trade unions.

The disagreements turned "on the different approach to the mass, the way of winning it over, and keeping in touch with it" (*Lenin*). The disagreements in the group were brought before the Central Committee Plenary Meeting. But Trotsky's December 24 speech before the delegates of the Eighth All-Russia Congress of Soviets and trade union activists carried the issue outside the Central Committee. On December 25, he published a pamphlet, which marked the formation of an anti-Party faction, and served as a signal for action by other anti-Party groups—"buffer", "Workers' Opposition", "Democratic Centralism", etc.

Lenin was against any discussion, realising that it distracted the Party's attention and forces from the immediate tasks of fighting the economic dislocation and the famine. But when the anti-Party groups came out, he attacked them, concentrating on the Trotskyites as the chief anti-Party force. In his speeches and articles—*The Party Crisis* and *Once Again on the Trade Unions, the Current Situation and the Mistakes of Trotsky and Bukharin*—Lenin showed the essence of the internal Party struggle and exposed the factional activity of the opposition groups, which tended to disrupt the Party's unity, and the great harm of the discussion imposed on it. He put forward and developed a number of important principles underlying the trade unions' role in the dictatorship of the proletariat and their tasks in socialist construction.

The discussion lasted more than two months. The overwhelming majority of the Party organisations approved Lenin's platform and rejected the opposition's. The results of the discussion were summed up at the Tenth Congress of the Party on March 8-16, 1921.

p. 19

[2] On its agenda were the current tasks of economic construction and the question of the trade union movement. It defined the short-term economic tasks and stressed the need for the trade

unions' active participation in socialist construction. It adopted
the following resolutions: "The Current Tasks of Economic Construction" and "The Trade Unions and Their Organisation".
See *K.P.S.S. v rezolutsiakh i resheniakh syezdov, konferentsi i
plenumov TsK* (The C.P.S.U. in the Resolutions and Decisions
of Congresses, Conferences and C.C. Plenary Meetings, Part 1,
1954, pp. 477-90, 490-94).   p. 22

3 The reference is to the Eighth All-Russia Congress of Soviets
of Workers', Peasants', Red Army and Cossack Deputies held
in Moscow on December 22-29, 1920. It was attended by 2,537
delegates, the greatest number ever. Of them 1,728 had voice and
vote, and 809, voice only. Of the total number of delegates
91.7 per cent were Communists; 2.7, Communist sympathisers;
3.9, non-party people; 0.3, Mensheviks; 0.3, Bundists; 0.15, Left
S.R.s; 0.15, anarchists, and 0.8, from other parties. It showed the
growing authority of the Communist Party and the political
bankruptcy of the petty-bourgeois parties, which had betrayed
themselves as anti-Soviet and counter-revolutionary.

The Congress met at a time when the war against the foreign
intervention and internal counter-revolution was coming to a
victorious end, and when the economic front stood out as "the
main and most important one" (*Lenin*). On its agenda there were
the following questions, the chief of which had been discussed
beforehand by the Communist group: report on the activity of the
All-Russia Central Executive Committee and the Council of
People's Commissars; electrification of Russia; rehabilitation of
industry and transport; development of agricultural production
and promotion of farming; efficiency of Soviet establishments
and the struggle against bureaucratic practices. These problems
were thrashed out in three sections: industry, agriculture and
Soviet administration.

Lenin guided the work of the Congress. At the plenary meeting
on December 22, he gave a report on the activity of the All-
Russia Central Executive Committee and the Council of People's
Commissars, and on December 23, he summed up the debate. He
spoke six times at the Communist group meetings on December
21, 22, 24 and 27 on the question of concessions and the draft
law on measures to consolidate and develop peasant farming.
By an overwhelming majority, the Congress adopted a resolution on Lenin's report, approving the government's activity,
and rejected a draft resolution motioned by the petty-bourgeois delegates, who had delivered anti-Soviet speeches.

The Congress adopted a plan for the electrification of the country (GOELRO), worked out on Lenin's initiative and instructions. This was the first long-range economic plan of the Soviet
state and Lenin called it "the second Party Programme". He also
wrote the resolution on Krzhizhanovsky's report.

Another major question on the agenda was a draft law on
measures to consolidate and develop peasant farming, which had
been adopted by the Council of People's Commissars on December

14, 1920. Lenin stressed that the law was "a kind of a focus around which hundreds of decrees and bills of the Soviet power were grouped". Lenin took part in the discussion of its principal clauses by the non-Party peasant delegates to the Congress at a special meeting on December 22, and by the Communist group on December 24 and 27. The draft law was adopted unanimously.

The Congress passed a comprehensive resolution to improve and reorganise the entire Soviet apparatus as required by the transition to peaceful economic construction. It regulated relations between central and local organs of power and administration. The Congress also discussed the reorganisation of the whole system of economic management in accordance with the new economic tasks, and approved a new statute of the Council of Labour and Defence.

It instituted the Order of the *Red Banner of Labour* as an award for dedication, initiative, efficiency and hard work in solving economic tasks.   p. 24

4 The reference is to the resolution of the Ninth All-Russia Conference of the R.C.P.(B.), "The Current Tasks of Party Organisation". See *K.P.S.S. v rezolutsiakh* . . . (The C.P.S.U. in the Resolutions and Decisions of Congresses, Conferences and C.C. Plenary Meetings, Part 1, 1954, pp. 506-12).   p. 27

5 *Izvestia* of the Central Committee of the Russian Communist Party was an information organ dealing with Party problems. It was published under a resolution of the Eighth Congress of the R.C.P.(B.) as a weekly supplement to *Pravda* from May 28, 1919, and as an independent organ from October 1920.

In 1929, it was transformed into a fortnightly, *Partiinoye Stroitelstvo* (Party Construction), and in June 1946 renamed *Partiinaya Zhizn* (Party Life).   p. 27

6 The *"buffer group"* took shape during the trade union discussion in 1920-21, as one of the anti-Party groups. It was headed by N. I. Bukharin and included Y. Larin, Y. A. Preobrazhensky, L. P. Serebryakov, G. Y. Sokolnikov, V. N. Yakovleva and others. They tried to reconcile Leninism and Trotskyism, acting as a "buffer" in disagreements on the question of the role and tasks of the trade unions. In fact Bukharin attacked Lenin and defended Trotsky. They did much harm to the Party by supporting the worst kind of factional activity. Lenin said Bukharin's theses were a "low in ideological disintegration". Bukharin soon abandoned his platform and openly sided with Trotsky.

Lenin characterised the "buffer" group and its anti-Party views in his article, "The Party Crisis", in the pamphlet, *Once Again on the Trade Unions, the Current Situation and the Mistakes of Trotsky and Bukharin*, and elsewhere.   p. 27

7 *The Council of Workers' and Peasants' Defence* was set up by the All-Russia Central Executive Committee on November 30, 1918, to implement its September 2, 1918 decree which proclaimed the Soviet Republic a military camp. Lenin was appointed

its Chairman. It was vested with extraordinary powers in mobilising the resources of the Soviet state for defence in that exceptionally difficult period.

The Council was the Republic's chief military-economic and planning centre during the intervention and Civil War and also controlled the activity of the Revolutionary Military Council and other military organs. Its decrees were binding on all Soviet citizens, as well as on central and local agencies. Early in April 1920, it was reorganised into the Council of Labour and Defence (C.L.D.) (*Soviet Truda i Oborony*—STO), and under a decision of the Eighth All-Russia Congress of Soviets in December 1920 it began to operate as a government commission responsible for co-ordinating the work of all economic departments. It was abolished in 1937.

p. 28

[8] *Glavpolitput*—the Chief Political Department of the People's Commissariat for Communications—was formed as a provisional organ under the direct leadership of the Party's Central Committee in February 1919, and in January 1920 it was renamed the Chief Political Administration. It took extraordinary measures to rehabilitate the railways that had been ruined in the imperialist war and the Civil War, to improve Party and political work among railway workers, and to strengthen and stimulate the activity of the railwaymen's trade union and make it an instrument for the further development of the railways. It introduced military discipline on the railways to gear them to the war effort. The measures effected by Glavpolitput saved the railways from utter ruin, but produced bureaucratic and undemocratic practices in the trade unions and a tendency to lose touch with the masses.

It was abolished by a Central Committee decision on December 7, 1920, at the end of the Civil War and the start of peaceful development.

p. 34

[9] *Tsektran*—the Central Committee of the Joint Trade Union of Rail and Water Transport Workers. In September 1920, the two unions were merged to set up a strong centralised administration capable of tackling the tasks of rapidly rehabilitating transport, whose stoppages tended to paralyse the national economy. Its extraordinary powers and military methods of work, which sprang from the enormity of the tasks before it, bred bureaucratic practices, the appointments system, administration by injunction, etc. It fell into the hands of the Trotskyites, who set the workers against the Party and split their unity. The plenary meetings of the C.C. on November 8 and December 7, 1920, condemned Tsektran's methods and adopted a decision to incorporate it into the general system of the All-Russia Central Council of Trade Unions on a par with other unions. Tsektran was advised to change its methods, develop trade union democracy, make all trade union bodies elective, reduce the appointments system, etc. The First All-Russia Congress of Transport Workers in March 1921 called by the Central Committee of the Party expelled the Trotskyites from the Tsektran leadership and outlined new methods of work.   p. 34

¹⁰ *Politvod*—the Chief Political Administration of Water Transport of the People's Commissariat for Communications—was set up in April 1920 as an agency of Glavpolitput to carry on political education among the workers and exercise political control over the technical and administrative personnel; to put water transport on its feet as soon as possible; to stimulate higher productivity and improve discipline. It was dissolved in December 1920.   p. 35

¹¹ The Party wanted the trade unions' work reorganised in accordance with the tasks of peaceful socialist construction, democracy developed and military methods of administration abolished. This was opposed by Trotsky, who demanded, at the Communist group meeting on November 3, a "shake-up" of the trade unions. He wanted "the screws tightened" and the trade unions governmentalised immediately. He disagreed on the "approach to the mass, the way of winning it over, and keeping in touch with it". His speech started the Party discussion on the trade unions, but the Communist delegates rejected his demands, for their realisation would have abolished the trade unions and undermined the dictatorship of the proletariat. That is why his theses were discussed by the Party Central Committee. At the November 8 C.C. Plenary Meeting, Lenin came out with his own theses which, when put to the vote, won 8 votes, as against 7 for Trotsky's. p. 37

¹² *The Workers' Opposition*—an anti-Party anarcho-syndicalist group under the leadership of A. G. Shlyapnikov, S. P. Medvedyev, A. M. Kollontai, I. I. Kutuzov, Y. K. Lutovinov, etc. It first came out under its demagogic name at the Ninth All-Russia Conference of the R.C.P.(B.) in September 1920.

In November the group launched a factional struggle undermining the unity of the Party and organised a special discussion at the Moscow Gubernia Conference of the R.C.P.(B.). It took final shape as the Workers' Opposition in 1920-21 during the discussion on the trade unions. Its views constituted an anarcho-syndicalist deviation within the Party and were expounded in full in Kollontai's pamphlet, *The Workers' Opposition*, published on the eve of the Tenth Party Congress, proposing that the national economy should be run by an All-Russia Congress of Producers organised in industrial trade unions. It wanted all economic bodies to be elected by the trade unions, with Party and Soviet organs having no power to reject the candidates nominated by the trade unions. It denied that the Party had the leading role to play in socialist construction and that the dictatorship of the proletariat was the Party's chief instrument. It said it was not the Party but the trade unions that were the highest form of workers' organisation.

The Workers' Opposition had some temporary support among workers swayed by petty-bourgeois influence and tried to use their vacillation to promote its narrow interests. It also had some sympathisers in central and local Party organisations. Thus, its platform won 21 per cent of the vote at the Moscow Gubernia Party

Conference in November 1920; 30 per cent at the Communist group meeting of the Second All-Russia Congress of Miners in early 1921, but less than 6 per cent at the Tenth Party Congress. The Congress completely defeated the Workers' Opposition; this was the result of the Party's educational work exposing the Opposition's demagogic anti-Party views. It lost ground among the rank and file and was heavily defeated at the Tenth Congress. Lenin's resolution, "On the Syndicalist and Anarchist Deviation in our Party", stressed that the views of the Workers' Opposition were wrong theoretically and "tended to weaken the Communist Party's consistent general line, actually helping the class enemy of the proletarian revolution". See *K.P.S.S. v rezolutsiakh* . . . (The C.P.S.U. in the Resolutions and Decisions of Congresses, Conferences and C.C. Plenary Meetings, Part 1, 1954, p. 532). The Congress decided that the propaganda of the Workers' Opposition ideas was incompatible with membership in the Party. Its resolution on the Party's unity demanded the immediate dissolution of all anti-Party groups, whatever their platforms. Most rank-and-file members of the Opposition broke with the group and gave sincere support to the Party's line. But Shlyapnikov and Medvedyev headed the remnants in an illegal organisation which continued to conduct anti-Party propaganda behind a façade of ultra-revolutionary phrases. In February 1922, they sent to the Executive Committee of the Comintern their "Declaration of 22", a slanderous attack on the Party. The Executive Committee studied the "Declaration", condemned the group, and warned that any further activity on their part would put them outside the Third International. Their organisational defeat was completed by the Party's Eleventh Congress in 1922.

p. 46

[13] At a joint meeting of the Party groups of the Eighth Congress of Soviets, the All-Russia Central Council of Trade Unions and the Moscow City Council of Trade Unions, an argument took place as to whether Y. E. Rudzutak was the author of the theses, *The Tasks of the Trade Unions in Production*. Lenin asked the Trade Union Central Council for documents on the origin of the theses. He was given an extract from record No. 44 of the minutes of November 1, and a covering note from S. A. Lozovsky. The extract proved that the Presidium had discussed and adopted Rudzutak's theses as a basis and had instructed M. P. Tomsky and Rudzutak to put finishing touches to the theses. The note said this was done by Rudzutak alone. The Fifth All-Russia Conference of Trade Unions heard Rudzutak's report, adopted his theses as a basis and elected a commission, consisting of G. V. Tsiperovich, A. A. Andreyev and Rudzutak, to edit them. They worked out several points and amplified the theses.

Lenin sent the documents and Rudzutak's theses to *Pravda* with his covering letter, which said: "I request the Editorial Board to publish Rudzutak's theses, which were adopted by the Fifth All-Russia Trade Union Conference of November 2-6, 1920,

and are indispensable to the discussion. I enclose additional
material on the disagreements in Party circles concerning the origin
of these theses." The documents and Lenin's letter were published
in *Pravda* No. 13 on January 21, 1921.   p. 47

14 The "Appeal to the Party" was adopted at a discussion meeting
of the representatives of Petrograd district Party organisations
on January 3, 1921. On January 6, it was approved by a city
meeting in People's House which was attended by over 4,000
Party members and candidates. Only 20 votes were cast against
it. When it was discussed in the district Party organisations it
had the support of 95-98 per cent of the membership.

The Petrograd Bolsheviks supported Lenin and opposed Trotsky
on the question of the trade unions' role and tasks. They called
the other Party organisations to follow Lenin and stressed the
danger of Trotsky's platform, for its realisation would have
abolished the trade unions and undermined the dictatorship of the
proletariat. *Pravda* No. 7 of January 13 published the Appeal
and also the counter-statement of the Moscow Party Committee,
which at that time took a "buffer" stand. In a resolution published
in the same issue of *Pravda* the Moscow Committee said that it
found "it absolutely impossible" to accept the Petrograd proposals; it said the Petrograd Party organisation's stand showed its
"extremely dangerous" tendency to become a special centre for
preparing the Party Congress; it did not condemn Trotsky's
establishment of a faction, thereby giving support to his anti-Party
struggle.   p. 48

15 *Draft Decision of the Tenth Congress of the R.C.P. on the Role
and Tasks of the Trade Unions* was Lenin's "Platform of 10"
tabled before the Central Committee by a group of members of
the C.C. and of the Central Committee's Trade Union Commission in opposition to the platforms of the anti-Party groups. It
defined the role of the trade unions in the light of the new tasks
connected with the end of the Civil War and transition to
peaceful socialist construction: the trade unions, being a school of
administration, a school of economic management, a school of communism, were chiefly to take part in government, train personnel for
government bodies and economic agencies, and help tighten labour
discipline. They were to base their work on education, persuasion
and democratic practices. The Tenth Congress's resolution on the
role and tasks of the trade unions was based on the "Platform
of 10", which during the discussion had been supported by a
majority of local Party organisations.   p. 48

16 An opportunist faction headed by M. S. Boguslavsky,
A. Z. Kamensky, V. N. Maximovsky, N. Osinsky, Raphail
(P. B. Farbman) and T. V. Sapronov. They first came out against
Lenin's line in Party and Soviet organisation at the Eighth Party
Congress. At the Ninth Congress, they had their own rapporteurs
on economic construction and organisational problems, but failed

to find any support among the Bolsheviks. On many questions they had backing only from the Mensheviks.

They denied the Party's leading role in the Soviets and trade unions and demanded freedom of factions and groups, and a merger of the Council of People's Commissars and the Presidium of the All-Russia Central Executive Committee; they opposed the subordination of local to central organs and wanted the Organisation Bureau of the Central Committee deprived of all say in political leadership, which would have split up the C.C.'s political and organisational unity. They opposed one-man management and the personal responsibility of managers in industry. In the Ukraine, they were against the "Poor Peasants' Committees" which were instruments of the proletariat's dictatorship in the countryside.

The group published its platform during the trade union discussion in 1920-21, but at the pre-Congress meetings it won only a handful of votes. At the Tenth Congress they withdrew their platform and allowed their members to vote freely. They continued to fight the Party on questions of organisation, on which V. N. Maximovsky delivered a co-report. After the Tenth Congress, only the leaders continued their anti-Party activity. In 1923, they joined the Trotskyites, and in 1926, formed the "Group of 15" headed by Sapronov and Smirnov, which was expelled from the Party by the Fifteenth Party Congress. p. 49

[17] *Ignatovites*, or "a group of activists of Moscow city districts", was an anti-Party anarcho-syndicalist group, headed by Y. N. Ignatov, during the trade union discussion of 1920-21. Its activity was limited to the Moscow Party organisation, because it had no influence among the city's workers and rank-and-file Party members. Before the Tenth Party Congress, it came out with two platforms: the current tasks of the trade unions, and Party organisation. The Ignatovites shared the anarcho-syndicalist views of the Workers' Opposition; they set the trade unions in opposition to the Soviet state; denied the Party's leadership in socialist construction: opposed democratic centralism; demanded freedom of discussions, and wanted the Party membership to consist of workers only. They also demanded the handover of the administration of the economy to an organ elected by the All-Russia Trade Union Congress, but in contrast to the Workers' Opposition, they wanted the organ confirmed by the All-Russia Central Executive Committee as well. At the Tenth Congress, Ignatov was the official rapporteur of the Workers' Opposition on problems of Party organisation. After the Congress, the group broke up. p. 49

[18] The reference is to the merger of the anti-Party *Vperyod* group (which consisted of otzovists, ultimatumists, and god-builders) with Menshevik liquidators and Trotskyites. They united after the Sixth (Prague) All-Russia Conference of the Russian Social-Democratic Labour Party to fight its decisions. They led a mali-

cious campaign against the Bolsheviks in an effort to split the workers' revolutionary movement and weaken the proletarian Party. They formed a bloc demanding the "transformation" of the Party, which, in fact, implied its liquidation. The bloc, which had no principles to hold it together, was unstable and soon fell apart.   p. 51

19 The reference is to the trade union discussion at an enlarged session of the Moscow Party Committee together with delegates from Party organisations of Moscow city districts and uyezds on January 17, 1921.

The session debated all the draft theses put forward by various groups during the discussion. In the preliminary voting, Lenin's theses got 76 votes; Trotsky's, 27; Bukharin's, 5; Shlyapnikov's, 4; Sapronov's, 11; Ignatov's, 25; Nogin's, none, and Ryazanov's, none. In the re-vote on the two main platforms, 84 votes were cast for Lenin's theses, and 27, for Trotsky's.

On January 18, the Moscow Party Committee adopted an appeal "To All Party Organisations" asking all Party members to give unanimous support to Lenin's platform.   p. 51

20 The Congress was held in Moscow's Trade Union House from January 25 to February 2, 1921. It was attended by 341 delegates, of whom 295 had voice and vote, and 46, voice only. They represented more than 332,000 members of the Miners' Trade Union. Lenin and Kalinin were Honorary Chairmen.

The items on its agenda were: report of the Miners' Trade Union Central Committee; reports of the Mining Council and its departments; fuel supply problems; tasks of the trade union; organisation of production; wage rates; organisation; cultural and educational work; labour safety measures; international ties; concessions, and election of a new Trade Union Central Committee. The Congress decided to issue an appeal for unity to the organised workers of all countries.

Prior to the Congress, on January 22-24, the R.C.P.(B.) group had four meetings to discuss the trade unions' role and tasks, which were addressed by Lenin, Trotsky and Shlyapnikov. The absolute majority of the group supported Lenin's platform, which won 137 votes; Shlyapnikov's received 61, and Trotsky's, 8.

The Congress helped to solve the fuel crisis and work out production programmes for the mining industry.   p. 54

21 The reference is to the resolution of the Second Congress of the Communist International, "On the Role of the Communist Party in the Proletarian Revolution". See *Vtoroi kongress Kominterna* (Second Congress of the Communist International, Moscow, 1934, pp. 640-46).   p. 62

22 The reference is to the Eighteenth Congress of the French Socialist Party in Tours, December 25-30, 1920. It was attended by

285 delegates with 4,575 mandates. The main question on the agenda was the Party's affiliation to the Communist International. The issue was a foregone conclusion because at the federation congresses held before the national Congress, an absolute majority had voted for immediate entry into the Third International on the basis of the 21 conditions. Still there was a bitter struggle at the Congress between supporters of affiliation (Paul Vaillant-Couturier, Marcel Cachin, Daniel Renoult) and its opponents (Léon Blum, Jean Longuet, Marcel Sembat and others). Clara Zetkin, who had come to the Congress in spite of the French Government's ban and police harassment, delivered a brilliant speech and conveyed greetings on behalf of the Communist International.

After a four-day debate, the delegates voted for affiliation by 3,208 mandates, or more than 70 per cent.

The majority set up the Communist Party of France, which was finally formed in May 1921. The minority, led by Léon Blum, aimed at splitting the workers' movement, and walked out of the Congress, forming their own reformist party, which retained the old name of the French Socialist Party.   p. 62

[23] The Workers' and Peasants' Inspection (Rabkrin) was set up in February 1920 on Lenin's initiative, on the basis of the reorganised People's Commissariat for State Control which had been formed in the early months of the Soviet power.

Lenin attached great importance to control and verification from top to bottom. He worked out in detail the principles of organising control in the Soviet state, kept an eye on Rabkrin's activity, criticised its shortcomings and did his best to make it more efficient. In his last articles, "How We Should Reorganise the Workers' and Peasants' Inspection" and "Better Fewer but Better", Lenin outlined a plan for reorganising Rabkrin. To merge Party and state control and to enlist more workers and peasants in its activity were the basic principles of Lenin's plan, and this he regarded as the source of the Party's and the state's inexhaustible strength. On Lenin's instructions, the Party's Twelfth Congress set up a joint organ, the Central Control Commission and the Workers' and Peasants' Inspection, to exercise Party and state control.

During Stalin's personality cult, these principles were violated, and Lenin's system of control was substituted by a bureaucratic apparatus. In 1934, Stalin secured a decision to set up two control centres—the Central Committee's Party Control Commission, and the Government's Soviet Control Commission. The People's Commissariat for State Control of the U.S.S.R. was set up in 1940; it was reorganised into the Ministry for State Control in 1946, and later, into the Commission for State Control. Pursuant to a decision of the Twenty-Second Congress, which stressed the importance of Party, state and mass control, the November 1962 Central Committee Plenary Meeting deemed it necessary to reorganise the system of control on Lenin's principles. The Party

and State Control Committee of the C.C. of the C.P.S.U. and the
Council of Ministers of the U.S.S.R. was set up under a decision
of the Central Committee of the C.P.S.U., the Presidium of the
Supreme Soviet and the Council of Ministers on November 27,
1962.   p. 68

[24] Lenin began writing the pamphlet on January 21 or 22, 1921,
in Gorki where he was taking a rest. Upon his return to Moscow
on January 22, he handed the greater part of the pamphlet to
his secretary for typing. He finished the work on January 25 and
had it sent to the printer's. Late on January 26, C.C. members who
were going to attend local discussions of the trade unions' role
and tasks were given copies of the printed pamphlet, while the
rest of the copies were ready on January 27.   p. 70

[25] *Petrogradskaya Pravda* (Petrograd Truth)—a daily published
from April 2, 1918, as the organ of the Bolshevik Central and
Petrograd Party Committees. Since January 1924, it has been
appearing as *Leningradskaya Pravda*.   p. 70

[26] V. I. Zoff's circular of May 3, 1920, was published in the *Bulleten
Mariinskogo Oblastnogo Upravlenia Vodnogo Transporta* (Bulletin of the Mariinsky Regional Water Transport Administration)
No. 5, 1920. It ran: "A great change is about to occur in the life
of water transport: primitive methods, committee treadmill, hap-
hazard work and anarchy are on the way out. Water transport
is becoming a state enterprise, headed by political commissars
with appropriate powers. Committees, trade unions and elected
delegates will no longer have the power to interfere in technical
and administrative matters."

The order was an example of administration by injunction
and bureaucratic practices, which Tsektran's Trotskyite leadership was introducing, and was evidence of their misunderstanding
of the trade unions' role in getting transport back on its feet. The
trade unions were equated with outdated army committees, and
barred by order from taking part in improving water transport
operations.   p. 79

[27] On December 24, 1920, in what used to be the Zimin theatre,
Trotsky gave a report on the trade unions' tasks in production
at a joint meeting of trade union activists and delegates to the
Eighth All-Russia Congress of Soviets, called by the Central
Committee of the Joint Union of Rail and Water Transport Work-
ers. It started the open Party discussion on the trade unions. p. 106

[28] The Conference was held in Trade Union House on February 4,
1921, and was attended by about 1,000 delegates from Moscow
and Moscow Gubernia. In view of the acute food crisis, the main
reports dealt with the food situation and the working-class attitude to the peasantry. Wage rates and the trade unions' role in
production were also discussed. A resolution adopted on the report
about the relations between the workers and the peasants stressed

the need to substitute a tax in kind for the surplus appropriation system. The Menshevik and S. R. delegates tried to use the country's difficulties to incite the delegates against the Soviet Government's economic policy and against the Communist Party but were rebuffed by the Conference. At the delegates' request, Lenin addressed the final sitting of the Conference.   p. 108

[29] The Congress was held in Moscow on February 1-6, 1921, and was attended by 287 delegates. The items on the agenda were: activity of the trade union's Central Committee; economic tasks; output norms; international trade union federation, etc. The Congress sent a message of greetings to Lenin.

Lenin addressed the ninth plenary sitting on the morning of February 6, and mentioned a conflict which had arisen at a Communist group meeting to discuss nominations for the new trade union Central Committee. The disagreements were so acute that the Party's C.C. deemed it necessary to step in.   p. 112

[30] The reference is to the newspaper *Volya Rossii* (The Will of Russia). It was the Central Organ of the Right Socialist-Revolutionaries, and was published in Prague from September 12, 1920, to October 9, 1921.   p. 115

[31] The reference is to the monarchist Kapp putsch in Germany in March 1920, organised by a reactionary military clique headed by Kapp. The Kapp government fell after a few days under pressure from the workers.   p. 117

[32] The Central Administration for the Distribution of Books under the State Publishing House was set up in December 1919 to work out a national plan for the stocktaking and distribution of literature.   p. 128

[33] F. Dobler's article "Modern Library Network" was published in *Pravda* No. 24, February 4, 1921.   p. 132

[34] Lenin wrote a rough draft of the theses on February 8, 1921, at a meeting of the Political Bureau of the Party's C.C., which dealt with the problems of the spring sowing campaign and the condition of the peasants. It was the first document defining the new economic foundation of the workers' and peasants' alliance, charting the transition from War Communism to the New Economic Policy. It was taken as a basis for the draft resolution on the substitution of a tax in kind for the surplus appropriation system, which was adopted by the Tenth Party Congress on March 15, 1921.   p. 132

[35] *Ekonomicheskaya Zhizn* (Economic Life)—a daily published from November 1918 to November 1937. It was initially the organ of the Supreme Economic Council and the economic People's Commissariats, and later, the organ of the People's Commissariat

for Finance of the U.S.S.R., the State Bank, other financial agencies and the Central Committee of the Bank Employees' Union.
p. 137

[36] *Bulleten Gosudarstvennoi Komissii po Elektrifikatsii Rossii* (Bulletin of the State Commission for the Electrification of Russia) was published by the State Publishing House of Technical Literature under the Science and Technology Department of the Supreme Economic Council in Moscow from April to August 1920. There were five issues in all.   p. 138

[37] The reference is to *Der Zukunftsstaat. Produktion und Konsum im Sozialstaat (The State of the Future. Production and Consumption in the Socialist State)*, a book by Karl Ballod, a professor of political economy, which was published in Germany in 1898. The second revised edition appeared in 1919, and a Russian translation, in Moscow, in 1920.   p. 140

[38] The quotations are from the resolution on electrification adopted by the Eighth All-Russia Congress of Soviets on December 29, 1920. The draft resolution was written by Lenin.   p. 141

[39] This and subsequent quotations are from the Party Programme adopted by the Eighth Party Congress in March 1919. See *K.P.S.S. v rezolutsiakh . . .* (The C.P.S.U. in the Resolutions and Decisions of Congresses, Conferences and C.C. Plenary Meetings, Part 1, 1954, p. 423).   p. 143

[40] *Tit Titych*—a rich tyrannical merchant in A. N. Ostrovsky's comedy, *Shouldering Another's Trouble*.   p. 145

[41] The Congress was held in Kharkov from February 25 to March 3, 1921. On its agenda were: a report by the Government of the Ukrainian Republic and reports on economic construction, electrification of the Ukraine, organisation of labour, rehabilitation of transport, food and land problems, and public education.

On February 25, the Presidium sent Lenin an invitation to attend the Congress. In reply, Lenin cabled a message of greetings, which was read out at the second sitting on February 26. Lenin was elected a member of the All-Ukraine Central Executive Committee.
p. 146

[42] The meeting was called by the Moscow Party Committee under a decision of an activists' meeting held on February 24, 1921. The plenary meeting heard a report on the food situation and Lenin's report on the international and domestic situation. It adopted a unanimous message to the workers, peasants and Red Army men of Moscow and Moscow Gubernia giving the reasons for the food crisis. It also called on them to fight the enemies, who tried to exploit these temporary food difficulties for their counter-

revolutionary aims. The message was published in *Pravda* No. 45,
on March 1, 1921.   p. 147

43 Negotiations between the governments of the R.S.F.S.R. and
the Grand National Assembly of Turkey opened in Moscow on
February 26, 1921, and ended with the signing, on March 16, of
a treaty of friendship and brotherhood between the R.S.F.S.R.
and Turkey. A treaty of friendship between Turkey and the Trans-
caucasian Soviet Republics, Armenia, Georgia and Azerbaijan,
was signed in Kars on October 13.   p. 147

44 The talks on the conclusion of a final peace treaty opened in Riga,
after the preliminary peace treaty between Poland, on the one
hand, and Soviet Russia and the Soviet Ukraine, on the other,
was signed on October 12, 1920. The talks went on for five months.
The Polish Government, instigated by France, continued its
aggressive acts against the Soviet Ukraine and Soviet Byelorussia
and hampered the peace conference in every way. Decisive
diplomatic action by the Soviet Government and the defeat of
Wrangel, who was an ally of bourgeois-landowner Poland, compelled the Polish Government to conclude peace. The final peace
treaty was signed in Riga on March 18, 1921, under which Western
Ukraine and Western Byelorussia were ceded to Poland.

The Riga Peace Treaty was abrogated by the Soviet Government on September 17, 1939, when Western Ukraine and
Western Byelorussia joined the Soviet Union in accordance with
the will of their peoples.   p. 148

45 The followers of B. V. Savinkov (1879-1925), a leader of the
counter-revolutionary revolts against the Soviet power in
1918-21.   p. 153

46 The reference is to the article *Surplus Appropriation or Tax* by
P. Sorokin and M. Rogov, published by way of discussion in *Pravda*
No. 35 and No. 43, on February 17 and 26, 1921. The discussion
in the press was started under the February 16, 1920 decision
of the C.C. Political Bureau.   p. 156

47 *The Tenth Party Congress* was held in Moscow on March 8-16,
1921. It was attended by 694 delegates with voice and vote and
296 with voice only. They represented 732,521 Party members.
The items on the agenda were: 1) Report of the Central Committee;
2) Report of the Control Commission; 3) The trade unions' economic role; 4) The Socialist Republic in a capitalist encirclement,
foreign trade, concessions, etc.; 5) Food supply, surplus-food
appropriation, tax in kind and fuel crisis; 6) Problems of Party
organisation; 7) The Party's current tasks in the nationalities
question; 8) Reorganisation of the army and the militia question;
9) The Chief Administration for Political Education and the Party's
propaganda and agitation work; 10) Report of the R.C.P.'s

representative in the Comintern, and its current tasks; 11) Report of the R.C.P.'s representatives in the International Trade Union Council; 12) Elections to the Central Committee, the Control Commission and the Auditing Commission. The Congress resolutions dealt with the key political and economic problems.

Lenin guided the entire work of the Congress: he delivered the opening and closing speeches and gave reports on the political activity of the C.C., the substitution of a tax in kind for the surplus appropriation system, the Party's unity and the anarcho-syndicalist deviation, the trade unions and the fuel crisis. He drafted the main resolutions. He gave a profound theoretical and political substantiation of the necessity of transition from War Communism to the New Economic Policy (NEP). The Congress adopted historic decisions on the substitution of a tax in kind for the surplus appropriation system, and the transition to NEP, which was designed to draw millions of peasants into socialist construction.

The Congress paid special attention to the Party's unity. Lenin exposed and sharply criticised the anti-Marxist views of the opposition groups. The resolution "On Party Unity" adopted on Lenin's motion ordered the immediate dissolution of all factions and groups which tended to weaken the Party's unity. The Congress authorised the Central Committee to apply, as an extreme measure, expulsion from the Party to C.C. members who engaged in factional activity.

The Congress also adopted Lenin's draft resolution "On the Syndicalist and Anarchist Deviation in our Party", which exposed the views of the Workers' Opposition as an expression of petty-bourgeois, anarchist vacillations. The propaganda of anarcho-syndicalist ideas was found to be incompatible with membership in the Party. With the country engaged in peaceful socialist construction, the Congress came down in favour of broader democracy within the Party.

The Congress summed up the discussion on the trade unions' role in economic development, condemned the ideas of the Trotskyites, the Workers' Opposition, the Democratic Centralism group and other opportunist trends, and approved Lenin's platform by an overwhelming majority, defining the trade unions as a school of communism, and suggesting measures to develop trade union democracy.

A commission headed by Lenin worked out the Congress's decisions on the Party's nationalities policy in the new conditions: to eliminate the actual inequality of peoples which had been oppressed in tsarist Russia, and draw them into socialist construction. The Congress condemned the anti-Party deviations on the nationalities question, great-power chauvinism and local nationalism, which were a grave danger to communism and proletarian internationalism.

On the newly elected 25-man Central Committee were Lenin, Artyom (F. A. Sergeyev), F. E. Dzerzhinsky, M. I. Kalinin, G. K. Orjonikidze, M. V. Frunze, Y. E. Rudzutak, J. V. Stalin,

Y. M. Yaroslavsky; S. M. Kirov, V. V. Kuibyshev, V. Y. Chubar were among the alternate members.

The historic decisions of the Tenth Congress charted the ways of transition from capitalism to socialism, and methods of construction of socialism in the new conditions; they stressed the importance of greater unity between the proletariat and the peasantry, and stronger Party leadership in the construction of socialism.   p. 165

⁴⁸ The Second Congress, which laid the programme, tactical and organisational foundations of the Comintern, was held from July 19 to August 7, 1920. It opened in Petrograd, but was transferred to Moscow on July 23. More than 200 delegates represented Communist Parties and workers' organisations from 37 countries.

At the first sitting, Lenin gave a report on the international situation and the main tasks of the Comintern. Later he made speeches on the Communist Party, the nationalities and colonial questions, parliamentarism and other questions. He took part in the work of most of the commissions.

The Congress adopted Lenin's 21 conditions of affiliation to the Communist International, which was of great importance for creating and strengthening the new type of workers' parties in the capitalist countries. The ideas in Lenin's classic *Left-Wing Communism, an Infantile Disorder* served as the basis of the Congress's resolutions. Lenin also took part in drafting a resolution "On the Role of the Communist Party in the Proletarian Revolution", which stressed that the Communist Party was the principal instrument in the liberation of the working class. Lenin's theses on the nationalities and colonial question and on the agrarian question were also adopted as resolutions.

The Congress stimulated the international communist movement. Lenin said that after the Congress "communism has become central to the working-class movement as a whole".   p. 167

⁴⁹ *The Ninth Congress* was held in Moscow from March 29 to April 5, 1920. It was attended by 715 delegates, the greatest number ever, who represented 611,978 Party members. Of them 553 had voice and vote, and 162, voice only. The delegates came from Central Russia, the Ukraine, the Urals, Siberia and other areas just liberated by the Red Army. Some delegates came straight from the front lines. The country was having a short respite after the defeat of Kolchak and Denikin.

Items on the agenda were: 1) Report of the Central Committee; 2) Current tasks of economic construction; 3) Trade union movement; 4) Organisational questions; 5) Tasks of the Communist International; 6) Attitude to co-operatives; 7) Transition to the militia system; 8) Election of the Central Committee; 9) Current business.

Lenin guided the work of the Congress. He made a report on the Central Committee's political activity and a summing-up speech; he spoke on economic construction and the co-operatives; he proposed a list of candidates for election to the Central Committee. He also delivered the closing speech of the Congress.

In the resolution, "The Current Tasks of Economic Construction", the Congress stated that "the main condition of the country's economic rehabilitation is the undeviating implementation of an integrated economic plan projected for the immediate historical period ahead". See *K.P.S.S. v rezolutsiakh . . .* (The C.P.S.U. in the Resolutions and Decisions of Congresses, Conferences and C.C. Plenary Meetings, Part 1, 1954, p. 478). Lenin considered its key item—electrification—to be a great programme for a period of 10 or 20 years. The Congress's directives served as the basis for GOELRO (the Plan of the State Commission for the Electrification of Russia), which was completed and adopted by the Eighth All-Russia Congress of Soviets in December 1920.

The Congress also dealt with industrial management. The resolution on this question stressed the need to develop competent, firm and vigorous administration on the basis of one-man management.

The anti-Party group of Democratic Centralism (T. V. Sapronov, N. Osinsky [V. V. Obolensky], V. M. Smirnov) came out against the Party's line in economic construction, but its proposals were condemned and rejected by the Congress.

The Congress discussed and approved the idea of labour emulation and communist *subbotniks.*

The Congress discussed the trade unions' activity in helping to fulfil the economic tasks. It defined their role, their relationship with the Party and the state, the forms and methods of the Party's leadership in the trade unions and their participation in economic construction.

At a closed session on April 4, the Congress elected 19 members and 12 alternate members of the new Central Committee.   p. 168

[50] The reference is to the Party discussion of the trade unions' role and tasks in socialist construction. Lenin analysed these problems and criticised the anti-Party groups in his articles: *The Trade Unions, the Present Situation and Trotsky's Mistakes*; *The Party Crisis*; *Once Again on the Trade Unions, the Current Situation and the Mistakes of Trotsky and Bukharin,* and also in his speeches at the Second All-Russia Congress of Miners and at the Tenth Party Congress.   p. 168

[51] The Soviet Government did its utmost to establish normal and good-neighbour relations with Poland. In 1919, it offered peace on many occasions, but received no answer from her bourgeois-landowner government, which continued in its hostile policy towards Soviet Russia.

On January 28, 1920, the Council of People's Commissars of the R.S.F.S.R. sent the Polish Government and people a message re-emphasising its recognition of Poland's independence and

sovereignty, and offering to make sizable territorial concessions
to Poland.

On February 2, 1920, the All-Russia Central Executive
Committee once again offered peace to the Polish people. Their
reactionary government was dependent on the imperialists of the
Entente and considered the Soviet concessions a sign of weakness.
It was preparing for aggression against the Soviet Republic and
the negotiations failed.   p. 171

⁵² *The 21 conditions for admission to the Comintern* were adopted
by its Second Congress on August 6, 1920. Lenin worked out 19
of the conditions, which were published before the Congress. He
submitted the 20th to the Congress commission on July 25, 1920,
and it was adopted. The 21st condition ran: "Members of the Party
who reject the obligations and theses of the Communist International in principle should be expelled from the Party. This also
applies to delegates of extraordinary Party congresses."   p. 180

⁵³ An international organisation set up at the Paris Peace
Conference of victor powers in 1919. The League's working organs
were its Assembly, Council and Permanent Secretariat headed by
a secretary-general. Its Covenant, a part of the Peace Treaty of
Versailles, was signed by 44 states. It was so couched as to create
the impression that the League served the purposes of peace and
security, worked for a reduction of armaments, and opposed
aggression. Actually, however, it pandered to the aggressors, and
encouraged the arms drive and preparations for the Second
World War.

From 1920 to 1934, the League's activity was hostile to the
Soviet state and in 1920 and 1921 the League was the organisational centre of armed intervention against it.

On September 15, 1934, on the initiative of French diplomats,
34 member-states sent the Soviet Union an invitation to join the
League. In joining, the U.S.S.R. tried to create a peace front,
but the reactionary circles of the Western powers resisted its
efforts. When the war broke out, the League actually ceased to
operate, although it was formally dissolved in April 1946, under
a special Assembly decision.   p. 180

⁵⁴ The trade agreement between Britain and Soviet Russia was
signed on March 16, 1921.   p. 181

⁵⁵ The counter-revolutionary mutiny in Kronstadt which began on
February 28, 1921, was organised by the S.R.s, Mensheviks and
whiteguards. It involved newly recruited sailors, most of whom
came from the countryside and were politically ignorant and
discontented with the surplus appropriation system. The mutiny
was sparked off by the economic hardships and facilitated by the
fact that the Kronstadt Bolshevik organisation was weakened.

The counter-revolutionary bourgeoisie did not dare come out
against the Soviet power openly and used a new tactic. In an

attempt to deceive the people the leaders of the mutiny put forward the slogan "Soviets without the Bolsheviks", hoping to drive out the Bolsheviks from the Soviets and re-establish capitalist rule in Russia.

On March 2, the mutineers arrested the fleet command and got in touch with foreign imperialists who promised them military and financial aid. The events in Kronstadt were a threat to Petrograd.

Red Army units under M. N. Tukhachevsky and over 300 delegates of the Tenth Party Congress who had military experience, led by K. Y. Voroshilov, were sent to storm Kronstadt. On March 18, the revolt was crushed.   p. 183

[56] On June 8, 1918, Samara was occupied by the mutinous Czechoslovak corps which set up a whiteguard-S.R.-Menshevik government, the so-called Komuch (A Committee of Members of the Constituent Assembly). By August 1918, Komuch had, with the aid of Czechoslovak units, occupied some gubernias on the Volga and in the Urals area, but that autumn it was defeated by the Red Army and ceased to exist.   p. 185

[57] The substitution of a tax in kind for the surplus appropriation system was discussed on February 8, 1921, at the C.C. Political Bureau, when N. Osinsky gave a report on "The Sowing Campaign and the Condition of the Peasants". A special commission was set up to work out proposals for improving the peasants' condition. For this commission Lenin wrote the *Rough Draft of Theses Concerning the Peasants* and defined the main principles on which the tax in kind was to be substituted for surplus appropriation.

Under a Political Bureau decision of February 16, a discussion on the question was started in *Pravda*, the first articles appearing on February 17 and 26.

On February 24, a C.C. Plenary Meeting approved a draft resolution on this question, which was then edited by a new commission. On March 3, Lenin tabled three amendments to it. On March 7, the C.C. Plenary Meeting discussed the draft once again and referred it for final editing to a commission headed by Lenin. It was adopted by the Tenth Congress on March 15, 1921.   p. 187

[58] The Central Committee's circular letter, "To All Party Organisations and Party Members", published in *Izvestia of the C.C., R.C.P.(B.)* on September 4, 1920, exposed the causes of the bureaucratic practices and other shortcomings in the Party, and outlined changes in Party work to develop inner-Party democracy. The measures were approved in a resolution, "The Current Tasks of Party Organisation", of the Ninth All-Russia Party Conference. See *K.P.S.S v rezolutsiyakh...* (The C.P.S.U. in the Resolutions and Decisions of Congresses, Conferences and C.C. Plenary Meetings, Part 1, 1954, p. 512). On December 28, the Eighth All-Russia Congress of Soviets discussed the report, "Improvement

of the Work of Central and Local Soviet Bodies and the Struggle
Against the Evils of Bureaucracy ".   p. 190

[59] *A Moscow Gubernia Conference of the R.C.P.(B.)* took place in
the Kremlin from November 20 to 22, 1920. It was attended by
289 delegates with voice and vote, and 89, with voice only. On
its agenda were reports on the activity of the Moscow Party Committee, the international and domestic situation and the Party's
tasks, the state of the country's economy, and production
propaganda.

The atmosphere at the Conference was very tense, because the
Bolsheviks had to fight against the anti-Party groups of Democratic Centralism, the Workers' Opposition and the Ignatovites,
who made demagogic attacks on the Party's policy. The Workers' Opposition tried to get as many of their supporters on the
Moscow Committee as possible and called a special meeting of
worker delegates in the Mitrofanyevsky Hall of the Great
Kremlin Palace, while the other delegates had a meeting in the
Sverdlovsky Hall.

At the afternoon sitting on November 21, Lenin spoke on the
international and domestic situation and the Party's tasks, and
later, on the elections to the Moscow Committee.

Led by Lenin, the Conference beat back the anti-Party attacks.
                                                                       p. 195

[60] *The Ninth All-Russia Conference of the R.C.P.(B.)* was held in
Moscow from September 22 to 25, 1920. Its 241 delegates (116
with voice and vote, and 125, with voice only) represented 700,000
Party members. On its agenda were: 1) Report by a representative
of the Polish Communists; 2) Political report of the C.C.; 3) Organisational report of the C.C.; 4) The current tasks of Party
organisation; 5) Report of a commission on the study of the history
of the Party; 6) Report on the Second Congress of the Comintern.

At the first sitting Lenin gave the political report of the
Central Committee, dealing mainly with peace negotiations with
Poland and preparations for defeating Wrangel. The Conference
adopted a unanimous resolution on the terms of a peace treaty
with Poland.

Having discussed the current tasks of Party organisation,
the Conference rejected the views of the Democratic Centralism
group, which tried to discredit the one-man management system
in industry, and to oppose Party discipline and the Party's
leading role in the Soviets and trade unions.

A resolution, "The Current Tasks of Party Organisation",
motioned by Lenin, outlined some measures for strengthening
the Party and its leading role in the Soviet state, and developing
inner-Party democracy, and also measures against the excesses
of bureaucracy in Soviet administrative bodies and economic
agencies. The Conference deemed it necessary to set up a Control
Commission alongside the Central Committee, and special Party
commissions under gubernia committees, to combat various abuses
and to inquire into complaints filed by Communists.   p. 195

[61] *The Second Congress of Miners* was held in Moscow's Trade Union House from January 25 to February 2, 1921. Its 295 delegates with voice and vote, and 46 with voice only, represented over 332,000 members of the Miners' Trade Union. Lenin and Kalinin were elected Honorary Chairmen.

The Congress heard and discussed a report of the Miners' Trade Union Central Committee and reports of the Mining Council and its chief administrations; discussed fuel supply, organisation of production and other problems.

From January 22 to 24, the R.C.P.(B.) group had four meetings to discuss the trade unions' role and tasks. Lenin gave a report on January 23 and the absolute majority of the group voted for his platform.

The Congress helped to mobilise the people to combat the fuel crisis and to work out production programmes for the mining industry.

Lenin is quoting a speech by a Siberian delegate from Kollontai's pamphlet, *The Workers' Opposition* (Moscow, 1921). The text quoted by Kollontai is not in the report of the Siberian delegate as it is given in the Minutes of the Second Congress of Miners.   p. 198

[62] The reference is to the speeches of Angel Pestana, of the Spanish National Confederation of Labour, and of Jack Tanner, of the British Shop Stewards Committee, at the sitting of the Second Congress of the Comintern of July 23, 1920.   p. 199

[63] The reference is to the Kharkov non-Party City Conference on March 5-6, 1921, on the food problem. It was attended by about 2,000 delegates. Left Socialist-Revolutionaries and Mensheviks sharply criticised the activity of economic and food supply bodies, but the Conference did not support their resolution. On the report of the Chairman of the Kharkov Gubernia Executive Committee it adopted a resolution mapping out concrete measures to improve the workers' food supplies.   p. 204

[64] The reference is to the anti-Soviet documents of the Kronstadt mutineers: a resolution of a general meeting of the battleships' 1st and 2nd brigades on March 1, and the provisional committee's appeal, "To the Population of the Fortress and the Town of Kronstadt", issued on March 2, 1921.   p. 204

[65] The Conference was held in Moscow from November 2 to 6, 1920, and was attended by 202 delegates with voice and vote, and 59, with voice only. The tasks of peaceful socialist construction demanded a reorganisation of trade union activity on the basis of greater democratisation, and this was opposed by Trotsky. At the Communist group meeting on November 3, he demanded the immediate "governmentalisation" of the trade unions, and the introduction of military methods of command and administration. His speech started the Party discussion on the trade unions, but his demands were rejected by the Communist delegates.

Y. E. Rudzutak gave a report on the trade unions' tasks in industry. The Conference adopted his theses, which were based on Lenin's ideas that it was necessary to enhance the role of the trade unions in industry, develop democratic principles in their work, and strengthen the Party's leadership in the trade union movement. These ideas were later developed in the resolution, "The Role and Tasks of the Trade Unions", adopted by the Tenth Party Congress. See *K.P.S.S. v rezolutsiakh* ... (The C.P.S.U. in the Resolutions and Decisions of Congresses, Conferences and C.C. Plenary Meetings, Part 1, 1954, pp. 534-49).   p. 210

[66] The reference is to Trotsky's speech at a joint meeting of Communist delegates to the Eighth Congress of Soviets and Communist members of the All-Russia Central Council of Trade Unions and the Moscow City Council of Trade Unions on December 30, 1920.   p. 211

[67] The resolution on railway and water transport and its further development was adopted by the Eighth All-Russia Congress of Soviets on December 29, 1920.   p. 211

[68] The *"Platform of Ten"* ("Draft Decision of the Tenth Congress of the R.C.P.(B.) on the Role and Tasks of the Trade Unions") was worked out during the trade union discussion in November 1920 and signed by V. I. Lenin, F. A. Sergeyev (Artyom), G. Y. Zinoviev, M. I. Kalinin, L. B. Kamenev, S. A. Lozovsky, J. V. Stalin, M. P. Tomsky, Y. E. Rudzutak and G. I. Petrovsky. The Tenth Congress's resolution on the role and tasks of the trade unions was based on the "Platform of 10", which was supported by the majority of Party members. See *K.P.S.S. v rezolutsiakh* ... (The C.P.S.U. in the Resolutions and Decisions of Congresses, Conferences and C.C. Plenary Meetings, Part 1, 1954, pp. 534-49).   p. 212

[69] See Engels, *The Origin of the Family, Private Property and the State* (Marx and Engels, *Selected Works*, Vol. II, Moscow, 1962, p. 322).   p. 212

[70] See *K.P.S.S. v rezolutsiakh* ... (The C.P.S.U. in the Resolutions and Decisions of Congresses, Conferences and C.C. Plenary Meetings, Part 1, 1954, p. 422).   p. 213

[71] Lenin's draft resolution on the co-operatives was adopted at the fourteenth sitting of the Tenth Party Congress, on March 15, 1921. See *K.P.S.S. v rezolutsiakh* ... (The C.P.S.U. in the Resolutions and Decisions of Congresses, Conferences and C.C. Plenary Meetings, Part 1, 1954, p. 564).   p. 221

[72] The Tenth Congress of the R.C.P.(B.) adopted a resolution "On the Substitution of a Tax in Kind for the Surplus Appropriation System". See *K.P.S.S. v rezolutsiakh* ... (The C.P.S.U. in the

Resolutions and Decisions of Congresses, Conferences and C.C.
Plenary Meetings, Part 1, 1954, pp. 563-64).   p. 222

[73] Clare Sheridan, an English sculptor, who visited Soviet Russia
in 1920.   p. 222

[74] *The Fifth All-Ukraine Party Conference* was held in Kharkov
in November 1920. Out of 316 delegates, only 23, or 7 per cent,
voted for the Workers' Opposition platform.   p. 241

[75] *Diskussionny Listok* (Discussion Bulletin)—a non-periodical
publication of the Party Central Committee, issued under a decision of the Ninth All-Russia Conference of the R.C.P.(B.) held
in September 1920. See *K.P.S.S. v rezolutsiakh* ... (The C.P.S.U.
in the Resolutions and Decisions of Congresses, Conferences and
C.C. Plenary Meetings, Part 1, 1954, p. 509).
    Two issues—in January and in February 1921—came out
before the Tenth Congress, and it was subsequently issued during
discussions and before Party congresses.   p. 243

[76] The resolution "On the Syndicalist and Anarchist Deviation in
Our Party". See *K.P.S.S. v rezolutsiakh* ... (The C.P.S.U. in the
Resolutions and Decisions of Congresses, Conferences and C.C.
Plenary Meetings, Part 1, 1954, pp. 530-33).   p. 243

[77] Under a decision of the Tenth Congress, Point 7 of the resolution, "On Party Unity", was not published at the time. The
Thirteenth Party Conference in January 1924 condemned the
factional activity of Trotsky and his supporters and decided to
make public Point 7. See *K.P.S.S. v rezolutsiakh* ... (The
C.P.S.U. in the Resolutions and Decisions of Congresses, Conferences and C.C. Plenary Meetings, Part 1, 1954, p. 785, item 14).
It appeared in the *Bulletin* of the Thirteenth Party Conference.
                                                              p. 244

[78] Lenin gave a report on Party unity and the anarcho-syndicalist
deviation at the final, sixteenth, sitting of the Congress on March
16, 1921. The Workers' Opposition and the Democratic Centralism groups came out against Lenin's draft resolutions on these
questions. But after Lenin's summing-up speech, his resolutions
were carried by an overwhelming majority.   p. 249

[79] See Marx, *Critique of the Gotha Programme*; Marx's letter to
J. Weydemeyer of March 5, 1852; and Engels, *Anti-Dühring*;
The Origin of the Family, Private Property and the State.   p. 250

[80] An anarchist "Leftist" group broke away from the German Communist Party and in April 1920 formed the so-called Communist
Workers' Party of Germany. The "Leftists" held petty-bourgeois,
anarcho-syndicalist views. Their representatives to the Second
Congress of the Comintern, Otto Rühle and A. Merges, failed to

win any support, and walked out. The party had no support within the working class and later degenerated into an insignificant sectarian group. p. 252

[81] Its resolution on the agrarian question adopted on August 4, 1920. See *Vtoroi kongress* ... (The Second Congress of the Communist International, July-August 1920, Moscow, 1934, pp. 522-31). p. 253

[82] The reference is to A. Z. Kamensky's speech. p. 258

[83] On behalf of the Workers' Opposition, S. P. Medvedyev motioned a resolution to counter Lenin's draft resolution "On Party Unity". The former was rejected by a majority of the Tenth Party Congress. p. 260

[84] The resolution was adopted, with some slight changes, by the Tenth Party Congress. See *K.P.S.S. v rezolutsiakh* ... (The C.P.S.U. in the Resolutions and Decisions of Congresses, Conferences and C.C. Plenary Meetings, Part 1, 1954, p. 533). p. 260

[85] D. B. Ryazanov motioned an amendment to Lenin's draft resolution "On Party Unity". It said: "While condemning all factional activity, the Congress vigorously opposes any election to the Congress by platform." *Desyaty syezd* ... (The Tenth Congress of the R.C.P.[B.], March 1921, Moscow, 1963, p. 539). On Lenin's motion, the amendment was rejected by the Congress. p. 261

[86] The draft instructions of the Presidium of the Tenth Congress to the delegates going to the localities are at the Central Party Archives of the Institute of Marxism-Leninism under the C.P.S.U. Central Committee. p. 267

[87] *Le Matin*—a French bourgeois daily, published in Paris from 1884. Its last issue appeared in August 1944. p. 268

[88] The Congress was held, under a decision of the Central Committee, in Moscow from March 22 to 31, 1921. Most of its 1,079 delegates were Communists. The items on the agenda were: report of Tsektran; report of the People's Commissar for Communications; report of the Central Board of the River Transport Workers section; wage rates; transport workers' food supplies, and international confederation of transport workers.

Lenin was elected Honorary Chairman of the Congress. On the eve of the Congress, on March 25, 1921, Lenin had a talk with V. V. Fomin, Deputy Commissar for Communications, about the work of the Congress and the composition of the next Tsektran. Lenin's speech at the March 27 afternoon sitting was published as a pamphlet in 1921.

The Congress drove out the Trotskyites from the Tsektran

leadership, and called on the transport workers to take an active part in the rehabilitation of the national economy.   p. 272

[89] Lenin's reply to a letter from the Trade Union Committee of the First State Motor Works informing him about the production of motors and inviting him to attend a ceremony on April 7, 1921.
Lenin sent his congratulations. Wishing his message to be cabled to the workers at the right time, he wrote: "To be sent at 12 o'clock."   p. 285

[90] The meeting was called by the Moscow Party Committee to explain the decisions of the Tenth Party Congress. It took place at Trade Union House, and was also attended by the Moscow Bolsheviks who had taken part in liquidating the Kronstadt counter-revolutionary mutiny, and the volost activists working among Moscow Gubernia peasant women. The report on the tax in kind was given by Lenin.   p. 286

[91] *The Poor Peasants' Committees* were set up under the June 11, 1918 decree of the All-Russia Central Executive Committee, "On the Organisation and Supply of Poor Peasants". They were to take stock of the food stored on peasant farms; to uncover surplus food on kulak farms, and to help the Soviet food supply bodies in requisitioning such surpluses and distributing them among the poor peasants. They were also to distribute farming machines, manufactured goods, etc. The committees actually became organs of the proletarian dictatorship in the villages. Their activity embraced all spheres of work and signified the further development of the socialist revolution in the countryside. At the end of 1918, after they had fulfilled their tasks, the committees were merged with volost and village Soviets.
In the Ukraine, they existed from 1920 to 1933, uniting land-starved and landless peasants.   p. 295

[92] *The Peace Treaty of Brest-Litovsk* between Soviet Russia and the powers of the Quadruple Alliance (Germany, Austria-Hungary, Bulgaria and Turkey) was signed in Brest-Litovsk on March 3, 1918, and ratified by the Extraordinary Fourth All-Russia Congress of Soviets on March 15. The terms of the treaty were extremely onerous for Soviet Russia: Germany and Austria-Hungary secured almost complete control over Poland, nearly the whole of the Baltic area, and a part of Byelorussia; the Ukraine seceded from Soviet Russia and became a German dependency; the cities of Kars, Batum and Ardagan were ceded to Turkey. In August 1918, Germany made Soviet Russia sign a supplementary treaty and a financial agreement whose terms were even more onerous.
The Brest Treaty was signed as a result of a great effort on Lenin's part, who had to fight Trotsky and the anti-Party "Left Communist" group. His wise and flexible tactics in extremely complicated conditions yielded the only correct policy: the Brest peace was a reasonable political compromise, which gave

the Soviet state a respite and an opportunity to demobilise the old
disintegrating army and to create a new one—the Red Army. It
allowed the country to get on with socialist construction and to
build up resources for the coming struggle against internal counter-revolution and foreign intervention. This policy generated
peaceful sentiments and promoted the growth of the revolutionary mood in the armies and the population of all the belligerent
countries. After the November 1918 revolution in Germany overthrew the monarchy, the Brest Treaty was annulled by the All-
Russia Central Executive Committee on November 13.   p. 295

[93] The conference was held in Moscow on April 5-7, 1921, as a
preliminary to the All-Russia Congress of Women of the East. It
was attended by 45 Communist delegates from Turkestan, Azerbaijan, Bashkiria, the Crimea, the Caucasus, Tataria, Siberia
and some gubernias with a Turkic and mountaineer population.
    It discussed the economic and juridical status of women in
the East, their organisation, and agitation and propaganda
among them.
    The delegates sent Lenin an invitation to attend the con-
ference, and in reply received the telegram in question. They sent
him another message of greetings at the close of the conference.
                                                      p. 299

[94] The meeting was held on April 11, 1921, to discuss the concessions
question, because some leading trade unionists were hesitant,
while A. G. Shlyapnikov and D. B. Ryazanov carried on demagogic propaganda against the idea of concessions.
    Lenin gave a report on the issue, argued against Shlyapnikov's
and Ryazanov's statements in the debate and made notes of all
the arguments, which he used in his summing-up speech. He
defined the essence of the concessions policy and its importance
for the Soviet state.   p. 300

[95] The reference is to the resolution of the Tenth Party Congress,
"The Soviet Republic in Capitalist Encirclement". See *K.P.S.S.
v rezolutsiakh* ... (The C.P.S.U. in the Resolutions and Decisions
of Congresses, Conferences and C.C. Plenary Meetings, Part 1,
1954, pp. 566-67).   p. 300

[96] On February 1, 1921, the Council of People's Commissars adopted
a decree on oil concessions in Baku and Grozny, which made it
necessary to work out the basic principles of concessions agreements. A. I. Rykov, Chairman of the Supreme Economic Council,
was assigned to draft the project. As the work dragged out, Lenin
studied the relevant material and in late March came out with
a project, "The Basic Principles of Concessions Agreements".
He made some additions and corrections (the document is at the
Central Party Archives of the Institute of Marxism-Leninism
under the C.C., C.P.S.U.) in the original (see *Lenin Miscellany
XX*, p. 148), and his draft project was adopted as the basis of the
March 29 resolution of the Council of People's Commissars. p. 302

[97] In March 1921, the workers of Mansfeld, led by Communists, went on strike against an order setting up police patrols at plants and factories in Central Germany. In some places there were armed clashes with the police. The workers of Berlin, Hamburg and several other towns expressed their solidarity with the heroic strikers, but the Communist Party of Germany failed to unite the working-class forces against the bourgeoisie because of the treacherous behaviour of Paul Levi and other opportunists in the party leadership.

The miners' strike in Britain lasted from April until June 1921, in protest of the mineowners' intention to cut wages. More than a million workers participated in the strike, with all the miners taking part. The miners' federation called on the executive committees of the transport and railway unions to strike in solidarity, but their reformist leaders were secretly negotiating with the government and the mineowners for a compromise to break up the strike. The miners had to return to work after a heroic three-month struggle.   p. 307

[98] The conference (April 10-20, 1921) was attended by over 1,000 delegates from Petrograd factories and plants. It discussed the following questions: 1) The tasks of the working class and its participation in the economic construction of Soviet Russia; 2) Workers' living conditions in connection with the tasks of organising production; 3) Problems of food and workers' supply. The Mensheviks who got in as non-party workers did not succeed in disrupting the meeting because the mass of workers expressed a desire to work with the Communist Party.

The delegates sent their greetings to Lenin and invited him to the meeting. Lenin's reply was read out at the final sitting on April 20.   p. 319

[99] The documents are preliminary material for Lenin's pamphlet, *The Tax in Kind (The Significance of the New Policy and Its Conditions)*.

The first document is an initial plan of the pamphlet; on its basis, Lenin worked out a more detailed plan—Document Two— and also Documents Three and Four. The third document also includes a summary of the part of the pamphlet dealing with state capitalism; and the fourth is an outline of its final part: "Political Summary and Deductions".   p. 320

[100] The reference is to Paragraph 2 of the economic section of the Party Programme adopted by the Eighth Party Congress. See *K.P.S.S. v rezolutsiakh ...* (The C.P.S.U. in the Resolutions and Decisions of Congresses, Conferences and C.C. Plenary Meetings, Part 1, 1954, p. 421).   p. 323

[101] Figures for 1920 showing the relative population of the imperialist countries and the colonies; out of the world's 1,750

million people, 250 million, or 1/7, lived in the imperialist countries, and 1,000 million, or 4/7, in the colonies.   p. 323

[102] Lenin began to work on *The Tax in Kind* pamphlet at the end
of March 1921, just after the Tenth Party Congress, and finished
it on April 21. He attached great importance to its earliest publication and distribution, because it explained the necessity of
transition to the New Economic Policy. In early May, it was
published as a pamphlet, and was soon after carried by the magazine *Krasnaya Nov* No. 1; it later appeared in pamphlet form in
many towns, and was reprinted in part and in full in central
and local papers. In 1921, it was translated into German, English
and French.
  A special resolution of the Central Committee instructed all
regional, gubernia and uyezd Party committees to use the pamphlet
to explain the New Economic Policy to the working people. p. 329

[103] *Novaya Zhizn* (New Life)—a daily published in Petrograd from
April 18 (May 1), 1917, to July 1918 by a group of Menshevik
internationalists and the writers who contributed to the
magazine *Letopis* (Chronicle).
  Lenin said their prevailing mood was one of intellectual
scepticism, which is an expression of and a cover up for lack of
principle.
  The newspaper was hostile to the October Revolution and the
Soviet power. From June 1, 1918, it appeared simultaneously
in Moscow and Petrograd but both editions were closed down in
July 1918.
  Vperyod (Forward)—a daily published in Moscow from March
1917, first by the Moscow Menshevik organisation and then as
the organ of the Moscow and Central Region Committees of the
R.S.D.L.P. (Mensheviks), and from April 2, 1918, as the organ
of the Central Committee of the Mensheviks. L. Martov, F. I. Dan
and A. S. Martynov were among its editors. On May 10, 1918,
it was closed down by the All-Russia Extraordinary Commission
(Cheka) for counter-revolutionary activity and its editors were
committed for trial. On May 14, the paper resumed publication
under the name *Vsegda Vperyod!* (Always Forward!) and was
finally closed down in February 1919 under an All-Russia C.E.C.
decision.   p. 335

[104] See Marx, *Critique of the Gotha Programme* (Marx and Engels,
Selected Works, Vol. II, Moscow, 1962, p. 24).   p. 335

[105] See Engels, *The Peasant Question in France and Germany*
(Marx and Engels, *Selected Works*, Vol. II, Moscow, 1962, p. 438).
                                                                  p. 337

[106] A paraphrase of Pushkin's words from his poem *A Hero*, in which
he says that he prefers the stimulating falsehood to a mass of
sordid truths.   p. 349

[107] *Oblomov*—a Russian landowner from I. A. Goncharov's eponymous novel, personifying sluggishness, stagnation and inertia. p. 350

[108] The reference is to the Plan for the Electrification of Russia worked out by a State Commission which consisted of the best scientists and specialists. It was the first long-range integrated state plan for laying the material foundation of socialism through electrification. The plan was published as a pamphlet for the Eighth All-Russia Congress of Soviets and was approved by it.
p. 350

[109] *The Eighth Party Congress*, held in Moscow from March 18 to 23, 1919, was attended by 301 delegates with voice and vote, and 102, with voice only. They represented 313,766 Party members.

The items on the agenda were: 1) Report of the Central Committee; 2) Programme of the R.C.P.(B.); 3) Formation of the Communist International; 4) The military situation and military policy; 5) Work in the countryside; 6) Organisational questions; 7) Election to the Central Committee.

Lenin delivered the opening and closing speeches at the Congress, gave the report of the Central Committee, and the reports on the Party Programme, work in the countryside, and military policy.

The key problem before the Congress was the new Party Programme, worked out under Lenin's guidance and with his participation. The Congress approved Lenin's draft Programme, and rejected Bukharin's anti-Bolshevik proposals.

The Congress also supported Lenin's programme on the nationalities question and rejected Pyatakov's and Bukharin's proposals to exclude from the Programme the paragraph on the right of nations to self-determination.

After Lenin's summing-up speech on the Party Programme, the Congress decided to "adopt the draft Programme as a whole" and refer it to a programme commission for final editing. The latter asked Lenin to write "The draft Third Paragraph of the Political Section of the Programme (For the Programme Commission of the Eighth Party Congress)", which it later adopted. On March 22, the Congress approved the final text of the Programme.

Another key problem was the attitude to the middle peasants. In his speeches, specifically in his report on work in the countryside, Lenin substantiated the Party's new policy: transition from the policy of neutralisation to solid alliance between the working class and the middle peasantry, based on support from the poor peasants and struggle against the kulaks, with the proletariat retaining its leadership of the alliance. Lenin first put forward the slogan in late November 1918. The Congress adopted Lenin's "Resolution on the Attitude Towards the Middle Peasantry".

While discussing the military situation, the Party's military policy and Red Army organisation, the so-called Military Opposition came out against the Central Committee's theses (the Opposition included former "Left Communists"—V. M. Smirnov,

G. I. Safarov, and G. L. Pyatakov—and some independents). The Military Opposition favoured retention of some guerrilla methods, and opposed strict discipline in the army and enlistment of the services of old military specialists. At a closed plenary session on March 21, Lenin spoke in defence of the C.C. theses, and was supported by most of the speakers, who denounced the Military Opposition. The mistakes and shortcomings of the Revolutionary Military Council of the Republic and its Chairman, Trotsky, were exposed and severely criticised in the military section and at plenary sessions.

The C.C. theses were assumed as a basis by a majority of 174 against 95, and a co-ordination commission worked out a resolution on the military question based on Lenin's directives, which was adopted by the Congress (with only one abstention).

Lenin's ideas on the military question were incorporated in the Party Programme and served as guidance in military organisation.

The resolution on the organisational question denounced the Sapronov-Osinsky opportunist group, which denied the Party's leadership within the system of the dictatorship of the proletariat.

The decision on Party organisation stressed the need to raise the standards for admission of non-worker and non-peasant elements into the Party, to maintain its social composition. It was decided to carry out a general registration of all Party members by May 1, 1919. The Congress rejected the federal principle of Party organisation and approved the principle of an integrated centralised Communist Party working under the guidance of a single Central Committee.

The newly elected Central Committee was headed by Lenin. The Congress welcomed the establishment of the Third (Communist) International and adopted its platform. p. 351

[110] An international association of Centrist parties and groups (temporarily made to leave the Second International by revolutionary-minded workers' masses) called the "Two-and-a-Half International". It was set up in Vienna in 1921 and broke up in 1923, when it rejoined the Second International. p. 356

[111] The Menshevik émigré journal, *Sotsialistichesky Vestnik* (Socialist Herald), was founded by L. Martov. It was published in Berlin from 1921, and later in Paris. It is now published in the United States. p. 359

[112] Sixteen of Lenin's speeches were recorded by the Central Periodicals Administration from 1919 to 1921. After the only record factory in Russia was restored, Lenin showed great interest in propaganda through records and in many ways helped to organise it. His first speeches were recorded in a specially equipped room at the Kremlin and the last, at the Central Periodicals Administration. Recording time was three minutes, and Lenin was always pleased when he managed to stay within limits. Sales ran to tens of thousands of records with special popularity enjoyed by his

speeches, "On the Middle Peasants", "What is the Soviet Power?"
and "On the Tax in Kind". The speeches published in this volume
were recorded on April 25, 1921.   p. 366

[113] Under a resolution of the Tenth Party Congress (March 21, 1921)
the All-Russia Central Executive Committee issued a decision
(March 23) on the substitution of a tax in kind for the surplus
appropriation system. In pursuance of that decision, the Council
of People's Commissars approved on March 28 and published on
March 29 two decrees: "The Amount of the Tax in Kind for
1921-22" and "On Free Exchange, Purchase and Sale of Farm
Produce in Gubernias Fulfilling Appropriations". On April 21
and later, the Council of People's Commissars adopted decisions
on the tax rate for grain, potatoes, oil seeds and other farm
produce.   p. 366

[114] Lenin worked on the draft Instructions at the same time as he
was preparing a draft decision of the C.L.D. (Council of Labour
and Defence), entitled "On Local Economic Meetings, Records
and Reports, and Guidance by the C.L.D.'s Instructions". Lenin
made a thorough study of local documents on economic meetings
and the first NEP measures. On May 20, 1921, the C.L.D. referred
the draft Instructions and the draft decision to a special commission,
which published the Instructions as a pamphlet because it was
important to discuss them immediately. Members of the Presidium of the State Planning Commission and officials of departments and local bodies were invited to help edit the two
drafts. On Lenin's proposal they were widely discussed by
the working people. On May 24, they were discussed by the
Fourth Congress of Economic Councils. On May 25, the Fourth
All-Russia Congress of Trade Unions instructed the newly
elected All-Russia Central Council of Trade Unions to consider
the drafts and to insert the necessary amendments and addenda.
The Tenth All-Russia Conference of the R.C.P.(B.) approved the
draft Instructions, authorising the All-Russia C.E.C. Communist
group to take steps to get them adopted as law. On May 30, both
drafts were discussed at the Third Session of the All-Russia
Central Executive Committee, where Lenin delivered a speech.
The session adopted them as a basis and referred them to a
commission. Lenin introduced a number of editorial amendments
to the C.E.C. decision, "On Local Economic Meetings", just
before its final approval. On June 30, both drafts were adopted
by the Presidium of the C.E.C. Because the Instructions defined
the tasks of recording and reporting for all Commissariats and
not only the economic ones, they were called "Instructions of
the Council of People's Commissars and the Council of Labour
and Defence".
    Lenin believed it was highly important to give the working
people a thorough explanation of these Instructions and put them
into practice as soon as possible.   p. 375

[115] An extraordinary conference, held in Moscow from May 26 to 28, 1921, was attended by 239 delegates from Party and Soviet organisations. On its agenda were the following questions: 1) Economic policy: a) tax in kind; b) co-operatives; c) financial reform; d) small industry; 2) The current role of the Socialist-Revolutionaries and Mensheviks; 3) The Third Congress of the Comintern; 4) Information on the Fourth Trade Union Congress; 5) Organisational question.

The Conference centred on the question of the New Economic Policy (NEP) because it was not yet clear enough to the people in the localities.

Lenin guided the work of the Conference: he delivered the opening speech, spoke on the agenda, was elected to the Presidium, gave a report and a summing-up speech on the tax in kind, and the closing speech of the Conference. Substantiating the New Economic Policy, he exposed the false rumours about NEP and distortions of this policy, and stressed that it was a policy whose aim was the construction of a socialist society; that it was to be carried out "in earnest and for a long time". The Conference adopted Lenin's draft resolution, "On Economic Policy", which confirmed NEP's basic principles and gave concrete instructions for their implementation. It said: "The basic political task of the moment is for all Party and Soviet workers to master and implement to the letter the New Economic Policy. See *K.P.S.S. v rezolutsiakh* ... (The C.P.S.U. in the Resolutions and Decisions of Congresses, Conferences and C.C. Plenary Meetings, Part 1, 1954, p. 574).

After the Conference had heard information on the work of the Fourth Trade Union Congress, Lenin sharply criticised the factional activity of the trade union leadership, first and foremost M. P. Tomsky, Chairman of the All-Russia Central Council of Trade Unions.

Another question of great importance was the organisational work of the Party, the report on which was given by V. M. Molotov. The Conference adopted a "Plan for the Work of the Central Committee of the R.C.P.(B.)" which demanded the training and promotion of new Party workers and activisation of all Party and Soviet work. Lenin stressed that Party organisations had to establish closer ties with the non-Party masses and that it was necessary to collect and study the experience of local Party organisations. His remarks were taken into account in the resolution.

Representatives of the Communist Parties of Germany and the United States conveyed greetings to the Conference, and, on the motion of the Presidium, the Conference cabled a message of greetings to workers detained in prison.   p. 399

[116] The reference is to the Fourth All-Russia Congress of Trade Unions, held in Moscow from May 17 to 25, 1921, and the Fourth All-Russia Congress of Economic Councils, held there from May 18 to 24, 1921.

The Fourth Congress of Trade Unions had the following items on its agenda: report of the All-Russia Central Council of Trade

Unions; report of the Presidium of the Supreme Economic Council; the role and tasks of the trade unions and economic development; organisational question; wage-rate policy and workers' supply; trade unions and co-operatives; labour protection, etc.

The Fourth Congress of Economic Councils had on its agenda: report of the Presidium of the Supreme Economic Council; economic policy of the S.E.C. in connection with the decree on the tax in kind and the co-operatives; S.E.C. organisation; report of the State Planning Commission; report on foreign trade; electrification of Russia; material resources of the Republic and organisation of supply in industry.

The most important questions were discussed at joint sittings of the two congresses with the participation of specialists and public figures.   p. 415

[117] Colonel of the gendarmerie Zubatov, Chief of the Secret Political Police, proposed the setting up of legal workers' organisations in 1901-03 to divert the workers from political struggle against the tsarist autocracy, and to switch their attention to narrow economic demands which the government, he asserted, was ready to meet. The Minister for the Interior, V. K. Plehve, approved Zubatov's activity and the first organisation, called "Workers' mutual aid in mechanical industries society", was set up in Moscow in May 1901, and later such societies made their appearance in Minsk, Odessa, Vilno, Kiev, and other towns.

The Second Congress of the R.S.D.L.P., in its resolution "On the Trade Union Struggle", defined Zubatovism as a policy of "systematic betrayal of working-class interests for the benefit of the capitalists", and in order to fight it, called on Party organisations to support and lead any strikes started by legal workers' organisations.

Revolutionary Social-Democrats made use of such organisations to draw the masses of working people into the struggle against the tsarist government, exposing the reactionary nature of Zubatov's policy. Lenin wrote in 1905: "And now the Zubatov movement is outgrowing its bounds. Initiated by the police in the interests of the police, in the interests of supporting the autocracy and demoralising the political consciousness of the workers, this movement is turning against the autocracy and is becoming an outbreak of the proletarian class struggle."

The tsarist government had to close down the Zubatov organisations in 1903 because of the mounting revolutionary movement.   p. 417

[118] *The Third Session of the All-Russia Central Executive Committee* met on May 30-31, 1921, to discuss M. I. Kalinin's report on the activity of its Presidium; the sowing campaign; agencies co-ordinating the activity of economic Commissariats and local economic bodies; substitution of a tax in kind for appropriation; Petrograd industry, and reorganisation of tribunals. It heard reports by the Tver Gubernia Executive Committee and the Siberian Revolutionary Committee.

Lenin spoke on local economic agencies at the afternoon sitting, and made notes of the debate on the question (see *Lenin Miscellany XX*, p. 91).   p. 438

[119] The Conference was held in Moscow from June 16 to 24, 1921, and was attended by 499 delegates: gubernia food commissars, members of gubernia food committee collegiums, and representatives of various food agencies and gubernia executive committees, co-operatives and trade unions.

The questions on the agenda were: 1) tax in kind; 2) commodity exchange; 3) relationship between the food agencies and co-operatives; 4) principles of the state supply, etc.

Lenin was elected an honorary member of the Presidium and spoke at the first sitting.

The Conference helped to improve the food situation in the country.   p. 441

[120] The reference is to the resolution of the Tenth All-Russia Conference of the R.C.P.(B.) "On Economic Policy". See *K.P.S.S. v rezolutsiakh* ... (The C.P.S.U. in the Resolutions and Decisions of Congresses, Conferences and C.C. Plenary Meetings, Part 1, 1954, pp. 574-76).   p. 444

[121] The Third Congress was held in Moscow from June 22 to July 12, 1921. Its 605 delegates (291 with voice and vote, and 314 with voice only) represented 103 organisations from 52 countries, namely: 48 Communist Parties, 8 Socialist Parties, 28 Youth Leagues, 4 syndicalist organisations, 2 opposition Communist Parties (the Communist Workers' Party of Germany and the Workers' Communist Party of Spain) and 13 other organisations. The 72 delegates from the Russian Communist Party of Bolsheviks were headed by Lenin.

The Congress discussed the world economic crisis and the new tasks of the Communist International; the report on the activity of the Executive Committee of the Communist International; the Communist Workers' Party of Germany; the Italian question; the tactics of the Communist International; the attitude of the Red International Council of Trade Unions to the Communist International; the struggle against the Amsterdam International; the tactics of the R.C.P.(B.); the Communist International and the Communist youth movement; the women's movement; the United Communist Party of Germany, etc.

Lenin directed preparations for and the activities of the Congress; he was elected its Honorary Chairman; he took part in drafting all the key resolutions; he gave a report on the tactics of the R.C.P.(B.); he spoke in defence of the Communist International's tactics; on the Italian question; in the commissions and at the enlarged sittings of the Executive Committee of the Comintern, and at the delegates' meetings. Before and during the Congress, Lenin met and talked with delegates about the state of affairs in the Communist Parties.

The Third Congress had a great influence on the formation and development of young Communist Parties. It paid great attention to the Comintern's organisation and tactics in the new conditions of the world communist movement. Lenin had to combat the Centrist deviation and "Leftist" dogmatism, pseudo-revolutionary "Leftist" cant and sectarianism. As a result, revolutionary Marxism prevailed over the "Leftist" danger.

In the history of the world communist movement the Third Congress is known for the following achievements: it worked out the basic tactics of the Communist Parties; it defined the task of winning the masses over to the side of the proletariat, strengthening working-class unity and implementing united front tactics. The most important aspect of its resolutions, Lenin said, was "more careful, more thorough preparation for fresh and more decisive battles, both defensive and offensive".   p. 451

122 On April 13, 1919, in Amritsar, an industrial centre in Punjab, India, British troops fired on a mass meeting of working people who were protesting against the colonialist reign of terror. About 1,000 were killed and 2,000 wounded. The massacre led to popular uprisings in Punjab and other provinces, which were ruthlessly suppressed by the British colonialists.   p. 455

123 *Posledniye Novosti* (The Latest News)—an émigré daily, the organ of the counter-revolutionary party of Constitutional-Democrats, published in Paris from April 1920 to July 1940. Its editor was P. N. Milyukov.   p. 460

124 *Kommunistichesky Trud* (Communist Labour)—a daily published by the Moscow R.C.P.(B.) Committee and the Moscow Soviet of Workers' and Peasants' Deputies from March 18, 1920. On February 7, 1922, it took the name of *Rabochaya Moskva* (Workers' Moscow); on March 1, 1939, *Moskovsky Bolshevik* (Moscow Bolshevik), and ever since February 19, 1950, has been appearing as *Moskovskaya Pravda* (Moscow Truth).   p. 461

125 *La Stampa* (Press)—an Italian bourgeois newspaper published in Turin since 1867.   p. 462

126 *Corriere della Sera* (Evening Courier)—an influential Italian bourgeois newspaper published in Milan since 1876.   p. 462

127 The conference of the reformist wing of the Italian Socialist Party, the so-called "socialist concentration" group, took place in Reggio Emilia on October 10-11, 1920. Lenin gave a detailed characteristic of it in his article, "On the Struggle Within the Italian Socialist Party" (*Collected Works*, Vol. 31, pp. 377-96).

The report on the conference mentioned by Lenin was published in *Corriere della Sera*.No. 244 and No. 245, of October 11 and 12, 1920, as well as in *Avanti!* No. 245 of October 13, 1920.   p. 462

[128] *Avanti!* (Forward!)—a daily, the Central Organ of the Italian Socialist Party, founded in Rome in December 1896. During the First World War, it took an inconsistently internationalist stand, and did not break with the reformists. In 1926, the paper was closed down by Mussolini's fascist government, but continued to appear abroad. It resumed publication in Italy in 1943. p. 462

[129] Lenin apparently refers to the conference of the "unitary" group (Serrati, Baratono and others) in Florence on November 20-21, 1920, which came out against the break with the reformists and, with this reservation, for the acceptance of the 21 conditions of affiliation to the Communist International.   p. 463

[130] In January 1919, the Ebert-Scheidemann government dismissed the Berlin police chief, Eichhorn (a Left-wing Independent) who was very popular with the workers. This sparked off a workers' protest demonstration on January 4, the day following Eichhorn's retirement, and later a general strike and an armed uprising to overthrow the Ebert-Scheidemann government. The Revolutionary Committee of Action which headed the uprising included some Independents and Karl Liebknecht and Wilhelm Pieck of the Communist Party of Germany. The Communist Party considered the uprising premature, but decided to support the revolutionary mass movement in every way. Berlin events fired the proletariat's revolutionary struggle in the Rheinland, the Ruhr, Bremen and elsewhere.

Alarmed by the scope of the movement, the Central Committee of the Independent Social-Democratic Party of Germany started negotiations with the government, who used them for preparing a counter-revolutionary offensive. On January 11, its forces, led by Noske, attacked the workers and drowned their uprising in blood. Karl Liebknecht and Rosa Luxemburg, the leaders of the German working class, were arrested and killed at the height of the counter-revolutionary reign of terror. Workers' action in other parts of the country was fiercely suppressed.   p. 463

[131] In September 1920, Italian steelworkers occupied their mills on the initiative of their trade union, which was in conflict with the association of industrialists. The movement started in Turin and Milan, then spread through Piedmont and Northern Italy across the country, from the metallurgical industry to other industries and to agriculture. In Sicily and in other areas peasants occupied the land. The scope of the movement jeopardised the capitalist regime, but the reformist leaders of the Socialist Party and the trade unions, terrified by the political character of the movement, adopted a decision to confine it to within the trade unions and prevent it from developing into a revolution. They also decided to start negotiations with the industrialists.

This was a hard blow at the Italian workers' movement and showed the leaders' inability to lead the mass forces. Fascism used the confusion within the working class to start its armed offensive in Italy. p. 465

132 The amendments were proposed by the German, Austrian and Italian delegations to the draft theses on tactics, motioned by the Russian delegation at the Third Congress of the Comintern. They were published in German in *Moskau*, the organ of the Third Congress. p. 468

133 The Open Letter (Offener Brief) of the Central Committee of the United Communist Party of Germany to the Socialist Party of Germany, Independent Social-Democratic Party of Germany, the Communist Workers' Party of Germany and all trade unions, was published in *Die Rote Fahne* (The Red Banner) on January 8, 1921. The U.C.P.G. called on all workers, trade unions and socialist organisations to unite their forces in combating reaction and the capitalists' offensive against the working people's vital rights. Their programme of joint action included demands for higher pensions for disabled war veterans; elimination of unemployment; improvement of the country's finances at the expense of the monopolies; introduction of factory and plant committee control over all stocks of food, raw materials and fuel; restarting of all closed enterprises; control over sowing, harvesting and marketing of farm produce by the Peasants' Councils together with the agricultural labourers' organisations; immediate disarming and dissolution of all bourgeois militarised organisations; establishment of workers' self-defence; amnesty of all political prisoners; immediate re-establishment of trade and diplomatic relations with Soviet Russia. Lenin said these tactics were *"quite correct"* (see *Lenin Miscellany XXXVI*, p. 221).

The Right-wing leaders of the organisations to whom the Open Letter was addressed rejected the proposal for joint action with the Communists, despite the fact that the workers came out for a united front of the proletariat. p. 470

134 The *theory of an offensive struggle* or "theory of the offensive" was proclaimed at the Unity Congress of the Communist Party of Germany and the Left-wing Independent Social-Democratic Party of Germany in December 1920. It envisaged that the party should conduct offensive tactics, regardless of whether there were any objective conditions for revolutionary activity or whether the working people supported the Communist Party. The theory found its followers among the "Leftists" in Hungary, Czechoslovakia, Italy, Austria, and France, and was one of the causes of the defeat of the March 1921 uprising in Germany. But the "Leftists" tried to justify the mistakes of the Central Committee of the U.C.P.G. The theses on the March uprising adopted by the U.C.P.G. Central Committee on April 8, 1921, reiterated that the

U.C.P.G. was always to "follow the line of revolutionary offensive" and that offensive tactics, "even when unsuccessful, were a prerequisite of future victory and the only means for a revolutionary party to win over the masses". At the Third Congress of the Comintern the followers of this theory fought to make it the basis of the Communist International's resolutions on tactics. Lenin proved this theory to be wrong and adventurous, and the Congress approved his line of patient preparation and winning over of the majority of the working class to the side of the communist movement. p. 471

[135] See Note 97 on the British miners' strike in April-June 1921. p. 476

[136] The reference is to the resolution of the Third Congress of the Communist International, "The International Situation and Our Tasks". See *Kommunistichesky Internatsional v dokumentakh. Resheniya, tezisy i vozzvaniya kongressov Kominterna i plenumov IKKI. 1919-1932* (The Communist International in Documents. Resolutions, Theses and Appeals of Congresses of the Comintern and Plenary Meetings of the Executive Committee of the Communist International. 1919-1932, Moscow, 1933, pp. 165-80). p. 478

[137] On May 26, 1921, in Vladivostok, the whiteguards, supported by the Japanese interventionists, overthrew the Maritime Regional Administration of the Far Eastern Republic and established a regime of bourgeois dictatorship and terror headed by industrialists, the Merkulov brothers. South Primorye became a springboard for continued imperialist intervention in the Far East.

The Revolutionary People's Army of the Far Eastern Republic, under V. K. Blyukher, and later I. P. Uborevich, defeated the whiteguards, liberating Khabarovsk on February 14, 1922, and Vladivostok on October 25, 1922. Japan had to withdraw her forces from the Far East. On November 14, 1922, the People's Assembly of the Far Eastern Republic set up the Far East Revolutionary Committee with plenipotentiary powers to implement the union of the Far East with Soviet Russia. On November 15, 1922, the Presidium of the All-Russia Central Executive Committee issued a decree proclaiming the Far Eastern Republic an inseparable part of the R.S.F.S.R. p. 479

[138] *The Czechoslovak Social-Democratic Party (Left) Congress* held in Prague from May 14 to 16, 1921, was the Inaugural Congress of the Communist Party of Czechoslovakia. It was attended by 569 delegates representing more than 350,000 Party members. The Congress adopted a resolution by acclamation on affiliation to the Third International. B. Smeral was the chief rapporteur at the Congress.

Lenin made a thorough study of the material of the Congress (see *Lenin Miscellany XXXVI*, pp. 288, 289, 311).

Vorwärts (Forward)—a newspaper published by the Austrian Left-wing Social-Democrats from May 1911 in Reichenberg. In

1921, it became the organ of the Czechoslovak Communist Party
(German group).   p. 488

139 The verbatim report then goes on to say (Lenin spoke in German):
"*als Glied der Weltwirtschaft*"; the French translation was:
"*comme membre de l'économie mondiale*"; and the English, "as
a member of the world's economy". The text in this volume is
taken from *Pravda*, July 9, 1921, which did not contain these
words.   p. 491

140 See Note 55 on the counter-revolutionary Kronstadt mutiny in
March 1921.   p. 495

141 The Congress, or the Third All-Russia Assembly of Tsentrosoyuz
Delegates, was held in Moscow from July 16 to 23, 1921, and
was attended by 384 delegates (250 with voice and vote, and 134
with voice only) from many parts of Russia. It discussed reports
and adopted decisions on the activity of Tsentrosoyuz; prospects
of the consumers' co-operative societies; trade and commodity
exchange of Tsentrosoyuz; workers' co-operative societies; the state
of and prospects for foreign trade and the role of co-operatives;
co-operative societies' assistance to areas hit by the crop failure,
and other questions. Lenin was elected Honorary Chairman,
and his message of greetings was read at the first plenary sitting on
July 16.   p. 499

142 The Congress took place in Moscow from July 3 to 19, 1921, and
was attended by 380 delegates from 41 countries of Europe, America and Asia, among them Russia, Britain, Italy, Spain, France,
Bulgaria, Yugoslavia, Germany, Czechoslovakia, Austria, Poland,
Finland, Korea, China and South Africa. The items on the agenda
were: 1) Report of the Provisional International Council of Trade
Unions, which was set up in July 1920; 2) The world economic
crisis and trade union tasks and tactics; 3) Trade unions and
parties. The Red International of Trade Unions and the Communist
International; 4) Trade unions, factory committees and shop
stewards; 5) Trade unions and workers' control over production;
6) Unemployment; 7) International trade and industrial unions;
8) Organisational question; 9) Women in production and trade
unions.
    It was the Inaugural Congress of the Red Trade Union Inter-
national, which existed till late 1937 and had a great influence
on the world trade union movement.
    The Congress adopted the Rules of the Red Trade Union
International, and elected its Central Council. It also adopted
resolutions on other questions.
    The Trade Union International fought for unity in the trade
union movement on the basis of the revolutionary struggle for
working-class demands; against the offensive of capital and

fascism, and the danger of an imperialist war. It worked for unity
with the working class of Soviet Russia.

Lenin's message of greetings, sent in reply to an invitation
from several delegations to attend, was read at the seventeenth
sitting on July 19.   p. 501

[143] Lenin's *Appeal to the International Proletariat* in connection
with the famine which hit almost 33 million people in the Volga
area and South Ukraine met with a broad response among the
working people of all countries. An "*Ad hoc* Foreign Committee
for Assistance to Russia" was set up on the initiative of the Comintern in August 1921. French revolutionary trade unions called
on the workers to contribute a day's earnings for the famine-
stricken population of Russia. Henri Barbusse and Anatole France
played an active part in organising assistance, and the latter
contributed to the fund the Nobel Prize he was awarded in 1921.
About one million francs were collected in France. Czechoslovakia
contributed 7.5 million korunas in cash and 2 million korunas'
worth of food; the German Communist Party collected 1.3 million
marks in cash and 1 million marks' worth of food; Dutch Communists collected 100,000 guilders; the Italians, about 1 million
liras; the Norwegians, 100,000 krones; the Austrians, 3 million
krones; the Spaniards, 50,000 marks; the Poles, 9 million marks;
the Danes, 500,000 marks, etc. By December 20, 1921, Communist
organisations had bought 312,000 poods of food and collected
1 million gold rubles. The organisations of the Amsterdam International bought 85,625 poods of food and collected 485,000 gold
rubles.   p. 502

[144] Lenin wrote the letter in connection with Myasnikov's article
"Vexed Questions", his memo to the Central Committee of the
R.C.P.(B.) and his speeches in the Petrograd and Perm Party
organisations. Myasnikov had set up an anti-Party group in the
Motovilikha District of Perm Gubernia which fought against
Party policy. A Central Committee commission investigated
his activity and proposed his expulsion from the Party for repeated breaches of discipline and organisation of an anti-Party group
contrary to the resolution "On Party Unity" of the Party's Tenth
Congress. His expulsion was approved by the Political Bureau
of the Central Committee of the R.C.P.(B.) on February 20, 1922.
                                                                     p. 504

[145] *The Communist Party of Britain* was founded at the Inaugural
Congress held from July 31 to August 1, 1920. It united the Left
wing of the British Socialist Party, the majority of the Scottish
Socialist Workers' Party, the Irish Socialists, the Communist
Unity Group of the Socialist Labour Party, the South Wales
Communist Council and a number of small socialist groups. In
January 1921, at the Unity Congress in Leeds, it was joined by
the Communist Workers' Party (consisting mostly of members
of the shop stewards movement in Scotland, headed by William

THE LIFE AND WORK

OF

V. I. LENIN

Outstanding Dates
(December 1920-August 1921)

1920

December 30   Lenin addresses a joint meeting of Communist delegates to the Eighth Congress of Soviets, Communist members of the All-Russia Central Council of Trade Unions and Communist members of the Moscow City Council of Trade Unions, and speaks on the trade unions, the present situation and Trotsky's mistakes.

December 31   The first sitting of the All-Russia Central Executive Committee, elected by the Eighth Congress of Soviets, unanimously confirms Lenin as Chairman of the Council of People's Commissars.

1921

January, not later than 22   Lenin is on vacation and lives at Gorki near Moscow, travelling to the city to attend meetings of the Central Committee of the R.C.P.(B.) and the Council of Labour and Defence.

January 4   Lenin presides at a plenary meeting of the Central Committee of the R.C.P.(B.).

January 6   Lenin has a talk with a peasant delegate from the village of Modyonovo, Bogorodsk Volost, Moscow Gubernia, about a reduction of the food levies.

January 9   Lenin gives a report at a meeting of peasants in the village of Gorki, Moscow Gubernia, on the international and domestic position of the Soviet Republic.

January 11   Lenin cables instructions to gubernia executive committees, gubernia food committees and gubernia land departments concerning the establishment of local sowing committees and the conduct of the sowing campaign.

January 12   Lenin presides at a plenary meeting of the Central Committee of the R.C.P.(B.).

January 14   Lenin takes part in drafting the decision of the Tenth Congress of the R.C.P.(B.) on the role and tasks of the trade unions.

January 19   Lenin writes the article, "The Party Crisis".

January 20   Lenin writes a letter to the factory and office workers of Proletarskaya Station on the Vladikavkaz Railway, who sent a delegation with wheat, barley and flour for the working people of Moscow. He gives them advice on how to organise their farming commune and establish correct relations with neighbouring peasants.

January 23   Lenin gives a report at a meeting of the Communist group of the Second All-Russia Congress of Miners on the role and tasks of the trade unions.

January 24   Lenin delivers the closing speech at a meeting of the Communist group of the Second All-Russia Congress of Miners about the role and tasks of the trade unions.

                Lenin meets Gorky to discuss ways of improving the living conditions of Academician Ivan Pavlov.

                Lenin signs a decision of the Council of People's Commissars on the conditions ensuring the scientific work of Academician Pavlov and his associates.

January 25   Lenin completes the pamphlet, *Once Again on the Trade Unions, the Current Situation and the Mistakes of Trotsky and Bukharin.*

January 26   Lenin presides at a plenary meeting of the Central Committee of the R.C.P.(B.), which approves a commission headed by Lenin to project the reorganisation of the People's Commissariat for Education.

January 27   Lenin receives Gorky and a delegation of the Joint Council of Scientific Institutions and Institutions of Higher Learning of Petrograd to discuss the creation of conditions for research in the Soviet Republic.

January 29-   Lenin chairs the commission to reorganise the
February 2   People's Commissariat for Education; writes the draft regulations of the Commissariat and the Central Committee's Instructions to Communists working in the Commissariat.

January 31   Lenin issues a directive to Baku leaders concerning the organisation of fisheries on the Caspian Sea.

Lenin is elected Chairman of the Grain Commission under the Council of Labour and Defence.

February 2   Lenin presides at a meeting of the Political Bureau of the Central Committee of the R.C.P.(B.), which examines the following questions: the theses for the Party's Tenth Congress on the Chief Administration for Political Education and on propaganda and agitation work; aid to the peasantry hit by the crop failure; producers' co-operatives, etc.

Lenin writes a letter to the Marx and Engels Institute, asking what has been done about the collection of letters and all the published works of Marx and Engels.

February 4   Lenin addresses an enlarged conference of Moscow metalworkers.

Lenin presides at a meeting of the Council of Labour and Defence to discuss the following questions: the progress of army demobilisation; measures to speed up the manufacture of electrical ploughing implements and motors, etc.

February 5   *Pravda* carries the Party Central Committee's Instructions, written by Lenin, to Communists working in the People's Commissariat for Education in connection with its reorganisation.

Lenin presides at a meeting of the Central Committee's Political Bureau to discuss the theses on "The Party's Immediate Tasks in the National Question" for the Party's Tenth Congress; various aspects of the sowing campaign; the work of the People's Commissariat for Nationalities, etc.

Lenin heads a commission set up for the final editing of the theses.

February 6   Lenin speaks at the Fourth All-Russia Congress of Garment Workers on the international situation and the tasks of the trade union movement.

February 7   Lenin writes the article, "The Work of the People's Commissariat for Education".

Lenin and other members of the commission edit the theses on the nationalities question for the Tenth Congress of the R.C.P (B.).

February 8   Lenin writes the "Rough Draft of Theses Concerning the Peasants".

Lenin presides at a government meeting to discuss the question of the losses caused by the foreign military intervention and blockade.

February 12   Lenin sends the members of the Political Bureau a memo and material on oil concessions and the state of the oil industry.

Lenin receives a Daghestan delegation and discusses the situation in the Daghestan Republic.

February 14   Lenin receives a peasant delegation from Tambov Gubernia and discusses the situation in the rural areas.

February 16   Lenin attends a meeting of the Moscow Committee with Party activists and gives a report on Party questions.

February 17   Lenin drafts a decision of the Council of Labour and Defence to set up a State Planning Commission and draws up a tentative list of its members.

February 19   Lenin presides at a discussion of questions for the forthcoming plenary session of the R.C.P.(B.) Central Committee at a session of the Central Committee's Political Bureau.

February 21   Lenin writes the article, "Integrated Economic Plan".

February 24-25 Lenin presides at a plenary meeting of the Party's Central Committee to discuss the following questions: the situation in Moscow; substitution of a tax in kind for the surplus appropriation system; oil concessions; fuel; operations of water transport; demobilisation of the army, etc.

February 25   Lenin visits the hostel of the All-Russia Art Studios and talks with students about art and literature.

February 26   Lenin addresses a Moscow Gubernia conference of working-class and peasant women.

Lenin receives a Turkish delegation and discusses the conclusion of a treaty with Turkey.

February 27   Lenin's message of greetings to the Fifth All-

Ukraine Congress of Soviets is carried in the
newspaper *Kommunist* (Kharkov).

February 28   Lenin presides at a meeting of the Political Bureau
of the Party's Central Committee to discuss the
fuel question, the situation in Moscow and
Petrograd, etc.

Lenin speaks at a plenary meeting of the Moscow
Soviet of Workers' and Peasants' Deputies on the
international and domestic position of the Soviet
Republic.

Lenin has a talk with peasants from Vladimir
Gubernia on the situation in the countryside and
the substitution of a tax in kind for the surplus
appropriation system.

March 1   Lenin writes a letter to the People's Commissariat
for Agriculture on recruiting non-Party peasants
with practical experience to help organise farming.

March 2   Lenin writes a letter to the Georgian Communists.

March 4   Lenin writes the article, "International Working
Women's Day".

March 7   Lenin presides at a plenary meeting of the Party's
Central Committee to discuss the draft resolution
on the substitution of a tax in kind for the
surplus appropriation system.

The Central Committee plenary meeting appoints
Lenin chairman of a commission to draft the
resolution for the Tenth Party Congress on the
switch to the tax in kind.

March 8-16   Lenin presides at the Tenth Congress of the
R.C.P.(B.).

March 8   Lenin delivers the opening speech at the Party's
Tenth Congress.

Lenin is elected to the Congress Presidium.

Lenin gives a report to the Congress on the political activity of the Party's Central Committee.

March 9   Lenin delivers the summing-up speech on the
Central Committee's political activity.

*March 12 and
13*   Lenin attends closed sittings of the Congress to
discuss the military question.

March 13 or 14	Lenin writes the Preliminary Draft Resolution of the Tenth Party Congress on Improving the Condition of Workers and Needy Peasants.
March 14	Lenin speaks at the Congress about the trade unions.
	A closed sitting of the Congress elects Lenin to the Party's Central Committee.
March 14 or 15	Lenin writes the preliminary draft resolutions of the Congress on Party unity, and the anarcho-syndicalist deviation in the Party.
March, not later than 15	Lenin writes the draft resolution of the Congress on co-operative societies.
March 15	Lenin gives a report and delivers the summing-up speech at the Congress on the introduction of the tax in kind.
March 16	Lenin gives a report and delivers the summing-up speech on Party unity and the anarcho-syndicalist deviation, and motions the draft resolutions on these questions.
	Lenin delivers a speech and motions a proposal on the fuel question.
	Lenin delivers the summing-up speech at the Tenth Party Congress.
March 17	Lenin's directive to the Revolutionary Military Council of the 11th Army on the establishment of contacts with the Revolutionary Committee of Georgia is published.
March, not later than 21	Lenin instructs the Petrograd Soviet to lift the state of siege in Petrograd and institute martial law.
March 22	Lenin has a talk with peasants from Ufa Uyezd and orders that they should each be issued a certificate testifying that he summoned them to Moscow to "discuss and give advice on an important matter relating to the peasant economy".
March 24	Lenin cables all front and army district commanders, instructing them to take urgent measures to help the land agencies in the sowing campaign.
March 27	Lenin speaks at the All-Russia Congress of Transport Workers on the external and internal position of the Soviet Republic.

End of March-   Lenin works on the plan for his pamphlet, *The*
early April   *Tax in Kind*.

April 7   Lenin sends a telephone message congratulating
                the Trade Union Committee and the workers of
                the First State Motor Works on ·their production
                of motors.

April 9   Lenin cables G.K. Orjonikidze about the steps
                taken to help Armenia and gives instructions on
                a number of measures to revive economic activity
                in the Transcaucasus.

                Lenin has a talk with a delegate from the workers
                of Ivanovo-Voznesensk on the condition of the
                textile factories in the gubernia.

                Lenin gives a report on the tax in kind at a meet-
                ing of secretaries and responsible representatives
                of R.C.P.(B.) cells of Moscow City and Moscow
                Gubernia.

April 10   Lenin's message of greetings to the conference of
                representatives of women's departments of the
                peoples of Soviet regions and republics in the
                East is published.

April 11   Lenin gives a report on concessions at a meeting
                of the Communist group of the All-Russia Central
                Council of Trade Unions.

April 14   Lenin writes a letter to the Communists of Azer-
                baijan, Georgia, Armenia, Daghestan, and the
                Mountaineer Republic, instructing them on the
                consolidation and development of the Soviet
                power in the Caucasus.

                Lenin sends a message of greetings to a Petrograd
                city conference of non-Party workers.

April 18   Lenin gives instructions to G. K. Orjonikidze
                about the preservation of the Georgia State Bank,
                and the need to wage a most determined struggle
                against the counter-revolutionary activity of the
                Georgian Mensheviks.

April 21   Lenin completes his pamphlet, *The Tax in Kind* (*The*
                Significance of the New Policy and Its Conditions).

April 25   Lenin writes three speeches for recording on the tax
                in kind; concessions and the development of capita-
                lism; and consumers' and producers' co-operative
                societies.

April 26   Lenin presides at a government meeting to discuss
               the questions of relationships between the Uzbeks
               and the Turkmens; the Karelian Labour Commune,
               etc.

End of April-   Lenin drafts a circular letter to the Party's guber-
early May   nia committees on their attitude to non-Party
                  workers.

May 10   Lenin presides at a meeting of the Central Commit-
               tee's Political Bureau to discuss the question of
               collective supplies.

               Lenin presides at a government meeting to dis-
               cuss the following questions: the state of workers'
               inspection in the localities, and appointment of
               a representative of the People's Commissariat
               for Nationalities to the "Narrow" Council of People's
               Commissars.

               Lenin writes his remarks on the theses for the
               Third Congress of the Communist International
               worked out by a commission.

May 14   In a letter "To Comrade Krzhizhanovsky, the
               Presidium of the State Planning Commission",
               Lenin outlines the principal questions for the
               drawing up of a nation-wide economic plan for the
               immediate period ahead.

May 18   On behalf of the Central Committee, Lenin speaks
               at a meeting of the Communist group of the Fourth
               All-Russia Congress of Trade Unions against the
               draft resolution motioned by the anarcho-
               syndicalist group on the report of the Presidium
               of the All-Russia Central Council of Trade Unions
               at the Congress.

May 21   Lenin completes his draft of the Instructions
               from the Council of Labour and Defence to local
               Soviet bodies.

May 22   Lenin drafts the Political Bureau's decision on
               the resolutions of the Communist group of the
               Fourth Congress of Trade Unions.

May 26-28   Lenin presides at the Tenth All-Russia Confer-
               ence of the R.C.P.(B.).

May 26   Lenin delivers the opening speech at the Conference.

               Lenin is elected to the Presidium of the Con-
               ference.

               Lenin gives a report on the tax in kind.

May 27   Lenin delivers the summing-up speech on the tax in kind.

Lenin delivers a report on the R.C.P.(B.) group of the Fourth Congress of Trade Unions.

May, not later than 28   Lenin drafts a resolution on the questions of the New Economic Policy (NEP).

May 28   Lenin speaks in support of the draft resolution on NEP.

Lenin delivers the summing-up speech at the Conference.

May 30   Lenin speaks on the tasks of local economic organs at a sitting of the third session of the Eighth All-Russia Central Executive Committee.

May   Lenin writes several letters to a Deputy People's Commissar for Education, requesting him to see what is being done to compile a dictionary of the Russian language (from Pushkin to Gorky).

June 5   Lenin instructs the Chairman of the State Commission for the Electrification of the R.S.F.S.R. to prepare material to acquaint delegates to the Third Congress of the Communist International with the electrification plan.

June 13   Lenin writes the theses of a report on the tactics of the R.C.P.(B.) to the Third Congress of the Communist International.

June 16   Lenin speaks on the New Economic Policy at the Third All-Russia Food Conference.

June 17   Lenin speaks at an enlarged meeting of the Executive Committee of the Communist International on the situation within the French Communist Party.

June 22- July 12   Lenin guides the work of the Third Congress of the Communist International.

June 22   Lenin is elected Honorary Chairman of the Third Congress of the Communist International.

June 28   Lenin speaks at the Third Congress of the Communist International on the Italian question.

June-July	Lenin issues instructions to provide manpower and all the necessary materials for the construction of the Kashira Electric Power Station.
July 1	Lenin speaks at the Third Congress of the Communist International in defence of the tactics of the Communist International.
July 4	Lenin writes a letter, "Ideas About a State Economic 'Plan'", containing instructions to the State Planning Commission under the Council of Labour and Defence in connection with the drawing up of the state plan.
July 5	Lenin gives a report at the Third Congress of the Communist International on the tactics of the R.C.P.(B.).
July 6	Lenin cables the People's Commissar for Food of the Ukraine, instructing him to take resolute steps to satisfy the needs of the Donets Basin.
July 11	Lenin speaks at a meeting of delegates to the Third Congress of the Communist International on revolutionary tactics.
July 13	Lenin takes a month's holiday on the advice of his doctors and goes to Gorki.
July 16	Lenin writes a message of greetings to the Delegate Congress of Tsentrosoyuz.
July 18	Lenin writes a message of greetings to the First International Congress of Revolutionary Trade and Industrial Unions.
July 19	Lenin gives instructions to M. I. Kalinin on measures to help the starving people in the Volga area.
	Lenin presides at a government meeting to discuss assistance to gubernias hit by the crop failure and other questions.
July 20	Lenin writes a message of greetings to the peasants of Gorki on the occasion of the first use of electricity in their village.
August 2	Lenin writes to V. V. Adoratsky concerning the foreword to a collection of letters of Karl Marx and Frederick Engels, and a book on the fundamentals of Marxism.

Lenin writes an appeal to the international proletariat for help to the population of the areas in
Soviet Russia hit by the crop failure.

Lenin writes an appeal to the peasants of the
Ukraine, asking them to help the workers and
peasants of the Volga area hit by the crop failure.

August 5   Lenin writes a letter to G. Myasnikov, exposing
the latter's anti-Party and anti-working-class
views.

August 13   Lenin writes a letter to the representative of the
British Communist Party on the Executive
Committee of the Communist International about
the tasks of the British Communist Party.

August 14   Lenin writes a letter to the German Communists
in connection with the forthcoming Congress of
the United Communist Party of Germany, advising
them to take guidance from the resolutions of the
Third Congress of the Communist International.

B. И. ЛЕНИН
СОЧИНЕНИЯ
Том 32

На английском языке